Information
for
Decision
Making

Information for Decision Making

quantitative and

behavioral dimensions

second edition

Alfred Rappaport
Northwestern University

Prentice-Hall, Inc., Englewood Cliffs, New Jersey

Library of Congress Cataloging in Publication Data

Rappaport, Alfred, comp.
    Information for decision making.

    Includes bibliographies.
    1. Decision-making—Addresses, essays, lectures.
2. Management information systems—Addresses, essays,
lectures. 3. Cost accounting—Addresses, essays,
lectures. I. Title.
HD69.D4R36 1974   658.4'03   74-17397
ISBN 0-13-464388-7

Printed in the United States of America

10   9   8   7   6   5   4   3   2   1

Prentice-Hall International, Inc., *London*
Prentice-Hall of Australia, Pty. Ltd., *Sydney*
Prentice-Hall of Canada, Ltd., *Toronto*
Prentice-Hall of India Private Limited, *New Delhi*
Prentice-Hall of Japan, Inc., *Tokyo*

CONTENTS

SEVEN   Decentralization and Transfer Pricing   295

EIGHT   Behavioral Aspects of Information   335

PREFACE

The subject matter of this book may be characterized by such labels as "management information systems," "management accounting," and "management decision making." More specifically, this book is addressed to the informational aspects of management systems. Information, that is, data organized to be useful for decision making, is essential to the survival of all goal-oriented organizations. Recent developments in information technology, quantitative methods, and the behavioral sciences have greatly expanded the potential of information for organizational decision making. Where once the financial accounting model served as *the* formal information system, we are now witnessing the emergence of management information systems emphasizing mathematical models, systems philosophy, *ex ante* measures, and non-financial as well as financial measures. Thus the primary objective of this text is to relate these advances in the management sciences, including the behavioral sciences, to the task of effectively designing and using decision-oriented information systems.

To facilitate this objective the articles have been carefully selected after an extensive search of the literature on the basis of relevance and clarity of exposition. Because the emphasis throughout the book is on concepts rather than techniques, students with only modest training in quantitative methods should be able to read the selections with relative ease and comprehension. As a further aid to the reader, a summary highlighting salient points precedes each selection. For student research projects or readers who wish to do further study, bibliographies appear at the end of each chapter.

The readings were selected and organized to enable the instructor to use the text as a supplement for the first course in cost or management accounting in either an undergraduate or an MBA curriculum. For those who find that time limits the introduction of additional material in the basic course, the text should prove a useful vehicle for a second-level readings and case course in management accounting.

Only ten of the articles appearing in this Second Edition were carried forward from the First Edition. This significant turnover reflects both the fast pace of the field and the greater emphasis placed on choosing readings which are most compatible with the manner in which cost and management accounting courses are typically designed.

The thirty-three readings are divided into eight chapters. The readings in Chapter 1, "An Overview of Information and Decisions," are primarily directed to developing a framework for viewing information systems and decision making. I have found that assigning the Ackoff article, in which he contends that managers suffer from information overload, and the Dana Corp. reading, which describes one company's way of dealing with information overload, invariably leads to good classroom discussion. Similar results can be expected in Chapter 2, "Budgeting and Financial Models," by the joint assignment of the Irvine reading, which focuses on the behavioral aspects of budgeting, and "Penney-Pinching," a detailed description of J. C. Penney's budgeting process.

In Chapter 3, "Cost-Volume-Profit Analysis," the readings extend beyond the normal textbook treatment of the topic by the explicit consideration of uncertainty and evaluation of the breakeven equation assuming absorption costing rather than direct costing. My favorite case for this section is Bill French (ICH-4C39R).

The readings on capital budgeting in Chapter 4 introduce the reader to three important dimensions of the subject—inflation, uncertainty, and the relationship between the discounted cash flow approach to capital budgeting and the accounting earnings reported to investors. I generally assign Molecular Compounds Corporation (ICH-10F 88 - Abr.) after the class has read the Lerner-Rappaport article.

The readings in Chapter 5 emphasize the role of cost information in management planning and control. Here the reader gains familiarity with the problems associated with estimating cost behavior patterns (Benston), the development of a PERT/Cost network (Ross), suggested improvements in the traditional standard costing model (Demski and Luh), and the usefulness of matrix cost allocation model (Livingstone).

The coverage of the topic of "decentralized financial control systems" has been expanded from the First Edition. The topic is covered in Chapters 6 and 7 under the titles "Decentralization and Performance Evaluation" and "Decentralization and Transfer Pricing," respectively. In Chapter 6, the two commonly used measures of return, the discounted cash flow rate of return and the book or accounting return, are analyzed and compared. The question of why companies use discounted cash flow models for capital budgeting purposes and an accounting return model for divisional performance evaluation is posed and an alternative approach is outlined. Two papers are devoted to the important problem of how to design a motivationally sound performance evaluation system when a single manager is responsible for both forecasting and decision making. Chapter 6 concludes with an innovative input-output approach to performance evaluation employed at Combustion Engineering. There is an abundance of good cases on decentralized performance evaluation in the leading case textbooks. Chapter 7 continues the consideration of decentralized financial control systems with an examination of the difficult problem of setting transfer prices. Goetz and Onsi differ on the usefulness of incremental costs for pricing transfer goods. Manes examines the possibility of using shadow prices to calculate transfer prices in an extension of the frequently used Birch Paper Company case. I have found this to be an excellent classroom vehicle for an immediate follow-up to the Birch Paper case.

The message which pervades all of the readings in Chapter 8, "Behavioral Aspects of Information," is that information systems designers must consider not only the problem the user is trying to solve and the data required to solve it, but they must also consider how the content and form of the information to be communicated may affect his behavior. Some instructors might prefer to assign this chapter before assigning the material in Chapters 6 and 7.

My thanks to the authors and copyright holders of the selections included in this book. I also wish to express my appreciation to the many professors who offered valuable feedback on the First Edition. My fondest thanks to my wife, Sharon for assisting in the laborious but essential task of proofreading the manuscript. Finally, special thanks go to Garret White and Cheryl Smith of Prentice-Hall.

Alfred Rappaport

AN OVERVIEW OF
INFORMATION
AND DECISIONS

CHAPTER ONE

Basic Concepts for Designing Management Information Systems

Richard O. Mason, Jr.

University of California, Los Angeles

Where should the information system leave off and the decision maker begin? The advantages, limitations and assumptions required are examined for four alternative approaches: (1) databank approach, (2) predictive information systems, (3) decision-making information system, and (4) decision-taking information system. An important task of the management information system designer is to establish the proper mix of the four approaches based on a study of the decision-making processes within the organization.

AIS. Research Paper No. 8, October 1969. Used by permission of Richard O. Mason, Jr.

The main distinguishing feature of a management information system is that it explicitly provides information for management decision-making. The paper begins by examining two approaches to the design of a MIS. One is to study and refine existing data flows. The other is to analyze management decision problems and to conceptualize and model their essential elements. The latter approach is proposed as better suited for the development of a MIS.

The key notion underlying the decision-oriented approach to MIS is that the parameters and variables included in the decision model serve to specify information requirements. This idea is carried further by proposing a categorization of the major components of an information/decision process. Decisions are said to consist of source, data, prediction and inference, value and choice, and action components. This analysis leads to a classification scheme consisting of databank, predictive, decision-making and decision-taking information systems. Feedback systems are treated as a special case.

All decisions and hence their supporting information systems are based on assumptions. Consequently a systemic information system design is proposed for the purpose of revealing and examining underlying assumptions and for developing new world views. A particular design for this purpose is reviewed.

INTRODUCTION

Management information systems should supply the basic information that managers need in order to make decisions. The more closely the information provided is attuned with the decision-maker's needs the better the decisions that will be made. This means that the designer of an information system must carefully analyze decision processes as well as existing information flows. For, in a *management* information system the two are essentially inseparable.

All too frequently, however, the approach used by designers has been limited to a study of existing forms, files, reports and procedures and an effort to determine ways in which they might be simplified, expanded, integrated and improved. Sometimes many useful and economical results are realized from this kind of study; but, they are generally in the area of increased efficiency of data flows or reduction in clerical staff, *not* in improved quality of decisions made.

In the decision-oriented approach the designer begins by identifying the range of alternatives open to the decision-maker, and the resources at his disposal. He then determines the kinds of data inputs which are necessary for choosing the best course of action and lays out a program for collecting, processing and disseminating that data to the appropriate decision-making party.

The decision-oriented approach raises two important and closely related questions which the designer must answer:

1. What is the best point of articulation between the information system and the decision-maker? That is, where should the information system leave off and the decision-maker begin?
2. What is the nature of the assump-

tions which are incorporated in the information system and which consequently influence the user's decision-making? Are they consistent with the decision-maker's needs?

Depending on how the designer resolves these questions a qualitatively different kind of information system will be specified. The designer's choice centers on the sequence of activities which begins with the state of the business itself and ends with the actual taking of a decision. This sequence of activities can be summarized as follows:

1. A *source* consisting of the physical activities and objects which are relevant to the business.
2. The observation, measurement and recording of *data* from the source.
3. The drawing of *inferences* and *predictions* from the data.
4. The evaluation of inferences with regard to the *values* (objectives or goals) of the organization and the *choosing* of a course of action.
5. The *taking* of a course of *action.*

The first natural point of articulation between the information system and the decision-maker occurs when they are separated between the process of collecting data (Item 2) and that of drawing inferences (Item 3). This design is sometimes referred to as the databank or data base approach.[1]

[1] This classification and subsequent development derives from an interpretation of a paper on measurement by C. West Churchman entitled "Suggestive, Predictive, Decisive and Systemic Measurements" which was prepared for the Second Congress on Industrial Safety, 1969.

DATABANKS

Graphically, the databank design appears as follows:

ator." The decision-maker must determine what "meaning" the data has for his decision problem and then act accordingly.

The databank approach makes a lot of sense for some kinds of applications,

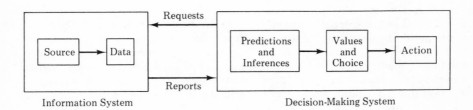

Information System   Decision-Making System

FIGURE 1

This design assumes the weakest link between the information system and the decision-maker. The responsibility of the information system is just to observe, classify and store any item of data which might be potentially useful to the decision-maker. It is incumbent on the user to request the data items he needs and to determine what their implication is for the decision problem he faces.

The information system's designer must specify the data inputs required for a variety of subsequent uses. For example, he might specify the various master files to be used in several applications. He then collects the master file data into a single pool that is keyed to the lowest common denominator of detail required for each of the decision-making applications. The information system, however, leaves off at this point.

The decision-maker utilizes the data pool by accessing those data items that are relevant to the problem at hand. He must determine which items he needs and secure them by placing retrieval requests or by establishing periodic reporting programs. This means that the databank information system is only a "fact gener-

especially in the general area of management control. Often, management control activity centers around queries in which the manager seeks to ask questions about the relationships between conditions and events occurring in one area and those in another, or between one particular point in time and some other time period. Since any combination or permutation of these data items might be requested (this results in an astronomical number of possibilities) it is not very efficient, if it is feasible at all, to program all of these possibilities into the system. In this case, it is better to let the decision-maker determine the kinds of predictions and inferences he wants to make and simply to inquire directly for the data he needs to do this.

Thus, in situations where the nature of the required inferences is not known with any precision beforehand, or where the structure of relationships and the assumptions about the system's preferences are changing rapidly, the databank approach is most effective. Moreover, it can prove to be economical as well. If properly implemented in an organization, a single databank can service a wide variety of decision-makers who face different decision problems and who have different but overlapping data requirements.

Used in this manner, the potential results from a well conceived databank can be phenomenal. For example, a large railway company has installed a communications and computer network that provides accurate and immediate data on the status of every railroad car on its lines. Dispatchers use this data to spot pileup areas and to determine which cars are available for reassignment. The dispatcher can then make a judgment as to which cars can be dispatched in order to economically or rapidly fulfill incoming demands. The car status databank aids him in making the associations necessary for arriving at these decisions. By means of the better dispatching decisions that this databank provides, the company expects to substantially reduce its investment in railroad cars—enough to more than recoup its $30 million expenditure for data processing and transmission equipment.

The railroad car status system serves to illustrate why databanks are, in Churchman's words, merely "suggestive." The manager who receives these car status reports must determine the cause and effect relationships between his actions and system and make judgments about which of the possible outcomes is preferred. He must, for example, trade-off the economic cost incurred in moving cars with the possible benefits gained by improving customer service. The databank does not make these predictions or decisions for him but by its very nature and availability it tends to *suggest* certain desirable alternatives to him.

It should be pointed out that most of the current discussions on databanks have centered on their implementation with computerized systems. The new third generation computers and the advent of relatively inexpensive mass memories have made it possible to consolidate highly fragmented data sources into a common data base that could be shared by many different computer programs. But in the broader sense in which the term is used in this paper, databanks are widespread and have been around for a long time. Almost all accounting systems are in reality databanks. The criterion of objectivity—"Verifiable, objective evidence has therefore become an important element in accounting and a necessary adjunct to the proper execution of the accounting function of supplying dependable information,"—has virtually assured this.[2] Following this criterion traditional accounting systems have incorporated little in the way of predictions or decision recommendations into the information system. Financial statements display data; the user determines what it means for him.

There are many other familiar examples of databanks. The large federal databanks being accumulated by the IRS and the Bureau of Census are exemplary of this design. So too, for that matter, is much of the information found in libraries, books, newspapers and most data storage and retrieval systems.

Two potential drawbacks pertain to databank systems and the designer should take them into account:

1. A failure to properly relate the databank to the decision process will result in both the collection of too much irrelevant data and the omission of many important, relevant items for decision-making. Moreover, a lack of decision orientation will result in data being collected which is not in the appropriate form for its subsequent use.

2. The decision-maker is left with the burden of performing the calculations and evaluations necessary for determining predicted outcomes and

[2]W. A. Paton, and A. C. Littleton; *An Introduction to Corporate Accounting Standards* (Columbus, Ohio: American Accounting Association, 1940), p. 18.

the best course of action. Quite often these manipulations are complex and illusive for the manager's unaided intuition; but, frequently they are amenable to a systematic logical inquiry and, eventually, programmable. When this situation occurs, predictive or higher order information systems can be designed.

PREDICTIVE INFORMATION SYSTEMS

The next class of information system extends the system forward from the activities of pure data collection and filing to include the drawing of the inferences and predictions that are relevant for decision-making. Prediction and inference making occur when the information system's processing passes from the basic data to conclusions about the source. In this process certain evidential relationships are assumed to exist. The decision-making system in effect inquires as to "what if?" certain actions are taken and these assumptions are true. The system responds in the vein of "if" he does that "then" this is what he can expect to occur. No attempt is made to evaluate the outcome. Diagrammatically a predictive information system is characterized as follows:

type. Financial planning simulation models are a good case in point.

Through the use of financial simulation techniques and timeshared computing technology it is possible for the manager of a business firm to sit down at a teletype console and call for the current status of his organization (as depicted by such databank type items as financial statements and charts of accounts). He then assumes forecasted levels for certain important economic indicators which affect his business such as population and GNP. He also assumes certain structural relationships between such items as sales and expenses, accounts receivable and collections, etc., and suggests internal policies for coping with them. For example, one policy might be to finance through equity and another to finance through borrowing. His considerations might include choices as to which divisions of the company will manufacture what products and by what methods they will distribute them. Alternative manufacturing techniques and their attendant cost equations might also be considered. Given these assumptions the simulation model then *predicts* the levels of sales, cost of materials and other variables by means of econometric methods and mathematical relationships. Then the program *infers* what the impact of these conditions will be on future financial statements and produces pro forma statements.

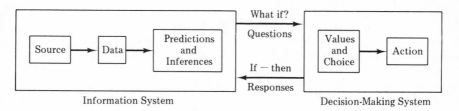

FIGURE 2

Much of the recent development in information systems tends toward this

These simulations inform the decision-maker as to what is predicted to happen under a given set of circumstances. The decision-maker may, of course, pose as many different conditions to the model as he thinks will be useful and obtain their separate implications. However, an evaluation of the outcomes—by applying the criterion or objective functions which ranks one potential outcome as being more preferable than another—remains with the decision-maker. It is not committed to the model. The decision-maker makes the ultimate choice based on predictions he receives about the alternatives tested.

It should be mentioned that predictive information systems need not be thought of strictly in computer or simulation terms. The president's advisory staff group, or a corporate market research group are also examples of predictive information systems embodied in the organizational design. The role of such organizational entities historically has been to intercede between the organization's databank and the final decision-making body for the explicit purpose of selecting and summarizing the data and drawing its implications. Most generally only the inferences are communicated to the manager.

This last observation leads to a consideration which is the underlying principle of this classification scheme. *As one moves from source to action (left to right on the diagram) more assumptions are introduced into the information/decision-making system.* And, at each step the assumptions built in are qualitatively different.

The predictive information systems require that additional aspects of the decision-maker's "relevant picture of the business" or "world view" be incorporated in the model. Relationships must be assumed. Specifically in the financial simulation illustration presented above the model has to include assumptions about the functional form of the forecasting equations, the cause and effect rela-

tionships between various activities within the firm and the functional form of the transformation from period to period. These assumptions are in addition to the assumptions built into the databank itself.

The advantages and disadvantages of the predictive information system center on the nature of the assumptions made. The predictive information system is particularly advantageous in those situations where the number of data items to be considered is large and their interrelationships are complicated (such as is the case with financial simulation). The resulting predictive model relieves the decision-maker of the burden of making these calculations and thereby frees him to consider other more important things. A well designed predictive system should be able to take into account more data items, make more accurate calculations, and produce predictions faster than the unaided manager's intellect permits. Moreover, it allows him to test many more alternatives quickly and economically than would be possible at the databank level.

Even if the required calculations are comparatively simple, the need for rapid response may marshal in favor of the predictive system. The investor who is contemplating a new stock purchase would like to know the effect of this action on his portfolio composition, on his projected cash flow and on his tax liability rather quickly. So, too, does the manager who is considering the effect of a proposed merger or acquisition want to know the impact of this move on his firm's future financial statements and reports of corporate performance. When the appropriate assumptions are incorporated in the information system design, these kinds of predictions can be obtained rapidly and they can substantially improve the quality of decision-making.

But there are also some serious dangers connected with use of predictive information systems. Predictive systems are realizations of what March and Simon refer to as "uncertainty absorption." "Uncertainty absorption takes place when inferences are drawn from a body of evidence (i.e., a databank) and the inferences, instead of the evidence itself, are then communicated."[3]

The danger lies in the possibility that the inferences are based on assumptions that are not in accord with the best judgment of the decision-maker and that these assumptions are "hidden" from him by the information system design. This point is of sufficient importance that an entire section will be devoted to it later in this paper.[4] For now, let us turn to the next class of information systems.

DECISION-MAKING INFORMATION SYSTEMS

Moving up the continuum, the next class of information systems includes those in which the organization's value system and the criteria for choice are incorporated into the information system itself. These can be referred to as *decision-making information systems* and are portrayed as follows:

The long range goal of many ardent practitioners of operations research and management science is to produce decision-making information systems. This kind of information system epitomizes these disciplines' major concern. But, it is only realizable when a full databank and prediction system supports an optimizing model.

A linear program for, say, production scheduling is one example of a decision-making information system. In developing this model the designer begins by specifying a group of functional relationships (e.g., "constraints") about machine output rates, cost coefficients, market demands, etc. This is the predictive or implicative aspect of the information system. But now the objective function (in this case to maximize profits) is added to the problem specification and it is built into the information system. In effect (although this is not precisely how the algorithms work) the objective function serves to "rank" the predicted outcome from each alternative and select the best or "optimal" policy. For this LP example the objective function determines the most profitable product mix for the company to produce.

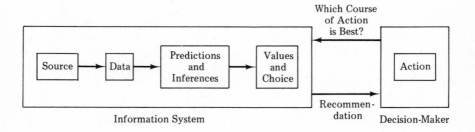

FIGURE 3

[3]March and Simon, *Organizations* (New York: John Wiley & Sons, 1958), p. 165.
[4]See the later section on Systemic Information Systems.

Mathematical programming models are not the only form that decision-making information systems can take. They are examples of what I have referred to elsewhere as "expert advice."[5] Their output is a single recommended course of action. The decision-maker retains just a "veto" power. In effect he either acts on the recommendation or he does not, although in some cases he may modify the original recommendation. There are several organizational entities that essentially operate in this manner. One is the "cost-effectiveness" study group; another is the decision-maker's advisory board.

An illustration of an advisory board form of decision-making information system was the operation of the National Security Council under President Eisenhower. Eisenhower believed that "good staff work means that the President should not be required to choose from among alternative policies, so that his job can instead be that of saying 'yes' or 'no' to the policy his advisors recommend to him."[6] Consequently, the National Security Council was used in this manner during the Eisenhower Administration. "Well-staffed" papers which argued for a single recommended course of action were the order of the day.

Cost-effectiveness studies have much the same flavor. Their mission is to determine benefits gained as compared with the resources expended for each alternative. If the benefits exceed cost an alternative is recommended or, alternatively, that alternative which gives the greatest contribution to effectiveness per unit of resource is advised.

The major difficulty facing all cost effectiveness studies is the problem of choosing the appropriate measure of effectiveness.[7] This same problem pervades every attempt to design a decision-making information system. *Most decision-making information systems assume the knowledge of a unidimensional scale for ranking the value of alternatives.*[8] Thus, decision-making information systems require the specification of an *acceptable* measure of value for the organization. If the proper measure is not found the decision-making information system's recommendations will be dysfunctional. They will be turned down or, worse yet, implemented blindly. One plausible answer to this problem is for the system to revert back to a predictive information system. A case history will serve to demonstrate the usefulness of this reversion strategy.

Several years ago a large corporation instituted a formal capital investment analysis procedure as part of their corporate planning function. Every proposed investment over $50,000 was to undergo a thorough discounted rate of return-on-investment analysis before it was presented to the board of directors for approval. The procedure was set up so that if the rate exceeded some benchmark rate, which reflected the corporation's cost of capital, the project would be recommended for action. In this particular decision-making information system the board received a comprehensive description of the technical aspects of the project but only the results of the discounted rate of return calculation.[9]

But much to the dismay of the board most of the discussion and debate about a proposed investment centered on ques-

---

[5]Mason, Richard O., "A Dialectical Approach to Strategic Planning", *Management Science*, Vol. 15, No. 8, April 1968.
[6]Gordon, Bernard K., "The Top of Policy Hill," *Bulletin of the Atomic Scientist*, Volume XVI, No. 7, September 1960, p. 289.
[7]See for example, P. M. Morse, and G. E. Kimbal, *Methods of Operations Research*, (Cambridge, Mass., MIT, 1951), pp. 52-53.

[8]Or, what amounts to much the same thing, they require some "decision rule" such as the minimax criterion or the "sure thing" principle.
[9]Actually for some projects the firm went so far as to estimate the probability distribution over various parameters of the project and then to calculate a cumulative distribution of rate of return. The procedure was similar to that described in David Hertz's article "Investment Policies that Pay Off", *Harvard Business Review*, Jan-Feb 1968, pp. 96-108.

tions of value. They found that there were many dimensions to these decisions which could not be specified in advance or adequately summarized on a single scale of value such as ROI. Questions on the possible effect of the proposed project on corporate image, management development and social responsibility arose.

One special concern, for example, was the timing of cash receipts and how it dovetailed with other corporate cash requirements. But, this information was not presented in the original recommending document. An acceptable solution to this problem was found when the corporate planning group decided to present the board with a summary report showing the key factors affecting the flow of cash receipts and disbursements and of expected profit for each period of the planning horizon. These predictions were performed for each of a variety of assumptions concerning costs, market demands, and alternative uses of the technology. The discounted ROI was still calculated but it became a less important factor in this new, predictive information system.

The principle illustrated by this case is that where some dimensions of the organization's value system can be specified but a single scale of value cannot be determined (or is unacceptable), a pre-

most appropriate design. The information system designer must make this judgment for each individual case.

The basic reason that the decision-making information system was deplored by the board of directors (i.e., the decision-makers) is that they had no *confidence* in the objective function it assumed. They also had some reservations about the assumptions underlying its predictions. Whenever general agreement and confidence in an objective function is present a decision-making information system may be converted into a decision-taking system.

DECISION-TAKING INFORMATION SYSTEM

A decision-taking information system is one in which the information system and the decision-maker are one. Management is so confident in the assumptions incorporated in the system that it sees fit to relegate even its veto power to the information system. For the sake of completion the schema for a decision-taking information system is presented below:

Process-control computer applications represent good examples of decision-taking information systems. The computer is programmed to know the pre-

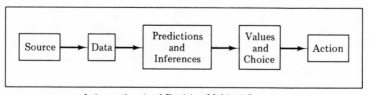

Information (and Decision-Making) System

FIGURE 4

dictive information—one which shows the impact in each dimension of value for each of several alternatives—may be the

ferred state of, say, a petroleum cracking process. For a rather large number of situations that can occur in the process the computer can "decide" which course of action to take and initiate action. It can, for example, change the temperature or regulate the flow of input materials. There is relatively little human intervention because the managing body for the organization has confidence in the premises upon which the computer acts.

The domain in which a process control computer operates, however, is rather small compared with the decision domain for the organization as a whole. Other attempts at decision-taking information systems are generally restricted to similarly small domains of influence. Some systems automatically initiate a purchase order when inventory has dropped below the reorder point, or send a dunn letter to a customer when he has been overdue for some prespecified period of time, or automatically create loans for bank customers who are overdrawn. But these are really trivial decisions within the overall context of management decision-making.

In a very real sense, decision-taking information systems are the computer scientist's dream for all of the decision-making process is relegated to the technology. But they will continue to escape his grasp until he determines a reliable and trustworthy method of incorporating management's values and basic underlying assumptions into his computer models. Unfortunately, or fortunately, this day is probably a long way off.

The road towards the development of decision-taking information systems has been opened up through the notion of *feedback* or of cybernetics. This idea is sufficiently unique so as to warrant special treatment.

FEEDBACK (CYBERNETIC) INFORMATION SYSTEMS: A SPECIAL CASE

Feedback or cybernetic systems can be formed through combinations of data-bank, predictive, decision-making and decision-taking information systems. The basic cybernetic model commences with some norm or target being set by a decision-making information system. Then action is taken pursuant to this goal. Subsequently, observations are made to measure the effect that the action has upon the source, and the resulting "feedback" is recorded in a databank. These databank items are then compared with the target to generate a variance, error or mis-match signal which shows the degree of deviation. (These signals are also databank type items.) The mis-match signal is, in turn, processed through the predictive-inferential and decision-making stages. Finally, action is taken with the intent of reducing the deviation to zero. This cycle is repeated to maintain the system "on course" (i.e., to keep the deviation from the goal near zero). A generalized diagram of a feedback system is presented following.

Various combinations of the components shown in the diagram above can be dedicated to the information system while the remaining are assigned to the decision-maker. In the classical example of a feedback system—James Watt's ball governor for controlling the speed of steam engines—all functions are assigned to the information system making it a complete decision-taking information system. The basic purpose of the steam engine, in terms of the equilibrium speed it is to achieve, is crystallized and built into the system. The system collects data and takes automatic action to achieve that speed thereafter. Servomechanisms and much in the way of automated equipment operate on this principle.

There are, however, several familiar examples of decision-making and databank information systems which also employ feedback. For example, most inventory control systems determine a "recommended" reorder quantity but the decision-maker has final veto power and

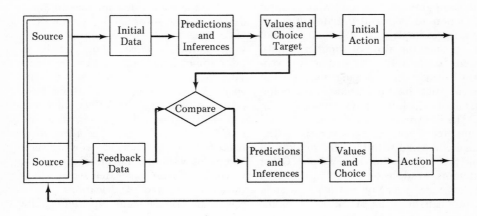

FIGURE 5.   Cybernetic Systems

the responsibility to take the action. Thus, they are decision-making information systems. Several managerial techniques provide what is in reality a kind of sophisticated databank information by relating current data to some previous goal. For example, budgetary planning systems produce data which describe the variance between budgeted and actual. But it is up to the decision-maker to make the appropriate predictions and inferences from this data and to reconsider the organizational values that apply before taking corrective action. Quality control methods are similar in this respect. The control chart reports the occurrence of an out-of-control state. The decision-maker must determine the cause of this deviation and then weigh the cost and benefits of several alternatives before taking action.

The designer of a feedback control system, as is true of the designer of any information system, has a choice as to where the decision-maker/information system interface will be placed. He may develop a databank, a predictive, a decision-making, or a decision-taking information system. His choice depends on the confidence he has in the assump-

tions upon which the decision-maker's ultimate action should be based. This concern leads us to a last category of information systems—systemic information systems.

SYSTEMIC INFORMATION SYSTEMS

Systemic information systems are those which apprise the manager or the information systems designer about the assumptions or view-of-the-world which underlie decisions. They are intended to test his judgment about the "whole system"; what it is and how it is to be defined. The purpose of a systemic information system is to expose these assumptions so that they may be examined and reconsidered.

Consideration of the other classes of information systems suggests the need to examine assumptions carefully. One point of emphasis in each of the preceding classes of information systems centers on the extent and kind of assumptions which are intrinsic to the information system. The key differentiating distinction between a databank information system and a predictive one is that additional managerial assumptions are built-in to the predictive system. The same principle holds as one moves along the continuum until in the decision-taking information system essentially all assumptions concerning the domain of choice are contained within the information system itself.

Each class of information system has quantitatively different kinds of assumptions incorporated. These differences are summarized in the diagram below:

Consider the accounting system for a financial institution such as a bank. Of the vast panorama of events that occur within the bank only those which are identifiable, objective, verifiable and which represent economic transactions measurable in monetary terms are observed and recorded. Furthermore, they are recorded as entries into a *pre-set* chart of accounts which reflects the aspects and distinctions among these items that the bank feels are important. (The degree of liquidity of an asset, for example.) These

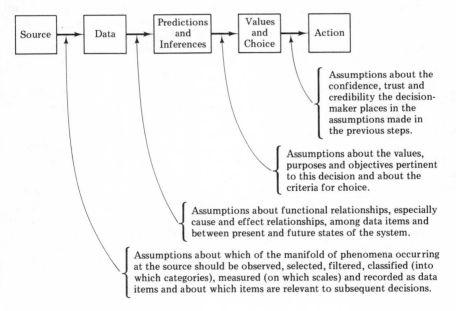

FIGURE 6

The diagram also reveals that all information systems contain assumptions. Since each step in the information/decision process uses the product of the previous step as its basic input, an assumption, once made, influences the subsequent operations and ultimately, the action taken. An illustration will serve to demonstrate the point.

constitute some of the assumptions about "item entry" that underlie the bank's databank.

It should be noted that the databank can be manipulated and summarized in various ways so as to produce financial statements and also certain status and performance indicators such as the loan to deposit ratio and the earnings per share. But these manipulations do not essentially change the databank quality.

The bank's management may, however, want to predict the effect that certain strategies and policies will have on future financial statements. Using the accounting system databank as a base, the bank might now begin to build a model which shows the assumed cause and effect relationship between actions taken and their outcome. This would include the effect of adding new loans, buying securities, adding or reducing deposits, etc. Using this model the bank may now set parameters to reflect a particular policy (e.g., make an increased percentage of new loans as commercial loans). The model then predicts the effects of these policies on the financial statements. These predicted financial outcomes are based on the databank and in conjunction with assumptions made about available alternative policies, future environmental conditions and the accounting relationships between policy actions and future financial statements.

But this kind of model is so far only predictive. If in addition, however, the model is designed to find that particular policy which maximizes an assumed objective function, such as earnings per share, then this becomes a decision-making information system because it yields just a single recommended course of action. Whenever the decision-maker has complete confidence in the assumptions underlying the model's recommendation and acts automatically on its conclusions, the information system becomes a decision-taking one.

Assumptions, however, are the product of management's judgment. They are not analytical nor can they be proven. But they may be *wrong*. And, incorrect assumptions lead to poor decisions. A systemic information system is one that attempts to guard against inappropriate assumptions. Its mission is to continue to

apprise the manager of the assumptions that are being made by his existing information system.

Very little is known about the best design for systemic information systems, but current research suggests that one approach offers promise.[10] The approach is dialectical and is based on the premise that "good" judgments on assumptions are derived in an atmosphere of opposition. An information system is said to be dialectical if it examines data completely and logically with at least two different and opposing sets of assumptions or from two different points of view. It is the conflict between the assumptions representing one point of view and those of the other that aids the manager in learning about his system, and hence, in developing new, more appropriate assumptions.

The dialectical model follows the scheme set forth by Hegel. The designer begins by identifying the existing information/decision system and asks, "What set of assumptions or view-of-the-world would make the existing information system an 'optimal' one"? To return to the banking example he might inquire, "How would one define the whole business of banking, this bank, its liquidity, its customers, its assets, its alternatives, its threats, etc., so that this information system is the best one for its users"? This question should penetrate each of the classes of assumptions underlying the databank, predictive, decision-making and decision-taking systems.

The intent of this inquiry is to develop the strongest argument as to why, say, earnings per share (if that is the stated objective of the bank) is more important than, for example, the number of individuals served (weighed perhaps as to their need). That is, the argument would show in what view of the bank, its

---

[10] This approach is discussed in more detail in Mason, "A Dialectical Approach to Strategic Planning", *op. cit.*

customers, suppliers and investors EPS was the best objective to pursue. The argument would go on to show in what view of the banking processes and of banking environment this basis for prediction and for data collection is best. The resulting set of arguments becomes the *thesis*.

The *antithesis* is developed by asking whether or not another opposing but credible conceptualization of a bank's business can be found. For example, a bank might be thought of as an information processor rather than a money depositor and lender. Or, it may define its objectives in terms of its contributions to society and its community (a goal for long-run survival) rather than strictly in economic terms (which is perhaps a short-run goal). It may also define honored concepts such as liquidity in terms of the number of days required to generate levels of cash (through cash on hand, sales or securities, loans, etc., and net of losses) rather than by means of a loan to deposit ratio. The conclusion of this *counter-argument* is that a different set of assumptions are best and consequently a different kind of information system should be designed.

In the dialectical design of a systemic information system these arguments and counter-arguments are presented to the manager via a *structured debate*. An advocate for each side presents his view of the business and argues for it. Hegel's theory, however, leads us to predict that the manager—observer of the conflict—will integrate and form a new and expanded world view, a better set of assumptions—the *synthesis*. The new insights gained from the synthesis serve as the premises for the design of a new data collection, prediction, evaluation, choice and action component of the management system.

What should the primary focus of the arguments and counter-arguments in a systemic information system be? I would propose that they should center around corporate or organizational strategy. A strategy is the most basic of organizational assumptions. It is a "pattern of objectives, purposes, or goals" that serve to define "what business the company is or is to be in and the kind of company it is or is to be."[11] As such it dictates kinds of assumptions about values, predictions and data collection that are appropriate for the organization. *In short, a statement of strategy is the unifying theme around which a management information system is based.*

One final comment about systemic information systems should be made. Their purpose is to promote learning. Contrary to decision-making and decision-taking information systems whose purpose is to bring closure to the debate about the appropriate course of action to be taken, systemic information systems serve to open these questions for a new examination. They are aimed at identifying the kinds of changes in environmental conditions, changing values and new conceptualizations that require new management assumptions. In this sense they are restless and never-ending. This may be a somewhat difficult role for the computer-oriented information scientist or the "green eyeshade" style of accountant who is accustomed to the certainty and security that the closure aspects of his technology provide. But he must reconsider, for change is the way of life in the business world.

CONCLUSION

The major thrust of this paper has been to clarify the differences between several alternative designs for management information systems. However, it is important

[11]Quoted from Learned, Christensen, Andrews and Guth, *Business Policy: Test and Cases,* (Homewood, Ill.: Richard D. Irwin, 1965), p. 17.

to stress the point that the designer must consider *all* aspects of the information/decision process. He then chooses the particular combination of designs which is best suited to the decision situation for which it is intended.

A design study for a management information system should proceed essentially in the reverse order of the decision sequence developed above. In the decision-oriented approach the researcher starts by examining the manager's action alternatives and the criteria for choosing from among them. He then specifies the kinds of predictions, forecasts, inferences and measurements that are required in order to render a choice. This, in turn, determines the nature of the data to be collected and recorded.

Throughout this process, however, the designer *and* the manager must continue to examine the assumptions being built into the system. Together they must strive for a structure of assumptions or *Weltanschauung* that integrates the system into one, coherent, cohesive whole—one which reflects the basic values of the participants involved. Without such an integrating structure a collection of data is little more than a potpourri of isolated fragments. The only way to interpret and interrelate such fragments is through some theory that binds them and gives them meaning.

For the business enterprise or government agency the central integrating theme is its strategy. A statement of strategy includes the values and purposes of the organization and identifies the critical and pivotal decisions the manager must take. Systemic information systems have as their purpose the development of strategy and an understanding of the assumptions which underlie it. Hence, the manager and the designer need to engage in the systemic information system process as a prerequisite to management information systems design. It is the only way to insure that the design is relevant to the problems at hand.

A Framework for Management Information Systems

G. Anthony
Gorry

Michael S.
Scott Morton

*Massachusetts Institute
of Technology*

Despite the importance and cost of information systems to many organizations, there is very little perspective on the field and the issues within it. A framework is needed to provide a more efficient allocation of resources in this area. In this paper, the authors present such a framework and show some implications of the framework for the implementation of management information systems.

Reprinted from *Sloan Management Review*, Fall 1971, 55-70. Used by permission of G. Anthony Gorry, Michael S. Scott Morton and *Sloan Management Review*.

INTRODUCTION

A framework for viewing management information systems (MIS) is essential if an organization is to plan effectively and make sensible allocations of resources to information systems tasks. The use of computers in organizations has grown tremendously in the 1955 to 1971 period, but very few of the resulting systems have had a significant impact on the way in which management makes decisions. A framework which allows an organization to gain perspective on the field of information systems can be a powerful means of providing focus and improving the effectiveness of the systems efforts.

In many groups doing MIS work, this lack of perspective prevents a full appreciation of the variety of organizational uses for computers. Without a framework to guide management and systems planners, the system tends to serve the strongest manager or react to the greatest crisis. As a result, systems activities too often move from crisis to crisis, following no clear path and receiving only *ex post facto* justification. This tendency inflicts an unnecessary expense on the organization. Not only are costly computer resources wasted, but even more costly human resources are mismanaged. The cost of systems and programming personnel is generally twice that of the hardware involved in a typical project, and the ratio is growing larger as the cost of hardware drops and salaries rise.[1] Competent people are expensive. More importantly, they exist only in limited numbers. This limitation actively constrains the amount of systems development work that can be undertaken in a given organization, and so good resource allocation is critical.

Developments in two distinct areas within the last five years offer us the potential to develop altogether new ways of supporting decision processes. First, there has been considerable technological progress. The evolution of remote access to computers with short turnaround time and flexible user interfaces has been rapid. Powerful mini-computers are available at low cost and users can be linked to computer resources through inexpensive typewriter and graphical display devices. The second development has been a conceptual one. There is emerging an understanding of the potential role of information systems within organizations. We are adding to our knowledge of how human beings solve problems and of how to build models that capture aspects of the human decision making processes.[2]

The progress in these areas has been dramatic. Entirely new kinds of planning and control systems can now be built— ones that dynamically involve the manager's judgments and support him with analysis, models, and flexible access to relevant information. But to realize this potential fully, given an organization's limited resources, there must be an appropriate framework within which to view management decision making and the required systems support. The purpose of this paper is to present a framework that helps us to understand the evolution of MIS activities within organizations and to recognize some of the potential problems and benefits resulting from our new technology. Thus, this framework is designed to be useful in planning for information systems activities within an organization and for distinguishing between the various model building activities, models, computer systems, and so forth which are used for supporting different kinds of decisions. It is, by defini-

[1] J. W. Taylor and N. J. Dean, "Managing to Manage the Computer," *Harvard Business Review*, Vol. 44, No. 5 (Sept. - Oct. 1966), pp. 98-110.

[2] See Scott Morton, *Management Decision Systems* (Boston: Harvard University Press, 1971) and P. O. Soelberg, "Unprogrammed Decision Making," *Industrial Management Review*, Vol. 8, No. 2 (Spring 1967), pp. 19-30.

tion, a static picture, and is not designed to say anything about how information systems are built.

In the next section we shall consider some of the general advantages of developing a framework for information systems work. We shall then propose a specific framework which we have found to be useful in the analysis of MIS activities. We believe that this framework offers us a new way to characterize the progress made to date and offers us insight into the problems that have been encountered. Finally, we shall use this framework to analyze the types of resources that are required in the different decision areas and the ways in which these resources should be used.

FRAMEWORK DEVELOPMENT

The framework we develop here is one for managerial activities, not for information systems. It is a way of looking at decisions made in an organization. Information systems should exist only to support decisions, and hence we are looking for a characterization of organizational activity in terms of the type of decisions involved. For reasons which we make clear later, we believe that an understanding of managerial activity is a prerequisite for effective systems design and implementation. Most MIS groups become involved in system development and implementation without a prior analysis of the variety of managerial activities. This has, in our opinion, prevented them from developing a sufficiently broad definition of their purpose and has resulted in a generally inefficient allocation of resources.

In attempting to understand the evolution and problems of management information systems, we have found the work of Robert Anthony and Herbert Simon particularly useful. In *Planning and Con-*

trol Systems: A Framework for Analysis,[3] Anthony addresses the problem of developing a classification scheme that will allow management some perspective when dealing with planning and control systems. He develops a taxonomy for managerial activity consisting of three categories and argues that these categories represent activities sufficiently different in kind to require the development of different systems.

The first of Anthony's categories of managerial activity is *strategic planning:* "*Strategic planning* is the process of deciding on objectives of the organization, on changes in these objectives, on the resources used to attain these objectives, and on the policies that are to govern the acquisition, use, and disposition of these resources."[4] Certain things can be said about strategic planning generally. First, it focuses on the choice of objectives for the organization and on the activities and means required to achieve these objectives. As a result, a major problem in this area is predicting the future of the organization and its environment. Second, the strategic planning process typically involves a small number of high-level people who operate in a nonrepetitive and often very creative way. The complexity of the problems that arise and the nonroutine manner in which they are handled make it quite difficult to appraise the quality of this planning process.

The second category defined by Anthony is *management control:* ". . . the process by which managers assure that resources are obtained and used effectively and efficiently in the accomplishment of the organization's objectives."[5] He stresses three key aspects of this area. First, the activity involves inter-

---

[3] R. N. Anthony, *Planning and Control Systems: A Framework for Analysis* (Boston: Harvard University Press, 1965).
[4] *Ibid.*, p. 24.
[5] *Ibid.*, p. 27.

personal interaction. Second, it takes place within the context of the policies and objectives developed in the strategic planning process. Third, the paramount goal of management control is the assurance of effective and efficient performance.

Anthony's third category is *operational control,* by which he means "the process of assuring that specific tasks are carried out effectively and efficiently."[6] The basic distinction between management control and operational control is that operational control is concerned with tasks (such as manufacturing a specific part) whereas management control is most often concerned with people. There is much less judgment to be exercised in the operational control area because the tasks, goals, and resources have been carefully delineated through the management control activity.

We recognize, as does Anthony, that the boundaries between these three categories are often not clear. In spite of their limitations and uncertainties, however, we have found the categories useful in the analysis of information system activities. For example, if we consider the information requirements of these three activities, we can see that they are very different from one another. Further, this difference is not simply a matter of aggregation, but one of fundamental character of the information needed by managers in these areas.

Strategic planning is concerned with setting broad policies and goals for the organization. As a result, the relationship of the organization to its environment is a central matter of concern. Also, the nature of the activity is such that predictions about the future are particularly important. In general, then, we can say that the information needed by strategic planners is aggregate information, and obtained mainly from sources external to

the organization itself. Both the scope and variety of the information are quite large, but the requirements for accuracy are not particularly stringent. Finally, the nonroutine nature of the strategic planning process means that the demands for this information occur infrequently.

The information needs for the operational control area stand in sharp contrast to those of strategic planning. The task orientation of operational control requires information of a well-defined and narrow scope. This information is quite detailed and arises largely from sources within the organization. Very frequent use is made of this information, and it must therefore be accurate.

The information requirements for management control fall between the extremes for operational control and strategic planning. In addition, it is important to recognize that much of the information relevant to management control is obtained through the process of interpersonal interaction.

In Table 1 we have summarized these general observations about the categories of management activity. This summary is subject to the same limitations and uncertainties which are exhibited by the concepts of management control, strategic planning, and operational control. Nonetheless, it does underscore our contention that because the activities themselves are different, the information requirements to support them are also different.

This summary of information requirements suggests the reason why many organizations have found it increasingly difficult to realize some of their long-range plans for information systems. Many of these plans are based on the "total systems approach." Some of the proponents of this approach advocate that systems throughout the organization be tightly linked, with the output of one becoming the direct input of another, and that the whole structure be built on the detailed data used for controlling opera-

[6] *Ibid.,* p. 69.

TABLE 1   Information Requirements by Decision Category

Characteristics of Information	Operational Control	Management Control	Strategic Planning
Source	Largely internal ⟶		➤ External
Scope	Well defined, narrow ⟶		➤ Very wide
Level of aggregation	Detailed ⟶		➤ Aggregate
Time horizon	Historical ⟶		➤ Future
Currency	Highly current ⟶		➤ Quite old
Required accuracy	High ⟶		➤ Low
Frequency of use	Very frequent ⟶		➤ Infrequent

tions.[7] In doing so, they are suggesting an approach to systems design that is at best uneconomic and at worst based on a serious misconception. The first major problem with this view is that it does not recognize the ongoing nature of systems development in the operational control area. There is little reason to believe that the systems work in any major organization will be complete within the foreseeable future. To say that management information systems activity must wait "until we get our operational control systems in hand" is to say that efforts to assist management with systems support will be deferred indefinitely.

The second and perhaps most serious problem with this total systems view is that it fails to represent properly the information needs of the management control and strategic planning activities. Neither of these areas *necessarily* needs information that is a mere aggregation of data from the operational control data base. In many cases, if such a link is needed, it is more cost effective to use sampling from this data base and other statistical techniques to develop the required information. In our opinion, it rarely makes sense to couple managers in the management control and strategic planning areas directly with the masses of detailed data required for operational control. Not only is direct coupling un-

necessary, but it also can be an expensive and difficult technical problem.

For these reasons it is easy to understand why so many companies have had the following experience. Original plans for operational control systems were met with more or less difficulty, but as time passed it became increasingly apparent that the planned systems for higher management were not being developed on schedule, if at all. To make matters worse, the systems which were developed for senior management had relatively little impact on the way in which the managers made decisions. This last problem is a direct result of the failure to understand the basic information needs of the different activities.

We have tried to show in the above discussion how Anthony's classification of *managerial* activities is a useful one for people working in information systems design and implementation; we shall return later to consider in more detail some of the implications of his ideas.

In *The New Science of Management Decision,* Simon is concerned with the manner in which human beings solve problems regardless of their position within an organization. His distinction between "programmed" and "nonprogrammed" decisions is a useful one:

"Decisions are programmed to the extent that they are repetitive and routine, to the extent that a definite procedure has been worked out for handling them so that they don't have to be treated *de novo* each time they

[7]See, for example, J. L. Becker, "Planning the Total Information System," in A. D. Meacham and V. B. Thompson (eds.), *Total Systems* (New York: American Data Processing, 1962), pp. 66-73.

occur. . . . Decisions are non-programmed to the extent that they are novel, unstructured, and consequential. There is no cut-and-dried method of handling the problem because it hasn't arisen before, or because its precise nature and structure are elusive or complex, or because it is so important that it deserves a custom-tailored treatment. . . . By non-programmed I mean a response where the system has no specific procedure to deal with situations like the one at hand, but must fall back on whatever *general* capacity it has for intelligent, adaptive, problem-oriented action."[8]

We shall use the terms "structured" and "unstructured" for programmed and nonprogrammed because they imply less dependence on the computer and more dependence on the basic character of the problem-solving activity in question. The procedures, the kinds of computation, and the types of information vary depending on the extent to which the problem in question is unstructured. The basis for these differences is that in the unstructured case the human decision maker must provide judgment and evaluation as well as insights into problem definition. In a very structured situation, much if not all of the decision making process can be automated. Later in this paper we shall argue that systems built to support structured decision making will be significantly different from those designed to assist managers in dealing with unstructured problems. Further, we shall show that these differences can be traced to the character of the models which are relevant to each of these problems and the way in which these models are developed.

This focus on decisions requires an understanding of the human decision making process. Research on human problem solving supports Simon's claim that all problem solving can be broken down into three categories:

"The first phase of the decision-making process—searching the environment for conditions calling for decision—I shall call *intelligence* activity (borrowing the military meaning of intelligence). The second phase—inventing, developing, and analyzing possible courses of action—I shall call *design* activity. The third phase—selecting a course of action from those available—I shall call *choice* activity. . . . Generally speaking, intelligence activity precedes design, and design activity precedes choice. The cycle of phases is, however, far more complex than the sequence suggests. Each phase in making a particular decision is itself a complex decision-making process. The design phase, for example, may call for new intelligence activities; problems at any given level generate subproblems that in turn have their intelligence, design and choice phases, and so on. There are wheels within wheels. . . . Nevertheless, the three large phases are often clearly discernible as the organizational decision process unfolds. They are closely related to the stages in problem solving first described by John Dewey: 'What is the problem? What are the alternatives? Which alternative is best?' "[9]

A fully structured problem is one in which all three phases—intelligence, design, and choice—are structured. That is, we can specify algorithms, or decision rules, that will allow us to find the problem, design alternative solutions, and select the best solution. An example here might be the use of the classical economic order quantity (EOQ) formula on a

---

[8]H. A. Simon, *The New Science of Management Decision* (New York: Harper & Row, 1966), pp. 5-6.

[9]*Ibid.*, pp. 2-3.

straightforward inventory control problem. An unstructured problem is one in which none of the three phases is structured. Many job-shop scheduling problems are of this type.

In the ideas of Simon and Anthony, then, we have two different ways of looking at managerial activity within organizations. Anthony's categorization is based on the purpose of the management activity, whereas Simon's classification is based on the way in which the manager deals with the problems which confront him. The combination of these two views provides a useful framework within which to examine the purposes and problems of information systems activity. The essence of this combination is shown in Figure 1. The figure contains a class of decisions we have called "semi-structured"—decisions with one or two of the intelligence, design, and choice phases unstructured.

Decisions above the dividing line in Figure 1 are largely structured, and we shall call the information systems that support them "Structured Decision Systems" (SDS). Decisions below the line are largely unstructured, and their supporting information systems are "Decision Support Systems" (DSS). The SDS area encompasses almost all of what *has* been called Management Information Systems (MIS) in the literature—an area that has had almost nothing to do with real managers or information but has been largely routine data processing. We exclude from consideration here all of the *information handling* activities in an organization. A large percentage of computer time in many organizations is spent on straightforward data handling with no decisions, however structured, involved. The payroll application, for example, is a data handling operation.

In Figure 1, we have listed some examples in each of the six cells. It should be stressed, however, that these cells are not well-defined categories. Although this may sometimes cause prob-

lems, the majority of important decisions can be classified into their appropriate cell without difficulty.

DECISION MAKING WITHIN THE FRAMEWORK

PLANNING AND RESOURCE ALLOCATION DECISIONS

An immediate observation can be made about the framework we have presented. Almost all the so-called MIS activity has been directed at decisions in the structured half of the matrix (see Figure 1), specifically in the "operation control" cell. On the other hand, most of the areas of greatest concern to managers, areas where decisions have a significant effect on the company, are in the lower half of the matrix. That is, managers deal for the most part with unstructured decisions. This implies, of course, that computers and related systems which have so far been largely applied to the structured operational control area have not yet had any real impact on management decision making. The areas of high potential do not lie in bigger and better systems of the kind most companies now use. To have all the effort concentrated in only one of the six cells suggests at the very least a severe imbalance.

A second point to be noted on the planning question is the evolutionary nature of the line separating structured from unstructured decisions. This line is moving down over time. As we improve our understanding of a particular decision, we can move it above the line and allow the system to take care of it, freeing the manager for other tasks. For example, in previous years the inventory reordering decision in most organizations was made by a well-paid member of middle management. It was a decision that involved a high degree of skill and

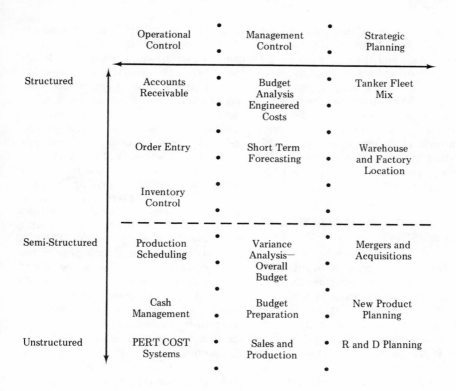

	Operational Control	Management Control	Strategic Planning
Structured	Accounts Receivable	Budget Analysis Engineered Costs	Tanker Fleet Mix
	Order Entry	Short Term Forecasting	Warehouse and Factory Location
	Inventory Control		
Semi-Structured	Production Scheduling	Variance Analysis— Overall Budget	Mergers and Acquisitions
	Cash Management	Budget Preparation	New Product Planning
Unstructured	PERT COST Systems	Sales and Production	R and D Planning

FIGURE 1. Information Systems: A Framework

could have a significant effect on the profits of the organization. Today this decision has moved from the unstructured operational control area to the structured. We have a set of decision rules (the EOQ formula) which on average do a better job for the standard items than most human decision makers. This movement of the line does not imply any replacement of managers since we are dealing with an almost infinite set of problems. For every one we solve, there are 10 more demanding our attention.

It is worth noting that the approach taken in building systems in the unstructured area hastens this movement of the line because it focuses our analytical

attention on decisions and decision rules. We would therefore expect a continuing flow of decisions across the line, or at least into the "grey" semi-structured decision area.

Through the development of a model of a given problem solving process for a decision in one of the cells, we can establish the character of each of the three phases. To the extent that any of these phases can be structured, we can design direct systems support. For those aspects of the process which are unstructured (given our current understanding of the situation), we would call on the manager to provide the necessary analysis. Thus a problem might be broken down into a set of related subproblems, some of which are "solved" automatically by the system and the remainder by the user alone or with varying degrees of computational and display support. Regardless of the resulting division of labor, however, it is essential that a model of the decision process be constructed *prior* to the system design. It is only in this way that a good perspective on the potential application of systems support can be ascertained.

STRUCTURED/UNSTRUCTURED DECISIONS

Information systems ought to be centered around the important decisions of the organization, many of which are relatively unstructured. It is therefore essential that models be built of the decision process involved. Model development is fundamental because it is a prerequisite for the analysis of the value of information, and because it is the key to understanding which portions of the decision process can be supported or automated. Both the successes and failures in the current use of computers can be understood largely in terms of the difficulty of this model development.

Our discussion of Structured Decision Systems showed that the vast majority of the effort (and success) has been in the area of structured operational control where there is relatively little ambiguity as to the goals sought. For example, the typical inventory control problem can be precisely stated, and it is clear what the criterion is by which solutions are to be judged. Hence we have an easily understood optimization problem. This type of problem lends itself to the development of formal "scientific" models, such as those typical of operations research.

Another important characteristic of problems of this type is that they are to a large extent "organization independent."

By this we mean that the essential aspects of the problem tend to be the same in many organizations, although the details may differ. This generality has two important effects. First, it encourages widespread interest and effort in the development of solutions to the problem. Second, it makes the adaptation of general models to the situation in a particular organizational setting relatively easy.

The situation with regard to areas of management decision making is quite different. To the extent that a given problem is semi-structured or unstructured, there is an absence of a routine procedure for dealing with it. There is also a tendency toward ambiguity in the problem definition because of the lack of formalization of any or all of the intelligence, design, or choice phases. Confusion may exist as to the appropriate criterion for evaluating solutions, or as to the means for generating trial solutions to the problem. In many cases, this uncertainty contributes to the perception of problems of this type as being unique to a given organization.

In general, then, we can say that the information systems problem in the structured operational control area is basically that of implementing a given general model in a certain organizational context. On the other hand, work in the unstructured areas is much more involved with model development and formalization. Furthermore, the source of the models in the former case is apt to be the operations research or management science literature. In the latter case, the relevant models are most often the unverbalized models used by the managers of the organization. This suggests that the procedure for the development of systems, the types of systems, and the skills of the analysts involved may be quite different in the two areas.

Although the evolution of information systems activities in most organizations has led to the accumulation of a variety of technical skills, the impact of computers on the way in which top managers make decisions has been minimal. One major reason for this is that the support of these decision makers is not principally a technical problem. If it were, it would have been solved. Certainly there are technical problems associated with work in these problem areas, but the technology and the technological skills in most large organizations are more than sufficient. The missing ingredient, apart from the basic awareness of the problem, is the skill to elicit from management its view of the organization and its environment, and to formalize models of this view.

To improve the quality of decisions, a systems designer can seek to improve the quality of the information inputs or to change the decision process, or both. Because of the existence of a variety of optimization models for operational control problems, there is a tendency to emphasize improvement of the information inputs at the expense of improvement in the decision making process. Although this emphasis is appropriate for structured operational control problems, it can retard progress in developing support for unstructured problem solving. The difficulty with this view is that it tends to attribute low quality in management decision making to low quality information inputs. Hence, systems are designed to supply more current, more accurate, or more detailed information.

While improving the quality of information available to managers may improve the quality of their decisions, we do not believe that major advances will be realized in this way.[10] Most managers do not have great informational needs. Rather, they have need of new methods to understand and process the information already available to them. Generally

speaking, the models that they employ in dealing with this information are very primitive, and as a result, the range of responses that they can generate is very limited. For example, many managers employ simple historical models in their attempts to anticipate the future.[11] Further, these models are static in nature, although the processes they purport to represent are highly dynamic. In such a situation, there is much more to be gained by improving the information processing ability of managers in order that they may deal effectively with the information that they already have, than by adding to the reams of data confronting them, or by improving the quality of those data.[12]

If this view is correct, it suggests that the Decision Support Systems area is important and that these systems may best be built by people other than those currently involved in the operational control systems area. The requisite skills are those of the model building based on close interaction with management, structuring and formalizing the procedures employed by managers, and segregating those aspects of the decision process which can be automated. In addition, systems in this area must be able to assist the evolution of the manager's decision making ability through increasing his understanding of the environment. Hence, one important role of a DSS is educative. Even in areas in which we cannot structure the decision process, we can provide models of the environment from which the manager can develop insights into the relationship of his decisions to the goals he wishes to achieve.

In discussing models and their importance to systems in the DSS area, we

[10]See R. Ackoff, "Management Misinformation Systems," *Management Science*, Vol. 11, No. 4 (Dec. 1967), B147-B156.

[11]W. F. Pounds, "The Process of Problem Finding," *Industrial Management Review*, Vol. 11, No. 1 (Fall 1969), pp. 1-20.

[12]G. A. Gorry, "The Development of Managerial Models," *Sloan Management Review*, Vol. 12, No. 2 (Winter 1971), pp. 1-16.

should place special emphasis on the role which the manager assumes in the process of model building. To a large extent, he is the source upon which the analyst draws. That is, although a repertoire of "operations research" models may be very valuable for the analyst, his task is not simply to impose a model on the situation. These models may be the building blocks. The analyst and the manager in concert develop the final structure. This implies that the analyst must possess a certain empathy for the manager, and *vice versa*. Whether the current systems designers in a given organization possess this quality is a question worthy of consideration by management.

This approach in no way precludes normative statements about decision procedures. The emphasis on the development of descriptive models of managerial problem solving is only to ensure that the existing situation is well understood by both the analyst and the manager. Once this understanding has been attained, various approaches to improving the process can be explored. In fact, a major benefit of developing descriptive models of this type is the exposure of the decision making process to objective analysis.

In summary then, we have asserted that there are two sets of implications which flow from our use of this framework. The first set centers on an organization's planning and resource allocation decision in relation to information systems. The second set flows from the distinction we have drawn between structured and unstructured types of decisions. The focus of our attention should be on the critical *decisions* in an organization and on explicit modeling of these decisions prior to the design of information systems support.

The second major point in relation to the structured/unstructured dimension that we have raised is that the kinds of implementation problems, the skills required by the managers and analysts, and

the characteristics of the design process are different above and below the dashed line in Figure 1. In discussing these differences, we have tried to stress the fundamental shift in approach that is required if Decision Support Systems are to be built in a way that makes them effective in an organization. The approach and technology that have been used over the last 15 years to build information systems in the structured operational control area are often inappropriate in the case of Decision Support Systems.

IMPLICATIONS OF THE FRAMEWORK

SYSTEM DESIGN DIFFERENCES

The decision categories we have borrowed from Anthony have a set of implications distinct from those discussed in connection with the structured and unstructured areas. The first of these has to do with the systems design differences that follow from supporting decisions in the three areas.

As was seen earlier, information requirements differ sharply among the three areas. There are few occasions in which it makes sense to connect systems directly across boundaries. Aggregating the detailed accounting records (used in operational control) to provide a base for a five-year sales forecast (required for a strategic planning decision) is an expensive and unnecessary process. We can often sample, estimate, or otherwise obtain data for use in strategic planning without resorting to the operational control data base. This does not imply that we should *never* use such a data base, but merely that it is not necessarily the best way of obtaining the information.

This point is also relevant in the collection and maintenance of data. Techniques appropriate for operational control, such as the use of on-line data collection terminals, are rarely justified for strategic planning systems. Similarly, elaborate environmental sampling methods may be critical for an operational control decision. In looking at each of the information characteristics in Table 1, it is apparent that quite different data bases will be required to support decisions in the three areas. Therefore, the first implication of the decision classification in our framework is that the "totally-integrated-management-information-systems" ideas so popular in the literature are a poor design concept. More particularly, the "integrated" or "company-wide" data base is a misleading notion, and even if it could be achieved would be exorbitantly expensive.

Information differences among the three decision areas also imply related differences in hardware and software requirements. On the one hand, strategic planning decisions require access to a data base which is used infrequently and may involve an interface with a variety of complex models. Operational control decisions, on the other hand, often require a larger data base with continuous updating and frequent access to current information.

DIFFERENCES IN ORGANIZATIONAL STRUCTURE

A second distinction is in the organizational structure and the managerial and analyst skills which will be involved across the three areas. The managerial talents required, as well as the numbers and training of the managers involved, differ sharply for these categories. The process of deciding on key problems that might be worth supporting with a formal system is a much smaller, tighter process in the strategic planning area than in the operational control area. The decision to be supported is probably not a recurring one and will normally not involve changes in the procedures and structure employed by the remainder of the firm. Because it is a relatively isolated decision in both time and scope, it need not involve as many people. However, the process of defining the problem must be dominated by the managers involved if the right problem and hence the best model formulation are to be selected. Similarly, the implementation process must be tightly focused on the immediate problem. The skills required of the managers involved are analytical and reflective, rather than communicative and procedural. In the strategic planning case, the manager must supply both the problem definition and the key relationships that make up the model. This requires an ability to think logically and a familiarity with models and computation. In the case of operational control, the particular solution and the models involved are much more the concern of the technical specialist. This is not to say that in unstructured operational control the manager's judgment will not be involved in the process of solving problems. However, his role in *building* that model can be much more passive than in the strategic area.

The decision process, the implementation process, and the level of analytical sophistication of the managers (as opposed to the staff) in strategic planning all differ quite markedly from their counterparts in operational control. The decision makers in operational control have a more constrained problem. They have often had several years in which to define the general nature of the problem and to consider solutions. In addition, to the extent that these managers have a technical background, they are more likely to be familiar with the analysis involved in solving structured and unstructured problems. In any event, the nature of the operational control problem, its size, and the frequency of the decision all combine to produce design and implementation problems of a different variety. The managers involved in any given problem tend to be from the decision area in question, be it strategic planning, management control, or operational control. As a result, their training, background, and style of decision making are often different. This means that the types of models to be used, the method of elucidating these from the managers, and the skills of the analysts will differ across these three areas.

As the types of skills possessed by the managers differ, so will the kinds of systems analysts who can operate effectively. We have already distinguished between analysts who can handle structured as opposed to unstructured model building. There is a similar distinction to be made between the kind of person who can work well with a small group of senior managers (on either a structured or unstructured problem) and the person who is able to communicate with the various production personnel on an unstructured job-shop scheduling problem, for example.

In problems in the strategic area, the analyst has to be able to communicate effectively with the few managers who have the basic knowledge required to define the problem and its major variables. The skills required to do this include background and experience which are wide enough to match those of the line executives involved. Good communication depends on a common understanding of the basic variables involved, and few analysts involved in current MIS activity have this skill.

A breadth of background implies a wide repertoire of models with which the analyst is familiar. In the operational control area, an analyst can usefully specialize to great depth in a particular, narrow problem area. The depth, and the resulting improvement in the final system, often pays off because of the frequency with which the decision is made. In the strategic area the coverage of potential problems is enormous and the frequency of a particular decision relatively low. The range of models with which the analyst is familiar may be of greater benefit than depth in any one type.

In addition to the managerial and analyst issues raised above, there is a further difference in the way the information systems group is organized. A group dealing only with operational control problems would be structured differently and perhaps report to a different organizational position than a group working in all three areas. It is not our purpose here to go into detail on the organizational issues, but the material above suggests that on strategic problems, a task force reporting to the user and virtually independent of the computer group may make sense. The important issues are problem definition and problem structure; the implementation and computer issues are relatively simple by comparison. In management control, the single user, although still dominant in his application, has problems of interfacing with other users. An organizational design that encourages cross functional (marketing, production, distribution, etc.) cooperation is probably desirable. In operational control, the organizational design should include the user as a major influence, but he will have to be balanced with operational systems experts, and the whole group can quite possibly stay within functional boundaries. These examples are merely illustrative of the kind of organizational differences involved. Each organization has to examine its current status and needs and make structural changes in light of them.

MODEL DIFFERENCES

The third distinction flowing from the framework is among the types of models involved. Again looking at Table 1 and the information differences, it is clear that model requirements depend, for example, on the frequency of decisions in each area and their relative magnitude. A strategic decision to change the whole distribution system occurs rarely. It is significant in cost, perhaps hundreds of millions of dollars, and it therefore can support a complex model, but the model need not be efficient in any sense. An operational control decision, however, may be made frequently, perhaps daily. The impact of each decision is small but the cumulative impact can involve large sums of money. Models for the decision may have to be efficient in running time, have ready access to current data, and be structured so as to be easily changed. Emphasis has to be on simplicity of building, careful attention to modularity, and so forth.

The sources of models for operational control are numerous. There is a history of activity, the problems are often similar across organizations, and the literature is extensive. In strategic planning, and to a lesser extent management control, we are still in the early stages of development. Our models tend to be individual and have to come from the managers involved. It is a model creation process as opposed to the application of a model.

In summary then, we have outlined implications for the organization which follow from the three major decision categories in the framework. We have posed the issues in terms of operational control and strategic planning, and with every point we assume that management control lies somewhere in between the two. The three major implications we have discussed are the advisability of following the integrated data base path; the differences in managerial and analyst skills as well as the appropriate forms of organizational structure for building systems in the three areas; and differences in the types of models involved. Distinguishing among decision areas is clearly important if an organization is going to be successful in its use of information systems.

SUMMARY

The information systems field absorbs a significant percentage of the resources of many organizations. Despite these expenditures, there is very little perspective on the field and the issues within it. As a result, there has been a tendency to make incremental improvements to existing systems. The framework we suggest for looking at decisions within an organization provides one perspective on the information systems issues. From this perspective, it becomes clear that our planning for information systems has resulted in a heavy concentration in the operational control area. In addition, there is a series of implications for the organization which flows from the distinction between the decision areas. Model structure and the implementation process differ sharply between the structured and unstructured areas. Data base concepts, types of analysts and managers, and organizational structure all differ along the Strategic Planning to Operational Control axis.

We believe that each organization must share *some* common framework among its members if it is to plan and make resource allocation decisions which result in effective use of information systems. We suggest that the framework that has been presented here is an appropriate place to start.

REFERENCES

Ackoff, R. "Management Misinformation Systems," *Management Science,* Vol. 11, no. 4 (December 1967), pp. B147-B156.

Anthony, R. N. *Planning and Control Systems: A Framework for Analysis.* Boston, Harvard University Graduate School of Business Administration, 1965.

Becker, J. L. "Planning the Total Information System." In: A. D. Meacham and V. B. Thompson (eds.), *Total Systems,* pp. 66-73. New York, American Data Processing, 1962.

Gorry, G. A. "The Development of Managerial Models," *Sloan Management Review,* Vol. 12, no. 2 (Winter 1971), pp. 1-16.

Pounds, W. F. "The Process of Problem Finding," *Industrial Management Review,* Vol. 11, no. 1 (Fall 1969), pp. 1-20.

Scott Morton, M.S. *Management Decision Systems.* Boston, Harvard University Graduate School of Business Administration, 1971.

Simon, H. A. *The New Science of Management Decision.* New York, Harper & Row, 1960.

Soelberg, P. O. "Unprogrammed Decision Making," *Industrial Management Review,* Vol. 8, no. 2 (Spring 1967), pp. 19-30.

Taylor, J. W., and Dean, N. J. "Managing to Manage the Computer," *Harvard Business Review,* Vol. 44, no. 5 (September-October 1966), pp. 98-110.

Management Misinformation Systems

Russell L. Ackoff

University of Pennsylvania

Five assumptions commonly made by designers of management information systems are identified. It is argued that these are not justified in many (if not most) cases and hence lead to major deficiencies in the resulting systems. These assumptions are: (1) the critical deficiency under which most managers operate is the lack of relevant information, (2) the manager needs the information he wants, (3) if a manager has the information he needs, his decision making will improve, (4) better communication between managers improves organizational performance, and (5) a manager does not have to understand how his information system works, only how to use it. To overcome these assumptions and the deficiencies which result from them, a management information system should be embedded in a management control system. A procedure for designing such a system is proposed and an example is given of the type of control system which it produces.

Reprinted from *Management Science,* XIV, No. 4 (December, 1967), 147-56. Used by permission of Russell L. Ackoff and *Management Science.*

The growing preoccupation of operations researchers and management scientists with Management Information Systems (MIS's) is apparent. In fact, for some the design of such systems has almost become synonymous with operations research or management science. Enthusiasm for such systems is understandable: It involves the researcher in a romantic relationship with the most glamorous instrument of our time, the computer. Such enthusiasm is understandable, but, nevertheless, some of the excesses to which it has led are not excusable.

Contrary to the impression produced by the growing literature, few computerized management information systems have been put into operation. Of those I've seen that have been implemented, most have not matched expectations and some have been outright failures. I believe that these near-and far-misses could have been avoided if certain false (and usually implicit) assumptions on which many such systems have been erected had not been made.

There seem to be five common and erroneous assumptions underlying the design of most MIS's, each of which I will consider. After doing so, I will outline an MIS design procedure which avoids these assumptions.

GIVE THEM MORE

Most MIS's are designed on the assumption that the critical deficiency under which most managers operate is the *lack of relevant information*. I do not deny that most managers lack a good deal of information that they should have, but I do deny that this is the most important informational deficiency from which they suffer. It seems to me that they suffer more from an *overabundance of irrelevant information*.

This is not a play on words. The consequences of changing the emphasis of an MIS from supplying relevant information to eliminating irrelevant information is considerable. If one is preoccupied with supplying relevant information, attention is almost exclusively given to the generation, storage, and retrieval of information: Hence emphasis is placed on constructing data banks, coding, indexing, updating files, access languages, and so on. The ideal which has emerged from this orientation is an infinite pool of data into which a manager can reach to pull out any information he wants. If, on the other hand, one sees the manager's information problem primarily, but not exclusively, as one that arises out of an overabundance of irrelevant information, most of which was not asked for, then the two most important functions of an information system become *filtration* (or evaluation) and *condensation*. The literature on MIS's seldom refers to these functions, let alone considers how to carry them out.

My experience indicates that most managers receive much more data (if not information) than they can possibly absorb even if they spend all of their time trying to do so. Hence they already suffer from an information overload. They must spend a great deal of time separating the relevant from the irrelevant and searching for the kernels in the relevant documents. For example, I have found that I receive an average of forty-three hours of unsolicited reading material each week. The solicited material is usually half again this amount.

I have seen a daily stock status report that consists of approximately six hundred pages of computer print-out. The report is circulated daily across managers' desks. I've also seen requests for major capital expenditures that come in book size, several of which are distributed to managers each week. It is not uncommon for many managers to receive an average of one journal a day or more. One could go on and on.

Unless the information overload to which managers are subjected is reduced, any additional information made available by an MIS cannot be expected to be used effectively.

Even relevant documents have too much redundancy. Most documents can be considerably condensed without loss of content. My point here is best made, perhaps, by describing briefly an experiment that a few of my colleagues and I conducted on the OR literature several years ago. By using a panel of well-known experts, we identified four OR articles that all members of the panel considered to be "above average," and four articles that were considered to be "below average." The authors of the eight articles were asked to prepare "objective" examinations (duration thirty minutes) plus answers for graduate students who were to be assigned the articles for reading. (The authors were not informed about the experiment.) Then several experienced writers were asked to reduce each article to two thirds and one third of its original length only by eliminating words. They also prepared a brief abstract of each article. Those who did the condensing did not see the examinations to be given to the students.

A group of graduate students who had not previously read the articles were then selected. Each one was given four articles randomly selected, each of which was in one of its four versions: 100 per cent, 67 per cent, 33 per cent, or abstract. Each version of each article was read by two students. All were given the same examinations. The average scores on the examinations were then compared.

For the above-average articles there was no significant difference between average test scores for the 100 per cent, 67 per cent, and 33 per cent versions, but there was a significant decrease in average test scores for those who had read only the abstract. For the below-average articles there was no difference in average test scores among those who had read the 100 per cent, 67 per cent, and 33 per cent versions, but there was a significant *increase* in average test scores of those who had read only the abstract.

The sample used was obviously too small for general conclusions, but the results strongly indicate the extent to which even good writing can be condensed without loss of information. I refrain from drawing the obvious conclusion about bad writing.

It seems clear that condensation as well as filtration, performed mechanically or otherwise, should be an essential part of an MIS, and that such a system should be capable of handling much, if not all, of the unsolicited as well as solicited information that a manager receives.

THE MANAGER NEEDS THE INFORMATION THAT HE WANTS

Most MIS designers "determine" what information is needed by asking managers what information they would like to have. This is based on the assumption that managers know what information they need and want it.

For a manager to know what information he needs, he must be aware of each type of decision he should make (as well as does), and he must have an adequate model of each. These conditions are seldom satisfied. Most managers have some conception of at least some of the types of decisions they must make. Their conceptions, however, are likely to be deficient in a very critical way, a way that follows from an important principle of scientific economy: The less we understand a phenomenon, the more variables we require to explain it. Hence, the manager who does not understand the phenomenon he controls plays it "safe" and, with respect to information, wants "everything." The MIS designer, who has even less understanding of the relevant phenomenon than the manager, tries to provide even more than everything. He thereby increases what is already an overload of irrelevant information.

For example, market researchers in a major oil company once asked their marketing managers what variables they thought were relevant in estimating the sales volume of future service stations. Almost seventy variables were identified. The market researchers then added about half again this many variables and performed a large multiple linear regression analysis of sales of existing stations against these variables and found about thirty-five to be statistically significant. A forecasting equation was based on this analysis. An OR team subsequently constructed a model based on only one of these variables, traffic flow, which predicted sales better than the thirty-five variable regression equation. The team went on to *explain* sales at service stations in terms of the customers' perception of the amount of time lost by stopping for service. The relevance of all but a few of the variables used by the market researchers could be explained by their effect on such perception.

The moral is simple: One cannot specify what information is required for decision making until an explanatory model of the decision process and the system involved has been constructed and tested. Information systems are subsystems of control systems. They cannot be designed adequately without taking control into account. Furthermore, whatever else regression analyses can yield, they cannot yield understanding and explana-

tion of phenomena. They describe and, at best, predict.

GIVE A MANAGER THE INFORMATION HE NEEDS AND HIS DECISION MAKING WILL IMPROVE

It is frequently assumed that if a manager is provided with the information he needs, he will then have no problem in using it effectively. The history of OR stands to the contrary. For example, give most managers an initial tableau of a typical "real" mathematical programming, sequencing, or network problem and see how close they come to an optimal solution. If their experience and judgment have any value, they may not do badly, but they will seldom do very well. In most management problems there are too many possibilities to expect experience, judgment, or intuition to provide good guesses, even with perfect information.

Furthermore, when several probabilities are involved in a problem, the unguided mind of even a manager has difficulty in aggregating them in a valid way. We all know many simple problems in probability in which untutored intuition usually does very badly (e.g., What are the correct odds that two of twenty-five people selected at random will have their birthdays on the same day of the year?). For example, very few of the results obtained by queuing theory, when arrivals and service are probabilistic, are obvious to managers; nor are the results of risk analysis where the managers' own subjective estimates of probabilities are used.

The moral: It is necessary to determine how well managers can use needed information. When, because of the complexity of the decision process, they can't use it well, they should be provided with either decision rules or performance feedback so that they can identify and learn from their mistakes. More on this point later.

MORE COMMUNICATION MEANS BETTER PERFORMANCE

One characteristic of most MIS's which I have seen is that they provide managers with better current information about what other managers and their departments and divisions are doing. Underlying this provision is the belief that better interdepartmental communication enables managers to coordinate their decisions more effectively and, hence, improves the organization's overall performance. Not only is this not necessarily so, but it seldom is so. One would hardly expect two competing companies to become more cooperative because the information each acquires about the other is improved. This analogy is not as far-fetched as one might first suppose. For example, consider the following very much simplified version of a situation I once ran into. The simplification of the case does not affect any of its essential characteristics.

A department store has two "line" operations: buying and selling. Each function is performed by a separate department. The Purchasing Department primarily controls one variable: how much of each item is bought. The Merchandising Department controls the price at which it is sold. Typically, the measure of performance applied to the Purchasing Department was the turnover rate of inventory. The measure applied to the Merchandising Department was gross sales; this department sought to maximize the number of items sold times their price.

Now by examining a single item, let us consider what happens in this system. The merchandising manager, using his knowledge of competition and consumption, set a price which he judged would maximize gross sales. In doing so he utilized price-demand curves for each type of item. For each price the curves show the expected sales and values on an upper and lower confidence band as well (see Figure 1).

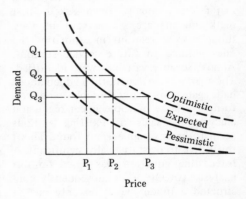

FIGURE 1.   Price-demand curve

When instructing the Purchasing Department how many items to make available, the merchandising manager quite naturally used the value on the upper confidence curve. This minimized the chances of his running short which, if it occurred, would hurt his performance. It also maximized the chances of being overstocked, but this was not his concern—only the purchasing manager's. Say, therefore, that the merchandising manager initially selected price P_1 and requested that amount Q_1 be made available by the Purchasing Department.

In this company the purchasing manager also had access to the price-demand curves. He knew the merchandising manager always ordered optimistically.

Therefore, using the same curve he read over from Q_1 to the upper limit and down to the expected value from which he obtained Q_2, the quantity he actually intended to make available. He did not intend to pay for the merchandising manager's optimism. If merchandising ran out of stock, it was not his worry. Now the merchandising manager was informed about what the purchasing manager had done, so he adjusted his price to P_2. The purchasing manager, in turn, was told that the merchandising manager had made this readjustment so he planned to make only Q_3 available. If this process—made possible only by perfect communication between departments—had been allowed to continue, nothing would have been bought and nothing would have been sold. This outcome was avoided by prohibiting communication between the two departments and forcing each to guess what the other was doing.

I have obviously caricatured the situation in order to make the point clear: When organizational units have inappropriate measures of performance which put them in conflict with each other, as is often the case, communication between them may hurt organizational performance, not help it. Organizational structure and performance measurement must be taken into account before opening the flood gates and permitting the free flow of information between parts of the organization. (A more rigorous discussion of organizational structure and the relationship of communication to it can be found in the Sengupta-Ackoff reference, listed at the end of this article.)

A MANAGER DOES NOT HAVE TO UNDERSTAND HOW AN INFORMATION SYSTEM WORKS, ONLY HOW TO USE IT

Most MIS designers seek to make their systems as innocuous and unobtrusive as possible to managers lest they become frightened. The designers try to provide managers with very easy access to the system and assure them that they need to know nothing more about it. The designers usually succeed in keeping managers ignorant in this regard. This leaves managers unable to evaluate the MIS as a whole. It often makes them afraid to even try to do so lest they display their ignorance publicly. In failing to evaluate their MIS, managers delegate much of the control of the organization to the system's designers and operators who may have many virtues, but managerial competence is seldom among them.

Let me cite a case in point. A chairman of a board of a medium-size company asked for help on the following problem. One of his larger (decentralized) divisions had installed a computerized production-inventory control and manufacturing-manager information system about a year earlier. It had acquired about $2,000,000 worth of equipment to do so. The board chairman had just received a request from the division for permission to replace the original equipment with newly announced equipment which would cost several times the original amount. An extensive "justification" for so doing was provided with the request. The chairman wanted to know whether the request was really justified. He admitted to complete incompetence in this connection.

A meeting was arranged at the division at which I was subjected to an extended and detailed briefing. The system was large but relatively simple. At the heart of it was a reorder point for each item and a maximum allowable stock level. Reorder quantities took lead-time as well as the allowable maximum into account. The computer kept track of stock, ordered items when required, and generated numerous reports on both the state of the system it controlled and its own "actions."

When the briefing was over I was asked if I had any questions. I did. First I asked if, when the system had been installed, there had been many parts whose stock level exceeded the maximum amount possible under the new system. I was told there were many. I asked for a list of about thirty and for some graph paper. Both were provided. With the help of the system designer and volumes of old daily reports I began to plot the stock level of the first listed item over time. When this item reached the maximum "allowable" stock level it had been reordered. The system designer was surprised and said that by sheer "luck" I had found one of the few errors made by the system. Continued plotting showed that because of repeated premature reordering, the item had never gone much below the maximum stock level. Clearly the program was confusing the maximum allowable stock level and the reorder point. This turned out to be the case in more than half of the items on the list.

Next I asked if they had many paired parts, ones that were only used with each other, for example, matched nuts and bolts. They had many. A list was produced, and we began checking the previous day's withdrawals. For more than half of the pairs the differences in the numbers recorded as withdrawn were very large. No explanation was provided.

Before the day was out it was possible to show by some quick and dirty calculations that the new computerized system was costing the company almost $150,000 per month more than the hand system which it had replaced, most of this in excess inventories.

The recommendation was that the system be redesigned as quickly as possible and that the new equipment not be authorized for the time being.

The questions asked of the system had been obvious and simple ones. Managers should have been able to ask them but—and this is the point—they felt themselves incompetent to do so. They would not have allowed a hand-operated system to get so far out of their control.

No MIS should ever be installed unless the managers for whom it is intended are trained to evaluate and hence control it rather than be controlled by it.

A SUGGESTED PROCEDURE FOR DESIGNING AN MIS

The erroneous assumptions I have tried to reveal in the preceding discussion can, I believe, be avoided by an appropriate design procedure. One is briefly outlined here.

1. Analysis of the Decision System

Each (or at least each important) type of managerial decision required by the organization under study should be identified, and the relationships between them should be determined and flow-charted. Note that this is *not* necessarily the same thing as determining what decisions *are* made. For example, in one company I found that make-or-buy decisions concerning parts were made only at the time when a part was introduced into stock and were never subsequently reviewed. For some items this decision had gone unreviewed for as many as twenty years. Obviously, such decisions should be made more often; in some cases, every time an order is placed in order to take account of current shop loading, underused shifts, delivery times from suppliers, and so on.

Decision-flow analyses are usually self-justifying. They often reveal important decisions that are being made by default (e.g., the make-buy decision referred to above), and they disclose interdependent decisions that are being made independently. Decision-flow charts frequently suggest changes in managerial responsibility, organizational structure, and measure of performance which can correct the types of deficiencies cited.

Decision analyses can be conducted with varying degrees of detail; that is, they may be anywhere from coarse to fine grained. How much detail one should become involved with depends on the amount of time and resources that are available for the analysis. Although practical considerations frequently restrict initial analyses to a particular organizational function, it is preferable to perform a coarse analysis of all of an organization's managerial functions rather than a fine analysis of one or a subset of functions. It is easier to introduce finer information into an integrated information system than it is to combine fine subsystems into one integrated system.

2. An Analysis of Information Requirements

Managerial decisions can be classified into three types:

1. Decisions for which adequate models are available or can be constructed and from which optimal (or near optimal) solutions can be derived. In such cases the decision process itself should be incorporated into the information system, thereby converting it (at least partially) to a control system. A decision model identifies what information is required and, hence, what information is relevant.

2. Decisions for which adequate models can be constructed but from which optimal solutions cannot be extracted. Here some kind of heuristic or search procedure should be provided, even if it consists of no more than computerized trial and error. A simulation of the model will, as a minimum, permit comparison of proposed alternative solutions. Here too the model specifies what information is required.

3. Decisions for which adequate models cannot be constructed. Research is required here to determine what information is relevant. If decision making cannot be delayed for the completion of such research or the decision's effect is not large enough to justify the cost of research, then judgment must be used to "guess" what information is relevant. It may be possible to make explicit the implicit model used by the decision maker and treat it as a model of type (2).

In each of these three types of situations it is necessary to provide feedback by comparing actual decision outcomes with those predicted by the model or decision maker. Each decision that is made, along with its predicted outcome, should be an essential input to a management control system. I shall return to this point below.

3. Aggregation of Decisions

Decisions with the same or largely overlapping informational requirements should be grouped together as a single manager's task. This will reduce the information a manager requires to do his job and is likely to increase his understanding of it. This may require a reorganization of the system. Even if such a reorganization cannot be implemented completely, what can be done is likely to improve performance significantly and reduce the information loaded on managers.

4. Design of Information Processing

Now the procedure for collecting, storing, retrieving, and treating information can be designed. Since there is a voluminous literature on this subject, I shall leave it at this except for one point. Such a system must not only be able to answer questions addressed to it; it should also be able to answer questions that have not been asked by reporting any deviations from expectations. An extensive exception-reporting system is required.

5. Design of Control of the Control System

It must be assumed that the system that is being designed will be deficient in many and significant ways. Therefore it is necessary to identify the ways in which it may be deficient, to design procedures for detecting its deficiencies and for correcting the system so as to remove or reduce them. Hence the system should be designed to be flexible and adaptive. This is little more than a platitude, but it has a not-so-obvious implication. No completely computerized system can be as flexible and adaptive as can a man-machine system. This is illustrated by a concluding example of a system that is being developed and is partially in operation (see Figure 2).

The company involved has its market divided into approximately two hundred marketing areas. A model for each has been constructed as is "in" the computer. On the basis of competitive intelligence supplied to the service marketing manager by marketing researchers and information

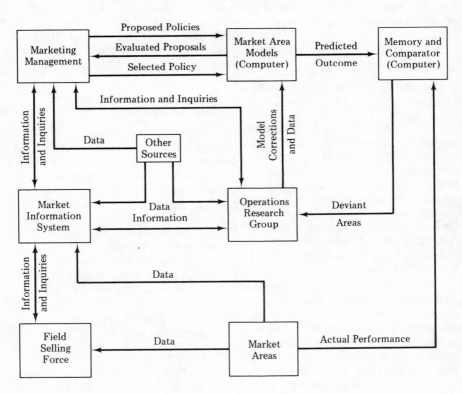

FIGURE 2.   Simplified diagram of a market-area control system

specialists, he and his staff make policy decisions for each area each month. Their tentative decisions are fed into the computer which yields a forecast of expected performance. Changes are made until the expectations match what is desired. In this way they arrive at "final" decisions. At the end of the month the computer compares the actual performance of each area with what was predicted. If a deviation exceeds what could be expected by chance, the company's OR group then seeks the reason for the deviation, performing as much research as is required to find it. If the cause is found to be permanent, the computerized model is adjusted appropriately. The result is an adaptive man-machine system whose precision and generality is continuously increasing with use.

Finally, it should be noted that in carrying out the design steps enumerated above, three groups should collaborate: information systems specialists, operations researchers, *and managers.* The participation of managers in the design of a system that is to serve them assures their ability to evaluate its performance by comparing its output with what was predicted. Managers who are not willing to invest some of their time in this process are not likely to use a management control system well, and their system, in turn, is likely to abuse them.

REFERENCE

1. Sengupta, S.S., and R.L. Ackoff, "Systems Theory from an Operations Research Point of View," *IEEE Transactions on Systems Science and Cybernetics,* I (November, 1965), 9-13.

Dana Corporation

Business Week

Management information systems should be uncomplicated. Witness the reduction of management staff and savings of millions of dollars when Dana Corporation replaced stacks of endless paperwork with television.

Reprinted from *Business Week,* January 30, 1971, 48 and 50. Used by permission of *Business Week.*

"When I threw all the paperwork away and threw out the procedure book, I was scared," admits Rene C. McPherson, the 45-year-old president of Dana Corp. "Would we lose control?"

For more than two years, McPherson has been injecting a bracing dose of autonomy into the 19 operating divisions of his Toledo-based truck and auto parts company. He has also beaten back a blizzard of paper that he felt had been snowing the company under. Control, however, has not been lost. A four-channel, closed-circuit television system has replaced the mounds of paperwork and gives top executives a simplified—though essentially complete—look at Dana's daily performance. The moves, if anything, have strengthened the control mechanism available to McPherson and his headquarters executives. The result is an uncomplicated management information system.

"Not only did we have the expense of doing all that paperwork," recalls McPherson, "it didn't solve any problems. We were so busy preparing figures that we weren't looking at them in time to take any remedial action."

New Tool

The new system is no piece of electronic wizardry tied on-line into the newest computer. Rather, the TV network that transmits vital company data onto screens in the offices of a dozen Dana executives is simply a tool to wean key managers away from heaps of paperwork, much of it computer-generated. McPherson estimates that executives used to have to wade through a stack of paper 20 feet high each year.

But that has changed. Now, the eight divisions that account for 80% of the company's volume telephone or teletype daily sales and cost totals to headquarters. Other divisions submit the same data monthly. The information is then transferred to charts, which together with monthly sales and profit forecasts, are flashed onto the screens. The panoply of continually updated charts, tracing the performance of each division, is closeted away with a TV camera in a small, locked control room. A chart can be called up with the flick of a switch. On other channels, the executives can get current market results, leading national economic indicators, balance sheet ratios, the company's cash balance, and can compare, at a glance, sales and profit performance with forecasts and the past year's results. With this information, they can also determine if a division's performance is below par. Only then do corporate officers call for an explanation.

"So long as a division hits its profit goals, we couldn't care less about things such as individual expenses," says Stanley W. Gustafson, 40, Dana's vice-president and treasurer. "Why get all the detail when you're only going to look at it when things go bad anyway?"

Common III

The situation at Dana was similar to that confronting other corporations. As small companies become big ones, their volume of paperwork can grow proportionately faster than sales. Computers condense the paperwork to punched cards, magnetic tape, and printouts, but the tendency to get the most out of these machines sometimes creates even more paper. In time, desks are stacked with more printed information than could ever be read, and the management information that really counts is buried somewhere in piles of minutiae.

As Dana grew in volume from $393-million in 1960 to $688-million in 1970, a neatly indexed, three-inch-thick procedure book became the symbol of the stranglehold that paperwork had on the corporation. Even worse, McPherson contends, the creative talents of division managers were being stifled. They spent most of their time submitting picayune forms to headquarters. "It all tended to throttle the entrepreneurship of division managers, and it kept the swingers from swinging," he asserts.

After taking on the presidency in July, 1968, McPherson soon junked the procedure book. And he quickly gave division heads greater authority to make decisions without first submitting detailed accounts to higher-ups. His reforms have paid off handsomely. Last year, inflation, combined with limited sales growth, reduced earnings of many auto parts producers. But in fiscal 1970, ending Aug. 31, Dana increased its profits by 4% on a sales advance of only 1%. Part of this was due to McPherson's cuts of paperwork and administrative personnel, which reduced expenses last year in that area alone by $2.3-million.

The pruning process has not been easy. Company accountants cringed when McPherson scuttled a 5-inch-thick annual budget, which listed, by hundreds of individual accounts, each division's projected expenditures for the coming year. McPherson insists it never was read. Moreover, even with computer assistance, the budget was never completed until the end of the first quarter, he says.

Dropping the budget also made it possible to scrap the nitpicking monthly expense reports that executives got from the division chiefs. Through some 140 separate accounts, each division's monthly expenditures were compared item by item with what the budget forecast. If an item was off target, the division manager had to explain why in his report. "We threw out the traditional budgets because they became excuse sheets," remarks Gustafson. "Going through all those explanations never made us a penny."

Simpler Plans

Division managers now submit annual plans in which projected total sales, operating expenses, profits, and capital expenditures are set forth in four or five concisely written pages. After getting higher-echelon approval, managers are free to spend the authorized sums virtually as they see fit. "Our point of control is in delegating big chunks of money to the divisions, and not determining if one needs a desk more than the other needs a drinking fountain," Gustafson insists.

For many of the same reasons detailed sales projections listing individual products and buyers also were shelved, along with the monthly personnel reports and itemized control reports. Corporate executives had considered the control reports especially annoying. They contained financial information—such as profit and loss statements, balance sheets, a detailed inventory listing, and a complete breakdown of capital spending and requests—spewed out every month by each of Dana's 35 plants. "Each officer had to read what amounted to a Sears, Roebuck catalogue each month," Gustafson muses.

Day-to-day requests for permission to buy equipment were also dropped. Dana had used about 300 such forms each month, and each had to be signed by 15 executives, including the president. William H. Schomburg, general manager of Dana's Spicer Transmission Div., says that managers used to spend much of their time explaining the written requests to their bosses. "The forms passed through so many hands that everyone could come up with a question on it—either to justify his own job or because he didn't understand the real need for the equipment," Schomburg recalls. Pushing less paper and providing fewer services has enabled Dana to trim its corporate staff from 390 to about 235 in the past 2½ years.

The reduction at headquarters went beyond anyone's expectations. When Dana moved into its new plush $4-million corporate offices last year, it found that, even with liberal grants of space to various departments, it had to leave one wing of the new building empty.

At the same time, Dana's divisions have also been cutting their own administrative personnel. In many cases, production foremen are now responsible for scheduling production runs and for personnel administration, purchasing, and quality control. Staff positions that handled those functions were eliminated. In the past five years, more than 500 non-production workers in the division have been let go.

Gustafson insists that Dana's administrative cuts cannot be lumped in the same bag with those made by conglomerates during the past decade, which often produced more management problems than they solved. "We're trying to shorten the lines of communication between the problem and the fellow who can solve it by eliminating the filtration system in the middle," he says. "In the case of the conglomerates, the group who made the cuts did not know anything about the businesses they were cutting."

Divisions Act

Following the headquarters lead, many divisions also have rid themselves of time-consuming paperwork and costly computer time. Divisions have been encouraged, for example, to project production for a full year based on customer forecasts and previous experience, instead of scheduling production by feeding orders and changes into the computer each day. Since the order changes tended to offset each other, tracking them by computer to adjust production created "literally miles of paperwork for absolutely no purpose," asserts Bud Giaque, manager of Dana's Spicer Axle Div. "All the computer work brought you back to where you started from." He estimates a 30% reduction in the amount of printout paper required for scheduling. Dana's data processing costs have tumbled from $4.2-million in 1969 to $3.4-million a year, which McPherson hopes soon to pare to about $2-million.

The computer was forced on people who could not handle it or it was used in situations where it did not apply, explains Gerald B. Mitchell, 43, Dana's executive vice-president. "There was no way we could avoid 'garbage in' since people were involved," he says, referring to several of the projects.

McPherson sees much more administrative lard that can be cut, especially in the divisions, where he says some managers let paperwork guide their operations. "Some still hold on to their security blankets," he says. "We haven't made one-third the dent we can still make, but we aren't going to jam this down their throats."

Although Gustafson had to assure his colleagues about not losing control with the new, abbreviated reporting system, he now thinks that Dana officers realize they have a surer grasp of what is going on in the divisions they monitor. Since the new system first went into operation two years ago—and perhaps because of it—some half-dozen division heads were shifted to other jobs because their performance was not considered satisfactory.

The new approach communicates only essential data, Gustafson says. "People don't have number acuity, and it's senseless to force them to pore over hundreds of numbers."

When the four-channel grid is enlarged to 10 channels later this year, the company can transmit video-taped highlights of corporate operations, such as construction progress on a new plant. Dana puts the cost of the completed TV system at only $30,000.

Gustafson sums up its contribution: "Now we get concentrated and meaningful information. We got the same information under the standard paperwork system, too, but it was without emphasis and buried in detail."

SELECTED REFERENCES FOR CHAPTER 1

BOOKS

Ackoff, Russell L., *Scientific Method: Optimizing Applied Research Decisions.* New York: John Wiley & Sons, Inc., 1962.

———, and Fred E. Emery, *On Purposeful Systems.* Chicago: Aldine Atherton, Inc., 1972.

Aguilar, Francis Joseph, *Scanning the Business Environment.* New York: The Macmillan Company, 1967.

Anthony, Robert N., *Planning and Control Systems: A Framework for Analysis.* Cambridge, Mass.: Harvard University Press, 1965.

Beckett, John A., *Management Dynamics: The New Synthesis.* New York: McGraw-Hill Book Company, 1971.

Beer, Stafford, *Cybernetics and Management.* New York: John Wiley & Sons, Inc., 1959.

———, *Decision and Control,* London: John Wiley & Sons, Ltd., 1966.

Bonini, Charles P., *Simulation of Information and Decision Systems in the Firm.* Englewood Cliffs, N.J.: Prentice-Hall, Inc., 1963.

———, Robert K. Jaedicke, and Harvey M. Wagner, *Management Controls: New Directions in Basic Research.* New York: McGraw-Hill Book Company, 1964.

Churchman, C. West, *The Systems Approach.* New York: Delacorte Press, 1968.

———, *The Design of Inquiring Systems.* New York: Basic Books, Inc., 1971.

Cooper, William W., Harold J. Leavitt, and Maynard W. Shelly II, eds., *New Perspectives in Organizational Research.* New York: John Wiley & Sons, Inc., 1964.

Cross, Hershner, Donald I. Lowry, A. R. Zipf, George Kozmetzky, and Robert N. Anthony, *Computers and Management.* Cambridge, Mass.: Harvard University Press, 1967.

Cyert, Richard M., and James G. March, *A Behavioral Theory of the Firm.* Englewood Cliffs, N.J.: Prentice-Hall, Inc., 1963.

Deming, Robert H., *Characteristics of an Effective Management Control System in an Industrial Organization.* Cambridge, Mass.: Harvard University Press, 1968.

Emery, James C., *Organizational Planning and Control Systems.* New York: The Macmillan Company, 1969.

Forrester, Jay, *Industrial Dynamics.* New York and Cambridge, Mass.: John Wiley & Sons, Inc., The M. I. T. Press, 1961.

Greenberger, Martin, ed., *Computers and the World of the Future.* Cambridge, Mass.: The M. I. T. Press, 1962.

Gregory, Carl E., *The Management of Intelligence.* New York: McGraw-Hill Book Company, 1967.

Ijiri, Yuji, *Management Goals and Accounting for Control.* Amsterdam: North-Holland Publishing Company, 1965.

———, *The Foundations of Accounting Measurement.* Englewood Cliffs, N.J.: Prentice-Hall, Inc., 1967.

Kirby, Warren E., *Long-Range Planning: The Executive Viewpoint.* Englewood Cliffs, N.J.: Prentice-Hall, Inc., 1966.

Mattesich, Richard, *Accounting and Analytical Methods.* Homewood, Ill.: Richard D. Irwin, Inc., 1964.

Miller, David W., and Martin K. Starr, *The Structure of Human Decisions.* Englewood Cliffs, N.J.: Prentice-Hall, Inc., 1967.

Morris, William T., *Management Science in Action.* Homewood, Ill.: Richard D. Irwin, Inc., 1963.

Murdick, Robert G., and Joel E. Ross, *Information Systems for Modern Management.* Englewood Cliffs, N.J.: Prentice-Hall, Inc., 1971.

Myers, Charles A., ed., *The Impact of Computers on Management,* Cambridge, Mass.: The M. I. T. Press, 1967.

Optner, Stanford L., *Systems Analysis for Business and Industrial Problem Solving,* 2nd ed. Englewood Cliffs, N.J.: Prentice-Hall, Inc., 1968.

Prince, Thomas R., *Information Systems for Management Planning and Control.* Homewood, Ill.: Richard D. Irwin, Inc., 1970.

Simon, Herbert A., *The New Science of Management Decision.* New York: Harper & Row, Publishers, 1960.

Wilensky, Harold L., *Organizational Intelligence.* New York: Basic Books, Inc., Publishers, 1967.

ARTICLES

Ackoff, Russell L., "The Evolution of Management Systems," *Canadian Operational Research Society,* (March 1970).

———, "Towards a System of Systems Concepts," *Management Science,* XVII (July 1971).

Ansoff, H. Igor, and Dennis P. Slevin, "An Appreciation of Industrial Dynamics," *Management Science,* XIV (March, 1968).

Beged-Dov, Aharon G., "An Overview of Management Science and Information Systems," *Management Science,* XIII, (August 1967).

Bertalanffy, Ludwig von, "General Systems Theory: A New Approach to Unity of Science," *Human Biology,* XXIII (December, 1951).

Boulding, Kenneth E., "General Systems Theory—The Skeleton of Science," *Management Science,* II (April, 1956).

Churchman, C. W., and R. L. Ackoff, "Operational Accounting and Operations Research," *The Journal of Accountancy,* CXII (February, 1955).

Daniel, D. Ronald, "Management Information Crisis," *Harvard Business Review,* XXXIX (September-October, 1961).

Dearden, John, "Can Management Information Be Automated?" *Harvard Business Review,* XLII (March, 1964).

———, "How to Organize Information Systems," *Harvard Business Review,* XLIII April, 1965).

———, "Myth of Real-Time Management Information," *Harvard Business Review,* XLIV (May-June, 1966).

Deutsch, Karl W., "The Evaluation of Models," *The Public Opinion Quarterly,* XVI (Fall, 1952).

Eilon, Samuel, "What Is a Decision?" *Management Science,* XVI (December 1969).

Ericson, Richard F., "The Impact of Cybernetic Information Technology on Management Value Systems," *Management Science,* XVI (October 1969).

Firmin, Peter A., "The Potential of Accounting as a Management Information System," *Management International Review,* II (1966).

Forrester, Jay W., "Industrial Dynamics—After the First Decade," *Management Science,* XIV (March, 1968).

Mason, Richard O. and Ian I. Mitroff, "A Program for Research on Management Information Systems," *Management Science,* XIX (January 1973).

————, "A Dialectical Approach to Strategic Planning," *Management Science,* XVI (April 1969).

"Report of Committee on Managerial Decision Models," *The Accounting Review,* XLIV (Supplement, 1969).

Swalm, Ralph O., "Utility Theory: Insights into Risk Taking," *Harvard Business Review,* XLIV (November-December 1966).

Wilson, Charles Z. and Marcus Alexis, "Basic Frameworks for Decisions," *The Journal of the Academy of Management,* V (August 1962).

BUDGETING
AND FINANCIAL
MODELS

CHAPTER TWO

Building a Corporate Financial Model

George W.
Gershefski

*Bonner & Moore
Associates*

This article summarizes the principal steps in the development of a corporate financial model at the Sun Oil Company. The model has proved extremely useful in profit planning, particularly when a "management by objectives" approach is employed. The corporate financial model is envisioned as the critical first step in building an effective management information system.

In 1965 the Sun Oil Company began to build a corporate financial model—the first step in the eventual development of a management information system for the entire enterprise. In its two years of operation, the model has enabled management to keep budgeted plans more in line with current results and to do more effective long-range planning through the simulation capacities of the computerized system.

No business executive needs to be told that the conditions under which he operates are always changing—and probably at a faster rate than ever before. The problem is how to cope with the changes, and a big part of solving the problem is developing the tools that help him to cope.

One tool that is certain to gain greater acceptance as uses of the computer become more sophisticated is the corporate model. A model enables management to:

Reduce the time required to react to change.

Evaluate alternative courses of action with a full knowledge of all pertinent factors.

Take longer looks into the future.

Certain kinds of models of course are a familiar part of the industrial scene. Engineers use them to test and modify new designs before committing themselves to production. Model aircraft in

Author's note: I wish to acknowledge the contributions of Irving Geller of the Sun Oil Company in preparing this article.

wind tunnels, model ships in test basins, and, on a larger scale, pilot plants are well-known examples.

These are special cases. There is one form of model, though, that, far from being special, is utilized by every company: the budget. The budget models a company's physical and financial operations. It summarizes strategies and activities, and projects the outcome. If the projected results are unsatisfactory, the top officers can either take corrective action to obtain results that will be in line with their goals or else modify their objectives.

As the modern corporation has grown, so has the complexity of the budget. Today the typical corporate budget is a ponderous document that is usually inaccurate and out of date soon after it appears. Many companies make an attempt to offset this drawback by scheduling a revision at midyear.

Unlike simpler models, such as those of airplanes or ships, however, management cannot readily modify or experiment with a budget to determine the impact of alternate courses of action or strategies.

The computer offers solutions to such a problem. Its speed, automatic documentation, flexibility, and accuracy have the power to tame the behemoth budget and make it a manageable beast once again. Many companies have undertaken to prepare computerized versions of the manual budget.

This entails converting a company's processes and accounting into a series of equations that can be run through the computer. Once this is done, it is feasible to keep the budget accurate and up to date and to develop revised projections of income whenever necessary. Management can also use the model to compare and evaluate alternate strategies, and to appraise the effects of different allocations of funds and resources.

This article describes the corporate financial model that the Sun Oil Company has built. Simulating as it does the company's entire physical operations to provide projections of financial performance, it may well be the largest and most complex corporate model yet developed.

The system is complex. Since Sun is a fully integrated petroleum enterprise, the model actually combines four different models—of production (finding and extracting oil), of transportation (tankers and pipelines), of manufacturing (refining), and of marketing (gasoline stations). The company has more than 30 subsidiaries which provide inputs into the model.

(The scope of the model is now being expanded to include the operations of the Sunray DX Oil Company, which were merged into those of Sun Oil in late 1968. Combined, they produced pro forma revenues of $1.8 billion in 1968. At the end of the year, combined assets were more than $2.4 billion, and the number of persons employed totaled more than 29,000.)

This article was written to inform and give guidance to executives who may wish to undertake a similar venture. Every company, of course, has its own characteristics, and companies that are not so large and complex as Sun would not require such a large (and expensive) system. But our experience can serve as a general guide to organization and approach.

WHAT THE MODEL CAN DO

The model incorporates all pertinent information about the company and puts it in an analytical framework that affords better-grounded decisions. The system accomplishes this with great speed: the central processor time required to simulate one year of operation is 14 seconds. Before the company launched the project a few years ago, it often made special studies as part of its financial planning and budgeting, as corporations routinely do. But the analyses based on these studies were made on information compiled by traditional hand methods and consequently could not be as complete as data derived from the model.

The model is extremely accurate in forecasting; if the forecasts specified as inputs are correct, Sun's net income can be estimated within 1% of the actual net for one year into the future. Errors do occur among the accounts making up the total, but the error is usually less than 3% for individual accounts.

The model has been used to prepare short-term profit plans and long-range projections, and to study specific problems of management interest.

It provides an independent projection of net income for the coming year and revises the projection at midyear. Before the advent of the model, Sun Oil customarily made a formal budget revision at midyear, a process that consumed much time and manpower. Now it is a relatively easy task.

The model has also proved useful when the new budget for the year is being prepared. It provides some departments with preplanning information. This information, recast into several case-study formats, is helpful in determining budget guidelines. Each case is based on a different set of assumptions about the future environment. Realistic revenue and profit projections for the department are then developed. These provide limits to the levels of expenses which could be incurred.

It also turns up some surprising information, such as the discovery that the company was failing to take construction lead time properly into account when planning new service stations.

As the year for which the forecast was made progresses, monthly data are collected and processed through two programs—the budget comparison program and the annual projection program. The former calculates the variance between budgeted and actual results for the year to date and for the current month. The latter forecasts a value for each major department for the year on the basis of past seasonal results.

Comparison of the budget with these projections determines whether the year is proceeding as planned. If significant deviations exist, it may be necessary to revise key forecasts. These forecasts are introduced into the corporate financial model to develop a revised projection of annual net income and other measures of financial performance.

This "early warning" system provides Sun's executives with a very powerful device for monitoring events that enables them to react swiftly to changes which affect the company.

To streamline the budget preparation, several auxiliary computer programs have been written. These programs take over most of the calculation work, reducing the time required to respond to management-directed changes in the budget. The programs develop directly the necessary inputs for the corporate model and provide analytical ratios and other comparisons.

PLANNING TOOL

In the area of long-range planning, the model has many uses. For instance, it developed 10-year projections of net income and cash flow for an operating division under varying conditions and following several investment strategies. In this case, there were three possible ways to achieve increased crude oil production, and each had different cash flow characteristics. The purpose of the search was to present management with information structured on a consolidated basis so that it could make a decision from a corporate point of view.

The model also has been used for special studies of the effects of interacting variables, or to see how changes in one area of the business would reverberate through the company and affect other areas. For example:

One goal was to determine the best timing, from a tax viewpoint, for recognizing additional taxes owed a foreign government as a result of post audits and the write-off of a foreign holding. The additional tax could have been recognized on the tax return in either of two years, and the abandonment could have been wholly recognized in either of the two years or partially in both years.

Six distinct cases could be formed from the various possibilities. For each case the model calculated the tax due in each of the two years. This information permitted management to select the strategy that would result in the least tax expense.

Another study concerned the breakeven point between a change in the price of one product and a change in the price of another product. This gave management an indication of relative product price sensitivity.

One of the greatest advantages of the model is the freedom it gives the company to experiment with ideas and alternatives without tying up a lot of manpower. Company operations are not interrupted, and results can be obtained in a shorter time—and much more cheaply, of course—than would be the case if facilities or procedures had to be installed and tested.

When the model was being constructed, the very act of gathering the necessary data provided management with a fresh look at the company's operations and accounting procedures. Departmental data were traced to their

sources, and data were "brought forward" as well to show how they contributed to the consolidated figures.

By strengthening the communication links throughout the company, the development of the model worked to neutralize the centrifugal forces that tend to fragment the corporation (like any large corporation) into separate, self-contained divisions and departments.

DEVELOPING THE SYSTEM

The project was launched in 1965, in cooperation with the Planning Executives Institute. By mid-1966 a working version was completed, but it took another year before the system was in full operation.

The working version required 13 man-years to complete—10 man-years of analytical time and 3 of computer coding. An additional 10 man-years were spent in familiarizing management at several levels with the operation of the model, soliciting comments and suggestions, and modifying the model accordingly.

Perhaps the most difficult problem in developing the corporate model was deciding where to start. The company undertook a feasibility study which set the direction for the entire program and to a great extent determined the final form of the model.

FEASIBILITY STUDY

Many critical decisions had to be made at the very beginning: the type of model, its scope in terms of how much of the company would be represented, its potential uses, the time period to be considered, and project organization. It was also necessary to plan a method of approach, determine if the necessary data were available, and assess what would be required of the computer. This phase took 10 persons about two months to complete.

There was a great deal of discussion—sometimes heated discussion—about what kind of model to use. We had a choice of an optimization (algorithmic or linear programming) model or a case-study (heuristic) model:

An optimization model is restricted to a single, predetermined objective, such as minimizing costs or maximizing profits, and it automatically selects the best of several given alternatives to reach the objective.

By simulating events, a case-study model displays the implications of two or more possible courses of action. The user searches through these alternatives on a "hunt and peck" basis and selects the one that is expected to produce the desired goals.[1]

The study team finally concluded that for the company's purposes the case-study type of model would be best. There were several reasons:

1. The case-study approach, unlike linear programming, makes it possible to develop a hierarchy of objectives, with the weights of emphasis on those objectives left up to management. The model provides management with the information to help it decide what trade-offs must be made in determining weights of emphasis.

2. It provides ease of communication. The statements produced by the case-study model are just like those that management is familiar with—income statements, source and use of

funds statements, rate of return analyses, and so on.

3. The case-study type is easier to develop. Linear programming requires a great deal more mathematical figuring, results are harder to interpret, and the details that caused the result are not spelled out (the "black box" situation). Simulation, however, follows a person's natural train of thought.

Next it was necessary to decide whether the model would be stochastic or deterministic:

A stochastic (conjectural) model is ideal for dealing with an operation that has a great amount of uncertainty associated with it; it automatically projects the results for a wide range of future conditions.

A deterministic model, on the other hand, projects results for only one given set of conditions; however, a deterministic model with a sufficient number of cases can be used to produce the same type of information that a stochastic model produces automatically.

The study team decided that it would be wiser to develop a deterministic-type model, on the ground that it would be easier to develop and at the same time would preserve all options. Variations in inputs could always be handled on a case-study basis.

It also was necessary to choose between an information compiler and an information generator:

An information compiler receives, as input, data collected from the various company departments and then performs the arithmetic necessary to consolidate these and develop an overview of the company.

[1] For fuller explanations of these techniques, see Alexander Henderson and Robert Schlaifer, "Mathematical Programing: Better Information for Better Decision Making," HBR May-June 1954, p. 73; and Jerome D. Wiest, "Heuristic Programs for Decision Making," HBR September-October 1966, p. 129.

Although an information generator model starts with only a few inputs, because of its internal makeup it can generate new information; however, it is much more difficult to develop, since the equations or mathematical logic used to generate information must be developed and tested for validity.

The study team decided that, wherever possible, an information generator should be constructed: though more difficult to develop, it would be easier to implement in the long run, since it would make fewer subsequent demands on operating departments for forecasts.

Scope and Use

We next had to decide on the scope of the model, choosing between the "forest" and the "tree" designs:

In the forest approach the model focuses on the entire company with little attention to detail.

In the tree approach it looks at a single segment in very fine detail.

The study team decided to develop initially a broad-scope model. The model as built considers the parent company in detail but treats subsidiaries' operations as gross inputs, to develop a consolidated outlook. Our experience during development and implementation confirmed the wisdom of our decision. The functional areas and departments already were preparing good analytical studies, but the company needed a better way to fit them into place to generate a consolidated budget and an overall plan.

Early in the model's development an attempt was made to define its potential uses. This was extremely difficult to do, since few persons knew what a corporate model was or how it could be of value. Left on its own, the study group defined the potential uses in terms of what it considered were management's information requirements. To make it most useful for top management, the model was designed to conform closely to Sun's existing accounting system and to produce financial reports following existing formats.

Finally, target dates were established. The deadline for the completion of a working model was set only one year ahead. This was done to maintain momentum and to avoid getting bogged down in unimportant details. Moreover, experience had shown that the model was a very difficult concept to explain, and the group decided that the best demonstration of its worth would be the completed system itself.

(During the model development phase, incidentally, we made extensive use of critical path scheduling. It was very useful for projecting completion dates and determining the principal scheduling problems.)

SYSTEM CONSTRUCTION

The company's annual report proved to be the ideal jumping-off point for developing the model. Everybody was familiar with it, and it provided data that were complete and usable as a base to build on.

We analyzed the income statement in detail to determine the main components of revenue and expense and the basic physical activities causing these items to increase or decrease. This involved tracing through several levels of detailed reports, and pinpointing the subaccounts and the underlying operational activities and their effects which caused the dollars to flow.

(In this effort to assign every data point to a function of the company, we spent a lot of time reconciling accounts. Other companies setting out to build a financial model may find that this has already been accomplished. Of the time spent in developing the model, about 70% was consumed in collecting and reconciling data from different sources and in determining how various reports were tied into the corporate books.)

Then we developed an appropriate model, or mathematical relationship, for each account. By means of an equation or a series of equations we related costs and revenues to the level of physical activity.

The amount of effort we devoted to "fix" each activity was governed by its significance, the data available, the relationship of the item to other variables, policy statements, and the ability of the user to forecast values for any independent variables that might be used.

The results of this analysis were summarized in a large input-output diagram, a condensed version of which is shown in Exhibit I. Various output items of revenue and expense are indicated along the top of this diagram; the independent variables which would be used to estimate each of these are listed on the side. The series of small "a"s represent coefficients of regression equations, which I shall go into more fully shortly.

This diagram provided a broad conceptual framework which showed how the various functions of the company were interrelated and how key variables affected performance within each area. In this manner we devised a complete set of simple algebraic equations to project and consolidate all costs and revenues. These equations, translated into computer instructions, became the heart of the model.

EXHIBIT I Condensed Input-Output Diagram

Columns RO_1, RO_2, RO_3, RO_{12} are grouped under O_4 (Refining expense).

INPUT \ OUTPUT	O_1 Selling expense	O_2 Cost of freight	O_3 Cost of packages	RO_1 Operating labor	RO_2 Chemicals, catalysts	RO_3 Taxes, insurance	RO_{12} Total refining expense	O_{29} Other outputs	O_{30} Total operating expense
a_1, a_2, a_3	○								○
Number of service stations	○	○							○
Gasoline sales	○	○							○
Advertising expense	○	○							○
Marketing depreciation expense	○								○
a_4, a_5, a_6		○					○		○
Time		○		○					○
Branch sales		○							○
a_7, a_8			○						○
Sales of grease, waxes, and motor oil			○						○
a_9, a_{10}, a_{11}				○			○		○
Operating labor pension cost				○			○		○
a_{12}, a_{13}, a_{14}					○		○		○
Plant throughput					○		○		○
Gasoline volume					○		○		○
a_{15}, a_{16}						○	○		○
Average refinery plant and equipment value						○	○		○
Other inputs								○	○

Regression Analysis

There are no set rules for developing these equations; a company's circumstances dictate the appropriate form. In our case, multiple regression analysis proved to be very useful in producing equations that permit accurate forecasts. It involved finding the correct independent variables and adding them to existing equations to form more complex and accurate ones.

Multiple regression analysis was particularly important in determining how costs relate to the level of physical operations. For example:

In deriving an equation for selling expense, we found that use of only one independent variable, gasoline sales, did not make the equation reliable enough as a predictive device. We improved the predictive accuracy greatly when we plotted these data against an additional independent variable—namely, the number of service stations.

Although we considered some 300 equations all told, only 60 are now being used. The others were found to have too large a standard error about the regression equation. Most of the regression equations we retained have a coefficient of determination of more than 90%, which indicates a very close relationship between the variables involved.

To develop meaningful regression equations, it is necessary to select valid independent variables, as well as to indicate the type of relationship that exists. Data must also be collected and analyzed to determine values for the regression coefficients.

Finally, it is necessary to determine how well the regression line fits the data. Usually a period of 10 years of data was used to determine the regression coefficients. When the model was being developed, 1963 was selected as the cutoff point. This enabled us to use 1964 and 1965 data to test the relationships developed; they were accurate within 3% for individual accounts and 1% for the total.

We monitor the regression equations at least once a year to determine whether the basic relationships of the variables should be changed. The regression coefficients are changed once a year. For flexibility, these values are specified as input, rather than becoming a fixed part of the model.

Let me illustrate these concepts by showing one equation formulated as part of a long series:

$$O_1 = \text{selling expense} = a_1 + (a_2 \times \text{number of service stations}) + (a_3 \times \text{gasoline sales}) + \text{marketing depreciation expense} + \text{advertising expense.}$$

This is one of the many equations representing expenses that are summed to make up Sun Oil's operating expenses (see Exhibit I). The inputs a_1, a_2, and a_3 are specified as coefficients of the regression equation. Advertising expense is an input, since it is discretionary in nature and can be increased or decreased as a matter of management policy. The marketing depreciation expense (depreciation of owned service stations) is calculated elsewhere in the model.

In addition to this kind of equation, we employed mathematical relationships to show the construction period required for capital investments. These equations take into consideration the fact that investments are made in one year, but results are not realized until the next year or even later.

The total number of equations necessary to translate Sun's complex, diversified operations into model form was some 2,000, with 1,500 inputs and 5,200 output items.

After we developed the equations, we converted them to computer instructions to form a computer program. We coded and separately tested each block of the program before assembling all of them into a single program for final testing.

ASCERTAINING ACCURACY

The next step was to ascertain the predictive accuracy of the model. Model accuracy is extremely difficult to define. The income projection for any year can be incorrect because of errors in the forecasted values of the inputs or errors in the model itself. The latter can result from a misrepresentation of the accounting system or random variations about the regression lines used.

To test accuracy, we specified the actual values for a previous year as inputs to the model and then used the model to project the level of the net income for the year. We compared this projection with actual net income.

Accuracy tests made for the last two years indicate that, if correct values are specified for all inputs, the model can project a level of net income within 1% of actual for one year into the future. The subaccounts making up net income also are estimated in a reasonably precise way so that overall accuracy is not due to large compensating errors among divisions.

It is important to realize that a model can be developed which is just as accurate as any of the analytical studies a company is making "by hand." Often a model is also expected to provide answers to a problem which conventional procedures cannot seem to solve. In some instances this can be done. But even if it cannot, the advantages of greater speed, automatic documentation, and flexibility are justification enough for using a model whose projections are as accurate as those of manual procedures.

BREAKING-IN PERIOD

As I mentioned earlier, we spent a year putting the model into full-scale operation after its completion. That period was used to familiarize management at various levels with its operation, soliciting comments and suggestions, and modifying it accordingly.

For example, we simplified the model's excessively detailed coverage of certain operations. However, there were exceptions. For instance, taxable income was initially represented as a percentage of reported net income. But the tax personnel wanted more detail, so the model now states precisely the additions and subtractions (Schedule M adjustments) for figuring taxable income.

After completing the project and reviewing the hazards and difficulties it encountered, the study team concluded that a steering committee, composed of top executives, and a task force is the best form of organization for overseeing and directing this kind of project.

The committee's main function would be to establish priorities and deadlines and give the project guidance. At the conclusion, management would not be "presented" with the project, since it had been involved all along. Our study team made periodic progress reports to the president, executive vice president, treasurer, and comptroller—to communicate what was happening.

The task force, consisting of persons from each major functional area of the company, would, in this scheme, have been the agent developing the model. Inasmuch as the basic concepts are extremely difficult to convey, it is important to educate executives and build up confidence in the project throughout the company, and the task force would have helped to accomplish this.

The steering committee—task force approach would have "greased the skids" for better and faster acceptance of the system. In any case, the model must be developed by a firmly directed, tightly controlled group which is motivated to do a good job.

PROFILE OF THE MODEL

I shall now give a rather brief description of the model as it operates at present. Since many aspects of it would be of interest principally to persons in the oil business, I shall leave out a number of the details here. Those wishing the details and a more technical discussion of modeling can obtain a pamphlet I wrote about the model.[2]

To represent the entire company, the equations in the model simulate the oil flow from production at the well to refined product sales at the service station, the revenues and expenses associated with it, and the impact of capital investments on volume of flow.

DATA REQUIRED

The model makes a projection based on certain assumptions or inputs, the values of which must be specified. They include:

Product prices and volumes.
Raw material costs.
Economic conditions.
Investments.
Subsidiary company income.
Discretionary expense items.

The general economic conditions specified as inputs are import restrictions, rates for U.S. taxes and mineral depletion allowance, and allowable levels of crude

oil production as set by state regulatory agencies. Although most investments must be specified beforehand, the model can determine the investment requirements in the marketing and production areas.

Subsidiary companies have not been modeled yet—they are all "bottom line" figures—so all projections regarding income have to be in the form of input to the model. Discretionary expense items include research and development, sales of securities, write-offs, and advertising. Since management has a great deal of control over these, it can plan strategies to increase or decrease them.

Some 1,500 items are required to simulate a year. These inputs can be divided into 2 categories: (a) 500 based on past averages, statistical relationships, or historic fact; and (b) 1,000 inputs as forecasts coming from the operating departments.

Exhibit II shows a sample of these forecasts coming from company departments. Of the 1,500 in the entire company, 50 are of major importance in effect on net income. All the inputs are classified according to department, and forms have been developed for each one to facilitate data collection.

The large number of inputs results from an early policy decision. As I have already indicated, when we found a statistical relationship (using regression analysis) that provided a reasonably accurate projection, the equation was put into the model. When it was not possible to find a good relationship, we specified the variable as an input. This was done, for example, with the oil-well-drilling success factor, which is extremely difficult to predict, even though it is based on statistics from past years.

An alternative would have been to construct the model on the basis of the average value over several past years and use this figure as the best forecast of future conditions. Specification of an

---

[2] *The Development and Application of a Corporate Financial Model* (published in 1968 by Planning Executives Institute, 16 Park Place, Oxford, Ohio 45056).

EXHIBIT II. SAMPLE OF DEPARTMENTAL FORECASTS USED AS INPUTS TO THE MODEL

Production department

Crude and condensate price
Natural gas price
Crude production from acquired properties
Nonassociated gas production
Gas plant revenue
Miscellaneous operating revenue
Development expense
Abandonment expense
Lease bonus investment
Producing property investment
Gas plant and facility investment
Drilling cost per well
Gas/oil ratio
Depreciation rate
Retirement rate

Marketing Department

Product prices
Product volumes
Gasoline sales by channel of distribution
New stations opened
New stations leased
Stations lost
Volume per station
Investment per station
Advertising expense
Rehabilitation expense
Bulk plant investment
Auto and truck investment
Depreciation rate

Treasury Department

Sale of securities
Treasury stock purchases or sales
Price/earnings ratio
Dividend rate
New long-term debt
Interest rate on debt
Debt repayment schedules

item as input, however, reminds the user that it may be appropriate to change the value on the basis of knowledge of future plans.

REPORTS GENERATED

The model simulates the operations of the company on the basis of the values of the inputs, and provides these key reports of projected data:

Income statement—indicates revenues, operating expenses, noncash charges, foreign and federal taxes, and net income after taxes for Sun Oil and each subsidiary.

Capital investment schedule—shows the capital expenditures to be made by each department. (The source and use of funds statement is based on these schedules. The sources consist of net income, recovery of capital, deferred taxes, borrowings, and reduction in working capital. The uses involve funds required for capital expenditures, cash dividends, purchases of treasury stock, repayment of debt, and increases in working capital.)

Statement of earnings employed and stockholders' equity—indicates the number of shares outstanding, stock and cash dividends payments, earnings employed, stockholders' equity, earnings per share, stock price, and the total common-stock market value.

Tax report—details the adjustments required to reconcile book income with taxable income, special deductions, handling of foreign taxes as credits or deductions against U.S. taxes, the investment credit, and the tax to be accrued.

Rate-of-return analysis—indicates the return on both gross and net operating investment, and provides an analysis in terms of profit margin and asset turnover.

Financial and operating summary—highlights financial items such as net income, revenue, total assets, long-term debt, return on stockholders' equity, and return on total assets employed. (Operational items highlighted are crude oil produced, crude oil to be run in the refineries, the level of crude oil reserves, gasoline sales, and market share.)

The model generates a number of supporting statements. Currently there are 142 pages of output making up 61 specific reports. In the future, when we are able to model working capital in more detail, we will prepare a balance sheet.

The reports are arranged so that summary information is shown first, and supporting detail follows. In all cases, the reports are based on the same accounting definitions as those already used by the company. This was decided in the planning stage so as to avoid having to "sell" both the model and new reporting procedures at the same time.

KEY DESIGN CHARACTERISTICS

The series of equations that represents the company is grouped to form "blocks" or subroutines, each one denoting an aspect of company operations. They take into account the activities performed and available alternatives, the relationship between costs and volume, and the accounting procedure followed.

Chosen for its flexibility and ease of use, the procedure permits construction of several blocks concurrently and simplifies model modification and extension. Each area of the company can be examined independently.

CALCULATIONS PERFORMED FOR CERTAIN OPERATION 'BLOCKS'

Here is a summary description of some of the calculations performed in certain blocks of the model:

The new investments block first determines the investment required for new service stations to achieve a specified market share for the coming year. This construction program is based on the expected performance of existing stations and those to be constructed. In the process, gasoline demand for the current year is estimated too.

The model will also ascertain the effects of a particular investment in this area; an investment level can be specified as input, and the model will then determine the associated gasoline volume. In addition, this block calculates the well-drilling program and the investment required in the production department to meet a specified crude oil production self-sufficiency goal and a desired ratio of crude reserves to production.

The production block determines the amount of crude oil and condensate production on the basis of the number of producing wells and allowables. In some areas the amount of crude oil production also depends on crude oil reserves. The block calculates natural gas production for gas wells, taking into consideration the level of natural gas reserves, and adds to this the gas associated with crude oil production.

The block figures certain expenses, such as lifting expense (the cost of getting hydrocarbons out of the ground), which is determined as a function of crude oil and natural gas production. Depreciation expense, retirement expense, and retirements and sales from the gross asset account are calculated by applying predetermined rates to the gross asset account.

The value of the gross asset account is updated by adding new investment to the gross asset value as of January 1 and deducting the retirements and sales from the account. A similar procedure for depreciation and retirement expense is followed for each functional area.

The boats and barges block estimates the amount of domestic crude carried by various-size tankers from the production fields on the Gulf Coast to Sun's refinery at Marcus Hook, Pennsylvania, and the direct costs of this transportation. Given information on the amount of crude to be carried and the capacity of the tanker fleet, the model also determines the amount of free time when ships are available for chartering to other companies and estimates the associated revenues and direct expenses. It calculates barge revenue and expenses too.

The other refining and marketing block projects selling expense and rental income on the basis of total gasoline sales and the number of service stations. Sales of tires, batteries, and accessories are determined as a percentage of the gasoline sales volume. The cost of freight from the refineries to the marketing warehouses is dependent on both branch sales of refined products and passage of time. Finally, the cost of packages and packaging of motor oil, industrial oils, and petrochemicals is determined by their sales.

The subsidiary company blocks are currently based on inputs of revenue, expenses, net income, and investments for each subsidiary. The framework is such that detailed simulation models of each of these can be added at a future date.

The source and use of funds and adjustments block compares the net income after taxes with a specified goal. If it is less than the goal, the model attempts to raise income by reducing certain expenses according to prespecified instructions. This block also determines the cash flow for the year and compares the sources and uses of funds.

The blocks, joined in the model according to their interrelationships, combine to determine consolidated net income. This is explained in the ruled insert above and portrayed schematically in Exhibit III.

The model is not capable of automatically searching through a large number of alternatives and choosing the best set, nor does it automatically consider variations in the forecasts submitted as inputs to the model. The model is used on a case-study basis. Alternative courses of action must be studied by running a series of cases.

Technically, the model can project 40 years into the future. The study team considered a 5- to 10-year period most useful, however, and developed the equations accordingly. The equations would probably have to be simplified for a longer-run forecast.

Since the constants for all regression equations are specified as inputs, cost structures can be changed easily without reprogramming. To determine if changes are necessary, we review the coefficients of the regression equations as data for each new year become available.

Even though predictive equations have been built into the model, the design of the model enables us to override any of them. Whenever a department decides that future conditions or policies are to be significantly different from before, the group can introduce the new values which it considers most appropriate.

The model design enables one to make several multiple-year runs or several sensitivity analyses (e.g., the sensitivity of net income to various wholesale gasoline prices) at one submittal of the program. This provision was made to simplify the case-study approach. If an identical value is to be used for input for successive years, it is necessary to specify the value for only the first year.

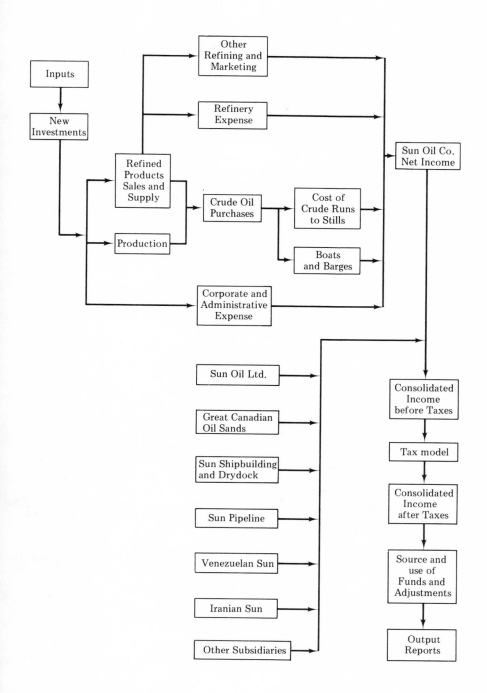

Exhibit III.   Financial Model Flow Chart

The model was originally designed for use by executive management, and therefore we employed summary reporting throughout. As the system gradually gained acceptance by middle management, it became necessary to include more detail on the operating departments. Also it became obvious that the program system needed the capability to change the content or arrangement of reports, so we developed a report-writing program that retrieves information from computer storage and specifies the format statements required for a report.

THE FUTURE

We plan soon to install budget assembly and analysis programs to eliminate much of the clerical work associated with budgeting. The programs will provide more analytical information in terms of ratios and trends, and develop directly the inputs required for the corporate model.

The model will also be extended and revised to determine the effects of such items as advertising, pricing, and research and development on operating departments, so that alternatives involving these expenditures can be incorporated directly into the model.

We will also build models for each functional area of the company. They are expected to be detailed enough to aid in operational decision making. These models will take over much of the detail that now is part of the corporate model, so that the latter's main function will be to consolidate the results of the functional models.

In addition, steps will be taken to model the capital budgeting process so that management can better compare alternative investments—from a total corporate point of view. Most capital evaluations do not provide management with information concerning the impact of an investment on short-term financial performance. The model will perform this function and will also provide information on the risk and uncertainty associated with an investment.

CONCLUSION

Those involved in the development of the corporate financial model at the Sun Oil Company envision it as the first step in building a management information system. A well-developed corporate financial model not only collects and stores data, but also processes and presents them in such a way that they are useful for decision making. For this reason, I think that the corporate financial model will be at the heart of future management information systems.

But the corporate model has become a powerful tool in its own right. It is extremely valuable for comparing and evaluating alternative courses of action that a company may take. The model is also useful in short-term profit-planning because it provides an independent estimate of net income for gauging how well current targets are being met. The model enables management to react quickly to events and to revise estimates of income and other aspects of performance.

The corporate model is most effectively employed in a company that has a "management by objectives" approach to its operations, and one in which planning is formalized. In a company where this style of management is not present, the computerized financial-model approach will likely have great difficulties gaining acceptance from top management.

In view of the rapid changes taking place in modern life and the increasing complexity of carrying on a business, the need for structured information is more vital than ever. The financial model, together with advanced computer technology and information systems, can provide management with a way to tackle these challenges.

Toward Probabilistic
Profit Budgets

**William L.
Ferrara and
Jack C. Hayya**

*Pennsylvania State
University*

Beginning with a conventional income statement with most likely values, the authors present three approaches for the construction of probabilistic profit budgets: the three-level, the probability-tree, and the continuous distribution approaches. In addition to the mean or expected value of each budget item, probabilistic budgets afford managers measures of variability such as the probability inverval, standard deviation, and the coefficient of variation.

Reprinted from *Management Accounting*, October 1970, 23-28. Used by permission of William L. Ferrara, Jack C. Hayya and the National Association of Accountants.

Practical techniques have recently been developed for business applications of probability concepts so that they can be easily integrated with profit planning. This paper shows how some of these techniques can be used in the construction of probabilistic profit budgets, i.e., budgets that display expected values and a probability interval for every item.

RELATED STUDIES
AND LITERATURE

The accounting literature does not specify how probabilistic profit budgets are constructed. A 1960 study on profit planning by executives, for example, makes no mention of probabilistic approaches to profit budgets.

The 1966 *Statement of Basic Accounting Theory*, encourages accountants to adopt probabilistic financial statements,

The authors are indebted to Joseph Mackovjak (now with General Electric) who provided simulation expertise and other valuable assistance.

but does not offer any guidelines.[1] Byrne, *et al*, offer similar encouragement when they state that decision-tree and network concepts "... may be a better way of utilizing the double-entry principle—at least when probability distributions are to be compounded for such purposes as ... projection of profit-and-loss statement categories along with related balance-sheet and flow-of-funds analysis."[2]

Magee,[3] Hertz,[4] and Jaedicke and Robichek[5] focus on issues related to

[1] A Statement of *Basic Accounting Theory*, American Accounting Association, 1966, pp. 38, 59, and 65.
[2] R. Byrne, A. Charnes, W. W. Cooper, and K. Kortanek, "Some New Approaches to Risk," *The Accounting Review*, January 1968, p. 33.
[3] John F. Magee, "How to Use Decision Trees in Capital Investment," *Harvard Business Review*, September-October 1964, pp. 79-96.
[4] David B. Hertz, "Risk Analysis in Capital Investment," *Harvard Business Review*, January-February, 1964, pp. 95-106, and "Investment Policies that Pay Off," *Harvard Business Review*, January-February 1968, pp. 96-108.
[5] R. K. Jaedicke and A. A. Robichek, "Cost Volume-Profit Analysis Under Conditions of Uncertainty," *The Accounting Review*, October 1964, pp. 914-926.

probabilistic profit budgets. Magee develops a detailed decision-tree in calculating the expected net present value of alternative capital investments. Hertz also deals with capital investments, but uses computer simulation to derive expected discounted return on investment and a probability distribution which expresses the variability of expected return on investment. Jaedicke and Robichek handle uncertainty in cost-volume-profit analysis by assuming that uncertainty is in the form of a normal probability distribution.

Coughlan,[6] Hespos and Strassman,[7] Springer, Herlihy, Mall and Beggs,[8] offer, in ascending order, some of the more detailed approaches to preparing probabilistic financial statements.

Coughlan uses discrete probability distributions to calculate expected net receipts. His treatment of probability intervals, however, is incomplete.

Hespos and Strassman, like some afore-mentioned authors deal with investment decisions. They expand the treatment of risk analysis in decision-trees by substituting continuous probability distributions for the discrete probabilities at the chance event nodes.

Springer, Herlihy, Mall and Beggs use an analytic technique and Monte Carlo to estimate probability intervals for net profit. In this respect, their work is similar to ours.

The intent of this paper is to integrate three probabilistic techniques suggested

in the literature with profit budgets. The PERT-like and probability-tree approaches used here emphasize most likely and mean values as well as measures of variability for each item in the income statement. Monte Carlo is used to simulate probability intervals for complex distributions that are too difficult to treat analytically.

THE TYPICAL PROFIT BUDGET

Let us assume that the profit budget in a single-product company is as shown in Exhibit 1. The direct-costing format of Exhibit 1 facilitates the use of break-even and cost-volume-profit analysis. Fixed costs are classified into managed and committed costs. Managed fixed costs are those costs which can be modified in the short run. Committed fixed costs are those which cannot be modified in the short run. The distinction between variable, managed and committed costs in this model is not only useful, it is particularly appropriate (as will become clear) in the preparation of probabilistic budgets.

The segregation of fixed costs into managed and committed fixed costs gives rise to the "short run margin." This margin is the contribution to earnings for which managers can be held accountable in a given budget period. The short-run margin further shows that committed costs are an obstacle which must be hurdled before a net profit is realized.

The weakness of Exhibit 1, and other models like it, is that they give no indication of the potential variability of the various estimates used. It is clear that the items in the budget are subjective estimates of most likely values, i.e., estimates of what is most probable in terms of revenues, costs and profits. The function of probabilistic profit budgets is to

[6] John W. Coughlan, "Profit and Probability," *Advanced Management Journal*, April 1968, pp. 53-69.

[7] Richard F. Hespos and Paul A. Strassman, "Stochastic Decision Trees for the Analysis of Investment Decisions," *Management Science*, August 1956, pp. 244-259.

[8] Clifford H. Springer, Robert E. Herlihy, Robert T. Mall, and Robert I. Beggs, *Probabilistic Models*, Richard D. Irwin, Inc., Homewood, Ill. 1968: Of particular relevance are Chapters 4 and 5.

EXHIBIT I   Profit Budget for Year Ending June 197X

Sales (100,000 units @ $10)		$1,000,000
Variable costs		
Manufacturing ($5 per unit)	$500,000	
Marketing ($.50 per unit)	50,000	550,000
Marginal contribution		$ 450,000
Managed fixed costs		
Manufacturing	$ 20,000	
Marketing	10,000	
Administrative	40,000	70,000
Short-run margin		$ 380,000
Committed fixed costs		
Manufacturing	$180,000	
Marketing	40,000	
Administrative	60,000	280,000
Net income before tax		$ 100,000
Tax — 50%		50,000
Net income after tax		$ 50,000

extend such models to indicate the variability of each budget item.

OPTIMISTIC, PESSIMISTIC AND MOST LIKELY VALUES

Consider first the "three-level" estimates referred to as optimistic, pessimistic and most likely values. Such a "three-level" profit budget can be easily prepared, as shown in Exhibit 2.

It is evident that the three-level estimates of Exhibit 2 are more informative than the most likely one of Exhibit 1. For example, Exhibit 2 shows that net income after tax may be as low as $13,500 or as high as $78,500. The lone use of the most likely estimate of $50,000, as in Exhibit 1, can therefore be misleading.

From the data of Exhibit 2, one can calculate means and standard deviations for sales, variable costs, and marginal contribution by using the PERT formulas[9] or through probability-tree analysis. If we are to use the PERT formulas, the person who is providing the estimates

must be made aware that a most likely estimate is a mode rather than a mean, and that the pessimistic and optimistic estimates are assumed to be six standard deviations apart.

PROBABILITY-TREE ANALYSIS: GENERAL

A more useful method for the preparation of probabilistic profit budgets is probability-tree analysis.[10] Probability-tree analysis is a generalization of the PERT method.

In using probability-tree analysis, probability estimates must be made for

$$\sigma = \frac{b-a}{6}$$

$$\mu = \frac{1}{3}\left[2m + \frac{1}{2}(a+b)\right]$$

Where "b" is the optimistic estimate, "a" is the pessimistic estimate and "m" is the most likely estimate.

[10] The probability-tree analysis used in this study differs from formal decision-tree analysis in that all nodes in the probability-tree are chance event nodes.

[9] The PERT formulas for the standard deviation (σ) and the mean (μ) are:

EXHIBIT 2   Profit Budget for Year Ending June 197X

	Pessimistic	Most Likely	Optimistic
Sales ($10 per unit)	$800,000	$1,000,000	$1,100,000
Variable Costs			
Manufacturing	408,000	500,000	528,000
Marketing ($.50 per unit)	40,000	50,000	55,000
Marginal contribution	$352,000	$ 450,000	$ 517,000
Managed fixed costs			
Manufacturing	10,000	20,000	30,000
Marketing	10,000	10,000	10,000
Administrative	25,000	40,000	40,000
Short-run margin	$307,000	$ 380,000	$ 437,000
Committed fixed costs			
Manufacturing	180,000	180,000	180,000
Marketing	40,000	40,000	40,000
Administrative	60,000	60,000	60,000
Net income before tax	$ 27,000	$ 100,000	$ 157,000
Tax — 50%	13,500	50,000	78,500
Net income after tax	$ 13,500	$ 50,000	$ 78,500

*The data are based on Exhibit 1 with optimistic, most likely, and pessimistic values for sales volume and variable costs being 110,000, 100,000, 80,000 and $4.80, $5.00, $5.10, respectively. Unit variable costs are assumed to vary inversely with volume. Committed costs and unit variable marketing cost are assumed to be certain; some managed costs are modified to reflect changing volume levels.

every level of volume and variable manufacturing cost considered. Thus, in our case, probabilities are assigned to each of the three sales and variable manufacturing cost levels as indicated in Exhibit 3. The probabilities (the p's and q's) assigned to each level are usually applicable to ranges whose mid-points are used in the calculations.

The budget variables under consideration in Exhibit 3 are sales, variable manufacturing cost, variable marketing cost, managed costs, committed costs, and net income after tax. The nine combinations in the Exhibit result by considering the three sales estimates to be independent of the three variable manufacturing cost estimates.[11]

In Exhibit 3 variable marketing costs, managed costs and committed costs are assumed to be non-probabilistic. The

[11] Exhibits 2 and 3 represent different models. The model of Exhibit 2 assumes that volume and variable manufacturing costs are inversely related. The model of Exhibit 3 assumes them to be independent.

Exhibit shows net income after tax (NIAT) for each of the nine combinations and the expected value (the average or mean value) of NIAT.

The expected value of NIAT in Exhibit 3 [Σ(NIAT)JP] is $44,710. On the other hand, the corresponding result for Exhibit 2 as calculated by use of the PERT formula for the mean turns out to be $48,666. The two results differ because they are based on two different models.

PROBABILITY-TREE ANALYSIS AND PROFIT BUDGETS

In Exhibit 4 the expected value (μ) and the standard deviation (σ) of every item in the income statement is presented. The normal distribution and probability intervals[12] of $\pm 2 \sigma$ or $\pm 3 \sigma$ from the mean cannot be used here since the probability

[12] Referred to as confidence intervals when the parameter to be estimated is not known.

EXHIBIT 3   Three Diagram of Basic Problem Including Expected Values

Volume (price = $10)	Variable Manufacturing Cost	Variable Marketing Cost	Managed Costs	Committed Costs	Net Income After Tax-50% (NIAT)	Joint* Probability (JP)	Combination	JP X NIAT
80,000	$5.10	$0.50	$45,000	$280,000	$13,500	0.06	1	$ 810
p = .3	q = .2 $5.00	$0.50	$45,000	$280,000	$17,500	0.18	2	3,150
	q = .6 $4.80	$0.50	$45,000	$280,000	$25,500	0.06	3	1,530
	q = .2							
100,000	$5.10	$0.50	$70,000	$280,000	$45,000	0.10	4	4,500
p = .5	q = .2 $5.00	$0.50	$70,000	$280,000	$50,000	0.30	5	15,000
	q = .6 $4.80	$0.50	$70,000	$280,000	$60,000	0.10	6	6,000
	q = .2							
110,000	$5.10	$0.50	$80,000	$280,000	$62,000	0.04	7	2,480
p = .2	q = .2 $5.00	$0.50	$80,000	$280,000	$67,500	0.12	8	8,100
	q = .6 $4.80	$0.50	$80,000	$280,000	$78,500	0.04	9	3,140
	q = .2				Expected Value of Net Income after Tax			$44,710

*Joint probabilities are calculated by multiplying the probabilities on the path (the succession of branches) moving toward each outcome.

67

EXHIBIT 4 Calculation of Expected Values, Standard Deviations and Coefficient of Variation for All Income Statement Items

Dollars in Thousands

Combination	1	2	3	4	5	6	7	8	9
Joint Probability	.06	.18	.06	.10	.30	.10	.04	.12	.04
Sales	$800	$800	$800	$1,000	$1,000	$1,000	$1,100	$1,100	$1,100
Variable Costs:									
Manufacturing	408	400	384	510	500	480	561	550	528
Marketing	40	40	40	50	50	50	55	55	55
Marginal contribution	352	360	376	440	450	470	484	495	517
Managed Costs:									
Manufacturing	10	10	10	20	20	20	30	30	30
Marketing	10	10	10	10	10	10	10	10	10
Administrative	25	25	25	40	40	40	40	40	40
Short-run margin	307	315	331	370	380	400	404	415	437
Committed costs	280	280	280	280	280	280	280	280	280
Net income before tax	$ 27	$ 35	$ 51	$ 90	$ 100	$ 120	$ 124	$ 135	$ 157
Tax @ 50%	13.5	17.5	25.5	45	50	60	62	67.5	78.5
Net income after tax	$ 13.5	$ 17.5	$ 25.5	$ 45	$ 50	$ 60	$ 62	$ 67.5	$ 78.5

In Dollars

	Expected value*	σ^{2}**	σ	Coefficient of Variation***
Sales	$960,000	$12,400,000,000,000	$111,400	11.6%
Variable Costs:				
Manufacturing	478,080	3,164,913,600	56,300	11.8%
Marketing	48,000	31,000,000	5,560	11.6%
Marginal Contribution	433,920	2,623,033,600	51,200	11.8%
Managed Costs				
Manufacturing	19,000	49,000,000	7,000	36.8%
Marketing	10,000	0	0	–
Administrative	35,500	47,250,000	6,870	19.4%
Short-run margin	369,420	1,462,363,600	38,250	10.4%
Committed costs	280,000	0	0	–
Net income before tax	89,420	1,462,363,600	38,240	42.8%
Tax @ 50%	44,710	365,590,900	19,120	42.8%
Net income after tax	44,710	365,590,900	19,120	42.8%

*$\Sigma\, x_1\, p(x_1)$ where the x_1 are the values of each combination and the $p(x_1)$ are the joint probabilities assigned to each x_1.

**$\Sigma\, [x_1^{2}\, p(x_1)] - \mu^{2}$ where μ is the expected value (mean).

***σ ... that σ is the mean

distributions under consideration are not normal. They are discrete probability functions, i.e., functions where the random variable must assume distinct values.

It may be preferable to use the coefficient of variation rather than a probability interval in describing variability for discrete probability distributions of the type shown in Exhibits 3 and 4. The coefficient of variation is the percentage relationship between the standard deviation and the mean. The calculated values of this coefficient are presented in Exhibit 4 for each item in the income statement.

The coefficient of variation is a useful tool for planning and control purposes. From the point of view of planning, the coefficient of variation predicts the potential variability of budgeted items. A high coefficient of variation, for example, indicates that an outcome (e.g., actual sales) has relatively large variations about the budgeted value. From the point of view of control, differences between budgeted and actual outcomes are understood more meaningfully when they are related to the coefficient of variation.

Exhibit 5 summarizes Exhibit 4 in the format of an income statement. The three columns provide the mean, the standard deviation and the coefficient of variation.

An alternative format is presented in Exhibit 6, which displays the 100 percent and the 90-percent probability intervals (or ranges) for the budget items. As the terms imply, the 100-percent probability interval includes all the elements in the distribution, whereas a 90-percent probability interval excludes five percent in each of the two tails of the distribution. Probability intervals are obtained from Exhibit 4 by inspection as explained below.

Clearly the highest and lowest possible values for an item would contain a 100-percent probability interval. This can be obtained readily from Exhibit 4. The 90-percent range, on the other hand, is

arbitrarily chosen in this instance because it fits the distribution of the nine possible values for each item shown in Exhibit 4. The highest value for each item has a probability of 0.04, while the lowest value for each item has a probability of 0.06. Thus the 90-percent range is determined by excluding the highest and lowest values for each item (with the exception of sales). By definition, the 90-percent probability interval as it has been presented here is slightly off center.

The probabilistic income statements of Exhibits 5 and 6 provide more information than the three-level format of Exhibit 2. The improvement results from attaching probabilities to sales and unit variable manufacturing cost. The choice of any of these formats, however, depends on managerial needs and preferences.

A MODEL WITH CONTINUOUS DISTRIBUTION

Thus far we have considered two general approaches to preparing probabilistic income statements, i.e., the three-level and the probability-tree approaches. We now consider the construction of a probabilistic income statement for a model with continuous probability distributions.

Description of the Model

The assumptions of the model are listed in Exhibit 7. Note that basic data (e.g., price, mean volume, or mean-unit variable manufacturing cost) similar to the previous illustrations are adopted. Again the model is for a single-product firm. The main variables (volume and unit variable manufacturing cost) are normally distributed and statistically independent with known means and standard deviations. A relevant range for volume $(80{,}000 \leqslant Q \leqslant 120{,}000)$, but not for unit

EXHIBIT 5   Profit Budget for Year Ending June 197X

	Expected Value	Standard Deviation	Coefficient of Variation
Sales	$960,000	$111,400	11.6%
Variable costs			
Manufacturing	478,080	56,000	11.8
Marketing	48,000	5,560	11.6
Marginal contribution	$433,920	51,220	11.8
Managed fixed costs			
Manufacturing	19,000	7,000	36.8
Marketing	10,000	0	0
Administrative	35,500	6,870	19.4
Short-run margin	$369,420	38,240	10.4
Committed fixed costs			
Manufacturing	180,000	0	0
Marketing	40,000	0	0
Administrative	60,000	0	0
Net income before tax	$ 89,420	38,240	42.8
Tax—50%	44,710	19,120	42.8
Net income after tax	$ 44,710	19,120	42.8

EXHIBIT 6   Profit Budget for Year Ending June 197X

	Expected Value	100% Range	90% Range
Sales	$960,000	$800,000 — $1,100,000	not applicable
Variable costs			
Manufacturing	478,080	384,000 — 561,000	400,000 — 550,000
Marketing	48,000	40,000 — 55,000	40,000 — 55,000
Marginal contribution	$433,920	352,000 — 517,000	360,000 — 495,000
Managed fixed costs			
Manufacturing	19,000	10,000 — 30,000	10,000 — 30,000
Marketing	10,000	—	—
Administrative	35,500	25,000 — 40,000	25,000 — 40,000
Short-run margin	$369,420	307,000 — 307,000	315,000 — 415,000
Committed fixed costs			
Manufacturing	180,000	—	—
Marketing	40,000	—	—
Administrative	60,000	—	—
Net income before tax	$ 89,420	27,000 — 157,000	35,000 — 135,000
Tax — 50%	44,710	13,500 — 78,500	17,500 — 67,500
Net income after tax	$ 44,710	13,500 — 78,500	17,500 — 67,500

variable manufacturing cost, is assumed. In addition, two costs are functions of volume. These are managed manufacturing cost and managed administrative cost. The former has a linear and the latter a quadratic relationship with volume. The other costs, and also unit price are constant.

The model presented may not be representative of the typical firm. Nevertheless, it is useful, for gaining insight into the construction of probabilistic profit budgets.

Difficulties Associated with the Construction of Probability Intervals When the Probability Distributions Are Not Readily Identifiable

To estimate a 95-percent probability interval for the various budget

EXHIBIT 7   Assumed One-Product Company Model

1. Volume (Q) is normally distributed with estimated mean, μ_Q = 100,000 units, standard deviation, σ_Q = 10,000 units, and relevant range 80,000 $\leqslant$ Q $\leqslant$ 120,000.
2. Sales price is constant at $10 per unit.
3. Unit variable manufacturing cost (v) is normally distributed with estimated mean, μ_v = $5.00 and standard deviation, σ_v = $0.20.
4. Volume (Q) and unit variable manufacturing cost (v) are statistically independent.
5. Managed manufacturing cost (Cm mfg) has the following linear relationship with volume (Q):
   Cm mfg = $20,000 + ½ (Q - 100,000),
   within a relevant range: 80,000 $\leqslant$ Q $\leqslant$ 120,000.
6. Managed administrative cost (Cm ad) has the following quadratic relationship with volume (Q):
   Cm ad = $40,000 + 0.25 Q + 0.64 $(10^{-5} Q^2)$
   within a relevant range: 80,000 $\leqslant$ Q $\leqslant$ 120,000.
7. All other costs are constant: managed marketing ($10,000),
   committed manufacturing ($180,000), committed marketing ($40,000),
   committed administrative ($60,000), and variable marketing ($0.50 per unit).

items, we must know how these items are distributed.[13] If these items are normally distributed, or if they belong to distributions that are tabulated, it would be a simple matter to obtain the desired distribution limits. However, in spite of the simplifying assumptions of our model, difficulties associated with identifying the proper distributions occur.

These difficulties increase as one progresses from the top to the bottom of the income statement. This is especially true with regard to the "short-run margin" and the "net income before and after tax" since these items are functions of a product of two normal variables, a linear function of a normal variable and a quadratic function of a normal variable.[14] Without knowing the specific or approximate distribution of these functions one cannot hope to obtain a probability interval for the items under consideration.

The distribution of these functions can be derived with involved numerical and mathematical techniques. By using simulation, however, we can more easily derive such probability intervals.

PROBABILISTIC INTERVALS THROUGH SIMULATION

The model described in Exhibit 7 was simulated by computer and the mean and a 95-percent probability interval for each budget item was determined. The result is the profit budget of Exhibit 8.

The simulation program involved 1000 iterations; for in this type of problem, experience indicated that 1000 iterations yields a reasonable approximation to the theoretical distribution.[15] We have partially verified this in our case as test runs of 3000 iterations did not produce significantly different results.

[13] The probability interval could be set at whatever level desired if 95 percent is considered inappropriate.
[14] The Short-Run Margin, SRM = 60,000 + Q $(8.75 - v) - .64(10^{-5})Q^2$, where Q is the volume, v is the unit variable manufacturing cost, and Q and v are independently and normally distributed. Net income before and after tax is of the same form.

[15] Additional information concerning how many iterations are appropriate in this type of problem is available in:
R. W. Conway, "Some Tactical Problems in Digital Simulation," *Management Science*, October 1963, p. 49.
Daniel Teichroew, "A History of Distribution Sampling Prior to the Era of the Computer and its Relevance to Simulation," *Journal of the American Statistical Association*, March 1965, pp. 27-49.

EXHIBIT 8   Profit Budget for Year Ending June 197X

	Expected Value	95% Probability Interval*
Sales	$1,002,146	$807,746 − $1,195,900
Variable costs		
Manufacturing	500,452	406,370 − 600,546
Marketing	50,123	40,387 − 59,795
Marginal contribution	$ 451,571	366,022 − 548,412
Managed fixed costs		
Manufacturing	20,111	10,387 − 29,795
Marketing	10,000**	−
Administrative	49,937	20,825 − 70,049
Short-run margin	$ 371,523	314,057 − 433,914
Committed fixed costs		
Manufacturing	180,000**	−
Marketing	40,000**	−
Administrative	60,000**	−
Net income before tax	$ 91,523	34,057 − 153,914
Tax − 50%	45,762	15,682 − 75,870
Net income after tax	$ 45,761	15,682 − 75,870

*Determined by dropping the upper and lower 2 1/2 percent of the 1000 iterations.
**Costs which are constant do not have a probability interval since they are considered "certain".

SUMMARY AND CONCLUSIONS

This paper presents three methods for the construction of probabilistic profit and loss statements: the three-level, the probability-tree and the continuous distribution approaches.

The paper begins with a typical profit and loss statement which displays most likely values. Valuable information, however, is added to budgeted profit and loss statements if every item in those statements displays a mean and a probability interval. The mean is an expected value—what the value of the item would be on the average if we are afforded a large number of trials. The probability interval, on the other hand, tells us that a stated percentage of the distribution of a budget item falls within a given range. Thus the probability interval serves as a measure of variability for the budget item. Other indices of variability suggested are, of course, the standard deviation and the coefficient of variation.

In models with continuous distributions, it is recommended that Monte Carlo simulation be used where the probability distributions in question are difficult to handle analytically. One thousand iterations usually yield an accurate approximation of the desired distributions.

Budgeting :
Functional Analysis and
Behavioral Implications *

**V. Bruce
Irvine**

*University of
Saskatchewan*

The budget can be a powerful tool for motivating people to
achieve the organization's objectives or it can be a positive
hindrance. This article analyzes the effects of budgeting on
people and shows how it can lead to either bad or good
consequences according to the way it is applied in various
types of organization.

Reprinted from *Cost and Management*, March-April 1970, 6-16. Used
by permission of V. Bruce Irvine and *Cost and Management*.

Many of those who have written about
budgets have emphasized the problems
resulting from typical budgeting systems.
Little enthusiasm has been voiced for the
practical effectiveness of budgets as a
means of obtaining the optimal benefits
of which such a device is capable.

A more positive approach might result
from a consideration of the control and
motivational effects of budgets on the
behavior of people. But an analysis of the
reactions of these people (supervisors,
foremen, laborers) to control devices
(such as budgets) has received little attention as a specific subject in the literature
of the past decade. The studies reported
have usually concentrated attention on
improving the usefulness of budgets from
a top management viewpoint and have

de-emphasized the subordinate positions.
Also, many of the studies have been
conducted by behavioral scientists and
have not been incorporated into accounting and management thought and teach-
ing. Consequently, although accountants
and management are aware that their
actions have behavioral implications, they
have not thoroughly understood what
these are. The result is uncertainty, confusion and indecision when human problems do arise.

The purpose of this article will be to
make a functional analysis of budgeting
towards the goal of maximizing long-run
profits (considered to be the present
value of the owner's net worth). An
analysis of reactions of the employees on
whom budgets are primarily exercised,
rather than a purely management viewpoint analysis, will be used to develop
basic propositions. Human behavioral

*Condensation of a thesis submitted for R.I.A.
qualification to the Society of Industrial Accountants of Saskatchewan.

aspects of budgets, therefore, become a very relevant factor in this approach. After investigation of why employees react as they do, the usefulness of budgets in view of such reactions and the implications of suggestions for making budgets more successful and acceptable can be considered within particular situations facing modern-day business.

DEFINITIONAL AND TECHNICAL CONSIDERATIONS

A functional analysis considers the various consequences of a particular activity and determines whether or not these consequences aid in the achievement of the organization's objective. According to Merton,[1] the consequences of an activity are functional if they increase the ability of a given system to achieve a desired goal. A consequence is dysfunctional if it hinders the achievement of the goal. Consequences of an activity may also be classified as manifest (recognized and intended by the participants in the system) or latent (neither intended nor recognized). Decisions based only on manifest consequences may often be incorrect because of latent consequences.

A budget is a device intended to provide greater effectiveness in achieving organizational efficiency. To be effective, however, the functional aspects must outweigh the dysfunctional aspects. Whether or not this will be true will depend upon many factors which will be discussed and summarized in a model of the elements of budgeting.

First, it is necessary to understand what a budget is. Although formal definitions of a budget exist, a definition is not always the most relevant aspect of understanding a concept.

Amitai Etzioni distinguishes between two types of models in organizational analysis.[2] The survival system consists of activities which, if fulfilled, allow a system to exist. Budgets are not part of such a system. Organizations in the past have functioned and in the future will function without the help of budgets. Budgets can be classified within an effectiveness system. These "define a pattern of interactions among the elements of the system which would make it more effective in the service of a given goal."[3]

A budget, as a formal set of figures written on a piece of paper, is in itself merely a quantified plan for future activities. However, when budgets are used for control, planning and motivation, they become instruments which cause functional and dysfunctional consequences both manifest and latent which determine how successful the tool will be.

Budgets mean different things to different people according to their different point of view. Accountants see them from the preparation aspect, managers from the implementation aspect, and behavioral scientists from the human implication aspect. All of these viewpoints must be melded together if budgets are to obtain the best functional results.

There are many types of budgets. The major purpose for having budgets, the type of organization using a budget, the personalities of people handling the budget, the personal characteristics of people subject to budget direction, the leadership style of the organization, and the method of preparing a budget are all

[1]Merton, R., "A Paradigm for Functional Analysis in Sociology" in *Sociological Theory: A Book of Readings* by L. Coser and B. Rosenberg, New York, MacMillan, 1957, pp. 458-467.

[2]Etzioni, Amitai, "Two Approaches to Organizational Analysis: A Critique and a Suggestion" in Bobbs-Merrill Reprint Series in the Social Sciences 8-80. Reprinted by permission of *Administrative Science Quarterly*, Vol. 5 (Sept. 1960), pp. 257-278.

[3]Ibid., p. 272.

factors accounting for budget type and style.

The technical procedures involved in the preparation and use of budget figures are similar for most organizations. People make estimates (standards) of what they expect should reflect future events. These estimates are then compared to what actually happened and the differences (variances) are studied.

THE FUNCTIONAL ASPECTS OF BUDGET SYSTEMS

In what specific way do budgets make management action more efficient and effective in maximizing the present value of the owners' worth?

Basically, a budget system enables management more effectively to plan, coordinate, control and evaluate the activities of the business. These are functional, manifest consequences in terms of their desirability.

Planning means establishing objectives in advance so that members of the organization will have specific, activity-directed goals to guide their actions. Budgets are quantitative plans for action. As such, they force management to examine the available resources and to determine how these can be used efficiently.

The point that budgets require this clarification and concrete quantification of ideas is not usually recognized directly by budgeting people as a benefit. As such, it could be considered functional and latent.

The planning aspect of budgeting has other latent functions. Planning requires that the plans be communicated to those involved in carrying them out. Communication is enhanced by distributing the budget to those responsible for various parts of it.

A budget makes lower level managers more aware of where they fit into an organization. Their budget indicates what is expected of them and that they have a goal towards which their activities are to be directed.

With a budget, junior (new) members of an organization have a better idea of where the company is going and are made to feel that the business is concerned about their future. This can affect both their own future plans and the company's recruitment policy and turnover problems.

When a person is given an objective, he is more likely to feel that he is part of the organization and that the upper echelons are interested in his work. Conversely, top management is likely to become more interested in, and aware of, the activities of lower level employees.

These latent, functional consequences of budgets create interest and, possibly, enthusiasm which increases morale and could result in greater efficiency and initiative.

Planning of departmental activities must be coordinated so that bottle-necks do not occur and inter-departmental strife can be limited. A budget system can assist in this coordination. By basing organizational activity on the limiting factor (such as sales, production, working capital), a comprehensive budget coordinating all of the firm's activities can be approved by top management and the controller. Such a budget permits these people to bring together their overall knowledge of the firm's abilities and limitations. By using budgets to coordinate activities, the organization is more likely to operate at an optimal level, given the constraints on its resources.

The control consequences are among the more important aspects of budgeting. Because a budget plan exists, decisions are not merely spontaneous reactions to stimuli in an environment of unclarified goals. The budget provides relevant information to a decision maker at the time he must choose between alternatives. Therefore, a budget implicitly incorporates control at the point of the decision. However, provision for taking advantage of unforseen situations should certainly be allowed even though a budget is violated.

A second type of control can be derived from budgets. A comparison of actual with budgeted performance after decisions have been made reveals to management the performance of the organization as a whole and of the individual responsible members.

A comparison merely reveals discrepancies. The action which is taken as a result of variances is in the hands of management. But the investigation of why there are variances, whether or not they are controllable, and the resulting control procedures is stimulated by the budgeting process. The result is the discovery of methods to save costs, improvement in the firm's efficiency, and better future planning.

Control of both types is important to top management because it cannot maintain personal contact with those in the lower management ranks. Devices such as budgets, employment contracts, job descriptions and rules are therefore necessary to direct subordinate behavior. In general, control is based on the assumption that individuals are motivated by their own security needs to fulfil the plans and obey the rules. To the extent that this is true, the benefits to be derived from the control aspects of budgeting can be deemed functional and manifest.

These benefits could be obtained only in the ideal situation where budgets work as they are intended to work. The theoretical benefits make budgets very appealing devices, but the practical problems of implementing and using them greatly affect their usefulness. Most of the problems arise from the difficulty of convincing people to accept and use a budget. Mechanical problems also exist. These difficulties create many possibilities for dysfunctional consequences to occur with the result that some functional consequences become difficult, if not impossible, to attain.

DYSFUNCTIONAL ASPECTS OF BUDGET SYSTEMS

Any system which involves motivation and control of individuals has dysfunctional aspects, simply because human behavior cannot be predicted or controlled with certainty. Frequently, activities by management to obtain desired functional results will actually lead to dysfunctional consequences. Management must understand why such a reversal can occur so that existing problems can be solved or an environment created which prevents problems arising.

This section will indicate how results of a budget system can be dysfunctional in nature. The basic approach will be to analyze the deterrents to achieving particular functional results. Within a particular organization, the dysfunctional aspects must be considered in relation to the functional aspects in order to evaluate the worthiness of a budget system. Obviously, if the dysfunctional consequences of an action outweigh the functional aspects, management should delete the activity. Because each business is unique, no attempt can be made to state that certain activities will be dysfunctional or functional in every situation.

Because factors which can lead to dysfunctional consequences are complex, each will be analyzed separately although it is realized they are usually inter-related.

A. THE TERM "BUDGET"

The first dysfunctional consequence of a budget system results from the name itself. Traditionally, budgets have carried a negative connotation for many:

> ... some of the words historically associated with the term budget are; imposed, dictated by the top, authorized. And what are the original purposes of control—to reduce, to eliminate, to increase productivity, to secure conformance, to assure compliance, to inform about deviation. An historical meaning of budget is to husband resources—to be niggardly, tight, Scrooge-like.[4]

If attitudes expressing such beliefs are not eliminated at the start, the budget will never get off the ground. One method of eliminating this problem is to refrain from calling the activity "budgeting."

B. ORGANIZATIONAL ARRANGEMENTS OF AUTHORITY AND RESPONSIBILITY

If a budget system is to be used to control and evaluate personnel, the persons involved must possess responsibility and authority over what is being assigned to them. Consequently a large and/or decentralized organization would probably have a greater potential use for budgeting than would a small, highly centralized business.

Centralized organizations may simply use budgets to plan and coordinate future activities. Because responsibility, control and authority rest with the top executives in such a business, any attempt to reward, punish or hold lower level employees responsible for variances would achieve nothing beneficial and would probably cause resentment. Any negative feelings

on the part of those who follow directives in carrying out operations would likely lead to less than optimal achievement of organizational objectives. Therefore, even though budgets can be used to improve planning and coordination, assignment of control responsibilities where there is no power to carry out those responsibilities could easily create dysfunctional, latent consequences.

On the other hand, over-emphasis on departmentalization can also have dysfunctional, latent effects:

> Budget records, as administered, foster a narrow viewpoint on the part of the user. The budget records serve as a constant reminder that the important aspect to consider is one's own department and not one's own plant.[5]

Over-emphasis on one's own department can lead to considerable cost in man hours, money and interpersonal relations when responsibility for variances, particularly large ones, is being determined. The result is a weakening of cooperation and coordination between departments.

C. ROLE-CONFLICT ASPECTS OF BUDGETING

Status differences, or more accurately role-conflict between staff and line personnel, are an important source of dysfunctional consequences. The problems created affect budget usefulness directly and also indirectly through their effect on communication, motivation and participation. The basic difficulties arise because of differences in the way budget staff people and line personnel under-

[4]Green, Jr., David, "Budgeting and Accounting: The Inseparable Siamese Twins," *Budgeting,* Nov. 1965, p. 11.

[5]Argyris, Chris, *The Impact of Budgets on People,* Ithaca, N.Y. Prepared for the Controllership Foundation, Inc. at Cornell University, 1952, p. 23.

stand the budgeting system and each other.

From Figure 1,[6] it can be seen how important budgets and the budget staff are in the supervisors' or foremen's working world. Ninety-nine per cent of the supervisors and foremen questioned in four companies stated that the budget department was either first or second in importance of impact on the performance of their activity.

FIGURE 1   Responses to the request "Name the departments affecting your actions most" asked of supervisors and foremen individually in four firms.

	Most Affect	2nd Most Affect	Total
Production Control	55%		
Budget Department	45%	54%	99%

From the supervisors' and foremen's follow-up comments, it was readily apparent that the budget department's influence was not only significant, it was usually considered troublesome as well. Why should this be so? Some suggested reasons are:

1. Line employees see budgets as providing results only and not the reasons for those results. Any explanations of variances by the financial staff, such as failure to meet expected production or inadequate use of materials, prove grossly insufficient. Causes behind these explanations still have to be determined before the supervisors and foremen could consider budget reports as being useful to them or presenting a fair appraisal of their activities to top management.

[6]The source of this figure and study is Argyris, C., op. cit., a summary of comments and statements, pp. 10-12.

2. Budgets are seen as emphasizing past performance and as a device for predicting the future. Supervisors and foremen are basically concerned with the present and with handling immediate problems. Budget figures would often be ignored in order to solve present difficulties.

3. Supervisors and foremen apparently see budgets as being too rigid. In some cases, budget standards have not been changed for two or three years. Even if they now met such a budget, they often would not be performing efficiently. Budget people would then adjust the budget. In such cases, those working under a budget would not really know what was expected of them until after they had submitted their cost reports and had received a control report.

4. Supervisors and foremen would also resent the opposite treatment of constantly changing a budget in the belief that increased efficiency would result. Such a procedure would lead them to believe, and often justly so, that budgets were unrealistically set. Budget men would be seen as individuals who could never be satisfied as they would raise the budget if a person made or came close to his previous budget. This would only result in frustration for the supervisor or foreman. The feeling that the company executives did not believe in the supervisor's own desire to do a good job could easily be implied when budgets are continually changing.

5. Thoughts about budgets are further aggravated when foremen and supervisors receive budget reports on their performance in a complicated format with an analysis that is incomprehensible to them. Supervisors felt that the job of budget people was to be critical and that the use of jargon

and specialized formats enabled them to justify their criticism of others without too much debate.

Whether or not these criticisms are logical and rational is not important. The point is that such feelings can and do exist. If the budget is regarded as merely emphasizing history, being too rigid, unrealistic, unattainable and unclear and if budget people are seen as over-concerned with figures, unconcerned with line problems and cut off by a language of their own, there can be no doubt that the effectiveness of a budget system would deteriorate.

The problems are compounded if the budget personnel's attitude is uncon-ducive to overcoming these opinions. Budget people should see their jobs as examining, analyzing and looking for new ways to improve plant efficiency. They should also think of a budget as an objective that should fairly challenge fac-tory personnel. Since it cannot be as-sumed that line personnel subscribe to or even recognize these ideas, the ideas should be impressed upon them directly through adequate budget introduction and education. Moreover, the effective use of budgets cannot be forced upon supervisors and foremen; it must be ac-cepted by them. This can only be accom-plished if budget people try to work constructively with line people as compa-triots rather than commanders. This ac-cord is usually very difficult to bring about. Often budget people will not even attempt it or simply give up on it because of lack of success. They conclude, cor-rectly or incorrectly, that the line person-nel's unsatisfactory use of budgets is due to their lack of education, understanding and interest.

Given this unwillingness to buck line opposition by the budget personnel and the line's viewpoint of budgeting as a hindrance to their performance, a classic role-conflict is created. The optimal bene-fits possible from budgeting cannot be obtained in such an environment.

Argyris also determined how foremen and supervisors felt the potential dysfunc-tional results of budgeting could be over-come. Suggestions dealt mainly with improving the outlook of budget men. According to the line personnel, bud-geting people should be taught that bud-gets are merely opinions, not the "be-all and end-all". They should also be taught, it was felt, that line employees are not inherently lazy, that budget men should learn to look at a problem from another's point of view, and that they are not superior to supervisory people. Also sug-gested were the use of timely and under-standable reports to foremen and super-visors, the practice of conferring with people who have variances so that the budget report indicates the real cause to top management, and the setting of real-istic budgets.

The problems arising are not, however, entirely the fault of the budget staff. Supervisors and foremen must put more effort into understanding the budget fig-ures, they must not be continually suspi-cious of budgets, and they should use budgets in performing their duties. Most important, they should alter their out-look toward budgeting. Budgets must be realistic and fair, but also foremen and supervisors should realize that the budget is designed to help them achieve the standards management expects of them.

How can these requirements be achieved? An educational program in-volving foremen, supervisors, middle and upper management, and budget personnel could help to clarify the different view-points and promote understanding of each other's objectives and difficulties. Such a program should precede the intro-duction of a budgeting system and continue after the system has been introduced.

D. BUDGETS AND NON-MANAGEMENT PEOPLE

The involvement of laborers (non-management personnel) in the budgeting process presents both functional and dysfunctional possibilities. Often, front-line supervisors who have a budget to meet do not use it as a device to spur their subordinates. According to the comments reported by Argyris, they fear that workers would look upon such action unfavorably and that no benefit would be received.

The proposition that workers would not respond to budgetary pressures is challenged by W. F. Whyte:

How do workers see budgets? They often recognize that management people are worried about costs, but with the foremen afraid to put the cost situation to them, they remain uninvolved in the struggle.[7]

Since workers generally have not been directly involved in budgetary systems, the question of whether or not such involvement would be functional is unresolved.

E. MOTIVATIONAL ASPECTS OF BUDGETING

The most controversial area of budgeting concerns its motivational implications.

The budget makes available information for comparison of expected with actual performance. When such an evaluation of performance is known to result

in rewards and punishments, people are expected to be motivated to do their best. Let us examine this assumption and its possible functional or dysfunctional consequences.

Argyris states that budgets are principal instruments for creating pressure which motivates individuals.[8] Budgets can also be seen as creating more pressure than they actually do. This "pressure illusion" is due to the fact that the budget is a concrete, quantitative instrument and managers and supervisors, feeling pressure from more abstract sources, place the blame for it on the concrete budget.

Factors directly related to budget pressures are budget "pep" talks (A), red circles around poor showings (B), production and sales drives using budgets (C), threats of reprimand (D), and feelings of failure if budgets are not met (E). These can all be considered as functional and manifest in terms of their motivational intent.

There are, however, counteracting effects which can be dysfunctional and latent in terms of budget effectiveness. These factors include informal agreements among managers and/or supervisors (V), fear of loss of job if efficiency increases but cannot be maintained (W), union agreements against speedups (X), performance abilities of individual employees (Y), and abilities of work teams as a whole (Z).

Equilibrium is attained when;

$$A + B + C + D + E = V + W + X + Y + Z$$

Management, by increasing one or more of the components on the left hand side of the relationship or by adding additional ones, can increase productivity. This increase is matched by an increase in tension, uneasiness, resent-

---

[7]Whyte, W. F., *Men at Work*, Richard D. Irwin, Inc. and The Dorsey Press, Inc., Homewood, Ill., 1961, p. 495.

[8]Op. cit., Argyris.

ment and suspicion on the part of the employees. This pressure increase is absorbed by joining groups which are strongly cohesive against top management and budget people. Again equilibrium is attained but each time pressures are increased by top management, they must become more intense as resistance is higher.

When and if management feels that the pressures are detrimental to the organization, it may attempt to reduce the causes on the left hand side of the equation. This does not result in decreased anti-management feeling because the groups have developed into relatively permanent social units and the individuals feel the pressures may occur again. Therefore, in the long run, increasing pressures may be very dysfunctional because of these latent features.

The rational way for management to approach this problem would be to concentrate its activities on reducing the forces that decrease efficiency rather than on increasing the factors that tend to increase efficiency.

Other dysfunctional ways of relieving motivational pressure could easily exist:

1. Interdepartmental strife could occur. A manager, supervisor or foreman could try to blame the variances on someone else. This would result in concentrated effort by individuals to promote only the cause of their own departments. The personal rivalries thus caused and the lack of co-operation among departments could mean decreased efficiency for the company in achieving its overall goals.

2. Another type of strife develops when the line employees blame the staff employees for their predicaments and absolve themselves of the responsibility for the variances. Budget people become scapegoats for problems and salesmen are blamed for incorrect pre-

dictions or orders that make the production process unstable.

3. An individual may internalize the personal pressure he feels. By not outwardly showing his problems, he would build up tension within himself. Eventually, frustration would develop and he would perform less efficiently in the long run.

4. If internal means of relieving pressure are used, manipulation of activities may result. Reporting sizable variances when one knows he will be over his budget may allow him to shift his costs so that he will easily make his budget in the next period. Saving easy jobs until just before the end of a budget period may enable a person to achieve the stipulated goal.

The point is that, in the short run, increasing motivational pressure through budgets may be functional but, in the long run, it may also be very dysfunctional.

Andrew C. Stedry postulates additional concepts concerning motivation through budgeting.[9] Through experiment, Stedry developed the findings shown in Figure 2.

The level of costs for which a person will strive (aspired costs) will be conceived by the individual in relation to past experience, confidence in his personal skills, expectation of future difficulties, and his feelings about the budget costs. Aspired and budget costs do not necessarily (or usually) coincide. The aspired costs are what the individual sets for himself. The budget costs are set by top management. When actual costs are compared to these two costs, the reaction of the employees depends on the discrepancies involved:

[9]Stedry, Andrew C., *Budget Control and Cost Behavior*, Englewood Cliffs, N.J., Prentice-Hall, Inc., 1960.

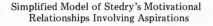

Simplified Model of Stedry's Motivational
Relationships Involving Aspirations

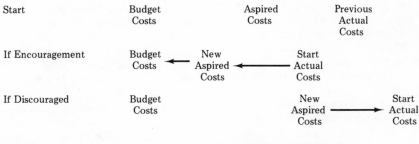

Start	Budget Costs	Aspired Costs	Previous Actual Costs
If Encouragement	Budget Costs	← New Aspired Costs ←	Start Actual Costs
If Discouraged	Budget Costs	New Aspired Costs →	Start Actual Costs
If Failure		Quit or a Change in the System such as a Lowering of the Budget	

FIGURE 2

1. Other things being equal, aspiration levels will move relative to the actual costs depending on the degree of discrepancy.

2. A person will be encouraged if the discrepancy between actual costs and aspired costs is not greater than an amount known as the discouragement point. Aspirations would be set higher on the next period of performance measurement.

3. A person will be discouraged if the discrepancy is greater than the discouragement point but less than a failure point. In this case, aspirations would move downward.

4. If the discrepancy is greater than the failure point, the system would cease to exist or a new one would be needed. Otherwise the individual concerned would resign.

Stedry concludes that management should set high, unattainable budgets to motivate individuals to achieve the greatest efficiency. "Unattainable" would have to mean that the discrepancy between aspired costs, formulated after the high budget was presented, and actual costs could not exceed the discouragement point. Such a policy would mean that individuals receiving separate budgets would be manipulated in accordance with the variances in the size of their discouragement points.

This may sound all right in theory but in practice the reactions of employees could make this a dangerous proposition for long-run efficiency. If individuals found out that they were the subjects of out-right manipulation, they could become rebellious and ignore future budgets whether they were fair or not. Other management control devices would probably be considered with unwarranted suspicion. Moreover, how is management going to determine the aspiration level and discouragement point of each individual, a necessary requirement for setting "personal" budgets? The use of individual budget standards would also have to be kept confidential. Otherwise, the resentment that employees would feel might lead them to resist all budgeting attempts and even to leave the organization.

Stedry's study suggests that participation in budget preparation is not as beneficial as having management set the budget. He points out, however, that participation may be desirable where low budgets are given as managers, supervisors and foremen would likely feel that they are capable of achieving greater efficiency and would say so.

Stedry's study is limited in that long-run results were not extensively examined. Also, the nature of his "laboratory" data leads to serious questions as to whether "real business world" conditions were reproduced.[10] However, his research on the reactions of lower level management to budgets does help to explain the behavior of these people. The study also indicates how management can improve a budgeting process where budgets are being ignored or causing personnel problems, because it shows why such situations exist.

Another consequence of budgetary motivation which has received little emphasis involves "a fear of failure" on the part of the individual. The failure to meet a budget or at least come close to it when it is accepted and fairly determined and when other members of a person's reference group are successful, represents a potential loss of status both within the group and the organization. A person's self-concept is also deflated in such circumstances.

The fear of such a loss may be a stronger motivating factor for a person to achieve his budget than any of the other pressures mentioned. "Fear of failure" then is a very powerful functional consequence of budgeting systems and, quite likely, is latent.

One of the major benefits of budgeting is motivation, explicitly incorporated in the use of standards. Budgets should reflect a goal which people can strive towards and achieve. To provide maximum motivation for employees, management should judge failure to achieve an objective in the context of the situation

causing failure and not merely in terms of a figure circled in red. All members of the organization must be aware of this basic principle.

F. PARTICIPATION IN BUDGETING

In a participatory system of budgeting, preparation of budget schedules would start at the lower levels of the hierarchy and move upward. As it moved upward, various people would make additional suggestions and some eliminations until the schedules reached the controller and top management. These people would analyze it and see that it was a coordinated plan in accordance with organizational goals before final approval would be given. Movement up and down the hierarchy could be made if drastic changes were necessary. By reciprocal communications, people would know why changes were justified and could constructively criticize them if they desired.

Behavioral scientists and accountants generally believe that such a system would be an improvement on imposed budgets. The functional, manifest results claimed for this system are:

1. It would have a healthful effect on interest, initiative, morale and enthusiasm.

2. It would result in a better plan because the knowledge of many individuals is combined.

3. It would make all levels of management more aware of how their particular functions fit into the total operational picture.

4. It would increase interdepartmental cooperation.

5. As a result of their direct involvement in the planning function, it would make junior management more aware of the future with respect to

[10] Becker, Selwyn and David Green, Jr., "Budgeting and Employee Behavior" in *Journal of Business*, Vol. 35 (1962). These are among the authors who debate the practical application of Stedry's conclusions.

objectives, problems and other considerations.

It is possible to achieve these benefits
through successful participation. There
are, however, factors that have a significant impact on whether or not participation can lead to successful results.

One essential requirement is that participation be legitimate. If participation
is allowed but top management continually changes the budgeted figures resulting from participation, legitimate participation does not exist. This might
better be described as a form of "pseudo-
participation." The supposed "participants" would likely resent such a policy
and the consequences would be dysfunctional. This is borne out by the
studies of V. H. Vroom who found
that productivity was higher when participation was viewed as legitimate, but
lower when it was viewed as not legitimate.[11]

Other factors limiting the usefulness of
budget participation are:

1. Personality differences of managers as reflected in their leadership
style are important. Aggressive managers can put forth their demands
more strongly than meek ones. Subordinates would view the latter as not
looking out for their interests and
antagonism between subordinates and
their superiors, and managers themselves, could easily develop.

2. An autocratic, centralized organization would have little use for a
participation policy whereas a democratic, decentralized organization
would likely benefit from, and almost
require, a participation policy.

3. Those allowed participation rights
must be positively oriented towards

the objectives of the firm. Only if the
group is cohesive in thought and desire
toward, and understands, the plan can
participation policy be functional.

4. The cultural setting of an organization and the background of employees should be considered. People in
rural areas or with a rural background
are more inclined to accept assigned
tasks. In such an atmosphere, a participation policy would probably meet
with little response.

Studies have been carried out showing
that participation in any situation is not
necessarily useful for increasing efficiency.[12] Other studies have reported that
when a non-participative group became
participative and was compared with an
existing non-participative or participative
group, the former never caught up in
terms of performance with the latter two
groups. These studies imply that the
introduction of a participation policy for
a formerly non-participative group would
not likely lead to increased efficiency and
may even result in decreased efficiency. If
this conclusion is accepted, a group
should be endowed with the right to
participate only when the group is created or the budget system is being implemented and not after either has previously been directed through decisions
made by superiors.

The most severe criticism offered
against participation is that the increased
morale which supposedly results does not
necessarily result in increased efficiency.
Is high morale a cause of increased
efficiency or is greater efficiency a cause
of high morale, or is there some inter-

[11]Stedry, Andrew C., "Budgeting and Employee Behavior: A Reply" in *Journal of
Business*, Vol. 37 (April 1964), p. 198.

[12]See Stedry, ibid., p. 196; also Morse, Nancy
and Reimer, E., "The Experimental Change of a
Major Organizational Variable" in *Journal of
Abnormal and Social Psychology*, Vol. LII
(1956), pp. 120-129; and French, Jr., J. R. P.,
Kay, E. and Meyer, H. H., *A Study of Threat
and Participation in a Performance Appraisal
Situation*, New York, General Electric Co.,
1962.

vening variable which must be present if a true causal relationship is to exist? Group cohesiveness seems to be the most significant of possible variables that have been examined although other variables are obviously involved. Figure 3 shows postulated relationships that could develop using group cohesiveness with regard to subordinate thoughts toward management.

upper management would be forced to revise them. Pseudo-participation would exist and likely result in the increase of negative attitudes toward management or budgeting.

If the atmosphere is favorable for allowing participation, group cohesiveness toward management and budgeting should be maintained and enhanced if possible. Group discussions led by an able

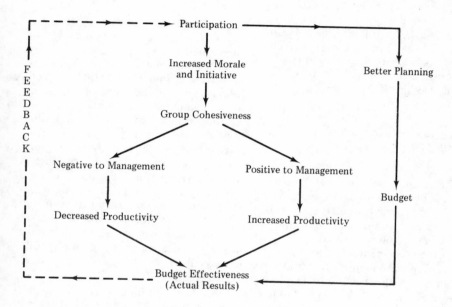

FIGURE 3. Participation and Budgets

As those participating in a budget (foremen and up) would be management-oriented, at least to some extent, they would probably have a positive approach to management activities and objectives. The previous discussion on role-conflict situations shows, however, that negative attitudes towards budgeting are quite possible.

If the group is anti-management or anti-budget, a participation policy would be of little use. Supervisors may even propose ridiculously low standards and

management man to inform *and* listen to supervisors, foremen and other management people could probably aid in implementing the budget. By listening to and taking action on suggestions made by the group, he would be able to indicate his and top management's sincerity in gaining successful participation in the budgeting system.

Undoubtedly, the evidence on the effectiveness of participation in budgeting is mixed. Supporters of participation readily admit that it is by no means a panacea for achieving the full motivational potential of the budget. The fact is that participation is not a segregated aspect of management but embraces several technical and behavioral concepts which make it more or less useful in different organizations. The organization's particular situation with regard to the development of these concepts must be recognized and thoughtfully considered when contemplating or evaluating a participation policy.

It should be noted that, even if productivity does not increase directly through participation, better planning and increased morale and initiative may, of themselves, justify such a policy.

G. COMMUNICATION ASPECTS OF BUDGETING

Researchers on control and motivation generally agree that information on planned and actual results should be communicated to the employee whose performance is being measured.

Nevertheless, many budget departments merely communicate the results to management with the result that the employee does not know how he has done until he is called up to discuss his performance report. Consequently, the individual may ignore the budget and perform without a guide, hoping for the best.

When results are communicated as rapidly as possible, an employee's mistakes can be associated with his recent actions and he is likely to learn more from the experience than if reports are received long after the action has been taken. This learning would likely result in improved performance on future budgets.

When reports given to management employees are timely, reasonably accurate and understandable, functional con-

sequences are more likely to occur than if the opposite exists. Figure 4 summarizes the effect of the communication system on the behavior of line people.

H. EMPLOYEE GROUP BEHAVIOR AND ITS EFFECTS ON BUDGETING

Peter Blau's study on the use of statistical measures in evaluating employee performance has implications for evaluating and understanding budgeting.[13] The study examined the effect of group cohesiveness, in the sense of willingness to cooperate among members, and the resulting productivity in different situations.

His findings showed that the group which cooperated was more productive than the group which did not cooperate but competed individually among themselves. He also discovered that highly competitive individuals in the latter group were more productive than any individual in the cooperative group. Blau's hypothesis was that a paradox existed:

> ... The resulting paradox is that competitiveness and productivity are inversely related for groups but directly related for individuals in the competitive group.[14]

In terms of the achievement of organizational objectives, the implication is that cooperative cohesiveness among group members assigned a particular task is most desirable. When this is achieved,

[13]Blau, Peter M., "Cooperation and Competition in a Bureaucracy" in Bobbs-Merrill Reprint Series in the Social Sciences, S-28. Reprinted by the permission of *The American Journal of Sociology*, Vol. LIX, May 1964.
[14]Ibid., p. 530.

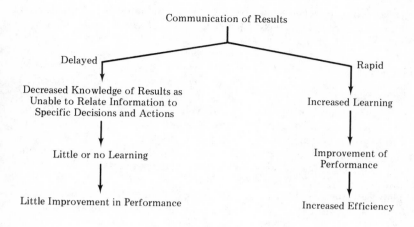

FIGURE 4. The Importance of the Communication Factor When Using Budgets to Control and Motivate Employees

cooperation will result in each member helping others in the group even though it may result in a decrease in the performance record of the assisting individual.

Applying this to budgeting, the suggestion is that individual performance should not be the ultimate objective in the eyes of top management or employees. Rewards and punishments should not be based entirely on an individual's performance as compared to the plan. The budget reports should be only one of many factors used for evaluation and superiors should recognize this fact. The result would be a decline in individual competition and greater cooperation towards the achievement of a goal. This environment could eliminate possible dysfunctional consequences. Group cohesiveness will be affected greatly by the leadership style of the group's superior. Whether he believes in rigidity or flexibility, whether he is authoritative or democratic, and the freedom granted him by the organizational structure and policies, will influence the way he controls his subordinates.

I. MECHANICAL CONSIDERATIONS OF BUDGETING

Dysfunctional consequences can arise from the mechanical aspects of budgeting.

Budgeting systems cost money to install and continue. These costs must always be considered in evaluating the worthiness of a system.

It must also be remembered that budgets are merely estimates or predictions. As such, they could be incorrect or inappropriate because of economic, technical and environmental changes. The estimating procedure itself may be inappropriate. If budgets are thought of as a goal rather than a means of reaching the goal, the emphasis on budgets cannot help but carry dysfunctional consequences, particularly when the estimates have been incorrectly computed.

A final mechanical problem involves the assignment of costs to the person deemed responsible for them. There is always a strong possibility that costs assigned to one person may have been caused by another. The subsequent bickering and ill-feeling would obviously be dysfunctional.

Budgets must be capable of flexibility. This is fundamentally the result of management attitudes and not inherent in the budget itself. Management must recognize that forced adherence to a plan could cause decisions to be made that are not in the long-run interest of the business. Unforeseen opportunities may arise which were not planned. A decision resulting in a significant, unfavorable variance on the short-range plan may be the best alternative in terms of long-range profitability. Failure to take advantage of such situations may result in adherence to the budget but also in dysfunctional consequences in terms of achieving the objectives of budgeting.

Alternatively, failure to adhere to budget figures when they are correct, merely to protect the individuals involved or their superiors, must also be avoided. Such an attitude would destroy one of the corner-stones of a successful budgeting system.

GENERAL MODEL OF THE CONSEQUENCES OF A BUDGETING SYSTEM

Figure 5 summarizes the factors which must be considered when determining the functional and dysfunctional consequences possible from a budgeting system.

The square immediately outside the BUDGET square indicates the potential benefits to be derived from a successful budgeting system. These benefits are functional to the more efficient achievement of an organization's goal of making profit. The next surrounding square indicates many of the factors which can aid

or prevent the achievement of the desired benefits. The descriptive model is arranged so that the effects of various environmental circumstances and managerial policies (participation, motivational intentions, organization structure, etc.) can be immediately related to a particular benefit (planning). The square at the top of the diagram includes factors which are not specifically related to any one particular benefit but which have an important influence on the success or failure of the overall budget system.

The points mentioned in the peripheral square and the top square cannot be clearly identified as either functional or dysfunctional. The relationship of these points to the benefits of budgeting depends upon the particular circumstances.

CONCLUSION

The model which has been developed to point out the functional possibilities of budgeting and to identify the sources of possible dysfunctional consequences represents a summary of relevant findings and statements by behavioral scientists, accountants and managers.

Budgeting is only one type of control technique used by top management. Many of the propositions developed are equally applicable to other types of quantitatively-oriented control techniques.

The points developed in this paper should be considered by any organization using or contemplating the introduction of a budgeting process. The importance of each point will vary, however, according to the particular organization, its strategy, history, organizational structure, reasons for using the system, the personalities involved, the leadership style of individuals in responsible positions, the general attitudes of employees toward the

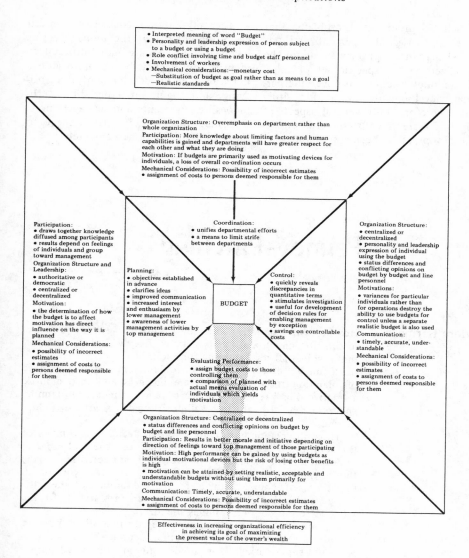

- Interpreted meaning of word "Budget"
- Personality and leadership expression of person subject to a budget or using a budget
- Role conflict involving time and budget staff personnel
- Involvement of workers
- Mechanical considerations:—monetary cost
  —Substitution of budget as goal rather than as means to a goal
  —Realistic standards

Organization Structure: Overemphasis on department rather than whole organization

Participation: More knowledge about limiting factors and human capabilities is gained and departments will have greater respect for each other and what they are doing

Motivation: If budgets are primarily used as motivating devices for individuals, a loss of overall co-ordination occurs

Mechanical Considerations: Possibility of incorrect estimates
- assignment of costs to persons deemed responsible for them

Participation:
- draws together knowledge diffused among participants
- results depend on feelings of individuals and group toward management

Organization Structure and Leadership:
- authoritative or democratic
- centralized or decentralized

Motivation:
- the determination of how the budget is to affect motivation has direct influence on the way it is planned

Mechanical Considerations:
- possibility of incorrect estimates
- assignment of costs to persons deemed responsible for them

Coordination:
- unifies departmental efforts
- a means to limit strife between departments

Planning:
- objectives established in advance
- clarifies ideas
- improved communication
- increased interest and enthusiasm by lower management
- awareness of lower management activities by top management

BUDGET

Control:
- quickly reveals discrepancies in quantitative terms
- stimulates investigation
- useful for development of decision rules for enabling management by exception
- savings on controllable costs

Organization Structure:
- centralized or decentralized
- personality and leadership expression of individual using the budget
- status differences and conflicting opinions on budget by budget and line personnel

Motivations:
- variances for particular individuals rather than for operations destroy the ability to use budgets for control unless a separate realistic budget is also used

Communication:
- timely, accurate, understandable

Mechanical Considerations:
- possibility of incorrect estimates
- assignment of costs to persons deemed responsible for them

Evaluating Performance:
- assign budget costs to those controlling them
- comparison of planned with actual means evaluation of individuals which yields motivation

Organization Structure: Centralized or decentralized
- status differences and conflicting opinions on budget by budget and line personnel

Participation: Results in better morale and initiative depending on direction of feelings toward top management of those participating

Motivation: High performance can be gained by using budgets as individual motivational devices but the risk of losing other benefits is high
- motivation can be attained by setting realistic, acceptable and understandable budgets without using them primarily for motivation

Communication: Timely, accurate, understandable

Mechanical Considerations: Possibility of incorrect estimates
- assignment of costs to persons deemed responsible for them

Effectiveness in increasing organizational efficiency in achieving its goal of maximizing the present value of the owner's wealth

FIGURE 5. General Model of the Factors to Consider When Determining the Functional and Dysfunctional Aspects of Introducing and Using a Budgeting System

organization and control devices, the cohesiveness of reference groups working on and with the budget, and the personal attitudes of employees regarding the justification of, and methods of achieving, organizational goals.

The major proposition suggested is that a budgeting system designed to accomplish the designated benefits is something more than a series of figures. Its origination, implementation, and degree of success are significantly related to the behaviorally-oriented problems that can easily arise. Management methods for solving these problems cannot be generalized into a specific set of rules. Definite rules can seldom cover the particular developments of unique situations. Therefore, only general aspects of budgeting systems with emphasis on behavioral topics have been considered.

The only absolute conclusion that can be proposed is that the human factors involved are generally more difficult to identify and deal with and more serious in nature than the development of quantifying and figure determination techniques. Accountants and managers must recognize this fact if they expect to perform their functions adequately.

Penney-Pinching

Isadore Barmash

The New York Times

How does the giant J. C. Penney Company select its priorities in drafting and updating its massive five-year plan, a project that involves all staff and line functions?

"Penney's doesn't have the problem some companies have of planning its way out of one business and into a more attractive one," replied N. Robert Maines, director of planning and research. "It's already well-positioned in a growth field," he said.

Thus, the planning problem is one of deciding how many of the corporate chips will be placed on each alternative opportunity for expansion, all of which are activities serving the consumer, he said. "The process of selection goes on all the time, of course, but is formalized annually when the five-year planning effort begins, this year on March 1, for the 1972-1976 period," Mr. Maines added.

Among this year's alternatives are continued high priority to full-line stores in major shopping centers; stores with or without supermarkets for small and medium-sized cities; selective expansion of the Treasury Stores, which compete with discount stores; expansion and modification of Thrift geographical catalogue coverages; and new ways of satisfying consumer convenience wants.

"Priority selections hinge on prospects for sales and profits but also on such factors as potential productivity improvements and what services consumers should expect from a major retail chain," he said.

Reprinted with permission from *The New York Times*, February 20, 1972.

Last September, Raymond L. Gill, manager of the J. C. Penney store in the Black Horse Pike Shopping Center, Audubon, N.J., stepped outside the store and sniffed at the air. It was promising for fall. Smiling, the 48-year-old West Virginian who had already spent 31 years with Penney, strolled for a few minutes and casually studied the traffic pattern in and around the shopping center.

The 10-year-old center, just across Route 168 from the Walt Whitman Bridge, which links South Jersey and Philadelphia, was beginning to fill up for the noon hour while the highway itself was brisk with traffic. Ordinarily, the sight of so many vehicles parked and on the move would have pleased the retailer, except that he knew that the portion of it that represented shoppers was as much attracted by other stores as by his own.

The store manager had just taken a few moments out from poring over an annual task, difficult because it meant he would have to look into every aspect of his store's retailing and catalogue operations and project his expectations for 1972 in sales, costs and profits for all categories of goods and services.

It was annual budgeting time once again for the J. C. Penney Company, a process almost 10 years old for the big New York-based retailer. Typical of well managed companies in many fields of endeavor, the Penney process, however, was atypical for the retail industry, more elaborate and refined than is the usual case in the country's multibillion-dollar distribution system.

Aimed at operating the company for the year ahead to achieve realistic and yet desirable results, the budget and profit plan, as it is termed, sets guideposts for delegated decision making. If followed correctly at the operating and lower levels, the budgeting program would result in the company's achieving its sales and profit goals in the new fiscal year, which began Feb. 1.

But nothing in the four-month process is as vital as the manner in which it is carried out in the individual Penney store or in the district and regional offices that supervise it.

Turning back to the store, Mr. Gill realized once again that the area, predominantly a white-collar residential one with a strong, secondary market of blue-collar families, inevitably had to draw competition. It had, in fact, become a magnet, with the center now competing with two newer ones 7 and 12 miles away while suburban branches of nearby and distant chains appeared to dot the countryside.

Returning to his desk, Mr. Gill picked up an elaborate form, known in the company as the "Profit Plan," and briefly considered 42 empty spaces calling for local store entries.

The form represented a compilation of estimates from more specific budget sheets and was, in effect, a set of guidelines and goals for a total Penney store operation. Alongside it, with tentative entries already penciled in, lay more detailed sheets from which the final results would be drawn. These had arrived only a few days before from Penney's parent office in New York.

He bent to the detail sheets, conscious that two major considerations would require his attention.

One was general expenses, which had changed significantly because of a recent remodeling and because the Audubon store only months before had started opening on Sundays. The other was control of markdowns, an item with which not only he but all other Penney managers have been grappling as a company-wide goal.

In his case, however, his store, known as Store 1473, was struggling with both these problems as a direct and indirect result of new competition in the immediate and nearby tri-county area.

Mr. Gill was hardly alone at the task. Across the country, at just about the same time, some 1,600 other Penney store managers were involved in the same routine. The effort was Penney's annual budget and profit-planning program, an activity that began last September, picked up in tempo through reviews and revisions during the winter and came to a close Jan. 26, 1972, after millions of sheets had been used and the work of several thousand Penney line-and-staff employes had ended.

The $4.6-billion company's budget-planning effort, one of the most elaborate in the retail industry, was especially complex this year because of Washington's new economic policy and consumer uncertainty resulting from it. Supervised by Kenneth S. Axelson, Penney's vice president for finance and administration, the 1972 plan represented company guidelines updated from an ongoing five-year plan.

In addition much of the underlying philosophy of the 1972 plan reflected an economic forecast of the year by N. Robert Maines, director of planning and research.

"We continue to be somewhat optimistic about the prospects for general merchandise retailing in 1972," said Mr. Maines, in recapping what he and his 20-man staff had told Penney's top management. "We have begun to see some signs of renewed confidence on the part of consumers.

"Any revival in buying enthusiasm would be reinforced by the highly liquid position of consumers, as indicated by the savings rate. General merchandise retailers should benefit greatly from such a change in buying attitude. All areas of our business, but especially hard goods, could be quite strong in 1972 if consumer confidence is restored."

Late in September, Oscar J. Hunter, vice president and Eastern regional manager of Penney who is based in Pittsburgh, wrote to all 14 district managers in 16 states in his region, listing budget guidelines. The region, which is Penney's largest in terms of sales, includes all of the industrial Northeast.

While initial sales estimates should be in line with current trends, he told the managers, they should recognize the extra sales opportunity that exists in the establishment in their areas of Penney's newer "full-line" as well as "limited-line" stores.

On markups, he said that the region's 352 stores "cannot expect markup improvement on individual items due to Phase Two guidelines." However, profit improvement will be possible through careful attention to merchandise assortments and continued tight expense control, Mr. Hunter said.

After increased sales, Mr. Hunter told the district managers, improved markdowns represent the greatest improvement opportunity in 1972. As a percentage of sales, the new year's advertising costs should be held to those of 1971, he added.

And what of the Linden, N.J., District 1109, with its 21 Penney stores, including Number 1473, Mr. Gill's ? Mr. Hunter, the Eastern regional manager, said:

"That district for us consists largely of two metropolitan areas, New York and Philadelphia, and it offers lots of merchandising opportunities, except that we have not had as many full-line department stores as we would like," Mr. Hunter said. "We are in the process of remedying that and of carrying on a substantial expansion program in New Jersey, as well as Long Island, Philadelphia and Connecticut from 1972 through 1975."

In mid-October in Linden, N.J., Raymond O. Wilson, district manager, perused the initial sales estimates submitted by his 21 stores for 1972 and dictated a memo to them: "We have just reviewed and approved the sales estimate questionnaires for all stores for fiscal 1972. In a couple of cases, we contacted the stores directly where we felt it was important enough to adjust their respective sales estimates for next year."

Then, after some thought, he added, "In general, the sales estimates for the district were set ultra-conservatively in nearly all the stores. This is probably all right for profit-planning purposes. It gives us a sound attainable base on which to build all of our budgets . . ."

Shortly afterward, in an interview, he said the Audubon store was "one of our better stores but is not in an up-to-date shopping mall." The center, however, was rapidly being encircled by other newer malls and "so we decided to remodel the store to meet the new competition. We have always had a favorable customer acceptance there and we felt that a new decor, a departmental realignment, expansion of the loading dock so we could handle more freight and a better mix of goods would help."

The moves, completed last year, immediately began to show results and the improved 143,000-square-foot unit, which includes a tire-battery-auto accessories center, appears poised for a new life.

However, the problem may be deeper than even Mr. Wilson indicated. Two years ago, or a year after Mr. Gill was transferred to Audubon from the Upper Darby, Pa., store, Store 1473 was the most profitable full-line store in the Penney chain. Although it is still a highly profitable store, it no longer ranks as No. 1. Newer and larger Penney stores have outstripped it in profits. But, as with many an older store throughout the country, both downtown and suburban, the trading market that Store 1473 thought was its own is no longer all its own.

The 45-story glass tower that Penney has occupied since 1964 at 1301 Avenue of the Americas in Manhattan is an imposing structure, housing the headquarters of the second largest American general merchandise company, second to Sears Roebuck & Co., Chicago. But impressive as is the building, its 4,000 headquarters employees and the concern's great success since the late James Cash Penney founded the concern in a tiny, one-room store in Kemmerer, Wyo., in 1902, its true strength probably rests in its far-flung network of 1,640 stores in 49 states and Puerto Rico.

Nine years ago, Penney started a formal five-year planning program, updating it annually. Thus, the 1972 budget and profit plan underwent five years of refinement before it was even re-referred to the field.

Since it deals with how each region, district and store will carry out the company's goals, the annual plan deals more with implementation than with any new structure. But since the process also calls for the individual setting of guidelines by regions and districts and takes into account the indigenous problems of the individual store, the annual budget and profit plan is clearly flexible.

Fifty-three copies of the five-year plan go to the company's senior executive group, spelling out the goals and needs for two major categories. One includes major company plans, 1971-1975; expected operating results, 1971-1975; financing, key projects and functional plans. The other category spells out goals and needs for the major Penney divisions, the stores, the catalogue operation, the Treasury stores, Thrift Drug stores, Supermarkets Interstate, consumer financial services, international operations, soft lines and hard lines.

The long-range analysis is prepared by Penney's planning and research department, reporting directly to the president. This process involved last year a study of the country's major 160 metropolitan markets, analyzing the marketing, location of stores and local demographics. It was backed up by a study by the company's real estate department, analyzing the large metropolitan markets to determine the effects of stores already opened and which and what types should be opened through the next five years.

Out of these two studies was extrapolated an expansion plan and from that plans for the capital outlays were drawn. But goal-strategies in terms of divisions and departments were developed on the basis of the planning department's economic forecast and prospects for business for the five years in major merchandise categories and services.

As far as the five-year plan was concerned, the advance 1972 updating of the 1971-1975 plan was developed late last spring and completed last August. From the long-range blueprint were drawn the budget guidelines to be presented to all operating divisions, including the stores in the field.

These guidelines included a schedule for the budget, the economic environment, the 1964-72 earnings trend for the company including Penney's goal for all but the last year and how closely it had come to it, the estimated profits for 1972 against what was expected in the year before and the sales forecast data by division in 1971 and what could be forecast for them in 1972.

As Mr. Axelson put it, the annual budget's guidelines seek to provide direction for the operating managers as to top management's expectations for the year ahead. Another goal is to provide standards to plan against in developing budget expectations for individual stores, depending on the type of store, the market it serves and the probable maturity of the store in penetrating its market.

But it is difficult to calculate a store's maturity, he noted. The company's first-full-line store, which was opened in 1963 at King of Prussia, Pa., and has twice been expanded, continues to show annual sales gains despite increased competition and shifts in local demographics. Stores opened in subsequent years are following a similar pattern.

In the budgeting process, of course, a different approach must be taken between profit-producing entities and those that are charged off to operations. Retail units, for example, budget their profits, income expense and volume, whereas non-retail units, such as the field administrative staff, central office, and buying offices are not called upon to account for such matters.

Once the guidelines were prepared in New York, a number of offices in the operating divisions then prepared the appropriate forms to be sent to the field. The scheduling strategy was mapped, and as Francis J. Depkovich, manager of operations in the regional operations department, put it, "The timing was established by looking at the calendar and asking how much time we need."

As this task was pursued, on Sept. 13 a letter was sent by Jack B. Jackson, vice president and director of regional operations, to the five regional managers and the 66 district managers informing them of a major change this year in the annual budgeting of large stores. Through 1970, the budgeting process called for a reworking of the budget-profit plan at the end of six months, but under the new system, unless there was a change in the sales and earnings of the six months then ended of 10 percent or more, it was no longer necessary to update the plan for the second half.

On Sept. 17, the budgeting plan took its first formal step with the mailing of a sales-estimate form to all stores from the regional offices. The same day, all stores were mailed a salary budget form from the main-office personnel department; budgets from the sales division; a catalogue unit budget from the catalogue division; a service budget from the controller's department, and a profit-planning package from the controller's department.

On Sept. 22, a general expense budget for larger stores went out from the controller's department.

After that, the reverse process began. On Oct. 1, the store manager returned his sales estimate forms to the district manager, and on Oct. 15 the district manager returned the approval sales estimate forms to the stores. On Oct. 29, the stores were called upon to mail their budgets to the district manager for review and approval. Copies of these in various colors were mailed by the store managers to the district manager, to the regional catalogue unit managers or retained in the store's file.

The process then picked up speed. By Nov. 12, all 66 district managers were compelled to mail certain copies of budgets and approval notices to all stores, with duplicates to various offices in New York. On Dec. 3, all stores had to mail their completed profit plans to the regional accounting office, the district manager and retain copies.

At this point, the budget committee in Penney's central office headed by C. L. Wright, president, began fulfilling its role in the overall process. Toward the end of December and in early January, the budget group reviewed in detail all budget proposals, including not only those from regional operations reflecting the work of the regions, districts and stores, but also all others from the corporate departments. Revisions were made during this stage of the process.

The budget committee then prepared its recommendations on the total budget, which was reviewed by the operating committee, another central-office group comprised of top company officers and department heads. And what had emerged as the final budget for 1972 was then submitted for approval by the firm's board of directors at its Jan. 26 meeting.

And, on the same day, the final step was reached when the controller's department provided Mr. Jackson's regional operations with approved recaps of district and regional profit plans.

Late in the process, as the data center was compiling tapes that were recast into one large and one small volume, Mr. Jackson said in an interview that the closing year would not only show gains in both sales and earnings but also an improved or lower rate of mark-downs.

"Fashions, an important part of our picture, are less confused this year, and that, plus the fact that we've just done a better job of planning our assortments is why our mark-down picture is brighter," he said.

Mr. Jackson, a career man at Penney's, added that the concern's buyers "have become proficient at seeing the trends six and eight months in advance, mainly because of experience and by keeping in close touch with the markets. You can't hit everything right when you work with our kind of lead time, but if in total it comes out right, that's enough reason to be happy. But, frankly, we'd like to beat our own budgets."

Mr. Jackson, a 30-year veteran of Penney's who came up through the store, district and regional manager route from his native Sherman, Tex., was elected Penney's president several weeks ago, effective April 1, succeeding Mr. Wright.

SELECTED REFERENCES FOR CHAPTER 2

BOOKS

Bonini, Charles P., *Simulation of Information and Decision Systems in the Firm.* Englewood Cliffs, N.J.: Prentice-Hall, Inc., 1963.

Boyd, D. F., *The Emerging Role of Enterprise Simulation Models.* Yorktown Heights, N.Y.: IBM Advanced Systems Development Division, 1964.

Forrester, Jay W., *Industrial Dynamics.* New York: John Wiley & Sons, Inc., 1961.

Gershefski, George W., *The Development and Application of a Corporate Financial Model.* Oxford, Ohio: The Planning Executives Institute, 1968.

Hofstede, G. H., *The Game of Budget Control.* Assen, Netherlands: Van Gorcum & Company, 1967.

Ijiri, Yuji, *Management Goals and Accounting for Control.* Amsterdam: North-Holland Publishing Company, 1965.

McMillan, Claude, and Richard F. Gonzalez, *Systems Analysis: A Computer Approach to Decision Models.* Homewood, Ill.: Richard D. Irwin, Inc., 1968.

Mattessich, Richard, *Accounting and Analytical Methods.* Homewood, Ill.: Richard D. Irwin, Inc., 1964.

Meier, Robert C., William T. Newell and Harold L. Pazer, *Simulation in Business and Economics.* Englewood Cliffs, N.J.: Prentice-Hall, Inc., 1969.

Schrieber, Albert N., editor, *Corporate Simulation Models.* Seattle: University of Washington, 1970.

Stedry, Andrew C., *Budget Control and Cost Behavior.* Englewood Cliffs, N.J.: Prentice-Hall, Inc., 1960.

ARTICLES

Charnes, A., and W. W. Cooper, "Some Network Characterizations for Mathematical Programming and Accounting Approaches to Planning and Control," *The Accounting Review,* XLII (January, 1967).

Charnes, A., W. W. Cooper, and Y. Ijiri, "Breakeven Budgeting and Programming to Goals," *Journal of Accounting Research,* I (Spring, 1963).

Damon, William W., and Richard Schramm, "A Simultaneous Decision Model for Production, Marketing and Finance," *Management Science,* XIX (October 1972).

Demski, Joel S., "An Accounting System Structured on a Linear Programming Model," *The Accounting Review,* XLII (October 1967).

Dunbar, Roger L. M., "Budgeting for Control," *Administrative Science Quarterly,* XVI, (March 1971).

Gunders, Henry, "Better Profit Planning," *Management Accounting,* XXXXVI, (August 1965).

Ijiri, Y., F.K. Levy and R.C. Lyon, "A Linear Programming Model for Budgeting and Financial Planning," *Journal of Accounting Research,* I (Autumn 1963).

Khoury, E. N., and H. Wayne Nelson, "Simulation in Financial Planning," *Management Services,* II (March-April 1965).

Krouse, Clement G., "A Model for Aggregate Financial Planning," *Management Science,* XVIII, (June 1972).

Lewin, Arie Y., and Michael Schiff, "The Impact of People on Budgets," *The Accounting Review,* XLV, (April 1970).

———, "Where Traditional Budgeting Fails," *Financial Executive,* XXXVI, (May 1968).

Mattessich, Richard, "Budgeting Models and System Simulation," *The Accounting Review,* XXXVI, (July 1961).

Novick, David, "Long-Range Planning Through Program Budgeting," *Business Horizons,* XII, (February 1969).

Wallace, Michael, "Behavioral Considerations in Budgeting," *Management Accounting,* XXXXVII, (August 1966).

COST-VOLUME-
PROFIT
ANALYSIS

CHAPTER THREE

Breakeven Analysis Under Absorption Costing

David Solomons

University of Pennsylvania

Conventional breakeven analysis is invariably based upon a direct costing approach to cost behavior. Financial statements, particularly those which management prepares for external parties, are typically developed using an absorption costing approach. In this article, the author presents the breakeven equation under absorption costing and contrasts it with results obtained under direct costing.

Reprinted from *The Accounting Review*, XLIII (July 1968), 447-452. Used by permission of David Solomons and *The Accounting Review*.

I gladly acknowledge my debt to my colleague, Dr. Matthew J. Stephens, Jr., who made several suggestions which enabled me to clarify the presentation in this paper.

The simplistic assumptions underlying the classical breakeven chart have long been recognized as unsatisfactory. Many of those who have felt this dissatisfaction have been content to apologize for the shortcomings of breakeven analysis. A few have labored to remove or minimize them.[1] The purpose of this article is to clarify these assumptions somewhat, and in particular to adapt the breakeven chart to a situation in which absorption costing is being used. It is important to recognize that, in its usual form, breakeven analysis is based on a direct costing approach to cost behavior, an approach which is by no means universally accepted.

[1]Three notable examples are A. W. Patrick's "Some Observations on the Break-Even Chart," *The Accounting Review* (October 1958), pp. 573- 580, about which more later; Rene Mane's "A New Dimension to Breakeven Analysis," *Journal of Accounting Research* (Spring 1966), pp. 87-100, which introduces the time-value of money into the analysis; and Jaedicke and Robichek's "Cost-Volume-Profit Analysis under Conditions of Uncertainty," *The Accounting Review* (October 1964), pp. 917-926.

Failure to grasp the implications of the direct cost philosophy for breakeven analysis leads to misunderstandings. For instance, it is commonly said that the classical breakeven chart assumes an identity of sales and production quantities. In fact, no such assumption is necessary, for under direct costing, all fixed costs are to be covered out of current revenue; no fixed costs are inventoriable. Once such a view has been accepted, a difference between the quantity produced and the quantity sold has no effect on the breakeven quantity or on the firm's profit, for any quantity of product put into inventory or taken out, being valued at variable cost only, has no effect on the (variable) cost of goods sold or on the fixed costs charged against current operations. It is because of this that the breakeven chart, as traditionally drawn assuming linear cost and revenue functions, has one and only one breakeven point.

As soon as adaptation of the chart to reflect conditions under absorption costing is attempted, the fact that fixed costs are no longer all non-inventoriable has to be faced. Absorption costing confines noninventoriable fixed costs to:

a. non-manufacturing expenses, and
b. under-absorbed fixed manufacturing expense, i.e., any unfavorable volume variance.

The second of these two categories is a function of actual output in relation to normal output. So, therefore, is noninventoriable fixed cost. It follows, then, that whereas the traditional breakeven chart points to a unique breakeven point and a unique profit figure for each level of sales (including zero profit at the breakeven level), breakeven analysis adapted to absorption costing must provide many breakeven production-sales combinations; for if production is high, the firm can break even with low sales, whereas if there is a lot of idle capacity (and consequently a large unfavorable volume variance) higher sales will be needed to generate enough contribution to cover this non-inventoriable cost.

Although, under direct costing, changes in inventory during a period do not affect the breakeven point, it does turn out that, under absorption costing, a firm can break even while achieving an identity of production and sales only at the traditional breakeven sales level. This will be demonstrated later. It is enough to note here that this is probably what is meant when it is said that an identity of sales and production is assumed in the traditional breakeven chart. In fact neither under direct costing nor absorption costing does such a condition need to be satisfied, unless the breakeven point under absorption costing is required to be the same as under direct costing.

The non-uniqueness of the breakeven point under absorption costing was discussed ten years ago by A. W. Patrick, in an outstanding article which has already been referred to. However, Patrick's analysis has three deficiencies:

1. It lacks generality, based as it is on an illustrative set of figures.
2. The position of the locus of breakeven points on his diagram is computed by use of the illustrative figures, and then put on to the diagram. It is not self-evident from the diagram itself.
3. It does not distinguish as clearly as could be wished between the two different influences on the breakeven point under absorption costing, namely the relationship of sales and production quantities on the one hand and the amount of idle production capacity on the other.

It is the aim of this paper to complete Patrick's work on breakeven analysis,[2] and incidentally to present a simple pedagogic aid to explain graphically how operating results differ under direct and absorption costing.

THE BREAKEVEN EQUATION UNDER ABSORPTION COSTING

Let

Q_s = Sales quantity (actual)

$Q_{ab\,(a)}$ = Sales quantity, at breakeven, under absorption costing

$Q_{sb\,(d)}$ = Sales quantity, at breakeven, under direct costing

Q_c = Production quantity at capacity[3]

Q_p = Production quantity (actual)

F_m = Total manufacturing fixed expense

F_s = Total selling and administrative fixed expense

v_m = Variable manufacturing cost per unit produced

v_s = Variable selling cost per unit sold

p = Selling price per unit.

Then under absorption costing, at breakeven, total revenue equals total non-inventoriable costs, i.e.,

What equation (1) says is that the breakeven sales quantity is determined by dividing total non-inventoriable fixed costs (made up of unabsorbed fixed manufacturing cost and all fixed non-manufacturing cost) by the net contribution per unit sold (after charging fixed costs at the standard rate). It is clear that, since the expression on the right contains Q_p, the quantity produced, there can be no unique value for $Q_{sb(a)}$, but only a set of values, one for each value of Q_p.

It is easy to see from equation (1) that if production is proceeding at capacity (i.e., if $Q_p = Q_c$), the first term in the numerator vanishes, and to break even under absorption costing it is only necessary to sell enough to generate net contribution to cover fixed selling and administrative expenses. If $Q_p = Q_s$ and F_s is zero, then, as was pointed out above, it is possible to break even with zero sales.

THE BREAKEVEN CHART UNDER ABSORPTION COSTING

The graphical representation in Figure 1 brings out these relationships, and some additional ones besides. The $Q_s(p - v_s)$ line shows total sales revenue (quantity sold × price) net of variable selling costs. The lower horizontal line represents total

$$Q_{sb(a)}(p - v_s) = Q_{sb(a)}v_m + Q_{sb(a)}\frac{F_m}{Q_c} + (Q_c - Q_p)\frac{F_m}{Q_c} + F_s$$

Net revenue from sales, after variable selling costs	Variable manufacturing cost of sales	Fixed cost of sales at standard overhead rate	Volume variance	Fixed Selling and Administrative Costs

$$(1)\;\therefore Q_{sb(a)}\,p - v_s - v_m - \frac{F_m}{Q_c} = (Q_c - Q_p)\frac{F_m}{Q_c} + F_s \quad\therefore Q_{sb(a)} = \frac{(Q_c - Q_p)\dfrac{F_m}{Q_c} + F_s}{p - v_s - v_m - \dfrac{F_m}{Q_c}}$$

---

[2] This is not to say that other dimensions do not need to be added also, but only that they will not be discussed in this paper. Articles which remove two other simplifications—cost-free capital and conditions of certainty—have already been cited.

[3] This leaves capacity to be defined in any one of a number of ways, e.g., normal capacity, practical capacity etc. The use of normal capacity makes favorable volume variances possible. Although not discussed below, the analysis for them is symmetrical with that for

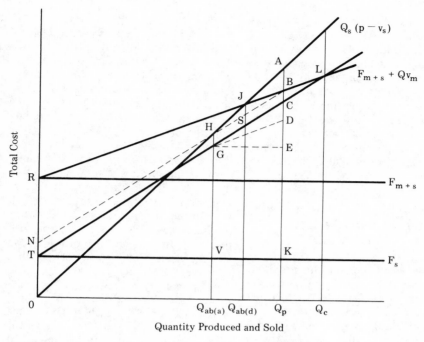

FIGURE 1

fixed selling costs, F_s, and to this is added total fixed manufacturing costs to give the upper horizontal line, F_{m+s}, total fixed costs. Variable manufacturing costs are added to give the total cost line, RL $(=F_{m+s} + Qv_m)$. Capacity output is Q_c and a vertical is erected at this point. Through L, the intersection of this vertical with the total cost line, a line is drawn to T, the Y intercept of the F_s line. The slope of this line represents the *standard* rate of fixed manufacturing overhead.

Everything on the chart so far represents budgetary information. If actual production is now added, the sales required to break even can easily be pointed to; and if actual sales are added, the result of selling more or less than the breakeven quantity can be indicated.

Let actual production be Q_p, and let a

vertical be erected at this point. Through B, the intersection of this vertical with RL, draw a line parallel to TL. The abscissa of the point H at which this line (drawn as a dotted line on Figure 1) cuts the net revenue line, OHA, gives the quantity of sales necessary to break even when production is equal to Q_p. The breakeven sales quantity is $OQ_{sb(a)}$. The net revenue generated, $HQ_{sb(a)}$ is just sufficient to cover the fixed selling expenses, $VQ_{sb(a)}$, the manufacturing cost of sales, GV, and the adverse volume variance, HG.

If a horizontal line is drawn through G to cut the Q_p vertical at E, it can be seen that, having accounted for $BC + EK + KQ_p$ $(=HG + GV + VQ_{sb(a)})$, when production is OQ_p, the only part of total cost of production, BQ_p, not yet accounted for is CE. And this, of course, is the manufacturing cost which, under absorption costing, would go into inventory

---

unfavorable variances, so long as they are regarded as (negatively) inventoriable.

with the unsold output, $OQ_p - OQ_{sb(a)}$, if sales were at breakeven.

It is worth noting that, under absorption costing, in the limit, if actual production equalled normal capacity so that there were no volume variance, and if there were no fixed selling and administrative expenses, a firm could break even if it sold nothing at all! All its production would go into inventory, and fixed manufacturing expense would go into inventory with it.

RESULTS UNDER ABSORPTION COSTING AND DIRECT COSTING COMPARED

The chart enables all the important differences between absorption costing and direct costing to be seen. Direct costing offers a unique breakeven point, J. A sales quantity $OQ_{sb(d)}$ is required to break even under direct costing, while only $OQ_{sb(a)}$ is required under absorption costing so long as production is OQ_p. By extending the dotted line BH to intercept the Y axis at N, it can be seen that even if nothing was sold at all, under absorption costing the loss would only be ON, equal to the adverse volume variance and fixed nonmanufacturing cost, whereas under direct costing with zero sales the loss would be equal to total fixed costs, OR.

Generalizing this relationship produces an interesting result. The profitability of sales above breakeven, under direct costing, is given by the angle AJB, and under absorption costing by the angle JHB, and correspondingly for losses when sales fall short of breakeven. The difference between these two angles is equal to the angle CGD, GD having been drawn through G parallel to RL. This can easily be proved geometrically,[4] but it is also intuitively obvious as soon as it is remembered that the slope of $GC = v_m + (F_m/Q_c)$, while the slope of GD,

parallel to JB, $= v_m$. The difference in slopes (angle CGD) $= F_m/Q_c$, the standard absorption rate of fixed manufacturing cost. The side opposite the angle CGD on the Q_p vertical, CD, measures the difference in profit under the two costing methods, absorption costing giving the bigger profit whenever production exceeds sales.

Quantitatively, the argument about the relative effect on profit of direct costing and absorption costing, which in the textbooks has taken so many tedious numerical illustrations to explain, can all be reduced to the triangle CGD. When production exceeds sales, absorption costing will give the greater profit by an amount equal to the fixed cost put into inventory, i.e., by $(Q_p - Q_s)(F_m/Q_c)$, and correspondingly when $Q_s > Q_p$, the profit under direct costing will be greater. It is obvious from the chart that as the gap between Q_s and Q_p closes, CD diminishes and eventually vanishes; and if the relative positions of Q_s and Q_p are transposed, CD re-appears with a changed sign.

It was pointed out at the beginning of this paper that the traditional breakeven chart, contrary to what is commonly said about it, does not need an assumption of identity between Q_s and Q_p. Referring to Figure 1, the traditional breakeven point is J. Assume that sales were $OQ_{sb(d)}$ and production OQ_p. Under direct costing, the products which are put into inventory, the excess of production over sales, go in at variable manufacturing unaffected. Now let us ask, assuming absorption costing to be used, at what level of sales the firm would break even

---

[4] $\angle JHB + \angle JBH = 180° - \angle HJB$
   $\angle AJB \qquad\quad = 180° - \angle HJB$
  $\therefore \angle JHB + \angle JBH = \angle AJB$
  $\therefore \qquad \angle JBH = \angle AJB - \angle JHB$
but, since $JB//GD$ and $HB//GC$, $\angle JBH = \angle CGD$
        $\angle CGD = \angle AJB - \angle JHB$

                       Q.E.D.

when a requirement is added that production must equal sales. The answer is that production and sales must both equal $OQ_{sb(d)}$. At that output, the adverse volume variance is JS, and to cover this and the other cost of production and selling, $SQ_{sb(d)}$, sales revenue must be $JQ_{sb(d)}$. This occurs only when sales are $OQ_{sb(d)}$—which is the traditional break-even sales volume also. As Patrick pointed out,[5] the traditional breakeven point, given the use of absorption costing, is *the* breakeven point only in the special circumstance that production and sales are required to be equal.

Before concluding this discussion, two gaps in it must be noted. First, throughout, the assumption has been that $Q_p \geqslant Q_s$. Hence, reductions in inventory have been ignored. The analysis above is quite symmetrical as between increases

[5] A. W. Patrick, *op. cit.*, p. 578.

and decreases in inventory *so long as there is no change in cost conditions from period to period*. But if the unit cost of last period's production should be different from this period's, the effect of a run-down of inventory will not be precisely the same, in the opposite direction, as an increase in inventory out of current production.

A second gap in the discussion is the neglect of variances other than volume variances. As non-inventoriable costs, these, too, need to be covered out of gross margin if the firm is to break even. But it would add little of value to the analysis to take this into account. Break-even analysis is concerned with projections into the future, it aims to answer the question "What would happen if . . . ?" From the consideration of such a question it seems reasonable to exclude departures from budget which are not of the first importance.

Cost-Volume-Profit Analysis Under Conditions of Uncertainty

Robert K. Jaedicke

Alexander A. Robichek

Stanford University

Traditional cost-volume-profit analysis is frequently used to make choices among alternative courses of action. The usefulness of this analysis is limited because the relative risk of various alternatives is not explicitly accounted for. When risk is introduced into the model, the resulting statement of probabilities with respect to various levels of profits and losses for each alternative should aid the decision maker, once his attitude toward risk has been defined. Illustrations are presented.

Reprinted from *The Accounting Review*, XXXIX (October, 1964), 917-26. Used by permission of Robert K. Jaedicke, Alexander A. Robichek, and *The Accounting Review*.

Cost-volume-profit analysis is frequently used by management as a basis for choosing among alternatives such decisions as: (1) the sales volume required to attain a given level of profits, and (2) the most profitable combination of products to produce and sell. However, the fact that traditional C-V-P analysis does not include adjustments for risk and uncertainty may, in any given instance, severely limit its usefulness. Some of the limitations can be seen from the following example.

Assume that the firm is considering the introduction of two new products, either of which can be produced by using present facilities. Both products require an increase in annual fixed cost of the same amount, say $400,000. Each product has the same selling price and variable cost per unit, say, $10 and $8, respectively, and each requires the same amount of capacity. Using these data, the break-even point of either product is 200,000 units. C-V-P analysis helps to establish the break-even volume of each product, but this analysis does not distinguish the relative desirability of the two products for at least two reasons.

The first piece of missing information is the *expected* sales volume of each product. Obviously, if the annual sales of A are expected to be 300,000 units and of B are expected to be 350,000 units, then B is clearly preferred to A so far as the sales expectation is concerned.

However, assume that the expected annual sales of each product is the same—say, 300,000 units. Is it right to conclude that management should be indifferent as far as a choice between A and B is concerned? The answer is *no, unless* each sales expectation is certain. If both sales estimates are subject to uncertainty, the decision process will be improved if the relative risk associated with each product can somehow be brought into the analysis. The discussion which follows suggests some changes which might be made

in traditional C-V-P analysis so as to make it a more useful tool in analyzing decision problems under uncertainty.

SOME PROBABILITY CONCEPTS RELATED TO C-V-P ANALYSIS

In the previous section, it was pointed out that *expected* volume of the annual sales is an important decision variable. Some concepts of probability will be discussed using the example posed earlier.

The four fundamental relationships used in the example were: (1) the selling price per unit; (2) the variable cost per unit; (3) the total fixed cost; and (4) the expected sales volume of each product. In any given decision problem, all four of these factors can be uncertain. However, it may be that, *relative to* the expected sales quantity, the costs and selling prices are quite certain. That is, for analytical purposes, the decision maker may be justified in treating several factors as certainty equivalents. Such a procedure simplifies the analysis and will be followed here as a first approximation. In this section of the paper, sales volume will be treated as the only uncertain quantity. Later, all decision factors in the above example will be treated under conditions of uncertainty.

In the example, sales volume is treated as a *random variable*. A random variable can be thought of as an *unknown quantity*. In this case, the best decision hinges on the value of the random variable, sales volume of each product. One decision approach which allows for uncertainty is to estimate, for each random variable, the likelihood that the random variable will take on various possible values. Such an estimate is called a *subjective probability distribution*. The decision would then be made by choosing that course of action which has the highest *expected monetary value*. This approach is illustrated in Table 1.

TABLE 1 Probability Distribution for Products A and B

Events (Units Demanded)	Probability Distribution— (Product A)	Probability Distribution— (Product B)
50,000	—	.1
100,000	.1	.1
200,000	.2	.1
300,000	.4	.2
400,000	.2	.4
500,000	.1	.1
	1.00	1.00

The expected value of the random variables, sales demand for each product, is calculated by weighting the possible conditional values by their respective probabilities. In other words, the expected value is a weighted average. The calculation is given in Table 2.

demand levels (events) are assumed to be mutually exclusive and also exhaustive. That is, the listing is done in such a way that no two events can happen simultaneously and any events *not* listed are assumed to have a zero probability of occurring. Herein are three important (basic) concepts of probability analyses.

Secondly, the probability distributions may have been assigned by using historical demand data on similar products, or the weights may be purely subjective in the sense that there is no historical data available. Even if the probability distributions are entirely subjective, this approach still has merit. It allows the estimator to express his uncertainty about the sales estimate. An estimate of sales is necessary to make a decision.

TABLE 2 Expected Value of Sales Demand for Products A and B

(1) Event	(2) P(A)	(1 × 2)	(3) P(B)	(1 × 3)
50,000	—	—	.1	5,000
100,000	.1	10,000	.1	10,000
200,000	.2	40,000	.1	20,000
300,000	.4	120,000	.2	60,000
400,000	.2	80,000	.4	160,000
500,000	.1	50,000	.1	50,000
	1.00		1.00	
Expected Value		300,000 units		305,000 units

Based on an expected value approach, the firm should select product B rather than A. The expected profits of each possible action are as follows:

Product A:
$2(300,000 units) - $400,000
= $200,000

Product B:
$2(305,000 units) - $400,000
= $210,000

Several observations are appropriate at this point. First, the respective probabilities for each product, used in Table 1, add to 1.00. Furthermore, the possible

Hence, the question is *not* whether an estimate must be made, but simply [what is] the best way to make and express the estimate.

Now, suppose that the expected value of sales for each product is 300,000, as shown in Table 3. In this example, it is easy to see that the firm would *not* be indifferent between products A and B, even though the expected value of sales is 300,000 units in both cases. In the case of product A, for example, there is a .1 chance that sales will be only 100,000 units, and in that case, a loss of $200,000 would be incurred (i.e., $2 × 100,000 units−$400,000). On the other hand, there is a .3 chance that sales will be

TABLE 3

Demand	P(A)	E.V.(A)	P(B)	E.V.(B)
100,000 units	.1	10,000	—	—
200,000 units	.2	40,000	—	—
300,000 units	.4	120,000	1.00	300,000
400,000 units	.2	80,000	—	—
500,000 units	.1	50,000	—	—
	1.00		1.00	
Expected Sales Demand		300,000		300,000

above 300,000 units, and if this is the case, higher profits are possible with product A than with product B. Hence, the firm's attitude toward risk becomes important. The expected value (or the mean of the distribution) is important, but so is the "spread" in the distribution. Typically, the greater the "spread," the greater the risk involved. A quantitative measure of the spread is available in the form of standard deviation of the distribution, and this concept and its application will be refined later in the paper.

THE NORMAL PROBABILITY DISTRIBUTION

The preceding examples were highly simplified and yet the calculations are relatively long and cumbersome. The possible sales volumes were few in number and the probability distribution was discrete, that is, a sales volume of 205,762 units was considered an impossible event. The use of a continuous probability distribution is desirable not only because the calculation will usually be simplified but because the distribution may also be a more realistic description of the uncertainty aspects of the situation. The normal probability distribution will be introduced and used in the following analysis which illustrates the methodology involved. This distribution, although widely used, is not appropriate in all situations. The appropriate distribution depends on

the decisions problem and should, of course, be selected accordingly.

The normal probability distribution is a smooth, symmetric, continuous, bell-shaped curve as shown in Figure 1. The area under the curve sums to 1. The curve reaches a maximum at the mean of the distribution, and one-half the area lies on either side of the mean.

On the horizontal axis are plotted the values of the appropriate unknown quantity or random variable; in the examples used here, the unknown quantity is the sales for the coming periods.

A particular normal probability distribution can be completely determined if its mean and its standard deviation, σ, are known. The standard deviation is a measure of the dispersion of the distribution about its mean. The area under any normal distribution is 1, but one distribution may be "spread out" more than another distribution. For example, in Figure 2, both normal distributions have the same area and the same mean. However, in one case the σ is 1 and in the other case the σ is greater than 1. The larger the σ, the more spread out is the distribution. It should be noted that the standard deviation is not an area but is a measure of the dispersion of the individual observations about the mean of all the observations—it is a distance.

Since the normal probability distribution is continuous rather than discrete, the probability of an event cannot be read directly from the graph. The unknown quantity must be thought of as

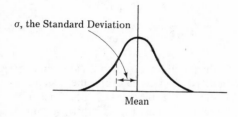

σ, the Standard Deviation

Mean

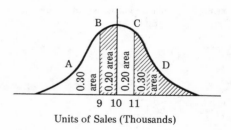

Units of Sales (Thousands)

FIGURE 1. The Normal Probability Distribution

FIGURE 3.

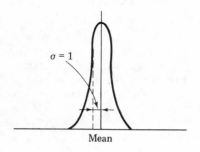

σ = 1

Mean

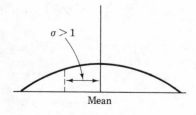

σ > 1

Mean

FIGURE 2. Normal Probability Distributions with Different Standard Deviations

between 9,000 and 10,000 is also .20. This is shown by shaded area B. These probabilities can be given a frequency interpretation. That is, area C indicates that the actual sales will be between 10,000 and 11,000 units in about 20 per cent of the cases.

2. The probability of the actual sales being greater than 11,000 units is .30 as shown by area D.

3. The probability of the sales being greater than 9,000 units is .70, the sum of areas B, C, and D.

Given a specific normal distribution, it is possible to read probabilities of the type described above directly from a normal probability table.

Another important characteristic of any normal distribution is that approximately .50 of the area lies within ±.67 standard deviations of the mean; about .68 of the area lies within ±1.0 standard deviations of the mean; .95 of the area lies within ±1.96 standard deviations of the mean.

As was mentioned above, normal probabilities can be read from a normal probability table. A partial table of normal probabilities is given in Table 4. This table is the "right tail" of the distribution; that is, probabilities of the unknown quantity being greater than X standard deviations from the mean are given in the table. For example, the probability of the unknown quantity being greater than the mean plus .35σ is .3632. The distribution

being in an interval. Assume, for example, that the mean sales for the coming period is estimated to be 10,000 units and the normal distribution appears as in Figure 3. Given Figure 3, certain probability statements can be made. For example:

1. The probability of the actual sales being between 10,000 and 11,000 units is .20. This is shown by area C. Because of the symmetry of the curve, the probability of the sales being

TABLE 4 Area Under the Normal Probability Function

X	0.00	0.05
.1	.4602	.4404
.3	.3821	.3632
.5	.3085	.2912
.6	.2743	.2578
.7	.2420	.2266
.8	.2119	.1977
.9	.1841	.1711
1.0	.1587	.1469
1.1	.1357	.1251
1.5	.0668	.0606
2.0	.0228	.0202

tabulated is a normal distribution with mean zero and standard deviation of 1. Such a distribution is known as a standard normal distribution. However, any normal distribution can be standardized and hence, with proper adjustment, Table 4 will serve for any normal distribution.

For example, consider the earlier case where the mean of the distribution is 10,000 units. The distribution was constructed so that the standard deviation is about 2,000 units.[1] To standardize the distribution, use the following formula, where X is the number of standard deviations from the mean:

$$X = \frac{\text{Actual sales} - \text{mean sales}}{\text{Standard deviation of the distribution}}$$

To calculate the probability of the sales being greater than 11,000 units, first standardize the distribution and then use the table.

[1] To see why this normal distribution has a standard deviation of 2,000 units, remember that the probability of sales being greater than 11,000 units is .30. Now examine Table 4, and it can be seen that the probability of a random variable being greater than .5 standard deviations from the mean is .3085. Hence, 1,000 units is about the same as ½ standard deviations. So, 2,000 units is about 1 standard deviation.

$$X = \frac{11,000 - 10,000}{2,000}$$

$$= .50 \text{ standard deviations.}$$

The probability of being greater than .50 standard deviations from the mean, according to Table 4, is .3085. This same approximate result is shown by Figure 3, that is, area D is .30.

THE NORMAL DISTRIBUTION USED IN C-V-P ANALYSIS

The normal distribution will now be used in a C-V-P analysis problem, assuming that sales quantity is a random variable. Assume that the per-unit selling price is $3,000, the fixed cost is $5,800,000, and the variable cost per unit is $1,750. Break-even sales (in units) is calculated as follows:

$$S_B = \frac{\$5,800,000}{\$3,000 - \$1,750} = 4,640 \text{ units.}$$

Furthermore, suppose that the sales manager estimates that the mean expected sales volume is 5,000 units and that it is equally likely that actual sales will be greater or less than the mean of 5,000 units. Furthermore, assume that the sales manager feels that there is roughly a 2/3 (i.e., .667) chance that the actual sales will be within 400 units of the mean. These subjective estimates can be expressed by using a normal distribution with mean $E(Q) = 5,000$ units and standard deviation $\sigma_q = 400$ units. The reason that σ_q is about 400 units is that, as mentioned earlier, about 2/3 of the area under the normal curve (actually .68) lies within 1 standard deviation of the mean. The probability distribution is shown in Figure 4.

The horizontal axis of Figure 4 denotes sales quantity. The probability of an actual sales event taking place is given by

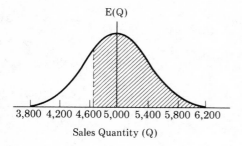

FIGURE 4.

the area under the probability distribution. For example, the probability that the sales quantity will exceed 4,640 units (the break-even point) is the shaded area under the probability distribution (the probability of actual sales exceeding 4,640 units).

The probability distribution of Figure 4 can be superimposed on the profit portion of the traditional C-V-P; this is done in Figure 5. The values for price, fixed costs, and variable costs are pre-

sumed to be known with certainty. Expected profit is given by:

$$E(Z) = E(Q)\,(P\text{-}V) - F$$
$$= \$450,000$$
$$E(Z) = \text{Expected Profit}$$
$$E(Q) = \text{Expected Sales}$$
$$P = \text{Price}$$
$$V = \text{Variable Cost}$$
$$F = \text{Fixed Cost.}$$

The standard deviation of the profit (σ_z) is:

$$\sigma_z = \sigma_q \times \$1{,}250 \text{ contribution per unit}$$
$$= 400 \text{ units} \times \$1{,}250 = \$500{,}000.$$

Since profits are directly related to the volume of sales, and since it is the level of profits which is often the concern of management, it may be desirable to separate the information in Figure 5 which relates to profit. Figure 6 is a graphical illustration of the relationship between profit level and the probability distribution of the profit level. A number of

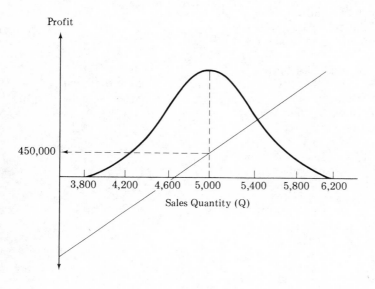

FIGURE 5.

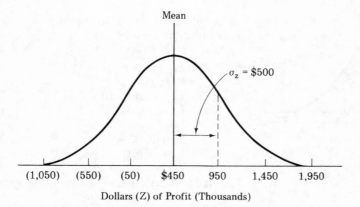

Dollars (Z) of Profit (Thousands)

FIGURE 6

important relationships can now be obtained in probabilistic terms. Since the probability distribution of sales quantity is normal with a mean of 5,000 units and a standard deviation of 400 units, the probability distribution of profits will also be normal with a mean, as shown earlier, of $450,000 and a standard deviation of $500,000.

Using the probability distribution shown in Figure 6, the following probabilities can be calculated (using Table 4)

1. The probability of at least breaking even: This is the probability of profits being greater than zero and can be calculated by summing the area under the distrubition to the right of zero profits. This probability can be calculated as 1−(the probability of profits being less than zero). Since the distribution is symmetric, Table 4 can be used to read left tail as well as right tail probabilities. Zero profits fall .9 standard deviations to the left of the mean

$$\left(\text{ie.,}\; \frac{\$450 - 0}{\$500} = .9\right)$$

Hence the probability of profits being less than zero is:

$P(\text{Profits} < .9\sigma \text{ from the mean}) = .184.$
Therefore
$P(\text{Profits} > 0) = 1 - .184 = .816.$

2. The probability of profits being greater than $200,000.

$P(\text{Profits} > \$200,000)$
$= 1 - P\left(\text{Profits} < \dfrac{450 - 200}{500}\sigma \right.$
$\left. \text{from the mean}\right)$
$= 1 - P(\text{Profits} < .5\sigma \text{ from the mean})$
$= 1 - .3085 = .692.$

3. The probability of the loss being greater than $300,000.

$P(\text{Loss} > \$300,000)$
$= P\left(\text{Loss} > \dfrac{450 - (-300),}{500}\right)$
$\text{or } 1.5\sigma \text{ from the mean}$
$P = .067.$

The question of how the above information can be used now arises. The manager, in choosing between this product and other products or other lines of activity, can probably improve his decision by considering the risk involved. He knows that the break-even sales is at a level of 4,640 units. He knows that the expected sales are 5,000 units which would yield a profit of $450,000. Surely, he would benefit from knowing that:

1. The probability of at least reaching break-even sales is .816.
2. The probability of making at least $200,000 profit is .692.
3. The probability of making at least $450,000 profit is .50.
4. The probability of incurring losses, i.e., not achieving the break-even sales volume, is (1 – .816, or .184).
5. The probability of incurring a $300,000 or greater loss is .067.

If the manager is comparing this product with other products, probability analysis combined with C-V-P allows a comparison of the risk involved in each product, as well as a comparison of relative break-even points and expected profits. Given the firm's attitude toward and willingness to assume risk (of losses as well as high profits), the decision of choosing among alternatives should be facilitated by the above analysis.

SEVERAL RELEVANT FACTORS PROBABILISTIC

It is evident from the above discussion that profit, Z, is a function of the quantity of sales in units (Q); the unit selling price (P); the fixed cost (F); and the variable cost (V). Up to this point P, F, and V were considered only as given constants, so that profit was variable only as a function of changes in sales quantity. In the following discussion, P, F, and V

will be treated in a manner similar to Q, i.e., as random variables whose probability distribution is known.[2] Continuing the example from the preceding section, let

Variable

Sales Quantity (Q)
Selling Price (P)
Fixed Costs (F)
Variable Costs (V)

Expectation (Mean)

$E(Q') = 5,000$ units
$E(P') = \$3,000^2$
$E(F') = \$5,800,000^2$
$E(V') = \$1,750^2$

Standard Deviation

$\sigma_Q' = 400$ units
$\sigma_P' = \$50^2$
$\sigma_F' = \$100,000^2$
$\sigma_V' = \$75^2$

For purposes of illustration, the random variables will be assumed to be independent, so that no correlation exists between events of the different random variables.[3] In this case, the expected profit $E(Z')$ and the related standard deviation σ_Z' can be calculated as follows[4]:

$$E(Z') = E(Q') [E(P' - E(V')] - E(F')$$
$$= \$450,000.$$
$$\sigma_Z' = \$681,500.$$

[2] The mean and standard deviation for P, F, and V can be established by using the same method described earlier. That is, the sales manager may estimate a mean selling price of $3,000 per unit and, given the above information, he should feel that there is roughly a 2/3 probability that the actual sales price per unit will be within $50 of this mean estimate.

[3] This assumption is made to facilitate com-

Note that when factors other than sales are treated as random variables, the expected profit is still $450,000 as in the previous cases. However, the profit's risk as measured by the standard deviation is increased from $500,000 to $681,500. The reason for this is that the variability in all of the components (i.e., sales price, cost, etc.) will add to the variability in the profit. Is this change in the standard deviation significant? The significance of the change is a value judgment based on a comparison of various probabilistic measures and on the firm's attitude toward risk. Using a normal distribution, Table 5 compares expected profits, standard deviations of profits, and select probabilistic measures for three hypothetical products.

factors are probabilistic. In the third case, the assumed product has the same expected values for selling price, variable cost, fixed cost, and sales volume, but the standard deviations on each of these random variables have been increased to $\sigma_Q'' = 600$ (instead of 400 units); $\sigma_{P''} = \$125$ (instead of $50); $\sigma_{F''} = \$200,000$ (instead of $100,000); and $\sigma_{V''} = \$150$ (instead of $75).

Table 5 shows the relative "risk" involved in the three new products which have been proposed. The chances of at least breaking even are greatest with product 1. However, even though the standard deviation of the profit on product 3 is over twice that of product 1, the probability of breaking-even on product 3

TABLE 5   Comparison of Expected Profits, Standard Deviations of Profits, and Probabilistic Measures*

	Products		
	(1)	*(2)*	*(3)*
Expected profit	$450,000	$450,000	$ 450,000
Standard deviation of profit	$500,000	$681,500	$1,253,000
The probability of:			
(a) at least breaking even	.816	.745	.641
(b) profit at least + $250,000	.655	.615	.564
(c) profit at least + $600,000	.382	.413	.456
(d) loss greater than $300,000	.067	.136	.274

*Note: The above probabilities, in some cases, cannot be read from Table 4. However, all probabilities come from a more complete version of Table 4.

In all three situations, the proposed products have the same break-even quantity—4,640 units. The first case is the first example discussed where sales quantity is the only random variable. The second case is the one just discussed; that is, all

---

putation in the example. Where correlation among variables is present the computational procedure must take into account the values of the respective covariances.

[4]For the case of independent variables given here, σ_Z' is the solution value in the equation:

$$\sigma_Z = \sqrt{[\sigma_Q^2\,(\sigma_P^2 + \sigma_V^2) + E(Q')^2}$$
$$(\sigma_P^2 + \sigma_V^2) + [E(P') - E(V')]^2$$
$$\sigma_Q^2 + \sigma_F^2\,]$$

is only .17 lower than product 1. Likewise, the probability of earning at least $250,000 profit is higher for product 1 (which has the lowest σ) than for the other two products.

However, note that the probability of earning profits above the expected value of $450,000 (for each product) is *greater* for products 2 and 3 than for 1. If the firm is willing to assume some risk, the chances of high profits are improved with product 3, rather than with 2 and 1. To offset this, however, the chance of loss is also greatest with product 3. This is to be expected, since product 3 has the highest standard deviation (variability) as far as profit is concerned.

The best alternative cannot be chosen without some statement of the firm's attitude toward risk. However, given a certain attitude, the proper choice should be facilitated by using probability information of the type given in Table 5. As an example, suppose that the firm's position is such that any loss at all may have an adverse effect on its ability to stay in business. Some probability criteria can, perhaps, be established in order to screen proposals for new products. If, for example, top management feels that any project which is acceptable must have no greater than a .30 probability of incurring a loss, then projects 1 or 2 would be acceptable but project 3 would not.

On the other hand, the firm's attitude toward risk may be such that the possibility of high profit is attractive, provided the probability of losses can be reasonably controlled. In this case, it may be possible to set a range within which acceptable projects must fall. For example, suppose that the firm is willing to accept projects where the probability of profits being greater than $600,000 is at least .40, provided that the probability of

a loss being greater than $300,000 does not exceed .15. In this case, project 2 would be acceptable, but project 3 would not. Given statements of attitude toward risk of this nature, it seems that a probability dimension added to C-V-P analysis would be useful.

SUMMARY AND CONCLUSION

In many cases, the choice among alternatives is facilitated greatly by C-V-P analysis. However, traditional C-V-P analysis does not take account of the relative risk of various alternatives. The interaction of costs, selling prices, and volume is important in summarizing the effect of various alternatives on the profits of the firm. The techniques discussed in this paper preserve the traditional analysis but also add another dimension—that is, risk is brought in as another important decision factor. The statement of probabilities with respect to various levels of profits and losses for each alternative should aid the decision maker once his attitude toward risk has been defined.

A New Application of Calculus and Risk Analysis to Cost-Volume-Profit Changes

Thomas A.
Morrison

Eugene Kaczka

*University of
Massachusetts*

Under traditional cost-volume-profit analysis, companies study-ing the effect that changes in selling prices will have on volume and profit are limited to a consideration of only a selected few alternatives. In this article, the authors offer an extension which takes into consideration a continuum of price changes and incorporates risk in the analysis as well.

Reprinted from *The Accounting Review*, XLIV (April 1969), 330-343. Used by permission of Thomas A. Morrison, Eugene Kaczka, and *The Accounting Review*.

Differential calculus has recently been applied to some cost-volume-profit situa-tions as an extension of breakeven anal-ysis to find maximum profit levels when cost and/or revenue behavior is curvi-linear.[1] However, there is another far more practical application that, for some unknown reason, has gone unrecognized up to now. It involves changes in selling prices and costs of changes in quality which result in changes in quantities demanded.

All companies consider the effect that changes in selling prices will have on the sales of their product. They are also laboring under a constant cost-push pres-sure to increase prices. Therefore, com-panies must forecast expected volume for the various changes in sales price. Then

they must determine whether or not such changes will be profitable. Finally, the most profitable combination of changes should be selected.

TRADITIONAL METHOD

The traditional method of approaching these problems is to select several discrete changes in sales prices, forecast new levels of sales at these points, and select the most profitable alternative. All manage-rial accounting texts explain this method but go no further. A recent article used the typical illustration shown in Exhibit A.[2] The traditional approach makes the

---

[1] Travis P. Goggans, "Break-even Analysis with Curvilinear Functions," *The Accounting Re-view*, (October 1965), pp. 867-871, and Hor-ace R. Givens, "An Application of Curvilinear Break-even Analysis," *The Accounting Review*, (January 1966), pp. 141-143.

[2] I. Wayne Keller, "Controlling Contribution," *Management Accounting*, (June 1967), p. 23, 28. Similar illustrations used by Walter B. McFarland, *Concepts for Management Account-ing*, (National Association of Accountants, 1966), p. 69, and Robert Beyer, *Profitability Accounting for Planning and Control*, (The Ronald Press Company, 1963) Chapter 7.

EXHIBIT A   Conventional Cost-Volume-Profit Analysis

Preliminary Budget for Period		
Net Sales		$200,000
Variable Costs		170,000
Variable Margin		30,000
Specific Capacity Costs		17,500
Product contribution to common capacity costs and profit		$ 12,500
Detail: Units		40,000
Unit rates: Selling price		$5.00
Variable costs		4.25
Contribution		.75

New Alternatives		Budget			
Price Increase		5%	10%	12.5%	15%
Unit Volume Reduction		10%	20%	30.0%	45%
Sales Price	$5.00	$5.25	$5.50	$5.63	$5.75
Variable Cost/unit	4.25	4.25	4.25	4.25	4.25
Variable Margin/unit	$.75	$1.00	$1.25	$1.38	$1.50
Sales Units	40,000	36,000	32,000	28,000	22,000
Variable Margin	$30,000	$36,000	$40,000	$38,640	$33,000

∴ Best solution = Increase sales price 10%

very substantial assumption that cost and demand functions are known. Since the data which are used in the analysis are in fact estimates, it is advisable to consider the accuracy of these estimates in making decisions. This article extends the usual approach by considering a continuum of price changes and incorporating risk in the analysis.

DEFECTS OF THE TRADITIONAL APPROACH

Unfortunately, the traditional approach fails to make full use of the relationships given. Once the original contribution is given (original selling price minus original variable costs) as well as the expected change in the quantity demanded as determined by marketing analysis, a maximum profit can be determined for *any* change in price (not merely for 3 or 4 given alternatives) where some explicit or implicit functional relationship is assumed between price and volume.

Also, some misleading inferences might be made from the use of a few discrete alternatives. In the preceding example, the ratio of volume reduction to price increase went from 2:1

$$\left(\text{i.e., } \frac{10\%}{5\%}, \frac{20\%}{10\%} \right)$$

$$\text{to } 2.4:1 \left(\text{i.e., } \frac{30.0\%}{12.5\%} \right)$$

$$\text{to } 3:1 \left(\text{i.e., } \frac{45\%}{15\%} \right)$$

Since the alternate selected was the last point at which the ratio was 2:1, it might be inferred that as long as the volume change relative to price change remained in the ratio of 2:1, the company should continue to raise the price. This is not true. It will be shown that even if the ratio remained constant at 2:1, the profits would start to decline after a 17.5% price increase had been reached. This is caused by the fact that the contribution per unit changes in a curvilinear fashion even though the price-volume relationship is linear.

THE CALCULUS APPROACH

The most important step is the development of a general formula which can be used for all changes in selling price and volume.[3]

The following notations will be used:

> a = constant intercept of Y axis
> b = constant slope of line
> OV = original volume in units
> OSP = original selling price per unit
> OVC = original variable cost per unit
> PCV = per cent change in volume
> PCP = per cent change in selling price
> OCP = original contribution as a per cent of selling price
> Z = variable margin divided by original revenue (original volume times original selling price)

When a per cent increase of selling price is associated with a per cent decrease in volume, variable margin can be determined as follows:

(1.1) Variable Margin = $[OV(1 - PCV)]$
$\cdot [OSP(1 + PCP) - OVC]$

Since original volume (OV) and original selling price (OSP) are irrelevant, divide both sides by these.

(1.2) $Z = (1 - PCV)$
$$\cdot \left[(1 + PCP) - \frac{OVC}{OSP} \right]$$

Since
$$OCP = 1 - \frac{OVC}{OSP},$$

then the general equation is:

[3] For explanatory purposes linear price-volume relationships are used over the relevant ranges. These may be assumed to be reasonable approximations of curvilinear relationships.

(1.3) $Z = (1 - PCV)(OCP + PCP)$

Since OCP is a constant only PCV and PCP remain as variables. Finally, when PCV is expressed linearly in terms of PCP, only one independent variable is left as follows:

since $PCV = a + b\,PCP$
$Z = [1 - (a + b\,PCP)]\,(OCP + PCP)$

This equation is identifiable as a parabola opening downward with its vertex a maximum, i.e., the second derivative is negative. The per cent price change at which the maximum occurs is determined by taking the first derivative and setting the resulting expression equal to zero and solving for PCP as follows:

$$Z = (1 - a)\,OCP + (1 - a)\,PCP$$
$$- b\,PCP \cdot OCP - b\,PCP^2$$
$$\frac{dZ}{d\,PCP} = 0 + (1 - a) - b\,OCP$$
$$- 2b\,PCP = 0$$
(1.4) $PCP = \dfrac{1 - a - b\,OCP}{2b}$

Example: If in the above example the price-volume relationship can be assumed to remain constant 2:1 up to $PCP = 10\%$, 2.4:1 when PCP lies between 10% and 12.5% and 3:1 when PCP is greater than 12.5%, three different linear relationships could be plotted (Exhibit B). The maximum profit points (which are the same as the maximum variable margin points) for the three separate lines can be computed by taking the first derivative of equation 1.3 after substituting the given relationships for PCV, or by using equation 1.4 directly as follows:
(a) When

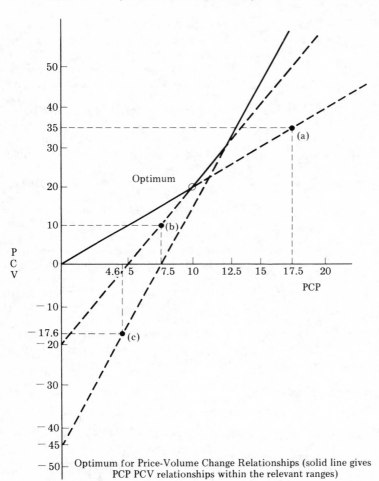

Optimum for Price-Volume Change Relationships (solid line gives
PCP PCV relationships within the relevant ranges)

$$PCV = 2\,PCP$$
$$a = 0$$
$$b = 2$$
$$OCP = \frac{.75}{5.00} = .15$$
$$\text{Maximum } PCP = \frac{1 - (.2) - 4(.15)}{4}$$
$$PCP = .175 = 17.5\%$$

Verification			
PCP	17%	17.5%	18%
PCV	34%	35%	36%
New selling price	$5.35	$5.875	$5.90
New contribution	$1.60	$1.625	$1.65
New volume	26,400	26,000	25,600
New variable margin	$42,240	$42,250	$42,240
		Max.	

This is above the relevant range 0-10%   (b) When

$$PCV = .2 + 4 (PCP - .1)$$
$$PCV = -.2 + 4 PCP$$
$$a = -.2$$
$$b = 4$$
$$OCP = .15$$

$$\text{Maximum } PCP = \frac{1 - (-.2) - 4(.15)}{8}$$

$$PCP = .075 = 7.5\%$$

This is below the relevant range 10%-12.5%.

This can be verified in a manner similar to (a).

(c) When

$$PCV = .3 + 6 (PCP - .125)$$
$$PCV = -.45 + 6 PCP$$
$$a = -.45$$
$$b = 6$$
$$OCP = .15$$

$$\text{Maximum } PCP = \frac{1 - (-.45) - 6(.15)}{12}$$

$$PCP = .046 = 4.6\%$$

This is below the relevant range 12.5% to ∞.

This can be verified in a manner similar to (a).

Answer to Example:

The maximum profit point is located exactly at $PCP = 10\%$, since a movement in either direction from this point is away from the maximum profit points of (a) and (b) above. The answer can easily be demonstrated by taking points just above and below the maximum as follows:

	9%	10%	11%
PCP	9%	10%	11%
PCV	18%	20%	24%
New selling price	$5.45	$5.50	$5.55
New contribution	$1.20	$1.25	$1.30
New volume	32,800	32,000	30,400
New variable margin	$39,360	$40,000	$39,520
		Max.	

The answer to this example is at a point of intersection. However, it should be emphasized that it is quite possible to have an optimum *not* falling at an intersection. If the relevant range in (a) had been from 0 to 20% (rather than from 0 to 10%) the maximum profit point would have been where $PCP = 17.5\%$ as computed in (a) above even though the intersection of the straight lines would have been at 20%.

The expressions developed up to this point have considered the typical product for which a downward sloping demand curve exists, but pertain only to that portion of the curve where prices are above the original (current) selling price. If we wish to consider decreasing the price, which for most products means an increase in volume, a slight modification is required in the general equation and its first derivative.

The basic variable margin expression (1.1) remains unchanged except for two signs as follows:

Variable Margin

$$(2.1) \quad = [OV(1 + PCV)]$$
$$\cdot [OSP(1 - PCP) - OVC]$$
$$(2.2) \; Z = (1 + PCV)$$
$$(2.2) \quad \cdot \left[(1 - PCP) - \frac{OVC}{OSP} \right]$$
$$(2.3) \; Z = (1 + PCV)(OCP - PCP)$$

Substituting for PCV by use of the same identity $PCV = a + bPCP$, and then taking the first derivative, setting the resulting expression equal to zero and solving for PCP, the following result is obtained:

$$(2.4) \; PCP = \frac{b \, OCP - 1 - a}{2b}$$

The same result could have been obtained by merely using the general equation of (1.3) and using negative values for PCV and PCP (i.e., $PCV = -a - bPCP$, and $PCP = -PCP$).

Example: If

$$PCV \text{ (increase)} = 10 \, PCP \text{ (decrease)},$$
$$a = 0$$
$$b = 10$$
$$OCP = .15$$

$$\text{Maximum } PCP = \frac{10(.15) - 1 - 0}{20}$$

$$PCP = .025 = 2.5\% \text{ (decrease)}$$
$$= - 2.5\%$$

Verification

PCP	2%	2.5%	3%
PCV	20%	25%	30%
New selling price	$4.90	$4.875	$4.85
New contribution	$.65	$.625	$.60
New volume	48,000	50,000	52,000
New variable margin	$31,200	$31,250	$31,200
		Max.	

CHANGES IN VARIABLE COSTS

A company may decide that a change in the quality of its product requiring an increase or decrease in variable costs may be appropriate.

An increase in variable costs which improves quality may increase sales. The following new notations are necessary:

PCC = Per cent change in variable costs

$OVCP$ = Original variable cost per cent Variable Margin

$$(3.1) = [OV(1 + PCV)] \cdot [OSP - OVC(1 + PCC)]$$

$$(3.2) \, Z = (1 + PCV) \cdot \left(1 - \frac{OVC}{OSP} - \frac{OVC \cdot PCC}{OSP}\right)$$

$$(3.3) \, Z = (1 + PCV) \cdot (OCP - OVCP \cdot PCC)$$

The only variables are PCV and PCC. When PCV is expressed in terms of PCC a

single variable equation remains and a maximum profit point can be found as follows:

$$\text{if } PCV = a + b \, PCC$$

$$Z = (1 + a + b \, PCC) \cdot (OCP - OVCP \cdot PCC)$$

$$Z = (1 + a) \, OCP - (1 + a) \cdot OVCP \cdot PCC + b \, OCP \cdot PCC - b \, OVCP \cdot PCC^2$$

$$\frac{dZ}{d \, PCC} = - (1 + a) \, OVCP + b \, OCP - 2b \, OVCP \cdot PCC = 0$$

$$PCC = \frac{b \, OCP - OVCP - a OVCP}{2b \, OVCP}$$

$$(3.4) \, PCC = \frac{b \dfrac{OCP}{OVCP} - 1 - a}{2b}$$

Also, if poorer quality decreases sales, the following maximum can be determined:

$$(4.1) \, PCC = \frac{1 - a - b \dfrac{OCP}{OVCP}}{2b}$$

The similarities between (3.4) and (2.4) and between (4.1) and (1.4) are due to the similarities in functional form describing the increase (or decrease) in volume associated with the decrease (or increase) in contribution.

CHANGES IN FIXED COSTS

A change in fixed costs does not lend itself to the above analysis. An infinite number of alternatives does not exist. If automation is being contemplated, a few machines may be considered resulting in only a few alternatives. Also, the contribution per cent does not vary directly with each incremental change in cost or selling price. There may be a reduction in variable costs when a machine is acquired, but any relationship between the reduction in variable costs and an increase in fixed costs is meaningful only at that one point. Furthermore, since with the acquisition of a new machine the fixed cost per period can vary according to the useful life and depreciation method selected, capital budgeting techniques using discounted cash flows are more meaningful for decisions among limited alternatives.

However, a portion of the analysis is pertinent when a change in fixed costs causes a change in variable costs. In the above formulas, a change in the original contribution per cent (*OCP*) would be made which would result in a different maximum point being attained.

INDIFFERENCE POINTS AND RISK

The usefulness of the determination of a maximum profit point hinges on the reliability of the changes in quantities demanded which have been assumed for different prices or quality improvements (cost changes). An important additional piece of information is the indifference point, i.e., the new volume level at which the company must operate in order to obtain the same total profit (or loss) as that obtained at the original volume level. Since this article assumes that there are an infinite number of possible volume levels, there are obviously an infinite number of indifference points.

In order to relate the indifference points to the volume and price changes when an increase in sales price causes a decrease in volume, the general equation (1.3) can again be used:

$$Z = (1 - PCV)(OCP + PCP)$$

The indifference point is by definition the point at which the changes in volume and price will result in the same profit. Assuming no change in fixed costs it would be where $Z = OCP$.

$$\therefore OCP = (1 - PCV)(OCP + PCP)$$

or

$$(5.1) \quad PCV = \frac{PCP}{OCP + PCP}$$

This profit indifference curve when plotted along with the original price-volume curve will result in portraying an "added profit" area expressed as a percentage relationship between price and volume changes (Exhibit C).[4] The exact added profit in dollars can be computed easily as follows:

$$(5.2) \text{ Profit} = \frac{\text{Added Profit Vol.\%}}{\text{Indifference Vol. \%}}$$
$$\times (\text{increase in contribution} \times OV)$$

Example: When *PCP* = 5%, indifference *PCV* = 25%

$$\text{Added profit} = \frac{15\%}{25\%} \times (.25 \times 40,000)$$
$$= \$6,000$$

The maximum profit point was previously found to be where *PCP* = 10%. By use of the above equation (5.2) the maximum added profit can be computed.

When *PCP* = 10%
$$\text{Added Profit} = \frac{20\%}{40\%} \times (.50 \times 40,000)$$
$$= \$10,000$$

Further confirmation that a maximum has been attained can be given by computing the added profit when *PCP* = 9% and *PCP* = 11%.

When *PCP* = 9% Added profit = \$9,360.

[4] For a decrease in selling price requiring an increase in volume to arrive at the same profit point the equation would be:

$$PCV = \frac{PCP}{OCP - PCP}$$

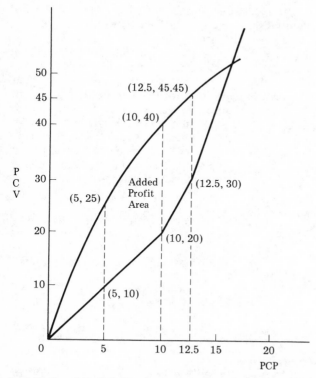

Introduction of Profit Indifference Curve (i.e., if price increases 10% and volume decreases 40%, the profit remains $12,500 as in Exhibit A)

EXHIBIT C.

When *PCP* = 11% Added profit
= $9,520.

Since both answers are less than $10,000, 10% appears as a maximum.

In every decision-making situation, risk must be weighed. The preceding example employs an estimate of how volume changes as price changes. Certainly, before taking action one would like to know the accuracy of the estimate and impact on profits that an error in this estimate will have. Whether the estimate was determined by classical statistical techniques or by subjective analysis, it is possible to ascertain the probability that a certain range of values about the esti-

mate will contain the true value. More specifically, if the error in the estimate of the slope of the line is normally distributed with a mean of zero and a standard deviation equal to σ_b, it is possible to indicate in probabilistic terms a level of confidence that a range which is equal to the estimated slope plus or minus any number of standard deviations will contain the actual slope. For example, there is a 95% chance that the range defined by the estimate plus or minus 1.96 standard deviations will contain the value which will in fact be realized.

The information about the slope of the line can be used to determine the probability that the per cent change in volume which occurs when price is changed will lie within a specified range. This in turn is used to establish a range about the estimated profits at the specified probability level.

For the purpose of clarification, this approach will be applied to the previous example.

The following notation is used:

σ_b = the standard deviation of the estimate of b

$Z\alpha$ = the number of standard deviations on each side of the mean which contain an area under the unit normal curve equal to the confidence level.

The confidence interval about the slope of the line for a specified α is thus

$$b \pm \sigma_b Z\alpha$$

which when substituted into the general linear expression for the per cent of volume change which results from a change in price yields

$$(5.3)\ PCV = a + (b \pm \sigma_b Z\alpha)\ PCP$$

If it is determined that σ_b = .5, the 95% confidence limits (i.e., $Z\alpha$ - - 1.96) about the change in volume are

$$PCV = a + (b \pm - .98)\ PCP$$

By substituting the values of a and b which are appropriate in the several ranges, Exhibit D can be generated. Notice that as the magnitude of the price change increases, the range of volume changes which may result in increases, and correspondingly the range of added profits increases. For a price change of 5% there is a 95% chance that added profits will fall between $7,960 and $4,040 while for a price change of 10%

there is a 95% chance that the added profits will fall between $14,900 and $5,100.

In addition to this information, it is possible to summarize in a general form the probability that profits are less than, or equal to, the original profits for any price change. This can be obtained by performing algebraic manipulations on the difference between the expression for the upper limit on the per cent change in volume and the indifference volume, (equation 5.1 minus equation 5.3).

$$0 \geqslant \frac{PCP}{OCP + PCP} - [a + (b - \sigma_b Z\alpha)PCP].$$

The probability statement that results is

$$\text{Prob}\left[Z\alpha \leqslant \frac{a}{\sigma_b\ PCP} + \frac{b}{\sigma_b} - \frac{1}{\sigma_b(OCP + PCP)} \right] = \alpha$$

Substituting the values from the previous example at the point where maximum profits are realized

$$\text{Prob}\left[Z\alpha \leqslant 0 + \frac{2}{.5} - \frac{1}{.5(.15+.10)} \right] = \alpha$$
$$\text{Prob}\ [Z\alpha \leqslant - 4] = \alpha$$
$$Z_{.000032} = - 4$$
$$\therefore \alpha = .000032$$

indicates that the chance of attaining less than the original profit is thirty-two millionths.

The types of problems which would seem to be of greatest practical interest are those which bear resemblance to the example depicted in Exhibit D. That is, situations where a change in price will result in an increase in expected profits. For the range of price changes (from the origin to point (a) on Exhibit D) which result in an increase in expected profits, some general statements can be made

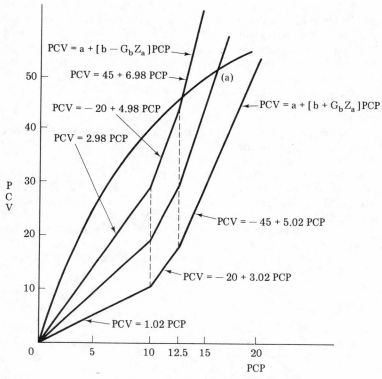

$$PCV = a + [b - G_b Z_a] PCP$$

$$PCV = 45 + 6.98\ PCP$$

(a)

$$PCV = -20 + 4.98\ PCP$$

$$PCV = a + [b + G_b Z_a] PCP$$

$$PCV = 2.98\ PCP$$

$$PCV = -45 + 5.02\ PCP$$

$$PCV = -20 + 3.02\ PCP$$

$$PCV = 1.02\ PCP$$

Introduction of Risk around Original
Price-Volume Change Line

EXHIBIT D.

about the effects which changes in parameters and variables have on the probability that profits will be less than indifference profits.

Returning to the probability statement, one finds, as might be expected, that the probability of profits falling below the indifference level increases if a, σ_b, PCP, or b increases. To partially demonstrate this, a modification is made in the example problem. The estimates of the slopes and the intercepts are assumed to remain the same; however, the accuracy of the estimate of the slopes is lower for values of PCP greater than 5%. Specifically for PCP less than or equal to 5%, σ_b is .5, while for values of PCP greater than 5%,

σ_b is 2.0. The price change at which maximum profits occur is unchanged, $PCP = 10\%$. However, from the probability statement

$$\text{Prob}\left[Z\alpha \leqslant \frac{2}{2} - \frac{1}{2(.15 + .10)} \right] = \alpha$$

$$\text{Prob}\ [Z\alpha \leqslant -1.0] = \alpha$$

$$Z_{.1587} = -1.0$$

$$\therefore \alpha = .1587$$

the chance of falling below the indifference profit is 15.87%. At $PCP = 5\%$,

$$\text{Prob}\ [Z\alpha \leqslant -6] = \alpha$$

indicates that the probability of obtaining less than the original profit is essentially zero. Given the probability information, the company may decide not to change prices to the point which would yield maximum profits, but may change to some point between PCP = 5% and PCP = 10%. Management may be willing to accept lower profits rather than risk the possibility that profits will fall below the original value.

It is also possible to treat the situation where there exists uncertainty about the points A and B where a change takes place in the relationship of PCP to PCV. The dotted lines in Exhibit E indicate the 95% confidence limits about the change in volume which results when price is changed, $PCV = -.1 + 4PCP$. Thus, when PCP = 10%, there is a 95% chance that added profits will lie between $100 and

$9900. Recall that when PCP = 5%, the confidence limits on added profits are $4,040 and $7,960. Given the increased risk of small profits which occurs the company may now decide not to change prices to the point where PCP = 10% but to some other point.

The sagacity of their decision is further supported when one realizes that change in the relationship between price and volume also changes the maximum profit point. If the change in the relationship takes place at PCP = 5%, as specified above the new optimum PCP = 6.25%. Should it be possible to specify a probability distribution about the point where the relationship changes, one could determine the price change which would yield the greatest expected added profits.

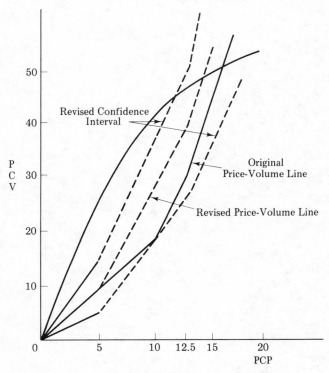

Introduction of Risk around Revised
Price-Volume Change Line

EXHIBIT E.

CONSTRAINTS AND OPPORTUNITY COSTS

Production of a product usually will be subject to various constraints such as limited raw materials, labor hours or machine hours. However, as soon as a constraint limits the company from attaining its maximum profit point a new alternative arises. How much should the company spend in order to eliminate the constraint? The lost profits (opportunity costs) should be weighed against the costs of eliminating the constraint.

Exhibit F shows how a constraint would operate. Any constraint above PCV = 20% would not bother manage-

ment since 20% is the maximum profit point. If the total number of machine hours available is 46,000 and it takes one machine hour to produce one unit, then the maximum volume possible is 46,000 units or PCV = 16% (i.e., 116% X 40,000).

The previously determined maximum added profit is $10,000 where *PCP* = 10%. Added profits of $8,640 are attainable where *PCP* = 8%. The difference of $1,360 represents the opportunity cost of not being able to move to the maximum point. Management can now evaluate the costs of eliminating the constraint (new machine, purchase semi-finished goods from outsiders, operate longer hours, etc.) against the lost profits.

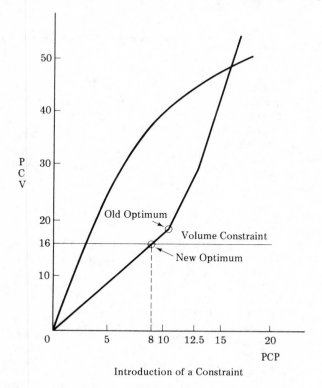

Introduction of a Constraint

COMPARISON WITH
LINEAR PROGRAMMING

Any method that considers finding maximum profit points for products whose production is subject to linear constraints invites comparisons with linear programming techniques. The analysis discussed here is concerned with a single variable problem with a nonlinear objective function. If one is faced with a situation where the optimal price changes for several products are desired and a number of constraints exist, then it may be approached as a general constrained maxima problem using Lagrangian multipliers or nonlinear programming as dictated by the form of the problem.

CONCLUSIONS

Decision making involving projected profits of product lines has traditionally required the breakdown of costs into fixed and variable costs as well as a projection of demand when selling prices or product quality involving variable costs are changed. Unfortunately businessmen have made only limited use of such valuable information.

Cost-volume-profit analysis in the past has been seriously handicapped by its consideration of only a selected few possible alternatives. By the introduction of a continuous price-volume relationship maximum profit points can be found. Even in linear breakeven analysis, volume changes related to price changes result in a quadratic equation whose shape, when plotted, is in the form of a parabola with its rounded top at the price-volume point which gives the maximum profit (easily computed by differential calculus by finding the point at which the slope of the curve is zero).

When finding the selling price change which will result in the maximum profit, only the following need be considered:

1. The original contribution per cent, (*OCP*),
2. the per cent change in volume for each change in price, (*b*),
3. and, only if the relationship changes, the point at which the change occurs and the *Y* axis intercept of the line expressing the new relationship (*a*).

When finding the variable cost change (quality change) which will result in the maximum profit only the addition of the following to the above three items need be considered:

4. the original variable cost per cent, (*OVCP*).

Much normally used but irrelevant data to the decision is disregarded, such as actual selling prices, actual volumes, actual variable costs or total profit at any point.

The analysis lends itself easily to further adaptations by using the simple general equation:

$$Z = (1 \pm PVC)\,(OCP \pm PCP)$$

1. Indifference points can be found for each change in price (or variable cost),
2. an "added profit" area can be found from which total profit for any given price can be determined,
3. risk can be introduced easily,
4. constraints can be applied, optimal product mix can be found (although not done here),
5. and even opportunity costs of not having adequate capacity to produce at the maximum profit point can be found.

SELECTED REFERENCES FOR CHAPTER 3

ARTICLES

Bell, Albert L., "Break-Even Charts Versus Marginal Graphs: A Case of Costs and Profits Versus Resource Allocation," *Management Accounting,* I, (February, 1969).

Charnes, A., W. W. Cooper, and Y. Ijiri, "Breakeven Budgeting and Programming to Goals," *Journal of Accounting Research,* I (Spring, 1963).

Devine, Carl T., "Boundaries and Potentials of Reporting on Profit-Volume Relations," *N.A.A. Bulletin,* XLII, (January, 1961).

Ferrara, William L., Jack C. Hayya and David A. Nachman, "Normalcy of Profit in the Jaedicke-Robichek Model," *The Accounting Review,* XLVII, (April, 1972).

Jaedicke, R. K., "Improving B-E Analysis by Linear Programming Techniques," *N.A.A. Bulletin,* XLII (March, 1961).

Manes, Rene, "A New Dimension to Breakeven Analysis," *Journal of Accounting Research,* IV (Spring, 1966).

Mitchell, G. B., "Breakeven Analysis and Capital Budgeting," *Journal of Accounting Research,* VI (Autumn, 1969).

Patrick, A. W., Some Observations on the Break-Even Chart," *The Accounting Review,* XXXIII, (October, 1958).

Soldofsky, Robert M., "Accountants' vs. Economists' Concepts of Break-Even Analysis," *N.A.A. Bulletin,* XLI (December, 1959).

Vickers, Douglas, "On the Economics of Break-Even," *The Accounting Review,* XXXV (July, 1960).

Wilson, James D., "Practical Applications of Cost-Volume-Profit Analysis," *N.A.A. Bulletin,* XLI, (March, 1960).

CAPITAL BUDGETING

CHAPTER FOUR

A Note on Biases in Capital Budgeting Introduced by Inflation

James C.
Van Horne

Stanford University

The cost-of-capital rate or discount rate used to compute net present value embodies anticipated inflation. Failure to take account of inflation in cash-flow estimates will result in a biased appraisal and, possibly, a less than optimal allocation of capital in the firm.

Reprinted from *Journal of Financial and Quantitative Analysis*, January-February 1971, 653-658. Used by permission of James C. Van Horne and *Journal of Financial and Quantitative Analysis*.

In the allocation of capital to investment projects, it is unlikely that optimal decisions will be reached unless anticipated inflation is embodied in the cash-flow estimates. Often, there is a tendency to assume that price levels remain unchanged throughout the life of the project. Frequently this assumption is imposed unknowingly; future cash flows are estimated simply on the basis of existing prices. However, a bias arises in that the cost-of-capital rate used as the acceptance criterion embodies an element attributable to anticipated inflation, while the cash-flow estimates do not. Although this bias may not be serious when there is modest inflation, it may become quite important in periods of high anticipated inflation. The purpose of this note is to investigate the nature of the bias and how it arises.

I. COST-OF-CAPITAL RATE

Consider a situation in which the cost-of-capital rate is used as the hurdle rate for project selection and there is no capital rationing. If a project meets the acceptance criterion, capital is available to finance it at the cost-of-capital rate. Suppose, also, that the acceptance of any investment project or group of projects will not alter the risk complexion of the firm as a whole. Finally, assume for simplicity that the firm has a capital structure consisting entirely of equity. Actually, the implications for the problem at hand are the same if debt is partially employed.

There is a general agreement that security prices depend not on past changes in prices, but on future anticipated ones.[1] Inflation is defined as a rise in the general level of prices for goods and services, which in turn results in a decline in the purchasing power of a unit of money. While there is disagreement as to what index is most representative of purchasing power,[2] we bypass this problem and assume that a single index exists that portrays effectively the general price level at various moments in time. The anticipated rate of inflation is defined as the expected annual rate of change in this index. For simplicity, we assume that this rate is the same for all future periods.

Generally, the market value of a share of common stock is considered to be the present value of all expected future dividends, discounted at a required rate of return, k, determined by the market. Thus,

$$(1)\ P_0 = \sum_{t=1}^{\infty} \frac{D_t}{(1+k)^t}$$

where:

P_0 = market price per share at time 0, and

D_t = the dividend expected by investors

at the margin to be paid at the end of period t.

For the continuous case, equation (1) becomes:

$$(2)\ P_0 = \int^{\infty} D_t e^{-kt} d_t$$

In the case of an all-equity capital structure, the required rate of return, k, becomes the cost of capital. This rate can be thought of as being comprised of two parts:

$$(3)\ k = i + \theta,$$

where:

i = the risk-free rate, and

θ = a risk premium to compensate investors for the uncertainty associated with their receiving the expected stream of dividends.

If the corporation were expected to exist in perpetuity, i might be represented by the current yield on a perpetual default-free bond.[3] As the rate is expressed in nominal terms, embodied in it is an element attributable to anticipated inflation from time 0 into perpetuity. Whether this element corresponds exactly to the rate of anticipated inflation, as denoted by changes in the price index, depends upon the preference functions of investors relative to the price index employed.[4]

---

[1] See Irving Fisher, *The Theory of Interest* (New York: The Macmillan Company, 1930), Chapter 2, from which most of the work on yields and inflation stems.

[2] See Martin Bronfenbrenner and Franklyn D. Holzman, "Survey of Inflation Theory," *American Economic Review*, LIII (September 1963), pp. 597-599.

[3] We assume that no call feature exists on the instrument and that investors pay no taxes on dividends and capital gains.

[4] In one study, Robert Mundell, "Inflation and Real Interest," *Journal of Political Economy*, LXXI (June 1963), pp. 280-283, contends that nominal rates of interest may contain less than the full rate of anticipated inflation. The reason is that inflation may influence wealth variables in such a manner as to lower the real rate of interest.

II. ESTIMATING CASH FLOWS

Having affirmed that anticipated inflation is embraced in the acceptance criterion—namely, the cost of capital, k—it is important to consider its impact on the project itself. The expected cash flows of a project are affected by anticipated inflation in several ways.[5] If cash inflows arise ultimately from the sale of a product, these inflows are affected by expected future prices. As for cash outflows, inflation affects both expected future wages and material costs. Note that future inflation does not affect depreciation charges on the asset. Once the asset is acquired, these charges are known with certainty.[6] The effect of anticipated inflation on cash inflows and cash outflows will vary with the nature of the project. In some cases, cash inflows, through price increases, will rise faster than cash outflows; while in other cases the opposite will hold. This phenomenon has given rise to the famous controversy of whether or not wages lag behind prices in times of inflation so that real wages decline and real profits increase.[7]

With the recognition of inflation, estimates of expected future cash flows must be modified to take account of the anticipated rate of inflation. One way is to adjust estimates made under an assumption of no future inflation by an inflation adjustment factor. The net-present value of a project then could be determined by:

$$(4) \ NPV_0 = \sum_{t=1}^{n} \frac{[I_t (1+\alpha\Gamma)^t - O_t(1 + \beta\Gamma)^t] \ [1-T] + F_t T}{(1 + k)^t} - C_0$$

where:

NPV_0 = the expected value of net-present value of the project at time 0,

n = final period in which cash flows are expected,

I_t = expected value of cash inflow in period t in the absence of future inflation,

Γ = anticipated rate of inflation as denoted by expected annual rate of change in the price index,

α = portion of Γ applicable to cash inflows,

O_t = expected value of cash outflows in period t in the absence of future inflation,

β = portion of Γ applicable to cash outflows,

T = corporate tax rate,

F_t = depreciation charges on the asset in period t, which are known with certainty, and

C_0 = cost of project at time 0, which is assumed to be known with certainty.

---

[5] Again, it is important to stress that we have assumed that the acceptance of the project does not alter the risk complexion of the firm as a whole.

[6] For further analysis of this point, see Brian Motley, "Inflation and Common Stock Values: Comment," *Journal of Finance*, XXIV (June 1969), pp. 530-535.

[7] Brofenbrenner and Holzman, "Inflation Theory," pp. 647-649; R. A. Kessel and A. A. Alchian, "The Meaning and Validity of the Inflation-Induced Lag of Wages Behind Prices," *American Economic Review*, L (March 1960), pp. 43-66; G. L. Bach and Albert Ando, "The Redistributional Effects of Inflation," *Review of Economics and Statistics*, XXXIX (February 1957), pp. 1-13; and Thomas F. Cargill, "An Empirical Investigation of the Wage-Lag Hypothesis," *American Economic Review*, LIX (December 1969), pp. 806-816.

The values α and β represent the expected sensitivity of cash inflows and outflows to inflation, assuming this sensitivity is invariant with respect to t. If the latter assumption does not hold, α and β can be made to vary with t. Added sophistication (in equation (4)) can be achieved by breaking down the cash inflows and cash outflows into individual components. For example, we might subdivide cash outflows into wages and material costs and calculate the sensitivity of each to Γ. If the project is expected to have a salvage value, the effect of inflation on this value must be recognized explicitly.

If a project has a net-present value greater than zero, as depicted by equation (4), it provides an inflation-adjusted return greater than that required by investors at the margin. As a result, its acceptance should result in a higher market price per share.[8]

The real problem, of course, is not in specifying an equation to deal with the impact of inflation, but in estimating the inputs that go into it. In some measure, price expectations appear to be related to past changes in price. Moreover, these expectations seem to be based more heavily on recent past price behavior than upon more distant past price behavior. Several empirical studies have documented these relationships.[9] If some weighted average of past changes in prices can be used to predict future changes, Γ in equa-

tion (4) can be estimated. Estimates of the expected sensitivity of cash inflows and outflows to Γ are best based upon past relationships between cash flows and actual inflation for similar types of projects. While we do not wish to belittle the difficulties associated with these estimates, our principal purpose is to point out the bias that arises if expected inflation is not incorporated in the cash-flow estimates for an investment project.

To illustrate this bias, assume that a project which cost \$100,000 at time 0 was under consideration and was expected to provide cash-flow benefits over the next 5 years. Assume further straight-line depreciation and a corporate tax rate of 50 per cent. Suppose that cash flows were estimated on the basis of price levels at time 0, with no consideration to the effect of future inflation upon them, and that these estimates were: [10]

If the firm's measured cost of capital were 12 per cent, the net-present value of the project would be −\$3,192. As this figure is negative, the project would be rejected.

| | *Period* | | | | |
	1	*2*	*3*	*4*	*5*
Expected cash inflow	\$30,000	\$40,000	\$50,000	\$50,000	\$30,000
Expected cash outflow	10,000	10,000	10,000	10,000	10,000
	20,000	30,000	40,000	40,000	20,000
Times 1-tax rate	.50	.50	.50	.50	.50
	10,000	15,000	20,000	20,000	10,000
Depreciation · tax rate	10,000	10,000	10,000	10,000	10,000
Net cash flow	\$20,000	\$25,000	\$30,000	\$30,000	\$20,000

[8] For the logic behind this statement, see James C. Van Horne, *Financial Management and Policy* (Englewood Cliffs, N. J.: Prentice-Hall, Inc., 1968), p. 130.
[9] See Phillip Cagan, "The Monetary Dynamics of Hyperinflation," in Milton Friedman, ed., *Studies in the Quantity Theory of Money* (Chicago: University of Chicago Press, 1956), pp. 23-117; and William E. Gibson, "Price-Expectations Effects on Interest Rates," *Journal of Finance*, XXV (March 1970), pp. 19-34.

However, the results are biased in the sense that the discount rate embodies an element attributable to anticipated future inflation, whereas the cash flow estimates do not. Suppose that the existing rate of

[10] Again, we have assumed that selection of the project will not affect the risk complexion of the firm as a whole.

inflation, as measured by changes in the price-level index, were 5 per cent, and that this rate was expected to prevail over the next 5 years. If both cash inflows and cash outflows were expected to increase at this rate, the net-present value of the project would be:

$$(5)\ NPV_0 = \sum_{t=1}^{5}$$

$$\frac{[I_t\,(1.05)^t - O_t\,(1.05)^t]\,[.5] + 20,000_t\,[.5]}{(1.12)^t}$$

$$- 100,000 = \$5,450$$

Because the net-present value is positive, the project would be acceptable now, whereas, before it was not. To reject it under the previous method of estimating cash flows would result in an opportunity loss to stockholders, for the project provides a return in excess of that required by investors at the margin.

The example serves to illustrate the importance of taking anticipated inflation into account explicitly when estimating future cash flows. Too often, there is a tendency not to consider its effect in these estimates. Because anticipated inflation is embodied in the required rate of return, not to take account of it in the cash-flow estimates will result in a biased appraisal of the project and, in turn, the possibility of a less than optimal allocation of capital. While our example has been framed in terms of a project whose acceptance does not alter the risk complexion of the firm, anticipated inflation can and should be recognized when this assumption is relaxed.[11]

[11]If expected cash flows are expressed as a probability tree reflecting series of conditional probabilities over time, each possible future cash flow should embody an assumption with respect to the rate of future inflation. This rate should be treated as stochastic. The project then could be evaluated according to the expected value of net-present value and the standard deviation of the probability distribution of possible net-present values, where the risk-free rate is used as the discount factor. This risk-return approach can be extended to handle the marginal impact of a project on the expected value and standard deviation of the probability distribution of net-present values for the firm as a whole. See James C. Van Horne, "The Analysis of Uncertainty Resolution in Capital Budgeting for New Products," *Management Science*, 15 (April 1969), pp. 376-382.

Stochastic Decision Trees for the Analysis of Investment Decisions

Richard F. Hespos

Dun & Bradstreet, Inc.

Paul A. Strassmann

Xerox Corporation

This paper describes an improved method for investment decision making. The method, which is called the stochastic decision tree method, is particularly applicable to investments characterized by high uncertainty and requiring a sequence of related decisions to be made over a period of time. The stochastic decision tree method builds on concepts used in the risk analysis method and the decision tree method of analyzing investments. It permits the use of subjective probability estimates or empirical frequency distributions for some or all factors affecting the decision. This application makes it practicable to evaluate all or nearly all feasible combinations of decisions in the decision tree, taking account of both expected value of return and aversion to risk, thus arriving at an optimal or near optimal set of decisions. Sensitivity analysis of the model can highlight factors that are critical because of high leverage on the measure of performance, or high uncertainty, or both. The method can be applied relatively easily to a wide variety of investment situations and is ideally suited for computer simulation.

Reprinted from *Management Science*, XI (August, 1965), 244-59. Used by permission of Richard F. Hespos, Paul A. Strassmann, and *Management Science*.

Investment decisions are probably the most important and most difficult decisions that confront top management, for several reasons. First, they involve enormous amounts of money. Investments of U.S. companies in plant and equipment alone are approaching $50 billion a year. Another $50 billion or so goes into acquisition, development of new products, and other investment expenditures.

Second, investment decisions usually have long-lasting effects. They often represent a "bricks and mortar" permanence. Unlike mistakes in inventory decisions, mistakes in investment decisions cannot be worked off in a short period of time. A major investment decision often commits management to a plan of action extending over several years, and the dollar penalty for reversing the decision can be high. Third, investments are implements of strategy. They are the tools by which top management controls the directions of a corporation.

Finally, and perhaps most important, investment decisions are characterized by a high degree of uncertainty. They are always based on predictions about the future—often the distant future. And they often require judgmental estimates about future events, such as the consumer acceptance of a new product. For all of these reasons, investment decisions absorb large portions of the time and attention of top management.

Investment decision-making has probably benefited more from the development of analytical decision-making methods than any other management area. In the past ten or fifteen years, increasingly sophisticated methods have become available for analyzing investment decisions. Perhaps the most widely known of these new developments are the analytical methods that take into account the time value of money. These include the net present value method, the discounted cash flow method, and variations on these techniques (4, 9).[1] Complementary to these time-oriented methods, a number of sophisticated accounting techniques have been developed for considering the tax implications of various investment proposals and the effects of investments on cash and capital position (2, 13, 16). Considerable thought has been given to the proper methods for determining the value of money to a firm, or the cost of capital (9, 13). The concepts of replacement theory have been applied to investment decisions on machine tools, automobile fleets, and other collections of items that must be replaced from time to time (16).

In a somewhat different direction, techniques have been developed for the selection of securities for portfolios.

[1]Note: The numbers in parentheses refer to the articles at the end of this reading.

These techniques endeavor to select the best set of investments from a number of alternatives, each having a known expected return and a known variability (12). In this context, the "best" selection of investments is that selection that either minimizes risk or variability for a desired level of return or maximizes return for a specified acceptable level of risk. (In general, of course, it is not possible to minimize risk and maximize return simultaneously.) The application of these techniques to corporate capital budgeting problems is conceivable but not imminent.

In the evolution of these techniques, each advance has served to overcome certain drawbacks or weaknesses inherent in previous techniques. However, until recently, two troublesome aspects of investment decision making were not adequately treated, in a practical sense, by existing techniques. One of these problems was handling the uncertainty that exists in virtually all investment decisions. The other was analyzing separate but related investment decisions that must be made at different points in time.

Two recent and promising innovations in the methodology for analyzing investment decisions now being widely discussed are directed at these two problems. The first of these techniques is commonly known as risk analysis (6, 8); the second involves a concept known as decision trees (10, 11, 15). Each of these techniques has strong merits and advantages. Both are beginning to be used by several major corporations.

It is the purpose of this article to suggest and describe a new technique that combines the advantages of both the risk analysis approach and the decision tree approach. The new technique has all of the power of both antecedent techniques, but is actually simpler to use. The technique is called the stochastic decision tree approach.

To understand the stochastic decision tree approach, it is necessary to understand the two techniques from which it was developed. A review of these two techniques follows.

A REVIEW OF RISK ANALYSIS

Risk analysis consists of estimating the probability distribution of each factor affecting an investment decision, and then simulating the possible combinations of the values for each factor to determine the range of possible outcomes and the probability associated with each possible outcome. If the evaluation of an investment decision is based only on a single estimate—the "best guess"—of the value of each factor affecting the outcome, the resulting evaluation will be at best incomplete and possibly wrong. This is true espicially when the investment is large and neither clearly attractive nor clearly unattractive. Risk analysis is thus an important advance over the conventional techniques. The additional information it provides can be a great aid in investment decision making.

To illustrate the benefit of the risk analysis technique, Figure 1 shows the results of two analyses of an investment proposal. First, the proposal was analyzed by assigning a single "best guess" value to each factor. The second analysis used an estimate of the probability distribution associated with each factor and a simulation to determine the probability distribution of the possible outcomes.

The best guess analysis indicates a net present value of $1,130,000, whereas the risk analysis shows that the most likely combination of events gives the project an expected net present value of only $252,000. The conventional technique fails to take into account the skewed distributions of the various factors and

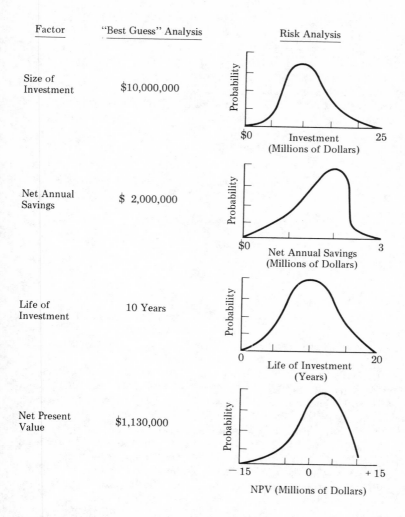

Factor	"Best Guess" Analysis	Risk Analysis

FIGURE 1. Two Analyses of an Investment Proposal

the interactions between the factors, and is influenced by the subjective aspects of best guesses. Furthermore, the conventional analysis gives no indication that this investment has a 48 per cent chance of losing money. Knowledge of this fact could greatly affect the decision made on this proposal, particularly if the investor is conservative and has less risky alternatives available.

The risk analysis technique can also be used for a sensitivity analysis. The purpose of a sensitivity analysis to determine the influence of each factor on the outcome, and, thus, to identify the factors most critical in the investment decision because of their high leverage, high uncertainty, or both. In a sensitivity analysis, equally likely variations in the values of each factor are made systematically to determine their effect on the outcome, or net present value. Table 1 shows the effect of individually varying each input factor (several of which are components of the net cash inflow).

This analysis indicates that manufacturing cost is a highly critical factor both in leverage and uncertainty. Knowing

analysis has been developed that can handle this problem well.

A REVIEW OF DECISION TREES

The decision tree approach, a technique very similar to dynamic programming, is a convenient method for representing and

TABLE 1   Use of Sensitivity Analysis to Highlight Critical Factors

An Unfavorable Change of 10 Percentiles from the Mean Value in This Factor	Which Corresponds to a Percentage Change of	Would Reduce NPV by
Annual net cash flow		
Sales level	12	17
Selling price	10	21
Manufacturing cost	18	58
Fixed cost	4	6
Amount of investment	5	12
Life of investment	12	30

this, management may concentrate its efforts on reducing manufacturing costs or at least reducing the uncertainty in these costs.

Risk analysis is rapidly becoming an established technique in American industry. Several large corporations are now using various forms of the technique as a regular part of their investment analysis procedure (1, 3, 7, 17, 18). A backlog of experience is being built up on the use of the technique, and advances in the state of the art are continually being made by users. For example, methods have been devised for representing complex interrelationships among factors. Improvements are also being made in the methods of gathering subjective probability estimates, and better methods are being devised for performing sensitivity analysis.

One aspect of investment decisions still eludes the capabilities of this technique. This is the problem of sequential decision making—that is, the analysis of a number of highly interrelated investment decisions occurring at different points in time. Until now no extension of risk

analyzing a series of investment decisions to be made over time (see Figure 2). Each decision point is represented by a numbered square at a fork or node in the decision tree. Each branch extending from a fork represents one of the alternatives that can be chosen at this decision point. At the first decision point the two alternatives in the example shown in Figure 2 are "introduce product nationally" and "introduce product regionally." (It is assumed at this point that the decision has already been made to introduce the product in *some* way.)

In addition to representing management decision points, decision trees represent chance events. The forks in the tree where chance events influence the outcome are indicated by circles. The chance event forks or nodes in the example represent the various levels of demand that may appear for the product.

A node representing a chance event generally has a probability associated with each of the branches emanating from that node. This probability is the likelihood that the chance event will assume the value assigned to the partic-

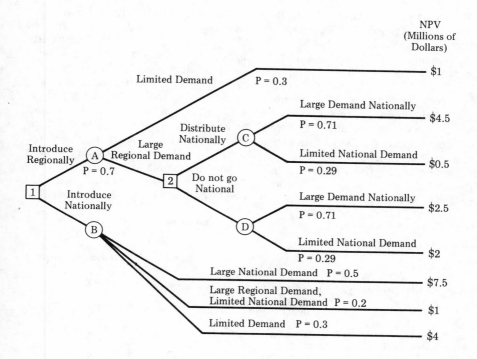

FIGURE 2. Use of Decision Tree to Analyze Investment Alternatives for a New Product Introduction

ular branch. The total of such probabilities leading from a node must equal 1. In our example, the probability of achieving a large demand in the regional introduction of the product is 0.7, shown at the branch leading from node A. Each combination of decisions and chance events has some outcome (in this case, net present value, or NPV) associated with it.

The optimal sequence of decisions in a decision tree is found by starting at the right-hand side and "rolling backward." At each node, an expected NPV must be calculated. If the node is a chance event node, the expected NPV is calculated for *all* of the branches emanating from that node. If the node is a decision point, the expected NPV is calculated for *each* branch emanating from that node, and the highest is selected. In either case, the expected NPV of that node is carried

back to the next chance event or decision point by multiplying it by the probabilities associated with branches that it travels over.

Thus in Figure 2 the *expected* NPV of all branches emanating from chance event node C is $3.05 million ($4.5 × .71 + $-0.5 × .29). Similarly the expected NPV at node D is $2.355 million. Now "rolling back" to the next node—decision point 2—it can be seen that the alternative with the highest NPV is "distribute nationally," with an NPV of $3.05 million. This means that, if the decision maker is ever confronted with the decision at node 2, he will choose to distribute nationally, and will expect an NPV of $3.05 million. In all further analysis he can ignore the other decision branch emanating from node 2 and all nodes and branches that it may lead to.

To perform further analysis, it is now necessary to carry this NPV backward in the tree. The branches emanating from chance event node A have an overall expected NPV of $2.435 million ($1 × 0.3 + $3.05 × 0.7). Similarly, the expected NPV at node B is $2.75 million. These computations, summarized in Table 2, show that the alternative that maximizes expected NPV of the entire decision tree is "introduce nationally" at decision point 1. (Note that in this particular case there are *no* subsequent decisions to be made.)

tion of all possible NPV's. However, it may vary somewhat from the expected NPV, depending on how the point estimates were selected from the underlying distributions and on the sensitivity of the NPV to this selection process. Furthermore, the decision tree approach gives *no* information on the range of possible outcomes from the investment or the probabilities associated with those outcomes. This can be a serious drawback.

In the example in Figure 2 and Table 2, the decision tree approach indicated that introducing the product nationally at

TABLE 2   Net Present Value of Investment Alternatives for a New Product Introduction

Alternative	Chance Event	Probability of Chance Event	Net Present Value	Expected NPV
Introduce product nationally	Large national demand	.5	$7.5	
	Large regional, limited national demand	.2	1.0	$2.75
	Limited demand	.3	−4.0	
Introduce product regionally (and distribute nationally if regional demand is large)	Large national demand	.5	4.5	
	Large regional, limited national demand	.2	−0.5	2.44
	Limited demand	.3	1.0	
Introduce product regionally (and do not distribute nationally)	Large national demand	.5	2.5	
	Large regional, limited national demand	.2	2.0	1.95
	Limited demand	.3	1.0	

One drawback of the decision tree approach is that computations can quickly become unwieldy. The number of end points on the decision tree increases very rapidly as the number of decision points or chance events increases. To make this approach practical, it is necessary to limit the number of branches emanating from chance event nodes to a very small number. This means that the probability distribution of chance events at each node must be represented by a very few point estimates.

As a result, the answers obtained from a decision tree analysis are often inadequate. The single answer obtained (say, net present value) is usually close to the expectation of the probability distribu-

once would be the optimal strategy for maximizing expected NPV. However, the NPV of $2.75 million is simply the mean of three possible values of NPV, which are themselves representative of an entire range of possible values, as shown in Figure 3a. Comparing the range of NPV's possible under each possible set of decisions shows a vastly different view of the outcome. (See Figures 3b and 3c.)

Although the first alternative has the highest expected NPV, a rational manager could easily prefer one of the other two. The choice would depend on the utility function or the aversion to risk of the manager or his organization. A manager with a linear utility function would choose the first alternative, as shown in

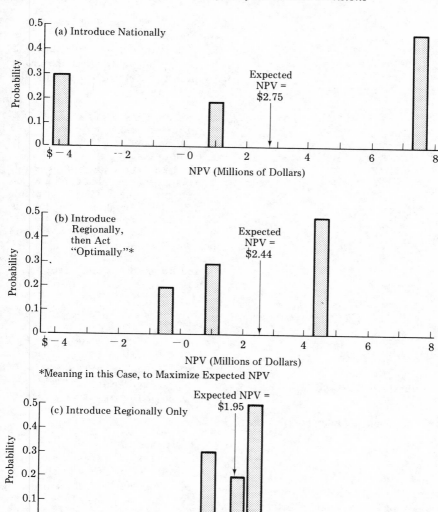

FIGURE 3. Range of Possible Outcomes for Each of Three Alternatives

Figure 4a. However, it is probably true that *most* managers would *not* choose the first alternative because of the high chance of loss and the higher utility value that they would assign to a loss, as shown in Figure 4b. This conservatism in management is, to a large extent, the result of the system of rewards and punishments that exists in many large corporations today. Whether it is good or bad is a complex question, not discussed here.

In spite of these shortcomings, the decision tree approach is a very useful analytical tool. It is particularly useful for conceptualizing investment planning and for controlling and monitoring an invest-

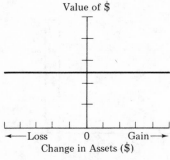

(a) Linear Utility Function

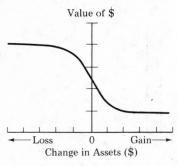

(b) More Typical
Nonlinear Utility Function

FIGURE 4.   Examples of Utility Functions

ment that stretches out over time. For these reasons, the decision tree approach has been, and will continue to be an important tool for the analysis of investment decisions.

COMBINING THESE APPROACHES: STOCHASTIC DECISION TREES

The complementary advantages and disadvantages of risk analysis and decision trees suggest that a new technique might be developed that would combine the good points of each and eliminate the disadvantages. The concept of stochastic decision trees, introduced in the remain-

der of this article, is intended to be such a combination.

The stochastic decision tree approach is similar to the conventional decision tree approach, except that it also has the following features:

1.   All quantities and factors, including chance events, can be represented by continuous, empirical probability distributions.
2.   The information about the results from any or all possible combinations of decisions made at sequential points in time can be obtained in a probabilistic form.
3.   The probability distribution of possible results from any particular combination of decisions can be analyzed using the concepts of utility and risk.

A discussion of each of these features follows.

REPLACEMENT OF CHANCE EVENT NODES BY PROBABILITY DISTRIBUTIONS

The inclusion of probability distributions for the values associated with chance events is analogous to adding an arbitrarily large number of branches at each chance event node. In a conventional decision tree, the addition of a large number of branches can serve to represent any empirical probability distribution. Thus in the previous example, chance event node B can be made to approximate more closely the desired continuous probability distribution by increasing the number of branches, as shown in Figures 5a and 5b. However, this approach makes the tree very complex, and computation very quickly becomes burdensome or impractical. Therefore, two or three branches are usually used as a coarse approximation of the actual continuous probability distribution.

Since the stochastic decision tree is to be based on simulation, it is not necessary to add a great many branches at the chance event nodes. In fact, it is possible to reduce the number of branches at the chance event nodes to *one*. (See Figure 5c.) Thus, in effect, the chance event node can be *eliminated*. Instead, at the point where the chance event node occurred, a random selection is made on each iteration from the appropriate probabilistic economic model such as the break-even chart shown in Figure 6, and the value selected is used to calculate the NPV for that particular iteration. The single branch emanating from this simplified node then extends onward to the next management decision point or to the end of the tree. This results in a drastic streamlining of the decision tree as illustrated in Figure 7.

REPLACEMENT OF ALL SPECIFIC VALUES BY PROBABILITY DISTRIBUTIONS

In a conventional decision tree, factors such as the size of the investment in a new plant facility are often assigned specific values. Usually these values are expressed as single numbers, even though these numbers are often not known with certainty.

If the values of these factors could be represented instead by probability distributions, the degree of uncertainty characterizing each value could be expressed. The stochastic decision tree approach makes it possible to do this. Since the approach is basically a simulation, any or all specific values in the investment analysis can be represented by probability distributions. On each iteration in the simulation, a value for each factor is randomly selected from the appropriate

frequency distribution and used in the computation. Thus, in the example, NPV can be calculated from not only empirical distributions of demand, but also probabilistic estimates of investment, cost, price, and other factors.

EVALUATING ALL POSSIBLE COMBINATIONS OF DECISIONS

Since this stochastic decision tree approach greatly simplifies the structure of the decision tree, it is often possible to evaluate by complete enumeration all of the possible paths through the tree. For example, if there are five sequential decisions in an analysis and each decision offers two alternatives, there are at most thirty-two possible paths through the decision tree. This number of paths is quite manageable computationally. And since most decision points are two-sided ("build" or "don't build," for example), or at worst have a very small number of alternatives, it is often feasible and convenient to evaluate all possible paths through a decision tree when the stochastic decision tree approach is used.

Why is it sometimes desirable to evaluate all possible paths through a decision tree? As the inquiry into the risk analysis approach showed, decisions cannot always be made correctly solely on the basis of a single expected value for each factor. The roll-back technique of the conventional decision tree necessarily deals only with expected values. It evaluates decisions (more exactly, sets of decisions) by comparing their expectations and selects the largest as the best, in all cases.

However, the stochastic decision tree approach produces *probabilistic* results for each possible set of decisions. These probability distributions, associated with each possible path through the decision

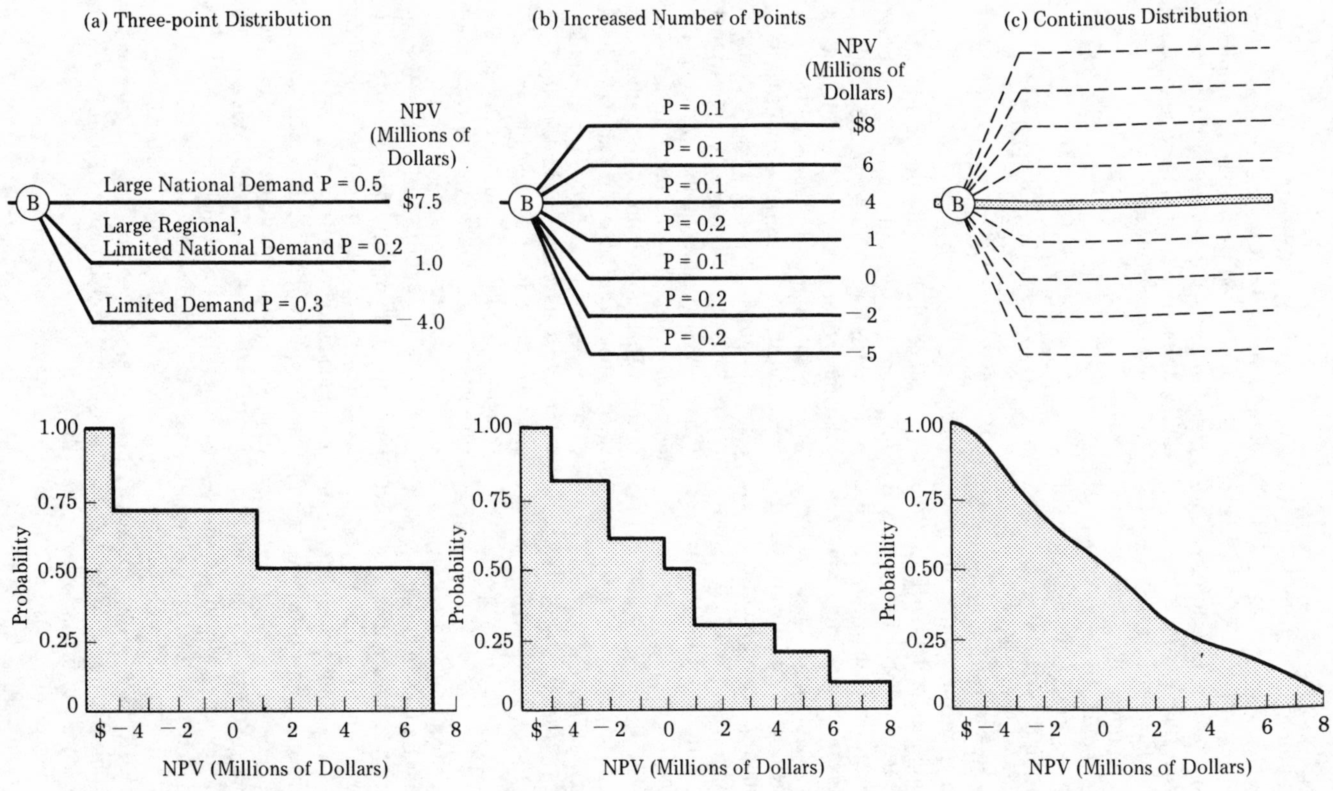

FIGURE 5. Probability Distributions at Chance Event Nodes

146

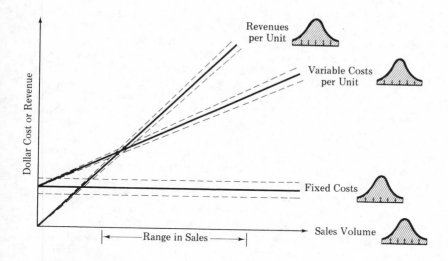

FIGURE 6. Typical Probabilistic Economic Model Used to Select Values of Factors at Chance Event Nodes

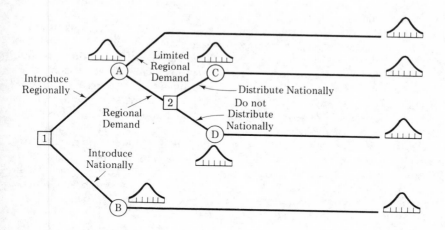

FIGURE 7. Simplified Decision Tree

tree, can be compared on the basis of their expectations alone, if this is considered to be sufficient. But alternative sets of decisions can *also* be evaluated by comparing the probability distributions associated with each set of decisions, in a manner exactly analogous to risk analysis. (The details of this technique are discussed in the next section.) Thus, the stochastic decision tree approach makes it possible to evaluate a series of interrelated decisions spread over time by the same kinds of risk and uncertainty criteria that one would use in a conventional risk analysis.

In a large decision tree problem, even with the simplifications afforded by the stochastic decision tree approach, complete enumeration of all possible paths through the tree could become computationally impractical, or the comparison of the probability distributions associated with all possible paths might be too laborious and costly.

In such a case, two simplifications are possible. First, a *modified* version of the roll-back technique might be used. This modified roll-back would take account of the probabilistic nature of the information being handled. Branches of the tree would be eliminated on the basis of dominance rather than simply expected value (7). For example, a branch could be eliminated if it had both a lower expected return and a higher variance than an alternative branch. A number of possible sets of decisions could be eliminated this way without being completely evaluated, leaving an efficient set of decision sequences to evaluate in more detail.

Computation could also be reduced by making decision rules before the simulation, such that if, on any iteration, the value of a chance event exceeds some criterion, the resulting decision would not be considered at all. This has been done in the example shown in Figure 2. If a limited demand appears at node A, national introduction of the product will not be evaluated. In the simulation, if demand were below some specified value, the simulation would not proceed to the decision point 2. This technique only saves computation effort—it does not simplify the structure of the tree, and if the criterion is chosen properly, it will not affect the final outcome.

RECORDING RESULTS IN THE FORM OF PROBABILITY DISTRIBUTIONS

It has already been shown that probability distributions are more useful than single numbers as measures of the value of a particular set of decisions. The simulation approach to the analysis permits one to get these probability distribu-

tions relatively easily. It is true that the method smacks of brute force. However, the brute force required is entirely on the part of the computer and not at all on the part of the analyst.

The technique is simply this: On each iteration or path through the decision tree, when the computer encounters a binary decision point node, it is instructed to "split itself in two" and perform the appropriate calculations along *both* branches of the tree emanating from the decision node. (The same logic applies to a node with three or more branches emanating from it.) Thus, when the computer completes a single iteration, an NPV will have been calculated for each possible path through the decision tree. These NPV's are accumulated in separate probability distributions. This simulation concept is illustrated in Figure 8.

At the completion of a suitable number of iterations, there will be a probability distribution of the NPV associated with each set of decisions that it is possible to make in passing through the tree. These different sets of decisions can then be compared, one against the other, in the usual risk analysis matter, as if they were alternative investment decisions (which in fact they are). That is, they can be compared by taking into account not only the expected return, but also the shape of each probability distribution and the effects of utility and risk. On the basis of this, one can select the single best set of decisions, or a small number of possibly acceptable sets. These sets of sequential decisions can then be evaluated and a decision whether or not to undertake the investment can be made by comparing it to alternative investments elsewhere in the corporation or against alternative uses for the money.

AN EXAMPLE

To illustrate the kinds of results that can be expected from a stochastic

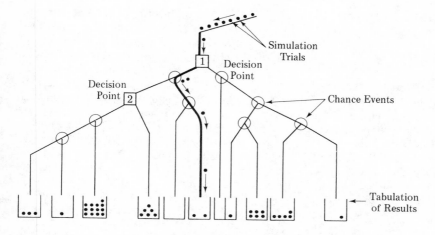

FIGURE 8. The GPSS Concept of Decision Trees with Risk Simulation

decision tree analysis, the new product introduction problem described earlier has been solved using this method. The results are shown in Figure 9.

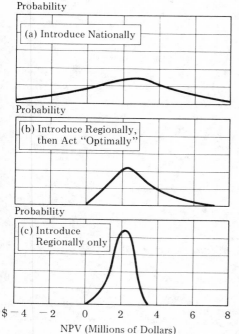

FIGURE 9. Results of Stochastic Decision Tree Analysis

The differences in the expected values of the outcomes can now be seen in proper perspective, since the results show the relationship of the expected values to the entire distribution of possible outcomes. Moreover, the expected values of these distributions will not necessarily be identical with expectations resulting from the conventional decision tree approach, because:

1. The interdependencies among the variables were not accounted for by the conventional approach.
2. The small number of point estimates used to approximate an entire distribution under the conventional approach did not utilize all the available information.

With the three alternatives presented in this form, it is easier to understand why a rational manager might choose an alternative other than the one with the highest expected value. Presented with the full range of possible outcomes related to each alternative, he can select that alternative most consistent with his personal utility and willingness to risk.

USING THE STOCHASTIC DECISION TREE APPROACH

Stochastic decision trees described here combine the best features of both risk analysis and conventional decision trees and are actually simpler to construct and use than either of these. The steps for collecting data and conceptualizing the problem are the same for the stochastic decision tree approach as they are for the risk analysis approach. These steps are:

1. Gather subjective probability estimates of the appropriate factors affecting the investment.
2. Define and describe any significant interdependencies among factors.
3. Specify the probable timing of future sequential investment decisions to be made.
4. Specify the model to be used to evaluate the investment.

The stochastic decision tree approach is ideally suited to the computer language known as General Purpose Systems Simulator (GPSS) (5, 14). Although this language is not now capable of handling very complex interdependencies without

certain modifications, it permits the solution of a very wide range of investment problems.

The structuring and solving of several sample problems have indicated that the stochastic decision tree approach is both easy to use and useful. The example in Table 2 and Figures 3 and 4 shows emphatically how the stochastic decision tree approach can detect and display the probable outcomes of an investment strategy that would be deemed optimal by the conventional decision tree approach, but that many managements would definitely regard as undesirable. Other work is being done on both sample problems and real-world problems, and on the development and standardization (to a limited extent) of the computer programs for performing this analysis.

SUMMARY

The stochastic decision tree approach to analyzing investment decisions is an evolutionary improvement over previous methods of analyzing investments. It combines the advantages of several earlier approaches, eliminates several disadvantages, and is easier to apply.

REFERENCES

1. Anderson, S. L., and H. G. Haight, "A Two-by-Two Decision Problem," *Chemical Engineering Progress,* LVII (May, 1961).
2. Anthony, Robert N., ed., *Papers on Return on Investment.* Boston: Harvard Business School, 1959.
3. *Chance Factors Meaning and Use,* Atlantic Refining Company, Producing Department, July, 1962.
4. Dean, Joel, *Capital Budgeting.* New York: Columbia University Press, 1951.
5. Gordon, G., "A General Purpose Systems Simulator," *IBM Systems Journal,* I (September, 1962).
6. Hertz, David B., "Risk Analysis in Capital Investment," *Harvard Business Review* (January-February, 1964).

7. Hess, Sidney W., and Harry A. Quigley, *Analysis of Risk in Investments Using Monte Carlo Technique,* Chemical Engineering Progress Symposium Series No. 42, Vol. LIX.

8. Hillier, Frederick, S., "The Derivation of Probabilistic Information for the Evaluation of Risky Investments," *Management Science* (April, 1963).

9. McLean, John G., "How to Evaluate New Capital Investments," *Harvard Business Review* (November-December, 1958).

10. Magee, John F., "Decision Trees for Decision Making," *Harvard Business Review* (July-August, 1964).

11. _____, "How to Use Decision Trees in Capital Investment." *Harvard Business Review* (September-October, 1964).

12. Markowitz, Harry, *Portfolio Selection, Efficient Diversification of Investments.* New York: John Wiley & Sons, Inc., 1959.

13. Masse, Pierre, *Optimal Investment Decisions.* Englewood Cliffs, N.J.: Prentice-Hall, Inc., 1962.

14. Reference Manual General Purpose Systems Simulator II, IBM, 1963.

15. Schlaifer, Robert, *Probability and Statistics for Business Decisions.* New York: McGraw-Hill Book Company, 1959.

16. Terborgh, George, *Business Investment Policy.* Washington, D.C.: Machinery and Allied Products Institute, 1958.

17. Thorne, H. C., and D. C. Wise. "Computers in Economic Evaluation," *Chemical Engineering* (April 29, 1963).

18. *Venture Analysis,* Chemical Engineering Progress Technical Manual, American Institute of Chemical Engineers.

Limit DCF in
Capital Budgeting

Eugene M. Lerner
Alfred Rappaport

Northwestern University

The failure of discounted cash flow methods to gain wider acceptance in industry may be because they do not incorporate the vital consideration of earnings to be reported to shareholders. The introduction of an earnings-growth constraint in a linear programming model allows a firm to choose a portfolio of projects which gives recognition to a minimal earnings growth rate deemed necessary to create increasing values for shareholders. The analytical merits, as well as possible conflicts, arising from the application of the model are discussed.

Reprinted from *Harvard Business Review,* XLVI (September-October, 1968), 133-39. Used by permission of *Harvard Business Review.* Copyright © 1968 by the President and Fellows of Harvard College. All rights reserved. *Authors' note:* We want to thank Joe Pellegrino, George Bruha, and the Vogelback Computing Center at Northwestern University for programming assistance.

During the past ten or fifteen years businessmen have witnessed a constant stream of articles, speeches, and conferences urging their companies to adopt a discounted cash flow approach for making capital budgeting decisions. And at the same time, widespread educational programs have been carried on by business schools, trade associations, and consulting firms to explain the advantages of DCF. Despite all this activity, a recent study indicates that of 163 companies selected from the *Fortune* list of 500 companies, less than half employ the DCF approach.[1]

Many writers attribute the relatively slow acceptance of DCF to either (a) a lack of understanding or a feeling of futility about projecting cash flows more than a few years into the future or (b) a preference for payback bench marks on the part of risk-conscious decision makers with strong liquidity preferences.

For a given company, both of these factors may well discourage the use of DCF. But they do not tell the whole story. We believe that a third, largely overlooked reason for the failure of DCF to gain wider acceptance is that management has found DCF does not successfully come to grips with the vital consideration of what earnings the company reports to shareholders. If the application of a DCF criterion results in an erratic earnings pattern, and if managers prefer to have a pattern of orderly and sustained earnings growth which they can report, then it is reasonable to suggest that this combination of facts may account for some of the reluctance to adopt the DCF approach for capital budgeting decisions.

ADVERSE EFFECT ON PRICES

The importance of earnings per share (EPS) is generally linked by management

to its broad objective of creating increasing value for the benefit of shareholders. In the survey referred to earlier, companies with multiple financial objectives were asked to rank the objectives in order of importance. EPS—in particular, its future level and/or growth rate—was indicated as the prime financial objective more often than was any alternative measure.

Let us suppose that a financial objective, such as maximizing the price of the corporation's shares, is the dominant organizing goal of a certain corporation, and that management uses reported growth in EPS to achieve its objective. How does adopting projects on the basis solely of DCF calculations affect the EPS the company reports to its shareholders?

To answer this question, we will assume that the corporate manager can solve all of the severe problems associated with the DCF method. This means, for example, that the company knows the appropriate cost-of-capital rate to use in discounting the cash flows of various projects, that the flows of various projects are known with certainty, and that the cash flows of each project are independent of the flows of the other projects. (None of these needs is easily met, as many financial executives know, and this fact alone weakens the case for the DCF approach.)

INVESTMENT OPPORTUNITIES

Let us now suppose that this corporation is faced with the opportunity of investing in fifteen different projects over the forthcoming five years. The economic lives of these assumed capital investments range from five years to as long as twelve years. The estimated cash flows associated with each project are presented in Table 1.

Let us further suppose that the company under consideration employs a for-

[1] See Alexander A. Robichek and John G. McDonald, *Financial Management in Transition* (Menlo Park, Calif.: Stanford Research Institute, 1965), p. 7.

TABLE 1 Estimated Cash Flows for Projects Under Consideration (in Hundreds of Dollars)

Project number	Year							
	1	2	3	4	5	6	7	8
1	$(239)	$ 45	$ 59	$ 64	$ 71	$ 70	$ 59	
2	(25)	$(40)	(30)	(10)	20	70	100	$ 150
3	(10)	(10)	(10)	20	30	50	40	20
4		(120)	25	25	30	35	30	25
5		(100)	(60)	(60)	80	74	66	56
6		(20)	80	100	(10)	50	(100)	50
7			(200)	(100)	0	50	200	300
8			50	100	(200)	100	150	
9			(10)	50	100	(200)	(100)	100
10				(80)	20	20	15	15
11				(300)	(50)	200	300	400
12				(50)	200	150	(100)	(100)
13					(300)	(50)	(100)	100
14					(200)	10	80	100
15					(100)	(50)	(50)	80

Project number	Year							
	9	10	11	12	13	14	15	16
1								
2	$150	$150	$100	$ 60				
3								
4	20	15	10	5				
5	44	30	14					
6	400	200						
7	200	50	50					
8								
9	300							
10	15	10	10	10				
11	200	0	100	100	$100			
12	100	200	150	100				
13	200	200	200	200	100			
14	300	500	300	200	(50)	$100	$100	$100
15	70	100	200	(50)	100	200	100	50

malized profit-planning system with a five-year time span. The estimated income flows or profit contributions associated with each of these projects during the planning period are shown in Table 2. It is also estimated that the five-year income flows that will result if the company makes no additional investments are $10,000, $9,500, $9,000, $9,000 and $8,000, respectively. Earnings in year 0 were $7,000.

Note that the estimated annual income and cash flows shown for the projects in Tables 1 and 2 do not coincide in all cases; Project 1 and others have different flows. The divergence is due to the employment of the accrual accounting model for measuring the company's operating results. The possible relationships between income flows (revenue and expense) and cash flows (receipts and disbursements) are summarized in Figure 1. To show how these estimated flows are derived for the fifteen projects, and also how the differences in income and cash flows arise, the detailed pro forma statements for Project 1 are presented in Table 3.

SELECTION OF PROJECTS

What projects will the company adopt if it uses the DCF approach and

TABLE 2   Estimated Income Flows for Projects (in Hundreds of Dollars)

Project number	Year				
	1	*2*	*3*	*4*	*5*
1	$(20)	$ 5	$ 15	$ 30	$ 50
2	(25)	(40)	(30)	10	20
3	(40)	(30)	(20)	100	120
4		(50)	5	20	25
5		(100)	(60)	(60)	80
6		(20)	80	100	(10)
7			(50)	(30)	(20)
8			(80)	100	200
9			(10)	50	100
10				(80)	50
11				(100)	(200)
12				(50)	200
13					(10)
14					(200)
15					(100)

TABLE 3   Calculation of Cash Flows and Income Flows for Project 1 (in Hundreds of Dollars)

Project description—expansion of machine capacity
Estimated investment cost—$280
Estimated economic life—7 years
Depreciation method—sum-of-the-years' digits

	Year						
	1	*2*	*3*	*4*	*5*	*6*	*7*
Cash receipts*	$ 21	$70	$104	$124	$151	$160	$139
Cash disbursements	280	20	30	30	30	40	40
	(259)	50	74	94	121	120	99
Federal income tax (50 per cent of income)	(20)	5	15	30	50	50	40
Net cash flow	$(239)	$45	$ 59	$ 64	$ 71	$ 70	$ 59
Revenue	$ 30	$90	$110	$130	$160	$160	$130
Depreciation	$ 70	$60	$ 50	$ 40	$ 30	$ 20	$ 10
Other operating expenses	0	20	30	30	30	40	40
	$ 70	$80	$ 80	$ 70	$ 60	$ 60	$ 50
Net income before tax	(40)	10	30	60	100	100	80
Federal income tax (50 per cent of income)	(20)	5	15	30	50	50	40
Net income	$(20)	$ 5	$ 15	$ 30	$ 50	$ 50	$ 40

*70 per cent of revenue collected in year of sales; 30 per cent during the following year.

what earnings will the company report to its shareholders?

If the discount rate that the firm employs is k per cent per annum, then the net present value, V, of each project's net cash flows, a, over the next n years is found by the expression:

$$v = \sum_{t=}^{n} \left[\frac{a_t}{(1+k)^t} \right]$$

In our case example, we assume that the manager of the company knows that the value of k is 20 per cent. Hence we can calculate the present value of each of the fifteen projects. These present values are listed in Table 4. If all of the projects that yield positive present values are purchased, the company will invest in ten projects and reject five. The present value of all of the projects purchased will be $97,513, and the earnings that the com-

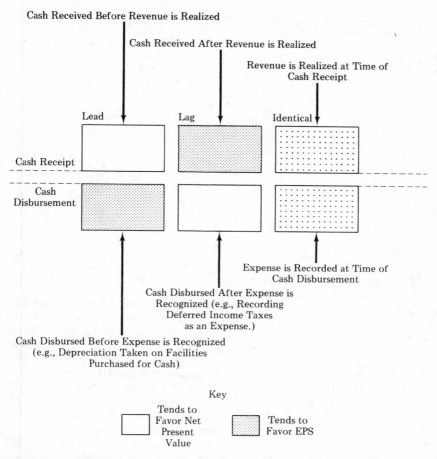

Cash Received Before Revenue is Realized

Cash Received After Revenue is Realized

Revenue is Realized at Time of Cash Receipt

Lead   Lag   Identical

Cash Receipt

Cash Disbursement

Expense is Recorded at Time of Cash Disbursement

Cash Disbursed After Expense is Recognized (e.g., Recording Deferred Income Taxes as an Expense.)

Cash Disbursed Before Expense is Recognized (e.g., Depreciation Taken on Facilities Purchased for Cash)

Key

Tends to Favor Net Present Value

Tends to Favor EPS

FIGURE 1. Possible Relationships Between Cash Flows and Income Flows

pany will report to its shareholders over the next five years will be:

Year	Earnings
1	$ 3,500
2	500
3	−2,000
4	27,000
5	19,000
	$48,000

If reported earnings to shareholders have a bearing on efforts to maximize share prices, and if a target of sustainable and orderly growth in earnings is established, then the foregoing figures show that the

DCF method leaves something to be desired. Surely the decline in earnings in Year 2 and the deficit reported in Year 3 will be viewed by the investment community at large as a failure of management to "use modern management tools to plan for contingencies." The dramatic rise in earnings in Year 4, followed by a decline in Year 5, will give rise to the speculation that the company is subject to severe cyclical swings. But whether it is believed that management fails to plan or that the company is subject to cyclical swings, investors are likely to respond by placing a low multiple on the reported

TABLE 4	Net Present Values of 15 Projects (in Hundreds of dollars)

Project Number	Net Present Value
1	$(35.75)
2	96.89
3	33.20
4	(10.67)
5	(29.82)
6	187.41
7	31.95
8	72.14
9	45.07
10	(9.21)
11	151.76
12	138.42
13	(12.19)
14	185.45
15	32.84

TABLE 5	Projects Adopted in Order to Assure a Growth Rate of 5 Per Cent per Year or More

Project Number	Proportion Adopted
1	100.00%
2	—
3	16.25
4	—
5	—
6	89.75
7	5.03
8	100.00
9	100.00
10	74.15
11	100.00
12	100.00
13	—
14	100.00
15	100.00

earnings. Hence share prices may be lower than they would be under another earnings pattern.

BETTER APPROACH

Let us now suppose that the corporate manager takes a different approach to the set of investment opportunities just described. Instead of adopting all of the projects that have a positive present value, he strives to maximize the present value of the investment projects *subject to the constraint that the earnings of the company must grow at a stipulated rate.*

If the stipulated growth rate is set at, let us say, 5 per cent per year, the manager would choose the ten projects indicated in Table 5. Some of these, it will be noted, are not completely adopted; for instance, only 89.75 per cent of Project 6 is adopted. In cases of this type we assume that the scope of the project can be reduced or, perhaps, that spending can proceed at a slower rate during the five-year period. If this is not the case, the project may be dropped completely, or perhaps adopted completely with an adjustment made either in

another investment or in the earnings target. If management wants a list of projects which are adopted completely or rejected completely, it can have the selection made through the use of a method known as integer programming.

(The mathematical statement of the new approach is shown in Table 6. Here we do not consider the question of what is the proper relationship between g, the growth rate, and k, the discount rate used to compute the present value of the cash flows; we assume that the rates are independent during the planning period.)

If we go back to Table 4 and find the present values of the ten projects adopted in whole or in part under the new approach, the total net present value is $71,800. This, of course, is well under the figure of $97,513 for the projects that would be chosen if the DCF approach were used. On the other hand, the new approach leads to a marked improvement in the consistency of reported earnings to shareholders during the five-year planning period. (Also, total earnings during the period are somewhat better.) The earnings are as follows:

Year	Earnings
1	$ 7,350
2	7,717
3	8,103
4	16,517
5	17,659
	$57,346

TABLE 6 Mathematical Statement of Approach Maximizing Present Value Subject to an Earnings-Growth Constraint

$$\text{Maximize} \sum_{j=1}^{15} \sum_{t=1}^{16} \frac{a_{jt}}{(1+k)^t} x_j$$

subject to:

$$\sum_{j=1}^{15} E_{jt} x_j - (1+g) \sum_{j=1}^{15} E_{j,t-1} x_j \geq 0,$$

for $t = 1,2,...,5$

$$x_j + q_j = 1, \text{ for } j = 1,2,...,15$$

$$x_j.q_j \geq 0$$

where a_{jt} represents the net cash flow of the jth project in period t, x_j represents the proportion of the jth project that is adopted, q_j represents the proportion that is not adopted, E_{jt} represents the earnings of the jth project in period t, and g represents the earnings-growth rate.

In this statement we ignore capital, labor, production, and other similar constraints because we wish to focus only on the relationship between earnings growth and the net present value of cash flows. Other constraints could, of course, be included if desired.

NEW CHOICES AND RESULTS

Examining the new list of projects in Table 5, we find several interesting variations from the set that would be adopted if the DCF approach were used:

1. Observe that the list includes the complete adoption of Project 1 and 74.15 per cent adoption of Project 10, both of which have negative net present values for their whole project lives

(see Table 4). The reason for their inclusion is that they enable the company to report relatively large earnings during the five-year planning period. 2. Projects 11, 14, and 15, which have negative earnings during the five-year planning period, are adopted. The reason for this is that their cash flows beyond the planning period are large enough to increase the present values of the portfolio of accepted projects, and yet they can be included without violating the earnings constraint.

Note that the earnings of the company increase each year at a rate equal to or greater than 5 per cent per annum. Thus, rather than being considered by investors as a poorly managed or cyclical company, the company may now be viewed by the investment community as one that is capable of maintaining orderly and sustainable growth. As a consequence, a high multiple may be placed on the earnings stream.

The company can, of course, experiment with other feasible earnings-growth rates to test their impact on both the earnings stream over the five-year planning period and the aggregate net present values of the fifteen projects.

CONCLUSION

The familiar present value approach to capital budgeting requires that the projects with the highest present values be adopted first, and that projects which lower the present value of the company not be adopted at all. The imposition of an earnings-growth constraint changes the approach to capital budgeting in two important ways:

1. It makes income flows as well as cash flows relevant to the investment decision. It therefore results in a portfolio of accepted projects that has a

lower present value than the uncon-
strained method allowed.

2. More important, it raises a policy
question of what planning horizon the
corporation should use in preparing its
capital budget.

Recall that under the new approach,
income flows are considered only for the
length of the company's formal profit-
planning period. In our example, this was
five years. The DCF calculations spanned
a longer time period, up to twelve years.
All present-value models are aimed at
creating increasing values for the share-
holder over some time span. The introduction of an earnings-growth constraint
emphasizes performance measured by
reported earnings over a chosen profit-
planning period, whereas the uncon-
strained DCF model considers the performance over the estimated economic life
of the portfolio of projects. If we eliminate, for practical reasons, alternatives to
the present accrual accounting system
used for public reporting, then an important aspect of the capital budgeting problem is balancing short-run and long-run
considerations.

SHORT-RUN VERSUS LONG-RUN

We do not propose a solution to the
policy question of what time horizon a
company should use for its capital budgeting planning period. At one extreme,
management may adopt the position that
market valuation based largely on investors' earnings expectations during a
limited time period is economically un-
sound. Hence management may ignore
interim market consequences in its pursuit of maximum long-run wealth. At the
other extreme, management's strategy
may be to create favorable market valuations during the short-run profit-planning
period. Neither alternative is sound.

Total disregard for short-run considerations could create adverse effects on
both the price of the company's shares
and its ability to exploit actual investment opportunities when they arise in the
future. The reason for this is that companies whose earnings and share prices are
subject to violent swings may be thought
of as being poorly managed, unreliable, or
speculative. Such a reaction could adversely affect the market for the company's products, the terms on which
suppliers will deal with it, the rate which
it must pay in the capital markets, and
other significant conditions.

At the other extreme, a strategy of
creating favorable market valuations during a limited profit-planning period can
also be unwise. The indiscriminate use of
an earnings-growth constraint can lead to
a serious questioning of management's
economic wisdom, and perhaps also its
standards of ethical behavior. The difficulty with an earnings-growth constraint
in capital budgeting is highlighted by our
example. The constraint may dictate that
a company deliberately bypass some of
its better opportunities for investment.
For a corporation to "manage" its earnings in this fashion, and thereby deceive
shareholders about real conditions and
potentials, is to engage in a questionable
practice. It is true that if a company has
rising investment opportunities in pros-
pect, it will be able to report higher
earnings in succeeding time periods, and
the price/earnings ratio will also likely
become higher. But the reporting of
higher earnings does not guarantee that
the company has a series of increasing
investment opportunities to exploit.

Undoubtedly, most managements
would recognize the wisdom of a mid-
course between the two extremes just
presented.

We do not propose a solution to the
question of what time horizon a company
should adopt, or of the price management

should pay for the company's reported earnings growth. However, the new approach we have described does allow management to deal explicitly with these questions. By contrast, the familiar DCF approach does not help management to come to grips with the issues raised. This is one of the reasons that the DCF approach has not gained wider acceptance in the financial community.

SELECTED REFERENCES FOR CHAPTER 4

BOOKS

Bierman, Harold, Jr., and Seymour Smidt, *The Capital Budgeting Decision,* 3rd ed. New York: The Macmillan Company, 1971.

Bower, Joseph L., *Managing the Resource Allocation Process.* Boston: Harvard Business School, 1970.

Farrar, Donald E., *The Investment Decision Under Uncertainty.* Englewood Cliffs, N.J.: Prentice-Hall, Inc., 1962.

Financial Analysis to Guide Capital Expenditure Decisions, N.A.A. Research Report 43, 1967.

Grayson, C. Jackson, Jr., *Decisions Under Uncertainty: Drilling Decisions by Oil and Gas Operators.* Boston: Harvard Business School, 1960.

Hanssmann, Fred, *Operation Research Techniques for Capital Investment.* John Wiley & Sons, Inc., 1968.

Istvan, Donald F., *Capital Expenditure Decisions: How They are Made in Large Corporations,* Indiana Business Report No. 33. Bloomington: Indiana University, Bureau of Business Research, 1961.

Lerner, Eugene M., and Willard T. Carleton, *A Theory of Financial Analysis.* New York: Harcourt, Brace Jovanovich, 1966.

Lesser, Arthur, Jr., *Decision-Making Criteria for Capital Expenditures.* Hoboken, N.J.: The Engineering Economist, 1966.

Markowitz, H. M., *Portfolio Selection: Efficient Diversification of Investments.* New York: John Wiley & Sons, Inc., 1959.

Merrett, A. J., and Allen Sykes, *The Finance and Analysis of Capital Projects.* London: Longmans, Green & Co., Ltd., 1963.

Pflomm, Norman E., *Managing Capital Expenditures,* Studies in Business Policy No. 107. New York: National Industrial Conference Board, Inc., 1963.

Porterfield, James T. S., *Investment Decisions and Capital Costs.* Englewood Cliffs, N.J.: Prentice-Hall, Inc., 1965.

Quirin, G. David, *The Capital Expenditure Decision.* Homewood, Ill.: Richard D. Irwin, Inc., 1967.

Robichek, Alexander A., and Stewart C. Myers, *Optimal Financing Decisions.* Englewood Cliffs, N.J.: Prentice-Hall, Inc., 1965.

Robichek, Alexander A., ed., *Financial Research and Management Decisions.* New York: John Wiley & Sons, Inc., 1967.

Solomon, Ezra, ed., *The Management of Corporate Capital.* New York: The Free Press, 1959.

Solomon, Ezra, *The Theory of Financial Management.* New York: Columbia University Press, 1963.

Weingartner, H. Martin, *Mathematical Programming and the Analysis of Capital Budgeting Problems.* Englewood Cliffs, N.J.: Prentice-Hall, Inc., 1963.

ARTICLES

Adelson, R. M., "Criteria for Capital Investment: An Approach Through Decision Theory," *Operational Research Quarterly,* XVI (March, 1965).

Berhard, Richard H., "Mathematical Programming Models for Capital Budgeting—A Survey, Generalization, and Critique," *Journal of Financial and Quantitative Analysis,* (June 1969).

Bierman, Harold, Jr., and Warren H. Hansman, "The Resolution of Investment Uncertainty Through Time," *Management Science,* XVIII (August 1972).

Bodenhorn, Diran, "On the Problem of Capital Budgeting," *Journal of Finance,* XIV (December, 1959).

Canada, John R., "Capital Budgeting: Its Nature, Present Practice and Needs for the Future," *Journal of Industrial Engineering,* XV (March-April, 1964).

————, "The Consideration of Risk and Uncertainty in Capital Investment Analyses," *Management International,* VII, No. 6 (1967).

Carter, E. Eugene, "A Simulation Approach to Investment Decision," *California Management Review,* XIII (Summer 1971).

Champion, Robert R., and R. George Glaser, "Sugar Cane Irrigation: A Case Study in Capital Budgeting," *Management Science,* XIII (August, 1967).

Charnes, A., W. W. Cooper, and M. H. Miller, "Application of Linear Programming to Financial Budgeting and the Costing of Funds," *Journal of Business,* XXXII (January, 1959).

Cohen, Kalmen J. and Edwin J. Elton, "Inter-Temporal Portfolio Analysis Based on Simulation of Joint Returns," *Management Science,* XIV (September 1967.

Donaldson, Gordon, "Financial Goals: Management vs. Stockholders," *Harvard Business Review,* XLI (May-June, 1963).

Dyckman, Thomas R. and James C. Kinard, "The Discounted Cash Flow Criterion Investment Decision Model With Accounting Income Constraints," *Decision Sciences,* IV, July 1973.

Fogler, H. Russell, Ranking Techniques and Capital Budgeting," *The Accounting Review,* XLVII (January 1972).

Foster, Earl M., "The Impact of Inflation on Capital Budgeting Decision," *Quarterly Review of Economics and Business,* Autumn 1970.

Hertz, David B., "Risk Analysis in Capital Investment," *Harvard Business Review,* XLII (January-February, 1964).

————, "Investment Policies That Pay Off," *Harvard Business Review,* XLVI (January-February, 1968).

Hillier, Frederick S., "The Derivation of Probabilistic Information for the Evaluation of Risky Investments," *Management Science,* IX (April, 1963).

Keeley, Robert H. and Randolph Westerfield, "A Problem in Probability Distribution Techniques for Capital Budgeting," *Journal of Finance,* (June 1972).

Kennedy, Miles, "A Critique of Game Theory for Capital Budgeting," *N.A.A. Bulletin,* XLIV (May, 1963).

————, "Risk in Capital Budgeting: An Interactive Sensitivity Approach," *Industrial Management Review,* IX (Fall 1968).

Klammer, Thomas, "The Association of Capital Budgeting Techniques With Firm Performance," *The Accounting Review,* XLVIII (April 1973).

Lerner, Eugene M., and Willard T. Carleton, "The Integration of Capital Budgeting and Stock Valuation," *American Economic Review,* LIV (September, 1964).

Magee, John F., "How to Use Decision Trees in Capital Investment," *Harvard Business Review,* XLII (September-October, 1964).

Mao, James C. F., "Survey of Capital Budgeting: Theory and Practice," *The Journal of Finance,* XXV, (May 1970).

Nelson, William G., IV, "Could Game Theory Aid Capital Budgeting?" *N.A.A. Bulletin,* XLIII (June, 1962).

Rappaport, Alfred, "The Discounted Payback Period," *Management Services,* II, (July-August 1965).

Robichek, Alexander A., Donald G. Ogilvie and John D. C. Roach, "Capital Budgeting: A Pragmatic Approach," *Financial Executive,* XXXVII, (April 1969).

Schiff, Michael, "Effect of Variations in Accounting Methods on Capital Budgeting," *Management Accountant,* XLVI (July, 1965).

Solomon, Martin B., Jr., "Uncertainty and Its Effect on Capital Investment Analysis," *Management Science,* XII, (April 1966).

Swalm, Ralph O., "A Review of 'Uncertainty and Its Effect on Capital Investment Analysis,' " *The Engineering Economist,* XII, (Winter 1967).

Tilles, Seymour, "Strategies for Allocating Funds," *Harvard Business Review,* XLIV (January-February, 1966).

Van Horne, James, "Capital-Budgeting Decisions Involving Combinations of Risky Investments," *Management Science,* XIII (October, 1966).

Walker, Ross G., "The Judgment Factor in Investment Decisions," *Harvard Business Review,* XXXIX (March-April, 1962).

Weingartner, H. Martin, "Capital Budgeting of Interrelated Projects: Survey and Synthesis," *Management Science,* XII (March, 1966).

COST:
ESTIMATION,
STANDARD, AND
ALLOCATION

CHAPTER FIVE

Multiple Regression Analysis of Cost Behavior

George J. Benston

University of Rochester

Information concerning the variability of cost with output and other decision variables is needed in a large number of managerial analyses. Multiple regression analysis is a valuable cost measurement tool particularly for recurring decisions. Data requirements related to (1) the length, (2) the number of time periods, (3) the range of observations, and (4) the specification of cost-related factors are described and implications for cost recording are outlined as well. The functional form of the regression equation is presented and followed by an illustration.

Reprinted from *The Accounting Review*, XLI (October, 1966), 657-72. Used by permission of George J. Benston and *The Accounting Review*.

Accountants probably have always been concerned with measuring and reporting the relationship between cost and output. The pre-eminence of financial accounting in this century resulted in directing much of our attention toward attaching costs to inventories. However, the recent emphasis on decision making is causing us to consider ways of measuring the variability of cost with output and other decisions variables. In this paper, the application, use, and limitations of multiple regression analysis, a valuable tool for measuring costs, are discussed.[1]

A valid objection to multiple regression analysis in the past has been that its computational difficulty often rendered it too costly. Today, with high speed computers and library programs, this objection is no longer valid: Most regression problems ought to cost less than $30 to run. Unfortunately, this new ease and low cost of using regression analysis may prove to be its undoing. Analysts may be tempted to use the technique without adequately realizing its technical data requirements and limitations. The "GI-GO" adage, "garbage in, garbage out," always must be kept in mind. A major purpose of this paper is to state these requirements and limitations explicitly and to indicate how they may be handled.

The general problem of cost measurement is discussed in the first section of this paper. Multiple regression analysis is considered first in relation to other methods of cost analysis. Then its applicability to cost decision problems is delineated. Second, the method of multiple regression is discussed in non-mathematical terms so that its uses can be understood better. The third section represents the "heart" of the paper. Here the technical requirements of multiple regression are outlined, and the implications of these requirements for the recording of cost data in the firm's accounting records are outlined. The functional form of the regression equation is then considered. In the final

section, we discuss some applications for multiple regression analysis.

THE GENERAL PROBLEM

In his attempts to determine the factors that cause costs to be incurred and the magnitudes of their effects, the accountant is faced with a formidable task. Engineers, foremen, and others who are familiar with the production process being studied usually can provide a list of cost-causing factors, such as the number of different units produced, the lot sizes in which units were made, and so forth. Other factors that affect costs, such as the season of the year, may be important, though they are more subtle than production factors. The accountant must separate and measure the effects of many different causal factors whose importance may vary in different periods.

COMMONLY USED METHODS OF COST ANALYSIS

Perhaps the most pervasive method of analyzing cost variability is separation of costs into two or three categories: variable, fixed, and, sometimes, semivariable. But this method does not provide a solution to the problem of measuring the costs caused by each of many factors operating simultaneously. In this "direct costing" type of procedure, output is considered to be the sole cause of costs. Another objection to this method is that there is no way to determine whether the accountant's subjective separation of costs into variable and fixed is reasonably accurate. Dividing output during a period into variable cost during that period yields a single number (unit variable cost), whose accuracy cannot be assessed. If the procedure is repeated for several periods, it is likely that different

[1] The use of statistical analysis for auditing and control is outside the scope of this paper. Excellent discussions of these uses of statistics may be found in Richard N. Cyert and H. Justin Davidson, *Statistical Sampling for Accounting Information* (Englewood Cliffs, N.J.: Prentice-Hall, Inc., 1962); and Herbert Arkin, *Handbook of Sampling for Auditing and Accounting*, Vol. I: *Methods* (New York: McGraw-Hill Book Company, 1963).

unit variable costs will be computed. But the accountant cannot determine whether the average of these numbers (or some other summary statistic) is a useful number. Another important shortcoming of this method is the assumption of linearity between cost and output. While linearity may be found, it should not be assumed automatically.

A variant of the fixed-variable method is one in which cost and output data for many periods are plotted on a two-dimensional graph. A line is then fitted to the data, the slope being taken as variable cost per unit of output. When the least-squares method of fitting the line is used, the procedure is called simple linear regression. Until the recent advent of computers, simple regression was considered to be quite sophisticated.[2] While it was recognized that its use neglects the effects on cost of factors other than output, it was defended on the then reasonable grounds that multiple regression with more than two or three variables is too difficult computationally to be considered economically feasible.

MULTIPLE REGRESSION

Multiple regression can allow the accountant to estimate the amount by which the various cost-causing factors affect costs. A very rough description is that it measures the cost of a change in one variable, say, output, while holding the effects on cost of other variables, say, the season of the year or the size of batches, constant. For example, consider the problem of analyzing the costs incurred by the shipping department of a department store. The manager of the department believes that his costs are primarily a function of the number of orders processed. However, heavier pack-

ages are more costly to handle than are lighter ones. He also considers the weather an important factor: Rain or extreme cold slows down delivery time. We might want to eliminate the effect of the weather, since it is not controllable. But we would like to know how much each order costs to process and what the cost of heavier against lighter packages is. If we can make these estimates, we can (1) prepare a flexible budget for the shipping department that takes account of changes in operating conditions, (2) make better pricing decisions, and (3) plan for capital budgeting more effectively. A properly specified multiple regression equation can provide the required estimates.

A criticism of multiple regression analysis is that it is complicated and so would be difficult to "sell" to lower management and supervisory personnel. However, the method allows for a more complete specification of "reality" than do simple regression or the fixed-variable dichotomy. Studies have shown that supervisors tend to disregard data that they believe are "unrealistic," such as those based on the simplification that costs incurred are a function of units of output only.[3] Therefore, multiple regression analysis should prove more acceptable to supervisors than procedures that require gross simplification of reality.

The regression technique also can allow the accountant to make probability statements concerning the reliability of the estimates made.[4] For example, he

---

[2]National Association of Accountants, *Separating and Using Costs as Fixed and Variable*, June, 1960.

[3]H. A. Simon, H. Guetzkow, G. Kozmetsky, and G. Tyndall, *Centralization versus Decentralization in Organizing the Controller's Department* (New York: The Controllership Foundation, 1954).

[4]This and the following statements are made in the context of a Bayesian analysis, in which the decision maker combines sample information with his prior judgment concerning unknown parameters. In the examples given, a jointly diffuse prior distribution is assumed for all parameters.

may find that the marginal cost of processing a package of average weight is $.756, when the effects on cost of different weather conditions and other factors are accounted for. If the properties underlying regression analysis (discussed below) are met, the reliability of this cost estimate may be determined from the standard error of the coefficient (say, $.032) from which the accountant may assess a probability of .95 that the marginal cost per package is between $.692 and $.820 (.756±.064).

Multiple regression analysis, then, is a very powerful tool; however, it is not applicable to all cost situations. To decide the situations for which it is best used, let us first consider the problem of cost estimation in general and then consider the subclass of problems for which multiple regression analysis is useful.

TYPES OF COST DECISION PROBLEMS

In general, cost is a function of many variables, including time. For example, the cost of output may be affected by such conditions as whether production is increasing or decreasing, the lot sizes are large or small, the plant is new or old, the White Sox are losing or winning, and so forth. Since there is *some* change in the environment of different time periods or in the circumstances affecting different decisions, it would seem that the accountant must make an individual cost analysis for every decision considered.

However, the maximization rule of economics also applies to information technology: The marginal cost of the information must not exceed the marginal revenue gained from it. The marginal revenue from cost information is the additional revenue that accrues or the losses that are avoided from not making mistakes, such as accepting contracts where the marginal costs exceed the marginal revenue from the work, or rejecting contracts where the reverse situation obtains. The marginal cost of information is the cost of gathering and presenting the information, plus the opportunity cost of delay, since measurement and presentation are not instantaneous.[5] Since these costs can be expected to exceed the marginal revenue from information for many decisions, it usually is not economical to estimate different costs for each different decision. Thus it is desirable to group decision problems into categories that can be served by the same basic cost information. Two such categories are proposed here: (1) recurring problems and (2) onetime problems.

Recurring decision problems are those for which the data required for analysis are used with some regularity. Examples are determining the prices that will be published in a catalog, preparation of output schedules for expected production, the setting of budgets and production cost standards, and the formulation of forecasts. These decisions require cost data in the form of schedules of expected costs due to various levels of activity over an expected range.

One-time problems are those which occur infrequently, unpredictably, or are of such a magnitude as to require individual cost estimates. Examples of these problems are cost-profit-volume decisions, such as whether the firm should take a one-time special order; make, buy, or lease equipment; develop a new product; or close a plant. These decisions require that cost estimates be made which reflect conditions especially relevant to the problem at hand.

These categories present different requirements for cost estimation. Recurring

[5]These two costs are related since delay can be reduced by expending more resources on the information system.

problems require a schedule of *expected* costs and activity. Since these problems are repetitive, the marginal cost of gathering and presenting data each time usually is expected to be greater than the marginal revenue from the data. Thus, while the marginal cost of additional production, for example, will differ depending on such factors as whether overtime is required or excess capacity is available, in general, it is more profitable to estimate the amount that the marginal cost of the additional production may be, on the average, rather than to take account of every special factor that may exist in individual circumstances.

In contrast, one-time problems are characterized by the economic desirability of making individual cost estimates. We do not rely on average marginal costs because the more accurate information is worth its cost. This situation may occur when the problem is unique, and average cost data are therefore not applicable. Or the decision may involve a substantial commitment of resources, making the marginal revenue from avoiding wrong decisions quite high.

MULTIPLE REGRESSION ANALYSIS

Regression analysis is particularly useful in estimating costs for recurring decisions.[6] The procedure essentially consists of estimating mathematically the *average* relationship between costs (the "dependent" variables). The analysis provides the accountant with an estimate of the expected marginal cost of a unit change in output, for example, with the effects on total cost of other factors accounted for. These are the data he requires for costing recurring decisions.

The usefulness of multiple regression analysis for recurring decisions of costs can be appreciated best when the essential nature of the technique is understood. It is not necessary that the mathematical proofs of least squares or the methods of inverting matrices be learned since library computer programs do all the work.[7] However, it is necessary that the assumptions underlying use of multiple regression be fully understood so that this valuable tool is not misused.

Multiple regression analysis presupposes a linear relationship between the contributive factors and costs.[8] The functional relationship between these factors, $x_1, x_2, \ldots, x_n$ and cost, C, is assumed in multiple regression analysis to be of the following form:

$$C_t = \beta_0 x_{0,t} + \beta_1 x_{1,t} + \beta_2 x_{2,t} + \ldots + \beta_n x_{n,t} + \mu_t \qquad (1)$$

where

β_0 is a constant term ($x_0 = 1$ for all observations and time periods),

the β's are fixed coefficients that express the marginal contribution of each x_i to C, and

μ is the sum of unspecified factors, the disturbances, that are assumed to be randomly distributed with a zero mean and constant variance, and

$t = 1, 2, \ldots, m$ = time periods.

The β coefficients are estimated from a sample of C's and x's from time periods 1 through m. For example, assume that the cost recorded in a week is a function of such specified factors as x_1 = units of

---

[6] Indeed, its use requires the assumption that the past costs used for a regressions analysis are a sample from a universe of possible costs generated by a continuing, stationary, normal process.

[7] The mathematics of multiple regression is described in many statistics and econometrics texts.

[8] A curvilinear or exponential relationship also can be expressed as a linear relationship. This technique is discussed below.

output, x_2 = number of units in a batch, and x_3 = the ratio of the number of "de luxe" units to total units produced. Then the right hand side of equation (2) is an estimate of the right hand side of equation (1), obtained from a sample of weekly observations, where the b's are estimates of the β's and u is the residual, the estimate of μ, the disturbance term:

$$C_t = b_{0,t} + b_1 x_{1,t} + b_2 x_{2,t} + b_3 x_{3,t} + \mu_t \qquad (2)$$

If the values estimated for coefficients of the three independent variables, x_1, x_2, and x_3, are b_0 = 100, b_1 =30, b_2 = −20, and b_3 = 500, the expected cost ($\hat{C}$) for any given week (t) is estimated by:

$$\hat{C} = 100 + 30_{x_1} - 20_{x_2} + 500_{x_3}$$

Given estimates of the β's, one has, in effect, estimates of the marginal cost associated with each of the determining factors. In the example given above, the marginal cost of producing an additional unit of output, x_1, is estimated to be $30, with the effects or costs of the size of batch (x_2) and the ratio of the number of de luxe to total units (x_3) accounted for. Or, β_2, the marginal reduction in total cost of increasing the batches by 3 units, given fixed values of the number of units and the relative proportions of de luxe units produced, is estimated to be −$60 (−$20 times 3).

It is tempting to interpret the constant term, b_0, as fixed cost. But this is not correct unless the linear relationship found in the range of observations obtains back to zero output.[9] This can be seen best in the following two-dimensional graph of cost on output.

[9] Fixed cost is defined here as avoidable cost related to time periods and not to output variables.

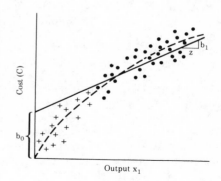

Output x_1

The line was fitted with the equation $C = b_0 + b_1 x_1$, where the dots are the observed values of cost and output. The slope of the line is the coefficient, b_1, an estimate of the marginal change in total cost (C) with a unit change (z) in output (x_1). The intercept on the C axis is b_0, the constant term. It would be an estimate of fixed cost if the range of observations included the point where output was zero, and the relationship between total cost and output was linear. However, if more observations of cost and output (the x's) were available, it might be that the dashed curve would be fitted and b_0 would be zero. Thus the value of the constant term, b_0, is not the costs that would be expected if there were no output; it is only the value that is calculated as a result of the regression line computed from the available data.

The data for the calculations are taken from the accounting and production records of past time periods. The coefficients estimated from these data are averages of past experience. Therefore, the b's calculated are best suited for recurring cost decisions. The fact that the b's are averages of past data must be emphasized, because their use for decisions is based on the assumption that the future will be like an average of past experience.

The mathematical method usually used for estimating the β's is the least-

squares technique. It has the properties of
providing best, linear, unbiased estimates
of the β's. These properties are desirable
because they tend "to yield a series of
estimates whose average would coincide
with the true value being estimated and
whose variance about that true value is
smaller than that of any other unbiased
estimators."[10] While these properties are
not always of paramount importance,
they are very valuable for making estimates of the expected average costs required for recurring problems.

Another important advantage of the
least-squares technique is that when it is
combined with the assumptions about the
disturbance term (μ_t) that are discussed
in Section 7, below, the reliability of the
relations between the explanatory variables and costs can be determined. Two
types of reliability estimates may be
computed. One, the standard error of
estimate, shows how well the equation
fits the data. The second, the standard
error of the regression coefficients, as-
sesses the probability that the β's estimated are within a range of values. For
example, if a linear cost function is used,
the coefficient (b_1) of output (x_1) is the
estimated marginal cost of output. With
an estimate of the standard error of the
coefficient, β_1, we can say that the true
marginal cost, β_1, is within the range b_1
$\pm s_{b_1}$, with a given probability.[11]

REQUIREMENTS OF
MULTIPLE REGRESSION AND
COST RECORDING
IMPLICATIONS

Although multiple regression is an excellent tool for estimating recurring costs,

it does have several requirements that
make its use hazardous without careful
planning.[12] Most of the data requirements
of multiple regressions analysis depend on
the way cost accounting records are
maintained. If the data are simply taken
from the ordinary cost accounting records of the company, it is unlikely that
the output of the regression model will be
meaningful. Therefore, careful planning
of the extent to which the initial accounting data are coded and recorded is necessary before regression analysis can be
used successfully; This section of the
paper is organized into four groupings
that include several numbered subsections
in which the principal technical requirements are described, after which the
implications for the cost system are discussed. In the first group, (1) the length
and (2) number of time periods, (3) the
range of observations, and (4) the specification of cost-related factors are described, following which their implications for cost recording are outlined.
In the second group, (5) errors of measurement and their cost recording implication are considered. The third group
deals with (6) correlations among the
explanatory variables and the important
contribution that accounting analysis can
make to this problem. Finally, (7) the
requirements for the distribution of the
nonspecified factors (disturbances) are
given. The implications of these requirements for the functional form of the
variables are taken up in the final section.

1. Length of Time Periods

a. The time periods $(1, 2, 3, \ldots,$
$m)$ chosen should be long enough to
allow the bookkeeping procedures to pair
output produced in a period with the cost

[10] J. Johnston, *Statistical Cost Analysis* (New
York: McGraw-Hill Book Company, 1960),
p. 31.
[11] The interpretation of the confidence interval
is admittedly Bayesian.

[12] Proofs of the requirements described may be
found in many econometrics textbooks, such as
Arthur S. Goldberger, *Econometric Theory*
(New York: John Wiley & Sons, Inc., 1964);
and J. Johnston, *Econometric Methods* (New
York: McGraw-Hill Book Company, 1963).

incurred because of the production. For example, if 500 units are produced in a day, but records of supplies used are kept on a weekly basis, an analysis of the cost of supplies used cannot be made with shorter than weekly periods. Lags in recording costs must be corrected or adjusted. Thus, production should not be recorded as occurring in one week while indirect labor is recorded a week later when the pay checks are written.

b. The time periods chosen should be *short* enough to avoid variations in production within the period. Otherwise, the variations that occur during the period will be averaged out, possibly obscuring the true relationship between cost and output.

2. Number of Time Periods. (Observations)

For a time series, each observation covers a time period in which data on costs and output and other explanatory variables are collected for analysis. As a minimum, there must be one more observation than there are independent variables to make regression analysis possible. (The excess number is called "degrees of freedom.") Of course, many more observations must be available before one could have any confidence that the relationship estimated from the sample reflects the "true" underlying relationship. The standard errors, from which one may determine the range within which the true coefficients lie (given some probability of error), are reduced by the square root of the number of observations.

3. Range of Observations

The observations on cost and output should cover as wide a range as possible. If there is very little variation from period to period in cost and output, the functional relationship between the two cannot be estimated effectively by regression analysis.

4. Specification of Cost-Related Factors

All factors that affect cost should be specified and included in the analysis.[13] This is a very important requirement that is often difficult to meet. For example, observations may have been taken over a period when input prices changed. The true relationship between cost and output may be obscured if high output coincided with high input due to price-level effects. If the higher costs related to higher price levels are not accounted for (by inclusion of a price index as an independent variable) or adjusted for (by stating the dependent variable, cost, in constant dollars), the marginal cost of additional output estimated will be meaningful only if changes in input prices are proportional to changes in output and are expected to remain so.

Implications for Cost Recording of 1, 2, 3, and 4

In general, the time period requirements (1a, 1b, and 2) call for the recording of production data for periods no longer than one month and preferably as short as one week in length. If longer periods are chosen, it is unlikely that there will be a sufficient number of observations available for analysis because, as a bare minimum, one more period than the number of explanatory variables is needed. Even if it is believed that only one explanatory variable (such as units of output) is needed to specify the cost function in any one period, requirement 4 (that all cost-related factors be specified) demands consideration of differences among time periods. Thus, such events as changes in factor prices

[13]Complete specification is not mandatory if requirement 7 (below) is met. However, requirement 7 is not likely to be fulfilled if the specification is seriously incomplete.

and production methods, whether production is increasing or decreasing, and the seasons of the year might have to be specified as explanatory variables.

The necessity of identifying all relevant explanatory variables, such as those just mentioned, can be met by having a journal kept in which the values or the behavior of these variables in specific time periods is noted. If such a record is not kept, it will be difficult (if not impossible) to recall unusual events and to identify them with the relevant time periods, especially when short time periods are used. For example, it is necessary to note whether production increased or decreased substantially in each period. Increases in production may be met by overtime. However, decreases may be accompanied by idle time or slower operations. Thus, we would expect the additional costs of increases to be greater than the cost savings from decreases.[14]

Other commonly found factors that affect costs are changes in technology, changes in capacity, periods of adjustment to new processes or types of output, and seasonal differences. The effect of these factors may be accounted for by including variables in the regression equation, by specific adjustment of the data, or by excluding data that are thought to be "contaminated."

The wide range of observations needed for effective analysis also argues against observation periods of longer than one month. With long periods, variations in production would more likely be averaged out than if shorter periods were used (which violates requirement 1b). In addition, if stability of conditions limits the

number of explanatory variables other than output that otherwise would reduce the degrees of freedom, this same stability probably would not produce a sufficient range of output to make regression analysis worthwhile. Thus, weekly or monthly data usually are required for multiple regression.

5. Errors of Measurement

It is difficult to believe that data from a "real life" production situation will be reported without error. The nature of the errors is important since some kinds will affect the usefulness of regression analysis more than others will. Errors in the dependent variable, cost, are not fatal since they affect the disturbance term, μ[15]. The predictive value of the equation is lessened, but the estimate of marginal cost (β_1) is not affected.

But where there are errors in measuring output or the other independent variable (x's), the disturbance term, μ, will be correlated with the independent variables.[16] If this condition exists, the sample coefficient estimated by the least-squares procedure will be an underestimate of the true marginal cost. Thus, it is very important that the independent variables be measured accurately.

The possibility of measurement errors is intensified by the number of observations requirement. Short reporting periods increase the necessity for careful

---

[14] A dummy variable can be used to represent qualitative variables, such as $P = 1$ when production increased and $P = 0$ when production decreased. From the coefficient of P, we can estimate the cost effect of differences in the direction of output change and also reduce contamination of the coefficient estimated for output.

[15] Let γ stand for the measurement errors in C:

$$C + \gamma = \beta_0 + \beta_1 x_1 + \mu$$
$$C = \beta_0 + \beta_1 x_1 + \mu - \gamma$$

[16] In this event, where ψ stands for the measurement error in x_1:

$$C = \beta_0 + \beta_1 (x_1 + \psi) + \mu$$
$$C = \beta_0 + \beta_1 x_1 + B_1 \psi + \mu$$

The new disturbance term $\beta_1 \psi + \mu$, is not independent of x_1 because of the covariance between these variables.

classification. For example, if a cost caused by production in week 1 is not recorded until week 2, the dependent variable (cost) of both observations will be measured incorrectly. This error is most serious when production fluctuates between observations. However, when production is increasing or decreasing steadily, the measurement error tends to be constant (either in absolute or proportional terms) and hence will affect only the constant term. The regression coefficients estimated, and hence the estimates of average marginal cost, will not be affected.[17]

Another important type of measurement error is the failure to charge the period in which production occurs with future costs caused by that production. For example, overtime pay for production workers may be paid for in the week following their work. This can be adjusted for easily. However, the foreman may not be paid for his overtime directly. Rather, many months after his work he might get a year-end bonus or a raise in pay. These costs cannot easily be associated with the production that caused them but will be charged in another period, thus making both periods' costs incorrect.[18] This type of error is difficult to correct. Usually, all that one can do is eliminate the bonus payment from the data of the period in which it is paid and realize that the estimated coefficient of output will be biased downward. Average marginal costs, then, will be understated.

A somewhat similar situation follows from the high cost of the careful record keeping required to charge such input factors as production supplies to short time periods. In this event, these items of cost should be deducted from the other

cost items and not included in the analysis. If these amounts are large enough, specific analysis may be required, or the decision not to account for them carefully may be re-evaluated.

This separation of specific cost items also is desirable where the accountant knows that their allocation to time periods bears no relation to production. For example, such costs as insurance or rent may be allocated to departments on a monthly basis. There is no point in including these costs in the dependent variable because it is known that they do not vary with the independent variables. At best, their inclusion will only increase the constant term. However, if by chance they are correlated with an independent variable, they will bias the estimates made (requirement 7a). This type of error may be built into the accounting system if fixed costs are allocated to time periods on the basis of production. For example, depreciation may be charged on a per unit basis. The variance of this cost, then, may be a function of the accounting method and not of the underlying economic relationships.[19]

6. Correlations among the Explanatory (Independent) Variables

When the explanatory variables are highly correlated with one another, it is very difficult, and often impossible, to estimate the separate relationships of each to the dependent variable. This condition is called multicollinearity, and it is a severe problem for cost studies. When we compute marginal costs, we usually want to estimate the marginal cost of *each* of the different types of output produced in a multiproduct firm. However, this is not always possible. For example, consider a manufacturer who makes refrigerators, freezers, washing

[17] If the error is proportionally constant (i.e., 10 per cent of production), transformation of the variables (such as to logarithms) is necessary.

[18] Actually, the present value of the future payment should be included as a current period cost.

[19] Depreciation is assumed to be time, not user, depreciation.

machines, and other major home appliances. If the demand for all home appliances is highly correlated, the number of refrigerators, freezers, and washing machines produced will move together, all being high in one week and low in another. In this situation it will be impossible to disentangle the marginal cost of producing refrigerators from the marginal cost of producing freezers and washing machines by means of multiple regression.[20]

Problems similar to that of our manufacturer can be alleviated by disaggregation of total cost into several subgroups that are independent of each other. Preanalysis and preliminary allocations of cost and output data may accomplish this disaggregation. This is one of the most important contributions the accountant can make to regression analysis.

If the total costs of the entire plant are regressed on outputs of different types, it is likely that the computed coefficients will have very large standard errors and, hence, will not be reliable. This situation may be avoided by first allocating costs to cost centers where a single output is likely to be produced. This allows a set of multiple regressions to be computed, one for each cost center. The procedure (which may be followed anyway for inventory costing) also reduces the number of explanatory variables that need be specified in any one regression.[21] Care must be taken to assure that the allocation of costs to cost centers is not arbitrary or unrelated to output. For example, allocation of electricity or rent on a square footage basis can serve no

useful purpose. However, allocation of the salary of the foremen on a time basis is necessary when they spend varying amounts of time per period supervising different cost centers.

A further complication arises if several different types of outputs are produced within the cost centers. For example, the assembly department may work on different models of television sets at the same time. In most instances, it is neither feasible nor desirable to allocate the cost center's costs to each type of output. Cost, then, should be regressed on several output variables, one for the quantity of each type of output. If these independent variables are multicollinear, the standard errors of their regression coefficients will be so large relative to the coefficients as to make the estimates useless. In this event, an index of output may be constructed in which the different types of output are weighted by a factor (such as labor hours) that serves to describe their relationship to cost. Cost then may be regressed on this weighted index. The regression coefficient computed expresses the average relationship between the "bundle" of outputs and cost and cannot be decomposed to give the relationship between one output element and cost. However, since the outputs were collinear in the past, it is likely that they will be collinear in the future, so that knowledge about the cost of the "bundle" of outputs may be sufficient.

A valid objection to the allocation of costs to cost centers is that one can never be sure that the allocations are accurate. Nevertheless, some allocations must be made for multicollinearity to be overcome. Therefore, the statistical method cannot be free from the accountant's subjective judgment; in fact, it depends on it.

A limitation of analysis of costs by cost centers also is that cost externalities among cost centers may be ignored. For example, the directly chargeable costs of

---

[20]However, the computed regression can provide useful predictions of total costs if the past relationships of production among the different outputs are maintained.

[21]The author used this procedure with considerable success in estimating the marginal costs of banking operations. See George J. Benston, "Economies of Scale and Marginal Costs in Banking Operations," *National Banking Review* (1965), 507-49.

the milling department may be a function of the level of operations of other departments. The existence and magnitude of operations outside of a particular cost center may be estimated by including an appropriate independent variable in the cost center regression. An overall index of production, such as total direct labor hours in total sales, is one such variable. Or, if a cost element is allocated between two cost centers, the output of one cost center may be included as an independent variable in the other cost center's regressions. The existence and effect of these possible intercost center elements may be determined from the standard error of the coefficient and sign of this variable.

Some types of costs that vary with activity cannot be associated with specific cost centers because it is difficult to make meaningful allocations or because of bookkeeping problems (as discussed above). In this event, individual regression analyses of these costs probably will prove valuable. For example, electricity may be difficult to allocate to cost centers although it varies with machine hours.[22] A regression can be computed such as the following:

$$E = b_0 + b_1 M + b_2 S_1 + b_3 S_2 + b_4 S_3$$
$$+ b_4 S_3 \qquad (3)$$

where

E = electricity cost

M = total machine hours in the plant

S = seasonal dummy variables

where

S_1 = 1 for summer, 0, for other seasons

S_2 = 1 for spring, 0 for other seasons

S_3 = 1 for winter, 0 for other seasons

b_0, b_1, b_2, b_3, and b_4 are the computed constants and coefficients.

If the regression is fully specified, with all factors that cause the use of electricity included (such as the season of the year), the regression coefficient of M, b_1, is the estimate of the average marginal cost of electricity per machine hour. This cost can be added to the other costs (such as materials and labor) to estimate the marginal cost of specific outputs.

For some activities, physical units such as labor hours can be used as the dependent variable instead of costs. This procedure is desirable where most of the activity's costs are a function of such physical units and where factor prices are expected to vary. Thus, in a shipping department, it may be best to regress hours worked on pounds shipped, percentage of units shipped by truck, the average number of pounds per sale, and other explanatory variables. Then, with the coefficients estimated, the number of labor hours can be estimated for various situations. These hours then can be costed at the current labor rate.

7. Distribution of the Nonspecified Factors (Disturbances)

a. Serial correlation of the disturbances. A very important requirement of least squares that affects the coefficients and the estimates made about their reliability is that the disturbances not be serially correlated. For a time series (in which the observations are taken at successive periods of time), this means that the disturbances that arose in period t are independent of the disturbances that arose in previous periods, t-1, t-2, etc. The consequences of serial correlation of the disturbances are that: (1) the standard errors of the regression coefficients (b's) will be seriously underestimated,

---

[22]Machine hours may not be recorded by cost center although direct labor hours are. If machine hours (M) are believed to be proportional to direct labor hours (L), so that $M_j = k_j L_j$ where k is a constant multiplier that may vary among cost centers, i, $k_j L_j$ is a perfect substitute for M_j.

(2) the sampling variances of the coefficients will be very large, and (3) predictions of cost made from the regression equation will be more variable than is ordinarily expected from least-squares estimators. Hence, the tests measuring the probability that the true marginal costs and total costs are within a range around the estimates computed from the regression are not valid.

b. Independence from explanatory variables. The disturbances which reflect the factors affecting cost that cannot be specified must be uncorrelated with the explanatory (independent) variables $(x_1, x_2 \ldots, x_n)$. If the unspecified factors are correlated with the explanatory variables, the coefficients will be biased and inconsistent estimates of the true values. Such correlation often is the result of bookkeeping procedures. For example, repairs to equipment in a machine shop is a cost-causing activity that often is not specified because of quantification difficulties. However, these repairs may be made when output is low because the machines can be taken out of service at these times. Thus, repair costs will be negatively correlated with output. If these costs are not separated from other costs, the estimated coefficient of output will be biased downward, so that the true extent of variableness of cost with output will be masked.

c. Variance of the disturbances. A basic assumption underlying use of least squares is that the variance of the disturbance term is constant; it should not be a function of the level of the dependent or independent variables.[23] If the variance of the disturbance term is nonconstant, the standard errors of the coefficients estimated are not correct and the reliability of the coefficients cannot be determined.

When the relationship estimated is between only one independent variable (output) and the dependent variable (cost), the presence of nonconstant variance of the disturbances can be detected by plotting the independent against the dependent variable. However, where more than one independent variable is required, such observations cannot be easily made. In this event, the accountant must attempt to estimate the nature of the variance from other information and then transform the data to a form in which constant variance is achieved. At the least, he should decide whether the disturbances are likely to bear a proportional relationship to the other variables (as is commonly the situation with economic data). If they do, it may be desirable to transform the variables to logarithms. The efficacy of the transformations may be tested by plotting the independent variables against the residuals (the estimates of the disturbances).

d. Normal distribution of the disturbances. For the traditional statistical tests of the regression coefficients and equations to be strictly valid, the disturbances should be normally distributed. Tests of normality can be made by plotting the residuals on normal probability paper, an option available in many library regression programs. While requirement 7 does not have implications for the accounting system, it does determine the form in which the variables are specified. These considerations are discussed in the following section.

FUNCTIONAL FORM OF THE REGRESSION EQUATION

Thus far we have been concerned with correct specification of the regression equation rather than with its functional form. However, the form of the variables must fit the underlying data well and be

---

[23]Constant variance is known as homoscedasticity. Nonconstant variance is called heteroscedasticity.

of such a nature that the residuals are distributed according to requirement 7 above.

The form chosen first should follow the underlying relationship that is thought to exist. Consider, for example, an analysis of the costs (C) of a shipping department. Costs may be a function of pounds shipped (P), percentage of pounds shipped by truck (T), and the average number of pounds per sale (A). If the accountant believes that the change in cost due to a change of each explanatory variable is unaffected by the levels of the other explanatory variables, a linear form could be used, as follows:

$$C = a + bP + cT + dA. \qquad (4)$$

In this form, the estimated marginal cost of a unit change in pounds shipped (P) is $\partial C/\partial P$ or b.

However, if the marginal cost of each explanatory variable is thought to be a function of the levels of the other explanatory variables, the following form would be better:

$$C = aP^b T^c A^d. \qquad (5)$$

In this case, a linear form could be achieved by converting the variable to logarithms:

$$\log C = \log a + b \log P + c \log T \\ + d \log A. \qquad (6)$$

Now, an approximation to the expected marginal cost of a unit change in pounds shipped (P) is $\partial C/\partial P = baP^{b-1} \bar{T}^c \bar{A}^d$ where the other explanatory variables are held constant at some average values (denoted by bars over the letters). Thus the estimated marginal cost of P is a function of the levels of the other variables.

The logarithmic form of the variables also allows for estimates of nonlinear relationships between cost and the ex-

planatory variables. The form of the relationships may be approximated by graphing the dependent variable against the independent variable. (The most important independent variable should be chosen where there is more than one, although in this event the simple two-dimensional plotting can only be suggestive.) If the plot indicates that a non-linear rather than a linear form will fit the data best, the effect of using logarithms may be determined by plotting the data on semi-log and log-log ruled paper.

If the data seem curvilinear even in logarithms, or if an additive rather than a multiplicative form describes the underlying relationships best, polynomial forms of the variables may be used. Thus, for an additive relationship between cost (C) and quantity of output (Q), the form fitted may be $C = a + bQ + cQ^2 + dQ^3$. If a multiplicative relationship is assumed, the form may be $\log C = \log a + \log Q + (\log Q)^2$. Either form describes a large family of curves with two bends.

When choosing the form of the variables, attention must always be paid to the effect of the form on the residuals, the estimates of the disturbances. Unless the variance of the residuals is constant, not subject to serial correlation, and approximately normally distributed (requirement 5), inferences about the reliability of the coefficients estimated cannot be made. Graphing is a valuable method for determining whether or not these requirements are met. (The graphs mentioned usually can be produced by the computers.) Three graphs are suggested. First, the residuals should be plotted in time sequence. They should appear to be randomly distributed, with no cycles or trends.[24] Second, the residuals can be

[24] A more formal test for serial correlation is provided by the Durbin-Watson statistic, which is built into many library regression computer programs. [J. Durbin, and G. J. Watson, "Testing for Serial Correlation in Least-Squares Regression," Parts I and II, *Biometrika* (1950 and 1951).]

plotted against the predicted value of the dependent variable. There should be as many positive or negative residuals scattered evenly about a zero line, with the variance of the residuals about the same at any value of the predicted dependent variable. Finally, the residuals should be plotted on normal probability paper to test for normality.

If the graphs show that the residuals do not meet the requirements of least squares, the data must be transformed. If serial correlation of the residuals is a problem, transformation of the variables may help. A commonly used method is to compute first differences, in which the observation from period t, $t-1$, $t-2$, $t-3$, etc., are replaced with $t-(t-1)$, $(t-1)-(t-2)$, $(t-2)-(t-3)$, and so forth. With first difference data, one is regressing the change in cost on the change in output, etc., a procedure which in many instances may be descriptively superior to other methods of stating the data. However, the residuals from first difference data also must be subjected to serial correlation tests, since taking first differences often results in negative serial correlations.[25]

When nonconstant variance of the residuals is a problem, the residuals may increase proportionally to the predicted dependent variables. In this event transformation of the dependent variable to logarithms will be effective in achieving constant variance. If the residuals increase more than proportionately, the square root of the dependent variable may be a better transformation.

AN ILLUSTRATION

Assume that a firm manufactures a widget and several other products, in

[25] If there are random measurement errors in the data, observations from period $t-1$ might be increased by a positive error. Then $t-(t-1)$ will be lower and $(t-1)-(t-2)$ will be higher than if the error were not present. Consequently, $t-(t-1)$ and $(t-1)-(t-2)$ will be negatively serially correlated.

which the services of several departments are used. Analysis of the costs of the assembly department will provide us with an illustration. In this department, widgets and another product, digits, are produced. The widgets are assembled in batches, while the larger digits are assembled singly. Weekly observations on cost and output are taken and punched on cards. A graph is prepared, from which it appears that a linear relationship is present. Further, the cost of producing widgets is not believed to be a function of the production of digits or other explanatory variables. Therefore, the following regression is computed:

$$\hat{C} = 110.3 + 8.21N - 7.83B$$
$$\quad\;\; (40.8) \quad (.53) \quad\; (1.69)$$
$$\quad + 12.32D + 235S + 523W$$
$$\quad\quad (2.10) \quad (100) \quad (204)$$
$$\quad - 136A$$
$$\quad\quad (154) \tag{7}$$

where
$\hat{C}$ = expected cost

N = number of widgets

B = average number of widgets in a batch

D = number of digits

S = summer dummy variable, where $S = 1$ for summer, 0 for other seasons

W = winter dummy variable, where $W = 1$ for winter, 0 for other seasons

A = autumn dummy variable, where $A = 1$ for autumn, 0 for other seasons

R^2 = .892 (the coefficient of multiple determination)

Standard error of estimate = 420.83, which is 5 per cent of the dependent variable, cost.

Number of observations = 156.

The numbers in parentheses beneath the

coefficients are the standard errors of the coefficients. These results may be used for such purposes as price and output decisions, analysis of efficiency, and capital budgeting.

For price and output decisions, we would want to estimate the average marginal cost expected if an additional widget is produced. From the regression we see that the estimated average marginal cost, $\partial C/\partial N$ is 8.21, with the other factors affecting costs accounted for. The standard error of the coefficient, .53, allows us to assess a probability of .67 that the "true" marginal cost is between 7.68 and 8.74 (8.21 ± .53) and .95 that it is between 7.15 and 9.27 (8.21 ± 1.06).[26]

The regression also can be used for flexible budgeting and analysis of performance. For example, assume that the following production is reported for a given week:

$W = 532$
$B = 20$
$D = 321$
$S = \text{summer} = 1$

Then we expect that, if this week is like an average of the experience for past weeks, total costs would be:

$$110.3 + 8.21\,(532) - 7.83\,(20)$$
$$+ 12.32\,(321) + 235\,(1) = 8511.14.$$

The actual costs incurred can be compared to this expected amount. Of course, we do not expect the actual amount to equal the predicted amount, if only because we could not specify all of the cost-causing variables in the regression equation. However, we can calculate the probability that the actual cost is within some range around the expected cost. This range can be computed from the

standard error of estimate and a rather complicated set of relationships that reflect uncertainty about the height and tilt of the regression plane. These calculations also reflect the difference between the production reported for a given week and the means of the production data from which the regression was computed. The greater the difference between given output and the mean output, the less confidence we have in the prediction of the regression equation. For this example, the adjusted standard error of estimate for the values of the independent variables given is 592.61. Thus, we assess a probability of .67 that the actual costs incurred will be between 7918.53 and 9103.75 (8511.14±592.61) and probability .95 that they will be between 9696.36 .and 7325.92 (8511.14 ± 2· 592.61). With these figures, management can decide how unusual the actual production costs are in the light of past experience.

The regression results may be useful for capital budgeting, if the company is considering replacing the present widget assembly procedure with a new machine. While the cash flows expected from using the new machine must be estimated from engineering analyses, they are compared with the cash flows that would otherwise take place if the present machines were kept. These future expected flows may be estimated by "plugging" the expected output into the regression equation and calculating the expected costs. While these estimates may be statistically unreliable for data beyond the range of those used to calculate the regression, the estimates may still be the best that can be obtained.

CONCLUSION

The assertion has been made throughout this paper that regression analysis is not

[26] The statements about probability are based on a Bayesian approach, with normality and diffuse prior distributions assumed.

only a valuable tool but a method made available, inexpensive, and easy to use by computers. The reader may be inclined to accept all but the last point, having read through the list of technical and book-keeping problems. Actually it is the ease of computation that the library computer programs afford which makes it necessary to stress precautions and care. It is all too easy to "crank out" numbers that seem useful but actually render the whole program, if not deceptive, worthless.

But when one considers that costs often are caused by many different factors whose effects are not obvious, one recognizes the great possibilities of regression analysis, limited as it may be. Nevertheless, it is necessary to remember that it is a tool, not a cure-all. The method must not be used in cost situations where there is not an ongoing stationary relationship between cost and the variables upon which cost depends. Where the desired conditions prevail, multiple regression can provide valuable information for solving necessary decision problems, information that can put "life" into the economic models that accountants are now embracing.

Pert/Cost Resource Allocation Procedure

W. R. Ross

University of Tulsa

The author presents a step-by-step approach to constructing a PERT/Cost network. After determining the lowest time/cost alternative for the directed date, the resource allocation procedure is extended by evaluating the effects of combination reductions of activities, critical path shifts, variable/ fixed cost relationships, and leveling over- and under-utilization of resources.

Reprinted from *The Accounting Review*, XLI, (July 1966), 464-473. Used by permission of W. R. Ross and *The Accounting Review*.

The Pert/Cost approach to managing large and complex programs of work—e.g., weapons systems, space ventures, etc.—is receiving considerable attention by industry, government, and in the literature. Structurally, the Pert/Cost system is based upon three interrelated components—a work breakdown structure, work packages, and the network—and is designed to provide management with the tools necessary to achieve schedule and cost planning, determination, and control in those instances for which conventional management systems are inadequate.

The "resource allocation procedure," a supplement to the basic Pert/Cost system. is concerned with the problem of efficient allocation of limited resources in accomplishing work programs, and is based on the premise that activities (work efforts; usually represented by arrows) on a network are subject to time/cost trade-offs.

This supplement is not considered an essential part of the Pert/Cost system. However, it serves to extend the usefulness and effectiveness of the Pert/Cost system as a management tool. While the concepts involved appear relatively simple, the implementation of the supplement usually requires considerable management education and understanding in order to insure its proper use. Maximum care is essential in the use of the resource-allocation supplement so as to obtain realistic results from its application.

The resource-allocation supplement is designed to assist the manager in the systematic development of an optimum assignment of men and equipment. This supplement is "a plan in which men and equipment are assigned to the project in such a way that the technical objectives are achieved at either the lowest cost for a specified time duration, or the shortest time within a specified cost limit."[1] To do this, the procedure calls for alternate time/resource estimates for performing each activity in the segment of the program under consideration. Provided an activity can be carried out in more than one way, it is assumed that these alternative approaches will produce different cost and time estimates.

Briefly, implementation of the resource-allocation supplement requires the following:

[1]DOD and NASA Guide: PERT/Cost— "Systems Design" (Washington, D.C.: Department of Defense and National Aeronautics and Space Administration, June 1962), p. 108.

Management first defines the project by a network of activities with technical specifications for the work. Alternative times and costs are then estimated for each of the activities. (Any number of meaningful time-cost combinations may be estimated.)

The duration of an activity is initially set at the time associated with its lowest cost alternative. Then, by selecting shorter time/higher cost points on certain critical-path activities, time is "bought" on the critical path until the project duration is equal to or slightly less than the target duration.[2]

It should be pointed out that while the overall Pert/Cost system is intended as a planning and control aid for entire work programs, the resource-allocation supplement can be used in planning small groups of associated activities from a larger network.

PRELIMINARY PROCEDURAL STEPS

The steps to be followed in the application of the time/cost trade-off portion of the resource-allocation supplement are summarized below and illustrated in Figure 1.

Step 1. Construct the network or portion thereof under consideration. For simplicity in illustration, a network of only three activities has been assumed with event C representing the desired end objective.

Step 2. Obtain alternate time/cost estimates for each activity. These are "discrete" time/cost intersect points for performing each activity. The manager may determine as many discrete intersect points as desired and practical. The graphs in Figure 1a show the alternative

[2]Ibid., p. 109.

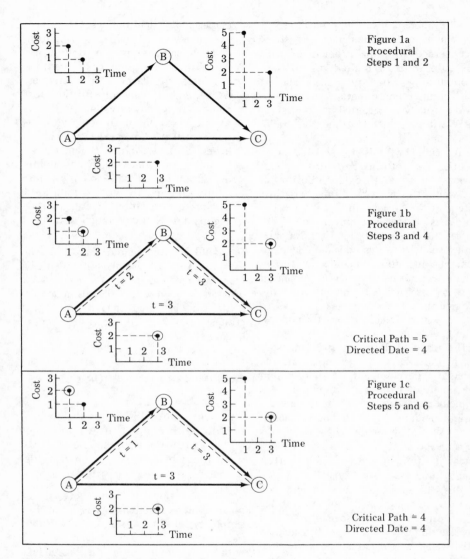

FIGURE 1. The Resource Allocation Procedure

Source: Adapted from *An Introduction to the PERT/Cost System for Integrated Project Management*, Special Projects Office, Department of the Navy, Washington, D.C., Figure 14.

times and costs estimated for each of the three activities. Where it is possible to extend the duration of a project it may be possible to reduce costs for a variety of reasons, including: (1) better preliminary planning, (2) reduction of overtime wages, (3) less premium purchasing, (4) less rework cost, or (5) a different approach in accomplishing the task. The alternative time/cost estimates submitted by the managers for the three activities in Figure 1 are as follows:

Activity A-B: 2 weeks/$1,000
1 week/$2,000
Activity B-C: 3 weeks/$2,000
1 week/$5,000
Activity A-C: 3 weeks/$2,000 (assumed
work can be accomplished
in only one way).

Step 3. Select the lowest cost alternate for each activity. For the illustrative example, this is the following:

Activity A-B	$1,000
Activity B-C	2,000
Activity A-C	2,000
Total Cost	$5,000

Step 4. Calculate the critical path, using the time values associated with the costs selected in Step 3, and compare to directed date. The critical path as indicated in Figure 1b is along activities A-B and B-C and has a duration of five weeks. The directed date calls for a maximum duration of four weeks; therefore, the critical path duration exceeds the necessary target date duration.

Step 5. If the critical path is too long, it must be compressed by shortening some or all of its component activities. Select the higher cost, shorter time alternates where the ratio of increased cost to decreased time is least. This is determined by dividing the increase in cost by the decrease in time as a result of moving to the next shorter time period. For the example these ratios are:

Activity A-B $\frac{1}{1} = 1$

Activity B-C $\frac{3}{2} = 1.5$

Activity A-B has the least increase in time associated with a decrease in cost; therefore, this activity should be shortened to its next shorter time alternate point or the one week/$2,000 cost intersect.

Step 6. Repeat Step 5 until the length of the critical path conforms to the directed date. In the example presented, iteration of Step 5 is unnecessary since the estimated duration has been reduced to four weeks and conforms to the directed date for the project (Figure 1c).[3]

In effect, if the critical path time exceeds the desired duration, time is "bought" until the required estimated duration is achieved. In buying this time, several additional important considerations must be kept in mind.

COMBINATION REDUCTION OF ACTIVITIES

First, where several alternate time/cost points exist for the critical path activities being operated on, a combination of reductions may be the best. This can be illustrated as follows. Suppose that the critical path consists of the three activities and their related time/cost estimates as presented in Figure 2. The lowest cost is $9,000 with a time duration of twenty-three weeks:

Activity	Lowest Cost	Related Time (Weeks)
A-B	$4,000	8
B-C	2,000	7
C-D	3,000	8
Totals	$9,000	23

Suppose that the directed date specifies a maximum duration of some number less that twenty-three weeks—in brief, that the critical path needs to be reduced. Application of the resource-allocation procedure calls for computing the ratio of

[3]These steps were adapted from Special Projects Office, Department of the Navy, *An Introduction to the PERT/Cost System for Integrated Project Management*, Sec. IV-B; and *DOD and NASA Guide: PERT Cost—"Systems Design,"* pp. 108-112.

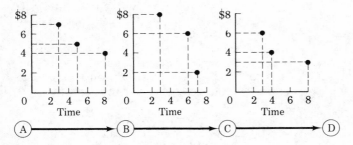

FIGURE 2. Three Activity Critical Path and Related Time/Cost Estimates

increased cost to decreased time for each of the alternative points other than those associated with the lowest cost (Figure 3). Now, the critical path can be systematically transformed from the minimum-cost, maximum-time plan to the minimum-time, maximum-cost plan, always making the optimum choice as illustrated in Figure 4.

the next plan shorter than the directed duration can be selected (e.g., if the directed duration is fifteen weeks, then it would be necessary to select Revised Plan C). With the desired duration determined in advance, it is unnecessary to complete the worksheet past the point of the revised plan that meets the duration criteria.

Activity	Lowest Cost	Second Lowest Cost			Third Lowest Cost		
	Cost/Time	Actual Cost/Time	Change Cost/Time	Ratio	Actual Cost/Time	Change Cost/Time	Ratio
A-B	$4 / 8	$5 / 5	$1 / 3	0.33	$7 / 3	$2 / 2	1.00
B-C	$2 / 7	$6 / 6	$4 / 1	4.00	$8 / 3	$2 / 3	0.67
C-D	$3 / 8	$4 / 4	$1 / 4	0.25	$6 / 3	$2 / 1	2.00

(Cost in Thousands of Dollars, Time in Weeks)

FIGURE 3. Computation of Activity Increased Cost/Decreased Time Ratios

With the information developed in the worksheet of optimal cost/time plans (Figure 4), management can select the plan that conforms to the directed date with assurance of minimum cost for such a plan. If there is no specific plan that meets exactly the directed duration, then

Care must be exercised to avoid buying excessive time when selecting the "cheapest time reduction" which finally reduces the duration to the desired plan. For instance, suppose that it becomes necessary to "buy" two weeks time, and further assume that movement to the

Description	A-B Time	A-B Cost	B-C Time	B-C Cost	C-D Time	C-D Cost	Total Time	Total Cost
Minimum cost, maximum time plan	8	$4	7	$2	8	$3	23	$ 9
Select cheapest time reduction (C-D = 0.25)					−4	+ 1	− 4	+ 1
Revised Plan A	8	$4	7	$2	4	$4	19	$10
Select next cheapest time reduction (A-B = 0.33)	− 3	+ 1					− 3	+ 1
Revised Plan B	5	$5	7	$2	4	$4	16	$11
Select next cheapest time reduction (A-B = 1)*	− 2	+ 2					− 2	+ 2
Revised Plan C	3	$7	7	$2	4	$4	14	$13
Select next cheapest time reduction (C-D = 2)					−1	+ 2	− 1	+ 2
Revised Plan D	3	$7	7	$2	3	$6	13	$15
Select next cheapest time reduction (B-C = 4)			−1	+ 4			− 1	+ 4
Revised Plan E	3	$7	6	$6	3	$6	12	$19
Select next cheapest time reduction (B-C = 0.67)			− 3	+ 2			− 3	+ 2
Minimum time, maximum cost plan	3	$7	3	$8	3	$6	9	$21

*Note that although activity B-C has a ratio of 0.67 associated with its "Third Lowest Cost," the ratio attributable to its "Second Lowest Cost" is 4 and has not been selected to this point. This illustrates that it is necessary to consider the shortest time periods for each activity in sequence. (Cost in thousands of dollars; time in weeks.)

FIGURE 4. Worksheet of Optimal Cost/Time Plans

next shorter times of two activities results in the following ratios:

Activity X-Y:

$$\frac{\text{Increase in Cost } \$4{,}000}{\text{Decrease in Time 5 weeks}} = .80$$

Activity Y-Z:

$$\frac{\text{Increase in Cost } \$3{,}000}{\text{Decrease in Time 2 weeks}} = 1.50$$

If the lower ratio (.80) is selected, then excessive cost of $1,000 is incurred because two weeks of time could have been bought on activity Y-Z for $3,000 as opposed to buying the excessive five weeks time at a cost of $4,000 on activity X-Y.

CRITICAL PATH SHIFT

A second consideration in "buying" time along the critical path is the possibility that another path may become critical as a result of shortening the original critical path. It may become necessary simultaneously to reduce the duration of two or more paths in such a situation. Also, since Pert/Cost is a dynamic management tool, certain critical path activities on which time is bought to reduce total duration in the original planning network may end up on a slack path as the network times are continuously subject to change. In this or any other case, the slack paths require review and, if possible, replanning at lower cost and longer duration so long as they do not become critical.

TIME AND FIXED-COST CONSIDERATIONS

While it may be possible to include fixed overhead in the estimates to determine the alternative time/cost points, this would likely prove to be a cumbersome and unnecessary task. Nevertheless, it is essential that fixed costs be scrutinized closely to determine their relationship to the over-all planning of a complex work program.

Figure 5 illustrates the effect that fixed overhead can have on total project cost. In this example, it is assumed that fixed overhead is one million dollars per year and that there are four feasible plans for completing the project. The five-year plan has a variable cost of $5.4 million and would be rejected since the four-year plan has a variable cost of only $5.2 million. The purpose for including the five-year plan is to demonstrate that there is a saturation point to variable cost reduction at which it becomes costlier to extend the duration.

The four-year plan has the lowest variable cost ($5.2 million), but a higher total cost than the three-year plan which has a variable cost of $5.6 million. The $0.6 million lesser total cost of the three-year plan over the four-year plan is attributable to the fact that the reduction in fixed cost of $1 million more than offsets the $0.4 million increase in variable costs.

Finally the two-year plan has $1 million less fixed cost than the three-year plan, but $1.4 million more variable cost for a net increase in total cost of $0.4 million. From strictly a total-cost point of view, the three-year plan is the best of those available.

It should be noted that the alternative feasible plans are at discrete time/cost intersects and that the dashed lines in Figure 5 are merely for readability and do not indicate continuous time/cost relationships. The value of calculating continuous time/cost curves for significant projects is doubtful. Whereas this is a reasonable approach to determining optimum quantities for continuous production, continuous time/cost curves are usually not applicable in the case of one-time programs of work.

Finally, the effect of optimizing one segment (activity or continuous group of activities) of the work program on other segments must be analyzed. Figures 6 and 7 can be used to illustrate this relationship. In both illustrations it is assumed that there are two work segments (A and B) to be completed and that the following time/cost alternatives have been determined:

| Duration | Segment A | | |
(years)	Variable	Fixed	Total
1	$16	$ 2	$18
2	11	4	15
3	8	6	14
4	7	8	15
5	11	10	21

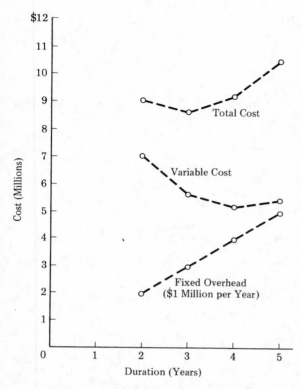

FIGURE 5. Fixed/Variable Cost Relationships

Duration	Segment B		
(years)	Variable	Fixed	Total
1	$31	$1	$32
2	31	2	33
3	24	3	27
4	18	4	22
5	12	5	17

These time/cost relationships are plotted in Figure 6. If A and B are completely independent of each other (one does not have to be completed before the other can start) and it is desirous to complete these at the lowest possible cost, then A would be performed in three years at a cost of $14 million and B would be performed in five years at a cost of $17 million—a total combined cost of $31 million. The maximum duration could be cut to four years, but at a cost increase of

$5 million (A in three years for $14 million + B in four years for $22 million = $36 million). Further time reductions at increased cost could similarly be made. If for technical reasons it is imperative that A and B be completed simultaneously, then a program of four years duration at a total combined cost of $37 million is optimal. Again, the duration could be reduced with increases in cost.

The effect of reducing time on the critical path must be measured not only on the critical path but on other paths as well. For example, to reduce a critical path by twenty weeks to the next discrete alternative may require an increase in cost along that path of only $50,000, and this may be desirable in management's judgment. However, if a reduction of twenty weeks in this path causes a

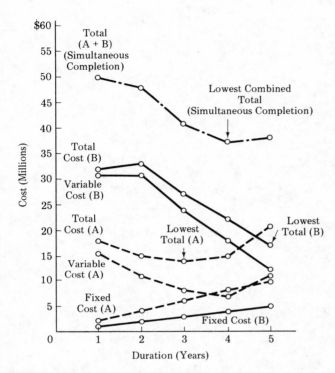

FIGURE 6. Time and Fixed/Variable Cost Relationships

Segment A	Segment B									
Year/Cost (Millions)	1	$32	2	$33	3	$27	4	$22	5	$17
	Total Time/Cost Plans where A Must be Complete Prior to Starting B									
	Years	Cost	Years	Cost	Years	Cost	Years	Cost	Years	Cost
1 $18	2	$50	3	$51	4	$45	5	$40	6	$35
2 $15	3	$47	4	$48	5	$42	6	$37	7	$32
3 $14	4	$46	5	$47	6	$41	7	$36	8	$31
4 $15	5	$47	6	$48	7	$42	8	$37	9	$32
5 $21	6	$53	7	$54	8	$48	9	$43	10	$38

FIGURE 7. Matrix of Total Time/Cost Combinations

second path to become critical, then a different decision may be forthcoming. If the second path becomes critical by sixteen weeks, then the real over-all time gained is only four weeks. Management may not be willing to spend $50,000 to gain four weeks. A further reduction in the second path may be extremely costly and thus undesirable, or it may be impossible.

Using the time/cost data for A and B presented above and assuming that A must be completed before B can commence, what is the optimal plan for various total durations? Figure 7 is a matrix of the various combinations of time/cost plans available.

A plan of eight years duration (A = 3; B = 5) provides the lowest possible cost of $31 million. Shorter durations and their associated lowest cost combinations are next listed:

| Duration | (Years) | | Combined Costs |
A + B	=	Total	(Millions)
2	5	7	$32
1	5	6	35
1	4	5	40
1	3	4	45
2	1	3	47
1	1`	2	50

The nine- and ten-year plans have total combined costs exceeding the costs for the eight-year plan and certain other combinations having a lesser duration. The matrix in Figure 7 provides data necessary to management in making the optimum combination choice for a given duration. As an example, if a six-year maximum duration is desired, then there are five combinations of A and B with the cost ranging from $35 million to $53 million. Using the matrix, the lowest cost combination of $35 million (A = 1; B = 5) can be determined; and it can also be ascertained that no shorter total duration plan provides a lower cost.

LEVELING RESOURCES UTILIZATION

After arriving at the desired plan, using the resource-allocation techniques described to this point, loading charts by resource categories and time periods should be developed. The purpose of these loading charts is to display the possible over- and under-utilization of resources. This will assist management in leveling out peaks and valleys in resource utilizations.

While graphs can be developed for various categories of resources, probably the most useful application of this leveling process is in manpower loading. This is illustrated in Figures 9 and 10, using the network in Figure 8. Suppose that two hundred hours of manpower skill "A" are required weekly for each activity in progress during that week. If each activity in the network is started as early as possible, the schedule of activities would appear as in Figure 9a and the manpower loading requirements for manpower skill "A" would appear as in Figure 9b. As can be seen in Figure 9b, the manpower requirements are quite erratic, ranging from a peak of 800 man-hours to a minimum of 200 man-hours per week. Needless to say, such a schedule of manpower requirements would create a number of problems relative to hiring, layoff, overtime, and idle time.

Figure 10 shows the effects of re-scheduling certain activities to smooth out the manpower requirements for skill "A". The schedule of activities in Figure 10a still permits completion in nineteen weeks, but starting times of certain activities on slack paths have been shifted in order to attain the leveling of manpower requirements as indicated in Figure 10b. Manpower skill "A" demands for this second schedule are much more compatible with the job of maintaining and scheduling a work force.

It is highly unlikely that the assumption of 200 skill "A" man hours per week for each activity in progress is a realistic one; certain activities might require varying quantities of this skill and some may require no skill "A" manpower

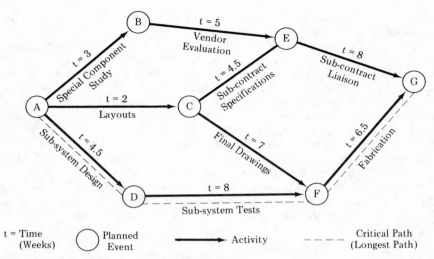

t = Time   Planned   Activity   Critical Path
(Weeks)   Event   (Longest Path)

FIGURE 8. Pert Network with Expected Times and Critical Path Indicated

Source: Adapted from *An Introduction to the PERT/Cost System for Integrated Project Management,* Special Projects Office, Department of the Navy, Washington, D. C.

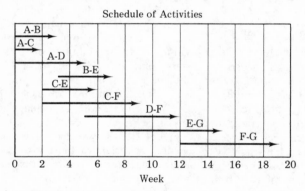

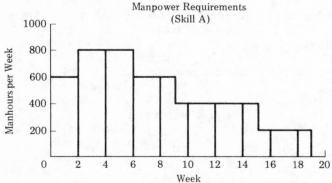

FIGURE 9. Schedule of Activities and Manpower Loading Requirements for Manpower Skill "A".
(Based on Network in Figure 8; each activity started as early as possible.)

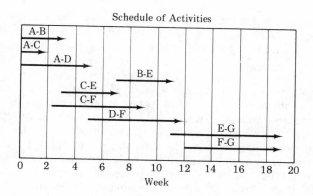

Schedule of Activities

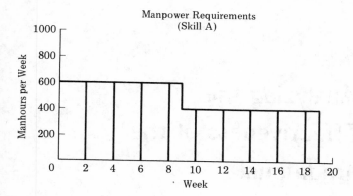

FIGURE 10. Schedule of Activities and Manpower Loading Requirements for Manpower Skill "A". (Based on Network in Figure 8; activities started so as to level manpower requirements.)

at all. The assumption, however, is a feasible one for explaining and illustrating simply the process of resource utilization leveling. In a real situation it may even become necessary to shorten or lengthen certain activities to attain the smoothing effects desired. Also there will undoubtedly be some compromise between the various resources involved in the leveling process.

RECAPITULATION

Commencing with the steps outlined under the caption "Preliminary Procedural Steps" above, which determine the lowest time/cost alternatives consistent with the directed date, application of the resource-allocation procedure is completed by evaluating the effects of (1) combination reductions of activities, (2) critical path shifts, (3) variable/fixed costs relationships, and (4) leveling over- and under-utilization of resources. The full utilization of this supplement requires both quantitative analysis and informed management judgment. Although the resource-allocation procedure is not considered absolutely essential in using the Pert/Cost system, the factors considered in its application must necessarily be an integral part of any well developed Pert/Cost plan. Therefore, where the procedure per se is not used, the factors involved must be considered by management even though this consideration may be an informal approach.

The application of the resource-allocation procedure to an entire network of several hundred or even thousands of activities would be a formidable task. As mentioned earlier, however, this supplement finds its primary usefulness in planning small groups of associated activities which represent only a minor portion of the over-all program of work. Formal application of the procedure may be restricted to work segments involving high costs and critical paths, and to work segments involving the use of substantial amounts of a certain resource where original network plans make some leveling of the planned requirements for this resource desirable. The effects of replanning one segment of work on other parts of the over-all project must be determined and evaluated when the resource-allocation procedure is applied on only selected portions of the entire network.

Analyzing the Effectiveness of the Traditional Standard Cost Variance Model

Joel S. Demski

Stanford University

The management control process is characterized as an adaptive process. The control process requires information flows related to planned results, actual results, and *ex post* optimum results. The traditional standard cost variance model ordinarily conveys only planned and actual results. An extension of the traditional model which takes into account what output should have been is proposed.

Reprinted from *Management Accounting* XLVIII (October 1967), 9-19. Used by permission of Joel S. Demski and the National Association of Accountants.

A fundamental, yet largely unexplored tenet in accounting is that accounting is utilitarian in nature. The implication is that both accounting theory construction and practice should be based on user requirements. Unfortunately, these requirements remain largely unknown. Two consequences follow: First, accounting—in both its external and internal versions—continues to rely on general purpose models for such activities as periodic income determination and profit variation analyses (to the extent that such models exist). Second, current empirical research is largely limited to defining utility in terms of predictive ability rather than in terms of specific decision consequences.[1]

In internal accounting, however, user requirements are now known to the extent that well-structured decision models are employed in certain managerial decision processes. It therefore becomes appropriate to examine the utility of the traditional accounting model in those situations. This paper conducts such an examination.

The analysis is divided into three sections. The first establishes a framework by viewing the management process as an adaptive control process. The second then contrasts the information provided by the traditional standard cost variance model with that required by the management process, as described in the first section. Finally, the third section suggests an operational extension of the traditional standard cost model, designed to provide superior control information.

THE MANAGEMENT CONTROL PROCESS

Jaedicke observes that:

A survey of the accounting and management literature seems to indicate that the control process is generally thought of in three ways. First, control is sometimes defined as the analysis of present performance in the light of some standard or goal in order to determine to what extent accomplishment measures up to the plan or standard ... An intermediate sort of concept defines control as a process of securing conformity to a plan. This concept holds that after the variance or deviation from the plan is discovered, the next step is to take corrective action ... A third concept of control stresses the idea of information *feedback*. That is, data collected as part of the control process might be systematically reported and used in future planning decision.[2]

The essential difference between the intermediate and broad conception is that the latter envisions the deviation data as being input both to the response decision—immediate corrective action—and to what might be termed the planning process. The former, however, concentrates only on the immediate corrective action. The narrow conception, on the other hand, concentrates only on the analysis of performance *per se*.

The broad response and feedback conception of the control process will be followed here. The reason for this preference is that the control system viewed in its entirety must encompass feedback and response considerations.

[1] See, for example, William H. Beaver, "Financial Ratios as Predictors of Business Failure" (unpublished Ph.D. dissertation, Graduate School of Business, University of Chicago, 1965) and Philip Brown, "The Predictive Abilities of Alternative Income Concepts: with Special References to Assets Amortized Under Certificates of Necessity" (paper presented to the Workshop in Accounting Research, Graduate School of Business, University of Chicago, Spring, 1966).

[2] R. K. Jaedicke, "Accounting Data for Purposes of Control," *Accounting Review*, April 1962, p. 181.

The narrow conception of the control process, being inadequate in its analytical implications, can be summarily dismissed as bordering on the naive. It is simply not possible to discuss the quality of information generated without considering the use to be made of that information.

The same argument can also be used to dispose of the intermediate conception, because it ignores the important use of current information as feedback into the planning model. For any deviation of an actual result from the expected result, the avoidability (or controllability) of the deviation must be assessed. If it were avoidable, it can be suppressed. Were it not avoidable, two further aspects must be considered: (1) Its statistical significance and (2) the (immediate) response—that is, should the existing program be altered?

If we are to be concerned with the "task of communicating information on the objectives to be accomplished, providing a means for evaluation of performance, learning and instigation of remedial action,"[3] we are compelled to look at this task in its entirety, including feedback into the planning model (learning and remedial action). The implication is that the traditional planning-control dichotomy is artificial and misleading to the extent that this feedback is important.

Perhaps enlisting the aid of a schematic representation of the control process being discussed will clarify this point. Consider Exhibit 1. The lower, individual task portion of the diagram depicts the usual interpretation of the control process. That is, control is usually viewed as being task oriented—where the term task is used in a broad sense (referring to any undertaking or piece of work). But in a strict literal sense we must also recognize the need for control

of this typical (task) control system—hence the diagram's upper portion.

The purpose of the multiple task control portion of the diagram, then, is to control the organization's set of task control systems. For example, the operation of an individual oil refinery in an integrated oil firm may be viewed in terms of the diagram's task control portion; but control of this individual refinery's management is exercised by the multiple task control portion.

As becomes obvious, the diagram in Exhibit 1 could easily be extended to represent each individual level in any organization. However, our objectives are adequately served by limiting the diagram as shown.

Given a set of objectives, the function of the planning model or adaptive controller is to receive environmental and feedback measures and determine the ideal or optimum output. This, in turn, is transmitted to the decision transformation process (via the controller) where the decision is transformed into instructions for the controlled system. Following this, actual results are measured and transmitted to the controller or response model where actual and optimum results are used as a basis for making a response decision which is transmitted, in turn, to the decision transformation process, and so on. But the optimum in this response decision need not be the one originally transmitted to the controller. The optimum may have changed as the result of further environmental measures and/or additional feedback from the controlled system and the purpose of the upper management control process is to make certain that all of this is done correctly.[4]

[3] Z. Zannetos, "Some Thoughts on Internal Control Systems of the Firm," *Accounting Review*, October 1964, p. 867-68.

[4] Further note in conjunction with the diagram that the term decision process is used in a broad sense. It refers either to quantitative, well-defined decision processes, or to qualitative, judgment oriented decision processes. Also, while the planning, response, behavioral and upper management processes are depicted as

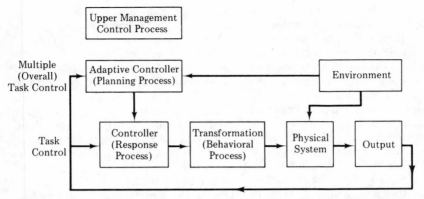

EXHIBIT 1. The Horizontal Line Indicates That Not All of the Usual Information Flows Between the Multiple and Task Control Processes Have Been Included

The adaptive controller's function, as indicated, is to receive environmental and feedback inputs and to generate an ideal or optimum program. In many instances today this type of decision process exists in well-defined form—that is, it

> ... is well structured to the extent that it satisfies the following criteria:
> 1. It can be described in terms of numerical variables, scalar and vector quantities.
> 2. The goals to be attained can be specified in terms of a well-defined objective function—for example, the maximization of profit or the minimization of cost.
> 3. There exist computational routines *(algorithms)* that permit the solution to be found and stated in actual numerical terms . . .[5]

separate decision processes in the diagram, this is an artifact. They are certainly not independent; in many instances, the same manager will make all four types of decisions. We separate them in the diagram in order to emphasize the fact that different information flows are associated with each of the processes and that different degrees of quantification may be associated with each.

[5]H. Simon and A. Newell, "Heuristic Problem Solving: The Next Advance in Operations Research," *Operations Research*, January-February 1958, p. 5.

Examples are provided by successful application of the inventory, linear programming, queuing, and linear decision rules for employment and production models (although this is not to deny that there are qualitative factors in these decision processes).

The function of the controller or response process is to make a decision in response to observed divergences between optimum and actual results. These divergences are the result of prediction errors, control failures (failures to maintain or obtain specific programs), measurement errors, model errors (errors or approximations in constructing and using the planning, response or transformation models), and/or the stochastic nature of some underlying variables. Because of the necessity of separating the impact of these various causal factors and of predicting the time path of the perceived deviation, the response decision is at once critical and difficult.

Work has been done in such areas as assessing the statistical significance of a given deviation,[6] making the decision to

[6]See, for example, A. J. Duncan, "The Economic Design of $\bar{x}$ Charts used to Maintain Current Control of a Process," *Journal of the American Statistical Association*, June 1956, pp. 228-242 or Z. Zannetos, "Standard Costs as a First Step to Probabilistic Control: A Theoretical Justification, an Extension and Implica-

investigate a deviation in the hope of determining the specific causal factors involved,[7] exploring the sensitivity of the planning model to estimation errors,[8] and simulating the transient characteristics of specified systems using certain decision rules.[9] The fact remains, however, that these items of research must be combined and supplemented before the response decision process can be synthesized to the extent that we are able to specify and successfully implement a well-defined response model. At present, these decisions remain in the realm of judgment or heuristic decision making.

The unfortunate implication for the present analysis is that in supplying control information, we must postulate the existence of some such heuristic response decision process and then indulge in the inextricable task of determining the inputs to this process.[10]

Once a response decision is made, it is relayed to the transformation process. In essence, the transformation process is a behavioral model; it takes an optimum plan or response and generates a set of specific instructions designed to achieve the plan or response.

Research has been done on such items as the motivational impact of budgets and

standards[11] and incentive systems.[12] However, we shall not be concerned with the behavior aspects of control theory, although the various components in the diagram are by no means independent. Major emphasis is placed instead on analyzing the nature of the data required for efficient control systems apart from the manner by which the data will or will not be used in the transformation process.

Finally, superimposed on this repeating sequence of decision-action-measurement-evaluation (the lower loop in the diagram), is a planning horizon. The planning model is constructed on the basis of some finite horizon and is periodically re-solved with these, periodic, results being used as the basis for a formal change (for example, a production run) in the specified program.

This task control system, in turn, is controlled or monitored by the upper management control process. This process is conceptually similar to the task control system's response process in that action is taken on the basis of divergences between optimum and actual results. This implies that the process requires as inputs what results were obtained by the task control system and what these results could have been according to the decision model. And, as in the case of the task system's response process, this upper-level process is regarded as being judgment or heuristic oriented. This, then, is the control process. It

> . . . encompasses the technique used to identify the need for action and to review possible action alternatives as

tions," *Accounting Review*, April 1964, pp. 296-304.

[7] See H. Bierman, Jr., *Topics in Cost Accounting and Decisions*, McGraw-Hill, New York, 1963.

[8] See C. Holt, J. Muth, F. Modigliani, and H. Simon, *Planning Production, Inventories, and Work Force*, Prentice-Hall, Englewood Cliffs, N.J., 1960 or C. Van de Panne and P. Bosje, "Sensitivity Analysis of Cost Coefficient Estimates: The Case of Linear Decision Rules for Employment and Production," *Management Science*, October 1962, pp. 82-107.

[9] See J. W. Forrester, *Industrial Dynamics*, McGraw-Hill, New York, 1964.

[10] As we shall see, while the response decision process has not been completely synthesized, we do know that one of the major inputs to the process is an analysis of the differences between actual and ideal results.

[11] See, for example, C. Argyris, "Human Problems with Budgets," *Harvard Business Review*, January-February 1953, pp. 97-110 and A. C. Stedry, *Budget Control and Cost Behavior*, Prentice-Hall, Englewood Cliffs, N.J., 1960.

[12] See M. Haire, "Psychological Research on Pay," *Management Controls: New Directions in Basic Research*, ed. C. P. Bonini, R. K. Jaedicke, and H. M. Wagner, McGraw-Hill, New York, 1964, pp. 277-81.

well as the ultimate control action itself ... Management has four basic methods of approaches to the control of internal operations.

1. Control by planning and decision making.

2. Control by scheduling, direction and supervision.

3. Control by follow-up response to feedback comparison.

4. Control by manipulation.[13]

The essential point to grasp in describing the firm's control system is that we are assuming a coupled organizational-environmental relationship which can be viewed in terms of what, in automatic control theory, is called a self-optimizing or adaptive control system. That is, we are describing a situation where

... the statistics of the inputs and the plant dynamics are not completely known or are gradually changing.[14]

THE TRADITIONAL ROLE OF ACCOUNTING IN THE CONTROL PROCESS

The traditional role of accounting in the control process centers around use of the standard costing and flexible budgeting techniques. Following the establishment of performance standards (for example, expected prices, labor time standards, and so on) and an optimum output program, the cost aspects of this program are used to establish the budget for the period. A

linear relation between total standard cost and some volume index of production is usually assumed. Actual cost is then compared with budgeted (standard) cost through the well-known techniques of standard cost variance analysis in order to isolate the effect of each specific deviation.

These techniques can be succinctly summarized by resorting to some algebraic notation. Omitting units, let

TC = total standard cost for the period,

F = standard fixed overhead cost for the period,

P_L = standard price of direct labor,

Q_L = standard quantity of direct labor,

P_M = standard price of direct material,

Q_M = standard quality of direct material,

V = standard volume for actual output, and

c = standard variable overhead per unit of volume

Then,

$$TC = F + P_L Q_L + P_M Q_M + cV$$

where we note that volume is the independent variable.[15] Now let primed ($'$) values denote actual results,

$$F' = F + \Delta F$$
$$P_L' = P_L + \Delta P_L$$
$$P_M' = P_M + \Delta P_M$$
$$Q_L' = Q_L + \Delta Q_L$$
$$Q_M' = Q_M + \Delta Q_M$$
$$V' = V + \Delta V$$
$$c' = c + \Delta c$$

---

[13]G. Shillinglaw, "Divisional Performance Review: An Extension of Budgetary Control," *Management Controls: New Directions in Basic Research*, ed. C. P. Bonini, R. D. Jaedicke, and H. M. Wagner, McGraw-Hill, New York, 1964, p. 152.

[14]S. Chang, *Synthesis of Optimum Control Systems*, McGraw-Hill, New York, 1961, p. 255.

[15]That is, total cost is assumed to be a function of volume. To be rigorous in our description, we should express the labor and material quantities as functions of volume. However, the exposition is facilitated by following the description presented.

The total difference between actual and standard cost *for the actual output is:*

$$TC' - TC = (F + \Delta F) + (P_L + \Delta P_L)$$
$$(Q_L + \Delta Q_L) + (P_M + \Delta P_M)$$
$$(Q_M + \Delta Q_M) + (c + \Delta c)$$
$$(V + \Delta V) - F - P_L Q_L$$
$$- P_M Q_M - cV = \Delta TC$$
$$= P_L \Delta Q_L + \Delta P_L Q_L$$
$$+ \Delta P_L \Delta Q_L + P_M \Delta Q_M$$
$$+ \Delta P_M Q_M + \Delta P_M \Delta Q_M$$
$$+ c\Delta V + \Delta cV + \Delta c\Delta V + \Delta F$$

$P_L \Delta Q_L$ is usually called the direct labor efficiency variance, $Q_L \Delta P_L + \Delta P_L \Delta Q_L$—the direct labor wage rate variance,[16] $P_M \Delta Q_M$—the direct material usage variance, $Q_M \Delta P_M + \Delta P_M \Delta Q_M$—the direct material price variance, $c\Delta V$—the overhead efficiency variance, and $\Delta cV + \Delta c\Delta V + \Delta F$—the overhead spending variance (using a three variance method of overhead analysis).

In an absorption costing system there would also be a volume or capacity variance arising from the difference between standard and absorbed fixed cost for the period. Such refinement, however, is not germane to the present analysis.

This is the essence of the traditional standard cost variance analysis technique. It subdivides the total difference between actual and standard cost for the standard amount produced and attempts to factor out the individual contributions to this difference of each deviation—that is, of ΔP_L, ΔQ_L, ΔP_M, ΔQ_M, Δc, ΔV and ΔF.

The factoring, of course, is limited by the existence of joint product terms.

This traditional role has also been expanded to include revenues of the products produced, as in the familiar break-even and cost-volume-mix (or profit variation) analyses. The latter is merely an extension of the above techniques to include product mix and selling price deviations, thereby focusing on the difference between actual and budgeted net income instead of between actual and budgeted cost.

As becomes obvious, the usefulness of these techniques is dependent upon, among other things, proper selection of the type of standard to be employed. Numerous types can be found in the literature. Horngren, for example, lists the three broad categories of basic, ideal, and currently attainable;[17] and for each category we could add *ex post* and *ex ante* versions. But much more important than the fact of variety is the fact that selection must be predicated on anticipated use of the resultant variance information. Here the distinction between the planning, response, behavioral and upper management decision processes being discussed becomes critical.

The planning model requires currently attainable inputs, where it is recognized that these data are *ex ante* in nature. They are also temporal in nature. As information in the form of feedback from current operations and additional environmental information is obtained, the *ex ante* data are either confirmed or altered. These confirmations and alterations then form part of the basis for the succeeding planning decisions.

As noted previously, explicit discussion of the inputs to the behavioral model is beyond the scope of this inquiry. There is sufficient evidence to suggest that

[16] This, of course, assumes that price variances are isolated as the materials are consumed, not when they are purchased. The latter situation is preferable from a control standpoint, but is not included in the algebraic description because of the notational burden that inclusion would impose.

[17] C. T. Horngren, *Cost Accounting: A Managerial Emphasis*, Prentice-Hall, Englewood Cliffs, N.J., 1962, pp. 138-39.

different types of standard may produce different results.[18] Therefore, we cannot argue in favor of some particular type without examining the behavioral process in detail.

Passing mention, though, should be made of the fact that one of the more common techniques used in the transformation process is performance evaluation where actual performance is compared with what it should have been in order to facilitate learning and motivation.[19] Exactly how and in what form this is accomplished is determined by the behavioral model; but whatever its form (for example, fictitious indicators of what should have been) *ex post* information is an input to the evaluation process.

The response and upper management decision processes require as inputs the results which were obtained (actual performance) and the results which could have been obtained. This implies that the proper standard to be used in supplying variance information for these two processes is a standard based on actual conditions—that is, ". . . those that would have been incorporated in the [original] plan if the actual conditions had been known in advance."[20] We shall call this an *ex post* (currently attainable) standard.

In order to fully describe what results could have been obtained, the response and upper management processes also require a determination of the optimum program implied by the *ex post* standards and decision model. We shall call this program the *ex post* (optimum) program. Its determination and synthesis, the tasks of *ex post* analysis, are discussed in the following section.

Thus, we see that the control process requires information flows related to planned results, actual results and *ex post*

optimum results. The traditional accounting model does not convey all of this information. It conveys planned and actual results; and, in addition, if the budget is revised to reflect actual events (that is, if *ex post* standards are used), it will also convey what performance should have been obtained for the output actually achieved. Otherwise, it will convey what performance was anticipated for the output actually achieved. In either event, the traditional variance model, because it treats volume as the independent or exogenous variable, reports divergencies between planned and actual output and between actual and (some definition of) standard cost for the actual output. It does not, however, report what output should have been. Explicit discussion of the proposed *ex post* system will further clarify this important distinction.

THE PREFERRED ROLE OF EX-POST ANALYSIS

Ex post analysis is an extension of the traditional accounting analysis to include program or output revisions. It is primarily concerned with linking the planning model to the response model through generation of an *ex post* optimum program. The net result is a system that simultaneously monitors both performance and the original plan.

This analysis differs from the traditional accounting technique in two important respects. First, actual results are compared with *ex post* optimum results instead of with either *ex post* or *ex ante* standard results for the output actually obtained. That is, output is viewed as an endogenous (internal) rather than exogenous (external) variable. Second, all the inputs to the planning model are incorporated into the analysis, not just those cost (or cost and revenue) factors present in the optimum program.

---

[18]See, for example, Argyris, *op. cit.*, Haire, *op. cit.*, and Stedry, *op. cit.*
[19]See, for example, Z. Zannetos, *op. cit.*, pp. 860-868.
[20]Shillinglaw, *op. cit.*, p. 151.

These two differences are not independent because all inputs to the planning model must be incorporated into the analysis in order to determine the *ex post* program. On the other hand, we could conceive of a system that formally reported only *ex post* optimum performance for certain inputs—for example, one that reported only the opportunity cost associated with variances in a traditional standard cost system. For this reason the two differences are treated somewhat independently in the following discussion.

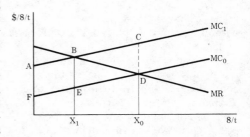

EXHIBIT 2.

IMPORTANCE OF PROGRAM ALTERATIONS

The importance of comparing actual performance with *ex post* optimum performance, instead of with standard performance for the standard volume produced, can be indicated by a brief review of some elementary aspects of the economic theory of the firm. In doing this we shall primarily concentrate on the relevance of the information for the response decision.

In economic theory the firm is viewed as determining its optimum output mix and quantities on the basis of its cost and demand functions. Consequently, when either of these functions changes (or differences between actual and predicted results are obtained), a new output decision is required: Whether to alter the optimum output and, if so, in what manner. Quite obviously this new output decision depends on the costs and benefits associated with alteration of the existing output.

Consider the typical marginal revenue vs. marginal cost situation give in Exhibit 2, where we assume that the firm produces a single product. (To rule out the possibility of measurement error, we shall also assume that the standard is the marginal cost curve.)

The maximizing firm, facing a marginal revenue curve of MR and a marginal cost curve of MC_0 will produce at output level X_0. If the marginal cost curve subsequently shifts unavoidably to MC_1, the firm will move from output level X_0 to X_1. Since it cannot now obtain its original cost curve, MC_0, the firm is maximizing profit by producing at level X_1. Hence, there is no foregone opportunity associated with the event. However, had the firm chosen to remain at X_0 in response to the unavoidable shift from MC_0 to MC_1, it would forego obtainable profit represented by area BCD. That is, the opportunity cost of this failure to move to the new optimum output level is represented by area BCD.

If, on the other hand, the shift to MC_1 had been avoidable, the firm would maximize profit by remaining at X_0 and suppressing the avoidable increase in marginal cost. If it does not suppress the increase and remains at X_0, it foregoes obtainable profit represented by area ACDF; if it moves to X_1, the opportunity cost is represented by area ABDF.

In contrast, regardless of whether the shift in marginal cost could have been avoided, the traditional accounting model produces a cost figure of ACDF if the firm remains at X_0 or ABEF if it moves to X_1.

Considering the various possible combinations of output level and avoidable shifts in the marginal cost curve we get the following variances provided by the traditional accounting model and opportunity cost variances provided by the proposed *ex post* model:

$$TR(100) - TC_0(100) = 500(100)$$
$$- (100)^2 - 100(100)$$
$$- (100)^2 - 1000 = \$19,000$$

If the cost curve now unavoidably shifts to $TC_1 = 300X + X^2 + 1000$, the new optimum output, X_1, would be:

Shift in MC_0	Actual output	Optimum output	Accounting variance	Opportunity cost
Avoidable	X_0	X_0	ACDF	ACDF
Avoidable	X_1	X_0	ABEF	ABDF
Unavoidable	X_0	X_1	ACDF	BCD
Unavoidable	X_1	X_1	ABEF	0

The *ceteris paribus* approach of the traditional accounting model does not consider optimum adjustment to the changed conditions; it merely says that the cost of the deviation is the difference between actual and standard results for the output produced. In contrast, the *mutatis mutandis* approach of *ex post* analysis does consider optimum adjustment; it gauges significance by determining the opportunities foregone as a result of the deviation and failure to respond to it.

Perhaps a numerical example will clarify these issues:

Example 1

Consider a firm with total revenue (TR) and total cost (TC_0) curves given by $TR = 500X - X^2$ and $TC_0 = 100X + X^2 + 1000$ units. Optimum output X_0 is determined as follows:

$$TR = 500X - X^2$$
$$MR = dTR/dX = 500 - 2X$$
$$TC_0 = 100X + X^2 + 1000$$
$$MC_0 = dTC_0/dX = 100 + 2X$$
Optimum output: $MR = MC_0$
$$500 - 2X = 100 + 2X$$
$$400 = 4X$$
$$X = 100 \text{ units}$$

The associated profit is $19,000

$$TR = 500X - X^2$$
$$MR = dTR/dX = 500 - 2X$$
$$TC_1 = 300X + X^2 + 1000$$
$$MC_1 = dTC_1/dX = 300 + 2X$$

Optimum output: $MR = MC_1$
$$500 - 2X = 300 + 2X$$
$$200 = 4X$$
$$X = 50 \text{ units}$$

and the maximum profit would be $4,000.

Suppose, now, that the firm does not respond to this shift in its cost function and remains at output level X_0. It will experience a loss of $1,000 instead of the $4,000 profit it could have obtained by moving to X_1. That is, the opportunity cost associated with not anticipating the shift and subsequent failure to respond to it is $5,000. The traditional accounting model, on the other hand, would report a variance of $20,000 under these circumstances.

The traditional opportunity cost variances associated with the various output level and avoidability possibilities are presented in Exhibit 3. Note that because actual and standard revenues are identical in the example, the accounting profit variance is the difference between actual and standard costs.

EXHIBIT 3

Shift in TC_0	Actual output	Optimum output	Standard cost	Actual cost
Avoidable	100	100	$21,000	$41,000
Avoidable	50	100	$ 8,500	$18,500
Unavoidable	100	50	$21,000	$41,000
Unavoidable	50	50	$ 8,500	$18,500

Shift in TC_0	Accounting variance	Optimum profit	Actual profit	Opportunity cost
Avoidable	$20,000	$19,000	($1,000)	$20,000
Avoidable	$10,000	$19,000	$4,000	$15,000
Unavoidable	$20,000	$ 4,000	($1,000)	$ 5,000
Unavoidable	$10,000	$ 4,000	$4,000	0

Thus, if our objective is to analyze differences between actual and ideal results, we need to consider *ex post* optimum performance instead of standard performance for the standard volume produced. Implied changes in output mix and quantities need to be explicitly recognized. Then, and only then, can we compare actual results with what these results should have been. Quite clearly such an approach requires that we monitor all inputs to the planning model and not just those cost (or cost and revenue) factors present in the optimum program.

IMPORTANCE OF MONITORING ALL PLANNING MODEL INPUTS

The effect of not monitoring all inputs to the planning model can be amply demonstrated with a simple example using the assignment model:[21]

Example 2

A department head has four subordinates and four tasks to be performed. The subordinates differ in efficiency, and the tasks differ in their intrinsic difficulty. His estimate of the times each man would take to perform each task is given in the effectiveness matrix below. How should the tasks be allocated, one to a man, so as to minimize the total man-hours?

		Man			
		I	II	III	IV
	A	8	26	17	11
Task	B	13	28	4	26
	C	38	19	18	15
	D	19	26	24	10

The optimum allocation is to make the following assignments:

A-I, B-III, C-II, D-IV

which results in 41 total labor hours.

[21]Adapted from M. Sasiene, A. Yaspen, and L. Friedman, *Operations Research*, John Wiley and Sons, New York, 1961, p. 185.

Assume, now, that the time for man II to do task D was erroneously estimated and should have been 3 hours. This implies that the assignment should have been:

A-I, B-III, C-IV, D-II

with a resultant labor hour total of 30 hours.

Under these circumstances a traditional standard cost system would report no variance whatever—in spite of the fact that 11 more labor hours than necessary were used to accomplish the four tasks. Expanding the scope of the traditional system to encompass all factors in the assignment decision would, on the other hand, result in a variance of 11 labor hours, appropriately costed.

SUMMARY

We see, then, that *ex post* analysis is an extension of traditional standard cost variance analysis techniques in two important related directions: (1) provision is made for revision of the (*ex ante*) optimum program and (2) all factors in the output decision are included in the analysis. It is anticipated, ignoring issues of the cost and value of information, that this extension will provide meaningful and valuable information for the managerial function of acting on exceptions which result from either the controlled process or established goals themselves falling outside of control limits.

By introducing into the analysis optimal variation of the planned output, the proposed *ex post* system establishes a framework which depicts the best that might have been done, given the actual circumstances encountered during the period. The resultant opportunity cost variances are potentially useful in such areas as (1) reviewing the period's operations, (2) future planning, (3) deciding if and how to alter a current program, (4) judging the effectiveness of the task control system and (5) evaluating performance.[22]

This suggested approach to generation of control information, of course, can be pursued only in those situations where a well-defined planning model is in operation. And, to be certain, the implications of such a combined approach are only beginning to be explored.[23]

[22] We should perhaps note that our description of the traditional accounting model, being strictly algebraic, does not give a true measure of the information provided by the system when the data are analyzed by a competent analyst. But this does not weaken the significance of the preceding discussion because our competent analyst is much better off with the *ex post* system than with the traditional system. The latter will signal certain deviations but in a complex model the accounting variables are likely to represent an aggregation of a number of individual model inputs. In such a situation, the analyst must search for causal deviations. Similarly, deviations signaled by the accounting model may, in part, be manifestations of deviations in elements not included in the accounting model; or worse yet, such deviations may not be signaled at all (as in Example 2). And, finally, even if the analyst could glean all deviations from the accounting model he would still be faced with the task of assessing their effect on the program. For example, he would have to assess the effect of a given deviation on other responsibility centers. The accounting model cannot provide this information.

[23] See J. S. Demski, "Variance Analysis: An Opportunity Cost Approach with a Linear Programming Application," (unpublished Ph.D dissertation, Graduate School of Business, University of Chicago, 1967).

Controlled Cost:
An Operational Concept
and Statistical Approach
to Standard Costing

F. S. Luh

Lehigh University

A cost control system based on the probability distribution of cost is proposed as an alternative to the conventional standard cost system based on a single value or a range of costs. The proposed system specifies explicitly the variability of costs and allows a more thorough analysis of performance than would be possible with single-value standard cost systems. The author shows how the concept of controlled cost can be operationalized by the use of basic statistical tests.

Reprinted from *The Accounting Review*, XLIII (January 1968), 123-132. Used by permission of F. S. Luh and *The Accounting Review*.

Cost control is a fundamental task of management. In order to acomplish the goal of long-run profit maximization, "cost control has as its objective production of the required quality at the lowest possible cost attainable under existing conditions."[1] The primary usefulness of a standard cost system is to facilitate cost control through identification of situations and investigation of performance when actual cost deviates significantly from standard cost. A level of cost that should be attained under efficient operation is specified and then compared with actual cost to measure operating efficiency and degree of control.

An effective system of cost control must be capable of achieving the following objectives:

1. Maintain current operating efficiency and identify deviations from it.
2. Disclose any sign of impending crisis.
3. Reveal any possibility of improving current operating efficiency.

Present practices of standard costing are based primarily on an assumption that the expected value of an efficient operation is stability and that any significant deviation of the mean of actual cost from the expected value indicates abnormality of operation requiring managerial attention. Such a system, at best, only accomplishes the first objective of cost control mentioned above.

Earlier works of cost accountants have extended the concept of standard cost from a single value comparison to a range

[1]National Association of Cost Accountants, "A Re-examination of Standard Costs," (Research Series No. 11), *N.A.C.A. Bulletin*, (February 1948), p. 703.

of control limits.[2] A range of costs is established by statistical control techniques, and when actual costs fall outside the control limits, managerial investigation is required. Recently, efforts have been made to use statistical sampling theory to limit managerial action to those situations where occurrence of actual cost outside the range is excessively frequent, while a limited number of out-of-the-range performances are recognized as chance variations and do not normally require managerial action.[3] This approach still overlooks the irregular performance within the control limits which may enable one to detect crises or guide us to improve operating efficiency.[4] Further-

more, the assumption of normal distribution of cost with a known mean and a known variance, and the selection of three standard deviations as control limits would appear to lack sound theoretical basis.[5]

The purpose of this paper is to propose a refinement of standard cost, to be called "controlled cost," using statistical techniques to evaluate operating efficiency and degree of control.

CONTROLLED COST[6]

VARIABILITY OF PERFORMANCE

It is well known that natural resources conventionally are not of uniform quality. For example, iron ore from different mines does not have identical chemical content or physical quality. Even ore from the same mine at a given time interval may vary in content or quality, and, consequently, material put into production often exhibits considerable variability of quality.

The variability of input is perhaps more obvious in respect to labor. Climatic conditions, atmospheric pressure, pollen count, etc. often influence the emotional, as well as the physical, well-being of workers. As a social being, a worker's alertness correlates highly with changes in social environment. These changing con-

[2]Edward H. Bowman, "Using Statistical Tools to Set Reject Allowance," *N.A.C.A. Bulletin*, (June 1954), pp. 1334-1342.

Edwin W. Gaynor, "Use of Control Charts in Cost Control," *N.A.C.A. Bulletin*, (June 1954), pp. 1300-1309.

Carl E. Noble, "Cost Accounting Potential of Statistical Methods," *N.A.C.A. Bulletin*, (August 1952), pp. 1470-1478.

————, "Calculating Control Limits for Cost Control Data," *N.A.C.A. Bulletin*, (June 1953), pp. 1309-1317.

L. Wheaton Smith, "An Introduction to Statistical Control," *N.A.C.A. Bulletin*, (December 1952), pp. 509-516.

James C. Stephenson, "Quality Control to Minimize Cost Variance," *N.A.C.A. Bulletin*, (October 1956), pp. 264-275.

[3]Harold Bierman, Jr., Lawrence E. Fouraker, and Robert K. Jaedicke, *Quantitative Analysis for Business Decisions*, (Richard D. Irwin, Inc., 1961). pp. 108-124.

Harold Bierman, Jr., *Topics in Cost Accounting and Decisions*, (McGraw-Hill Book Company, 1963). pp. 9-26.

Charles T. Horngren, *Cost Accounting: A Managerial Emphasis*, (Prentice-Hall Inc., 1962). pp. 746-760.

[4]Dudley J. Cowden points out in his *Statistical Method in Quality Control*, (Prentice-Hall, 1957), p. 230, that in addition to distinguishing between points within and outside the control limits, observations of several points which are close together, a run of successive points or a larger number of points on one side of the central value, or a trend in the points may provide warning signals of abnormality of performance.

[5]Noble believes that cost accountants will find two standard deviation control limits more practical. (*op. cit.,* p. 1471).

Richard M. Cyert and G. Myers advocates in their "Statistical Techniques in the Control of Labor Performance" in Robert M. Trueblood and Richard M. Cyert, *Sampling Techniques in Accounting*, (Prentice-Hall, Inc., 1957). p. 145, that "specified" probability limits be used in lieu of standard deviation control limits.

[6]The term "controlled cost" is favored to describe what cost should be when a process is in control and to distinguish from the conventional single value concept of standard cost.

ditions are quite naturally reflected in job performance. The non-uniformity of mental capacity and physical ability among individuals is ubiquitous. Education and other training merely intensify otherwise innate differences. Accordingly, it may be expected that the output of different individuals on a given job, or process, will display a considerable degree of variation. It is evident that manufacturing activities combine, directly or indirectly, natural resources and human efforts, and that the performance of a production process is patently subject to much fluctuation and variation.

CHARACTERISTICS OF A CONTROLLED PROCESS

Having recognized the inherent variability of performance, it is necessary to provoke a workable distinction between controlled performance and noncontrolled performance. Quality control engineers define a controlled process in terms of the constancy of the probability distribution of the outcome of operation.

Cowden states that when a process is under control, it is governed by a constant system of causes operating in a random manner. Thus, the probability distribution of an item can be discovered if all nonrandom types of variation either have been eliminated or have been taken into consideration quantitatively.[7] Deming notes that there is no constancy in real life, but that there may be "constant cause systems" in the sense that they produce varying results which exhibit a constant or stable distribution.[8]

Therefore, when a manufacturing process is under control, it is not that the result is free from variation, but rather it is that the result displays a distinctive pattern of probability distribution.

[7]Cowden, *op. cit.*, p. 2.
[8]W. E. Deming, "Some Principles of Shewhart Method of Quality Control," *Mechanical Engineering*, (March 1944), p. 173.

SPECIFICATION OF CONTROLLED COST

With a fixed quantity of input, the output varies. Conversely, if the output is held constant, input will vary. When a manufacturing process is under control, the probability distribution of output displays a stable pattern. This is another way of saying that the probability distribution of input also has a similar characteristic. Hence, when a process is under control, the amount of labor and quantity of material required for a given unit of product exhibit a distinctive pattern of probability distribution.

If one assumes that dollar cost is a linear function of the number of physical units of input, the analysis of cost in terms of physical units is usually sufficient for control purpose. Furthermore, the price of labor or materials is often predetermined by external environments, and those who are in charge of operations normally only have authority or control over utilization of resources; control must emphasize the physical unit aspect of cost. Therefore, controlled cost will be defined here only with respect to physical units. Controlled cost is defined as the probability distribution of a collection of input costs in physical units required for the production of a given unit of output when a process is under control. The amount of labor or the quantity of materials required for the production of one unit of intermediate or finished product may vary when a process is under control, but there exists a definite pattern of variation in the required input. This pattern of variation, stated in terms of a probability distribution function, is used to specify controlled cost. Controlled cost defined in this manner not only fully describes the characteristic of inherent variability of performance but also encompasses the conventional single value standard cost implicitly by its expected value. It will be convenient to use a frequency function or a distribution function to describe controlled cost.[9]

UNIVERSE VS. SAMPLE OF CONTROLLED PERFORMANCE

Under a given state of technology, some performances will be controlled. Let us call the aggregate of the performance considered under control the universe of controlled performance. Although this universe theoretically exists, and ideally the probability distribution of the cost of this universe should be used to establish controlled cost, complete knowledge of this universe is unattainable.

Accordingly, the knowledge about the universe of controlled performances must be inferred from limited and selective observations of a sample, presumably from the universe of controlled performance. The probability distribution of the cost of a sample performance thus establishes the controlled cost.

An Example

Assume that, after appropriate and sufficient number of observations, management decides that in Table 1 the production data tabulated in Columns 1 and 2 represent the controlled cost distribution for labor time per unit of finished product. Controlled cost for the assembly labor may then be stated in frequency function or distribution function as given in Columns 3 and 4, or shown graphically in Figures 1 and 2.

In terms of frequency function, the process is under control when one-half per cent of the units are assembled in 45 to 46 minutes, another one-half per cent of the units are assembled in 46 to 47 minutes and so on. Similarly, in terms of distribution function, one-half per cent of the units are assembled in less than 46 minutes, one per cent of the units are

assembled in less than 47 minutes and so on.

COST DEVIATION[10]

SAMPLE OF ACTUAL PERFORMANCE

Because of possible limited availability of managerial time, fluctuation of performance, and the impractibility of evaluating performance by elements, it is the general practice of management to evaluate performance in groups of a functional unit (e.g., a worker, a group of workers, a department) for a given period of time. Such evaluation units are simply a limited collection of observations from a vast number of performances. In other words, performance evaluation must be conducted through a sample of actual performance.

COST DEVIATION DEFINED

When an actual performance is under control, the sample of actual performance is a sample from the universe of controlled performance. Since the sample of controlled performance is also presumably a sample from the universe of controlled performance, both samples are from the same universe. The probability distribution of a sample is approximately the same as its universe most of the time. Hence, the probability distribution of actual cost and that of the controlled cost are both approximately the same as the probability distribution of cost of the universe of controlled performance. This is merely another way of saying that when a process is under control, the

[9]This may either be a parametric or nonparametric function.

[10]The term "cost deviation" is used to denote the deviation of actual cost from controlled cost to distinguish from the term cost variance in the conventional standard cost system.

TABLE 1   Assembly Labor Time Controlled Cost

Assembly Time (minutes) (1)	Frequency of Occurrence (2)	Frequency Function (3)	Distribution Function (4)
45	2	.005	.005
46	2	.005	.010
47	4	.010	.020
48	4	.010	.030
49	6	.015	.045
50	8	.020	.065
51	16	.040	.105
52	24	.060	.165
53	40	.100	.265
54	60	.150	.415
55	80	.200	.615
56	60	.150	.765
57	40	.100	.865
58	24	.060	.925
59	14	.035	.960
60	6	.015	.975
61	4	.010	.985
62	2	.005	.990
63	2	.005	.995
64	2	.005	1.000
Total	400	1.000	

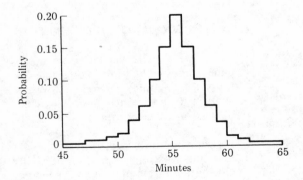

FIGURE 1. Controlled Assembly Time Frequency Function

probability distribution of actual cost being evaluated is approximately the same as that of the controlled cost established previously. On the other hand, when a process is not controlled, the sample of actual performance and the sample of controlled performance are samples from different universes having different probability distributions. The probability distribution of actual cost is accordingly different from the probability distribution of the controlled cost.

To determine whether an actual performance is under control, in essence, is to determine whether actual performance is a sample from the universe of controlled performance. Since complete knowledge of the universe is unattainable,

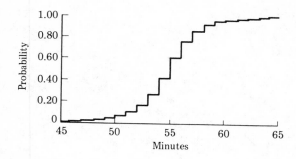

FIGURE 2. Controlled Assembly Time Distribution Function

we may accomplish our purpose by comparing the probability distribution of actual cost with that of the controlled cost. The deviation between the two probability distributions will be called "cost deviation." For a nonparametric distribution, the cost deviation may be expressed by the arithmetic differences in frequency functions or distribution functions (Appendix-part I); for parametric distribution, we may express cost deviation by ratios or some functions of the parameters of probability distributions. (Appendix-part II) When cost deviation is small, i.e., when the probability distribution of actual cost is approximately the same as that of controlled cost, the actual performance is considered under control, and vice versa.

An Example

Assume that we wish to evaluate the performance of a group of assembly workers for a certain day whose actual assembly time, a frequency function and distribution function are given in Table 2. Assume that we do not know the parametric distribution function of the universe; then we may express cost deviation in terms of arithmetic differences in frequency function or distribution function as shown in Table 3, or Figures 3 and 4.

QUANTITATIVE EVALUATION

PROCEDURES OF IMPLEMENTATION[11]

It is necessary to develop a scientific method of evaluating the significance of cost deviation as defined in the preceding section. The author favors a probabilistic significance over the simple use of absolute figures.

There are numerous theorems in mathematical statistics which concern testing the hypothesis that two samples are drawn from the same universe.[12] In general, these theorems state that, given sizes of samples, we can mathematically derive the probability that the deviations, which are computed differently in different theorems,[13] fall within a certain specified value. Thus it is possible to reach a conclusion with a certain degree of assurance whether two samples are from the same universe by comparing the actual deviations of the probability distribution of

---

[11] Only a general procedure is given in this section. The specific detailed procedure is left to the reader.

[12] For example, see Appendix at the end of this reading. These are the most suitable theorems for performance evaluation purposes.

[13] For example, see Appendix at the end of this reading.

TABLE 2   Assembly Labor Time Actual Cost

Assembly Time (minutes)	Frequency of Occurrence	Frequency Function	Distribution Function
45	1	.005	.005
46	1	.005	.010
47	2	.010	.020
48	3	.015	.035
49	4	.020	.055
50	6	.030	.085
51	12	.060	.145
52	16	.080	.225
53	24	.120	.345
54	32	.160	.505
55	34	.170	.675
56	26	.130	.805
57	17	.085	.890
58	10	.050	.940
59	5	.025	.965
60	2	.010	.975
61	2	.010	.985
62	1	.005	.990
63	1	.005	.995
64	1	.005	1.000
Total	200	1.000	

TABLE 3   Controlled vs. Actual Assembly Labor Time Probability Distributions

Assembly Time (minutes)	Frequency Function			Distribution Functions		
	Controlled	Actual	Deviation	Controlled	Actual	Deviation
45	.005	.005	—0—	.005	.005	—0—
46	.005	.005	—0—	.010	.010	—0—
47	.010	.010	—0—	.020	.020	—0—
48	.010	.015	.005	.030	.035	.005
49	.015	.020	.005	.045	.055	.010
50	.020	.030	.010	.065	.085	.020
51	.040	.060	.020	.105	.145	.040
52	.060	.080	.020	.165	.225	.060
53	.100	.120	.020	.265	.345	.080
54	.150	.160	.010	.415	.505	.090
55	.200	.170	.030	.615	.675	.060
56	.150	.130	.020	.765	.805	.040
57	.100	.085	.015	.865	.890	.025
58	.060	.050	.010	.925	.940	.015
59	.035	.025	.010	.960	.965	.005
60	.015	.010	.005	.975	.975	—0—
61	.010	.010	—0—	.985	.985	—0—
62	.005	.005	—0—	.990	.990	—0—
63	.005	.005	—0—	.995	.995	—0—
64	.005	.005	—0—	1.000	1.000	—0—
Total	1.000	1.000				

two samples with the mathematically derived deviation.

Applying the theorems to performance evaluation, management must first determine a desired degree of assurance that it wishes to have from the results. This desired degree of assurance is best specified in terms of probability. From the desired

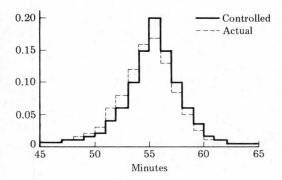

FIGURE 3. Controlled vs. Actual Assembly Time Frequency Function

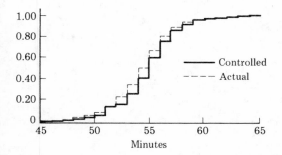

FIGURE 4. Controlled vs. Actual Assembly Time Distribution Function

assurance, the size of the sample used in establishing controlled cost, and the size of the sample of actual performance to be evaluated, a corresponding "allowable deviation" between the probability distribution of controlled cost and that of actual cost is either computed using a mathematical function, or merely extracted from a mathematical table. Meanwhile, the "actual deviation" is computed directly from the probability distribution of actual cost and that of the controlled cost. Finally, the actual deviation is compared with the allowable deviation to determine whether two samples are from the same universe. In other words, we conclude whether the actual performance is under control. These procedures are presented in a flow chart in Figure 5.

INTERPRETATION OF THE RESULTS

In the process of using samples to test the truth of a hypothesis—two samples are from the same universe—there is no certainty that a mistake will not be made unless the sizes of sample are equal to the size of the universe. Since the probability of making errors is inherent in the conclusion, it is important that the significance of the decision be fully understood.

When the actual deviation computed from actual cost and controlled cost falls within the allowable precision computed using a mathematical function or taken from a table, the actual performance

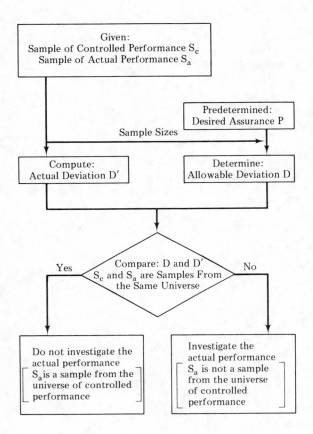

FIGURE 5. Flow Chart of General Test Procedure

should be accepted as under control and corrective managerial action is not required. The acceptance of actual performance as under control may result from:

1. The probability distribution of actual cost falling within the allowable deviation limits of the probability distribution of controlled cost, or

2. Chance variation causing the probability distribution of actual cost to fall within the allowable deviation limits of the probability distribution of controlled cost, in which case unsatisfactory performance in this category will be overlooked. (Type II error)

When the actual deviation exceeds the allowable deviation, the actual performance will be rejected and considered to be not under control. Managerial investigation of the performance is then necessary.

Rejection of the actual performance may be the result of:

1. The probability distribution of actual cost deviating from the probability distribution of controlled cost in excess of allowable deviation; managerial investigation will reveal the irregularity of operations; or

2. Chance variation causing the probability distribution of actual cost to exceed the allowable deviation from the controlled cost; investigation by management will not disclose any operating deficiencies. (Type I error)

Type I error may cause undesirable process changes and unjustifiable criticism of personnel, tools or materials. Type II error may result in overlooking evidence of impending actual problems and making it difficult to attain the best performance. Given a set of sample sizes, a decrease in one type of error must inevitably be accompanied by an increase in the other type; therefore, an economic balance in both types of error must be maintained to avoid frequent occurrence of errors.

ADVANTAGES OF THE CONTROLLED COST SYSTEM

The proposed controlled cost system is based on the probability distribution of cost and is aimed at correcting inadequacies of the conventional standard cost system based on a single value or a range of costs. The advantages of the proposed system are summarized as follows:

1. Realistic specification of controlled cost is achieved. Because of the variability of performance, it is impossible to attain uniform performance or confine performance to a certain narrow range as postulated under the conventional single value or range standard cost system. The proposed controlled cost system specifies what cost should be in terms of a probability distribution of cost, thus properly reflects the variability of cost. Occasional extreme fluctuations due to chance causes are also an integral part

of controlled cost. The result is a more realistic and attainable specification of a cost objective.

2. It avoids unrealistic assumptions. The single value standard cost system assumes that a perfectly controlled operation should yield uniform performance. The range concept standard cost system assumes that a controlled operation will fluctuate only within a certain specific narrow range. Variability of performance and inevitable presence of chance causes indicate that these assumptions are contrary to facts. On the other hand, the sole assumption in the controlled cost system is the tendency of cost toward a stable pattern of probability distribution when a process is under control. This assumption is well recognized by quality control engineers. Instead of making assumptions as to the knowledge of the universe, the controlled cost system recognizes that both controlled cost *and* actual cost are merely samples and proceeds with the analysis accordingly.

3. Thorough analysis of cost is achieved. The conventional single value standard cost system limits the analysis of cost to the arithmetic mean of cost. The range concept standard cost system simply distinguishes cost existing within the control limits from cost falling outside the control limits. Even the modified range concept standard cost system mentioned earlier in this paper fails to consider the irregular pattern of variation within the control limits. The result is an oversimplification of the problem and insufficient analysis of cost. Through comparison of probability distribution of costs, the controlled cost system extends the analysis of cost from the mean to variance, median, mode, skewness, kurtosis, etc. Such an analysis may disclose discrepancies that would be overlooked from sole reli-

ance on the arithmetic mean or separation of cost between those within the control limits and those outside the control limits.

4. Quantitative evaluation of results is achieved. Except in the initial selection of the desired assurance, the implementation of the controlled cost system is based on probability, statistics and sampling theory. The use of judgment and intuition is minimized, and the probability of making erroneous decisions due to human errors is reduced.

APPENDIX

I. Kolmogorov-Smirnov Limit Theorem

Let $(X_{11}, X_{12} \ldots, (X_{1n_1})$ and $(X_{21}, X_{22}, \ldots, X_{2n_2})$ be two sets of random samples size n_1, and n_2 from the same universe. The empirical distributions of the two samples are $S_{1n_1}(x)$ and $S_{2n_2}(x)$, respectively. Consider the random variable:

$$Dn_1 n_2 = \max | S_{1n_1}(x) - S_{2n_2}(x) |$$

Let $n = n_1 n_2 / (n_1 + n_2)$ and $Qn_1 n_2(\lambda)$ be the distribution function of the random variable $\sqrt{n} Dn_1 n_2$ thus

$$Qn_1 n_2(\lambda) = P(Dn_1 n_2 < \lambda/\sqrt{n})$$

then $Qn_1 n_2(\lambda)$ has the limiting distribution function:

$$Qn_1 n_2(\lambda) = \sum_{k=-\infty}^{\infty} (-1)^k \exp(-2k^2\lambda^2)$$

For details of the theorem and table values of $Qn_1 n_2(\lambda)$, see Marek Fisz, *Probability Theory and Mathematical Statistics*, Third Edition: (John Wiley & Sons, Inc., 1963), pp. 394-405, 664.

In short, the theorem states that if two samples are taken from the same universe, the maximum of the absolute values of the differences in the distribution functions of the two samples has a known limiting distribution function. If the distribution function of the universe of controlled performance is not known, we may use this theorem. Actual cost deviation is the maximum of the absolute values of the differences in the distribution functions of controlled cost and actual cost, which is compared with the allowable deviation $Dn_1 n_2$. Note that this is a non-parametric theorem.

II. Sampling Distribution of Means and Variances:

Assume that two sets of random samples $(X_{11}, X_{12}, \ldots, X_{1n_1})$ and $(X_{21}, X_{22}, \ldots, X_{2n_2})$, size n_1, and n_2, are taken from a normally distributed universe with an unknown mean and variance. The means and variances of the two samples are these:

$$\bar{X}_1 = \frac{\Sigma X_{1i}}{n_1} \quad S_1^2 = \frac{\Sigma(X_{1i} - \bar{X}_1)^2}{n_1 - 1}$$

$$\bar{X}_2 = \frac{\Sigma X_{2i}}{n_2} \quad S_2^2 = \frac{\Sigma(X_{2i} - \bar{X}_2)^2}{n_2 - 1}$$

Then, the statistic given by the formula

$$F = \frac{S_1^2}{S_2^2}$$

has an F-distribution with $n_1 - 1, n_2 - 2$ degrees of freedom. And the statistic given by the formula

$$t = \frac{\bar{X}_1 - \bar{X}_2}{S_p \sqrt{(1/n_1) + (1/n_2)}}$$

where

$$S_p^2 = \frac{(n_1 - 1)S_1^2 + (n_2 - 1)S_2^2}{n_1 + n_2 - 2}$$

has a t-distribution with $n_1 + n_2 - 2$ degrees of freedom. For details of the theorem and table values, see Wilfrid J.

Dixon and Frank J. Massey, Jr., *Introduction to Statistical Analysis,* Second Edition: (McGraw-Hill Book Company, Inc., 1957), pp. 103-104, 121-122, 390, 403. In short, the theorem states that if two samples are selected from a normally distributed universe, then certain values computed from means, variances, and sizes of samples have known probability distributions. Note that the theorem does not presume knowledge of the values of the mean and variance of the universe, although the universe is known to have a normal distribution.

The elements of cost data may sometimes be the mean of some random variables. For example, a weekly performance may consist of forty elements of hourly average performance. The central limit theorem of mathematical statistics tells us that data of this type will be approximately normally distributed. Thus we may use the theorem given above for cost evaluation. Allowed deviations are the F and t table values and the actual deviations are computed from the means and variances of actual cost and controlled cost.

Input - Output Analysis for Cost Accounting, Planning and Control

John Leslie Livingstone

Georgia Institute of Technology

Input-output analysis is shown as a general model of which the matrix cost allocation model is a special case. A comprehensive example is presented to illustrate the use of the input-output model in cost allocation, planning and control. Input-output analysis is particularly useful in situations characterized by a high degree of interaction because the model affords a basis for segmenting and analyzing such interactions.

The author wishes to express appreciation to Gerald L. Salamon, doctoral candidate at The Ohio State University, for helpful comments on this paper.

Reprinted from *The Accounting Review*, XLIV (January 1969), 48-64. Used by permission of John Leslie Livingstone and *The Accounting Review*.

Several articles in the recent accounting literature have dealt with the allocation of costs among interacting departments in an organization.[1] The term "interacting departments" is used here to describe departments which both make and receive allocations of costs to and from other departments. An example would be a service department which supports several operating departments and which in

[1]Thomas H. Williams and Charles H. Griffin, "Matrix Theory and Cost Allocation," *The Accounting Review* (July 1964), pp. 671-78. Neil Churchill, "Linear Algebra and Cost Allocations: Some Examples," *The Accounting Review* (October 1964), pp. 894-904. Rene P. Manes, "Comment on Matrix Theory and Cost Allocation," *The Accounting Review* (Teachers' Clinic) (July 1965), pp. 640-43.

turn receives support from other service departments.

The articles cited make use of simultaneous linear equation systems and linear algebra to handle the interactive cost allocation problems. The purpose of this paper is to present some more powerful extensions of these techniques and to show their uses for planning and decision-making. This will be done through input-output analysis. It will be shown that input-output analysis is a general model, of which the matrix cost allocation model is a special case.

MATRIX COST ALLOCATION

To show the link between matrix cost allocation and input-output analysis it is convenient to borrow the example used by Williams and Griffin.[2] This example is based on five interacting service departments and three operating departments, and is summarized as follows.

Cost Allocation Percentage

	Allocations from Service Departments				
	1	*2*	*3*	*4*	*5*
To Service Departments					
1	0	0	5	10	20
2	0	0	10	5	20
3	10	10	0	5	20
4	5	0	10	0	20
5	10	10	5	0	0
To Operating Departments					
A	25	80	20	0	10
B	25	0	30	40	5
C	25	0	20	40	5
	100%	100%	100%	100%	100%

Direct costs of each department, before any allocations are:

Service Departments	
1	$ 8,000
2	$ 12,000
3	$ 6,000
4	$ 11,000
5	$ 13,000

[2]Williams and Griffin, *op. cit.*, p. 675.

Operating Departments	
A	$120,000
B	$200,000
C	$ 80,000

The following system of simultaneous equations is formed:

$$(1) \quad X_1 \qquad -.05X_3 - .10X_4 \\ -.20X_5 = 8,000$$

$$(2) \qquad X_2, -.10X_3 - .05X_4 \\ -.20X_5 = 12,000$$

$$(3) -.10X_1 - .10X_2, +. \quad X_3 - .05X_4 \\ -.20X_5 = 6,000$$

$$(4) -.05X_1 \qquad -.10X_3 + \quad X_4 \\ -.20X_5 = 11,000$$

$$(5) -.10X_1 - .10X_2 -.05X_3 \\ + \quad X_5 = 13,000$$

Where X_i is the redistributed cost of the ith service department after receiving cost allocations from the other service departments. In matrix form these equations are expressed as $Ax = b$, where A is the matrix of cost allocation percentages, x is the vector of redistributed service department costs with elements X_1, X_2, ..., X_5, and b is the vector of service departments' direct costs.

The system is solved for x by premultiplying $Ax = b$ by the inverse of A, so that $x = A^{-1}b$. The result is:

$$\chi = \begin{bmatrix} X_1 \\ X_2 \\ X_3 \\ X_4 \\ X_5 \end{bmatrix} = \begin{bmatrix} 13,657.46 \\ 17,503.59 \\ 13,290.64 \\ 16,368.06 \\ 16,780.64 \end{bmatrix}$$

By summing equations (1) through (5) we get:

$$.75X_1 + .80X_2 + .70X_3 + .80X_4 \\ + .20X_5 = \$50,000$$

so that a total of $50,000 (which is the total of service department direct costs, ΣB_i) is allocated to the operating departments.

The X_i are now distributed to operating departments, by using the matrix of percentages of service department costs allocable to operating departments to premultiply the x vector, as follows:

$$\begin{bmatrix} .25 & .80 & .20 & 0 & .10 \\ .25 & 0 & .30 & .40 & .05 \\ .25 & 0 & .20 & .40 & .05 \end{bmatrix} \begin{bmatrix} 13,657.46 \\ 17,503.59 \\ 13,290.64 \\ 16,368.06 \\ 16,780.64 \end{bmatrix}$$

$$= \begin{bmatrix} 21,755 \\ 14,787 \\ 13,458 \end{bmatrix}$$

which, subject to some small rounding errors, gives the allocation to the three operating departments of the $50,000 of service department costs.

multiplication instead of the three sets of matrix operations used above.

INPUT-OUTPUT REPRESENTATION

Input-output analysis summarizes transactions between all possible economic units involved, in a square matrix. For this reason we express our example in such a manner below, adding zeros to indicate the absence of cost flows from operating to service departments.

We refer to the above matrix as A^* and, as before, we use the vectors x (now 8 by 1, to include all departments—both service and operating) and b (also now 8 by 1).

In our matrix formulation of equations 1 through 5 earlier, the matrix A actually consisted of the service department reciprocal cost allocation percentages subtracted from an identity matrix

| | | Allocations from Departments | | | | | | | |
		1	2	3	4	5	A	B	C
	(1)	0	0	.05	.10	.20	0	0	0
	(2)	0	0	.10	.05	.20	0	0	0
	(3)	.10	.10	0	.05	.20	0	0	0
	(4)	.05	0	.10	0	.20	0	0	0
To Departments	(5)	.10	.10	.05	0	0	0	0	0
	(A)	.25	.80	.20	0	.10	0	0	0
	(B)	.25	0	.30	.40	.05	0	0	0
	(C)	.25	0	.20	.40	.05	0	0	0

To the vector of redistributed service department costs we add the vector of direct costs of operating departments and arrive at the total costs—both allocated and direct—of operating departments, as follows:

$$\begin{bmatrix} 21,755 \\ 14,787 \\ 13,458 \end{bmatrix} + \begin{bmatrix} 120,000 \\ 200,000 \\ 80,000 \end{bmatrix} = \begin{bmatrix} 141,755 \\ 214,787 \\ 93,458 \end{bmatrix}$$

We now recast the same example in terms of input-output analysis and show the same result achieved in a single matrix

of the same dimensions. This is seen in equations 1 through 5 by the unity coefficients along the main diagonal and negative or zero coefficients elsewhere.

We now formalize this procedure and define:

$$A = I - A^*.$$

The input-output conditions[3] for clearing

[3]See R. G. D. Allen, *Mathematical Economics* (Macmillan, 1963), p. 483. Our formulation is of an open (rather than closed) system.

all costs out of service departments into operating departments are:[4]

$$Ax = b.$$

Since we are given b and want to find x, we have:

$$x = A^{-1}b$$

and the reader who makes this computation will find that:

$$\chi = \begin{bmatrix} 13,658 \\ 17,503 \\ 13,290 \\ 16,368 \\ 16,780 \\ 141,755 \\ 214,787 \\ 93,458 \end{bmatrix}$$

which is the same result that we previously obtained in three steps of matrix operations.

In our example so far we have made no distinction between fixed and variable costs. Suppose that certain service departments have both fixed and variable costs. In particular, let us assume that the direct costs of departments 1 and 4 include fixed costs of $2,000 and $5,000, respectively. We can separate the fixed cost allocations by redefining the b vector for fixed costs only as:

$$b^T = [2,000 \ 0 \ 0 \ 5,000 \ 0 \ 0 \ 0 \ 0]$$

and recomputing x, which we rename x'. Then:

[4] Readers can, of course, verify from our example that this equation holds.

$$\chi' = A^{-1}b = \begin{bmatrix} 2,624 \\ 393 \\ 631 \\ 5,261 \\ 333 \\ 1,130 \\ 2,967 \\ 2,903 \end{bmatrix}$$

Now the last three elements of b total $7,000 and represent the fixed cost portion of the aggregate costs of operating departments. It is vitally important that the fixed cost portion be separated, otherwise the model automatically unitizes fixed costs as in absorption costing but does not allow for under- or overabsorption when activity levels change. Of course, the first five elements of b represent fixed cost components of service departments' total costs. By subtracting x' from x the variable costs of each department can be found.

With this information, unit fixed and variable costs can be computed by dividing these respective costs for each department by its unit output.

From these unit variable costs, and unit fixed costs computed for varying volumes of output, there can be developed breakeven analyses, flexible budgets and absorption rates for overhead for each department and the system as a whole.

In the above example we were given b, the vector of direct cost inputs, and solved for x, the output vector. Usually the input-output model is used for the opposite purpose. Given the output vector, it is sought to determine the inputs required. The model is briefly described below, after which we will again apply it to our example—this time as a planning technique to compute input resource requirements from an expected level of outputs.

THE BASIC INPUT-OUTPUT MODEL

The input-output model, which is due to Leontief,[5] analyzes transactions between economic activities, where an activity may represent an industry, a firm, or—as in our case—a single department or cost center. It is assumed that there is only one primary input (usually labor) and only one output for each activity. There are n activities and n output commodities, each of which may comprise a final product or an intermediate product serving as input for other activities. Production takes place through processes with fixed technological yields of constant proportionality. There is only one process used with no substitution in each activity. The use of only one process does not necessarily imply that alternative processes are non-existent. It may be that an activity has a production function that includes alternative processes, each with constant technological yields, and then elects a single, perhaps optimal, process for use. In this case the process selected is preferred only for a given set of prices.

The basis of the input-output model is a matrix of transactions (presently assumed to be in monetary terms), with a row and a column for each activity. The transactions matrix can be summarized as:

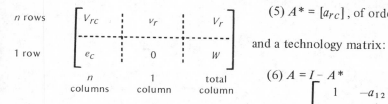

n rows	V_{rc}	v_r	V_r
1 row	e_c	0	W
	n columns	1 column	total column

[5]Wasily W. Leontief, *The Structure of American Economy 1919-1939*, second edition (Oxford University Press, 1951). A very good, concise description of the model is given in Richard Mattessich, *Accounting and Analytical Methods* (Richard D. Irwin, Inc., 1964), pp. 295-311.

The amounts V_{rc}(with $r, c = 1, 2, \ldots, n$) are the monetary values of output of the rth activity used as input by the cth activity. The rows thus represent distribution of the output of each activity, while the columns represent sources of the inputs of activities. The n dimensional vector, v_r, shows the final demand for each commodity (or the "bill of goods") and $V_r(n$ by 1) is the total output column so that:

(1) $V_r = v_r + \sum_c v_{rc}, r = 1, 2, \ldots, n.$

The n dimensional row vector e_c represents the costs of the primary input (say labor) to the activities, with a total of W, and thus:

$$W = \sum_c e_c$$

Fixed technological coefficients are assumed:

(3) $a_{rc} = v_{rc}/V_c \ r, c = 1, 2, \ldots, n$

which are the $(n + 1)$ elements of each column, respectively, divided by their sum, V_c, which is:

(4) $V_c = e_c + \sum_r v_{rc}.$

These give an input coefficient matrix:

(5) $A^* = [a_{rc}]$, of order n by n

and a technology matrix:

(6) $A = I - A^*$

$$= \begin{bmatrix} 1 & -a_{12} & \cdots & -a_{1n} \\ -a_{21} & 1 & \cdots & -a_{2n} \\ \hline -a_{n1} & -a_{n2} & \cdots & 1 \end{bmatrix}$$

The solution to the system, expressing the condition that all output is exactly distributed over uses (both final and intermediate) is:

(7) $A V_r = v_r$.

Note that equation (7) does not directly give us e_c which can be derived as follows: Given v_r, final demand, we compute V_r, total output, and then calculate e_c. From (7) we compute V_r,

(8) $V_r = A^{-1} v_r$.

Since all output is exactly distributed over uses, total inputs equal total output for each activity, i.e.,

(9) $V_r = V_c$ for all $r = c$

in other words, the row total for any activity equals its column total.

Now consider any column, with subscript $c = 0$. We can rewrite (3) as:

(10) $a_{ro} = v_{ro}/V_0$

and sum both sides over rows:

(11) $\sum_r a_{ro} = \sum_r v_{ro}/V_0$.

Similarly, (4) can be rewritten as:

(12) $V_0 = e_0 + \sum_r v_{ro}$.

Then, we divide (12) by V_0 and obtain:

(13) $1 = e_0/V_0 + \sum_r v_{ro}/V_0$

and substitute from (11) into (13):

(14) $1 = e_0/V_0 + \sum_r a_{ro}$

which can be rearranged into:

(15) $e_0 = V_0 \left(1 - \sum_r a_{ro} \right)$

Since V_0 is known to us from (8) and (9), and $\sum_r a_{ro}$ is given, e_0 can be computed from (15). Having set up the basic input-output model, we now apply it to our example as a planning technique to compute requirements for primary inputs from a given level of outputs.

INPUT-OUTPUT APPLIED TO PLANNING

Input-output applications normally proceed by gathering the data for the transactions matrix and then computing the technological coefficients from these data. We will follow this procedure, using the same example as before. The dollar transactions matrix in canonical (or standard) form is shown in Table 1.

The transactions matrix in Table 1 requires some explanation. Note that it differs in form from the cost allocation model where outputs were stated in columns and inputs along rows as shown above. The standard transactions matrix is the transpose of that arrangement, with outputs stated rowwise and inputs columnwise.

The vector V_r

$$V_r = \begin{bmatrix} 13,658 \\ 17,503 \\ \cdot \\ \cdot \\ \cdot \\ 93,458 \end{bmatrix}, 8 \text{ by } 1.$$

is seen to be identical with the vector x which we computed previously in the one-step procedure for cost allocation. Note that the vector V_c of column totals is simply the transpose of the V_r vector, so that the row and column totals for any activity are equal.

The V_r vector of final demand shows the output of operating departments

TABLE 1

			Inputs		
	1	*2*	*3*	*4*	*5*
(1)			1,366	683	1,366
(2)			1,750		1,750
(3)	655	1,329		1,329	665
(4)	1,637	818	818		
Outputs (5)	3,356	3,356	3,356	3,356	
(A)					
(B)					
(C)					
e_c	8,000	12,000	6,000	11,000	13,000
Total (V_r)	13,658	17,503	13,290	16,368	16,781

	A	*B*	*C*	v_r	Total (V_r)
(1)	3,415	3,414	3,414		13,658
(2)	14,003				17,503
(3)	2,658	3,986	2,658		13,290
(4)		6,548	6,547		16,368
Outputs (5)	1,679	839	839		16,781
(A)				141,755	141,755
(B)				214,787	214,787
(C)				93,458	93,458
e_c	120,000	200,000	80,000		450,000
Total (V_r)	141,755	214,787	93,458	450,000	977,600

which, as expected, totals $450,000 and equals the scalar, W, which is the total value of primary inputs (the elements of the e_c vector). It is worth pointing out that the overall total of the table, namely $977,600, amounts to twice the total of primary inputs ($450,000) or final demand, plus the sum of interactivity transfers ($77,600), i.e.:

$$2(450,000)+13,658+17,503+13,290$$
$$+ 16,368 + 16,781 = 977,600.$$

Thus the table adds to the aggregate value of all transactions of all activities in the system. The familiar macroeconomic quantities of gross national product, national income, consumption and so on that are used in national income accounting have their analogies at the micro level of our system of activities.

Payments to primary factors, or gross system product at factor prices, is $450,000—the sum of the e_c row, which is also gross system income, or total consumption—the sum of the v_r *column.* This is the fundamental identity of the product and expenditure sides in national (or here, system) income accounting. Interactivity transactions would, of course, be excluded as double-counting since they do not represent any value added. Thus, input-output analysis can be regarded generally as a double-entry accounting technique for recording and analyzing transactions between activities in an economic system.

Finally, in explanation of Table 1, it remains to show the derivation of the v_{rc}, i.e., the amounts in the upper left hand part of the transactions matrix. These are obtained by applying the cost allocation percentages previously given to the total redistributed cost of each service department. For instance, of service department #2's total redistributed costs of $17,503, 10% (or $1,750) each is allocated to departments 3 and 5 and the remaining 80% (or $14,003) to operating department A. We now calculate the a_{rc} to obtain A^*. Applying (3) to column 1 of the transactions matrix we have:

$$v_r = \begin{bmatrix} 0 \\ 0 \\ 0 \\ 0 \\ 0 \\ 14{,}176 \\ 21{,}479 \\ 9{,}346 \end{bmatrix}$$

$$V_1 = 13{,}658$$
$$a_{31} = v_{31}/V_1 = 665/13{,}658 = 0.0487$$
$$a_{41} = v_{41}/V_1 = 1{,}637/13{,}658 = 0.1199$$
$$a_{51} = v_{51}/V_1 = 3{,}356/13{,}658 = 0.2457$$
$$\frac{e_1/}{V_1} = \qquad = 8{,}000/13{,}658 = \underline{0.5857}$$
$$\text{Total} = \overline{1.0000}$$

The remaining columns are treated in the same way to compute A^* and then A, which is:

Then, from (8),

$$V_r = A^{-1} v_r = \begin{bmatrix} 1{,}359 \\ 1{,}742 \\ 1{,}326 \\ 1{,}636 \\ 1{,}668 \\ 14{,}176 \\ 21{,}479 \\ 9{,}346 \end{bmatrix}$$

$$\begin{bmatrix} 1 & & & -.1028 & -.0417 & -.0814 & -.0241 & -.0159 & -.0365 \\ & 1 & & -.1317 & & -.1043 & -.0988 & & \\ -.0487 & -.0759 & 1 & & -.0812 & -.0396 & -.0188 & -.0186 & -.0284 \\ -.1199 & -.0467 & -.0616 & 1 & & & & -.0305 & -.0701 \\ -.2457 & -.1918 & -.2525 & -.2050 & 1 & & -.0118 & -.0039 & -.0090 \\ & & & & & 1 & & & \\ & & & & & & 1 & & \\ & & & & & & & 1 & \\ & & & & & & & & 1 \end{bmatrix}$$

and

$$A^{-1} = \begin{bmatrix} 1.0386 & .0319 & .1391 & .0737 & .0934 & .0319 & .0217 & .0471 \\ .0424 & 1.0378 & .1734 & .0402 & .1186 & .1082 & .0056 & .0094 \\ .0767 & .0947 & 1.0410 & .0995 & .0573 & .0314 & .0238 & .0394 \\ .1312 & .0581 & .0889 & 1.0169 & .0203 & .0108 & .0348 & .0786 \\ .3096 & .2427 & .3485 & .2594 & 1.0643 & .0506 & .0235 & .0403 \\ & & & & & 1 & & \\ & & & & & & 1 & \\ & & & & & & & 1 \end{bmatrix}$$

Now, for any given final demand vector v_r we can compute e_c, the primary input resource requirements. For instance, consider a final demand one-tenth as large as before, so that:

Note that rounding error impairs the accuracy of the computation. We know from Table 1 that the elements of V_r should be (to the nearest dollar) 1,366, 1,750 and so on rather than the 1,359,

1,742, etc., above. This is due to the use of only four decimal places in setting up the A^* matrix, a nearest-dollar v_r vector, and use of a single-precision computer routine for the inversion of A.[6] The inaccuracy is of the order of one-half of one percent. Users wishing superior accuracy may be well-advised to resort to double-precision routines.[7]

Having determined V_r, the next step is to compute e_c, the primary input resource requirements. We use expression (15), which can be expressed in matrix form as:

$$(16)\ e_c = V_r^T Z$$

where Z is a matrix with elements

$$(1 - \sum_r a_{r0})$$

on the main diagonal and zeros elsewhere:

$$Z = \begin{bmatrix} \left(1 - \sum_r a_{r1}\right) & 0 \dots\dots 0 \\ 0 & \left(1 - \sum_r a_{r2}\right) \dots 0 \\ \hline 0 & 0 \quad \left(1 - \sum_r a_{rn}\right) \end{bmatrix}$$

In our example we have:[8]

$$Z = \begin{bmatrix} .5857 & 0 & 0 & 0 \\ 0 & .6856 & 0 & 0 \\ 0 & 0 & .4514 & 0 \\ 0 & 0 & 0 & .6721 \\ 0 & 0 & 0 & 0 \\ 0 & 0 & 0 & 0 \\ 0 & 0 & 0 & 0 \\ 0 & 0 & 0 & 0 \end{bmatrix}$$

$$\begin{bmatrix} 0 & 0 & 0 & 0 \\ 0 & 0 & 0 & 0 \\ 0 & 0 & 0 & 0 \\ 0 & 0 & 0 & 0 \\ .7747 & 0 & 0 & 0 \\ 0 & .8465 & 0 & 0 \\ 0 & 0 & .9311 & 0 \\ 0 & 0 & 0 & .8560 \end{bmatrix}$$

and using V_r corrected for rounding error,

$$e_c = [800\ \ 1{,}200\ \ 600\ \ 1{,}100\ \ 1{,}300 \\ 12{,}000\ \ 20{,}000\ \ 8{,}000],$$

which we can see from Table 1 is correct, being one-tenth of the primary input requirements in the table.

Expression (16) can be generalized and used to find any desired row of the dollar transactions matrix. The Z matrix applied to find e_c can be subscripted e. A Z matrix, Z_r, can be formulated to find any row r as follows:

$$Z_r = \begin{bmatrix} a_{r1} & 0 \dots 0 \\ 0 & a_{r2} \dots 0 \\ \hline 0 & 0 \dots a_{rn} \end{bmatrix}$$

and then (16) in general form becomes:

$$(17)\ r = V_r^T Z_r.$$

For instance let $r = 2$. Then:

$$Z_{33} = .1317, Z_{55} = .1043 \text{ and}$$
$$Z_{66} = .0988$$

with all other $Z_{ij} = 0$, and:

---

[6] Inversion was done using the General Electric Time-Sharing Service and one of its library routines called MATRIX***. Even though this program requires a redundant (for this purpose) matrix multiplication, its run time was 7 seconds. This run time (inefficiently used) for an 8 by 8 matrix inversion, is interesting to compare with the 10 seconds reported by Manes (*op. cit.*, p. 641) for a 5 by 5 matrix, which resulted in a loss of one-third of one percent average accuracy.

[7] See Manes, *op. cit.*, p. 641, for a report on the use of a double-precision routine.

[8] Note that the $(1 - \sum_r a_{r0})$ can be obtained by summing the columns of the A matrix.

row 2 $= V_r^T Z_2$

$= [0 \ 0 \ 175 \ 0 \ 175 \ 1400 \ 0 \ 0]$

which, it is seen from Table 1, is correct.

To summarize, it has been shown how any vector of expected final demand can be translated into the required vector of primary inputs. In addition, we have shown how to derive the associated inter-activity transactions. Once the A^{-1} and Z matrices have been computed, so long as the mix of services is constant, they can be used again and again for any values of expected final demand, and the computational load of evaluating the effects of various final demand vectors is quite light. Therefore, the technique has advantages for planning and resource allocation purposes, and also for ensuring proper coordination of input and output requirements. In fact, it conforms to the normal budgeting procedure of commencing with expected sales and then working back to determine production and other budgets consistent with the sales forecast. However, in the standard budget procedure this internal consistency is not assured as it is in input-output analysis—where the output of any activity is consistent with the demands, both final and from other activities, for its product.

The illustration above is only the most obvious application of input-output analysis for planning. Before proceeding to more sophisticated levels, however, it is necessary to examine the model in greater detail.

PHYSICAL COEFFICIENTS AND THE NUMERAIRE

The transactions matrix has so far been dealt with in terms of dollars. It can, however, be broken down into physical quantities and unit costs or prices which enables more precise planning use. The effects of price and quantity changes can then be separated in similar fashion to standard cost variance analysis.

Let there be n activities plus a final demand vector and a vector of primary inputs. Let x_{rc} be the physical amount of the input quantity X_r of the rth activity used by the cth activity. Then the physical transactions matrix is composed of elements x_{rc} and sums across rows to the vector X_r of total physical output. Let f_c be the vector of primary input quantities (say labor hours), summing to Y for all activities. Thus, the physical transaction matrix is:

$$
\begin{array}{c}
n \text{ rows} \\
\\
1 \text{ row}
\end{array}
\left[
\begin{array}{c:c:c}
x_{rc} & x_r & X_r \\
\hdashline
f_c & 0 & Y
\end{array}
\right]
$$

$$
\begin{array}{ccc}
n & 1 & \text{total} \\
\text{columns} & \text{column} & \text{column}
\end{array}
$$

Fixed physical coefficients, t_{rc}, are assumed:[9]

(18) $t_{rc} = x_{rc}/X_r$,

for all $r = c = 1, 2, \ldots, n$.

The t_{rc} comprise an input coefficient matrix, T^*, and a technology matrix $T = I - T^*$ which is n by n in dimension. The T matrix can be expanded by adding a bottom row of labor input coefficients, $-d_c$, where:

(19) $d_c = f_c/X_r$, for all $c = r$.

Finally we need two vectors of prices: p is the row vector of unit commodity prices, and w is the row vector of labor cost per unit of output, and both are n-dimensional.

The system takes as given T, x, and w. For all output to be exactly distributed over final and intermediate uses, the conditions are:

[9] These are analogous to physical standards for material and labor usage in a standard cost system.

(20) $TX_r = x_r$

(21) $pT = w$.

Note from (21) that the prices, p, are dependent on unit labor costs, w, just as in a standard cost system amounts transferred to work-in-process and finished goods depend on standard material, labor and overhead unit costs. In other words, output prices are determined by cost-based primary input prices, as is generally the case in accounting. In addition we can compute Y, total labor hours, and S, total labor costs (which equals system gross income or aggregate final demand), as follows:

(22) $Y = d_c X_r$

$= dcT^{-1}x_r$, substituting from (20)

and

(23) $S = px_r$

$= wX_r$

$= wT^{-1}x_r$, substituting from (20).

As mentioned before, prices of outputs are cost-determined by the w vector of labor unit costs (or—more generally—unit costs of whatever the primary input happens to be, say computer time for that matter). Since specification of w determines p, w can be called the numeraire vector, or common denominator for assigning value. Thus, w serves the same purpose as a set of standard costs, which are also exogenous, or given, in an accounting system.

Although perhaps theoretically less acceptable, it should be noted that there is no mathematical reason for w to be given. If p is given, equation (21) is then:

(24) $v_{rc} = p_r x_{rc}$

recalling that the v_{rc} are the dollar elements of the dollar transactions matrix and the x_{rc} are the elements of the physical transactions matrix. From (3) we have the dollar technological coefficients, a_{rc}:

(25) $a_{rc} = v_{rc}/V_c$

$= P_r x_{rc}/V_c$

$= (p_r/p_c)t_{rc}$

since for any $c = r$, $P_c X_r = V_c$.

Thus the relationship between a_{rc} and t_{rc} is determined by the ratio of the respective row and column unit prices. Then, given v_{rc}, the system can be solved as shown previously.

Up to now, we have followed the usual input-output approach of determining primary inputs given final demand, i.e., the last column vector of the transactions matrix is treated as exogenous (or given) and it is desired to find the last row vector (of primary inputs). However, any column vector and any row vector of the transactions matrix can be made exogenous, say the ith row and the jth column. Then the technical matrix A is reduced, by elimination of the ith row and the jth column, to order $(n-1)$, and the vector V_r of total output also becomes $(n-1)$ dimensional by elimination of the ith row. Expression (7) may then be generalized to :

(26) $A V_r = v_j$

where v_j is the given column vector of inputs to the jth activity.[10]

ANALYSIS OF INCREMENTAL AND OPPORTUNITY COSTS

In order to illustrate the analysis in terms of physical inputs and outputs, a new example is required. This is as follows:

[10] Allen, *op. cit.*, pp. 486-488.

		Process Inputs			Final Demand x_r	Total Output X_r
		1	2	3		
Process Outputs	(1) (lbs.)	0	14	30	36	80
	(2) (gals.)	4	0	48	18	70
	(3) (cu. ft.)	16	28	0	56	100
	Labor (hrs.)	20	98	72	0	190

Using (18) we compute the t_{rc}, for instance:

$$t_{21} = 4/80 = .05, \qquad t_{31} = 16/80 = .20.$$
$$t_{12} = 14/70 = .20, \qquad t_{32} = 28/70 = .40.$$

and then the technology matrix, T:

$$T = \begin{bmatrix} 1 & -.20 & -.30 \\ -.05 & 1 & -.48 \\ -.20 & -.40 & 1 \end{bmatrix}$$

Computation of the inverse results in:

$$T^{-1} = \begin{bmatrix} 1.13356 & .448934 & .555556 \\ .204826 & 1.31874 & .694444 \\ .308642 & .617284 & 1.38889 \end{bmatrix}$$

From (20) we have:

(27)
$$X_r = T^{-1} x_r = \begin{bmatrix} 80 \\ 70 \\ 100 \end{bmatrix}$$

which agrees with the transactions matrix above.

We now consider what it takes to produce one pound of final output from process 1. This is best shown by setting final demand accordingly, i.e.:

$$x_r = \begin{bmatrix} 1 \\ 0 \\ 0 \end{bmatrix}$$

Then:

$$X_r = T^{-1} x_r = \begin{bmatrix} 1.13356 \\ .204826 \\ .308642 \end{bmatrix}$$

which is simply the first column of T^{-1}. Thus, the columns of T^{-1} show the total production required to end up with a single unit of output from each activity. For instance, to produce one gallon from process 2 requires 0.448934 pounds from process 1, 1.31874 gallons from process 2 and 0.617284 cubic feet from process 3.

Note that 1.31874 gallons from process 2 are needed as intermediate output, since this process requires inputs from processes 1 and 3—both of which in turn, require inputs from process 2. Note also that the T matrix does not give this information. It shows inputs of 0.20 pounds, from process 1 and 0.40 cubic feet from process 3 to produce 1 gallon from process 2. However, these are simply the direct or "first round" inputs and not the total additions to production after allowing for indirect effects through the system. The cumulative results, after all the feedback effects have worked themselves out, are therefore shown in the T^{-1} matrix. In other words, the analysis is not *ceteris paribus* but *mutatis mutandis*.[11]

By use of the T^{-1} matrix *mutatis mutandis* physical standards become available, relating the work loads of the respective process to the demands im-

[11] For further discussion and illustration of *mutatis mutandis* vs. *ceteris paribus* approaches see Yuji Ijiri, Ferdinand K. Levy and R. C. Lyon, "A Linear Programming Model for Budgeting and Financial Planning," *Journal of Accounting Research* (Autumn 1963), pp. 208-210.

posed by exogenous activities.[12] These standards are useful tools in planning for the logistics of changes in the future levels of activities, in budgeting for processes, activities and products, and in appraising performance for control purposes.

We now introduce monetary values to the system. It is convenient to take as given the price vector p, rather than the more usual step of determining p from a given w, the unit wage cost. Let:

$$p = [5 \quad 10 \quad 15]$$

with elements representing the dollar cost per pound, gallon and cubic foot, respectively, of the output of each process.[13] Then, from (21):

$$(28)\ w = pT = [1.5 \quad 3 \quad 8.7].$$

Using (19) we compute the labor input coefficients:

$$(29)\ d_c = [20/80\ 98/70\ 72/100]$$
$$= [0.25 \quad 1.4 \quad 0.72]$$

and from (22) we set Y, total labor hours:

$$(30)\ Y = d_c X_r = 190$$

which is also verified as correct from the transactions matrix. Finally, from (23), S, total labor cost is:

$$(31)\ S = w X_r = \$1,200.$$

Now the dollar transactions matrix can be completed:

	Process Inputs		
	1	*2*	*3*
Outputs (1)	0	70	150
(2)	40	0	480
(3)	240	420	0
e_c	120	210	870
Total V_c	400	700	1,500

	Final Demand v_r	Total Output V_r
Outputs (1)	180	400
(2)	180	700
(3)	840	1,500
e_c	0	1,200
Total V_c	1,200	3,800

The v_{rc} were computed as in (24), by multiplying the x_{rc} by their unit prices and similarly for the v_r *and* V_r vectors. The labor costs, e_c, were inserted as balancing figures,[14] which sum to $1,200 as shown in (31) above.

We now consider the effects of changes in prices. Suppose that a wage rate increase takes place in process 1. Previously, as shown in the physical and dollar transactions matrices, 20 hours of labor cost $120 giving an average wage rate of $6 an hour. Say that this average now becomes $10 an hour.

From (29) we computed the labor input coefficient[15] for the process 1, d_1:

$$d_1 = 0.25$$

and multiplied d_1 by the wage rate to calculate w, the vector of labor cost per unit of output. Previously W_1 (the first element of w) was 0.25 times $6 or 1.5. Now, with an average wage rate of $10 an hour:

$$W_1 = 0.25\ (\$10) = 2.5$$

---

[12] For discussion of the dependent nature of service departments on the volume demands of other activities, and for exposition of budgeting and control techniques with respect to non-interactive departments, see Gordon Shilling-law, *Cost Accounting*, revised edition (Richard D. Irwin, Inc., 1967), pp. 481-494.

[13] Given the direct linear proportionality of cost and volume in the system, p and w represent both average and incremental unit costs.

[14] They could be directly derived by multiplying each W_r (elements of w) with the corresponding X_r element, for instance $W_1 = 1.5, X_1 = 80$ and $e_1 = W_1 X_1 = 1.5(80) = \$120.$

[15] Representing the hours of labor required to produce one unit of output in that process.

and

$$w = [2.5 \quad 3 \quad 8.7].[16]$$

From (23) we compute S, total labor costs:

$$S = wX_r$$
$$= \$1,280$$

which have increased from the previous \$1,200 in the dollar transactions matrix. The increase of \$80 is, of course, the 20 hours in process 1 multiplied by the rise of \$4 an hour in the wage rate. This can be computed directly by using the change in w, which we designate w'. Then:

$$w' = [1 \quad 0 \quad 0]$$

and

$$w'X_r = \$80 = S'$$

which is the increment to the total wage bill.

From the new value of w a revised dollar transactions matrix can be derived. First, from (21),

$$(32)\ p = wT^{-1} =$$
$$[6.13356 \quad 10.448934 \quad 15.555556].$$

By multiplying the x_{rc}, the x_r and the X_r by these new unit prices, the revised dollar transactions matrix is found to be:

wages increased by \$80, total output increased by \$90.69 in process 1, \$31.42 in process 2, and \$55.56 in process 3, amounting to \$177.67 altogether. This illustrates the multiplier (or amplification) effect in the interactive system. It can be more directly analyzed by again taking the incremental approach with respect to p, where we use p' to designate the change or difference between the old and revised p vectors. From (32):

$$(33)\ p' = w'T^{-1} =$$
$$[1.13356 \quad .448934 \quad .555556].$$

Using p' to multiply the x_{rc}, x_r and X_r we can compute the changes in the dollar transactions matrix. These changes are, of course, the increments resulting in each input-output element of each process in the dollar transactions matrix due to the change in wage rate in process 1. Thus, for each increment in the cost of primary inputs, there is a complementary set of process opportunity costs arising in the interactive system.

It is worth glancing back at (33) and noting that the elements of p' are identical to the first row of T^{-1}. The reason for this is as follows: labor costs in process 1 went up by \$4 an hour. Since 4 pounds of output are produced per hour in process 1, the increase in labor costs per pound, is \$1. In other words, $W_1' = 1$ as we previously found.

		Process Inputs		Final Demand v_r	Total Output V_r
	1	2	3		
(1)	0	85.87	184.01	220.81	490.69
Outputs (2)	41.79	0	501.55	188.08	731.42
(3)	248.90	435.55	0	871.11	1,555.56
e_c	200.00	210.00	870.00	0	1,280.00
Total V_c	490.69	731.42	1,555.56	1,280.00	4,057.67

A comparison with the previous dollar transactions matrix shows that while total

Now the first row of T^{-1} shows the inputs in pounds, from process 1 required to produce one unit of output in each process. Equivalently, this row shows the increase in cost per unit of each process

[16]Note, by comparison with (28), that remaining elements of w are unchanged.

from a \$1 per pound increase in the costs of process 1. Therefore, given the strict linear proportionality of the system, we can generalize that the ith row of T^{-1} shows the unit opportunity cost in each process per \$1 increment in the unit cost of the ith process. Thus by using (33), the effects on the system of any labor rate change in any process can easily and speedily be computed. Where labor rates vary in more than one process, the effects of individual changes can be computed separately if desired and then in the aggregate.

It should be emphasized that this analysis of cost changes and their effects was made without any need to adjust the T matrix. Any adjustments to T would, of course, have required the computation of a new inverse, T^{-1}, to be used in the analysis. This is an advantage of basing the system on physical relationships and explicit independent price vectors, rather than using monetary values as the original basis.[17] If the system had been built from scratch on a dollar transactions matrix, any change in wage rates (or in any other prices) would have altered the input-output coefficients and thus required computation of a new inverse.

Note that we refer to a change in the unit cost of a primary input as an incremental cost, and to its effect on the costs of the system as the associated opportunity cost. It was also shown that the interactive nature of the system amplified the incremental cost into a larger cost[18]—which we termed opportunity cost. This is a true opportunity cost since it reflects the total sacrifice associated with the wage rate increase on a *mutatis mutandis* (rather than a *ceteris paribus*) basis. In other words, it takes into account the effects on every other activity resulting from the single change in wage rate, as opposed to the more usual approach of assuming that only one or a few effects are considered, while all others are treated as constant.

EXPANDING THE TRANSACTIONS MATRIX

The analysis can be extended to take into account factors not yet considered. For instance, the notion of beginning and ending inventories has not explicitly been considered. Implicitly, however, there has been an unstated inventory assumption made in the following sense. Given a system of interacting activities, many or most of which use each other's outputs as inputs, it seems very unlikely that the system could start up or continue to operate without inventories. In the absence of inventories the situation may be likened to attempting to produce a chicken without an egg or vice versa.[19]

Extension of the system can be accomplished to include inventories and other factors by expanding the transactions matrix. Instead of a single vector for final demand it is possible to have a series of column vectors such as the following, one for each component of final demand:

Additions to Inventory	*Outputs Sold Outside Without Further Processing*

---

[17] For a more general and complete discussion of separating physical measurement and monetary valuation in accounting see Yuji Ijiri, "Physical Measures and Multi-Dimensional Accounting," in *Research in Accounting Measurement*, R. K. Jaedicke, Y. Ijiri and O. Nielsen, editors (American Accounting Association, 1966), pp. 150-164.

[18] In our example, for instance, incremental cost of the wage rate increase in process 1 was \$80, while the cost of total output went up by \$177.67.

[19] It is possible for activities to use their own output as input. Usually self-consumption is offset against output. For the opposite approach see Yuji Ijiri, "An Application of Input-Output Analysis to Some Problems in Cost Accounting," *Management Accounting*, (April 1968), pp. 60-61.

*Outputs
for Use
Elsewhere
in Firm*

*Sales to
Customer
Classes
A, B, . . . N*

Similarly, the vector of primary inputs can be expanded into a series of row vectors such as:

Inventory Depletion
Direct Outside Purchases
Depreciation Allowances
Materials
Labor
Variable Overhead
Fixed Overhead
Profit Margin

Thus, the expanded transactions matrix (in either physical or money terms) now consists of multiple vectors of final demand and of primary input components, in addition to the sector which states the input-output flows between processes or activities.[20] The latter sector is normally termed the processing sector.

For the purposes of performing any computations it is necessary to collapse the multiple vectors of final demand and primary input components into single vectors by addition. Then the computation is carried out as previously shown. However, after computation the computed vector (usually that of primary inputs) can be disaggregated again into its components, so that an expanded transactions matrix is made available. The disaggregation may be done by using previously established ratios between various components (such as proportionalities between materials, labor, variable overhead and profit) and/or use of constraints (such as a limit to the quantities of

beginning inventory available, or a constant amount as in the case of fixed costs). A component such as inputs purchased direct from outside may serve as a slack, to provide for demands in excess of available inventory quantities.

With respect to lump sum constant items such as fixed costs and possible depreciation and profit (unless treated as factors directly varying with output volume) the cautions previously noted must be observed. Also, it should be remembered that the transactions matrix is required to meet a symmetry condition: that total inputs match total outputs. Thus, primary input components, such as depreciation and profit for example, must have their theoretical output complements—such as "Outputs Used Elsewhere in the Firm" (perhaps in capital investment) and "Sales," respectively. Of course, the dollar totals of aggregate final demand and primary inputs must be the same.

CONCLUSIONS

As in the case of every model, input-output analysis is conditioned on strict assumptions. These were previously described, but will be briefly noted below. The would-be user is cautioned to ensure that the assumptions are met by the situation in which the model is hoped to be applied. Three critical assumptions may be summarized as follows.

(a)   *One standard output for each activity:* it is required that each activity produces a single, standardized output. If individual activities were to vary their commodities produced, we would not be able to specify the fixed input-output coefficients needed to form the technology matrix. If there are joint or by-products it is necessary for them to be produced in constant

---

[20] An example of a transactions matrix expanded to include ending inventories, overhead, and profit, appears in Shawki M. Farag, "A Planning Model for the Divisionalized Enterprise," *The Accounting Review*, (April 1968), pp. 317-318.

combination, so that a fixed ratio exists between the quantities of each product of a process and thus this combination can be specified as a standardized single output. Also, the same commodity should not be produced by two or more processes, since this creates alternative rather than unique input-output coefficients.

(b) *Fixed input-output coefficients:* it is not permissible for the proportions among inputs used in a process to be varied. If such input substitutions are allowable it again becomes inpossible to specify fixed input-output coefficients from which to derive the technology matrix.

(c) *A linear homogenous production function:* this requires the relations between inputs and outputs not only to be linear, which follows from (b) above, but also to be homogenous. The mathematical condition for linear homogeneity is:[21]

$$f(kx_1 \ kx_2, \ldots, kx_n)$$
$$= kf(x_1, x_2, \ldots, x_n)$$

[21] See Allen, *op. cit.,* p. 335.

For instance the function $y = a_1 x_1 + a_2 x_2$ meets this condition since:

$$a_1 k x_1 + a_2 k x_2 = k(a_1 x_1 + a_2 x_2)$$

However, the function $y = c + a_1 x_1 + a_2 x_2$ does not since:

$$c + a_1 k x_1 + a_2 k x_2$$
$$\neq k(c + a_1 x_1 + a_2 x_2)$$

In the model, each column of the technological matrix represents a process in the firm's production function. If any process is not linear homogeneous due to the presence of a constant term, a different input-output coefficient would be needed for each value of the x_1 (i.e., for every possible volume of operation the technological yield would vary). Therefore, once again, we would not have fixed input-output coefficients for the technology matrix.

Subject to the assumptions outlined above, input-output analysis may usefully be applied as shown in this paper. There seems to be no reason why it cannot be as valuable a technique for intrafirm as it has been for interfirm and interindustry economic analysis.

SELECTED REFERENCES FOR CHAPTER 5

BOOKS

Butler, William F., and Robert A. Kavesh, eds., *How Business Economists Forecast.* Englewood Cliffs, N. J.: Prentice-Hall, Inc., 1966.

Fisher, Gene H. *Cost Considerations in Systems Analysis.* New York: American Elsevier Publishing Company, Inc., 1971.

Johnston, J., *Statistical Cost Analysis.* New York: McGraw-Hill Book Company, 1960.

Staubus, George J., *Activity Costing and Input-Output Accounting.* Homewood, Ill.: Richard D. Irwin, Inc., 1971.

Vatter, William J., *Standards for Cost Analysis,* A Report to the Comptroller General of the United States. Washington, D. C.: General Accounting Office, 1969.

ARTICLES

Bailey, Andrew D., Jr., "A Dynamic Approach to the Analysis of Different Costing Methods in Accounting for Inventories," *The Accounting Review,* XLVII (July 1973).

Bailey, F. A., "A Note on PERT/Cost Resource Allocation," *The Accounting Review,* XLII (April 1967).

Bentz, William F., "Input-Output Analysis for Cost Accounting, Planning and Control: A Proof," *The Accounting Review,* XLVIII (April 1973).

Bierman, Harold, Jr., Lawrence E. Fouraker and Robert K. Jaedicke, "A Use of Probability and Statistics in Performance Evaluation," *The Accounting Review,* XXXVII (July 1961).

Davis, Gordon B., "Network Techniques and Accounting—with an Illustration,"*N.A.A. Bulletin,* XLIV (May, 1963).

Demski, Joel S., "An Accounting System Structured on a Linear Programming Model," *The Accounting Review,* XLII (October 1967).

————, "Optimizing The Search for Cost Deviation Sources, *Management Science,* XVI (April 1970).

Dopuch, Nicholas, Jacob G. Birnberg and Joel Demski, "An Extension of Standard Cost Variance Analysis," *The Accounting Review,* XLII, July 1967.

Duvall, Richard M., "Rules for Investigating Cost Variances," *Management Science,* XII (June 1967).

Dyckman, T. R., "The Investigation of Cost Variances," *Journal of Accounting Research,* VII (Autumn 1969).

Fekrat, M. Ali, "The Conceptual Foundations of Absorption Costing," *The Accounting Review,* XLVII (April 1972).

Feltham, Gerald A., "Some Quantitative Approaches to Planning for Multiproduct Systems," *The Accounting Review,* XLV (January 1970).

Gambling, Trevor E., "A Technological Model for Use in Input-Output Analysis and Cost Accounting," *Management Accounting,* L (December 1968).

Gordon, Myron, "Cost Allocations and the Design of Accounting Systems for Control," *The Accounting Review,* XXVI (April 1951).

Hill, Laurence S., "Some Cost Accounting Problems in PERT/Cost," *Journal of Industrial Engineering,* XVII (February, 1966).

Hirschmann, Winfred B., "Profit from the Learning Curve," *Harvard Business Review,* XLII (January—February, 1964).

Jensen, Robert E., "A Multiple Regression Model for Cost Control—Assumptions and Limitations," *The Accounting Review,* XLII (April, 1967).

————, "Sensitivity Analysis and Integer Linear Programming," *The Accounting Review,* XLIII (July, 1968).

Kaplan, Robert S. and Gerald L. Thompson, "Overhead Allocation Via Mathematical Programming Models," *The Accounting Review,* XLVI (April, 1971).

Knapp, Robert A., "Forecasting and Measuring with Correlation Analysis," *Financial Executive,* XXXI (May, 1963).

Kotler, Julian L., "The Learning Curve—A Case History in Its Application," *Journal of Industrial Engineering,* XV (July-August, 1964).

LaValle, Irving H. and Alfred Rappaport, "On the Economics of Acquiring Information of Imperfect Reliability," *The Accounting Review,* XLIII (April, 1968).

Leontief, Wassily W., "Proposal for Better Business Forecasting," *Harvard Business Review,* XLII (November-December, 1964).

Lev, Baruch, "An Information Theory Analysis of Budget Variances," *The Accounting Review,* XLIV (October, 1969).

Levy, Ferdinand K., Gerald L. Thompson, and Jerome D. Wiest, "The ABC's of the Critical Path Method," *Harvard Business Review,* XLI (September-October, 1963).

Livingstone, J. Leslie, "Input-Output Analysis of Cost Accounting, Planning and Control: A Reply," *The Accounting Review,* XLVIII (April 1973).

McClenon, Paul R., "Cost Finding Through Multiple Correlation Analysis," *The Accounting Review,* XXXVIII (July, 1963).

Paige, Hilliard W., "How PERT/Cost Helps the General Manager," *Harvard Business Review,* XLI (November-December, 1963).

Probst, Frank R., "Probabilistic Cost Controls: A Behavioral Dimension," *The Accounting Review,* XLVI (January 1971).

Rappaport, Alfred, "Sensitivity Analysis in Decision Making," *The Accounting Review,* XLII (July 1967).

Ross, W. R., "Evaluating the Cost of PERT/Cost," *Management Services,* III (September-October, 1966).

———, "Accounting Aspects of PERT/Cost," *Management Accounting,* XLVII (April, 1967).

Schoderbek, Peter, P., "PERT-Cost: Its Values and Limitations," *Management Services,* III (January-February, 1966).

Vazsonyi, Andrew, "Statistical Techniques for Financial Planning and Forecasting," *The Controller,* XXV (May, 1957).

Zannetos, Zenon S., "Toward a Functional Accounting System: Accounting Variances and Statistical Variance Analysis," *Industrial Management Review,* VII (Spring 1966).

DECENTRALIZATION AND PERFORMANCE EVALUATION

CHAPTER SIX

Return on Investment: The Relation of Book-Yield to True Yield

Ezra Solomon

Stanford University

Using the internal rate-of-return variant of DCF, the relationship between it (true yield) and book yield and the ratio of book income to net book value of assets is examined. Variations in project life, capitalization policy, depreciation methods, timing of cash inflows, and investment growth rates are tested to establish the effect on the relationship between book yield and true yield. Implications of this relationship are discussed briefly.

Reprinted from *Research in Accounting Measurement*, eds. Robert K. Jaedicke, Yuji Ijiri, and Oswald Nielson (Chicago: American Accounting Association, 1966), pp. 232-44. Used by permission of Ezra Solomon and The American Accounting Association. This article is a development of an earlier paper presented in 1963 at the 38th Annual Meeting of the Society of Petroleum Engineers. I am indebted to two doctoral students, Jaime C. Laya and Robert Carlson, for many of the formulations contained in this essay—E.S.

This paper analyzes the relationship between the *book yield* on investment (measured as the ratio of net book income to net book value of assets) and the *true yield* on investment. It examines the effect on this relationship of variation in capitalization policy, depreciation methods, revenue patterns, and growth rates. It considers the implications of the potential error in the conventional book measure of rate of return for managerial evaluation and government regulation of private business.

The rate of return on investment is a key concept which is widely used for a number of significant business and financial purposes. It is of central importance for the evaluation of an individual investment project, the financial evaluation of a company's performance, the evaluation of managerial efficiency for a division or a product line and, finally, as a guide for establishing ceiling prices in the regulated industries.

The most commonly used multipurpose measure for return on investment is the ratio of net book income, as this is conventionally measured by the accounting process, to net book value of assets employed, similarly measured. The measure has several names such as "the accounting rate of return," "the book rate of return," "the conventional rate of return," but for the purpose of this paper we will refer to it as "book yield," defined here as follows:

$$a = \frac{F_t - D_t}{K_t} \tag{1}$$

where

> a = book yield in period t
>
> F_t = funds flows from operations, before taxes, in period t
>
> D_t = depreciation charges in period t
>
> K_t = net book value of assets as of the beginning of period t
>
> $F_t - D_t$ = reported before-tax operating profits in period t

One reason for the widespread use of the book yield as a measure of return on investment is that it ties in directly with the accounting process. A second and

even more important reason is that it is the only approach available for measuring the ongoing return on investment for a collection of assets which together comprise a division or a company.

In spite of the wide use of the book yield ratio, surprisingly little work has been done on its validity and accuracy as a measure of rate of return. Does it correctly measure the actual yield on investment? Is it a consistent general yardstick in the sense that it provides comparable measures as between divisions, companies, and industries? These questions have been asked but they have not been answered systematically.

For at least one class of purposes for which return on investment is used, the book yield measure has been questioned and found wanting. I refer to single investment projects or acquisitions. In this situation the size and timing of all investment outlays and of all net cash receipts flowing from these outlays are available, or can be estimated either retrospectively or prospectively. Given these data, there is an alternative method available for measuring return on investment. This measure is the true or exact yield; i.e., that annual rate of discount at which the present value of investment outlays is just equal to the present value of cash receipts flowing from the investment.

This approach to the measurement of return on investment also has several names. In the financial world, where it is now universally used for the purpose of measuring bond yields, it is called "the effective yield to maturity." Economists have referred to it as "the marginal productivity of capital," "the marginal efficiency of capital," and the "internal rate of return." In the industrial world, where it is being used with increasing frequency to measure the rate of return on single investment projects it has been called, "the discounted cash flow method," the investor's method," the "scientific method," and the "profitability index." We will refer to it as "true yield."

The nature of the measure does not permit an explicit algebraic definition. However, for a single investment project, in which input takes place at one point of time and output flows occur at annual intervals, the true yield r can be defined implicitly as the rate r which satisfies the following relationship:

$$I_O = \sum_{t=1}^{n} R_t (1 + r)^{-t} \qquad (2)$$

where

I_O = investment in year zero

R_t = net receipts arising out of project I_O received in period t

n = length of the investment's productive life.

For the special case in which the investment generates uniform receipts over the life of the project, equation 2 may be restated as:

$$R = I_O \left[\frac{r(1 + r)^n}{(1 + r)^n - 1} \right] \qquad (3)$$

For single investment projects it is now well known that project book yield and project true yield may differ, and that the difference between the two measures can be quite large. It is also widely recognized and provable that the answer provided by the true yield method is the correct one and that it is the book yield measure which is in error. Because of this the financial world long ago abandoned the book yield measure in favor of the true yield approach as a measure of bond yields. A similar move is now going on in the industrial world as far as single project analysis is concerned.

In contrast to the single project situation, a company or division is a collection of ongoing projects, and we have neither data nor estimates of all cash flows, past and future, associated with this collection of assets. Hence, we have no direct way of measuring or estimating the true yield for a company. In contrast, the book yield is conveniently available.

However, if the book yield approach produces incorrect results for a single investment outlay it must follow that the book yield measure for a company is also subject to error. The main purpose of the analysis which follows is to explore the size and nature of the potential error inherent in the book yield measure.

METHODOLOGY

Since it is not possible to get a direct measure of the true yield for an ongoing company, it is not possible to check directly on the accuracy or error of the observable book yield measure.

What we can do is to develop hypothetical models of a company using a given true yield on investment and then test the book yield as it would appear from the *pro forma* income statements and balance sheets of such a company.

This is what is done in the models contained in this paper. All of them assume a hypothetical company that invests in a series of identical projects, each of which has an assumed true yield. The purpose of each test is to establish how the book yield measure differs from the known true yield when certain basic parameters are changed. The principal parameters are:

1.   Length of project life
2.   The timing and configuration of cash inflows relative to the timing of cash outlays
3.   Accounting policy with respect to

the capitalization and depreciation of investment outlays

4. The rate at which outlays grow over time

It is convenient to divide the overall analysis into two parts: (a) the static or zero-growth situation in which a company's annual investment outlays are constant over time and (b) the dynamic situation in which the growth rate is something other than zero.

THE BASIC ZERO-GROWTH MODEL

Assuming that all projects generate uniform and identical cash inflows per dollar of investment equal to R per period per project, then for any given period subsequent to n (if the investment process starts at period zero), we have:

$$a = \frac{2(nR - D)}{I(n + 1)} \quad (4)$$

nR = the total funds inflows from operations of all n projects operating in period t.

D = total depreciation expense during the period

$I(n + 1)$ ($\frac{1}{2}$) = net book value as of the beginning of period t:

$$K_t = \frac{I}{n} [n + (n - 1) + \ldots + 2 + 1]$$

$$= \frac{I(n + 1)}{2}$$

For example, consider a company that acquires homogeneous investments each of which requires an outlay of $1,000 in year 0 and generates a cash flow of $229.61 a year for six years beginning exactly one year after the outlay is made.

The true yield on each investment is exactly 10 per cent per annum. The fact that it is 10 per cent and exactly 10 per cent can be easily demonstrated by

placing a similar amount in a bank which pays 10 per cent interest on unwithdrawn balances, and by withdrawing $229.61 each year. The sixth withdrawal will exactly exhaust the balance. (See Table 1.)

Assume that the company in question acquires one such investment each year. Since each investment yields 10 per cent we know that the company's true yield must also be 10 per cent.

What would the book yield be for such a company? This depends of course on the depreciation method used, and on whether we use beginning-of-year, mid-year or end-of-year net book value.

Using straight line depreciation and beginning-of-year net book values, it is easy to show that the company's net income will grow as it acquires new investments but that net income will settle at $377.66 from year 6 onward. The beginning-of-year net book value of assets will also rise as new investments are acquired, but this will also settle at $3,500 from year 6 onward. Thus from year 6 onward the book yield will stabilize at $377.66/$3,500.00 or 10.79 per cent. (See Table 2.)

In this particular instance the observable book yield overstates the true yield by some 8 per cent of the true yield, a not insignificant error. The error stems from the fact that, when cash inflows are level, the use of straight line depreciation reduces net book value at a faster rate than economic value declines.

If the basic characteristics of the model are held constant (i.e., if we continue to assume constant cash flows, no time lag between investment and the flow of benefits, complete capitalization of all investment outlays, and zero salvage at the end of each project's life), the error in the book yield changes with the duration of each underlying project. For example, for a 10 per cent true yield project which paid off in fifteen installments of $131.50 instead of six install-

TABLE 1　　Basic Model: Constant Cash Flows

Initial investment outlay $1,000 (all capitalized)
Constant cash flows for six years
Zero salvage value at the end of the sixth year
Known true yield of 10 per cent per annum

Year	Actual Investment of Year	Interest at 10 Per Cent	Balance at End of Year	Cash Withdrawal at End of Year	Ending Value
1	$1,000.00	$100.00	$1,100.00	$229.61	$870.39
2	870.39	87.04	957.43	229.61	727.82
3	727.82	72.78	800.61	229.61	571.00
4	571.00	57.10	628.10	229.61	398.50
5	398.50	39.85	438.35	229.61	208.74
6	208.74	20.87	229.61	229.61	—

TABLE 2　　Basic Model: Net Income, Net Book Value and Book Yields

Project: Single Investment of $1,000

Year	Cash Flow	Depreciation (Straight Line)	Net Income	Beginning of the Year Net Book Value	Project Book Yield (Per Cent)
1	$ 229.61	$ 166.66	$ 62.95	$1,000.00	6.30
2	229.61	166.66	62.95	833.33	7.55
3	229.61	166.66	62.95	666.67	9.44
4	229.61	166.66	62.95	500.00	12.59
5	229.61	166.66	62.95	333.33	18.89
6	229.61	166.66	62.95	166.67	37.77

Project: Company's Successive Investment of $1,000 a Year*

Year	Cash Flow	Depreciation (Straight Line)	Net Income	Beginning of the Year Net Book Value	Project Book Yield (Per Cent)
1	$ 229.61	$ 166.66	$ 62.95	$1,000.00	6.30
2	459.22	333.32	125.90	1,833.33	6.82
3	688.83	500.00	188.83	2,500.00	7.55
4	918.44	666.67	251.77	3,000.00	8.39
5	1,148.05	833.33	314.72	3,333.33	9.44
6	1,377.66	1,000.00	377.66	3,500.00	10.79
onward	1,377.66	1,000.00	377.66	3,500.00	10.79

*Company true yield—10 per cent; Company book yield—10.8 per cent.

ments of $229.61, the observable book yield would be 12.16 per cent rather than 10.79 per cent. The error in the book yield measure rises as project life is lengthened. At the limit of very long life projects the observable book yield will approach twice the level of the known true yield. (See Table 3.)

CAPITALIZATION POLICY

A second factor which has a major influence on the difference between the observable book yield and the true yield is accounting policy with respect to the capitalizing or expensing of initial investment outlays.

If the fraction c of each gross outlay is capitalized on the company's books, with the fraction $(1-c)$ being written off as expense during the current period, then the net book value would be accordingly reduced such that:

$$a = \frac{2(nR - I)}{cI(n + 1)} \tag{5}$$

TABLE 3   Basic Model: Variation of Book Yield with Project Duration

Initial investment outlay $1,000 (all capitalized)
Constant cash flows
Zero salvage value at end of project life
Known true yield of 10 per cent per annum
Straight line depreciation

Project Life (Years)	Annual Cash Flow (Dollars)	Annual Depreciation (Dollars)	Annual Net Income (Dollars)	Average Net Book Value (Dollars)	Average Apparent Rate (Per Annum)	True Yield (Per Annum)
6	$229.6	$166.7	$ 62.9	$583.33	10.8	10.0
10	162.7	100.0	62.7	550.00	11.4	10.0
15	131.5	66.7	64.8	533.33	12.2	10.0
20	117.5	50.9	67.5	525.00	12.9	10.0
25	110.2	40.0	70.2	520.00	13.5	10.0
30	106.1	33.3	72.8	516.67	14.1	10.0
40	102.3	25.0	77.3	512.50	15.1	10.0
50	100.8	20.0	80.8	510.00	15.8	10.0
100	100.0	10.0	90.0	505.00	17.8	10.0
	100.0	0	100.0	500.00	20.0	10.0

In the no-growth case, total annual deductions from net operating cash inflow nR remains equal to I, thus:

$$D = cI + (1 - c)I$$

where cI = depreciation expense for the period on capitalized investments, and $(1-c)I$ = portion of current investment charged off to expense.

For example, if we take the investment assumed in the basic model, i.e., a $1,000 outlay and $229.61 cash inflows for six periods, but introduce the assumption that $600 of the outlay is capitalized and $400 expensed in the first year, we get the following results. True yield (before taxes) remains at 10 per cent, but book yield (before taxes) rises to 17.9 per cent.

If we take the secondary effect of income taxes into account, the relationship between book yield and true yield again changes. For example, assuming a 50 per cent corporate income tax rate in the model just preceding, the true yield after taxes would be 6 per cent, and the book yield after taxes would be 9 per cent.

DEPRECIATION POLICY

A change in the rate at which book depreciation is taken will also change the relationship between the observable book yield and the true yield. On a before-tax basis the depreciation rate has no effect on true yield, but it does have a significant effect on observable book yield.

To illustrate this point, let us return to the basic full capitalization model, and replace the straight line depreciation used in it with the sum of years' digits depreciation schedule.

Total depreciation expense for each period is the same for both methods. Under the straight line method we have:

$$D = \frac{I}{n} + \frac{I}{n} + \ldots + \frac{I}{n} = I$$

and under the sum of years' digits method of depreciation, D is also equal to I.

$$D = \frac{nI}{\sum_{t=1}^{n} t} + \frac{(n-1)I}{\sum_{t=1}^{n} t} + \ldots + \frac{I}{\sum_{t=1}^{n} t}$$

$$= \left[\frac{I}{\sum\limits_{t=1}^{n} t}\right]\left[\sum\limits_{t=1}^{n} t\right]$$

In the zero-growth case, the real impact of the depreciation method is on the amount reported as net book value. Since relatively larger fractions of initial investment are written off early in a project's life, book values will be lower for more rapid depreciation methods than for the straight line calculation. For the sum of years' digits method, the net book value of all operating projects will be:

$$K_t = \frac{I\sum\limits_{t=1}^{n} t}{\sum\limits_{t=1}^{n} t} + \frac{\sum\limits_{t=1}^{n-1} t}{\sum\limits_{t=1}^{n} t} + \ldots + \frac{I\sum\limits_{t=1}^{2} t}{\sum\limits_{t=1}^{n} t}$$
$$+ \frac{I}{\sum\limits_{t=1}^{n} t}$$

This reduces to

$$K_t = \frac{I(n + 2)}{3}$$

Hence, when the sum of years' digits depreciation is employed, the book yield is given by:

$$a = \frac{3(nR - I)}{I(n + 2)} \qquad (6)$$

A change in the depreciation method used will leave the true yield (before tax) unchanged at 10 per cent. Net income will also remain unchanged at $377.66 for year 6 onward. (See Table 2.) But the net book value of assets will fall from $3,500 to $2,666.65. Thus the observable pre-tax book yield will rise from 10.8 per cent to 14.2 per cent.

RISING CASH FLOWS

A major variable which influences the size of the book measure relative to the true yield measure is the general timing of cash inflows relative to the timing of investment outlays.

A time lag between outlays and inflows can take one of three general forms: (a) The investment process itself may involve varying amounts of time. For example, the acquisition of a bond or a piece of equipment takes very little time. In contrast, the development of a producing oil well could involve a five-year lag between the inception of initial outlays and the time the project is complete. (b) There can be a lag between the completion of a project and the initial inflow of cash from operations. (c) The equivalent of a lag may exist when the inflows of cash are distributed over time in a rising pattern so that the bulk of the inflows occur further from the outlay point.

Assuming once again a total outlay of I, the effect of the first type of lag is to require larger cash receipts in order to maintain an effective true yield of 10 per cent. If the investment consists of installments of P dollars per period over a total of $(m + 1)$ periods before the project is finally operational, the true yield can be defined as:

$$\sum\limits_{t=-m}^{0} P_t(1 + r)^{-t} = \sum\limits_{t=1}^{n} R_t(1 + r)^{-t}$$

It would be acceptable accounting practice to consider the total investment in this project as:

$$\sum\limits_{t=-m}^{0} P_t = I.$$

But R would be greater here than was true in the basic model discussed above. For example, if the investment outlay for each project consists of two installments of $500, one in year 1 and the other in year 0, the annual receipts required for each project to yield 10 per cent would be $241.09. Using equation 4, the book yield is seen to be 11.16 per cent.

The second kind of lag occurs when, say, an investment made at the beginning of period 1 produces its first cash inflow at the end of period $(1 + p)$. In this case, true yield can be defined as:

$$I_O = \sum_{t=p+1}^{p+n} R_t(1 + r)^{-t}$$

$$R = I_O \left[\frac{r(1 + r)^{n+p}}{(1 + r)^n - 1} \right] \qquad (8)$$

if R is uniform over project life.

All the other elements required to find book yield would be the same as in the basic model if we assume, reasonably, that no depreciation is charged off until receipts take place. For example, if there is a lag of two years between the year of investment and the year of the first cash inflow (note that lag = 0 when investments produce a first receipt in year 1), book yield may be seen to be 12.13 per cent.

The third type of lag involves the configuration of cash receipts. A cash inflow pattern which rises over time will produce a higher book yield because the absolute size of dollar inflows generated by a project of given outlay and of given true yield are greater when inflows are delayed in time. If the cash inflows from each project rise logarithmically at the rate h, we have:

$$I_O = A \frac{(1 + h)}{(1 + r)} + A \frac{(1 + h)^2}{(1 + r)^2}$$

$$A \frac{(1 + h)^3}{(1 + r)^3} + \cdots$$

$$+ \frac{(1 + h)^n}{(1 + r)^n}$$

(where A is some constant satisfying the above conditions), and hence we have:

$$a = \frac{A \sum_{t=1}^{n} (1 + h)^t - I}{K_t} \qquad (9)$$

If $r = 10$ per cent and $h = 12$ per cent, then cash flows from the project would be as follows:

Year	Cash Inflows
1	$ 175.24
2	196.26
3	219.81
4	246.19
5	275.74
6	308.82
	$1,422.06

After year 6, the total company cash flows will be $1,422.06. From equations 1 or 9 it may be seen that the book yield is 12.06 per cent.

Conversely, it is possible to envisage an investment project which contains the opposite of this type of time lag, i.e., a project which offers large early returns that decline over time.

An example of such a project with $r = 10$ per cent and $h = -12$ per cent, would be:

Year	Cash Inflows
1	$ 298.15
2	262.38
3	230.89
4	203.18
5	178.80
6	157.35
	$1,330.75

The company book yield would then be 9.45 per cent.

To summarize, as far as the zero-growth case is concerned, the major findings are: (1) the book yield is not an accurate measure of true yield, (2) the error in the book yield is neither constant nor consistent. Indeed it is fairly capricious measure which may sometimes underestimate true yield, but which more generally overstates true yield.

The degree of potential overstatement ranges from slight under certain circumstances to very gross and misleading overstatements in others.

Specifically, the degree to which book yield overstates true yield is a complex function of four basic factors. These are: (a) Length of project life—the longer the project life, the greater the overstatement. (b) Capitalization policy—the smaller the fraction of total investment capitalized on the books, the greater will be the overstatement. At the limit for investments which are expensed 100 per cent, the observable book yield will rise toward infinity. (c) The rate at which depreciation is taken on the books—depreciation procedures faster than a straight line basis will result in higher book yields. At the limit the most rapid method of depreciation is, of course, tantamount to 100 per cent expensing of outlays and hence leads to the same result. (d) The greater the lag between investment outlays and the recoupment of these outlays from cash inflows, the greater the degree of overstatement.

Since no two investments and, hence, no two companies or industries are likely to hold investments that are identical with respect to all of these variables, it must follow that observable book yields do not provide a consistent measure of return on investment or even a consistent *ranking* of the underlying true yields actually being earned by such companies or industries.

GROWTH SITUATIONS

We now lift the assumption that the company's growth rate is zero, and we will find that the rate at which a division or a company or an industry acquires new investments is a major variable affecting the size of the error contained in the observable book yield.

So long as the investments being acquired are homogeneous, i.e., each year's investment produces the same true yield on that investment, it is easy to see that the rate at which investment outlays are made over time has no effect on the true yield being earned by the company as a whole. This will be equal to the true yield on each investment regardless of the rate at which investment outlays grow or decline over time.

However, the book yield is significantly affected by the pace at which investment outlays are made.

In order to see why this is the case it is useful to return to the basic model. In this model the $1,000 investment in year 1 produces a cash flow of +299.61 each year for six years. Using straight line depreciation, the depreciation allowance is $166.66 a year, leaving net income of $62.95 per year for six years.

Although annual net income is constant over the life of each investment, the net book value of assets employed is not constant. Rather, it declines steadily from year 1 until it reaches zero at the end of year 6.

This means that on a year-to-year basis the ratio of net income to net book value for each individual investment rises. In year 1 of the project's life the beginning of year net book value is $1,000 and, hence, the project book yield during year 1 is 6.3 per cent. (See Table 2).

In the second year of the project's life it has a book yield of 7.5 per cent. By the sixth year, the value of net book assets has fallen to $166, and the project's sixth year book yield is 37.8 per cent.

When a company acquires investments at a constant rate, the overall book yield for the company is simply the weighted average of the year-by-year project book yields, with the appropriate net book values used as weights. Thus in Table 2 the overall book yield of 10.8 per cent is equal to (6.3 per cent × 1,000 + 7.5 per cent × 833 + ... + 37.77 per cent × 166.67) ÷ 3,500.

If, however, a company acquires new investments at a rising pace, the overall company yield in any year will be more heavily weighted with investment projects which are in their early phase of development and for which net book values are high relative to net income. Thus, the observable book yield for a growing company will be smaller than the observable yield for a nongrowing company, even though both hold essentially identical investments.

The opposite is true for a company which commits a smaller amount each year to new investments. For such a company the observable book yield is more heavily weighted with investment projects which are in their late phase of development and for which net book values are very low relative to net income. For such a company observable book yield will be higher than for a nongrowth company even though both companies hold identical investments.

In general, if the observable book yield is higher than true yield for a nongrowth situation, the introduction of positive growth will tend to lower book yield relative to true yield. The faster the growth, the more will book yield decline relative to true yield.

It is necessary to distinguish between two kinds of growth: (a) real growth in investment outlays (with no change in prices) and (b) money growth in investment outlays due entirely to inflation. Assuming a consistent true yield on each investment and a uniform rate of growth over time in investment outlays, it follows that net book value, cash receipts, depreciation expense, and the reserve for depreciation also grow at the rate at which investment outlays are growing.

REAL GROWTH

When a company's real growth rate is g, book yield is given by:

$$a = g \left[\cfrac{\cfrac{(1+g)^n - 1}{1 + (1+g)^n (gn - 1)}}{\cfrac{1 + (1+r)^n (rn - 1)}{(1+r)^n - 1}} \right] \quad (10)$$

This is derived from equation 1 and the following relationships; for $t = n$

$$F_n = I_0 [1 + (1+g) + (1+g)^2 + \ldots$$
$$+ (1+g^{n-1}] \left[\frac{r(1+r)}{(1+r)^n - 1} \right]$$

$$D_n = I_0 \left[\frac{1}{n} + \frac{(1+g)}{n} + \frac{(1+g)^2}{n} \right.$$
$$\left. + \ldots + \frac{(1+g)^{n-1}}{n} \right]$$

$$K_n = I_0 \left[\frac{n}{n} (1+g)^{n-1} + \frac{(n-1)}{n} \right.$$
$$(1+g)^{n-2} + \ldots + \frac{2}{n} (1+g)$$
$$\left. + \frac{1}{n} \right]$$

If the book yield a is higher than the true yield r in the zero-growth case, then as g increases the book yield falls continuously toward r.

In the special situation where the growth rate just equals true yield, the book yield is also just equal to true yield.

In other words, when $g = r$, a is equal to r. The proof of this fundamental and important equality condition is as follows:

TABLE 4   Basic Model with Inflation

Real investment outlay $1,000 (all capitalized)
Constant real cash flows
Zero salvage at end of project life
Known real true yield at 10 per cent per annum
Money true yield 13.30 per cent
Inflation rate 3 per cent per annum
Straight line depreciation

Investments Made in Year	Money Investment	Money Inflows in Year 6	Annual Depreciation Expense	Profits in Year 6	Net Book Value in Year 6
0	$1,000.00	$ 274.18	$ 166.67	$107.51	$ 166.67
1	1,030.00	274.18	171.67	102.51	343.33
2	1,060.90	274.18	176.82	97.36	530.46
3	1,092.73	274.18	182.12	92.06	728.48
4	1,125.51	274.18	185.58	86.60	937.90
5	1,159.27	274.18	193.21	80.97	1,159.27
	$6,468.41	$1,645.08	$1,078.07	$567.01	$3,866.11

By definition,

$$aK_t = F_t - D_t \tag{11}$$

and

$$gK_t = I_t - D_t \tag{12}$$

Now, the condition $g = r$ exists only when all company receipts are reinvested, i.e., when $F_t = I_t$. In this case:

$$aK_t = gK_t$$

Hence if $g = r$, $a = g = r$.

It can also be seen directly from equation 10 that $a = r$ if $g = r$, regardless of n. Furthermore, it can be proved that as long as depreciation method, capitalization practice, time lags, and cash flow patterns are consistent over time, the growth rate of all items remains the same as the growth rate in investment, and the $r = g = a$ equality holds.

INFLATIONARY GROWTH

The existence of inflation in the economy would directly alter the cash flow pattern from individual projects. Assuming for simplicity that inflation has an equal effect on the price level of investment input and cash flow output, we have:

$$I_o = \sum_{t=1}^{n} \frac{R_t(1 + i)^t}{(1 + m)^t} \tag{13}$$

where

m = money true yield
i = inflation rate
R = receipts in dollars of period zero.

On the basis of equation 2, equation 13 may be restated as:

$$I_o = \sum_{t=1}^{n} \frac{R_t (1 + i)^t}{(1 + i)^t \ (1 + r)^t} \tag{14}$$

Thus we have money true yield $m = i + ri + r$.

Another way of looking at the effect of inflation is to say that all real cash receipts are multiplied by $(1 + i)^t$ in order to obtain the actual cash inflow in period *t.* At the same time, actual investment, and, hence, depreciation expense and net book value are themselves affected by the inflationary process. The various elements of equation 1 are therefore affected such that:

$$F_t = nI_o \left[\frac{r (1 + r)^n (1 + I)^t}{(1 + r)^n - 1} \right]$$

$$D_t = \frac{I_{t-n}}{n} \; [1 + (1 + i) + \ldots + (1 + i)^n] = \left[\frac{I_o (1 + i)^{t-n}}{n} \right] \left[\frac{(1 + i)^n - 1}{i} \right]$$

$$K_t = I_{t-n} \left[\frac{n}{n} (1 + i)^{t-1} + \frac{(n - 1)}{n} (1 + i)^{t-2} + \ldots + \frac{1}{n} (1 + i)^{t-n} \right]$$

which simplifies to

$$K_t = I_o \left[\frac{(1 + i)^{t-n}}{ni^2} \right] [1 - (1 + i)^n (1 - ni)]$$

Thus, the book yield *a* may be computed, using equation 1, as follows:

$$a = \left[\frac{nr (1 + r)^n}{(1 + r)^n - 1} - \frac{(1 + i)^n - 1}{ni (1 + i)^n} \right] \cdot \left[\frac{ni^2 (1 + i)^n}{1 - (1 + i)^n (1 - ni)} \right] \quad (15)$$

Using the above equation, it can be seen that the introduction of a 3 per cent inflation rate in the basic model would produce a book yield of 14.7 per cent. (See also Table 4.)

IMPLICATIONS

If the findings above are valid, and there is no reason to believe that they are not, they present financial analysis with a serious dilemma. On the one hand, the ratio of net income to net book assets is not a reliable measure of return on investment. On the other hand, analysis definitely requires some measure of return on investment and there appears to be no other way in which this concept can be measured for an ongoing division or company.

The pragmatic answer is that book yield will continue to be used, but that its use must be tempered by a far greater degree of judgment and adjustment than we have employed in the past, and in extreme cases the measure may have to be abandoned altogether in favor of an alternative measure, such as the ratio of cash flow before depreciation to gross book value.

Adjustments are also required whenever book yields are used for the purpose of making interdivisional, intercompany, or interindustrial comparisons. While we have as yet no precise basis for making these necessary adjustments, the use of models does provide an approximate basis for doing so. It is probably better to use adjusted book yields even if the adjustments are imprecise than to use the unadjusted book yield figures, which we know are subject to error.

A final implication is that the conventional rate-base approach commonly used in rate regulation should be amended to take into account the fact that companies and industries differ widely with respect to the basic parameters that affect the accuracy of the book yield measure. For industry situations in which book yield is

equal to true yield, multiplying an intended cost of capital rate by an original
cost net book value rate base produces
meaningful and intended results. However, for situations in which the book

yield is higher than the true yield on
invested funds, such a procedure will in
fact provide a true yield significantly
lower than the cost of capital rate being
aimed at.

A Capital Budgeting Approach to Divisional Planning and Control

Alfred Rappaport
Northwestern University

Companies are increasingly using discounted cash flow techniques to evaluate capital expenditures and also employing the
investment center approach for decentralized performance
evaluation. The dysfunctional behavioral implications of using
contradictory planning and performance evaluation models are
enumerated. A new performance evaluation system based
directly on a discounted cash flow planning model is proposed.
Advantages as well as limitations of this system are discussed.

Reprinted from *Financial Executive* October 1968, 61-63. Used by
permission of *Financial Executive*.

During the past ten to fifteen years
decentralized profit responsibility has
gained widespread acceptance in American industry. More recently a large
number of companies have decided that
divisional performance measurements
would be more useful if they were related
in some way to a division's investment
base. The significant and surprising extent
to which this investment-center concept
is replacing the profit-center notion
is indicated by the results of the recent
Mauriel-Anthony survey.[1] Based on responses from 75 per cent of 3,525 of the

largest companies in the United States,
the survey reports that almost 60 per cent
of the respondents employ a return-on-
investment (ROI) criterion for their
evaluations of divisional performance.

The Mauriel-Anthony survey disclosures
concerning methods used to calculate
ROI are both interesting and disquieting.
The essential conclusion reached is that:

[1] John J. Mauriel and Robert N. Anthony,
"Misevaluation of Investment Center Performance," *Harvard Business Review*, March-April,
1966, pp. 98-105.

... generally accepted accounting principles, including any internal company rules and procedures intended to govern the reporting to outsiders of financial data on the firm as a whole, tend to influence very strongly the methods used in calculating an investment center's profit and investment base. Thus, most companies use net book value in determining the amount of an asset included in the investment base, and almost all companies (97 per cent of the respondents) report using the same method for figuring depreciation for purposes of investment-center profit calculations as that used for their external accounting reports.[2]

DCF MODELS

Many of the same companies that use such "book ROI" performance measurement systems employ discounted cash flow (DCF) models as a basis for capital budgeting decisions. Using a planning model (DCF) which takes into account the time value of money, and then evaluating subsequent results with a model (book ROI) that accords no such recognition, inevitably leads to serious contradictions. If one accepts the basic premise that DCF planning models which incorporate a time preference for money are an appropriate expression of management criteria, then what are the potential consequences of using models without a time-preference function for purposes of divisional performance evaluation? Undoubtedly, the consequences are far-reaching and significant. Consider, for example, the following:

1. Many companies use division ROI rates as a basis for executive promotion and compensation plans.

2. Top management decisions concerning appropriation of funds for expansion purposes can be influenced by comparisons of book ROI ratios among the divisions of the company. The credibility of this supposition is enhanced by the fact that 38 per cent of the Mauriel-Anthony respondents report that they use a single ROI target rate for all investment centers.

3. Book ROI, when used as a performance evaluation measurement, may actually force a division manager to employ strategies contrary to the long-run interest of the company. Since "book ROI" is measured in terms of accounting periods rather than long-range periods, the division manager is naturally motivated to seek optimal divisional results for the period he expects to retain his current position. Under these conditions, the division manager may well forego highly profitable projects that will show only modest returns during his expected tenure in favor of much less profitable projects with earlier returns.

The disparity between DCF capital investment planning and divisional control based on "book ROI" measurements suggests a need for a re-examination of conventional approaches to divisional planning and control. In this article we shall propose a divisional planning and control model, which we believe offers important advantages over existing systems.

DIVISIONAL PLANNING

The superiority of discounted cash flow (DCF) over other criteria—such as urgency, payback, and "book ROI"—for measuring the economic worth of capital projects has been convincingly argued

[2]*Ibid.*, p. 99 and p. 103.

many times in the literature.[3] In essence, DCF superiority is attributable to two principal factors:

1. DCF explicitly recognizes the time value of money.
2. DCF recognizes that the relevant flows are cash flows; hence capitalization and depreciation policies are irrelevant for capital budgeting decisions except as they affect taxes.

If DCF is truly the most reasonable measure of capital productivity, would it not be reasonable to extend this concept to *all* cash flows traceable to an investment center such as a division? In short, this simply involves determining the time-adjusted rate-of-return (TAROR) for the division's long-range cash forecast.[4]

Let us consider briefly the following simplified illustration. The management of a highly decentralized conglomerate corporation is deliberating the wisdom of establishing a new division for the manufacture and sale of a consumer product line not related to any of the company's existing lines, but one with promising growth potential. Assume that an initial investment of $700,000 in depreciable assets and $300,000 in working capital is required. The time span used in long-range planning for this prospective division is seven years. Seven years was chosen because management believed it would take about this length of time to

accomplish its principal marketing objectives. Also, the confidence factor for forecasts beyond this period substantially decreases. It should be noted, however, that length of the planning period not only differs among organizations, but should be responsive to changes affecting any one organization over time.[5]

CASH FLOW FORECAST

A seven-year forecast of cash flow before taxes is presented as Exhibit 1. Note the rows are to accommodate the formal chart of accounts or any other system of classification designed to enumerate budgeted cash inflows and outflows in a manner consistent with the planner's approach. Each column designates a year within the long-range planning span. To illustrate, the cash flow denoted as C_{12} may represent cash receipts in year 2 resulting from sales of product class 1. The total cash flow for each year, appearing as the last row of Exhibit 1, is then used as a point of departure in calculating the after-tax cash flow in Exhibit 2. Note that by the end of the seventh year divisional working capital has grown to $1,797,000; i.e., the initial $300,000 working capital investment plus cumulative after-tax cash flows of $1,497,000. The divisional terminal value of $1,797,000 represents a TAROR of 8.7 per cent since each dollar invested at that rate will yield $1.80 at the end of seven years.[6]

[3] For example see Joel Dean, "Measuring the Productivity of Capital," *Harvard Business Review*, January-February, 1954; John G. McLean, "How to Evaluate New Capital Investments," *Harvard Business Review*, November-December, 1958; Harold Bierman, Jr. and Seymour Smidt, *The Capital Budgeting Decision*, second edition, New York: The Macmillan Company, 1966.

[4] See Billy E. Goetz, *Quantitative Methods: A Survey and Guide for Managers*, New York: McGraw-Hill Book Company, 1965, pp. 271-328 for a detailed discussion of a comprehensive planning budget incorporating the notion of discounted cash flows.

[5] To obtain meaningful results for the proposed divisional planning model, care must be exercised to incorporate a time span of sufficient length to include the major returns expected from large expenditure programs. If the illustration were concerned with an existing rather than a new division, beginning investment should be valued at the current market value of the division.

[6] Note the significant increase in working capital balances over the seven-year period. Given that working capital requirements are responsive to

EXHIBIT 1   Seven-year Cash Flow from Operations Forecast (000 Omitted)

Year \ Account	↑1	↑2	↑3	↑4	↑5	↑6	↑7	Totals
A_1	C_{11}	C_{12}	—	—	—	—	C_{17}	
A_2	C_{21}	C_{22}	—	—	—	—	C_{27}	
—	—	—						
—	—	—						
—	—	—						
—	—	—						
—	—	—						
—	—	—						
A_n	C_{n1}	C_{n2}					C_{n7}	
TOTALS	\$382	\$542	\$867	\$712	\$822	\$892	\$1,047	\$5,264

EXHIBIT 2   Seven-Year After-Tax Cash-Flow Forecast (000 Omitted)

Year	Cash Flow from Operations	Depreciable Investment Outlays	Depreciation[a]	Taxes[b]	Required Increase in Working Capital	Cash Transfers Avail. for or Reqd. from Hdqtrs.[c]
0		\$700				
1	\$ 382	70	\$100	\$141	\$ 171	\$0
2	542	105	110	216	221	0
3	867	175	125	371	321	0
4	712	210	150	281	221	0
5	822	280	180	321	221	0
6	892	385	220	336	171	0
7	1,047	490	275	386	171	0
					\$1,497	

[a]Straight-line depreciation, seven-year life, and no residual value for tax and book purposes. Note that since all cash outlays as well as receipts are assumed to take place at the end of the year, depreciation charges are not recorded until the subsequent period.

[b]50% of income or cash flow from operations less depreciation.

[c]Cash flow from operations less the sum of depreciable investment outlays, taxes, and required increase in working capital.

While in the foregoing example headquarters has permitted the new division to reinvest all its cash flows, this assumption can be easily relaxed to take into account transfers of cash between the division and corporate headquarters. How would TAROR be affected by a requirement that the division transfer varying sums of cash to headquarters each year? If we make the simplifying assumption that divisional working capital requirements will not be significantly altered during the forthcoming period by the transfer of cash to headquarters, then it is clear that the division must reduce its development expenditures (whether administratively classified as capital or ex-

sales levels, the reader may properly question why the cash-flow trend did not correspond to the increases in working capital. This is explained by the fact that despite significant increases in sales and working capital, cash flows were adversely affected by large expense outlays for product and market development.

pense projects) by the amount of the transfer. This reduction in cash expenditures will presumably be offset by a related reduction in cash benefits in future periods. The impact of the transfer on divisional TAROR thus depends upon the marginal productivity rate of the funds. Headquarters, on the other hand, can test the estimated sensitivity of divisional TAROR's, and more importantly, total firm TAROR, to alternative cash-transfer plans that effectively govern the allocation of limited investment funds among divisions.

Let us reconsider the 8.7 per cent TAROR. The value of the division at the end of the seventh year was equated to the forecasted working capital. Working capital, however, represents but one factor in estimating the market value of a division. Going concern valuations take into account customer relations, patents, technology, management skill, and other factors likely to affect future earnings. Consideration of these factors, along with a seven-year history of sound profit performance, would suggest that our illustrative division has value far beyond its working capital balance. The sensitivity of the TAROR to some alternative valuations at the seventh year is shown in Exhibit 3.

tivity of capital, presumably a prime factor in management's long-range system.

2.   The proposed model is particularly useful for establishing a judicious balance between short-range and long-range considerations.

3.   The model is easy to operate and understand. Indeed its requirement for cash-flow data only effectively bypasses the nagging problems associated with alternative accrual accounting procedures for depreciation, inventory costing, pensions, leasing, and various other divisional transactions.

4.   The proposed model is not intended to replace existing planning statements such as forecasted income statements and balance sheets, but rather serves to supplement and test the reasonableness of these statements in terms of the capital productivity criterion.

5.   As is the case with other planning models, sensitivity analysis may be employed to test the responsiveness of model results to changes in the variables which are subject to control by division or headquarters executives, and thereby facilitate the choice among alternative strategies.

EXHIBIT 3   TAROR for Various Divisional Valuations at the End of the Seventh Year (000 Omitted)

Working Capital	Estimated Additional Value	Total Estimated Value	TAROR
$1,797	—	$1,797	8.7%
1,797	$ 500	2,297	12.6
1,797	1,000	2,797	15.8
1,797	1,500	3,297	18.5
1,797	2,000	3,797	21.0

The advantages as well as limitations of the proposed planning model can now be summarized briefly:

1.   First and foremost, the proposed model properly measures the produc-

6.   The deterministic, "best estimate" model presented earlier does not recognize explicitly the uncertainty surrounding the forecasted cash flows. An explicit recognition of uncertainty —"risk analysis"—would require a

range of estimates and associated probabilities for each estimated cash flow. If the planning team is willing and able to develop the probable input data, the model results can then be expressed as a TAROR probability distribution.[7]

CONVENTIONAL PLANNING AND CONTROL

The most carefully conceived plans are inadequate without the exercise of management control. By management control is meant the process by which managers provide for the effective achievement of planned objectives. Perhaps the most important tool serving management control is a sound measurement and reporting system. In a divisional context, such a reporting system generally exists for three main purposes:

1. To guide divisional executives toward actions that are in the best interests of the company.
2. To assess the performance of divisional executives.
3. To evaluate the productivity of capital invested in the division.

The Mauriel-Anthony survey cited earlier clearly indicates the current popularity of the investment-center concept in American industry. The notion of return on investment (ROI) is at the foundation of investment-center planning and control systems. In calculating so-called "book ROI," companies use balance-sheet asset amounts in the investment denominator and profits calculated in accordance with generally accepted accounting principles in the numerator. The importance attributed to "book ROI" systems by some

managements is illustrated by the statement of an officer of the Armstrong Cork Company:

Our company adopted the return-on-investment measurement in 1950. Today it is our basic working tool in planning and striving for the best results possible. All other working tools and controls in our business, such as those provided by production and inventory planning, engineering of all kinds, accounting, purchasing, and sales promotion, are designed to improve the return on investment. Since they are so designed, we would stand to lose a major part of their effectiveness if objectives were to be stated in terms of growth, share of markets, or well-rounded lines, or in any other terms rather than return on investment.[8]

Do "book ROI" systems meet the three proposed objectives served by divisional reporting? Consider the first, the guidance of divisional executives toward actions in the best interests of the company. That performance measurement systems, formal and informal, influence behavior is a widely recognized phenomenon. Division managers, just like others in the organization, are motivated to optimize those indices upon which their evaluations depend. The attempt to optimize "book ROI," however, may not necessarily be in the company interest. Because "book ROI" emphasizes current period results, it tends to promote short-range thinking which often discourages growth and the acceptance of reasonable risk. A few examples should serve to illustrate this point more clearly.

---

[7]See David B. Hertz, "Investment Policies That Pay Off," *Harvard Business Review,* January-February, 1968, pp. 96-108.

[8]F. J. Muth, "Return on Investment—Tool of Modern Management," in #*III, Financial Management Series,* New York: American Management Association, p. 9.

Case 1—After a careful study of a proposed capital expenditure, the division manager decided not to forward it to headquarters. The DCF-calculated return of 20 per cent after taxes was significantly above the company's cost of capital. However, the increase in balance-sheet assets and the adverse effect of accelerated depreciation on accounting profits would in all probability lower the division's "book ROI" for the next year or two. Note that the "book ROI" control model is incompatible with the DCF planning model. The division manager's attitude may be neatly summed up by a familiar thought: It's fine to talk about the long-run, but I won't be here in the long-run if I don't do something about the short-run.

Case 2—A division manager struggling for personal survival perceives that he must show some immediate results. To show such results he employs a potpourri of actions counter to the company's best interest. Under the guise of "cost reduction" he defers preventative maintenance programs previously established as most economical; employee training and development programs are severely reduced; leasing decisions are favored over more economical purchase plans to avoid adding to the ROI investment base; an unwarranted number of subcontracting agreements are signed as a further means of bypassing current investment outlaws. The unfortunate consequences of his actions will appear in future divisional statements to the great distress of the current division manager or his unsuspecting successor.

Case 3—The extremes to which a "book ROI" control system can drive a manager is vividly portrayed by a case recently reported by Henderson and Dearden.[9] They relate an incident where the division manager, in his anxiety to reduce his investment, scrapped some machinery not currently in use. When the machinery was needed at a later date, he purchased new equipment.

Case 4—Consider the case of the ambitious division manager hoping to be promoted to a headquarters position in the next two or three years. He has developed two main guidelines for decisions concerning discretionary outlays of funds. First, the risk involved must be low, and secondly, the significant portion of the returns from the project should be forthcoming within the next two- or three-year period. Any control system which compels a manager to suppress intelligent risk-taking surely is costly to the company that has lost the discarded opportunities.

Other illustrations could be presented. However, the foregoing should suffice to underline the essential point that "book ROI" can influence divisional decisions in a manner contrary to the best interests of the company.

DEFECTS OF 'BOOK ROI'

In assessing "book ROI" as an index of executive performance, it should be pointed out that the problem of establishing what is controllable investment and what are the controllable elements that govern profit calculation is one concerned with gaining an improved understanding of the complex behavior of

[9]Bruce D. Henderson and John Dearden, "New System for Divisional Control," *Harvard Business Review,* September-October, 1966, p. 150.

organizational systems, and hence would be common to all measurement methods developed to appraise executive performance. The most serious defect of "book ROI" is that it focuses on current period results, and consequently tells us little about how well the manager is providing for future needs. In short, the current performance of a manager should be measured by current *and* future results. There is no assurance that even the division manager who meets or exceeds his "target book ROI" is providing wisely for the future growth and profitability of operations. Indeed, one is led to suspect a performance measurement system that can "reward" a manager who pays inordinately for improved short-run results at the expense of strategic long-run considerations.

MEASURING PRODUCTIVITY

How well does "book ROI" measure the productivity of capital invested in a division? Despite the fact that it is the most widely used measure of profitability, its use in many situations must be viewed with serious reservations. Earlier, we noted that "book ROI" suffers from an important deficiency, namely its neglect of the time value of money. We further noted that DCF models which do in fact recognize the magnitude and time pattern of cash flows have found increasing acceptance among those responsible for capital budgeting decisions. If the DCF approach is indeed the "true" measure of capital productivity, then it seems reasonable to examine the disparities between it and the model under consideration, "book ROI."

Ezra Solomon[10] has shown that the

degree to which "book ROI" improperly estimates a known TAROR for a given project is a complex function of five basic variables:

1. Length of project life.
2. Accounting policy concerning capitalization versus expensing of outlay.
3. Accounting policy concerning alternative depreciation methods.
4. The timing and configuration of cash inflows relative to that of cash outlays.
5. The rate at which investment outlays grow over time.

To illustrate this difference, let us reconsider the seven-year cash flows presented earlier as Exhibit 2. Assume that these divisional cash flows no longer represent a forecast, but that we are now at the end of the seventh year and wish to measure the actual productivity of capital invested in the division.

Since the actual cash-flow data are identical to the forecasted cash flows, TARORS as presented in Exhibit 3 would hold. The "book ROI" results are presented as Exhibit 4. Note that within individual years the "book ROI" ranges from 13.2 per cent to 23.9 per cent. The average "book ROI" for the period is 16.4 per cent, as opposed to the TARORS in Exhibit 3. The magnitude of the variance between these two measurements will of course differ from situation to situation. The important point to be recognized is that "book ROI," and hence its variance from TAROR, is affected by factors (e.g., accounting policy for capitalization and depreciation) that should have no bearing on a productivity of capital measurement except as they relate to possible tax consequences.

---

[10] Ezra Solomon, "Return on Investment: The Relation of Book-Yield to True Yield," in *Research in Accounting Measurement* edited by Robert K. Jaedicke, Yuji Ijiri and Oswald Nielsen, American Accounting Association, 1966, pp. 232-244. Solomon uses the internal rate-of-return variant of DCF in his illustration.

EXHIBIT 4   Seven-Year "Book ROI" Results (000 Omitted)

Year	Cumulative Depreciable Investment	Cumulative Depreciation	Net Book Value of Depreciable Investment	Working Capital*	Total Investment	Net Income	"Book ROI"
1	$ 700	$ 100	$600	$ 471	$1,071	$141	13.2%
2	770	210	560	692	1,252	216	17.3
3	875	335	540	1,013	1,553	371	23.9
4	1,050	485	565	1,234	1,799	281	15.6
5	1,260	665	595	1,455	2,050	321	15.7
6	1,540	885	655	1,626	2,281	336	14.7
7	1,925	1,160	765	1,797	2,562	386	15.1
Average					1,795	294	16.4

*Represents $300,000 initial investment in working capital plus incremental cash flow for each period. For example, the period 1 balance of $471,000 is the sum of the initial investment and the $171,000 after-tax cash flow of the first year.

What are the implications of using a "book ROI" measurement which improperly estimates a known "true yield," i.e., TAROR? The answer lies in the degree to which capital productivity measurements affect corporate as well as divisional decisions. Where such measurements affect the appropriation of funds among divisions, product decisions, or other key decisions concerning the future of divisions, there is a real danger that "book ROI" measurements may be misleading. This is particularly true when great importance is attached to shorter period "book ROI" results.

In designing control systems, management may choose to measure the performance of people and invested resources directly—in terms of the organizational objective function—or, alternatively, a surrogate index with fewer measurement problems may be used. Neither of these two alternatives provides any guarantees for success or failure. In choosing between the two basic design approaches, we seek that control system that holds the greatest promise of facilitating the effective achievement of planned objectives.

PROPOSED CONTROL SYSTEM

The hypothesis that management is, or at least should be, interested in long-run profitability underlies the entire discussion. Accordingly, we have advocated a planning model (TAROR) that mirrors this interest. Conventional control systems are not structured directly in terms of management's objective function. Instead, these surrogate systems emphasize current profitability, often at the expense of long-run profitability. Unquestionably, a control system that restricts its focus to current activity involves fewer measurement problems than a system that also incorporates measurements of current contributions to the future profitability of the organization. Nevertheless, we would challenge the former system on its limited usefulness for management control.

We advocate a divisional control system based directly on the planning model proposed earlier. After a brief extension of the earlier illustration, the proposed control system will be evaluated on the same three criteria used to evaluate conventional control systems.

Exhibit 5 depicts the flow of the divisional planning and control activities. After the divisional plan has been approved by headquarters, the stage is set for execution. Feedback or control is established first by a comparison of planned versus actual results for the current period. This comparison in turn serves as a point of departure for planning for the next period.

CONTROL LINK

A summary of the financial plan for the first seven years, prepared at the end of year zero, was presented earlier as Exhibit 2. To illustrate the control link to the recommended planning model, a performance report prepared at the end of the first year is presented as Exhibit 6. Note that there are two distinct parts to the performance report: (1) planned versus actual results in current year and (2) TAROR (18.5 per cent) based upon a seven-year forecast at the beginning of the year versus TAROR (12.7 per cent) based upon a seven-year forecast at the end of the year. The difference in these two TARORS could be related to some or all of the following factors:

1. Since there was a $21,000 defi-

EXHIBIT 6   Performance Report for the First Year (000 Omitted)

	Planned	Actual	Difference— Favorable (Unfavorable)
Receipts:			
Product sales	$1,600	$1,750	$ 150
Other	37	30	(7)
	1,637	1,780	143
Disbursements			
Product costs:			
Material	150	200	(50)
Labor	300	320	(20)
Manufacturing overhead	300	350	(50)
	750	870	(120)
Division-managed costs:			
Manufacturing	50	100	(50)
Marketing	140	155	(15)
New-product development	200	140	60
Administrative	100	150	(50)
Other	10	10	
	500	555	(55)
Cash flow on division-managed costs	387	355	(32)
Non-division managed costs	75	75	—
	312	280	(32)
Taxes on income	141	130	11
Cash flow after taxes	$ 171	$ 150	$ (21)

Planned cash flows—beginning of year											
1	2	3	4	5	6	7	DV₇[1]	TAROR	8	DV₈[1]	TAROR

Planned cash flows—beginning of year

1 2 3 4 5 6 7	DV₇ [1]	TAROR	8	DV₈ [1]	TAROR
$171 221 321 221 221 171 171 1,500		18.5%	—	—	—
Planned cash flows—end of year					
150* 200 300 200 200 200 250		—	(200)	1,000	12.7%

[1] DV = estimated value of division beyond working capital balance at the end of years seven and eight, respectively.
*Actual.

Divisional Planning and Control Cycle

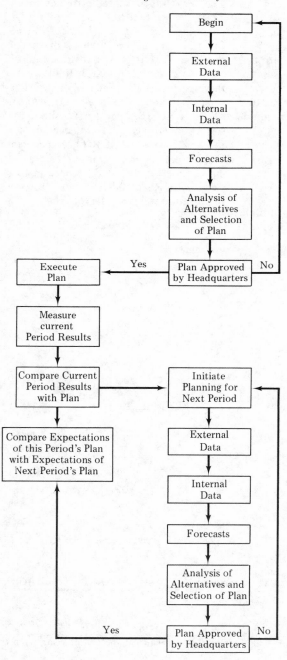

EXHIBIT 5. Divisional Planning and Control Cycle

ciency in cash generated in year 1, the reduction in planned reinvestment adversely affected cash flow in subsequent years. If, however, headquarters decided to provide the $21,000 to the division, this explanation would be invalidated.

2. Based upon the first-year performance report as well as other relevant information, the division's plans and/or expectations for years 2-7 may be modified.

3. The TAROR forecasted at the end of the year incorporates consideration of an additional year, the eighth year.

4. Due to the changes enumerated above, the forecasted value of the division may also change. In the example there is a decrease from $1.5 million to $1 million.

EVALUATING PROPOSED SYSTEM

The reader will recall that conventional control systems were evaluated on their ability to (1) provide appropriate decision-making guidance and motivation to divisional executives; (2) measure performance of divisional executives; (3) measure the productivity of capital invested in the business. Let us consider the proposed system in light of the capital productivity criterion.

The superiority of TAROR methods for determining the productivity of invested resources was discussed earlier. Subsequently, differences in TAROR and "book ROI" results were illustrated. There is no need to belabor these points. A word about the applicability of the proposed TAROR model to a special category of firms would, however, be timely. Solomon describes this set of firms and underlines the shortcomings of conventional "book ROI" measurements for these firms.

... category of firms for which the return on capital has less than normal significance is made of those using relatively little capital, and whose ability to make profits is much more a function of technical skill or research than of the capital investment they command. Such industries as publishing and pharmaceuticals may perhaps be taken as representatives of this group.

The existence of this last class, which relies less on its physical equipment than on its technical skill, serves to remind us of what is, perhaps, the most serious deficiency in rate of return calculations—namely, that most computations of 'capital employed' or 'investment' limit themselves to tangible investment. Because expenditure on research is not usually capitalized (even when results are evidenced by patents), no intangible assets are deemed to result from it. The same thing is true of the initial expenditures which a company makes to bring itself into existence, and to get itself organized to do business. Similarly, money spent over the years in developing harmonious relations with customers, suppliers and employees—the constituents of valuable goodwill—does not enter into investment computations.[11]

These deficiencies of "book ROI" are absent from the proposed TAROR model. Note that because the relevant flows are cash flows, TAROR results, unlike "book ROI" results, are unaffected by *accounting* capitalization-versus-expense-decisions. Further, unlike conventional calculations, the TAROR calculation gives recognition to both development expenditures and the related benefits

[11]David Solomons, *Divisional Performance: Measurement and Control*, New York: Financial Executives Research Foundation, 1965, p. 124.

reflected as increases in divisional terminal value over a period of time.

The proposed model offers important potential advantages as a motivational and guidance system for divisional executives. TAROR results are affected by both current or this year's operations as well as operation up to management's planning horizon. The long-run perspective of the model is no justification for poor short-run performance. To the contrary, because of the discounting function, the TAROR is more sensitive to short-run than long-run results of operations. Unlike conventional models, the proposed model can be used to test explicitly the estimated capital productivity trade-offs between alternatives emphasizing short-range versus long-range considerations. It seems reasonable to suggest that any well-conceived multi-period model should have this strategic facility.

POSITIVE FORCE

As vividly portrayed by the four illustrative cases presented earlier, short-run thinking and unreasonable risk aversion can emerge as unwelcome products of conventional control systems. While the proposed system cannot guarantee company-oriented behavior by divisional executives, it surely has no apparent characteristics that would discourage such behavior. We would at present tentatively hypothesize that the proposed model can serve as a positive motivational force in divisional planning and control. A more confident assessment, however, must await the results of implementation.

The third, and final, criterion for judging the proposed model involves the question of how well does it measure the performance of divisional executives. We hasten to repeat that the problem of developing sound and acceptable guidelines for distinguishing between controllable versus non-controllable transactions is common to all control models. The proposed TAROR model claims no special advantage on this count. It does, however, overcome the most serious shortcoming of conventional control systems.

As stated earlier, conventional systems focus on current period results, but fail to examine how well the divisional executive is providing for the future. Whether we are evaluating performance of managers, whole divisions, products, or markets, the fact remains that no meaningful conclusions can be reached unless consideration is extended to the end of the planning period. Just as in capital expenditure analysis current outlays are considered in light of prospective returns for the life of the project, performance measurements require that current and past outlays be evaluated in relation to their expected benefits in forthcoming periods. It is important to recognize that many current period decisions by divisional executives affect not only results in this period, but alter the magnitude and timing of net receipts for future periods as well. The proposed model which gives explicit recognition to the impact of current decisions on future period results should serve the purposes of performance measurement most capably. Indeed, it may serve as a basis for rewarding managers for their contribution to the long-term growth and development of the company as well as for their more immediate contributions.

LEARNING TOOL

The discipline required by the proposed system should prove to be an important "learning" tool for headquarters and division executives alike. By a period-to-period comparison of operating results and revised forecasts, headquarters has some broad indication of how well division managers conduct the search for opportunities, how well they implement decisions to undertake selected opportunities, and how well they adapt to unforeseen changes in the environment.

The projected TAROR, when compared with industry benchmarks, may provide a point of departure for the quality of the division manager's opportunity search. The control report which compares planned versus actual results for the period may serve as an indication of how well decisions are implemented. This control report, including the seven-year forecast at the beginning and the ending of the year, may also provide insight into the adaptiveness of divisional executives to unforeseen events. As Anthony observes, the aim of control is not necessarily to gain operating results that conform as closely as possible to plans.

Since no one can foretell the future precisely—that is, since people are not clairvoyant—it follows that in some respects actual events will differ from the assumed events that the plans were designed to meet. Even if plans are revised frequently, the preparation and communication of revisions take time, and the revised plans therefore cannot be up-to-date in the literal sense of this term. Top management wants middle management to react to the events that actually occur, not to those that might have occurred had the real world been kind enough to conform to the planning assumptions. Therefore top management does not necessarily want operations to conform to plans.

ANTICIPATING ERRORS

Furthermore, since people are not omniscient, their plans do not necessarily show the best course of action; they merely show what was thought of as best when the plan was made.

Subsequently, someone may think of a way to improve on the plan; indeed, it is quite likely that he will do so as the facts and alternatives become clearer. If he does, he should act accordingly. For this reason, also, top management does not necessarily want operations to conform to plans.[12]

It should be recognized that large and consistent variations in period-to-period forecasts may well be a manifestation of unsatisfactory opportunity search, poor decision-implementation, and an inability to adapt to unforeseen changes in a timely fashion. A careful review of planning assumptions and estimating procedures serves to develop information about the pattern of errors associated with different divisional executives. This, in turn, serves as an essential prerequisite for improving the accuracy of future estimates.

IMPLEMENTATION CHALLENGES

Analogous to the young candidate who campaigns against the well-entrenched incumbent, the proposed system must hold extraordinary promise to gain even initial attention. Furthermore, as would be the case with any new system, certain risks must be forthrightly faced. In our judgment, the proposed system has one major obstacle to overcome before it can be expected to gain widespread acceptance. Notwithstanding this obstacle, to be discussed, support for the proposed system rests on the proposition that its benefit-to-risk ratio is substantially more favorable than that of its competitors, the conventional systems.

[12] Robert N. Anthony, *Planning and Control Systems: A Framework for Analysis*, Boston, Division of Research, Harvard Business School, 1965, pp. 28-29.

The principal risk involves the use of projections of an uncertain future for purposes of evaluating current performance. There is first the question of the sensitivity of TAROR results to projections that ultimately prove to be inaccurate. There is the further concern about where in the organization the responsibility for forecasting should reside. The former question centers on the issue of whether more objectively determined, but largely irrelevant and often misleading measurements, are to be preferred to relevant measurements subject to varying degrees of accuracy because of uncertain predictive inputs. Any generalization must await the test of empirical evidence, but it certainly would not be surprising to find that in most cases differences due to choice of measurement method (TAROR versus "book ROI") would exceed differences between estimated and actual TAROR due to the use of inaccurate projections. It should be further noted that TAROR need not be expressed as a deterministic output. Using risk analysis techniques, it may instead be expressed as a TAROR probability distribution.

The question of where in the organization responsibility for divisional budget projections should be placed involves two basic choices: within the division or outside the division—presumably corporate headquarters. To suggest the latter alternative would be contrary to the tenets of decentralized profit responsibility as well as potentially damaging to company interests. On the other hand, the suggestion that budget projections remain within the jurisdiction of the divison introduces the possibility of a conflict situation for divisional executives. The potential conflict emerges from the fact that given the proposed model, the divisional executive can to some degree bias his performance measurements by virtue of his control over budgetary projections. While we acknowledge that this can become a problem in some instances, the following safeguards should tend to minimize its seriousness:

1. A comprehensive educational program explaining the proposed new approach to divisional planning and control should precede its implementation. The advantages as well as the key role of divisional executives should be stressed.

2. Corporate management and staff should carefully review the explicit planning premises underlying budgetary projections.

3. Corporate management and staff should compare actual versus budgeted results and evaluate the reasonableness of past projections as a basis for encouraging improvement in future projections.

CONCLUSION

The joint effect of the accelerated trends toward merger and decentralization has further increased the critical need for divisional planning and control systems that facilitate the integration of corporate and divisional goals, and also provide a balance between short- and long-range considerations. We believe that the system proposed in the article offers great promise as a first step toward accomplishing these two key objectives of management control. Because of its demonstrable superiority to conventional systems, we hope that it will become a widely and profitably applied tool for divisional planning and control.

An Integrated Evaluation System for Budget Forecasting and Operating Performance

Y. Ijiri

Carnegie-Mellon University

J. C. Kinard

Ohio State University

F. B. Putney

Columbia University

This article presents a performance evaluation system which measures a manager both as a forecaster and as an operating decision maker. The evaluation system is applicable to situations in which the individual who prepares the forecast is also responsible for the forecasted operations. The difficult behavioral problems associated with developing penalty coefficients for misestimation are pointed out.

Reprinted from the *Journal of Accounting Research*, Spring 1968, 1-11. Used by permission of Y. Ijiri, J. C. Kinard, F. B. Putney and the *Journal of Accounting Research*.

This study was supported, in part, by funds made available by the Ford Foundation to the Graduate School of Business, Stanford University. The authors are indebted to the participants of the Accounting Colloquy at the Graduate School of Business, Stanford University for their helpful comments and suggestions.

The bibliography was compiled by F. B. Putney and J. C. Kinard.

Planning may be described as the process of developing a strategy for changing or responding to changes in one's environment; however, few responses can be made instantaneously; most require lead time. For example, a firm must plan the size of its sales force, funds, plant capacity, etc., since they cannot be significantly changed overnight. Accurate forecasting is important because critical and irrevocable present actions depend upon such forecasts. Even where effective instantaneous response is possible, it is often more efficient to select the eventual response prior to the actual event.

Consider the Pik Corporation which produces a perishable product that must be sold no later than the day after production since it becomes valueless at the end of that day. It can be produced on the day before sale at a variable cost of $2 per unit or, on the day of sale, by a crash program at a variable cost of $3 per unit; in the latter case, it perishes at the end of the day of production. The per unit selling price is $6. Thus, any overestimation of sales on the following day will cost the firm $2 per unit and any underestimation of sales on the following day will cost the firm (in the form of extra cost) $1 per unit.[1] If a forecaster's estimates on 10 trials are as shown in Table 1, the average cost due to forecasting error is $140 per day.

of forecasts may not be necessary, as Stedry (1960) observed, but in budgetary planning it is crucial to obtain accurate forecasts to minimize the forecasting displacement cost.[2]

An accounting and evaluation system of forecaster's performance is therefore as essential as the control of operator's performance. Such an evaluation system may be used as a basis for monetary of

TABLE 1

		Underestimation		Overestimation	
Difference between estimate and actual	−200	−100	0	+100	+200
Frequency	1	2	3	3	1
Total units of over- and underestimation	200	200	0	300	200
		400		500	
Cost per unit of misestimation		$1		$2	
Total cost due to forecasting errors		$400		$1,000	
			$1,400	(or $140 per day)	

We call this cost of forecasting error "forecasting displacement cost"; in the example, this means perishable inventory unsold because of overestimation and extra production cost because of underestimation. There are many cases which involve forecasting displacement cost. Overestimation can result in out-of-pocket costs for excess production capacity as well as its cost of capital, spoiled perishable inventory, excess inventory carrying cost, etc. Underestimation can result in lost profit from sales not made, emergency production and purchases at extra costs, etc. Forecasting displacement cost includes both opportunity and actual costs; from the standpoint of optimization, all of these costs represent inefficiency resulting from forecasting error. Thus, in budgetary control the accuracy

nonmonetary incentive systems, although accounting and reporting of forecasting performance alone may provide motivation for forecaster accuracy.

The evaluation of a forecaster's performance is based primarily on his estimates as compared with actual results. Theoretically, it may be argued that his performance should be evaluated in terms of the difference between his estimate, E, and the best estimate, E^*, that any forecaster can ever make ex ante under the given circumstances. Since there may be many factors which are unforeseeable to all forecasters and since it is difficult

[1] See Chapter 1 of Pratt, Raiffa, and Schlaifer (1965) for more examples of this type.

[2] Here, by the accuracy of a forecast we mean the degree to which an estimate of a factor in the future differs from the actual result. The degree of deviation may be measured in many different ways such as $E - A$ or $(E - A)^2$, where E is the estimate and A is the actual.

to segregate foreseeable from unforeseeable factors, we do not derive E^* operationally. But, in the long run, luck in forecasting should even out. Thus, among forecasters who are estimating the same factor, one who can do better than the others when compared with the ex ante best estimate will be expected to do better than the others, on the average, when compared with the ex post actual.

A more complicated problem arises when an operator is asked to forecast factors under his control. The responsibility for forecasting can be placed either on staff or operating personnel. The trend, however, seems to be to assign the primary responsibility for forecasting to operating personnel with assistance provided by staff personnel specializing in forecasting. For example, the vice-president in charge of marketing, divisional or district sales managers, or salesmen are often responsible for sales forecasting although they may obtain help from a marketing research staff group.[3] The primary advantage of letting operating personnel forecast the factors related to their operations is that, in general, they know more about these factors than others. In this situation, we have an interaction of forecasting and operating which an evaluation system must take into account.

An integrated evaluation system based on the desired properties can be developed. Let P denote the performance measure (the larger the P, the better the performance), let E denote the amount of the factor estimated, and let A be the actual amount of the factor attained; thus, P is dependent upon both E and A. Next, impose the following two conditions on the way in which P is derived

from E and A; these assume that a larger A is more desirable from the organizational standpoint:[4] for any given level of A, P must be greater if E is closer to A, and for any given level of E, P must be greater if A is greater.[5]

To illustrate the first condition, suppose the sales manager of the Pik Corporation sold 1.5 million cases in each of two consecutive years. In the first year, he forecast sales at 1 million cases; in the second, at 1.4 million cases. His performance measure in the second year should be higher than the first. The highest performance measure for any given actual sales occurs when the estimate is exactly equal to the actual. To illustrate the second condition, suppose the sales manager estimated the sales in each of two consecutive years to be 1 million cases. He actually sold 1 million cases in the first year and 1.5 million cases in the second. His performance measure in the second year should be higher than in the first.

We now explore a simple example of the application of such an evaluation system. A salesman for the Pik Corporation is asked to estimate the level of sales for a product for the next period. His performance evaluation as a forecaster-operator is computed as follows. The estimated number of units will be sold to him at a per unit cost of $10.00. The market price is $15.00 per unit. If he

---

[3] For example, the study by the American Management Association (1956) indicated that the sales department is mentioned most frequently as the primary source of sales forecasting. See also the National Industrial Conference Board (1963).

[4] In the economics and accounting literature, the point is often made that both an upper and lower bound will exist for desirable levels of the operation due to diminishing returns. The lower bound is that level of operations below which the operations would be discontinued, while the upper bound represents the point at which marginal cost exceeds marginal benefit. In many situations, however, the range of actual operations does not approach either bound.

[5] A mathematical statement of these conditions may be as follows: Forecasting-Evaluation Condition: $\partial P/\partial E > 0$ for $E < A$, $\partial P/\partial E = 0$ for $E = A$, $\partial P/\partial E < 0$ for $E > A$. Operating-Evaluation Condition: $\partial P/\partial A > 0$ for all A, providing, of course, the partial derivatives exist.

does not sell his estimated quantity he can sell back the remaining units at $8.00 per unit. If he can sell more than his original estimate he may purchase his additional needs at $12.00 per unit. His performance measure is given by the profit calculated on the basis of these costs and revenues.[6]

To illustrate the calculation procedure, suppose the salesman estimates sales volume to be 50 units and subsequently sells 60 units. His profit would be calculated as given in Situation 1 below. However, with the same actual sales volume and an estimate of 80 units, his profit would be calculated as given in Situation 2 below.

condition. Figure 1 shows how performance measure P changes as A changes for various given values of E, and Figure 2 shows how P changes as E changes for various given values of A.

Incentive systems based on an evaluation system similar to the one proposed above can be found in negotiated incentive-fee contracts used in Department of Defense (DOD) procurement. Basically, government procurement falls into two categories—competitive bidding and negotiated contracts. Within both of these, increasing use is being made of incentive-fee based contracts. In the DOD, significant contracts are awarded

		Situation 1	Situation 2
Revenue	60 units @ $15	$900	$900
Costs	60 units @ $10	600	600
		300	300
Less: Penalties for misestimation			
Underestimation	10 units @ $2	20	
Overestimation	20 units @ $2		40
Profit		$280	$260

However, on his accounting record the penalties may be entered implicitly as follows:

Revenue 60 units @ $15 = $ 900

Costs   50 units @ $10 = (500)
         10 units @ $12 = (120)   (620)
Profit $ 280

on a negotiated basis; for example, 55% of all prime contracts awarded in fiscal year 1965 were negotiated contracts.[7]

60 units @ $15 = $900
20 units @ $ 8 = 160 $1,060
80 units @ $10 =   (800)
                       $260

Table 2 shows the salesman's profit for various combinations of estimate and actual. Notice from the underlinings in Table 2 that the salesman's profit is at a maximum for any actual volume of sales (a row) when the actual equals his estimate. For any given estimate (a column), profit increases for each additional unit sold, satisfying the operating-evaluation

[6]Note that all transactions between the salesman and the company are hypothetical and need not involve actual transfers of goods and cash. In addition, the amount of costs and revenues need not have external validity.

Although most, if not all, negotiated contracts could use an incentive system, we find the application of a system similar to the one discussed above only in those cases utilizing an incentive-fee. For these, the DOD procedure has two basic stages—the negotiation stage (which corresponds to our forecasting stage) and the performance stage (which corresponds to our operating stage). At the negotiation stage, the contractor and contracting

[7]See Office of the Secretary of Defense (1965), p. 8.

TABLE 2

Actual market sales (in units)	Estimated market sales (in units)									
	0	10	20	30	40	50	60	70	80	90
0	0	−20	−40	−60	−80	−100	−120	−140	−160	−180
10	30	50	30	10	−18	−30	−50	−70	−90	−110
20	60	80	100	80	60	40	20	0	−20	−40
30	90	110	130	150	130	110	90	70	50	30
40	120	140	160	180	200	180	160	140	120	100
50	150	170	190	210	230	250	230	210	190	170
60	180	200	220	240	260	280	300	280	260	240
70	210	230	250	270	290	310	330	350	330	310
80	240	260	280	300	320	340	360	380	400	380
90	270	290	310	330	350	370	390	410	430	450
100	300	320	340	360	380	400	420	440	460	480

agency develop a target cost, target fee, plus a cost/profit sharing ratio. At the operating stage, the contractor's fee is adjusted by applying the sharing ratio to any decreases (increases) in costs and adding (deducting) this amount from the target fee.[8] A numerical example illustrates this basic procedure.

$$E = \text{Target Cost} = \$10,000,000$$
$$P = \text{Target Fee} = \$1,000,000$$
$$\text{Sharing Ratio} = 80/20 \quad (80\%\text{-government}/20\%\text{-contractor}).$$

Case 1: A = Actual costs = $12,000,000

Net fee = $1,000,000 − .20(12,000,000 − 10,000,000) = $600,000.

Case 2: A = Actual costs = $9,000,000

Net fee = $1,000,000 + .20(10,000,000 − 9,000,000) = $1,200,000.

The evaluation system discussed earlier differs from the DOD procedure in only

one material respect—the target fee (payoff) is modified not only by operations but also by any misestimation. The extension of the incentive system to include the effects of misestimation could be considered a formal extension of the negotiation process. However, the estimation responsibility falls upon the contractor since he chooses the proper payoff function. The contracting agency's estimation is done separately and in advance by selecting a family of payoff functions based on prior information. The payoff functions then serve as the mediating or negotiating function. Using the same numerical example, assume the contractor selected the payoff function which has a target fee of $1,000,000 with a sharing ratio for misestimation (k_1) of .05 and a sharing ratio for costs (k_2) of .1. In equation form the net fee would equal:

$$P = \$1,000,000 - k_1 \,|\, E - A \,| + k_2(E - A)$$
$$= \$1,000,000 - .05 \,|\, E - A \,| + .1(E - A).$$

Case 1: A = Actual costs = $12,000,000
$$P = \$1,000,000 -$$
$$.05 \,|\, - 2,000,000 \,| +$$
$$.1(-2,000,000)$$
$$= \$700,000.$$

---

[8]The structure, provisions, and calculation procedures are discussed in detail in Office of Assistant Secretary of Defense (1965).

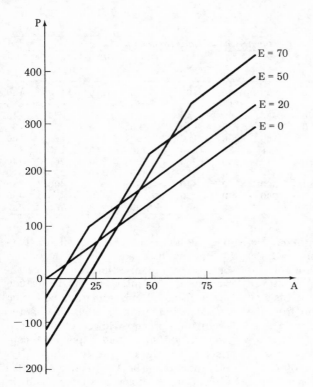

FIGURE 1.

Case 2: A = Actual costs = \$9,000,000
P = \$1,000,000 –
.05 | 1,000,000 | +
.1(1,000,000)
= \$1,050,000

Of course, factors other than costs could readily be included in these incentive systems. Many incentive-fee contracts awarded by the DOD utilize multiple incentives such as cost, schedule, and quality.[9] Also a specific range or boundaries for the fee may be established, but these are only modifications of the basic form. If multiple incentives are desirable, more terms are added to the fee calculation, thus requiring estimation of more factors. For example, it would be possible to expand the payoff equation as follows:

$$P = \$1,000,000 - k_1 \; | E - A |$$
$$+ k_2 \; (E - A) - k_3 \; | E_s - A_s |$$
$$+ k_4 (E_s - A_s) - k_5 \; | E_q - A_q |$$
$$+ k_6 \; (E_q - A_q),$$

where the s and q subscripts indicate schedule (in days) and quality standards (in terms of performance).

The performance evaluation model discussed above can also be applied to responsibility accounting. Each responsibility center submits its budget which provides a basis for the central planning group. The performance of the responsibility center is then evaluated by using the accounting figures calculated on ordinary accounting methods plus a penalty for misestimation. For example, if we let P be the profit, R_e and R_a be estimated

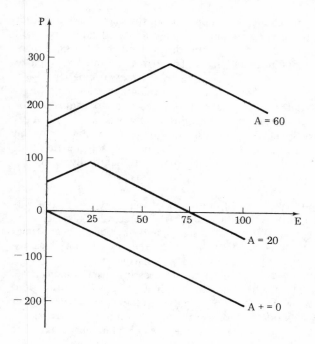

FIGURE 2.

and actual revenue, C_e and C_a be estimated and actual cost, and k_r and k_c be penalty coefficients, then P, which is ordinarily calculated by $R_a - C_a$, is determined as

$$P = R_a - C_a - k_r \mid R_e - R_a \mid -$$
$$k_e \mid C_e - C_a \mid {}^{10}$$

The penalty for misestimation is especially important when the forecast made by one responsibility center affects the performance of another. A typical example is the case where the production volume is based on the sales forecast made by the sales division.

The penalty coefficients for misestimation must be determined after careful

study of the forecasting displacement costs involved, as well as other factors such as profit margins. It is difficult to make a general statement about how one should actually calculate the penalty coefficients; however, in general, we can say that (1) if the forecasting displacement costs involved are large, the penalty coefficients should also be made large relative to the operating performance measure (making the angle of the lines in Figure 2 more acute), (2) the penalty coefficients should not be made so large as to discourage operations beyond the estimated level insofar as such operations are desirable from the standpoint of the organization as a whole. For example, the penalty per unit of misestimation in sales should not be greater than the profit margin.[11] Of course, the penalty coeffi-

[10] Of course, as mentioned in footnote 2, the accuracy may be measured not only by the absolute value of the difference between estimate and actual, but also its square or any other transformations of the difference.

[11] This is simply a restatement of the conditions set forth in footnote 5.

cients need not be constant throughout the range of misestimation. (If we vary the coefficients, the lines in Figure 2 are replaced by stepwise-linear or non-linear curves.) Or they may differ between overestimation and underestimation.

The difficulty of determining precisely how the forecasting displacement cost should be reflected in the penalty coefficients for misestimation is further compounded by two factors. One is the utility which the forecaster-operator attaches to the various values of performance measure. It is this utility that ultimately affects the behavior of the forecaster-operator rather than any external performance or incentive measure. Since utility is a personal matter, the optimum alignment of the penalty coefficient with the forecasting displacement cost differs from person to person and causes the difficulty in creating an operational evaluation system.

The second problem is that of personal bias in estimation.[12] Knight and Weinwurm state:

[12] If we let E_i and A_i be the estimate and the actual in the ith trial, the forecaster's *bias* shown in the past n trials may be quantified by

$$\text{Bias} = \frac{1}{n}\sum_{i=1}^{n} (E_i - A_i).$$

Alternatively, we may define the forecaster's *precision* to mean the degree of variability of $E_i - A_i$, with the idea that if the variability of $E_i - A_i$ is smaller, the forecast is more useful since after adjusting for the bias, E_i will be closer to A_i. One possible measure of precision is:

$$\text{Precision} = \frac{1}{n}\sum_{i=1}^{n} [(E_i - \text{Bias}) - A_i]^2.$$

Interested readers may verify that if we use $1/n[\sum_{i=1}^{n} (E_i - A_i)^2]$ as the measure of the forecaster's accuracy (see footnote 2), we have the following relation between the three measures defined above:

Reports from the salesmen in a district are then accumulated and forwarded to the district and regional sales managers. These men ... are expected to draw upon their own experience as a basis for evaluating sales conditions and prospects and for adjusting or correcting the reports of the individual salesmen, some of whom may be known to be over-optimistic ..., while others may habitually make pessimistic forecasts.[13]

Of course, bias itself may not be undesirable; where the forecasting displacement cost is significantly higher for overestimation than for underestimation, bias toward underestimation may be desirable. Given the forecasting displacement costs and the personal tendency in estimation, it may be desirable for the central planner to adjust the subordinate's forecast for use in the overall plan and retain the original forecasts for evaluations.

Consider the example given in Table 1 and assume that the forecaster's tendency in estimation is expected to remain as given in Table 1, i.e., 10% and 20% chances of underestimation by 200 units and 100 units, 30% chance of accurate estimation, and 30% and 10% chances of overestimation by 100 units and 200 units. Then, from the viewpoint of the central planner it is desirable to reduce the forecaster's estimate by 100 units. To show this point, let us note that the chances of misestimation after the adjustment are changed to 10%, 20%, and 30% chances of underestimation by 300, 200, and 100 units, respectively, 30% chance of accurate estimation, and 10% chance of overestimation by 100 units. Since each unit of underestimation costs $1 while each unit of overestimation costs

$$\text{Accuracy} = \text{Precision} + (\text{Bias})^2.$$

See also Cochran and Cox (1957), p. 16.

―――――――――――――――――

[13] Knight and Weinwurm (1964), p. 73.

$2, the expected forecasting displacement cost of the firm when the adjustment is made is given by:

$$\$1 \times [.1 \times 300 + .2 \times 200 + .3 \times 100 + .3 \times 0] + [.1 \times 100] \times \$2 = \$120.$$

This is $20 per day savings compared to the case where the firm makes no adjustment, assuming the forecaster's tendency in estimation will remain as given in Table 1.[14]

[14] It can easily be verified from Table 1 that the firm's expected forecasting displacement cost is a stepwise-linear function of the amount the firm subtracts from (or adds to) the forecaster's estimate and that the minimum expected displacement cost is $120 which is given when 100 units are subtracted from the forecast.

The problems mentioned above are not easy to solve; however, the efforts to develop a proper evaluation system of budget forecasting and planning seem warranted. It took many decades to develop reasonable evaluation and incentive systems on operating performance; much experimentation is probably necessary to develop reasonable evaluation and incentive systems on forecasting performance as well as systems which integrate the two types of performance.

REFERENCES

American Management Association, *Sales Forecasting, Special Report No. 16* (New York: 1956).

Elmer C. Bratt, *Business Forecasting* (New York: McGraw-Hill Book Company, 1958).

A. Charnes and A. C. Stedry, *The Attainment of Organization Goals through Appropriate Selection of Sub-Unit Goals* (unpublished paper, August 5, 1964).

William G. Cochran and Gertrude M. Cox, *Experimental Design,* 2d. ed. (New York: John Wiley and Sons, Inc., 1957).

Yuji Ijiri, *Management Goals and Accounting for Control* (Amsterdam: North-Holland Publishing Co.; Chicago: Rand McNally, 1965).

W. D. Knight and E. H. Weinwurm, *Managerial Budgeting* (New York: The Macmillan Co., 1964).

James G. March and Herbert A. Simon, *Organizations* (New York: John Wiley and Sons, Inc., 1958).

National Industrial Conference Board, *Forecasting in Industry, Studies in Business Policy No. 77* (New York: 1956).

Office of Assistant Secretary of Defense (Installations and Logistics), *Incentive Contracting Guide, 1965* (Washington, D.C.: Department of Defense, 19 January, 1965).

Office of the Secretary of Defense, *Department of Defense Cost Reduction Program—Third Annual Progress Report* (Memorandum for the President) (Washington, D.C., 12 July, 1965).

John W. Pratt, Howard Raiffa, and Robert Schlaifer, *Introduction to Statistical Decision Theory* (New York: McGraw-Hill Book Company, 1965).

Andrew C. Stedry, *Budget Control and Cost Behavior* (Englewood Cliffs, N.J.: Prentice-Hall, Inc., 1960).

Comments on a Measure of Forecasting Performance

**Russell M.
Barefield***

University of Arizona

The author offers some observations on the previous article by
Iriri, Kinard and Putney.

Reprinted from the *Journal of Accounting Research*, Autumn 1969,
324-327. Used by permission of Russell M. Barefield and the *Journal of
Accounting Research.*

*The author appreciates comments made on this paper by Professors
J. L. Livingstone, Y. Ijiri, and J. C. Kinard.

In a previous issue of this journal, Ijiri,
Kinard, and Putney[1] propose a performance measure which takes both forecasting accuracy and actual level of operations into account. The purpose of this
note is to elaborate on the possible
effects of such a performance on the
behavior of a forecaster.

A specific algebraic formulation of
their performance measure is

$$P = -k_1 |A - F| + k_2 A$$

where P = the level of performance
attained

A = actual level of operations in
units

F = expected or forecasted level
of operations in units[2]

k_2 = the contribution or profit
margin per unit

k_1 = the penalty coefficient for
misestimation.

In the general formulation of the
performance measure, k_1 could be either
a constant function or a function which
varies with the magnitude of the forecast
error. Regarding k_1, the authors state:

The penalty coefficients for misestimation must be determined after careful
study of the forecasting displacement
costs involved, as well as other factors
such as profit margins. It is difficult to
make a general statement about how
one should actually calculate the
penalty coefficients; however, in general, we can say that (1) if the forecasting displacement costs involved are
large, the penalty coefficients should
also be made large relative to the
operating performance measure . . .
(2) the penalty coefficients should not
be made so large as to discourage
operations beyond the estimated level

[1]Y. Ijiri, J. C. Kinard, and F. B. Putney, "An
Integrated Evaluation System for Budget Forecasting and Operating Performance with a
Classified Budgeting Bibliography," *Journal of
Accounting Research*, 6 (Spring, 1968), 1-28.
[2]Ijiri, Kinard, and Putney originally used E to
denote the expected level of operations in
units. E is used here to denote the expectation
operator in statistics.

insofar as such operations are desirable from the standpoint of the organization as a whole.[3]

Two questions arise about the case where k_1 is a constant:

1. What value in a normative sense should the forecaster predict?
2. In practice, can we expect the performance measure, $-k|A - F|$, to encourage the forecaster to predict the value that the normative theory specifies?

QUESTION 1

There are different measures which can lead to optimal forecasting, depending on the nature of the penalty assessment. To illustrate, assume a forecast represents a choice of a measure of central tendency from the subjective probability density function $f(x)$ of unit operations x.[4] The penalty for forecast errors is measured by the portion of the formula $-k_1 |A - F|$. If we assume that the forecaster wants to maximize his performance measure, then the forecaster should forecast $x = b$ such that the expected value of $k_1 |x - b|$ is a minimum. As is well known in statistics, $E(k_1 |x - b|) = k_1 E(|x - b|)$ is a minimum when b is the median value of the probability density function $f(x)$.[5]

The mode of the distribution will be an optimal prediction when the performance measure is of the form:[6]

$$P = \begin{cases} -\$100 \text{ if } A \neq F \\ \$0 \quad \text{ if } A = F \end{cases} + k_2 A.$$

As an example, assume that the forecaster feels that operations will consist of 0 to 3 units of product being sold and that the probability of each level of sales occurring can be described by the probability distribution $f(x)$:

x	$f(x)$
0	8/20
1	4/20
2	4/20
3	4/20

To maximize P, the forecaster should predict b such that $\$0 \ f(b) - \$100 [1 - f(b)]$ is a maximum. The modal value $b = 0$ maximizes the portion of the performance measure which relates to forecasting accuracy:[7]

b	$\$0 f(b) - \$100 [1 - f(b)]$
0	$\$-60.00
1	$-80.00
2	$-80.00
3	$-80.00

Alternative measures of performance can be devised which make the optimal choice in prediction the mean. As a general rule concerning measures of central tendency, we should predict the mode if we want to be right as often as possible, predict the median if we are

[3] See Ijiri, Kinard, and Putney, *op. cit.*, p. 9.
[4] We assume $f(x)$ satisfies the requirements of a probability density function. A list of these requirements may be found in R. V. Hoag and A. T. Craig, *Introduction to Mathematical Statistics* (New York: The Macmillan Co., 1965), p. 11. We should point out that experimental tests frequently show that subjective probability distributions violate some of these requirements. See W. Edwards, "Behavioral Decision Theory," *Annual Review of Psychology*, 12 (1961), 473-98.
[5] For example, see E. Parzen, *Modern Probability Theory and Its Applications* (New York: John Wiley and Sons, 1960), p. 213.

[6] This performance measure is the one measure discussed in this paper which does not satisfy the conditions specified by Hoag and Craig, *op. cit.*, p. 3. Their conditions require that the degree of error affect the performance measure P.
[7] Implicit in this discussion is the assumption that the forecaster's choice of a value of x to predict has no influence on the value of x which actually occurs.

trying to minimize absolute error, and predict the mean[8] in order to minimize squared error.

In some cases, the optimal prediction may not even be one of the three common measures of central tendency mentioned above. For example, this will occur when the value of k_1 depends on the direction or sign of forecast error. An example of such a value of k_1 might be:

$$P = -k_1 \, |A - F| + k_2 A \text{ where } k_1$$
$$= \begin{Bmatrix} \$2 \text{ when } A < F \\ \$1 \text{ when } A \geqslant F \end{Bmatrix}.$$

In this case, specific knowledge of the probability density function of operations, $f(x)$, would be required before the optimal prediction strategy could be specified.

As an illustration, consider the probability density function $f(x) = (1/50)x$, $0 \leqslant x \leqslant 10$. The mean, median, and mode of this distribution are 6.67, 7.07, and 10.0, respectively.[9] To find the optimal strategy, we must choose b such that $E(k_1|x - b|)$ is a minimum.

$$E(k_1 \, |x - b \,|) = \int_0^{10} k_1 \, |x - b \,| f(x)\, dx$$

[8]See W. L. Hays, *Statistics for Psychologists* (New York: Holt, Rinehart and Winston, 1963), p. 165.
[9]The mean, median and mode are derived as follows:

$$\text{Mean} = E(x) = \int_0^{10} xf(x)\, dx = \int_0^{10} \frac{1}{50} x^2 \, dx$$

$$= \frac{1}{150} x^2 \, \Big|_0^{10} = 6.67.$$

$$\text{Median} = \int_0^{m} \frac{1}{50} x \, dx = \frac{1}{2} \text{ or } \frac{1}{2} = \frac{1}{100} x^2 \, \Big|_0^{m}$$

$$= \frac{m^2}{100} \quad m = 7.07.$$

$$= \int_0^{10} k_1 \, |x - b \,| \frac{1}{50} x\, dx$$

$$= \int_b^{10} \$1 \, (x - b) \frac{1}{50} x\, dx$$

$$+ \int_0^{b} \$2 \, (b - x) \frac{1}{50} x\, dx$$

which simplifies to $(b^3/100) - b + (20/3)$.

Setting the first derivative with respect to b equal to zero, we find an extreme value, $b*$, which satisfies $(3b*^2/100) - 1 = 0$, or $b* = 5.77$.[10] Note that the optimal prediction in this case is lower than any of the three measures of central tendency discussed above.

QUESTION 2

The second question deals with whether a performance measure like $P = -k_1 | A - F | + k_2 A$ will actually encourage the forecaster to predict the value which is specified by our normative theory. There is some evidence that it may not. Peterson and Miller[11] in a sequence of two laboratory experiments using students as subjects tested the subject's ability to adopt optimal prediction strategies. Each of three groups of subjects had either the mean, median, or mode as an optimal prediction strategy. They summarized their results as follows:

The clear conclusion from Experiment I is that Ss are surprisingly accurate in minimizing expected cost under mode and median cost conditions, but not under mean cost conditions.[12]

[10]The second derivative is $(6b/100)$ which is positive for values of b in the domain of $f(x)$, so $B* = 5.77$ is a minimum.
[11]See C. Peterson and A. Miller, "Mode, Median, and Mean as Optimal Strategies," *Journal of Experimental Psychology*, 6 (October, 1964), 366.
[12]*Ibid.*

One possible explanation offered for the failure of subjects to adopt the mean prediction strategy was that the "apparatus [used in the experiment] emphasized error too much and cost not enough."[13] A second experiment provided only a small amount of support for this explanation. In both of these experiments, subjects whose optimal strategy was to predict the mean consistently erred in the direction of the median. Apparently, more complex measures hinder a subject's ability to develop optimal strategies.[14]

[13] *Ibid.*
[14] One such measure might be $P = -k_1(A - F)^2 + k_2A$.

SUMMARY

This note has pointed to the need to examine the possible conditions under which optimal performance measures can be identified and implemented. Although we must be careful in applying the results of laboratory experiments, they might be used to determine characteristics which make the measures appear more complex. One might also investigate further the relationship between performance measure complexity and tendency to minimize error rather than cost.

Using Input/Output Analysis for Evaluating Profit Center Performance

S. W. Yost

Combustion Engineering, Inc.

C. E. Stowell

Combustion Engineering, Inc.

The authors begin with a review of the fundamentals of input-output analysis. They proceed to show how an input-output model of the U.S. economy combined with a detailed product-industry consumption matrix relevant to a specific profit center are used at Combustion Engineering. Specifically, the input-output methodlogy has been employed for making improved product forecasts, testing the sensitivity of product forecasts to the more variable elements of GNP, allocating resources to most promising markets, and providing a basis for performance evaluation by factoring out those external elements which were not encompassed in the original forecast.

Presented at The Institute of Management Sciences, XVII International Conference, London, July 1-3, 1970. Reprinted with permission of Combustion Engineering, Inc.

"There was a young lady from Natchez
Whose garments were always in patches
When comment arose
On the state of her clothes
She said 'When Ah itches, Ah scratches!' "

anon.

Like the young lady in the limerick, when a corporation itches, it too scratches. To put it another way, commercial enterprises are problem-oriented rather than technique-oriented. The successful management scientist recognizes this and avoids letting any personal penchant influence him in his search for the methodology that will solve the problem.

The itch that we are attempting to scratch in this paper is that of evaluating profit center performance. How do you measure a profit center's performance? This is really a loaded question. The easy way out is to answer "Look at the bottom line and maybe the return on investment." But, of course, these measures are relative—relative to a plan or budget, to other corporate profit centers, to other corporate investments. More importantly, why ask the question? What does top management really want to know? What decisions will be based on the answers?

What we want to know at Combustion Engineering is: how effective is the management of a profit center in doing its job? It is not the center's performance, but rather management's performance that we would like to get a fix on, and you can't do it simply by looking at the "bottom line" or the return on investment. These measures reflect what *has happened* rather than what *was possible*. They measure the immediate consequences of operating decisions, but they do not measure the *quality* of those decisions.

In our approach to the evaluation problem, we begin by defining management as the process by which the destiny of an enterprise is controlled or shaped. An effective management is one which recognizes changes in its environment quickly and moves to meet them in a way that the profit center's objectives are met or bettered.

We believe that fundamentally there are two aspects to this process. One is managing internal operations in a way that permits a firm to fit into its environment in the most effective manner. This is meant to imply efficient operations in terms of the trade-off between cost and adaptability, or flexibility if you prefer. These are areas over which management has direct control.

A simple example of this is the decision whether to install special purpose or general purpose machinery. The former will result in the lowest cost production runs as long as the product does not change often. General purpose machines, however, can handle a variety of products, or product changes, with relatively smaller set-up costs, but with a higher unit cost. The proper decision takes into account market and technical trends affecting its products as well as production efficiency in order to place the firm in the best *overall* competitive position.

On the other hand, management usually has little control over the environment external to the firm. Consequently, to exert control over the destiny of the firm, management must be able to perceive the nature of its external environment, now and in the future, and take such action as needed to permit the firm to capitalize on this knowledge. For example, this may involve such strategic decisions as determining the rate and direction of diversification in markets and products.

Taking this as our definition of what effective management is all about, how do we evaluate profit center performance? Again, we see two areas. One is the traditional measurement of actual performance against planned performance, but with the latter adjusted to take into account the impact of economic factors external to the profit center and beyond management's control.

The second area is that of measuring management's ability to perceive the profit center's environment and to adapt to it. This involves evaluating the soundness of their plans and contingency plans and their means for monitoring the environment—economic, customer, and competitor. To evaluate these activities, we shift some of our attention away from the end results of our manager's performance and instead look at the underlying *means* to that end. Among other things, this approach has the advantage of helping us to avoid the situation where high short-term gains may result in long-term disaster. An example of this is described later in the article. Also, our approach gives us some assurance that profit center decisions are based on an explicit analysis of conditions that are likely to prevail in the future and not on a simple extrapolation of the past.

With both of the above evaluation objectives, we have found that an econometric technique known as Input/Output analysis has important advantages. The concept of Input/Output (I/O) was developed by Wassily Leontief of Harvard University several decades ago. Based on a systematic representation of all interindustry business transactions and tied to national income accounting *vis a vis* the gross national product (GNP), this method of representing the entire economy has interested both government and industry economists in recent years. Several published I/O tables, or "models", of the U.S. economy now exist. The most ambitious, in terms of detail, is one recently prepared by the U.S. Department of Commerce. A number of research institutes and consulting firms have also developed I/O models which they utilize in making forecasts of industry markets.

Three years ago Combustion Engineering, as a diversified supplier of many industries, became interested in this potentially powerful tool. Ultimately a model was developed, checked against government and consulting models, and placed in service.

In the balance of the article. we will summarize briefly the logic of the basic Input/Output model and how we have adapted it for use in a profit center at Combustion Engineering. We will then describe the overall methodology developed for evaluating profit center performance.

THE FUNDAMENTALS OF INPUT/OUTPUT ANALYSIS

The Input/Output (I/O) model essentially represents a blueprint of the way the entire economy is linked together. Each industry sells certain products to other industries to support the production of their final product. For instance, in order to make each automobile, industries sell to the auto manufacturer certain amounts of steel, plastic, glass, etc. The I/O model is simply a means of storing these sales in the form of ratios which reflect, for example, the dollars of steel sold to the auto industry per output of automobiles. Then the model links these interindustry sales to the U.S. GNP by allocating to the industries the various categories of GNP such as new construction and durable goods, by means of historical observations.

In linking each industry's output to the GNP, the model is able to show how the sales of each industry will be affected by each dollar change in GNP. This is accomplished by means of matrix algebra which allows a change in an input to the model to be easily multiplied throughout the system. With this kind of manipulation, it is possible to make assumptions of what the GNP will be in the future and cycle these forecasts back through the model to determine the amount of sales each industry will receive under different conditions.

Figure 1 constructs a hypothetical economy of 800 units divided among three industries. As can be seen, the I/O diagram breaks the total gross output of the economy into two parts, that produced for industry use (listed as "total intermediate output") and that produced for final consumption (listed as "final demand"). Each industry's output produced for itself and the other two industries is listed in the center of boxes 1, 2, and 3 in the *rows,* while the purchases from other industries to support the industry's output is listed in the center of boxes 1, 2, and 3 as *columns.* The sum of these numbers in boxes 1, 2, and 3 represents the intermediate inputs and outputs or the total amount of inter-industry transactions needed to support the level of consumer purchases (i.e., the level of GNP).

For example, when the amount Industry 1 produces for itself and other industries is added to the amount it produces for final sales, the resulting total is the gross output of that industry, in this case 492 units. Looking at Industry 1 as a purchaser instead of as a producer, it is seen (in Column 1) that Industry 1 buys 161 units from itself, no units from Industry 2, and 95.6 units from Industry 3 to make up a total of 256 units purchased. In addition to purchasing from other industries, Industry 1 also purchased labor and capital, and pays taxes and profits which totaled 236 units and is listed as primary inputs (often referred to as "value added"). The addition of the intermediate input and the primary input equals the total gross input for any given industry, in this case 492 units. The sum of the final demand

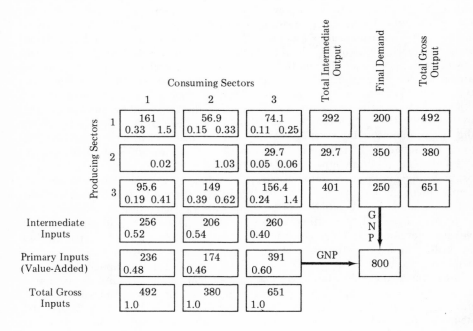

FIGURE 1. Illustration of I/O Model

purchases of goods and services ("final demand" column) equals the cost of producing goods plus the profit ("primary inputs" row) which represents the double accounting method of computing the gross national product, in this example 800 units.

Once we have agreed to model the economy in this manner, two sets of ratios or co-efficients evolve which are basic to the functioning of an Input/Output model

The number in the lower left corner of each industry box represents the amount that the industry must produce to support the *gross output* of an industry divided by the total output of the producing industry. This ratio is called a direct, or technological co-efficient. For example, Industry 1 must produce 161/492 or .33 units to support each unit of its own production.

The number in the lower right corner of each box represents the amount of production needed to support each industry's *final sales*. This number is termed the "indirect co-efficient" and is derived from the I/O table by matric inversion (a mathematical procedure for solving the simultaneous equations represented by the I/O table). For example, Industry 1 must produce 1.5 units per unit of its own final sales (200 units), .33 units per unit of the final sales of Industry 2 (350 units), and .25 units per unit of final sales of Industry 3 (250 units).

To check the results, we can sum the products of each indirect co-efficient multiplied by final sales of each industry:

1.5 x 200 = 312
.33 x 350 = 116
.25 x 250 = 64
Total   = 492 units of GNP

The result is the gross output of Industry 1.

I/O as a forecasting technique separates the sales to other industries from the sales to the ultimate consumer. It has been shown that this is useful for two reasons. One of these is ease in handling numbers. The I/O model permits derivation of the two sets of ratios necessary for rapid mathematical manipulations and calculations, a feature very necessary considering that I/O tables can be set up to handle as many industries as the data available allows. In other words, if the user wishes to know the effect on plastic production of consumers buying $10 million more cars, I/O provides the means for a quick determination.

Secondly, and more importantly from a management point of view, the I/O approach of separating intermediate from final sales offers a way to handle the tough problem of synthesizing economic forecasts with product forecasts. This is the job frequently left up to the line manager when he is given corporate "economic assumptions" with which to plan. I/O allows management attention to be focused separately: (1) on the relationship of its product to other industrial customers, and (2) on consumer sales or the GNP of the economy. Defining one's customer/industry usage patterns is a natural activity for line marketing personnel while economic forecasting is the normal domain of professional economists. A combination of these two activities in an Input/Output model such as the one described below, yields both product and market forecasts for any future year desired in terms that are meaningful to the profit center manager.

ADAPTING THE I/O MODEL TO PROFIT CENTER OPERATIONS

Following the U.S. Bureau of Census practices, many different, but hopefully related, products are aggregated into "industry" classifications. The problem to date with a firm's use of an Input/Output table is that in order to generate product-level forecasts, the model must have data for industries defined very narrowly in terms of specific products. However, none of the I/O models have reached this disaggregated state for the very good reason that a tremendous amount of work and knowledge is required to generate internally consistent sales/output ratios for specific products and their consuming industries. Figure 2 illustrates the kinds of aggregate forecasts currently possible versus those needed by profit center management. We have bypassed this temporary lag in the state-of-the-art

published I/O models by: (1) using the aggregate models to forecast the size of the industries to which a product is sold (Table 1) and (2) developing a separate detailed table for the ratios of the product to each consuming industry (Tables II and III).

Table I represents the use of the Combustion Engineering aggregate I/O model in determining the size of the producing sectors to which refractories are sold.

Out of the 90 total sectors, it was found that refractories were sold to seven sectors. The identification of markets for

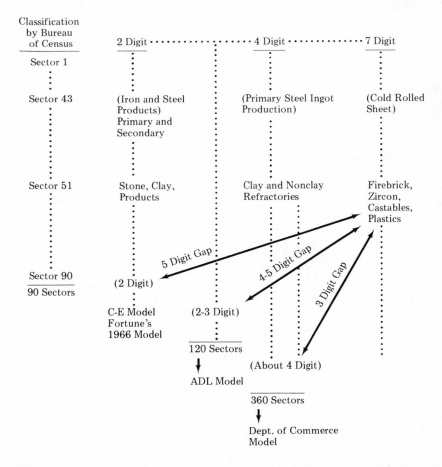

FIGURE 2. Gap Between Product Level Information and State-of-the-Art of I/O Model Output

TABLE I

	Sector 1 . . . . Sector 90	1968 Sales (Billions Current $)
Sector 1		.
.		
.		.
Sector 43	Primary Steel Production	16 (equal to 131 million tons)
.		.
.		.
Sector 45	Stone and Clay Products (cement & ceramics only)	3.5
.		.
.		.
Sector 49	Glass and Glass Products	4
.		.
.		.
Sector 67	Industrial Chemicals	22
.		.
.		.
Sector 69	Petroleum Products	22
.		.
.		.
Sector 72	Nonferrous Metals, Primary & Secondary	15.5
.		.
.		.
Sector 75	Public Utilities	18.5
.		.
.		.
Sector 90		.

refractories, as defined by SIC classification and confirmed by the refractory industry association and the correlation of these markets to the C-E I/O model definition of sectors offers a means of determining the size of the markets to which refractories are sold in any future year.

Once we have the size of the markets to which we sell, the other step needed to arrive at product forecasts is to develop the ratios for the amount of our product sold per output of the market to which we sell (the "direct co-efficient").

Table II illustrates the approach taken to forecast the future direct co-efficient to the primary steel sector 43 shown in Table I.

The refractories sold to steel (line C) divided by the tons of steel produced

TABLE II

	1953	1958	1963	1968 (Estimate in 1963)
A. Total primary steel production (millions of tons)	112	82	109	131
B. Direct co-efficient (1968 dollars of refractories per ton steel processed)	$2.40	$2.05	$1.75	$1.53
C. Total refractories sales for steel processing (millions of dollars)	290	175	190	200m

(line A) equals the co-efficient (line B). By looking at the trend of past co-efficients in Fig. 3, and by interviewing steel technologists, a reasonable future co-efficient can be determined. The 1968 co-efficient estimated originally in 1963 turned out to be off by $.07 ($1.53 vs. $1.60), mostly based on more rapid than expected price increases which resulted in refractory sales totalling 210 million dollars versus the estimate of 200 million dollars.

or whatever is the customary language of the user. This flexibility makes I/O an easy system to install and operate.

Figure 4 represents a simplified scheme which illustrates the parameters used in the C-E matrix.

It shows, for example, the I/O forecast of fireclay (one of the 24 refractory products) in constant and current dollars. The table also indicates the various market sizes such as the open hearth steel processing market and the total primary

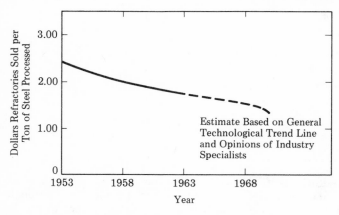

FIGURE 3. Plot of Direct Coefficients (Line B of Table 2)

Table II illustrates the derivation of the total refractory sales to the entire primary production steel market. C-E profit center personnel, however, need much more specific forecast information. For instance, the C-E refractories profit center wanted the amounts of individual refractory products sold to each steel making process. Furthermore, they have particular ways of grouping products in their accounting which are not always compatible with the Bureau of Census Standard Industrial Classification. A great deal of the time spent in setting up an I/O forecasting system, therefore, involved designing the table to meet the needs of operating personnel. The point is that I/O is completely adaptable to whatever format the line people desire and the output can be expressed in tons, barrels, dollars,

steel market which can, in turn, be checked against trade association data to determine the accuracy of the co-efficients. C-E updates its co-efficients both formally and informally through the use of consulting firms and marketing personnel. Yearly I/O forecasts are made each quarter with latest GNP changes, inventory levels, and competitive imports reflected in the forecast.

It should be stressed at this point, however, that the numbers and forecasts emanating from the I/O model are by themselves of limited value. They must be combined with sound market research such as keeping up with technological developments in consuming industry, analyzing the trends which the I/O output indicates, and developing a feel for the movement of key indicators of each

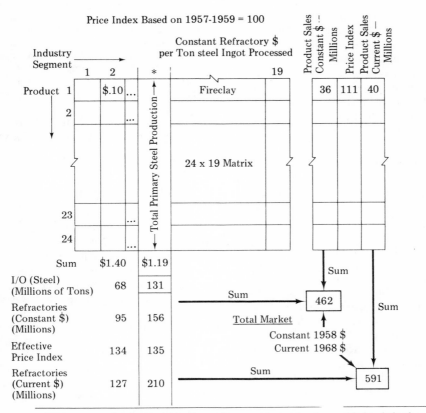

*This column does not exist in the working matrix but has been added to help the reader relate the aggregated primary steel production (Sector 45) figure, used in Tables I and II to the matrix figures.

FIGURE 4. 1968 Matrix of Technology Coefficients for Refractories

product. In other words, the I/O output is only as valid and current as the quality of information which serves as inputs. The model may quickly become obsolete if it is not updated by market specialists as new information becomes known.

The virtue of using the model is that it facilitates and encourages the profit center manager to focus on an important aspect of the business—customer usage of his product. This focus not only enables him to get a better handle on his future market share from a technological standpoint, but the customer usage approach demands a thorough knowledge of each customer, his needs, and how those needs are changing.

Personal contact and detailed knowledge of customer plans are the obvious ingredients of a strong and comprehensive marketing program. Product-level Input/Output analysis demands this kind of attention.

Earlier we said that I/O is an effective tool for evaluating managerial performance both in internal operations and in the environment. The above demonstration of how an I/O model is set up makes it obvious that our definition of performance evaluation is very broad, including not only forecast versus actual results, but the whole methodology of planning.

We are concerned not just that the manager did what he said he would do, but that he has a clear and consistent approach in his practice of management. The next section illustrates how the I/O methodology strengthens the process of forecasting and planning.

FORECASTING WITH I/O

I/O is essentially a longer term forecasting tool (over six months) which is based on identifying technological trends and estimates of the various components of final demand. Because it concentrates on the future industry usage patterns, is comprehensive in its scope, and offers consistency (independently derived steel and automobile industry forecasts may be found to be *simultaneously* impossible through I/O analysis), I/O is likely to be more accurate than other long-range forecasting methods. For instance, the trend line approach applied to the steel market would produce a 1968 sales estimate of significantly less than actual refractories to steel sales of $210 million. Alternatively judging 1968 sales on the basis of percentage growth of steel production would have produced an estimate considerably above $210 million. To get an accurate forecast, the industry to which the product is sold must be correctly estimated along with the industry usage patterns of the product. The I/O method of forecasting has, with the same data base used in other methods, tended to make more accurate forecasts. In the refractory case the I/O figure was more accurate because:

1. The steel processing used less refractories per unit output in 1968 than in 1963 although selective prices went up sharply (Fig. 3 illustrated this changing relationship).

2. The steel industry grew at a slower rate from 1963 to 1968 than the previous five year period. I/O was able to detect the slowdown because of its approach of tracing out each industry's customers and the future needs.

A relatively more accurate forecast resulted from treating these factors explicitly.

SENSITIVITY ANALYSIS

No manager is, or should be, comfortable with a point forecast. Only at his own peril does he base his expansion plans, new product decisions, or changes in his sales force on one number. The 1968 I/O forecast of $200 million was based on two factors: (1) the interrelations of each industry and (2) the effect of each consumer dollar spent on each industry. The direct co-efficients which make up the first category probably will not vary significantly over a one year planning period, but the GNP consumer elements which make up the second factor are subject to wide fluctuations based on such broad economic variables as consumer taste, the world economy, Government spending policy, and so forth. Certain elements of the GNP are going to have more effect on sales of refractories than others. The I/O approach to sensitivity analysis is to trace each market of refractories, or any other product, out to its most sensitive (largest) element of the GNP. Then attention is focused on those elements of GNP which particularly affect refractory sales. When reasonable limits are determined, between which each of the sensitive GNP components may vary, the original assumptions in the model are replaced by the extreme assumptions. The result is: first, a "most likely" forecast based on the original GNP assumptions; and second, high and low forecasts which provide upper and lower "limits".

An example of using I/O for sensitivity analysis for the refractories industry follows. Figure 5 shows the I/O approach for determining which GNP elements are key to refractory sales, and Table III presents the use of the key GNP elements in Fig. 5 to arrive at a high and low forecast of refractories consumption by the steel industry in 1968.

ments affecting his customers (steel in this case) and, hence, indirectly affecting his product (refractories in this case).

After tracing out all buyers to GNP in the above figure it is evident that three GNP components strongly affect refractory customers and, hence, refractory sales. Table III portrays the results of focusing closer attention in the area of personal consumption expenditures, new construction, and steel imports.

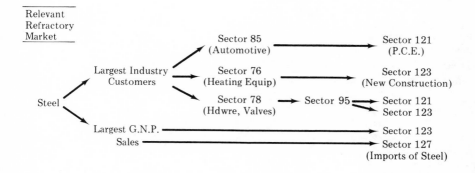

FIGURE 5. Sensitivity Analyses on the Refractory Steel Market

The I/O table, because it blueprints all industry transactions and each industry's link to GNP is able to show the analyst which are the largest industry customers and GNP consumers of the refractory market users, such as the steel and glass industries. The I/O analast simply documents the linkage from his industry customers to final demand sales and, thereby, identifies the largest GNP ele-

EVALUATING PROFIT CENTER PERFORMANCE

Having described our methodology for employing I/O as a planning tool, we will illustrate with a specific example how these concepts bear on Combusion Engineering's use of I/O in evaluating profit center performance. As mentioned ear-

TABLE III   GNP Element Changes*

Total GNP for 1968 Assumed to be $945B	Adverse Limit	Original Assumption (millions of current $)	Favorable Limit
Components of GNP Assumptions			
1. Personal consumption expenditures	622	710	710
2. New construction	24	29	29
3. Steel imports (millions of tons)	(8% of total steel shipments)		(5% of total steel ship.)
	10	10	6
Effects			
a) Effect on steel shipment production (millions of tons)	−15	0	+4
b) Tonnage co-efficient, 1968	$1.53/ton	$1.53/ton	$1.53/ton
c) Effect on refractories forecast from steel production changes	−$30 million	0	+$8.0 million
d) Resulting size of refractories forecast from steel production	170	200	208
e) Effect on total refractories forecast from GNP changes	465	515	530

*Each GNP component (top 3 rows of table) was reviewed to determine reasonable limits between which it might vary. Then those limits of GNP adverse to refractory sales were used to determine the low limit of the refractory forecast; conversely, the extremes of GNP which boosted refractory sales were used to determine the high side of the refractory forecast. It can be seen that the original forecast can vary downward from $200 m to $170 m or up to $208 m if either of the extreme set of assumptions is realized (Row (d)). The effect of the changes in GNP components on steel production (Row (a)) is shown as a point of reference. From the table it is evident that "adverse limit" assumptions cut steel production 15 million tons which, in turn, cuts refractory sales to steel by $30.0 million which is most of the $50 m cut (515-465 in Row (e)).

lier, we will be using I/O to help us judge the manager's internal operating results and his plans for coping with the environment external to the profit center.

INTERNAL OPERATIONS AND I/O—LINKING THE FORECAST TO RESULTS

Typically operational performance is measured against a standard derived from the annual budget or plan. These standards usually are based on projected sales for the period and use cost price extrapolations to predict expenses and profit for that level of operations.

Monthly or quarterly reviews of the budget are made which compare actual with planned. There may also be a comparison with the previous year for the same time period.

One thing we can be sure of, the plan and the actual will never be the same except by coincidence. We can expect unforeseen changes in economic conditions, changes in customer buying patterns, changes in competitor activity, and changes in prices, wages, and products. In reflecting on these changes, it is clear that most of them are outside the control of the business unit—and yet our standards are internally preset. To simply reset them every month certainly does not solve the problem. It is equally clear that in order to be realistic and fair, performance standards must take into account changes in the environment which are beyond the control of those being measured.

For example, the "fixed" budget or standard alluded to above provides for setting a forecast sales dollar total and the expenses that should be incurred at that level of attainment. The actual sales may turn out to be 85% of the standard and the expenses 90% of standard. The expense variance will then be shown as favorable, i.e., below budget, whereas in reality the variance may be unfavorable in relation to the actual sales volume.

I/O may be used to address this internal problem of working from a fixed budget and the external problem of changes in the economy (and hence sales) by facilitating the use of flexible budgets. I/O can readjust the original forecast to take into account the actual economic conditions that prevailed during the period being evaluated. Taking the earlier case of 1963-1968 refractory sales to the

the economic assumptions and the refractory to steel ratios (co-efficients) used.

Step 2: Testing Forecast (Sensitivity Analysis)

Procedure: Obtain forecast range for refractory sales to steel industry

Result: Optimistic, 208; Original, 200; Pessimistic, 170; (taken from I/O sensitivity analysis example in Table III). This range was determined through identification and further analysis of key indicators through the I/O model.

Step 3: Flexible Budgets Based on Sensitivity Analysis

Procedure: Set up a flexible budget with the parameters set by the forecast ranges and adjusted for the company's predicted share of market (S.O.M.).

Result:

	Optimistic (millions $)	%	Original (millions $)	%	Pessimistic (millions $)	%
Gross Industry Sales	208		200		170	
Firm's Sales Based on Obtaining 10% S.O.M.	20.8	100	20.0	100	17.0	100
Cost of Goods Sold	15.6	75	15.0	75	12.8	75
Gross Margin	5.2	25	5.0	25	4.2	25
Selling & G & A	2.0		2.0		1.8	
Profit before Tax	3.2		3.0		2.4	

steel industry, we now will illustrate the approach step by step.

Step 1: Forecasting

Procedure: Generate forecast for refractory sales to steel industry

Result: $200 million (taken from Table II)
The accuracy of this forecast depends on

Step 4: Evaluating Internal Operations

Procedure: After the results for the period which is to be evaluated come in, develop a new budget based on actual sales for the period and compare it with operating results.

Result: $19 million of refractories were sold by C-E to steel processors.

	New Flexible Budget (millions $)	%	Actual Expenditures (millions $)	%	Variance
C-E Sales	19.0	100	19.00	100	
C.G.S.	14.2	75	14.0	74	—
G.M.	4.8	25	5 0	26	+
Selling & G & A	1.9		1.8		—
Profit before Tax	2.9		3.2		+

The new flexible budget was obtained by interpolation between the budgets shown in Step 3. It can be seen that although the manager did not reach the *targeted* market of 20 million dollars he obtained the 19 million in sales with less expenditure than planned to support that level of sales, thereby yielding better than expected profit.

Step 5: Evaluating Response to Environment

Procedure: Estimate the external economic effects on profit center sales and adjust any key indicators (i.e., those derived in Fig. 5) which were different from the forecast assumptions.

Result:

fall, his total market share falling in the process from 10% to 9% (21 million versus 19 million dollars).

If for example, he had been watching current personal consumption statistics during the year he would have observed the unexpected large increase and recognized its impact on his market. Now his decision to cut selling and G & A expenses by $200,000 becomes open to question. Did, in fact, this action cripple his chances of maintaining his market share? Once lost, will his share of market be easily regained by increasing his selling expense again in the future? These questions will make for interesting discussions when the profit center's performance is reviewed. We will return to this case in the next section.

Key Indicators	(Made Prior to Period) Forecast Assumption	(Adjusted after Period) Actual
P.C.E.	710	730
New Construction	29	26
Steel Imports	10	12
Resulting Sales to Steel	200	210
10% S.O.M.	20.0	21.0

By running the actual GNP results back through the I/O model, we find that total refractory sales and C-E's sales should have been $210 and $21.0, respectively. Although the manager in our example managed his budget well, he should have received $1 million extra sales (21 minus 20) from unanticipated changes in the economy. Thus, I/O has shown that although he has done well internally he must account for the fact that he didn't capitalize on the external economic wind-

We should not forget, of course, that when we adjust for external economic factors the reverse case may be true. The adjustment may show that our share of market actually increased even though the profit center sales volume was lower than predicted. In this case we may have a hero on our hands given the same internal operating performance described above.

The procedures laid out in these five steps have the great virtue of making explicit the impact of various possibilities that could affect operations and of forcing management to consider the actions necessary to perform effectively within the range of possibilities. Equally important, this exercise can improve the timing of operational decisions by identifying for management the critical indicators affecting their environment. Once identified, management is in a position to monitor these indicators and put contingency plans into effect in a timely fashion. Lastly, this approach gets the assumptions and numbers out in the open where they can be reviewed after the fact, and thereby stimulate continued improvement.

THE EXTERNAL ENVIRONMENT AND I/O— PLANNING FOR CHANGED CONDITIONS

When a profit center manager reads in the *Wall Street Journal* that "housing starts are down sharply" or "consumer durables appear weak for near term", how can he determine the specific impact of such information on his sales? Because the I/O methodology separates the economic assumptions from the inter-industry assumptions, information like the above can be immediately substituted in the model and related to the strategy being pursued by the manager.

Indeed, the most significant feature of I/O analysis and one which makes it such a powerful management tool is that it allows the user to make whatever hypothesis he wishes about social, political, and economic developments. He can then vary those components of GNP which are most affected by these hypotheses, and determine the effect of his product sales. This concept of synthesizing economic/political analysis with product forecasts can be used still more broadly to include a whole host of interrelated events in the

future. Figure 6 presents this feature of I/O analysis.

Taking our example of refractory sales to the steel industry, consider the hypothesis of a Viet Nam phase out. Capital expenditures, at least in defense industries, may be assumed to decrease. Net exports and personal consumption expenditures may or may not be directly affected, while Federal, state, and local expenditures would probably go up in domestic programs. The linkage between these GNP categories to steel production and finally to refractory sales is at once solved with I/O. The real argument is, of course, just how a Viet Nam phase-out might affect the various GNP categories. The use of I/O in this example, however, has reduced the issue to a number over which arguments, research, and consultation can be generated. To put the question in manageable form goes a long way toward establishing the dimensions of a problem and the magnitude of its impact on operations and strategy.

A final aspect of using I/O to evaluate a manager's strategic position to exploit future opportunities involves assessing whether his present time, effort, and money are directed toward capturing profitable markets. It is entirely possible for a manager to have increased his market share in an industry and look good in the short term, while the future returns from the industry do not warrant the time and effort spent.

We demonstrate this point by looking again at our example of refractories sales to the steel industry. The refractories manager, it will be recalled, suffered a reduction in his steel market share but did so in a way that improved his profit margin for refractories sold to steel companies. As it turns out, the reduction of emphasis on steel market was the result of a conscious decision to shift marketing dollars into the aluminum industry. When current operations were reviewed on a product line basis, this action showed

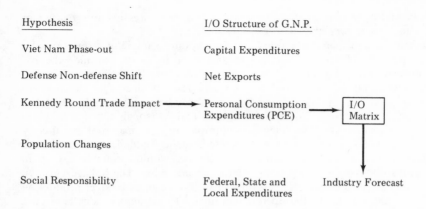

Hypothesis	I/O Structure of G.N.P.
Viet Nam Phase-out	Capital Expenditures
Defense Non-defense Shift	Net Exports
Kennedy Round Trade Impact ⟶	Personal Consumption Expenditures (PCE) ⟶ I/O Matrix
Population Changes	
Social Responsibility	Federal, State and Local Expenditures Industry Forecast

FIGURE 6. Synthesizing Economic/Political Analyses with Product Forecasts

high profits for refractories sold to steel companies because marketing expenses had been reduced. Of course, the converse was true with respect to the aluminum industry refractories where profits were lower than planned.

Taking this data alone, the manager's action of moving away from an apparently more profitable industry would seem peculiar at best. However, I/O forecast analysis made it clear that the aluminum industry's use of refractories would be the fastest growing market over the next five years (Fig. 7). So, although our manager lost market share in steel, he had taken steps to place the company in excellent position to exploit the fast growing aluminum market. Clearly, it is important to encourage this kind of investment in the future and not simply reward past and possibly misleading, results.

GENERAL COMMENTS

A significant value of any mathematical model is that it offers a useful way to store and interrelate data. The Input/Output model is particularly valuable in this respect because it has the dynamic quality of forcing management to look at important interrelationships in industry—updating these relationships as they change — and of allowing management to see what specific effect certain changes would have on their markets. Using Input/Ouptut analysis demands total commitment because it requires inputs from all levels and involves people in generating information which they will have to "live with".

For instance, the firm's economic analysts must not only "hang their hats" on general economic indicators, but, for example, are forced to predict the very specific makeup of GNP. At a different level, market researchers must answer how their industry is related to its various markets in such specific terms as "dollar of their product sold per unit of product in each market". In other words, the model requires information at each level of expertise and then synthesizes the inputs of all levels. Thus, the manager in making his investment or acquisition plans can bring all the relevant information to bear on his decision through use of the model. He can use broad economic forecasts taken, for example, from an interesting article he reads in *The Wall*

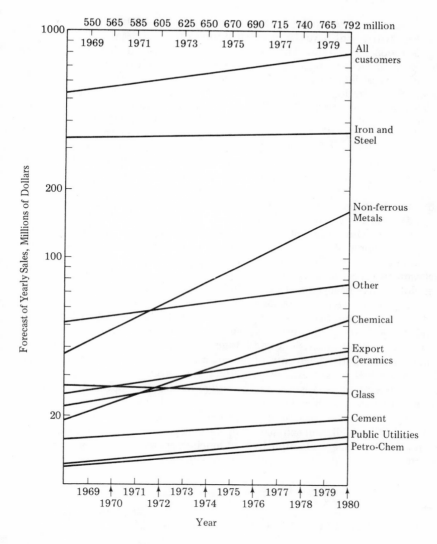

FIGURE 7. Current Dollar Sales of Refractories to Each Customer, 1968 to 1980

Street Journal to see how they affect his market. The model not only bridges the gap between economic analysis and individual market forecasting and planning, but also offers specific numbers in a format to which each group can relate and over which each level of management can argue. This becomes important when a certain number has a high probability of variance. Management can perform sensitivity analysis to see what impact different assumptions would have whether they be durable good orders or pounds of refractories sold per ton of steel shipments. Input/Output, of course, highlights the numbers management may want to vary because it blueprints how all variables are interrelated and, hence, provides a head start on determining which factors in the environment have the most effect on a product's market. And, of course, once these factors are identified management knows what to monitor in order to change operations in a *timely* manner. That is to say, *faster* than the competition!

SUMMARY

At Combustion Engineering we have developed and applied a methodology which uses an Input/Output model of the U.S. economy combined with a very detailed product-industry consumption matrix relevant to a specific profit center. The methodology has been valuably employed in the following steps: (1) making forecasts for products and the markets of those products, (2) aiding in sensitivity analysis which consists of establishing and varying the most sensitive elements of GNP affecting product sales to establish a likely range of operations, (3) assisting in planning by demonstrating which markets and industries deserve the most dollars and effort, and (4) providing bench mark forecasts for performance evaluation by factoring out those external elements which were not encompassed in the original forecast.

We hope it is clear that this I/O based methodology is not limited to the refractories industry, but can be usefully extended to any industry selling some of their output to other industries rather than directly to end users. The value of utilizing the Input/Output approach is that it provides a complete, consistent, and systematized way of cataloging and using information and encourages management to focus on the all-important relationship of customer usage. We have found that it is not the numbers themselves emanating from the Input/Output model which are invaluable; rather it is the mental process and associated activities which each manager must go through in order to develop the input for the model. In the successful application of Input/Output analysis the manager must ultimately develop both excellent customer relations and a feeling for those elements in the economy which strongly affect his product sales, and concomitantly, his level of operations. Further, the documentation of assumptions together with the range of their impact on operations provides top management with a much-improved basis for evaluating profit center performance.

SELECTED REFERENCES FOR CHAPTER 6

BOOKS

Anthony, Robert N., John Dearden, and Richard F. Vancil, *Management Control Systems.* Homewood, Ill.: Richard D. Irwin, Inc., 1972.

Bierman, Harold, Jr., *Topics in Cost Accounting and Decisions.* New York: McGraw-Hill Book Company, 1963.

Bonini, Charles P., Robert K. Jaedicke, and Harvey M. Wagner, *Management Controls: New Directions in Basic Research.* New York: McGraw-Hill Book Company, 1964.

Jerome, William Travers, III, *Executive Control—The Catalyst.* New York: John Wiley & Sons, Inc., 1961.

Morris, William T., *Decentralization in Management Systems,* Columbus:Ohio State University Press, 1968.

Solomons, David, *Divisional Performance: Measurement and Control.* New York: Financial Executives Research Foundation, 1965. See also the comprehensive bibliography on pp. 287-301.

Warren, E. Kirby, *Long-Range Planning: The Executive Viewpoint.* Englewood Cliffs, N.J.: Prentice-Hall, Inc., 1966. See also the bibliography on pp. 92-101.

Williamson, Oliver E., *Corporate Control and Business Behavior.* Englewood Cliffs, N.J.: Prentice-Hall, Inc., 1970.

ARTICLES

Barefield, Russell M., "A Model of Forecast Biasing Behavior," *The Accounting Review,* XLV, (July 1970).

Berg, Norman, "Strategic Planning in Conglomerate Companies," *Harvard Business Review,* XLIII (May-June, 1965).

Birnberg, Jacob G., Louis R. Pondy and C. Lee Davis, "The Effect of Three Voting Rules on Resource Allocation Decisions," *Management Science,* XVI (February 1970).

Dearden, John, "Problem in Decentralized Profit Responsibility," *Harvard Business Review,* XXXVIII (May-June, 1960). Other Dearden articles on decentralized profit systems appear in (May-June, 1961), (July-August, 1962), (November-December, 1962), (May-June, 1968), and (May-June, 1969), issues.

Demski, Joel S., "Decision—Performance Control," *The Accounting Review,* XLIV, (October 1969).

————, "The Decision Implementation Interface: Effects of Alternative Performance Measurement Models," *The Accounting Review,* XLV, (January, 1970).

Heflebower, R. B., "Observations on Decentralization in Large Enterprises," *Journal of Industrial Economics* (November, 1960).

Henderson, Bruce D. and John Dearden, "New System for Divisional Control," *Harvard Business Review,* XLIV (September-October, 1966).

Kensey, John P., "Dividing the Incentive Pie in Divisionalized Companies," *Financial Executive,* XXXVIII, (September, 1970).

Livingstone, John Leslie and Gerald L. Salamon, "Relationship Between the Accounting and the Internal Rate of Return Measures: A Synthesis and an Analysis," *Journal of Accounting Research,* VIII, (Autumn, 1970).

Ma, Ronald, "Project Appraisal in a Divisionalized Comapny," *Abacus,* V, (December, 1969).

MacGregor, Douglas, "An Uneasy Look at Performance Appraisal," *Harvard Business Review,* XXXV (May-June, 1957).

Mauriel, John J., and Robert N. Anthony, "Misevaluation of Investment Center Performance," *Harvard Business Review,* XLIV (March-April, 1966).

Schwayder, Keith, "A Proposed Modification to Residual Income—Interest Adjusted Income," *The Accounting Review,* XLV (April, 1970).

Shillinglaw, Gordon, "Toward a Theory of Divisional Income Measurement," *The Accounting Review,* XXXIX (April, 1962).

Shubik, Martin, "Incentives, Decentralized Control, the Assignment of Joint Costs and Internal Pricing," *Management Science,* VIII (April, 1962).

Staubus, George J., "Plant Financing, Accounting, and Divisional Targetry," *California Management Review,* X (Summer, 1968).

Stephenson, G. G., "A Hierarchy of Models for Planning in a Division of I.C.I." *Operational Research Quarterly,* XXI, No. 2.

Vatter, William J., "Does the Rate of Return Measure Business Efficiency?" *N.A.A. Bulletin,* XL (January, 1959).

———, "Income Models, Book Yield, and the Rate of Return," *The Accounting Review,* XLI (October, 1966).

DECENTRALIZATION AND TRANSFER PRICING

CHAPTER SEVEN

Transfer Prices: An Exercise in Relevancy and Goal Congruence

Billy E. Goetz

Florida Atlantic University

The author argues that incremental cost, not market price or accounting costs, is the proper and unique transfer price to use in information systems which seek decentralized decision making directed toward congruent goals. An example involving the decisions of divisional managers to buy computer time internally versus externally is used to demonstrate the superiority of incremental cost transfer prices.

Reprinted from *The Accounting Review,* July 1967, 435-440. Used by permission of Billy E. Goetz and *The Accounting Review.*

The recent *Statement of Basic Accounting Theory* postulates a number of criteria that accounting data should satisfy. Among these, relevancy is ranked first among unequals.[1] This dominant position seems justified to me. Certainly I would prefer a rough approximation, vaguely verified, of a truly relevant datum to perfectly precise, perfectly verified irrelevant data. At best, irrelevant data are useless; at worst, irrelevant data can lead managers into serious error. If data are irrelevant, perfection in all other criteria leaves the data useless or harmful. If data are relevant, serious deficiencies with respect to all other criteria still may leave a considerable value.

In the recent past, accountants and especially cost accountants have often behaved as if relevancy were irrelevant and

[1] American Accounting Association, 1966.

the criterion of objective verifiability alone had any significance. The obsessive preoccupation with historical original cost seems to support this judgment conclusively. Certainly, all those sunk costs have little relevancy to managerial problems. The result has necessarily been an ever-increasing reliance by managers on engineering cost estimates, and a strong tendency for both managers and engineers to ignore the irrelevant, fully-allocated, original, historical cost data reported by cost accountants.

There is evidence that many present-day accountants, espousing the cause of managerially useful data, are still erroneously pushing irrelevant data. Take the matter of transfer pricing.[2] It is alleged that, if an external market price exists, arrived at by competitive, arm's-length bargaining between independent buyers and sellers, such a market price is a valid transfer price.[3] Such a transfer price tends to be irrelevant, and tends to lead to lack of goal congruence. Such transfer prices may strongly motivate divisional managers to make decisions bad for the company.

Goal congruence is important. So is motivation. I want my managers strongly motivated toward congruent goals. If the subgoals of divisional managers conflict with global corporate goals, I would like as little motivation as possible! I propose to prove that use of incremental costs as transfer prices is the unique way to congruence of goals. This has the interesting consequence of invalidating the concept of "profit centers" and of "financial responsibility centers" wherever and whenever goods or services are transferred within an enterprise.

[2]"Transfer prices" are the intra-company charges at which goods or services are "sold" by one organizational unit to another in the same company.
[3]Anthony, Dearden, and Vancil, *Management Control Systems* (Irwin, 1965), pp. 259, 269.

DECISIONS TO MAKE, BUY, CHANGE, OR DISCONTINUE

It is all too easy to get lost in an argument pitched on highly abstract levels. A reasonably believable specific case has advantages in this respect. Consequently, I will proceed by the case method, which will amuse my friends, particularly when used in the present context.

We assume a company with four divisions, *A, B, C,* and *D*. Division *D* operates a computer, which it rents from the manufacturer for $4,000 per week plus $50 per hour for hours in excess of 40 per week. (These bills are rendered and paid weekly.) Divisions *A, B,* and *C* have computer jobs done for them by Division *D*. Division *A* has 15 jobs, each of which requires one hour of computer time every week. Division *C* has two jobs, each of which requires 6 hours of computer time each week. This totals 42 hours per week, and consequently the computer manufacturer is paid $4,100 per week.

There are, of course, other costs involved: labor, supplies, power, space, etc.; but, to keep calculations simple, we will confine our analysis to transfer prices for computer services—assuming that parallel transfer prices can be constructed whereby Division *D* can charge Divisions *A, B,* and *C,* and/or the jobs performed, for the services rendered. To keep the case simple, we will assume that the company does no work in any way related to cost-plus or renegotiable contracts; we assume a clean and static situation: no random variation, no cyclical or secular factors; just one week like another, endlessly and unchangingly repeated.

We also assume that such computer services are available in the open market. Service companies, using the same kinds of computer equipment, paying rent to a computer manufacturer on the same terms, and seeking a reasonable profit, charge prices that work out to a charge of $120 per hour for the computer component of their services. Of course, their actual charge will be enough larger to cover their labor, supplies, and such.

Our question is, what should be the transfer prices for Division *D's* computer services to Division *A, B,* and *C*, itemized for each job? More precisely, what should Division *D* charge for computer time, to which other charges will be added to cover other ingredients of the service?

I contend that both market price and average historical cost, with or without a markup, will be both (1) irrelevant and (2) mischievous in that either will motivate divisional managers to make decisions inimical to the welfare of the company. The unique correct transfer price here, and everywhere in intracompany transfers, is incremental cost.

This implies that "financial responsibility centers" (or "profit centers") have no validity, are worse than useless, wherever one organizational subdivision does work for another; that divisional managers cannot be evaluated in terms of "profits" made by their divisions. Such appraisals of managerial efficiency should be made solely in terms of a comparison of standards of accomplishment, of costs, and of investments with actual subsequent performance, that is, through a properly conceived system of budgetary control. Such a system would make much use of physical as well as financial standards and performance measurements.

THE FRICTIONLESS, NOISELESS, CHANGELESS CASE

Incremental cost, in this and all other cases, is ascertained by finding the answer to the appropriate one of two questions: (1) How much will total enterprise costs be increased if this contemplated job (activity) is added to the present mix? or (2) How much will total enterprise costs be reduced if this job (activity) is discontinued? It is essential to note that incremental costs cannot be added or subtracted according to the rules of fourth-grade arithmetic. To find the incremental cost of two additional jobs, we treat the two as one—as a package—and ask: How much will total enterprise costs increase if this package of two activities are added to the present mix? No matter how complex a mixture of added and discontinued activities is conceived, its incremental cost (which may be positive or negative) is found by budgeting the present mix, budgeting the contemplated mix, and subtracting the total of a second budget from the total of the first.

With the assumptions given, Division *D* should charge Division *A* $50 for each of Division *A's* 15 jobs, or $100 for any package of two or more (or even all 15) of these jobs. The company's total cost for computer hire is reduced by $50 if any one of these jobs is discontinued (or contracted out), or by $100 if any package of two or more of these jobs is discontinued. Similarly, Division *D* should charge Division *B* $100 for its one 15-hour job, and Division *C* $100 for each of its two jobs, or for a package of the two. This is the reduction in the weekly bill from the computer manufacturer if such discontinuances occur.

If we use the recommended[4] practice of using competitive market prices as transfer prices, Division *D* will charge Division *A* $120 for each job, $240 for any package of two jobs, $360 for any package of three, and so on; and will charge Division *B* $1800 for its one 15 hour job; and Division *C* $720 for each of its 6 hour jobs or $1440 for a package of the two. If the Division *C* manager believes one of his jobs is worth $650, or can be performed by some alternative means for $650, and the other is worth

[4]See footnote 3.

$300, he will discontinue both. This will "improve" his "profit" by 1440−(650 + 300) = $490. However, the company will get a reduction of $100 in its computer bill in return for discontinuing jobs worth $950, or possibly in return for spending $950 to do these same jobs some other way. And this recommendation comes from authors who quite properly champion the cause of goal congruence!

If we follow the traditional cost accountant as a guide we arrive at a similar lack of goal congruency. Now, each job is charged at a rate of $97.62 per hour. The manager of Division *C* finds that the job he values at $650 (or can get done elsewise for $650) costs him $583.72, so he decides to continue the service. But the job he values at $300 also costs him $583.72, so he discontinues it (or has it done by an alternative means costing $300). This "saves" him $283.72. And it reduces the computer bill paid by the company by $100—at a cost of $300. Moreover, having discontinued this job, the cost accountant finds it necessary to recompute costs. Since the company pays $4,000 for a computer used 36 hours, each hour now costs $111.11 and the other Division *C* job is now charged at $666.66. Since it is deemed to be worth only $650, Division *C's* manager will discontinue it, saving Division *C* $16.66, reducing the computer bill paid by the company by precisely zero dollars, and increasing company costs by $600 to have the job done by alternate means.

Neither "cost" (as traditionally computed) nor market produces goal congruence. Both strongly motivate divisional managers to make decisions contrary to the welfare of the company. However, if Division *D* charges a transfer price precisely equal to incremental cost, divisional managers can be trusted to make decisions in harmony with company profit goals. Thus, and only thus, can the advantages of decentralized decision-making be obtained without paying an unnecessary price of bad decisions arising from erroneous data producing noncongruent goals.

Nor can the concept of "profit centers" or "financial responsibility centers" be rescued, by incremental costing or however. Assume the manager of Division *C* finds an alternative means of doing one of his jobs that costs only $40. Consequently, he discontinues that job. This reduces the weekly load on the computer to 36 hours, and the weekly computer bill to $4,000. Now discontinuing any job will reduce the computer bill by zero dollars. Consequently, the transfer price for all present jobs to all divisions is zero dollars. This apparently means that the "profits" for which managers of Divisions *A* and *B* are "responsible" have been changed by a unilateral decision by the manager of Division *C.*

My recommendation is to put all these managers on the same team and charge them as a team—with responsibility for company profits. Award bonuses based on company profit to assure goal congruence. Judge each manager individually by how his performances compare with expected performance; as to achievement, as to cost, and as to investment utilized. Any or all of these outputs may be measured in dollars or in physical terms, or both. He can be budgeted 1,000 hours of time on a machine or of a particular class of workman, and the number of hours actually taken to perform the job can be compared with this standard. This is a less debatable measure of efficiency than dollars cost, at least when the latter is contaminated by doubtful allocations or transfer prices.

DECISION TO DISCONTINUE THE COMPUTER

If Division *D* does charge incremental costs, and if a naive bookkeeper-accountant analyzes Department *D*'s "profit and loss account" in defiance of the principles demonstrated above, the division will show a whopping loss, leading to proposals to get rid of the division and its money-losing computer. However, if a mildly sophisticated managerial accountant is available, he will approach the problem of continuing or discontinuing Division *D* rather differently. He will ask each division manager to estimate the value of each of his jobs—that is, of the computer time he uses. This is an estimate of the *value* which would be lost, not of the *cost* which would be saved, by discontinuance of the job. These values would then be summed. If the sum exceeds the $4,100 per week paid for the computer, Division *D* and its computer would be retained.

Note that this decision did not require allocation of costs. Nor did it require use of transfer prices. Use of either, however arrived at, would strongly tend to produce the wrong decision.

Nor are any managerial decisions at any level improved by treating any or all of the divisions as profit centers or as centers of financial responsibility. Each decision should be made at the appropriate level, and the information which guides decentralized decisions should incorporate incremental costs as transfer prices. The decision to keep or to discontinue the computer is a top-level, corporate-wide decision, and consequently no transfer prices of any kind are involved.

NOISELESS AND FRICTIONLESS CHANGE

It is time to relax our tight, simplified, unrealistic assumptions a bit. We change our illustrative case. The computer manufacturer offers his wares at the same contractual $4,000 per week plus $50 per hour in excess of 40 hours per week. But the company has not yet rented a computer. It hasn't even considered renting one.

Division *B* discovers the 15 hour per week job it would like to put on a computer. It can be done outside for $1,800 or inside for $4,000. If Division *B*'s manager estimates the value of the job at less than $1,800, he should decide, at least temporarily, not to have it done. He should not forget it. If it is judged to be worth more than $1,800, say $6,000, he should contract it out for $1,800.

As other divisional managers discover their jobs, they should estimate the value of each job. They should contract out any jobs worth more than $120 per hour.[5] When the total values of jobs contracted out (figured at $120 per hour) or held in abeyance exceeds $4,000, without exceeding 40 hours per week computer load, the computer should be acquired and the subcontracted jobs transferred to the newly acquired computer.

Let us assume that the $4,000 total value is exceeded and the computer is acquired when the weekly load accumulates to 35 hours. As new jobs are discovered, if they have any value they are added (at zero incremental cost) until the 40 hour per week total is reached. If other new jobs are discovered, the value of each job, old and new, is estimated and the less valuable per hour are bumped by the more valuable until all jobs continued have values greater than $50 per hour (assuming total hours exceed 40 per week). Jobs worth more than $50 per hour can now be added until a total of 168 hours per week is reached.

Now, as more jobs are discovered, the more valuable per hour supplant the less valuable until a backlog of rejected and stockpiled jobs, each worth more than $50 per hour, has accumulated to a total

[5]The assumed external market price.

value of $2,000. Then a second computer is acquired, and sufficient jobs transferred from the first to the second computer to leave both operating more than 40 hours per week.

If the size of the computer bill is graphed against hours per week, a nice series of clean, sharp steps is obtained. The first computer hour purchased produces a giant $4,000 step in the graph. There follows a horizontal line at the $4,000 level until 40 hours is reached. Each additional hour adds a $50 step increase until the 169th hour, which adds a $2,000 step.[6] Subsequent hours add $50 step increases with a $2,000 step every 168 hours.

FRICTION

Jobs are not easily put on and taken off computers. There are costs of converting records from files to punched cards or to magnetic tapes, or vice versa if the computer is being exorcized. Consequently, jobs should not be transferred to computers if they are likely soon to be bumped by new jobs of greater hourly value. Managers should predict changes in computer loads and hold low-value jobs off the computer until increasing load makes possible permanent rather than transient status.

NOISE

Almost every datum and estimate in such computer utilization problems (or any other problem calling for a managerial decision) is subject to random variation and uncertainties both as to magnitudes and as to timing. Estimates of the values of jobs, in anticipation or even in retrospect, are particularly difficult. Estimates of costs—computer hours and associated labor, supplies, etc.—are only somewhat less hazardous. The estimates

of the timing of the discoveries of new jobs (and their values), needed to decide whether low-value jobs should be stockpiled, are uncertain. All prediction involves uncertainty, and many estimates of values must be estimates of expected values. Most estimates of probabilities are probably properly estimated as probability frequency distributions, since most values or costs or times don't just happen or not happen. They happen more or less, sooner or later.

The result is to blur all the nice clean step functions we have been hypothesizing. Instead of clean lines and sharp steps, a graph of a projected function of cost against time would consist of probability density bands, with greatest probability down the center of the band or zone and probabilities thinning out toward both edges. Substitution of such blurred zones for the sharp clean lines of perfect prediction tends to round the corners, and to slope and spread the steps. If the graph be of incremental cost per hour, instead of total costs, the corners become rounded, the steps up and down become slopes, the peaks are lowered and spread out, and the troughs become somewhat filled in.

A large number of managerial judgments are needed as to values and costs, as to timing, and as to probability distributions accompanying the spectra of possible magnitudes of values, costs and times. All of these estimates should be reduced to mathematical expected values. If any time horizons are relatively distant, the more distant expected values and costs may need compound discounting to make them comparable with more immediate anticipated cash receipts and disbursements.

CONCLUSIONS

It is an ambitious program. Perhaps its greatest value lies in giving managers a clearer picture of the nature of the

---

[6]This is $4,000 for the second computer, minus $2,000 saved on the first computer by transferring 40 hours of overtime to the second.

decisions they are called upon to make. This should improve their judgment—the excellence of their estimates. It should focus their aim on preferred targets, make their predictions of inputs and of outputs more relevant to their goals.

However, neither change, nor friction, nor noise seems to upset our conclusions that incremental cost is the unique proper transfer price to use in information systems which seek to make possible decentralized decision making directed toward congruent goals. Change, friction, and noise make decision problems enormously more complex and difficult. They may make necessary an almost universal reliance on managerial estimates instead of objective observations and measurements. But they do not justify a use of market prices nor of traditional costs as transfer prices.

Relevancy and goal congruence demand that incremental costs be used as transfer prices.

A Transfer Pricing System Based on Opportunity Cost

Mohamed Onsi

Syracuse University

In direct contrast to Goetz, the author argues that using variable or incremental costs to price transfer goods has several important limitations. In the absence of a market price, the transferred goods should be priced equal to the opportunity cost of diverting divisional resources into producing such goods, instead of producing another good that has an outside market. "Motivation costs" can be employed to reduce the level of conflict which might arise from the transfer pricing system.

Reprinted from *The Accounting Review,* July 1970, 535-543. Used by permission of Mohamed Onsi and *The Accounting Review.*

With decentralization of decision-making and creation of profit centers in multi-product organizations, the transfer pricing system becomes an acute problem. To arrive at an optimal solution, or at an approximation to it, both accounting and economic thought have recommended certain solutions.[1] However, some of the suggested solutions have shortcomings that cannot be ignored or assumed to be insignificant. The problem is material when the performance of a divisional manager is measured based on profit, and incentive compensation is so determined.

In this paper, the economic foundation of a transfer pricing system and its limitations will be briefly presented. A new transfer pricing system is suggested, based on an opportunity cost concept. The advantages of this approach, compared to others, will be discussed.

THE ECONOMIC TRANSFER PRICING SYSTEM

When there is a market price for intermediate goods, they are transferred according to such a price, assuming that the goods transferred are produced in a competitive market where the supplying center cannot influence the sales price in the open market by its own output decision. Pricing intermediate goods according to market price has the advantage of motivating the supplying center to reduce its cost as much as possible and emphasize innovation and research and development, since it will be to its advantage.

However, if there is no market price for the intermediate goods, then the

[1]See: David Solomons, *Divisional Performance* (Financial Executives Research Foundation, 1965), pp. 212-228, and Jack Hirshleifer, "Internal Pricing and Decentralized Decisions," in *Management Controls*, ed. by C. P. Bonini, R. K. Jaedicke and H. M. Wagner, (McGraw-Hill, 1964), pp. 27-37.

volume which Profit Center A should produce and that which Profit Center B should demand, ideally, is at that level, where the MC_A is equal to the NMR_B. Operationally, however, the profit center manager, in this case, may behave according to one of two possibilities: (1) as *a simple maximizer* of his own profit, or (2) as a *cooperator* who is concerned with maximizing total joint profits.

THE SIMPLE MAXIMIZER CASE

If the selling profit center (A) is in a monopolistic position, he will keep the price of the intermediate goods at P_2 (Exhibit I) and will produce at a level equal to that demanded, OBd_2; that is, the volume where the buying center equates its own $NMR_B = P_2$. The profit area of Center A lies between the P_2 line and his MC_A line. This area is larger than his profit if he accepts lowering the price to P^*, where $MC_A = NMR_B$ and corresponds to the ideal volume X. On the other hand, if the buying profit center (B) is in a monopsonistic position, it will force the selling center (A) to set the price at P_1 and produce a volume OAS_1, where it equates its own $MC_A = P_1$. This results in a maximization of profit for center B, as shown in the areas between the NMR_B line and P_1. This profit area is larger than that of a transfer price set at P^*. The total profit of both centers, however, is smaller than the joint profit that can be achieved if both centers set the transfer price at P^*.

THE COOPERATIVE CASE

In this second case, in which the profit center manager is a *cooperator* concerned with maximizing total joint profits; the volume produced will be optimal from the corporate point of view.

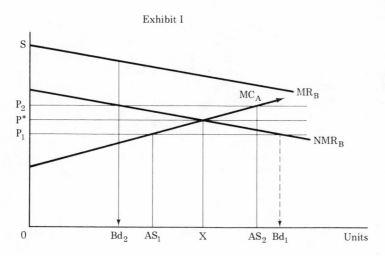

EXHIBIT 1. Transfer Price Is Equal to $MC_A = NMR_B$

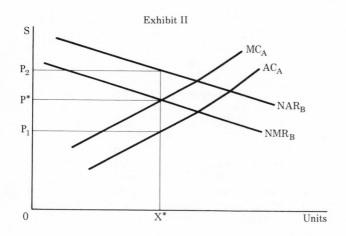

EXHIBIT 2. The Paretian Optima Solution

Total profit will be a maximum and larger than that under the first case, but the distribution of such profits is not clear-cut (see Exhibit II).

If Profit Centers A and B are conceived to maximize their combined profits, the volume of transferred goods is the quantity OX^*, for which $MC_A = NMR_B$, and the ideal price is P^*. However, in such a situation where the buyer is obliged to buy from within, there is no guarantee that the price is going to be P^*, even if they are cooperative. The transfer price, in other words, is indeterminate, i.e., between P_1 and P_2. That is to say, the transfer price can be negotiated somewhere between ANR_B and AC_A (e.g., the average net revenue for Center B and the average cost of Center A for the volume OX^*).

If the transfer price is negotiated at P_1 for the optimal volume OX^*, Center A receives zero profits and Center B receives the total joint profit. If the transfer price is negotiated at P_2, Center A will receive the total joint profit and Center B receives zero. So, operationally, the negotiated transfer price is in a range with P_2 as an upper limit and P_1 as a lower limit, and the actual transfer price somewhere in between. This negotiated transfer price is set after reaching the optimal product volume and not before.

To overcome such a limitation, it is believed that the budget committee should be in a position to receive the necessary information from each profit center, establish the volume which maximizes corporate profit (OX^*), and set the price at P^*. The accounting practice of pricing the transfer goods as equal to variable costs, approximating marginal costs, is felt to yield such an optimal volume. However, imposing a transfer price does not guarantee on optimal solution. The reason is that the selling profit center knows the rules of the game and, as a result, it adjusts its level of accuracy in estimating variable costs according to its belief in the accuracy of other centers' estimations. This managerial response is feasible especially when the selling profit center is not given the option to produce another product that is more profitable.

Another weakness in the economic transfer system is its failure to provide incentive for a center manager to reduce his MC below the determined level $(MC_A = NMR_B)$. Suppose that the transfer price of intermediate goods is

$8.00/unit.[2] If the supplying profit center discovers a new method for producing such goods at $7.00/unit, should this be the new price for transferred goods according to the $MC_A = NMR_B$? If the answer is yes, there is no motivation or reward for the innovating supplying profit center, since the receiving profit center will reap all the profit increment, while the supplying center breaks even. Should the transfer price remain at $8.00/unit, the receiving profit center will find no incentive to remix its production or increase its output to take advantage of the relatively cheaper input prices. As a solution to this problem, it is suggested, violating the main principle of $MC_A = NMR_B$, that the supplying profit center should charge $8.00/unit for additional units over that budgeted volume. Another solution is that the supplying center will negotiate a lump sum grant or subsidy from the receiving center as a condition for continuous cost reduction and innovation.[3] While this is a deviation from the theoretical principle (e.g., P is determined having $MC = MR$), its purposes are motivationally oriented.

Another operational difficulty stems from the assumption that there are no constraints (physical or monetary) on the resources available for each profit center in producing the volume OX^* that is optimal based on $MC = MR$. This assumption is not realistic, because each profit center has certain constraints, either manpower, capacity, etc. If these

[2] Remember that we are assuming, in the entire discussion, no cost interdependence, i.e., MC_A is dependent from the MC_B. If the marginal cost of (A) (which is P^*) depends also on the volume of output of the final product (B), through common cost savings, the level of over-all marginal costs of the final product B for the organization is not equal to the sum of MC_A & MC_B. The analysis in such a case will be different.

[3] Jack Hirshleifer, "On the Economics of Transfer Pricing," *Journal of Business* (July 1956), pp. 172-184.

constraints are not explicitly dealt with in the system, the theoretical solution is no longer a pragmatic one.

To solve these problems, a new approach to solving the transfer price problem based on an opportunity cost concept is needed. Opportunity cost is used here with cost accounting derived surrogates. This approach takes into consideration in arriving at the optimal solution the physical and financial constraints that exist at divisional levels and at the top corporate level. While the transfer price under this system is determined based on the decomposition principle, the final suggested price is not necessarily equal to it as we will show later. Since we will not discuss the mathematical operational steps of solving a case using the decomposition principle, a bibliography at the end of this article is a representative reference for this purpose. In addition, we will show how this approach, with some motivational factors, can induce a profit center manager to act in the right direction and lessens his reason to manipulate cost estimates. This approach works as follows.

TRANSFER PRICE AND OPPORTUNITY COST

If Profit Center (*A*) transfers a part of its goods to Profit Center (*B*), and there is an outside market price, the transferred goods are priced equal to the market price, which represents the opportunity cost of not selling to outsiders.

If there is no market price, the transferred goods still should be priced equal to the opportunity cost of diverting divisional (*A*) resources into producing such goods, instead of producing another kind of goods that has an outside market. In developing the framework of this system, two cases will be differentiated.

I. Profit Center (A) Transfers Product X_1, That Has No Outside Market Price, to Profit Center (B). However, Profit Center (A) Also Produces X_2, Which Has a Known Market Price.[4]

In this case, the price of the transferred product X_1 is equal to the opportunity cost or the shadow price of resources utilized in its production instead of being used to produce X_2. The following example is written in a linear programming model:

$$\text{Max } \pi = C_1 X_1 + C_2 X_2 = ?X_1 + 8X_2$$

subject to:

Process I $3X_1 + 6X_2 \leqslant 60$

Process II $2X_1 + 4X_2 \leqslant 40$

$$X_1, X_2 \geqslant 0$$

Since the market price of product X_1 is unknown, we will first *a priori* assume that Profit Center *A* will maximize its profit by producing only X_2. The optimal solution is to produce 10 units of X_2, yielding a contribution margin of \$80.00 and shadow price of $W_1 = 8/10$. No idle capacity is available.

If Profit Center *A* is to produce X_1, it will divert a portion of its resources devoted to producing X_2 to produce X_1. For example, to reduce X_2 by 1 unit, it will increase X_1 by 2 units. Such a substitution rate will maintain the total contribution margin (\$80.00) at the same level. This means that if Profit Center *A* is to produce (X_1), it should charge Profit Center *B*, \$7.00/unit in order to maintain its profitability intact. The \$4.00/unit represents the opportunity cost of profit foregone by not producing X_2, calculated as follows:

[4]This is assuming that X_2 has a free competitive market, and that the organization will be able to sell all its produces of X_2. If this assumption is released, the analysis still can be applied, although it gets complicated.

$$C_1 = a_{11}W_1 + a_{12}W_2$$

$$= (3 \times \frac{8}{10}) + (2 \times \frac{8}{10})$$

$$= \frac{24}{10} + \frac{16}{10} = \frac{40}{10} = \$4.00$$

Sales price = Variable costs + Contribution Margin = 3.00 + 4.00 = \$7.00.

If the preceding example had resulted in idle capacity with the optimal solution, it would create motivational problems that the operating manager of Profit Center A may find difficult to ignore. For example, assume that the preceding example is the same except for a change of the coefficient a_{22}.

$$\text{Max} = CX_1 + C_2X_2$$
$$?X_1 + 8X_2$$
$$\text{subject to:} \quad 3X_1 + 6X_2 \leqslant 60$$
$$2X_1 + 3X_2 \leqslant 40$$
$$X_1, \quad X_2 \geqslant 0$$

The solution is to produce 10 units of X_2, with a contribution margin of \$80.00. However, process II has an idle capacity of 10 hours and, accordingly, $W_2 = 0$. Process I has dual evaluator of $W_1 = 1\ 1/3$. The substitution rate is still 2 units of X_1 for 1 unit of X_2, requiring X_1 to be priced at \$7.00/unit. However, if Profit Center A is being asked to completely divert its resources into producing X_1, it will produce 20 units of X_1, yielding the same contribution margin of \$80.00. There is no idle capacity in process II, however. The center manager will hardly accept the utilization of all of his center's resources and still receive the same contribution margin. Theoretically, this is explainable on the grounds that the idle capacity of a slack variable is considered cost-free, assuming that such idle capacity cannot be leased, rented, or have its utilization deferred to next year without a reduction in its value. If these

conditions are not met, the opportunity cost concept will require that the transfer price of X_1 be more than \$7.00/unit to account for such additional profit foregone. If this is not accounted for, the manager of Profit Center A may believe that top corporate policy favors Profit Center B, because it does not reward his profit foregone.

The previous example also raises a crucial problem operationally. The shadow price value of W_1 and W_2 depends on the contribution margin of X_2 per unit and its required $[A]$ coefficients. If the CM is high, the values of the dual evaluators will be high, and vice versa, assuming that the $[A]$'s are the same. If it happens that X_2 is the most profitable product for Center A, the transfer price for X_1 will be so high that Profit Center B may not be able to pay. The opposite may also be possible, leaving Profit Center A at a disadvantage. While such operational problems have long-run implications for policy planning, in the short-run it is a situation to reckon with! A suggested solution is that the corporate level may use dual pricing for motivating reasons, since its total profit is still optimal because the volume of both centers is determined by the system.

It is not advisable to obtain the optimal solution for Profit Center A first, and then that of Profit Center B.[5] This procedure usually leads to diseconomies or a suboptimal solution for the company as a whole. To overcome such a difficulty, a solution for the combined efforts of both centers has to be obtained. If such an optimal solution, company-wise, put Profit Center A at a disadvantage, the system should provide a motivational solution to induce and maintain the divisional manager's motivation in the right direction, or at

[5]This is due to the fact that Profit Center A acts as a simple maximizer, and, as such, forces Center B to behave in the same way, leading to suboptimization. See the example illustrated above.

least minimize the chance of moving in the wrong motivational direction. Motivation costs (the difference between the center's maximization figure and that resulting from the corporate optimal solution) should be credited to Center A's profitability plan. If this is not done, conflict between the division's goal and that of the corporation moves into full gear, especially when the reward system is based on each center's profit. These points are illustrated in the following example:

Profit Center A	Profit Center B
Max $C_1X_1+C_2X_2$	$C_3Y_1+C_4Y_2$
$?X_1+8X_2$	$(10-C_1X_1)Y_1+5Y_2$

subject to:

$3X_1+6X_2 \leqslant 60$	$4Y_1+5Y_2 \leqslant 28$
$2X_1+4X_2 \leqslant 40$	$3Y_1+2Y_2 \leqslant 14$
$X_1, X_2 \geqslant 0$	$Y_1, Y_2 \geqslant 0$

To solve this problem, maximizing profit from a corporate point of view, assume that the variable cost of X_1 is $3.00/unit, and that one unit of X_1 is needed to produce one unit of Y_1. This makes the net contribution margin of $Y_1 = \$7.00$/unit.

A linear programming model based on decomposition is as follows:[6]

Max $\pi (X, Y) =$

$$
\left.
\begin{array}{l}
0X_1 + 8X_2 + 7Y_1 + 5Y_2 \\
-X_1 \quad\quad + Y_1 \quad\quad\quad \leqslant 0 \\
3X_1 + 6X_2 \quad\quad\quad\quad \leqslant 60 \\
2X_1 + 4X_2 \quad\quad\quad\quad \leqslant 40 \\
\quad\quad\quad 4Y_1 + 5Y_2 \leqslant 28 \\
\quad\quad\quad 3Y_1 + 2Y_2 \leqslant 14 \\
X_1, \quad X_2, \quad Y_1, \quad Y_2 \geqslant 0.
\end{array}
\right\} \text{Master Budget}
$$

The mathematical solution of such a case is illustrated in Exhibit III, where the feasible plans and optimal one are

[6]See: George Dantzig and Philip Wolf, "Decomposition Principles for Linear Programming, *Operations Research* (February 1960); and George Dantzig, *Linear Programming and Extensions* (Princeton University Press 1963); Chapters 22-24.

EXHIBIT III

Different Operating Profitability Plans

Plan I		
Production	*Center (A)*	*Center (B)*
$Y_2 =$ 5 units		$25.00
$Y_1 =$ 0 units		0
$X_1 =$ 10 units	0	
$X_2 =$ 10 units	$80.00	
$S_1 =$ 0 hours		
$S_2 =$ 0 hours		
$S_3 =$ 3 hours		
$S_4 =$ 4 hours		
Divisional Profit	$80.00	$25.00
Corporate Profit	$105.00	

Plan II		
Production	*Center (A)*	*Center (B)*
$Y_2 =$ 1 units		$ 5.00
$Y_1 =$ 4 units		28.00
$X_1 =$ 4 units	0	
$X_2 =$ 8 units	$64.00	
$S_1 =$ 0 hours		
$S_2 =$ 0 hours		
$S_3 =$ 7 hours		
$S_4 =$ 0 hours		
Divisional Profit	$64.00	$33.00
Corporate Profit	$97.00	

Plan III		
Production	*Center (A)*	*Center (B)*
$Y_2 = 4$		$20.00
$Y_1 = 2$		14.00
$X_1 = 2$		
$X_2 = 9$	$72.00	
$S_1 = 0$		
$S_2 = 0$		
$S_3 = 0$		
$S_4 = 0$		
Divisional Profit	$72.00	$34.00
Corporate Profit	$106.00	

shown.[7] The slack variables (S_1, S_2, S_3, S_4) corresponding to each plan are also shown, indicating any idle capacity in the corresponding process of each profit center.

For the corporation as a whole, plan III is optimal. However, if we look at the solution from the point of view of each profit center, do we reach the same conclusion?

From the profit Center *B*'s point of view, plan III is optimal. From Profit Center *A*'s point of view, it is not, since plan I is its optimal program. Would the manager of Profit Center *A* accept plan III, knowing what this means for his incentive compensation at the end of the year? Will the rate of return on his divisional investment reflect a fair measure of his performance if he accepts plan III?

What is the source of the problem and how should it be solved? The problem arises from the fact that the intermediate good X_1 is priced equal to its marginal (variable) costs. No contribution margin is given to Profit Center *A*, meaning that Profit Center *B* has captured all the gains yielded from this process itself, without sharing it with Profit Center *A*. This reflects unfair treatment. Accounting literature argues for the distribution of the joint profit of $7.00/unit of (X_1, Y_1) between both centers, either through bargaining or by means of an equalization rate based on the ratio of production cost

in both centers related to (X_1, Y_1). This accounting solution, as seen in this example, leads to suboptimization.[8] If a fair and equitable distribution is to be followed, Profit Center *A* should be given the profit foregone as a result of producing X_1. This means that the operating budget of Center *A*, if plan III is adopted, should be increased by $8.00 as motivation costs. Profit Center B's additional contribution as a result of further processing X_1 to Y_1, is $1.00. This is the additional gain the company obtained by encouraging the production of (X_1, Y_1). If the corporate level does not adhere to such an opportunity cost approach, budgetary conflict arises between the profit center managers and the corporate level.

The previous solution in general, however, raises two important implications:

1. If product X_2 is highly profitable, the opportunity cost of producing X_1 is high. If product Y_1, which uses X_1 as input, is not so profitable as to afford paying such opportunity costs, the company as a whole will be better off by not producing Y_1. However, if product Y_1 should be produced in order to meet a contract commitment, or as a result of a policy decision, this decision is a top corporate decision and not a center one. The profit (or loss) consequence of such a decision should be isolated. Center *A* should not be penalized by a decision not of its own.

2. If product X_2 is not highly profitable, the opportunity cost of pro-

---

[7]No top corporate constraints are assumed. If any exist, the problem can still be solved, using the decomposition principle. The operating costs of each center are assumed to be independent of the level of activity of the other center and linear. Also, any additional sales of Y's will not reduce the external demand for X_2. These two conditions are called technological independence and demand independence consecutively. However, there is a demand interdependence for Y_1 and X_1; the demand of X_1 is derived from that of Y_1. If the demand for X_2 and Y_2 is interrelated, the problem still can be solved, although it gets complicated.

[8]If Center *A* charges *B* a sales price of $8.00/unit of X_1, using the accounting equalization method, Center *B* finds it in its best interest not to buy X_1 and not to produce T_1. Center *B* will produce 5 units of T_2 and yield CM of $25.00, and Center *A* will then produce 10 units of X_2 yielding CM of $80.00. The total of $105.00 (equal to plan I) is a suboptimization case.

ducing X_1 will be less, and Profit Center B may be in an advantageous position. Profit Center A should not blame Profit Center B for this condition. Profit Center A would be well advised, if the demand for X_2 is decreasing and profitability is declining, to shift its resources to a new product. In the short run, however, Profit Center A should not ask Profit Center B to subsidize its operation and increase its profits.

These two implications do not necessarily require that the top corporate level use motivation costs in profitability planning, as in the case above.

II. Profit Center A Produces Both Product X_1 and Product X_2 for Profit Center B, and There Are No Market Prices for Either Product.

In this case, Profit Center A, in reality, is not a profit center. It will function the same if it is treated as a cost center,[9] or is joined with Profit Center B to compose one large profit center. The latter may require a change in the organization's structure, which may be justifiable to minimize the undesirable motivational consequence of a system based on "games" if the price of suboptimization is too high for the company to bear!

[9]If it is treated as a cost center, it will have a zero marginal contribution which a budgetary system should accept. Its performance can be evaluated in terms of cost control and volume attainment.

SUMMARY

Under the assumption $MC_A = NMR_B$, the supply profit center is not motivated to change the relative use of various factors of production in response to changes in factor prices, since these favorable effects will pass over to the buying profit center. In addition, the profit center selling the final product will be motivated either to manipulate its sales by delaying them to next year, if this year is especially profitable, or to increase its production inventory level so that a part of its overhead will be capitalized, leading to an increase of its profit if it is originally unfavorable. This will affect the production of intermediate goods. To prevent this, the corporate level watches the inventory level and asks for an explanation if it exceeds a certain level. Another solution is that the buying division commits itself to acquire a certain volume. These methods are partial solutions to the problem.

We have shown that using variable costs, approximating marginal costs, to price transfer goods has several limitations since this approach ignores several strategic factors. Also, we have shown that using the accounting equalization method leads to suboptimization and that any solution to a transfer pricing system cannot ignore the motivational conflict that is pertinent. We have used "motivation costs" to reduce the level of conflict due to the transfer pricing system. As a result, arriving at an optimal solution based on opportunity costs from the company's point of view, accepted by profit centers, is feasible.

SELECTED REFERENCES

A. Charnes, and W. W. Cooper, *Management Models and Industrial Application of Linear Programming*, Vol. I, II (John Wiley & Sons, 1961).

G.B. Dantzig, *Linear Programming and Extensions* (1963).

———— and P. Wolfe, "The Decomposition Principle for Linear Programs," *Operations Research*, Vol. 8 (1960), pp. 101-111.

Warren E. Walker, "A Method for Obtaining the Optimal Dual Solution to a Linear Program Using the Dantzig-Wolfe Decomposition," *Operations Research* (March-April 1969), pp. 368-370.

Adi Ben-Israel and Philip D. Roberts, "A Decomposition Method for Interval Linear Programming," *Management Science* (January 1970), pp. 374-387.

David P. Rutenberg, "Generalized Networks, Generalized Upper Bounding and Decomposition for the Convex Simplex Method," pp. 396-401.

William J. Baumol and Tibor Fabin, "Decomposition Pricing for Decentralization and External Economics," *Management Science* (September 1964), pp. 1-32.

Jerome E. Hass, "Transfer Pricing in a Decentralized Firm," *Management Science* (February 1968), pp. 310-331.

C. S. Colantoni, R. P. Manes and A. Whinston, "Programming, Profit Rates and Pricing Decisions," *The Accounting Review* (July 1969), pp. 467-481.

Andrew Whinston, "Pricing Guides in Decentralized Organization," *New Perspective in Organizational Research,* edited by W. W. Cooper, et al., (John Wiley and Sons, 1964), pp. 405-448.

Edwin V. W. Zschau, *A Primal Decomposition Algorithm for Linear Programming,* Ph. D. Thesis (Graduate School of Business Stanford University, December 1966).

Birch Paper Company Revisited: An Exercise in Transfer Pricing

Rene P. Manes

University of Arizona

This exercise examines the possibility of using shadow prices to calculate transfer prices between divisions of the multi-division or conglomerate firm and of basing divisional profit statements on transfer prices derived in this way. In order to demonstrate the proposal, a well known Harvard Business School case is modified in two ways so that two different linear programming solutions can be derived. Divisional income statements are then computed which indeed do exactly distribute the total profit of the firm each time, but these statements are found to have several unsatisfactory features for purposes of income determination. The exercise concludes by suggesting extensions for study and problem solving for the student.

Reprinted from *The Accounting Review,* July 1970, 565-572. Used by permission of Rene P. Manes and *The Accounting Review.*

This note will examine the proposal advanced by several economists[1] and a few accountants[2] that intra-firm transfer prices might be based on "shadow" prices, i.e. the "dual" variables of linear programming models. First the note will point out some of the operational difficulties of preparing divisional income statements when shadow prices have been used to calculate transfer prices. Then more fundamental conceptual questions will be raised with regard to the approach. As a vehicle for the exercise, Birch Paper Company, a well known Harvard Business School case[3] has been

[1] Baumol, *Economic Theory and Operations Analysis*, Chapter 6, Sections 2-4, Prentice-Hall 2nd Edition; A. Whinston "Price Guides in Decentralized Operations", pp. 420-424, *New Perspectives in Organization Research*, J. Wiley and Sons 1962, "Thus if the jth constraint is applied to a transfer of a good between various organization units then λj would be referred to as a "transfer price"; Whinston is careful to qualify this statement "for separable criterion functions and no externalities in the x_js."

[2] J. M. Samuels, "Opportunity Costing: An Application of Mathematical Programming," *Journal of Accounting Research*, (Fall 1965). It should be pointed out that although he discusses "transfer prices", Samuels does not illustrate a problem where "the output of one activity is the input of another."

[3] This case, copyrighted in 1957 by the President and Fellows of Harvard College and revised in 1964 was written by William Rotch and Professor N.E. Harlan. A recent survey by Professor T. Burns found Birch to be "the most frequently used case." (*The Accounting Review*, January 1968, p. 138). In a far more technical paper by A. Charnes, R. W. Clower and K. O. Kortanek, "Effective Control Through Coherent Decentralization with Pre-emptive Goals" (*Econometrica*, April 1967, pp. 305-307), The Birch Paper case was used to illustrate other problems of decentralization. The thrust of this article was that price guides from linear programming models would not in and of themselves lead divisions to proper action, i.e. overt cost minimization of the firm. Refer also A. Charnes and K. O. Kortanek "On the Status of Separability and Non-Separability in Decentralization Theory," *Management Science* Application Series, October 1968.

modified in two successive ways so that simple linear programming solutions of the firm's operations can be obtained. These modifications are interesting in and of themselves, since they highlight countervailing effects, on the one hand the rigorous need of the operations researcher for more data and on the other hand his complete abstraction of behavioral, personnel and organization issues. In the two modifications, specific plant capacity limits, technological coefficients and product prices are furnished and one major assumption of the original case is changed in that Birch Paper's activities (products) now are made to constitute significant proportions of the capacities of the respective divisions. The first modification of the Birch Paper case follows in problem form.

BIRCH PAPER REVISITED NO. 1

Birch Paper Company is an integrated paper company producing 1) paperboard (by its Southern Division) 2) corrugated boxes (by its Thompson Division) and 3) specialized paper products (by its Northern Division). Each division is judged independently on the basis of its profit and return on investment even though much of the business of the three divisions is intra company. Specifically, Northern has designed special display boxes for its products in conjunction with the Thompson division, which spent months perfecting design and production methods and which equipped itself for the work. Thompson, which sells boxes both to Northern and to outside firms, is required to buy its paperboard from Southern, which in turn is free to market either to Thompson or to other manufacturers.

Southern has quoted market prices to Thompson of $280, about 60% of which covers its out-of-pocket costs. Thompson incurs an additional $120 to process paperboard into boxes. The market price of its boxes is $450. Northern values the special display boxes at $480[4] and it is at this price that Thompson offers to transfer then to Northern. A controversy develops over this price and as an alternative to the fully integrated process described above, a proposal is made that Southern sell "outside" liner to Thompson at a price equivalent of $90; that the outside liner be colored and printed by Thompson for $30 ($25 of which is out-of-pocket) and then delivered to Eire Company, a firm outside of the Birch Paper complex. Eire has offered to pay the $120 for the prepared liner and to resell it in box form to Northern for $432.00. Given its plant costs and capacities,[5] Birch Paper's top management must decide 1) whether to go outside the firm and give business to Eire or 2) whether to keep all of the work within the firm; and if it elects the latter, it must determine what prices its decentralized divisions will charge each other.

Figure 1 represents the pattern of activities open to Birch Paper and Table 1 recapitulates the data on market prices, variable costs and plant capacities in this first version of the problem.

The linear programming problem which can be formulated from *Birch Paper Revisited No. 1* is:

$$\text{Max.} \quad 112x_1 + 162x_2 + 192x_3 + 89x_4$$

S.T.
1) $x_1 + x_2 + x_3 + 1/3x_4$
$\leqslant 100$ Capacity constraint on Southern

2) $x_2 + x_3 + 1/7x_4$
$\leqslant 100$ Capacity constraint on Thompson

3) $x_3 + x_4$
$\leqslant 150$ Capacity constraint on Northern

$+ x_i \geqslant 0$

The solution to this problem is $x_2 = 50$ and $x_4 = 150$. Total gross margin is $21,450. Southern and Northern both operate at full capacity of 100 units each but 28 4/7 units of Thompson's plant are idle. The shadow prices attaching to capacity constraints are:

$W_1 = +162$ on constraint #1, i.e. Southern's capacity, over a range of 28-4/7 units of Thompson's idle plant
$W_3 = +35$ on constraint #3, i.e. Northern's capacity (35 = 89 from activity 4 less 1/3 of 162 from x_2)
$W_2 = 0$

Budgeted income statements based on a direct cost approach[6] and using these shadow prices are developed for each division in Exhibit I.

TABLE I

Activity	Selling Division's Outside Price/Unit		Selling Division's Variable Cost/Unit	Forwarded Variable Cost/Unit	Contribution Margin/ Unit	Capacity Utilization/Unit	Total Capacity
x_1	Southern	$280	$168	—	$112	1/Unit	100
x_2	Thompson	450	120	$168	162	1/Unit	100
x_3	Northern	480	—	288	192	1/Unit	150
x_4	Northern	480	312	54 } 25 }	89	1/3/Unit Southern } 1/7/Unit Thompson } 1/Unit Northern }	150

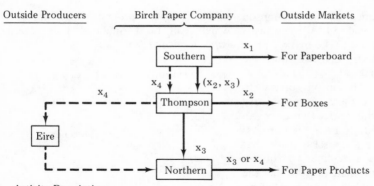

Outside Producers   Birch Paper Company   Outside Markets

Activity Description:

x_1 = Southern sale of paperboard to outside paperboard markets
x_2 = Sale by Southern of paperboard to Thompson for processing and sale to
         outside box markets
x_3 = Sale by Southern of paperboard to Thompson for processing of specially
         designed boxes for Northern's account and sale to paper products market
x_4 = Sale by Southern to Thompson of outside liners for printing only, transfer to Eire
         for conversion into boxes and delivery to Northern and ultimate sale to paper
         products market

FIGURE 1.

Some considerable changes both in optimal activities and derived income statements will result however if we relax the rules on Thompson and assume the existence of intercompany markets. Let us suppose that the Thompson Division has the opportunity and permission of Birch Paper's corporate headquarters to buy paperboard for $10 less from a rival firm and that Southern agrees to absorb this $10 (a transportation difference, for example) in any of its sales to Thompson. Now we must consider a new problem, Birch Paper Revisited No. 2; Figure 1 must be changed to Figure 2, and Table 1 is replaced by Table 2.

Note that only activities x_1 and x_4 are still the same. Activity x_2 of Figure 1 has been decomposed into x_2 and x_3 whereas activity x_3 of Figure 1 is now represented by x_2 and x_5. It proves redundant to add the constraint but now, because Thompson may acquire paperboard from the outside, $x_2 - x_4 - x_5 \leqslant 0$.[7]

However, further consideration of this type of constraint is enlightening. There are several levels of complexity in the shadow-transfer price suggestions. At the first level illustrated by Samuels, various products utilize joint or common services and are costed up to the extent that they make use of scarce, fixed plant. Except possibly where operations are organized by product under a system of product managers ("Department responsibility relates to a specific product, not to separate resources"[8]), there could be some question whether Samuels' "opportunity costs" are transfer prices as commonly understood.

At the second level in vertically integrated firms such as Birch Paper Company, alternative intermediate products flow through the company chain and must be priced if separate divisional profits are to be computed. Finally at a third level of complexity, a vertical chain is combined with horizontal extensions.

[7]Another variation of the problem which was not considered here and which would lead to still another optimal solution would permit

Thompson to buy both paperboard and outside liner from outside suppliers.
[8]Samuels, *op. cit.* p. 184.

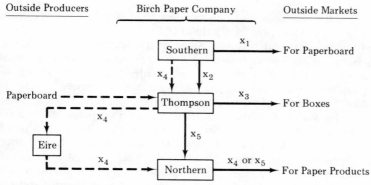

Revised Activity Description:

x_1 = Southern sale of paperboard to outside paperboard markets
x_2 = Sale by Southern of paperboard to Thompson
x_3 = Sale by Thompson to outside box markets
x_4 = Sale by Southern to Thompson for printing only, transfer to Eire for conversion into
 boxes and delivery to Northern and ultimate sale to paper products market
x_5 = Processing by Thompson of specially designed boxes for Northern's account and
 sale to paper products market

FIGURE 2.

TABLE 2

Activity	Selling Division's Outside Price/Unit		Selling Division's Variable Cost/Unit	Variable Costs Forwarded/ Unit	Contribution Margin/ Unit	Capacity Utilization/Unit	Total Capacity
x_1	Southern	$280	$168	—	$112	1/Unit	} 100
x_2	Southern	270	168	—	102	1/Unit	
x_3	Thompson	450	120	$270*	60	1/Unit	100
x_4	Northern	480	312	79	89	1/3/Southern 1/7/Thompson } 1/Northern	} 150
x_5	Northern	480	—	390	90	1/Unit	

* Whether Thompson buys from Southern or from outside sources, this market price must now be viewed as a forwarded variable cost.

In the Birch paper context such a situation would exist if Birch owned two or more box plants, each competing for the limited output of Southern as follows.

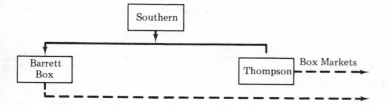

Now, if Southern is the only source of inputs for Barrett Box and Thompson, a stricter material balance constraint may be required such as $x_1 - x_2 - x_3 = 0$. In such systems shadow prices will take account not only of the bottlenecks in the vertical chain but also of the alternative opportunities available at the levels of horizontal integration.

At each of the three levels of complexity, the problem solver must consider whether or not outside purchases of inputs to divisions or sales of outputs by divisions are permissible. And if outside purchases and sales are permitted, their prices must be known and often material balance equations, including upper and lower market constraints, must be provided.

To return to our own problem, the only change in Birch Paper Revisited No. 1 which we have made is that we have allowed Thompson to buy paperboard from an outside supplier.

The linear programming problem for Birch Paper Revisited No. 2 can be stated now as

$$\text{Max } 112x_1 + 102x_2 + 60x_3 + 89x_4 + 90x_5$$

$$\begin{aligned}
\text{S.T.1)} \quad & x_1 + x_2 + \tfrac{1}{3}x_4 \leqslant 100 \\
\text{2)} \quad & x_3 + \tfrac{1}{7}x_4 + x_5 \leqslant 100 \\
\text{3)} \quad & x_4 + x_5 \leqslant 100 \\
& + x_i \geqslant 0
\end{aligned}$$

The solution to this problem is $x_1 = 50$, $x_3 = 78\,4/7$, $x_4 = 150$. Total gross margin is increased to $23,664\,2/7 and all three divisions are now at full capacity operation. The shadow prices attaching to capacity constraints are (Southern + 112, Thompson + 60, and Northern + 43 2/21).

$W_1 = +112$ (Southern's capacity)

$W_2 = +60$ (Northern's capacity)

$W_3 = +43\,2/21$ (Thompson's capacity $[+89 - 1/3(112) - 1/7(60)]$.

The preparation of budgeted income statements based on direct costing and using these shadow prices is furnished in Exhibit II.

Some of the operational difficulties of using shadow prices as transfer prices can now be pointed out. 1) As shown by Solomons,[9] shadow prices must be supplemented by the variable costs incurred up to the point of transfer. Strictly speaking then, the proposition is to base transfer prices on "shadow prices plus variable costs to point of transfer." 2) As pointed out by Dopuch and Drake[10] whenever market prices intrude in the system, difficulties arise in determining appropriate transfer prices. In Birch Paper Revisited, both in Exhibits I and II we have a mixed system containing both out-of-pocket market prices and internal transfer prices. The question can be asked whether Thompson's revenue from activity x_4 is recorded consistently in Exhibits I and II. In Exhibit I, with a zero shadow price on Thompson's capacity, the agreed-on cash price of $120 from Eire was used to record revenue. Alternatively, Thompson's price for x_4 could have been calculated at $133 ($109 shadow price forwarded from Southern plus $25 variable costs), but then an adjustment

[9]*Divisional Performance: Measurement and Control*, Financial Executives Research Foundation, 1965. Refer especially Chapter VI, p. 187-198. Solomons also furnishes an example of how shadow prices might be converted into transfer prices. Division A produces three intermediate products which are required in varying proportions by Division B to make two final products. There are capacity limits on Division A's intermediate products. No outside transactions other than final product sales are allowed and one possible criticism of the example is that there is no production substitutability within A for its three intermediate outputs. Solomons should be referred to for the most extensive discussion on transfer pricing in the accounting literature and for his thorough bibliography on the subject.

[10]N. Dopuch and D. Drake, "Accounting Implication of a Mathematical Programming Approach to the Transfer Price Problem", *Journal of Accounting Research*, Autumn, 1963, pp. 12-16.

EXHIBIT I

Divisional Income Statement — Birch Paper Company Revisited No. 1 — Year Ending December 31, 19xx

Southern	Thompson	Northern
Sales:	Sales:	Sales:
50 x2 units @ $\left\{\begin{array}{l}\text{162 Shadow Price} \\ \text{168 Variable Cost}\end{array}\right.$ $330 each $16,500	50 x2 units @ $450 $22,500	
150 x4 units @ 54 (1/3X162) Shadow Price 54 Variable Cost $108 each 16,200 $32,700	150 x4 units @ 120 18,000 $40,500	150 x4 units @ $480 $72,000
Less Cost of goods sold:	Less Cost of goods sold:	Less Cost of goods sold:
50 @ $168 $8,400	50 @ $\left\{\begin{array}{l}\text{330 Southern Transfer} \\ \text{120 Variable}\end{array}\right.$ 450 each $22,500	
150 @ 54 8,100 16,500	150 @ $\left\{\begin{array}{l}108 \\ 25\end{array}\right.$ 133 each 19,950 42,450	150 @ $432 Eire 64,800
Southern Contribution Margin $16,200	Thompson Contribution Margin $(1,950)	Northern Contribution Margin $ 7,200
		Total Birch Paper Co. Contribution Margin:
		Southern Division $16,200
		Thompson Division (1,950)
		Northern Division 7,200
		$21,450

EXHIBIT II

Divisional Income Statement — Birch Paper Company Revisited No. 2 — Year Ending December 31, 19xx

Southern	Thompson	Northern
Sales:	Sales:	Sales:
50 x_1 @ $\begin{cases}112 \text{ Shadow Price} \\ 168 \text{ Variable Cost}\end{cases}$	78 4/7x_2 units @ 450 $35,357 1/7	
280 each $14,000		
37 1/3 Shadow Price	150 x_4 @ 124 19/21	
(112X1/3)	units (see below) 18,735 5/7	150 x_4 units @ 480 $72,000
150 x_4 @ $\begin{cases}54 & \text{Variable Cost} \\ 91\ 1/3 \text{ each}\end{cases}$		
13,700 $27,700	$54,092 6/7	
Less Cost of goods sold:	Less Cost of goods sold:	Less Cost of goods sold:
50 @ $168 $8,400	78 4/7 @ 390 91 7/21 $30,642 6/7	150 @ 432 $64,800
150 @ 54 8,100 (same as Exhibit I)	150 @ $\begin{cases}25 \\ 116\ 7/21 \text{ ea.}\end{cases}$ 17,450 48,092 6/7	150 @ 4 19/21 734 5/7*
16,500		65,535 5/7
Southern Contribution Margin $11,200	Thompson Contribution Margin $ 6,000	
		Northern Contribution
	91 7/21 Southern transfer	Margin $ 6,464 2/7
	25 Variable Cost	
	8 12/21 Shadow Price	Total Birch Paper
	(1/7X60)	Contribution Margin:
		Southern Div. $11,200
	124 19/21 each	Thompson Div. 6,000
		Northern Div. 6,464 2/7
		$23,664 2/7

*Difference between transfer price Thompson receives for x_4 and payment by Eire.

318

would have to be made to Northern's unit Cost of Goods Sold. This approach is taken in Exhibit II. Here the costs of paperboard from Southern, 91 7/21 plus Thompson's variable costs of 25 plus its own shadow price of 8 12/21 indicated a total transfer price of $124 19/21 on x_4, which price was used instead of $120. Having used $124 19/21, of course, we must then adjust Northern's cost of goods sold on x_4 up by $4 19/21 per unit. This relatively simple example illustrates, then, the problem of such a transfer pricing scheme in a mixed system, that is, one where some outside market prices exist side by side with intra divisional transfer charges. 3) A third problem not illustrated in either variation of the Birch Paper case but touched on above involves shadow prices related to constraints other than capacity constraints. Conceivably we could have upper limits on activity levels due to marketing or institutional limitations, to which positive shadow prices would attach. The question would arise then as to which division should be credited with this shadow price.

These are operational difficulties which might be resolved in each instance without too much difficulty. More serious conceptual problems, however, suggest themselves from a study of Exhibits I and II. Although permitting Thompson to buy paperboard on the outside increased Birch Paper's overall profit by only about 10%, it caused dramatic intra-firm fluctuations in the reported gross margins of the three divisions, two of which (Southern and Northern) performed exactly the same kind and amount of work in each instance. If one were to probe more deeply into a situation such as reflected by Exhibit I, he might find that the reason Thompson was not permitted to buy outside paperboard was because Southern had been organized only to supply Birch Paper divisions and had no

marketing staff. Yet the failure to seek out outside marketing opportunities is not reflected in Exhibit I's linear programming model and the whole burden of this failure falls on Thompson instead of on Southern (or even on Birch's central management itself).

Another serious problem which suggests itself revolves around planning for excess capacity. Under a system which strictly translates shadow prices into transfer prices, no divisional manager will ever willingly plan to have excess plant capacity. Long-range planning and the provision of extra plant for peak loads or anticipated growth of future demand might be severely penalized, and a "grasshopper" philosophy developed among divisional managers. On the same point, the sudden and dramatically large changes in shadow prices (and thus transfer prices) which would occur as divisions reached or receded from capacity limits might well make the interpretation of direct costing income statements meaningless, particularly where return on investment analyses were involved. Finally the transfer prices based on shadow prices would have to be developed "ex ante." The difficulties of changing these prices whenever operations did not conform exactly to plans are obvious but will not be dwelt on here.

All in all, we must conclude that whenever centralized planning is indicated as here in the modified Birch Paper Company case, the determination of output levels and intra-divisional pricing decision cannot be delegated to divisional managers. Decentralization, if it is deemed desirable, should take the direction of variable cost minimization and seeking out other criteria for measuring performance. These would include readings on success 1) in dealing with the public, with unions and community leaders 2) in maintaining custody of elaborate plant installations 3) in meeting centralized schedules and 4) in upholding quality levels. Where intra firm activities are dependent these are duties enough. If the firm still wishes to establish profit centers (or is required to do so by future SEC/AICPA opinions on conglomerate activities) transfer prices should be negotiated in advance and management incentive schemes developed to a greater extent on the basis of agreed percentages of overall company profit. It is difficult to see how we shall ever be able to consider seriously the use of linear programming shadow prices as intra-divisional transfer prices. There are too many operational difficulties and conceptual objections to such a proposition. This conclusion is in no way intended to derogate the "meaningfulness" or the intrinsic analytic worth of the "shadow price." It is just another illustration of a common dictum in accounting: "No one accounting report or approach can serve all of the information or motivational needs of the firm."

Transfer Prices of the Multinational Firm: When Will They Be Arbitrary?

Arthur L. Thomas[1]

McMaster University, Ontario

Transfer prices can be used by multinational firms to minimize taxes or otherwise adversely affect the interests of the host company. Unless the transfer price approximates an equivalent arm's length price, it will be arbitrary. The arbitrariness of the transfer price problem is shown to be part of the larger allocation problem in accounting. Whenever transfer prices are arbitrary, the host country may have to introduce non-accounting considerations to influence a more favorable outcome.

[1]This article was inspired by Litvak and Maule [9]; I wish to thank its authors, as well as Mrs. Nancy Vichert, Mr. Earl K. Littrell and Professor L. G. Eckel, for their generous assistance and criticism during the writing of this paper. An earlier version was presented at the 1970 annual meeting of the Association of Canadian Schools of Business, University of Manitoba. 7-9 June 1970.

All international firms as defined here are, by definition, integrated across national frontiers either horizontally or vertically or both ... A high degree of integration inevitably introduces an important element of arbitrariness in the allocation of overhead costs to different operations and in the setting of the prices at which goods and services are transferred between the subsidiary entities of the firm. If we assume that firms attempt to minimize taxes in their efforts to maximize retained earnings, we can infer that they will attempt to use the scope thus provided to allocate overhead costs among their foreign branches, subsidiaries and affiliates, and to adjust their transfer prices, in order to reduce their total tax outlays . . .[2]

A giant multinational firm based in another country operates a manufacturing subsidiary in your country. This subsidiary purchases services and component parts from its foreign parent. Subsidiary sales have been high, but its profits have been low. As a responsible official of the host country, you suspect that the prices of the services and components that are purchased from the parent have been inflated arbitrarily.

The firm claims, however, that these transfer prices merely reflect the cost of the services and components, plus a modest mark-up to cover general overheads and profit. Although the firm has impressively complicated records and calculations to support this claim, your suspicions persist—if only because you know that a variety of alternative recording procedures are available to accountants, leading to many conflicting figures for the 'cost' of a manufactured good. Is there a simple way to determine whether such transfer prices are arbitrary? The answer to this question should be stated at the outset.

We will contend that, as far as affected parties in the host country are concerned, the transfer price will be arbitrary unless it approximates an equivalent arm's-length price. To some degree, of course, all transfer prices are arbitrary, for they depend upon the discretion of management. But Section III of this paper will show that a narrower definition of 'arbitrariness' is preferable here, one which is consistent with the lay sense in which a price is arbitrary if it is 'subject

to manipulation'. Thus, the main conclusion of this paper may be rephrased as follows: unless a transfer price approximates an arm's-length price, it will be subject to manipulation.

It is important to know this, for the multinational firm often will try to argue otherwise; after all, it is the party doing the manipulating.[3] While denials of arbitrariness are apt to be elaborate and well-buttressed by authoritative opinion, nevertheless a high proportion of international transfer prices may be found to be arbitrary.

Various parties in the host country are affected by the choice of international transfer prices: revenue and customs officials, minority and joint-venture investors in the subsidiary, union leaders and the employees they represent, members of the subsidiary company's management, etc. Arbitrary transfer prices may further the interests of at least some affected parties in host countries if these interests are consistent with the goals of the multinational firm. But often an arbitrary transfer price will harm the interests of the host country. The implications of 'arbitrariness' here are that, within what seem to be broad limits, any alternative price which an affected party in the host country might prefer will be just as defensible as the one chosen by the multinational firm. Affected parties in host countries should closely watch arbitrary transfer prices, and defend their own interests as best they can.[4]

[2] Penrose (10), p. 43. Numbers in parentheses refer to works which are at the end of this article.

[3] An alleged example of this received wide coverage in the Canadian press at the time that this paper was being put into its final form—see press coverage of the preliminary report of the Barber Royal Commission, and subsequent reactions beginning during the latter half of January 1970. The Barber report indicated that transfer prices of tractors imported into Canada were set arbitrarily high. The manufacturers issued vigorous denials.

[4] Such a defense of a party's own interests involves dynamic considerations which go beyond the limitations of this paper. The discus-

The arguments supporting these conclusions are sufficiently complicated to make desirable some guide to the organization of the rest of this paper. Section II is a brief discussion of the tax effects of transfer prices on host countries. The Appendix sketches other effects on host countries, as well as the main *internal* goals of the multinational firm that might be furthered by appropriate manipulation of transfer prices. Section III is a detailed discussion of the sense in which many transfer prices may be said to be 'arbitrary'. The main reason why transfer prices usually are arbitrary is that allocations in accounting usually are arbitrary. Accordingly, Section IV takes what might seem to be a detour; it deals with the general problem of allocations in accounting. Section V examines the various transfer pricing approaches currently used in accounting; it is contended that they are arbitrary, except when they yield the equivalent of an arm's-length price for the same goods or services. Section VI sketches the implications of all this for host country officials. Finally, following the Appendix, there is a list of works cited in this study.

THE EFFECTS OF TRANSFER PRICES ON HOST COUNTRY INTERESTS

Manipulation of transfer prices to advance firm interests. Affiliated units of a multinational firm often have transactions with each other, transactions which may involve the purchase and sale of services as well as goods; it is commonplace for affiliated companies to perform management, research, mar-

keting and other services for each other, and to charge each other service fees. The transfer prices at which these transactions are recorded are often selected by the parent company to best advance the interests of the firm as a whole. This self-interest implies that arbitrary international transfer prices for goods or services may be either advantageous or disadvantageous to the host country in which the subsidiary is located.

Most discussions of transfer price manipulation by the multinational firm focus on the ways in which skilful choice of transfer prices may minimize total taxes paid by the company.[5] For example, Rutenberg (12)* has developed a model in which transfer prices for goods and services, short-term intersubsidiary loans, and dividend payments are employed to make optimal use of tax havens, bilateral tax treaties, non-uniform treatments of income received from abroad, and national differences in income tax rates and import and export duties.[6] As Rutenberg's model indicates, such tax minimization efforts inevitably become extremely complicated. But, *ceteris paribus,* it will be to the firm's advantage to choose transfer prices that result in low taxable magnitudes (such as net incomes and invoice values for goods subject to border taxes) in countries where income taxes or border tax rates are high, and high taxable magnitudes where tax rates are low.[7]

---

sion which follows is deliberately restricted to statics—to the specific transfer prices employed by individual firms at particular points in time. The reason for this restriction is that most of the theories which are used to justify such transfer prices are also restricted to statics, and it is the purpose of this paper to provide affected parties in host countries with a defence against such justifications.

[5]Although throughout this paper the discussion is confined to firms operating in two or more countries, even those operating in a single country also try to minimize provincial or state taxes. Most of what follows is just as significant for provincial or state taxation authorities as it is for officials of the national government of the host country.

*Numbers in parentheses refer to selected references at the end of this reading.

[6]*See* Penrose (10) pp. 43-6 for additional examples.

[7]'In principle, if vertically integrated international firms were maximizing consolidated profits and could freely determine their internal

In advanced countries, authorities are alert to the possibilities of various kinds of manipulation through transfer prices, and may intervene.[8] In fact, with a low transfer price more than one government may intervene: first, the authorities in the importing country who are responsible for the prevention of dumping would be concerned; second, the government to which the exporting affiliate pays income taxes would object.[9] Although underdeveloped nations may be less able to defend their interests, most advanced countries have tariff laws which insist on the use of arm's-length prices for imports whenever these are available, and which otherwise try to set a floor below which transfer prices may not fall.[10]

Effects on the host country. There are no simple guides to what the effects of transfer price manipulation will be on the host country. One might initially believe that if transfer prices were being used to divert taxable magnitudes from one country to another, the country in which the tax was paid would benefit and the country in which the tax was avoided would suffer. But things are not always this simple. For one thing, different parties within a single country may have conflicting interests. Perhaps the most common example of this is the differing interests of customs and internal revenue authorities with regard to imports. Both to raise revenue and to prevent dumping, customs authorities generally will wish

transfer prices on imported goods to be as high as possible.[11] But the higher import prices are, the higher will be the expenses of the affiliated company and therefore the lower its net income and its income tax.[12] Nor are the effects of transfer price manipulation the concern only of tax authorities. Local minority investors, joint-venture investors,[13] and local customers of the affiliate are among the various parties who, with taxation authorities, have interests affected directly by the amounts chosen for transfer prices. Also, as the Appendix to this paper indicates, in addition to tax minimization there are various internal goals of the multinational firm which can be furthered by transfer price manipulation.

All in all, since an arbitrary transfer price may be either advantageous or disadvantageous to a host country, clearly a host country should not object to a transfer price just because it is arbitrary. But, just as clearly, since an arbitrary transfer price which benefits the host country does so only by a kind of coincidence, officials of host countries should, at least, have some way of telling when a transfer price is arbitrary and when it is not.[14]

TRANSFER PRICES AND ARBITRARINESS

Where transfer prices are based on costs of production or other magnitudes yielded by accounting processes, there is always the possibility that they will be arbitrary. The numbers of dollars generated by accounting rules for costs of goods, transfer prices, profits, and so on, are significant only insofar as they affect

---

pricing structure without fear of political repercussions or of government pressures ... then the inter-affiliate price structure adopted by any firm would be such as to leave zero profit ... in those countries in which the effective tax rates were highest, after making allowance for the effects of any offsets against their home tax liability that their home government allows ...' Penrose (10) p. 45.

[8] For examples, *see* Penrose (10) pp. 44*n* and 260-1; Rutenberg (10) pp. 7-8; Tuckerman (18) p. 35; and Stone (16).

[9] Rutenberg (12), p. 7.

[10] Stone (16), pp. 40-1.

[11] Stone (16), p. 40.

[12] Given, of course, certain assumptions as to the elasticity of demand for the affiliate's products.

[13] For example, *see* Penrose (10), p. 265.

[14] For a discussion of conflicts of interest between host countries and multinational firms, *see* Penrose (10) pp. 260-2, 264-6.

decisions made or to be made by users of accounting reports. But it is well known that a large number of different assumptions may be made and a large number of different formulae may be used in making cost and other calculations, and hence in deriving any transfer price based on these calculations. Any such transfer price will be arbitrary unless it can be defended decisively against all other possible, and materially different, transfer prices. And, decisive defense requires more than the mere assertion or fiat of one party to the transaction.

If any object or event can be represented by many possible magnitudes, it is possible for those responsible for reporting on it to choose a magnitude on grounds of self-interest or on any other grounds. To describe the product of such a choice as arbitrary corresponds with one of the ways in which 'arbitrary' is commonly used; as meaning 'subject to manipulation'.[15]

Of course many magnitudes appearing in accounts or accounting statements are not arbitrary. For example, if a firm determines the total amount owing to materials suppliers at a year's end and none of the constituent amounts is in dispute, the aggregate is not arbitrary; it can be defended against any other amount by recourse to the impersonal evidence. An equally conclusive defence may be given to the use, as a transfer price, of the arm's-length price of an equivalent good where such a price is obtainable; there is independent evidence of its propriety.

On the other hand, some magnitudes now reported in accounting statements cannot be so defended; they are arbitrary. We have argued elsewhere[16] that most allocations made by accountants are arbitrary in this sense. When allocations are arbitrary, transfer prices based on them are also arbitrary. One or more parties of interest may challenge these prices on the ground that they serve, in a biased fashion, the interest of the firm which chooses them.

THE ALLOCATION PROBLEM IN ACCOUNTING

Most numerals generated by accounting systems result from allocations. When, for instance, a company buys a building with a thirty-year useful life, under conventional accounting rules, during each of the next thirty years part of that building's cost will be charged—allocated—as that year's depreciation. This is but one example of a general class of magnitudes. A *nonmonetary input* to a firm is any economic good acquired by the firm other than cash or legally enforceable claims to receive cash. Nonmonetary inputs include such things as raw materials inventories, services provided by office and factory employees, utilities and advertising services, machinery, etc.—i.e., the bulk of the inputs to the firm. Accountants always allocate the costs of nonmonetary inputs to one or more years, and to one or more activities of a firm.

In the same sense, the accountant allocates profits (and related revenues, cost savings, etc.). When efforts are made to determine the contributions to profits

---

[15]This definition of 'arbitrariness' differs from the one used in Thomas (17). That work is exclusively concerned with the numerals reported in published financial statements. These statements are general-purpose reports going to a great variety of readers, and used in making many different kinds of decisions. In contrast, however, this paper is concerned to establish whether, from the standpoint of a specific user such as an affected party in a host country, transfer price numerals are arbitrary.

[16]Thomas (17) (For further discussion of the points raised here and in the next two notes, see also this work's sequel, *The Allocation Problem: Part Two*, American Accounting Association, 1974—Ed.)

made by individual inputs to the firm, calculation of these contributions requires taking the total profits of the firm as a whole, and allocating them to the individual inputs. Because this can be done at any of a variety of different levels of aggregation, profits may be allocated to one specific machine, to the combination of inputs in a particular department of the firm, and to the individual parent and subsidiary companies of a multinational firm. It should be stressed that if individual net incomes are calculated for the affiliated companies which make up a multinational firm, the accountant *is* thereby allocating the total profit of the multinational firm to the individual parent and subsidiary companies.

An implicit assumption regarding allocation. Accountants have developed a rich variety of rule-of-thumb allocation systems, most of them notoriously in conflict with each other. Within the accounting profession, one result has been considerable concern over the inconsistent treatment given by different companies to certain allocations—such as the depreciation allocation. Much of the theoretical literature of accounting consists of attempts both to defend particular allocation schemes and to damn others. An implicit assumption in almost all this literature is that there is *some* way of allocating *which is defensible* against alternatives.

There is, however, persuasive evidence that this assumption often will be invalid.[17] Although a large number of allocation methods is available and is discussed in the literature, there has been no demonstration of the conclusive defence of any of them against all others. Further, the range of ambiguity (the range of the products of all possible allocation methods) may easily exceed the limits of the immaterial. For instance,

for a long-lived depreciable asset the range of ambiguity in the depreciation allocation for any one year may be a substantial fraction of the original purchase price of that asset. Similarly, the writing off of R & D costs in the year of their incurrence, and the allocation of them to future years according to one of a limitless variety of allocation schemes, may be equally defensible; and equally indefensible. Once again, the range of ambiguity may be very large. And when one passes from the individual input to consider sets of inputs (such as the set of all inputs contributing to the manufacture of a product for which a transfer price is calculated), the range of ambiguity is correspondingly magnified.

Allocation theory and interaction. These ambiguities arise because the individual inputs to the firm interact with each other, so that the linkage between particular outputs is not directly discernible. Contemporary allocation theory cannot cope with input interactions, except by arbitrary fiat. There usually is no way in which costs and profits may be allocated so that the result can be conclusively defended against the result obtained by other modes of allocation. Nor is there usually even any way to narrow down the possibilities.[18]

Allocations and transfer prices. These conclusions have great significance for any allocations to be employed in calculating (or defending) international transfer prices. Conflict of goals is common between multinational firms and affected parties in host countries. If a transfer price depends upon one or more allocations of costs or profits, usually many conflicting allocations will be possible and will result in a range of alternative transfer prices, with no possibility of narrowing this range nor of con-

[17] *See* Thomas (17).

[18] *See* Thomas (17).

clusively defending a single transfer price against all others.

THE IMPLICATIONS OF THE ALLOCATION PROBLEM FOR TRANSFER PRICING

Because transfer prices are often determined according to plausible formulas supported by voluminous statistical and accounting data, expert testimony and other authoritative opinion, it is easy to believe that many kinds of internally calculated transfer prices would be hard to challenge. One is even apt to feel intimidated by the complexity or overawed by the ingenuity of transfer price calculation schemes. What is more, transfer prices often result from prolonged and delicate negotiations among the various components of the total firm, each wishing to maximize its own profits. Once these components have finally reconciled themselves to a particular negotiated formula, there is a tendency to resist change. The most arbitrary formula may be sincerely defended by both parent and subsidiary as the only 'right' way to calculate a transfer price.

Nonetheless, this section will argue that such internally calculated transfer prices are arbitrary and may properly be rejected as irrelevant by host country officials, joint-venture investors, and other parties external to the multinational firm. Moreover, no matter how complicated the internal calculations are, nor how firmly supported by expert opinion, their details may be ignored by all external parties. Instead, external parties may rely upon a simple rule of thumb: if a transfer price does not demonstrably approximate an arm's-length price resulting from an equivalent transaction with an independent third party, the transfer price is arbitrary, and the external party may be confident that any plausible alternative which he might prefer will be at least equally defensible.

Transfer prices of goods. Suppose that a subsidiary of a multinational firm which makes certain regular products selling directly to wholesalers, retailers, and other independent external parties, also manufactures certain transfer products selling to a parent in a foreign country. (The following argument applies, *mutatis mutandis,* to all intra-group sales.) The parent sells some of the transfer products directly to other independent external parties, using the remaining transfer products internally (as component parts, etc.).

The regular products sold by the subsidiary to independent external parties present no difficulties, beyond those typical of accounting in general.

Transfer products sold to outsiders. When the parent sells transfer products to outsiders, the selling price to the outside purchaser is easily determined. The difference between this selling price and whatever is calculated to be the manufactured cost of the product to the subsidiary will be the gross profit recorded by the multinational firm as a whole. Since the transfer price between parent and subsidiary automatically serves to allocate the total gross profit between the two affiliated companies, if this allocation is arbitrary, the same arbitrariness is implied for the related transfer price. In the extreme case, if the transfer price equals the selling price to outside purchasers, the entire gross profit will have been allocated to the subsidiary.

It was emphasized above that contemporary accounting allocation procedures will usually give arbitrary results if there is interaction among inputs. Also, it was pointed out that division of the total multinational enterprise into component parent and subsidiary companies is merely one of many possible ways of grouping the activities of the multinational firm as a whole. Accordingly, allocations of the total profits of the multinational firm to its affiliated companies usually *will* be arbitrary if the affiliated companies interact; and unless they can be defended in some other way (such as by demonstrating that they approximate equivalent arm's-length prices), the transfer prices will be arbitrary too.[19] Moreover, the subsidiary's cost figures (upon which the gross profit is calculated) will also be arbitrary unless the subsidiary's nonmonetary inputs do not interact with each other.

Transfer products consumed by the parent. If anything, the situation is even worse for those transfer products used internally by the parent, for there is no final selling price to independent purchasers to work from. Here are the main ways in which transfer prices are determined for such internally consumed products:[20]

1. At a known market price for the product, based on arm's-length purchases of equivalent products in equivalent circumstances by independent purchasers.

2. At such an arm's-length price, minus certain adjustments relating to the special relationship between the affiliated companies. For example, since the subsidiary will have negligible marketing costs *vis-à-vis* the parent, estimated average marketing costs may plausibly be subtracted from the arm's-length price. Similarly, if the parent company is acting as the selling agent for the subsidiary, a sales commission may be deducted from the arm's-length price. Almost all such adjustments reflect the general problem

(discussed below) of determining 'comparable circumstances'.

3. At an arm's-length price adjusted for a modification of the product. This is a special case of the foregoing, occurring when the parent subjects the product to additional processing or incorporates it as a component in another product, selling the new product to outsiders. Here, the transfer price may be determined by subtracting all costs incurred by the parent in completing the new product from the price to outsiders. If things are left at this, the entire gross profit on the sale to outsiders will be implicitly allocated to the subsidiary, unless, as often happens, the transfer price is reduced still further, either to provide a 'normal' gross profit to both companies or according to some other rationale.

4. At the 'cost' of the product to the subsidiary. In practice, there are four main meanings that may be given to 'cost' here:

(a) Marginal cost to the subsidiary. When an external market exists for the product, this will be the market price less selling expense. Otherwise, 'marginal cost' is usually taken as the variable cost incurred by the subsidiary (and thus involves the usual implied assumptions of the linearity of the cost curve over the relevant range of output).

(b) Variable cost of the subsidiary, adjusted by a subsidy (often calculated as a total figure once a year) to provide for fixed manufacturing costs. Such a subsidy implies an allocation of total fixed manufacturing costs; costs that pertain to work done for the parent are differentiated from those that do not.

(c) Full cost to the subsidiary. This is made up of variable costs plus allocated fixed manufacturing costs. This corresponds to what an

---

[19] CF. Penrose (10), pp. 43-4.
[20] A good textbook summary of the various different approaches used in practice for determination of transfer prices may be found in Shillinglaw (13). *See also* Henderson and Dearden (5), and Bierman (1), pp. 89-93.

economist would call the product's internally calculated 'average' cost. It is similar to (b) if the figures are viewed from the standpoint of the year as a whole.

(d)   Full cost to the subsidiary, plus a 'normal' profit (or other allocation of total profits earned by the multinational firm as a whole). Since this 'normal' profit is apt to be a gross profit, it is likely to include an allowance for general (non-factory) overheads.

Finally, 'cost' under any one of these approaches may be either an actual historical cost or a standard cost.

5.   At a negotiated price. These negotiations may involve reference to other market prices, to gross profits allowed to other subsidiaries, and to a variety of other things, but the final transfer price is arrived at by bargaining. Although it is of course possible that bargaining could result in one of the previously mentioned kinds of transfer prices, this 'negotiated price' category is intended to cover all *other* kinds of negotiated transfer prices.

Many of these transfer price methods are arbitrary. From the earlier discussion, it is easily seen that most of these methods generate arbitrary transfer prices.

Because negotiated transfer prices (method 5) are ultimately subject to dictation by the parent company, the subsidiary is never in a position to conduct true arm's-length bargaining; accordingly, unless the negotiated transfer price approximates some other kind of transfer price, it will be arbitrary.

Method 3, in which the transfer price is based on the selling price of the new product completed by the parent, suffers from all the arbitrariness already present in those cases where the parent, without further processing, sells the transfer product directly to outsiders. In addition,

since determination of the parent's cost of completing the new product involves additional allocations of nonmonetary inputs, there is arbitrariness from this source, except in the highly unlikely case in which the parent's inputs (including the products from the subsidiary) do not interact with each other.

While one or another type of full-cost transfer pricing (methods 4(c) or 4(d)) is common in practice,[21] one or another type of variable-cost transfer pricing (methods 4(a) or 4(b)) is often recommended by theorists.[22] In each case, since the calculation of product costs will involve allocations of nonmonetary inputs, these allocations will be arbitrary, unless the subsidiary's inputs do not interact. In method 4(d), described as cost plus a 'normal' profit, an additional allocation must be performed of the total profit of the whole multinational firm. Unless the parent and subsidiary companies do not interact, this will be arbitrary. Since both kinds of interactions almost always will be present, the 'cost' approaches to transfer pricing almost always will be arbitrary.

It should be emphasized again that this arbitrariness has nothing whatever to do with whether a particular transfer price method can be defended for use *within* the multinational firm. For example, given certain assumptions, use of equilibrium-output marginal costs as transfer prices will tend to maximize total firm profits.[23] But the marginal-cost transfer price would still be an arbitrary one unless maximization of total firm

[21]*See,* for example, Horngren (8) p. 349.
[22]*See* Horngren (8) pp. 349-50; Shillinglaw (13) pp. 824-8; and Solomons (15) Chapter VI, all of which are based in turn on the work done by Hirshleifer in (6) and (7).
[23]*See* Solomons (15) Chapter VI, and Hirshleifer (6). However, *see also* Wells' arguments (19) that transfer prices will be meaningless within the firm except when, in effect, they are arm's-length prices.

profits is the goal of all parties to the transfer price. Actually these parties include taxation and other governmental authorities of the host country, minority host-country stockholders in the subsidiary, and others (such as host-country union officials) whose interests conflict in one way or another with profit maximization by the multinational firm as a whole.

Arm's-length prices. This leaves arm's-length transfer prices (methods 1 and 2) in the field. But at least three circumstances may make supposedly arm's-length prices arbitrary, too.[24]

1. The price must be for equivalent goods, sold under equivalent conditions. Transfer products frequently are slightly different in grade or design from those traded in a competitive market because the affiliated company may have unique specifications. Since the transfer product would not be sold to outsiders in its present form or without promotional effort, some adjustment of arm's-length prices is necessary to reflect completion or selling costs, an adjustment usually involving arbitrary allocations of nonmonetary inputs (for reasons discussed earlier).

To some extent, even among independent companies, most market prices are negotiated, while published prices give little information concerning such things as delivery terms, cash discounts, discounts for large and continuing orders, service and warranty terms. Since many goods are purchased only after competitive bids have been sought by the company, resulting prices are very difficult to learn.

2. If the transfer product is so specialized that either there is no market or only a very thin market, any supposed arm's-length price may be arbitrary. For example, if a subsidiary produces most of the total world supply of the particular good, and sells most of its output to its parent, the world market price simply does not reflect a potential price to third parties. Cases of no markets and thin markets are probably very common.

3. The market in which arm's-length prices are sought may have characteristics which violate other classical requirements of free competition. For example, the market prices of many raw materials are administered by a few large producers, often with the co-operation of certain governments—crude oil prices are a standard example.[25] Or, in order to manipulate the market price, governments may deliberately alter supply or demand conditions through their tariff policies.

In any of these circumstances, arm's-length prices may be impossible to calculate, and if some calculation *is* made, the resulting figure may be arbitrary.[26]

Transfer prices for services. Transfer prices are charged not only for products but also for various services performed for other affiliates by one affiliate of the multinational firm. These include management services, research and development,

---

[24] For background to the following discussion, *see* Solomons (15) pp. 177-8; Shillinglaw (13) pp. 829-30; Penrose (10) pp. 50-2, 177-8, 260-2; and Bierman (1) pp. 90-1.

[25] For example, *see* Penrose (10) pp. 50, 261-2.
[26] Dearden (3) discusses many of the practical details of determining arm's-length prices and approximations thereto for transfers between divisions. Although the implications of this article might suggest that plenty of cases exist in which satisfactory arm's-length prices can be calculated, the article shows that a fairly wide range of prices for the same product could each claim to be 'arms-length'. On the practical level, the concept of an arm's-length price often will be ambiguous. Compare Henderson and Dearden (5).

marketing services, royalties on patents and trademarks, and allocated head-quarters overheads. As Rutenberg points out, such services are 'very elusive and difficult to price'.[27] While on the one hand this situation makes transfer prices for services especially popular objects of manipulation,[28] on the other hand an equivalent arm's-length price for such services is especially difficult to determine. Lacking an arm's-length price, transfer prices for services will be arbitrary for exactly the same reasons as will transfer prices of tangible products.

Transfer prices for services usually are set either at estimated full cost with an added 'normal' profit—possibly including a general allowance for overheads not explicitly traced to performance of the service—or at a negotiated price. The quality of the allocations required is, if anything, even lower than when a tangible product is involved. But the main point is that, with either cost or negotiated- price bases, the transfer prices of services will be arbitrary.

IMPLICATIONS FOR HOST COUNTRY OFFICIALS

For host country officials, the implications of the foregoing are twofold. A high proportion of transfer prices will be arbitrary, subject to manipulation by the multinational firm. A claim that a particular transfer price is *not* arbitrary should always be supported by a convincing demonstration that it approximates an equivalent arm's-length price. Lacking such a demonstration, the host country official need inquire no further and need pay no attention to any other arguments raised by the firm, no matter how elaborate these arguments

are, nor how massively based on expert opinion. For it is a sound rule of thumb that if such a demonstration is not feasible, the transfer price is arbitrary. The implications of 'arbitrariness' here are that, within what appear to be broad limits, any alternative price which the host country official might prefer will be just as defensible as the one chosen by the multinational firm. This rule of thumb greatly simplifies the task of evaluating transfer prices.

What then? In theory, whenever transfer prices *are* arbitrary, host country officials will wish to influence their determination. The extent to which this is possible will depend upon a number of non-accounting considerations. For example, host countries are often in poor bargaining positions. But at least host country officials need not be confused by accounting calculations which, although they may be useful to the multinational firm itself, are of no significance to outsiders.

APPENDIX

GOALS OF THE TOTAL FIRM THAT CAN BE FURTHERED BY APPROPRIATE CHOICE OF TRANSFER PRICES

Various goals of the multinational firm may be furthered by an appropriate choice of transfer prices. These goals, which fall into two broad categories, pertain first to the firm's relationship with outsiders (external goals), and second to the firm's general control over its affiliated components and employees (internal goals).[29] Shulman's excellent summary[30] of external goals which may be furthered by appropriate choice of transfer prices includes:

---

[27] Rutenberg (12) p. 8. *See also* Penrose (10) pp. 43-4, and Tuckerman (18) pp. 34 and 35.
[28] Cf. Rutenberg (12) p. 8.

[29] Cf. Penrose (10) pp. 177, 265.
[30] Shulman (14); *see also* Tuckerman (18) p. 35.

1. Tax reduction as it applies to income taxes, customs duties, and various other kinds of taxes which may be 'managed'.[31]
2. Reduction of the share of profits going to local minority-interest investors (or joint-venture-partnership investors) in the host country subsidiary.
3. Defeat or blunting of economic restrictions imposed by the host country (for example, repatriation of profits despite host country controls over dividend remittances).
4. Improvement of an affiliated company's credit status or general ability to raise capital extending to provision of reinvestment funds when there are barriers both to raising capital locally and to transferring it from abroad.
5. Subsidizing of the activities of a new venture, including general strengthening of the competitive position of the total firm.

To these might be added the benefits of price discrimination, when sales are made both to affiliates and to outsiders.

Furtherance of internal goals[32] Shillinglaw has summarized the internal goals that may be furthered by appropriate choice of transfer prices:

The prices used to record transfers of goods between divisions serve two main purposes:

1. Before the fact, to guide division managers toward decisions

that will lead to an economic allocation of resources.
2. After the fact, as one determinant of the profit attributed to each profit center.[33]

An example of the first kind of internal use has already been mentioned. Under certain conditions pricing transfers at their marginal costs may lead to optimum short run use of total firm resources.[34] As an example of the second kind of internal use, if one subsidiary is operating in adverse circumstances, transfer prices may be manipulated until its rate of return on invested capital compares favourably with the rates of other subsidiaries.

While appropriate choice of transfer prices may help the multinational firm advance both its internal and its external purposes, clearly it is the *firm's* goals that are being furthered, and although the goals of the host country may be furthered, too, often the firm's goals will be opposed, and in consequence the related transfer prices may conflict with the host country's interests.

---

[31] Rutenberg (12) has developed an unusually detailed deterministic model of this, and indicates that a stochastic model is forthcoming.
[32] For background to the following, *see* Shillinglaw (13) Chapter 26; Solomons (15) Chapter VI; Horngren (8) pp. 348-52; Dopuch and Drake (4) pp. 10-15; Henderson and Dearden (5); and Hirshleifer (6). Hirshleifer (7) should also be read by those who wish to go into this topic in detail.

[33] Shillinglaw (13) p. 817. As noted earlier, Wells (19) argues that transfer prices are meaningless (and useless) for these purposes, except when divisions are autonomous, trading freely in the market place—i.e., except when they are arm's-length prices. This conclusion, which would reinforce those reached in this paper, is consistent with the analysis in (17). However, Well's arguments need not be examined here, since my arguments already indicate that non-arm's-length transfer prices—even should they be meaningful to the firm itself—are meaningless from the standpoint of host country officials.
[34] The rules are very complicated for selecting transfer prices which will result in the maximization of total firm profits. Hirschleifer, (6), a summary of whose conclusions appears on p. 183, is still the standard detailed discussion. Bierman (1), though differing somewhat in detail and method, provides on pages 93-102 a good introduction to Hirshleifer's writings. For additional complications, *see* Cook (2).

LIST OF WORKS CITED

The literature of transfer pricing is extensive; no attempt is made here to offer a comprehensive bibliography. The reader who wishes to pursue transfer pricing further may begin with the selected references in Rappaport (11) pp. 359-60, continuing with the bibliography in Solomons (15) pp. 287-301.

No work which came to notice after the end of 1969 is cited.

1. Harold Bierman, Jr., *Topics in Cost Accounting and Decisions,* New York 1963, pp. 88-102.

2. Paul W. Cook, Jr., 'New Technique for Intracompany Pricing', *Harvard Business Review,* Vol. 35 (July-August 1957), pp. 74-80.

3. John Dearden, 'Interdivisional Pricing', *Harvard Business Review,* Vol. 38 (January-February 1960), pp. 117-25.

4. Nicholas Dopuch and David F. Drake, 'Accounting Implications of a Mathematical Programming Approach to the Transfer Price Problem', *Journal of Accounting Research,* Vol. 2 (Spring 1964), pp. 10-24; reprinted in Rappaport (11) pp. 340-51.

5. Bruce D. Henderson and John Dearden, 'New Systems for Divisional Control', *Harvard Business Review,* Vol. 44 (September-October 1966), pp. 144-60; reprinted in Rappaport (11) pp. 326-39.

6. Jack Hirshleifer, 'On the Economics of Transfer Pricing', *Journal of Business,* Vol. 29 (July 1956), pp. 172-84.

7. Jack Hirshleifer, 'Economics of the Divisionalized Firm', *Journal of Business,* Vol. 30 (April 1957), pp. 96-108.

8. Charles T. Horngren, *Cost Accounting: A Managerial Emphasis,* Englewood Cliffs, N.J. Prentice-Hall, Inc., 2nd edition, 1967, pp. 348-52.

9. I. A. Litvak and C. J. Maule, 'What Price Sovereignty? The American Impact on Canada', (Paper presented to the Policy Conference of the Progressive Conservative Party of Canada, Niagara Falls, 10 October 1969). This paper will be published in a forthcoming book, to be edited by Professor T. Symons.

10. Edith T. Penrose, *The Large International Firm in Developing Countries: The International Petroleum Industry,* Cambridge, Mass., 1968.

11. Alfred Rappaport (ed.), *Information for Decision Making: Quantitative and Behavioral Dimensions,* Englewood Cliffs, 1970.

12. David P. Rutenberg, Maneuvering Liquid Assets in a Multi-National Company: Formulation and Deterministic Solution Procedures', *Management Sciences Research Report* No. 154, Carnegie-Mellon University, February 1969.

13. Gordon Shillinglaw, *Cost Accounting: Analysis and Control,* Homewood, Ill. Revised edition 1967, Chapter 26.

14. James Shulman, 'When the Price is Wrong—By Design', *Columbia Journal of World Business,* Vol. 11 (May-June 1967), pp. 69-76.

15. David Solomons, *Divisional Performance: Measurement and Control,* Homewood, Ill. 1965, Chapter VI.

16. Williard E. Stone, 'Legal Implications of Intracompany Pricing', *Accounting Review,* Vol. XXXIX, (January 1964), pp. 38-42.

17. Arthur L. Thomas, *The Allocation Problem in Financial Accounting Theory*, American Accounting Association, Evanston, Ill. 1969.
18. Bert Tuckerman, 'Objective Consolidation Standards for Foreign Subsidiaries', *Accounting Review*, Vol. XXXIX (January 1964), pp. 32-7.
19. M. C. Wells, 'Profit Centres, Transfer Prices and Mysticism', *Abacus*, Vol. 4, (De-(December 1969), pp. 174-81.

SELECTED REFERENCES FOR CHAPTER 7

BOOKS

Solomons, David, *Divisional Performance: Measurement and Control.* New York: Financial Executives Research Foundation, 1965.

ARTICLES

Baumol, William J., and Tibor Fabian, "Decomposition, Pricing for Decentralization and External Economics," *Management Science*, XIII (September, 1964).

Bernhard, Richard H., "Some Problems in Applying Mathematical Programming to Opportunity Costing," *Journal of Accounting Research*, VI (Spring, 1968).

Cook, Paul W., Jr., "New Technique for Intracompany Pricing," *Harvard Business Review*, XXXV (July-August, 1957).

Dean, Joel, "Decentralization and Intracompany Pricing," *Harvard Business Review*, XXXIII (July-August, 1955).

Dopuch, Nicholas and David F. Drake, "Accounting Implications of a Mathematical Programming Approach to the Transfer Price Problem," *Journal of Accounting Research*, II (Spring, 1964).

Goetz, Billy E., "The Effect of a Cost-Plus Contract on Transfer Prices," *The Accounting Review*, XLIV, (April, 1969).

Gould, J. R., "Internal Pricing in Firms When There Are Costs of Using an Outside Market," *The Journal of Business*, XXXVII (January, 1964).

Hirshleifer, Jack, "On the Economics of Transfer Pricing," *The Journal of Business*, XXIX (July, 1956).

———, "Economics of the Divisionalized Firm," *The Journal of Business*, XXX (April, 1957).

Philippakis, Andreas S. and Howard E. Thompson, "Reward Functions, Transfer Prices, and Decentralization," *The Quarterly Review of Economics and Business*, X (Spring, 1970).

Ronen, Joshua and George McKinney, III, "Transfer Pricing for Divisional Autonomy," *Journal of Accounting Research*, VIII (Spring, 1970).

Samuels, J. M., "Opportunity Costing: An Application of Mathematical Programming," *Journal of Accounting Research*, III (Autumn, 1965).

Thomas, Arthur L., "Transfer Prices of the Multinational Firm: When Will They be Arbitrary?" *Abacus*

Wells, M. C., "Profit Centres, Transfer Prices and Mysticism," *Abacus*, IV (December, 1969).

BEHAVIORAL
ASPECTS OF
INFORMATION

CHAPTER EIGHT

The Role of
the Firm's
Accounting
System for
Motivation

**George J.
Benston**

*University of
Rochester*

An overview of research findings from the behavioral sciences and organization theory as they relate to motivation is presented. A critical examination of accounting systems in light of these findings concludes that responsibility accounting systems are likely to be an incentive for the effective motivation of managers. Depending upon how budgets are developed, they may serve the purposes of positive motivation in certain instances and lead to a reduction in effective motivation in other cases. Participation budgets, a clear expression of goals, and timely performance reports are key factors in increasing positive motivation.

Reprinted from *The Accounting Review*, XXXVIII (April, 1963), 347-54. Used by permission of George J. Benston and *The Accounting Review*. "Grateful acknowledgement is due the members of the Workshop in Accounting Research of the Institute of Professional Accountancy at the University of Chicago for their helpful (though often devastating) criticism, and especially to Professor Charles Horngren for his encouragement and aid. Regrettably, they cannot be held responsible for errors in fact or opinion." —G.J.B.

INTRODUCTION

Motivating employees to work for the goals of the firm has long been one of management's most important and vexing problems. The search for methods that motivate effectively, that induce the employee to work harder for the firm's goals, led to experimentation with a wide diversity of devices.[1] In recent years, several writers emphasized that the firm's accounting system has a direct influence on the motivation of managers.[2] This paper (a) surveys the available findings of research done in the behavioral sciences and organization theory as they bear on motivation and (b) critically examines the accounting system and reports in the light of such findings.

Part I surveys the literature related to motivation and organizational structure and concludes that the decentralized[3] form of organization provides the conditions in which effective motivation can occur. In the light of Part I and other evidence, the accounting system and reports are critically evaluated in Part II. The major conclusions of Part II are that:

1. The empirical research reinforces and justifies the recent emphasis on the virtues of responsibility accounting. Responsibility accounting provides an effective overall aid to decentralization and, hence, while indirect and not as dramatic as some proposed direct uses (such as "proper" budgets or standards), perhaps is more important for effective motivation.

2. The evidence does not support the unqualified use of accounting reports as direct motivating factors. Indeed, there is evidence that the direct use of budgets can lead to a reduction in effective motivation. Nevertheless, there are positive aspects to the direct use of accounting reports.

I. MOTIVATION AND ORGANIZATIONAL STRUCTURE

The motivation of employees may be attempted by the use of a very large variety of techniques, applied in a number of ways. Among these techniques are direct wage incentives, participation schemes, goal setting, and morale boosters. These may be offered directly to the employee by the firm in a centralized fashion (by the personnel department, for example), or indirectly, by the department head in a decentralized firm.[4] Since even a cursory examination of the literature on motivation leads to the realization that the specific techniques of motivation are of almost infinite variety, this paper will concentrate on the problem of application. Indeed, the survey of the literature presented below led the writer to conclude that the organizational structure of the firm is very important for the successful application of motivation

[1] See M. S. Viteles, *Motivation and Morale in Industry* (New York: W. W. Norton and Company, Inc., 1953).

[2] C. Argyris, *The Impact of Budgets on People* (New York: The Controllership Foundation, 1952). "Tentative Statement on Cost Accounting Concepts Underlying Reports for Management Purposes," *The Accounting Review*, XXXI (1956), p. 188; R. Anthony, "Cost Concepts for Control," *The Accounting Review*, XXXII (1957), pp. 229-34; N. Bedford, "Cost Accounting as a Motivation Technique," *N.A.C.A. Bulletin* (1957), 1250-57; and A. Stedry, *Budget Control and Cost Behavior* (Englewood Cliffs, N.J.: Prentice-Hall, Inc., 1960).

[3] *Decentralization*, as used in this paper and in organization theory generally, refers to the vesting of authority and responsibility in the department manager or supervisor for the day-to-day conduct of departmental operations. The department in question need not be physically or organizationally separate from the rest of firm. The title "department manager" and the organizational grouping "department," then, signify any supervisory position and work group for which authority and responsibility over specific tasks are delegated and for which accounting reports are prepared. With this system of organization, the department manager is given the authority to operate his department and supervise his employees as he would do if he were an individual entrepreneur.

[4] In a small firm, these two procedures of application may merge, since the central decision maker is in direct contact with the employees.

techniques, especially with respect to the ordinary worker.[5] The influence of organizational structure on motivation, then, is examined below.

DECENTRALIZATION AND CENTRALIZATION

The organizational structure of decentralization is one in which managers and employees are in direct and continuous contact. This face-to-face relationship facilitates the manager's perception of the needs and goals of his workers. With the authority given him by decentralization, the manager can provide those specific rewards and penalties that are effective for motivating individual workers and groups. Thus, he is in a good position to persuade them to accept the goals of the firm as their own (or as not opposed to their goals) and work to achieve these ends.

In contrast, centralization and large size make perception of the workers' needs difficult. Communication between the decision makers and those who carry out their decisions becomes complicated and subject to more interference ("noise").[6] And, as a study of ten voluntary associations revealed, ordinary members become more passive and disassociated from the central purposes of the organization and leaders become further removed from the activities they plan.[7]

In addition, research at Sears, Roebuck and Co. revealed that organizational size alone unquestionably is one of the most important factors in determining the quality of employee relationships: "the smaller the unit, the higher the morale and vice versa."[8] And, a study of two British motor car factories demonstrated that the size factor affects productivity directly. Significant (though low) correlations were found between output and size, the smaller work groups showing consistently larger output in each factory.[9]

However, the existence of small groups, per se, is not a sufficient condition for motivation. Workers may feel a greater sense of belonging if they work in smaller, more cohesive groups, but they will not necessarily be motivated toward fulfilling the goals of the organization. Some writers, notably Argyris (who has done extensive research at Yale's Labor and Management Center), believe that it is inevitable that the ordinary worker fight the organization. He writes that the organization characterized by ". . . task specialization, unity of direction, chain of command, and span of control . . . may create frustration, conflict, and failure for the employee. He may react by regressing, decreasing his efficiency, and creating informal systems against management."[10]

This tendency for informal organizations to be created has been explored extensively.[11] Sleznick, for example,

[5]The motivation of managers and other executives similarly is affected by organizational structure. However, since published findings that dealt with the motivation of executives specifically could not be found, the major emphasis in this paper is on the motivation of the ordinary worker.

[6]T. M. Whitin, "On the Span of Central Direction," *Naval Research Logistics Quarterly*, I (1954), 27.

[7]F. S. Chapin and J. E. Tsouderos, "Formalization Observed in Ten Voluntary Associations: Concepts, Morphology, Process," *Social Forces*, XXX (1955), 306-9.

[8]J. C. Worthy, "Organizational Structure and Employee Morale," *American Sociological Review*, XV (1950), 173.

[9]R. Marriott, "Size of Working Group and Output," *Occupational Psychology*, XXIII (1949), 56.

[10]C. Argyris, "The Individual and Organization: Some Problems of Mutual Adjustment," *Administrative Science Quarterly*, II (1957), 1.

[11]For example, see C. I. Barnard, *The Functions of the Executive* (Cambridge, Mass.: Harvard University Press, 1938); J. A. March and H. A. Simon, *Organizations* (New York: John Wiley & Sons, Inc., 1958); P. Selznick,

writes that "In every organization, the goals of the organization are modified (abandoned, deflected, or elaborated) by processes within it. The process of modification is effected through the informal structure."[12] After reviewing several empirical studies, he concludes that "the day-to-day behavior of the group becomes centered around specific problems and proximate goals which have primarily an internal relevance. Then, since these activities come to consume an increasing proportion of the time and thoughts of the participants, they are—from the point of view of actual behavior—*substituted* for the professed goals.[13]

THE MOTIVATION OF SMALL GROUPS

There also is ample evidence that these informal groups can work to increase or decrease productivity, depending on whether or not the workers perceive that the organization's goals are not contrary to theirs.[14] Two types of procedures have been proposed to cope with this problem. One, the direct approach, involves an immediate attempt by top management to influence the worker through direct wage incentive plans, companywide incentive plans, and group discussions. The other, the indirect approach, gives primary responsibility and authority to the department manager to motivate his workers effectively.

The direct approach is often effective, but it is also difficult to administer successfully. Direct incentive plans are not feasible generally unless a homogeneous product is produced under repetitive conditions.[15] Also, attempts to promote individual increases in productivity usually are disruptive and detrimental to efficiency where the employees' tasks are interrelated.[16] Companywide incentive plans have had a spotty record of success.[17] They seem to work best where there is a long history of trust between labor and management or an unusual person as chief executive of the company.[18] However, efforts to impose companywide incentive plans in other situations have been generally unsuccessful. Group discussions also do not appear to be reliable. A famous experiment conducted in an American plant on the effect of group discussions on productivity and worker acceptance of change produced negative results when replicated in Norway.[19]

"An Approach to a Theory of Organization," *American Sociological Review*, VIII (1943), 47-54; and H. A. Simon, *Administrative Behavior* (New York: The Macmillan Company, 1947).

[12] *Ibid.*, p. 47.

[13] *Ibid.*, p. 48. (Emphasis appears in the original.)

[14] For example, see L. Berkowitz, "Group Standards, Cohesiveness and Productivity," *Human Relations*, VII (1954), 509-19; D. Cartwright and A. Zander, "Group Pressures and Group Standards," in *Group Dynamics*, 2nd ed., eds. D. Cartwright and A. Zander (New York: Harper & Row, Publishers 1960), pp. 165-88; S. Schacter, N. Ellertson, D. McBride, and D. Gregory, "An Experimental Study of Cohesiveness and Productivity," *Human Relations*, IV (1951), 229-38; and W. F. Whyte *et al.*, *Money and Motivation* (New York: Harper & Row, Publishers, 1955).

[15] W. B. Wolf, *Wage Incentives as a Management Tool* (New York: Columbia University Press, 1957).

[16] P. M. Blau, *The Dynamics of Bureaucracy* (Chicago: University of Chicago Press, 1955), Chap. IV; M. Deutch, "The Effects of Cooperation and Competition Upon Group Process," in *Group Dynamics*, 2nd ed., *op. cit.*, footnote 14, pp. 414-48; and E. J. Thomas, Effects of Facilitative Role Interdependence of Group Functioning," *Human Relations*, X (1957), 347-66.

[17] J. N. Scanlon, "Profit Sharing: Three Case Studies," *Industrial and Labor Relations Review*, II (1948), 58-75.

[18] See J. F. Lincoln, *Lincoln's Incentive System* (New York: McGraw-Hill Book Company, 1946).

[19] L. Coch and J. R. P. French, Jr., "Overcoming Resistance to Change," *Human Relations*, I (1948), 512-32; and J. R. P. French, Jr.,

The indirect approach makes the informal group's goals synonymous with the organization's goal through effective company leadership of the informal group. The firm then can take advantage of the demonstrated positive relationship between group goals and productivity (cited above).[20] Also, this approach does not rule out the use of direct techniques when and where they are deemed feasible.

THE ROLE OF THE DEPARTMENT MANAGER

The indirect approach can be effected most readily in the decentralized firm. The department manager, who is likely to understand and accept the firm's goals,[21] can be assigned the task of leading the informal group. In assigning the department manager this role, the departmentalized firm can take advantage of the probability that the informal grouping of workers will follow the formal department organization. Task specialization and frequent interaction provide this cohesiveness.[22]

It is very important that the organization-oriented manager assume the leadership role, for when he abdicates or

is incapable in his role as leader, an informal leader arises.[23] Without a management-oriented leader, the drives of workers for satisfaction are often channeled into nonproductive or destructive practices.[24] This behavior is to be expected, since the effort necessary for high production rarely is satisfying in itself. Indeed, many empirical investigations have shown that there seldom is positive, but occasionally negative, correlation between productivity and job satisfaction.[25]

The factors that are likely to make the department manager an effective leader also are a product of decentralization. Bass, who considers much of the literature on leadership, concludes that the effective supervisor satisfies the needs of his subordinates.[26] Since these needs are diverse, any number of leadership styles have been found to work in a variety of situations. Thus, the organizational structure must allow the manager the freedom and authority to reward his workers. Freedom is necessary so that the manager can adapt his methods to the particular needs of his group. And, the employees will respond to the demands of the manager only if he has enough influence to make the employees' behavior pay off in terms of actual benefits.[27]

J. Israel, and D. Ås, "An Experiment on Participation in a Norwegian Factory," *Human Relations*, XXX (1960), 3-19.

[20] See footnote 14.

[21] Research that examined the motivation of managers, as distinct from production workers, could not be found. However, managers are in more direct and continual contact with the firm's policy makers than are ordinary workers. Hence, they are likely to assume the goals of top management (see evidence cited in footnotes 14 and 22). Also, top management can exercise control over the performance and possibly the motivation of department managers through budgets and accounting reports of performance (as discussed below).

[22] J. M. Jackson, "Reference Group Processes in a Formal Organization," *Sociometry*, XXII (1959), 307-27. Also reprinted in *Group Dynamics*, 2nd ed., *op. cit.*, footnote 14.

[23] R. L. Kahn and D. Katz, "Leadership Practices in Relation to Productivity and Morale," in *Group Dynamics*, 2nd ed., *op. cit.*, footnote 14, pp. 554-70.

[24] W. F. Whyte *et al.*, *op. cit.*, footnote 14.

[25] A. H. Brayfield and W. H. Crockett, "Employee Attitudes and Employee Performance," *Psychological Bulletin*, LII (1955), 396-424; and R. L. Kahn and N. C. Morse, "The Relationship of Productivity to Morale," *Journal of Social Issues*, VII (1951), 8-17.

[26] B. M. Bass, *Leadership, Psychology, and Organizational Behavior* (New York: Harper & Row, Publishers, 1960). The bibliography of this work includes 1155 items.

[27] D. C. Petz, "Influence: A Key to Effective Leadership in the First Line Supervisor," *Personnel*, XXIX (1952). A similar conclusion is reached by Fiedler for military and sports groups. He concludes that ". . . leadership traits

Decentralization also is effective in encouraging the manager to use a style of leadership that promotes effective motivation. It was found in several empirical studies that the fewer the restraints put upon a group (within limits), the more it produced.[28] Kahn and Katz have done extensive research on this aspect of motivation. They find that "Apparently, close supervision can interfere with the gratification of some strongly felt needs."[29] They go on to observe that

There is a great deal of evidence that this factor of closeness of supervision, which is very important, is by no means determined at the first level of supervision. . . . The style of supervision which is characteristic of first-level supervisors reflects in considerable degree the organizational climate which exists at higher levels in the management hierarchy.[30]

Thus decentralization, which is characterized by the autonomy of action given the department manager by top management, serves both to allow the managers the necessary freedom and authority needed for motivation and to encourage them to supervise their workers effectively.

II. ACCOUNTING SYSTEMS AND MOTIVATION

Decentralization, which provides the motivational advantages described above, is aided by the firm's accounting system. In fact, many students of decentralization agree with E. F. L. Brech's conclusion (in a review of British experience with decentralization):

By whatever arrangements and procedures, decentralization necessitates provision for the periodic review of performance and progress and the expression of approval.[31]

This need is met by the firm's accounting system. Top management can afford to give authority to the department manager, since it can control the basic activities of the department with the help of accounting reports of performance. Furthermore, accounting reports and budgets may serve as reliable means of communication, wherein top management can inform the manager of the goals of the firm that it expects him to fulfill.

RESPONSIBILITY ACCOUNTING

More specifically, the findings surveyed above reinforce the recent emphasis on responsibility accounting. In making the smallest areas of responsibility the fundamental building blocks of the accounting system, accountants facilitate effective motivation. With a system of responsibility accounting, top management can afford to widen its span of control and allow operating decisions to be made on a decentralized basis. Correlatively, assigning costs to the individual

---

can become operative in influencing group productivity only when the leader has considerable power in the group." (F. E. Fiedler, "The Leader's Psychological Distance and Group Effectiveness," in *Group Dynamics*, 2nd ed., *op. cit.*, footnote 14, p. 605). Kahn and Katz also reach this conclusion (*op cit.*, footnote 23, p. 561), as do W. S. High, R. D. Wilson, and A. Comrey, "Factors Influencing Organizational Effectiveness," *Personnel Psychology*, VIII (1955), 368.

[28] R. M. Stogdill, *Individual Behavior and Group Achievement* (New York: Oxford University Press, Inc., 1959), p. 272.

[29] R. L. Kahn and D. Katz, *op. cit.*, footnote 23, p. 560.

[30] *Ibid.*, p. 560.

[31] E. F. L. Brech, "The Balance Between Centralization and Decentralization in Managerial Control," *British Management Review*, VII (1954), 195.

managers who have control over their incurrence is a factor in encouraging these managers to exercise effectively their authority to motivate their supervisees. The managers' performance in this regard is measured by the accounting reports, which are likely to be an incentive for the effective motivation of the managers.

BUDGETS AND MOTIVATION

Indeed, several writers have proposed that accounting reports be used as a direct factor for effective motivation. The most extensive examination of the use of budgets as a tool for motivation was made by Stedry, who measured the effect of various budgets on an individual's level of aspiration as a method of determining the differences in motivation on these budgets.[32] His experiment, in which the subjects attempted to solve problems for which they received budgets and were rewarded for achievement, resulted in the following determinations:

> The experimental results indicate that an "implicit" budget (where the subject is not told what goal he must attain) produced the best performance, closely followed by a "medium" budget and a "high" budget. The "low" budget, which was the only one which satisfied the criterion of "attainable but not too loose," resulted in performance significantly lower than the other budget groups.
>
> However, there is a strong interaction effect between budgets and the aspiration level determination grouping. The group of "high" budget subjects who received their budgets prior to setting their aspiration levels performed better than any other group, whereas the "high" budget

group who set their aspirations before receiving the budget were the lowest performers of any group.[33]

After presenting arguments to the effect that firms probably do not operate at optimal efficiency, Stedry concludes that:

> ... it seems at least reasonable to suppose that it is a proper task of budgetary control to be concerned with strategies for constant improvement in performance.[34]

He implies that the budget should be used to motivate department managers. The function of the budget would be to raise the manager's level of aspiration and thereby increase his level of performance, rather than to inform him of top management's goals and decisions.

Stedry briefly notes, but does not really consider, the effects of accounting reports on the setting of aspiration levels. His experiment was deliberately designed so that the subjects would not have knowledge of their performance.[35] The budget then became their primary point of reference.[36] But would this happen where the managers had knowledge of their previous performance to compare with the budget that is supposed to motivate them to new productive heights?

It is likely that department managers can make a fairly accurate estimate of their performance. The experience of time study engineers can be noted, since the setting of a rate for a particular job is analogous to the setting of a budget for a department. In both situations the attempt is made to motivate the worker to produce more by setting high standards. But, as many articles, texts, and case studies attest, the worker almost always

---

[32] A. Stedry, *Budget Control and Cost Behavior* (Englewood Cliffs, N.J.: Prentice-Hall, Inc., 1960).

[33] *Ibid.*, pp. 89-90.
[34] *Ibid.*, p. 147.
[35] *Ibid.*, p. 71.
[36] *Ibid.*, p. 82.

can gauge his performance. The worker generally will fight a "tight" rate by refusing to produce efficiently, because of his fear that the "carrot" will always be pushed ahead every time he attempts to overtake it.[37] There is no reason to expect department managers to be less perceptive than factory workers.

In an actual situation, the department manager probably would compare his estimate of his performance with the budget to see how well he did. This means that the manager would have knowledge of his success or failure. Several experimenters have examined the effect of this knowledge on aspiration levels. Lewin, Dembro, Festinger, and Sears, in an often quoted review and analysis of the literature to 1944, conclude that "... generally the level of aspiration will be raised and lowered respectively as the performance (attainment) reaches or does not reach the level of aspiration."[38]

The effects of success and failure are difficult problems for the would-be budget manipulator. Stedry's findings indicate that a high budget (one technically impossible of attainment) produced the best performance where the subject received it before setting his level of aspiration. The attainable low budget produced the worst results. But in working

conditions, assuming knowledge, the high budget probably will result in failure for the department manager and, consequently, in lowering his level of aspiration (motivation) and performance.[39] The budget manipulator, then, must either give the manager false reports about his performance or attempt to set the budget just enough above the manager's perception of his performance to encourage him.

The first alternative, false reports, is a potentially dangerous procedure and is likely to be quite expensive. Performance reports would have to be secretly prepared. This would make accounting data on the department's actual operations (needed for economic decisions) difficult to obtain, since the department manager could not be consulted. Also, this procedure must be based on the assumption that the manager will believe a cost report, even if it conflicts with his own estimates. The validity of this assumption is denied in a study by Simon, Guetzkow, Kozmetsky, and Tyndall:

> Interview results show that a particular figure does not operate as a norm, in either a score card or attention-directing sense, simply because the controller's department calls it a standard. It operates as a norm only to the extent that the executives and supervisors, whose activity it measures, accept it as a fair and attainable yardstick of their performance. Generally, operating executives were inclined to accept a standard to the extent that they were satisfied that the data were *accurately recorded*, that the standard level was *reasonably attainable*, and that the variables it measured were *controllable* by them.[40]

[37] See W. F. Whyte *et al.*, *op. cit.*, footnote 14, Chap. 3, "Setting the Rate," for a delightful description of this practice.

[38] K. Levin, T. Dembro, L. Festinger, and P. Sears, "Level of Aspiration," in *Personality and the Behavioral Disorders*, Vol. 1, ed. J. McV. Hunt (New York: The Ronald Press Company, 1944), p. 337. A comprehensive test of the hypothesis stated by Lewin *et al.*, which confirmed it, was made by I. L. Child and J. W. M. Whiting, "Determinants of Level of Aspiration: Evidence from Everyday Life," *Journal of Abnormal and Social Psychology*, XLIV (1949), 314. Similar results are reported by I. M. Steisel and B. D. Cohen, "Effects of Two Degrees of Failure on Level of Aspiration in Performance," *Journal of Abnormal and Social Psychology*, XLVI (1951), 78-82.

[39] This may have happened even in Stedry's experiment, since he found that the poorest performance occurred where the subjects determined their aspiration levels before they were given the high budget.

[40] H. A. Simon, H. Guetzkow, G. Kozmetsky,

The second alternative open to the budget manipulator is rather difficult to effect. The manager's level of aspiration must be measured and *his* perception of his performance level must be estimated. However, measurement of an individual's aspiration level is not a well-developed science. Some fairly successful, though crude, procedures for measuring level of aspiration have been developed. Unfortunately, they depend on the subject's verbal response to questions about the goal explicitly to be undertaken, such as the score expected (not hoped for) in a dart throwing contest.[41] The usefulness of this technique for a work situation is limited, since the employee has an incentive to state a false, low goal and, thus, avoid failure. A more precise measure has been developed by Siegel,[42] but the technique itself restricts it to highly artificial conditions. Thus, it is doubtful that the use of budgets for motivation can be effective except in carefully selected situations.

The direct influence of the budget on motivation may be more effective than is indicated above if the budget is a participation budget, rather than an imposed budget of the type used by Stedry. In a [recent] article, Becker and Green present evidence and arguments to show that participation in budget making in conjunction with the comparison and reviewing process may lead to increased cohesiveness and goal acceptance by the participants.[43] If this goal acceptance is at a higher level than previous goals, the aspiration level of the participants has been raised and should lead to increased production.[44]

ACCOUNTING REPORTS OF PERFORMANCE AND MOTIVATION

Budgets are not the only accounting reports that may be used for motivation. Accounting reports of performance also have a direct effect on motivation by giving the department manager knowledge of his performance. Most of the published experiments on this subject consider the effects of knowledge on the learning or performance of physical tasks. However, the general findings reported ought to be relevant to the effect of accounting information on the manager's performance. Ammons surveyed most of the literature in this area (to 1956) and reached the following generalizations that seem applicable to the present problem:

1. Knowledge of performance affects rate of learning and level reached by learning.
2. *Knowledge of performance affects motivation.* The most common effects of knowledge of performance is to increase motivation.
3. The more specific the knowledge of performance, the more rapid improvement and the higher the level of performance.
4. The longer the delay in giving knowledge of performance, the less effect the given performance has.
5. When knowledge of performance is decreased, performance drops.[45]

and G. Tyndall, *Centralization vs. Decentralization in Organizing the Controller's Department* (New York: The Controllership Foundation, 1954), p. 29. (Emphases appear in the original.)

[41] K. Levin, T. Dembro, L. Festinger, and P. Sears, *op. cit.,* footnote 38.

[42] S. Siegel, "Level of Aspiration and Decision Making," *Psychological Review,* LXIV (1957), 253-63.

[43] S. Becker and D. Green, Jr., "Budgeting and Employee Behavior," *The Journal of Business,* XXXV (1962), 392-402.

[44] For a fuller treatment of this subject see the Becker and Green paper, in which is discussed the conditions under which cohesiveness, goal acceptance, and productivity can be lowered as well as increased.

[45] R. B. Ammons, "Effects of Knowledge of

However, overemphasis of departmental cost reports may have undesirable effects, since accounting data often do not measure fulfillment of the firm's goals. Ammons notes that, "It is very important to keep in mind *what* the subject is motivated to do when knowledge of performance increases his motivation. Often he is motivated to score higher, not necessarily to learn the task faster and better. He may then resort to taking advantage of weaknesses in the apparatus, learning habits which are of no value or actually lead to poorer performance when he later attempts to learn a similar task."[46] Overemphasis of accounting reports has been found to result from this behavior.[47] Where the reports became the sole criteria for evaluating performance, managers resorted to such anti-productive techniques as delayed maintenance, bickering over cost allocations, and even falsification of inventories.

Thus, recognition of the positive motivational aspects of accounting reports should not lead to the conclusion that they can be used without limits. Indeed, the history of the search for "the key to motivation" indicates that people's needs are too diverse and changeable to be satisfied by any single device or mechanically applied procedure.

CONCLUSION

Decentralization contributes to effective motivation. The firm's accounting system facilitates decentralization and hence has an indirect but important impact on motivation. The direct use of accounting reports, such as budgets, for motivation can result in reduced performance if the budget is imposed on the department manager. However, a participation budget may be effective in increasing motivation. Also, accounting reports of activities aid motivation by giving the manager knowledge of his performance.

In short, the accounting system facilitates decentralization, which is conducive to effective motivation. Furthermore, the careful use of accounting reports can directly contribute toward effective motivation by expressing goals and by supplying knowledge of performance.

Performance: A Survey and Tentative Theoretical Information," *Journal of General Psychology* (1956), pp. 283-90. (Emphasis appears in the original.)

[46]*Ibid.*, p. 280.

[47]See C. Argyris, *op. cit.*, footnote 10; P. W. Cook, Jr., "Decentralization and the Transfer Price Problem," *The Journal of Business,* XXVII (1955), 87; and V. F. Ridgway, "Dysfunctional Consequences of Performance Measurements," *Administrative Science Quarterly,* I (1956), 240-47.

Dysfunctional Consequences of Performance Measurements

V. F. Ridgway

*College of Business
Colorado State
University*

Although quantitative measures of performance are undoubtedly useful, their behavioral side effects should be carefully considered to gauge their net benefits. The consequences of using single, multiple, and composite criteria for performance measurement are examined. Each of these three types of criteria can lead to undesirable consequences for overall organizational performance. Further research is required if we are to understand the motivational potentials of various performance measurement systems.

Reprinted from *Administrative Science Quarterly*, I (September, 1956), 240-47. Used by permission of V. F. Ridgway and *Administrative Science Quarterly*.

There is today a strong tendency to state numerically as many as possible of the variables with which management must deal. The mounting interest in and application of tools, such as operations research, linear programming, and statistical decision making, all of which require quantifiable variables, foster the idea that if progress toward goals can be measured, efforts and resources can be more rationally managed. This has led to the development of quantitative performance measurements for all levels within organizations, up to and including measurements of the performance of a division manager with profit responsibility in a decentralized company. Measurements at lower levels in the organization may be in terms of amount of work, quality of work, time required, and so on.

Quantitative measures of performance are tools, and are undoubtedly useful. But research indicates that indiscriminate use and undue confidence and reliance in them result from insufficient knowledge of the full effects and consequences. Judicious use of a tool requires awareness of possible side effects and reactions. Otherwise, indiscriminate use may result in side effects and reactions outweighing the benefits, as was the case when penicillin was first hailed as a wonder drug. The cure is sometimes worse than the disease.

It seems worthwhile to review the current scattered knowledge of the dysfunctional consequences resulting from the imposition of a system of performance measurements. For the purpose of analyzing the impact of performance measurements upon job performance, we can consider separately single, multiple, and composite criteria. Single criteria occur when only one quantity is measured and observed, such as total output or profit. Multiple criteria occur when several quantities are measured simultaneously, such as output, quality, cost, safety, waste, and so forth. Composite criteria occur when the separate quantities are weighted in some fashion and then added or averaged.

SINGLE CRITERIA

A single criterion of performance was in use in a public employment agency studied by Peter M. Blau.[1] The agency's responsibility was "to serve workers seeking employment and employers seeking workers." Employment interviewers were appraised by the number interviews they conducted. Thus the interviewer was motivated to complete as many interviews as he could, but not to spend adequate time in locating jobs for the clients. The organization's goal of placing clients in jobs was not given primary consideration because the measurement device applied to only one aspect of the activity.

Blau reports another case in a federal law enforcement agency which investigated business establishments. Here he found that work schedules were distorted by the imposition of a quota of eight cases per month for each investigator. Toward the end of the month an investigator who found himself short of the eight cases would pick easy, fast cases to finish that month and save the lengthier cases till the following month. Priority of the cases for investigation was based on length of the case rather than urgency, as standards of impartiality would require. This is one of many instances in which the existence of an "accounting period" adversely affects the overall goal accomplishment of the organization.

Chris Argyris also reports this tendency to use easy jobs as fillers toward the end of a period in order to meet a quota.[2] In this case, a factory supervisor reported that they "feed the machines all the easy orders" toward the end of the month, rather than finish them in the sequence in which they were received. Such a practice may lead to undue delay of the delivery of some customers' orders, perhaps the most profitable orders.

David Granick's study of Soviet management reveals how the attention and glory that accrue to a plant manager when he can set a new monthly production record in one month lead to the neglect of repairs and maintenance, so that in ensuing months there will be a distinct drop in production.[3] Similarly, the output of an entire plant may be allowed to fall off in order to create conditions under which one worker can make a production record, when the importance of such a record is considered greater than overall plant production.

Joseph S. Berliner's report on Soviet business administration points out sharply how the accounting period has an adverse effect upon management decisions.[4] The use of monthly production quotas causes "storming" at the end of the month to reach the quota. Repairs and maintenance are postponed until the following month, so that production lags in the early part of the month, and storming must again be resorted to in the following month. This has impact upon the rate of production for suppliers and customers who are forced into a fluctuating rate of operations with its attendant losses and wastes.

Standard costs as a criterion of performance is a frequent source of dissatisfac-

[1] Peter M. Blau, *The Dynamics of Bureaucracy* (Chicago: The University of Chicago Press, 1955).

[2] Chris Argyris, *The Impact of Budgets on People* (New York: The Controllership Foundation, 1952).

[3] David Granick, *Management of the Industrial Firm in the U.S.S.R.* (New York: Columbia University Press, 1954).

[4] Joseph S. Berliner, "A Problem in Soviet Business Management," *Administrative Science Quarterly*, 1 (1956), 86-101.

tion in manufacturing plants.[5] The "lumpiness" of indirect charges that are allocated to the plants or divisions (indirect charges being unequal from month to month), variations in quality and cost of raw materials, or other factors beyond the control of the operating manager, coupled with inaccuracies and errors in the apportionment of indirect charges, cause distrust of the standards. A typical reaction of operating executives in such cases seems to be to seek explanations and justifications. Consequently, considerable time and energy is expended in discussion and debate about the correctness of charges. Only "wooden money" savings accrue when charges are shifted to other accounts, and there is no increase in company profits. It should be pointed out, however, that having charges applied to the proper departments may have the advantage of more correctly directing attention to problem areas.

Granick discusses two measures of the success of the Soviet firm which have been considered and rejected as overall measures by Soviet industrial leaders and economists.[6] The first, cost reduction per unit of product, is considered inadequate because it does not provide a basis for evaluating new products. Further, variations in amount of production affect the cost reduction index because of the finer division of overhead costs, quality changes, and assortment. The second overall measure of a firm's performance, profitability, has been rejected as the basic criterion on the grounds that it is affected in the short run by factors outside the control of management, such as shortages of supplies. Profitability as a measure of success led to a reduction in experimental work and deemphasized the importance of production quantity,

quality, and assortment. Neither cost reduction nor profitability was acceptable alone; each was only a partial index. The Soviets had concluded by 1940 that no single measure of success of a firm is adequate in itself and that there is no substitute for genuine analysis of all the elements entering into a firm's work.

Difficulties with single criteria have been observed in operations research, where one of the principal sources of difficulty is considered to be the choice of proper criteria for performance measurement.[7] The difficulty of translating the several alternatives in their full effect upon the organization's goal forces the operations researcher to settle for a criterion more manageable than profit maximization, but less appropriate. The efficiency of a subgroup of the organization may be improved in terms of some plausible test, yet the organization's efficiency in terms of its major goal may be decreased.

In all the studies mentioned above, the inadequacy of a single measure of performance is evident. Whether this is a measure of an employee at the work level or a measure of management, attention is directed away from the overall goal. The existence of a measure of performance motivates individuals to effort, but the effort may be wasted, as in seeking "wooden money" savings or may be detrimental to the organization's goal, as in rushing through interviews, delaying repairs, and rejecting profitable opportunities.

MULTIPLE MEASUREMENTS

Recognition of the inadequacies of a single measure of success or performance

[5]H. A. Simon, H. Guetzkow, G. Kosmetsky, G. Tyndall, *Centralization vs. Decentralization in Organizing the Controller's Department* (New York: The Controllership Foundation, 1954).
[6]Granick, *op. cit.*

[7]Charles Hitch and Roland McKean, "Suboptimization in Operations Problems," in *Operations Research for Management*, eds. J. F. McCloskey and Flora F. Trefethen (Baltimore: Johns Hopkins Press, 1954).

leads organizations to develop several criteria. It is felt then that all aspects of the job will receive adequate attention and emphasis, so that efforts of individuals will not be distorted.

A realization in the employment office studied by Blau that job referrals and placements were also important led eventually to their inclusion in measuring the performance of the interviewers.[8] Merely counting the number of referrals and placements had led to wholesale indiscriminate referrals, which did not accomplish the employment agency's screening function. Therefore, to stress the qualitative aspects of the interviewer's job, several ratios (of referrals to interviews, placements to interviews, and placements to referrals) were devised. Altogether there were eight quantities that were counted or calculated for each interviewer. This increase in quantity and complexity of performance measurements was felt necessary to give emphasis to all aspects of the interviewer's job.

Granick relates that no single criterion was universally adopted in appraising Soviet management.[9] Some managers were acclaimed for satisfying production quotas while violating labor laws. Others were removed from office for violating quality and assortment plans while fulfilling production quotas. Apparently there is a ranking of importance of these multiple criteria. In a typical interfirm competition, the judges were provided with a long list of indexes. These included production of finished goods in the planned assortment, an even flow of production as between different ten-day periods and as between months, planned mastery of new types of products, improvement in product quality and reduction in waste, economy of materials through improved design, and changing of technological processes, fulfillment of labor productivity tasks, and lowering of

unit cost, keeping within the established wage fund, and increase in the number of worker suggestions for improvements in work methods and conditions and their adoption into operation. But no indication of how these indexes should be weighted was given. The pre-eminence of such indexes as quantity, quality, assortment of production, and remaining within the firm's allotment of materials and fuels, brought some order into the otherwise chaotic picture. The presence of "campaigns" and "priorities" stressing one or more factors also has aided Soviet management in deciding which elements of its work are at the moment most important.

Without a single overall composite measure of success, however, there is no way of determining whether the temporarily increased effort on the "campaign" criteria of the month represents new effort or merely effort shifted from other criteria. And the intangibility of some of these indexes makes it impossible to judge whether there has been decreased effort on other aspects. Hence even in a campaign period the relative emphases may become so unbalanced as to mitigate or defeat the purpose of the campaign.

The Soviet manager is working then under several measurements, and the relative influence or emphasis attached to any one measurement varies from firm to firm and from month to month. Profits and production are used, among other measurements, and these two may lead to contradictory managerial decisions. Granick hypothesizes that some managers have refused complicated orders that were difficult to produce because it would mean failure to produce the planned quantities. Acceptance of these orders would have been very profitable, but of the two criteria, production quantity took precedence.

Numerous American writers in the field of management have stressed the importance of multiple criteria in eval-

[8]Blau, *op. cit.*
[9]Granick, *op. cit.*

uating performance of management. Peter Drucker, for example, lists market standing, innovation, productivity, physical and financial resources, profitability, manager performance and development, worker performance and attitude, and public responsibility.[10] This list includes many of the same items as the list used by Soviet management.

The consensus at a round-table discussion of business and professional men[11] was that although return on investment is important, additional criteria are essential for an adequate appraisal of operating departments. These other criteria are fairly well summed up in Drucker's list above.

Thus we see that the need for multiple criteria is recognized and that they are employed at different levels of the organization—lower levels as in the employment agency, higher levels as considered by Granick and Drucker. At all levels these multiple measurements or criteria are intended to focus attention on the many facets of a particular job.

The use of multiple criteria assumes that the individual will commit his or the organization's efforts, attention, and resources in greater measure to those activities which promise to contribute the greatest improvement to overall performance. There must then exist a theoretical condition under which an additional unit of effort or resources would yield equally desirable results in overall performance, whether applied to production, quality, research, safety, public relations, or any of the other suggested areas. This would be the condition of "balanced stress on objectives" to which Drucker refers.

Without a single overall composite measure of performance, the individual is forced to rely upon his judgment as to whether increased effort on one criterion improves overall performance, or whether there may be a reduction in performance on some other criterion which will outweigh the increase in the first. This is quite possible, for in any immediate situation many of these objectives may be contradictory to each other.

COMPOSITES

To adequately balance the stress on the contradictory objectives or criteria by which performance of a particular individual or organization is appraised, there must be an implied or explicit weighting of these criteria. When such a weighting system is available, it is an easy task to combine the measures of the various subgoals into a composite score for overall performance.

Such a composite is used by the American Institute of Management in evaluating and ranking the managements of corporations, hospitals, and other organizations.[12] These ratings are accomplished by attaching a numerical grade to each of several criteria, such as economic function, corporate structure, production efficiency, and the like. Each criterion has an optimum rating, and the score on each for any particular organization is added to obtain a total score. Although there may be disagreement on the validity of the weighting system employed, the rating given on any particular category, the categories themselves, or the methods of estimating scores in the A.I.M. management audit, this system is an example of the type of overall performance measurement which might be developed. Were

[10] Peter M. Drucker, *The Practice of Management* (New York: Harper & Row, Publishers, 1954).
[11] William H. Newman and James P. Logan, *Management of Expanding Enterprises* (New York: Columbia University Press, 1955).
[12] *Manual of Excellent Managements* (New York, 1955).

such a system of ratings employed by an organization and found acceptable by management, it presumably would serve as a guide to obtaining a balanced stress on objectives.

A composite measure of performance was employed in Air Force wings as reported by K. C. Wagner.[13] A complex rating scheme covering a wide range of activities was used. When the organizations were put under pressure to raise their composite score without proportionate increases in the organization's means of achieving them, there were observable unanticipated consequences in the squadrons. Under a system of multiple criteria, pressure to increase performance on one criterion might be relieved by a slackening of effort toward other criteria. But with a composite criterion this does not seem as likely to occur. In Wagner's report individuals were subjected to tension, role and value conflicts, and reduced morale; air crews suffered from intercrew antagonism, apathy, and reduced morale; organization and power structures underwent changes; communications distortions and blockages occurred; integration decreased; culture patterns changed, and norms were violated. Some of these consequences may be desirable, some undesirable. The net result, however, might easily be less effective overall performance.

These consequences were observable in a situation where goals were increased without a corresponding increase in means, which seems to be a common situation. Berliner refers to the "ratchet principle" wherein an increase in performance becomes the new standard, and the standard is thus continually raised.

Recognition of the operation of the "ratchet principle" by workers was documented by F. J. Roethlisberger and William J. Dickson.[14] There was a tacit agreement among the workers not to exceed the quota, for fear that the job would then be rerated. Deliberate restriction of output is not an uncommon occurrence.

Although the experiences reported with the use of composite measures of performance are rather skimpy, there is still a clear indication that their use may have adverse consequences for the overall performance of the organization.

CONCLUSION

Quantitative performance measurements—whether single, multiple, or composite—are seen to have undesirable consequences for overall organizational performance. The complexity of large organizations requires better knowledge of organizational behavior for managers to make best use of the personnel available to them. Even where performance measures are instituted purely for purposes of information, they are probably interpreted as definitions of the important aspects of that job or activity and, hence, have important implications for the motivation of behavior. The motivational and behavioral consequences of performance measurements are inadequately understood. Further research in this area is necessary for a better understanding of how behavior may be oriented toward optimum accomplishment of the organization's goals.

[13] Kenneth C. Wagner, "Latent Functions of an Executive Control: A Sociological Analysis of a Social System under Stress," *Research Previews*, vol. 2 (Chapel Hill, N.C.: Institute for Research in Social Science, March, 1954), mimeo.

[14] F. J. Roethlisberger and William J. Dickson, *Management and the Worker* (Cambridge, Mass.: Harvard University Press, 1939).

Behavioral Assumptions of Management Accounting

Edwin H. Caplan

*The University of
New Mexico*

Assumptions concerning organization goals, behavior of participants, behavior of management, and the role of management
accounting are postulated both from the standpoint of the
"traditional" management accounting view of the firm and
that of modern organization theory. Well-conceived empirical
research to measure the effectiveness of these alternative
systems is urged. If the modern organization theory model
proves to be a more realistic view of human behavior, then
management accounting systems should be designed with
greater awareness of and sensitivity to the complex social and
psychological motivations and limitations of organization
participants.

Reprinted from *The Accounting Review*, XLI (July, 1966), 496-509.
Used by permission of Edwin H. Caplan and *The Accounting Review*.

Accounting has been closely associated with the development of the modern business organization. Thus, we might expect accountants to show a strong interest in recent contributions to organization theory which increase our understanding of the business firm and how it functions. An examination of accounting literature, however, suggests that (despite the steadily increasing flow of accounting articles and texts incorporating the words *management* and *decisions* in their titles) accountants have been relatively unconcerned with current research in organization theory. Although the past few years have witnessed the beginnings of an effort to bridge this gap, much still remains to be done.[1] This paper attempts to demon-

strate that an understanding of behavioral theory is relevant to the development of management accounting theory and practice.

The discussion to be presented here may be summarized as follows:

1. The management accounting function is essentially a behavioral function, and the nature and scope of management accounting systems is materially influenced by the view of human behavior which is held by the

[1] See, for example, Robert T. Golembiewski,

"Accountancy as a Function of Organization Theory," *The Accounting Review* (April, 1964), pp. 333-41; and John J. Willingham, "The Accounting Entity: A Conceptual Model," *The Accounting Review* (July, 1964), pp. 543-52.

accountants who design and operate these systems.

2. It is possible to identify a "traditional" management accounting model of the firm and to associate with this model certain fundamental assumptions about human behavior. These assumptions are presented in Table 1.

3. It is also possible to postulate behavioral assumptions based on modern organization theory and to relate them to the objectives of management accounting. A tentative set of such assumptions appears in Table 2.

4. Research directed at testing the nature and validity of accounting assumptions with respect to human behavior in business organizations can be useful in evaluating and, perhaps, improving the effectiveness of management accounting systems.

MANAGEMENT ACCOUNTING AS A BEHAVIORAL PROCESS

The management of a business enterprise is faced with an environment—both internal and external to the firm—that is in a perpetual state of change. Not only is this environment constantly changing, but it is changing in many dimensions. These include physical changes (climate, availability of raw materials, etc.), tech-

---

TABLE 1.   Behavioral Assumptions of "Traditional" Management Accounting Model of the Firm

Assumptions with respect to organization goals
  1. The principal objective of business activity is profit maximization (economic theory).
  2. This principal objective can be segmented into subgoals to be distributed throughout the organization (principles of management).
  3. Goals are additive—what is good for the parts of the business is also good for the whole (principles of management).

Assumptions with respect to the behavior of participants
  1. Organization participants are motivated primarily by economic forces (economic theory).
  2. Work is essentially an unpleasant task which people will avoid whenever possible (economic theory).
  3. Human beings are ordinarily inefficient and wasteful (scientific management).

Assumptions with respect to the behavior of management
  1. The role of the business manager is to maximize the profits of the firm (economic theory).
  2. In order to perform this role, management must control the tendencies of employees ro be lazy, wastful, and inefficient (scientific management).
  3. The essence of management control is authority. The ultimate authority of management stems from its ability to affect the economic reward structure (scientific management).
  4. There must be a balance between the authority a person has and his responsibility for performance (principles of management).

Assumptions with respect to the role of management accounting
  1. The primary function of management accounting is to aid management in the process of profit maximization (scientific management).
  2. The accounting system is a "goal-allocation" device which permits management to select its operating objectives and to divide and distribute them throughout the firm, i.e., assign responsibilities for performance. This is commonly referred to as "planning" (principles of management).
  3. The accounting system is a control device which permits management to identify and correct undesirable performance (scientific management).
  4. There is sufficient certainty, rationality, and knowledge within the system to permit an accurate comparison of responsibility for performance and the ultimate benefits and costs of that performance (principles of management).
  5. The accounting system is "neutral" in its evaluations—personal bias is eliminated by the objectivity of the system (principles of management).

TABLE 2.   Some Behavioral Assumptions from Modern Organization Theory

Assumptions with respect to organization goals
1. Organizations are coalitions of individual participants. Strictly speaking, the organization itself, which is "mindless," cannot have goals—only the individuals can have goals.
2. Those objectives which are usually viewed as organizational goals are, in fact, the objectives of the dominant members of the coalition, subject to whatever constraints are imposed by the other participants and by the external environment of the organization.
3. Organization objectives tend to change in response to: (1) changes in the goals of the dominant participants, (2) changes in the relationships within the coalition, and (3) changes in the external environment of the organization.
4. In the modern complex business enterprise, there is no single universal organization goal such as profit maximization. To the extent that any truly overall objective might be identified, that objective is probably organization survival.
5. Facing a highly complex and uncertain world and equipped with only limited rationality, members of an organization tend to focus on "local" (i.e., individual and departmental) goals. These local goals are often in conflict with each other. In addition, there appears to be no valid basis for the assumption that they are homogeneous and thus additive—what is good for the parts of the organization is not necessarily good for the whole.

Assumptions with respect to the behavior of participants
1. Human behavior within an organization is essentially an adaptive, problem-solving, decision-making process.
2. Organization participants are motivated by a wide variety of psychological, social, and economic needs and drives. The relative strength of these diverse needs differs among individuals and within the same individual over time.
3. The decision of an individual to join an organization and the separate decision to contribute his productive efforts once a member are based on the individual's perception of the extent to which such action will further the achievement of his personal goals.
4. The efficiency and effectiveness of human behavior and decision making within organizations is constrained by: (1) the inability to concentrate on more than a few things at a time, (2) limited awareness of the environment, (3) limited knowledge of alternative courses of action and the consequences of such alternatives, (4) limited reasoning ability, and (5) incomplete and inconsistent preference systems. As a result of these limits on human rationality, individual and organizational behavior is usually directed at attempts to find satisfactory—rather than optimal—solutions.

Assumptions with respect to the behavior of management
1. The primary role of the business manager is to maintain a favorable balance between (1) the contributions required from the participants and (2) the inducement (i.e., perceived need satisfactions) which must be offered to secure these contributions.
2. The management role is essentially a decision-making process subject to the limitations on human rationality and cognitive ability. The manager must make decisions himself and must effectively influence the decision premises of others so that their decisions will be favorable for the organization.
3. The essence of management control is the willingness of other participants to *accept* the authority of management. This willingness appears to be a nonstable function of the inducement-contribution balance.
4. Responsibility is assigned from "above" and authority is accepted from "below." It is, therefore, meaningless to speak of the balance between responsibility and authority as if both of these were "given" to the manager.

Assumptions with respect to the role of accounting
1. The management accounting process is an information system whose major purposes are: (1) to provide various levels of management with data which will facilitate the decision-making functions of planning and control and (2) to serve as a communications medium within the organization.
2. The effective use of budgets and other accounting control techniques requires an understanding of the interaction between these techniques and the motivations and aspiration levels of the individuals to be controlled.
3. The objectivity of the management accounting process is largely a myth. Accountants have wide areas of discretion in the selection, processing, and reporting of data.
4. In performing their function within an organization, accountants can be expected to be influenced by their own personal and departmental goals in the same way as other participants are influenced.

nological changes (new products and processes, etc.), social changes (attitudes of employees, customers, competitors, etc.), and financial changes (asset composition, availability of funds, etc.).

An important characteristic of "good" management is the ability to evaluate past changes, to react to current changes, and to predict future changes. This is consistent with the view that management is essentially a decision-making process and the view that accounting is an information system which acts as an integral part of this decision-making process. It is inconceivable, however, that any workable information system could provide data relative to all, or even a substantial portion, of the changes occurring inside and outside of the organization. There are several reasons for this. Many changes—particularly those that occur in the external environment—are simply not available to the information system of the firm. These changes represent "external unknowns" in a world of uncertainty and limited knowledge. Further, a substantial number of changes that occur within the firm itself may not be perceived by the information system. Thus, there exist "internal" as well as "external" unknowns.

Even if accountants were aware of all the changes which are taking place—or if they could be made aware of them—they still would not be able to reflect them all within their information system. There must be a selection process, explicit or implicit, which permits the gathering and processing of only the most critical information and facilitates the screening out of all other data. In the first place, many items of information would cost more to gather and process than the value of the benefits they would provide. Also, an excessive flow of data would "clog" the system and prevent the timely and efficient passage and evaluation of more important information.[2] Therefore, only

a certain, very limited, set of data (i.e., observations about changes) can be selected for admission into the system. The essential point to be noted here is that decisions regarding what information is the most critical, how it should be processed, and who should receive it are almost always made by accountants. In addition, they are often directly involved, as participants, in the management decision-making process itself.

In carrying out these activities, accountants utilize a frame of reference that is, in effect, their view of the nature of the firm and its participants. The operation of their system requires them to be constantly abstracting a selected flow of information from the complex real world and using these selected data as the variables in their "model" of the firm. It seems clear that accountants exercise choice in the design of their systems and the selection of data for admission into them. It also seems clear that the entire management accounting process can be viewed from the standpoint of attempting to influence the behavior of others. It follows, therefore, that they must perform these functions with certain expectations with respect to the reactions of others to what they do. In other words, their model of the firm must involve some set of explicit or implicit assumptions about human behavior in organizations.

THE "TRADITIONAL" VIEW OF BEHAVIOR

Once it has been demonstrated that the management accounting function does, by necessity, involve assumptions about

---

[2]This is the "capacity problem" discussed by

Anton. See Hector R. Anton, *Some Aspects of Measurement and Accounting*, Working Paper No. 84 (Berkeley, Calif.: Center for Research in Management Science, University of California, 1963).

behavior, the next task is to identify these assumptions. Our investigation is complicated by the fact that nowhere in the literature of accounting is there a formal statement of the behavioral assumptions of the management accounting model of the firm. It is necessary, therefore, to attempt to construct such a statement. We begin with the premise that present-day management accounting theory and practice is the product of three related conceptual forces, namely, industrial engineering technology, classical organization theory, and the economic "theory of the firm." An examination of the literature of management accounting suggests that accountants may have avoided the necessity of developing a behavioral model of their own by borrowing a set of assumptions from these other areas. If this thesis is valid, an appropriate point to begin the search for such assumptions is by an examination of the assumptions of these related models. Since much of the engineering view appears to be incorporated in the classical organization theory model,[3] it can probably be eliminated from this analysis without significant loss. Further, it appears that classical organization theory and economics do not represent two completely different views of human behavior, but rather that they share essentially a single view.

The following paragraphs will attempt to demonstrate that—with the exception of the modern organization theory concepts of recent years—there has been a single view of human behavior in business organizations from the period of the industrial revolution to the present and that management accounting has adopted this view without significant modification or serious question as to its validity.

THE ECONOMIC THEORY OF THE FIRM

It has been suggested that, from the beginnings of recorded history, the traditional determinants of human behavior in organizations have been either custom or physical force.[4] As long as this was the case, there was no real need for an organization theory or economic theory to explain how and why human beings worked together cooperatively to accomplish common goals. However, the changing structure of society, which accompanied—and to an extent caused—the industrial revolution, destroyed much of the force of these traditional determinants of behavior. The new entrepreneurial class of the eighteenth century sought not only a social philosophy to rationalize its actions, it also sought practical solutions to the immediate problems of motivating, coordinating, and controlling the members of its organizations. The second of these needs resulted in the development of the classical organization theories which will be discussed in the following section. The first need, i.e., the quest for a rationalization, ultimately led to the incorporation of the economic theory of the firm into the logic of the industrial society.

The economic theory of the firm can be summarized as follows. The entrepreneur is faced with a series of behavior alternatives. These alternatives are limited by the economic constraints of the market and the technological constraints of the production function. Within these constraints he will act in such a way as to maximize his economic profit. This behavior is facilitated by the personality characteristic of complete rationality and the information system characteristic of perfect knowledge. Finally, the individual so described is one who is entirely moti-

---

[3]One of the earliest, and perhaps the best, example of this consolidation can be found in the work of Taylor. See Frederick W. Taylor, *Scientific Management* (New York: Harper & Row, Publishers, 1911).

[4]Robert L. Heilbroner, *The Worldly Philosophers*, rev. ed. (New York: Simon and Schuster, Inc., 1961), pp. 7-8.

vated by economic forces. A more subtle elaboration of this last point is the view that leisure has value and that a person will not work except in response to sufficient economic incentives. Thus, the classical economist specifically assumed that man was essentially "lazy" and preferred to minimize his work effort.[5]

Most modern economists would agree that the classical theory of the firm is based on several rather severe abstractions from the real world of business enterprise.[6] Nevertheless, despite these criticisms there can be little doubt that it has had a substantial influence on the development of management philosophy and practice. The explanation of human behavior offered by economists—i.e., economic motivation and profit maximization—was incorporated into the patterns of thought of the merging industrial community where it not only became established in its own right but also provided the philosophical and psychological foundations of the scientific management movement.

CLASSICAL ORGANIZATION THEORY

At the turn of the century, Fredrick W. Taylor began a major investigation into the functioning of business organizations, which became known as the scientific management movement. Taylor's approach combined the basic behavioral assumptions of the economic theory of the firm with the viewpoint of the engineer seeking the most effective utilization of the physical resources at his disposal. He was concerned with men

primarily as "adjuncts to machines" and was interested in maximizing the productivity of the worker through increased efficiency and reduced costs. Implicit in this approach was the belief that if men who might otherwise be wasteful and inefficent could be instructed in methods of achieving increased productivity and, at the same time, provided with adequate economic incentives and proper working conditions, they could be motivated to adopt the improvements, and the organization would benefit accordingly.[7]

March and Simon have noted that the ideas of the scientific management movement are based predominantly on a model of human behavior which assumes that "organization members, and particularly employees, are primarily *passive instruments,* capable of performing work and accepting directions, but not initiating action or exerting influence in any significant way."[8]

The scientific management movement flourished and rapidly became an important part of the business enterprise scene: in fact, for many years it virtually dominated this scene. Furthermore, even a brief glance at current management literature and practices should satisfy the reader that most of Taylor's views are still widely accepted today. Newer theories of management may have supplemented, but they have never entirely replaced, the scientific management approach.

About 1920 a second major pattern of organization theory, usually referred to as "principles of management" or "administrative management theory," began to develop. This body of doctrine adopted what was essentially a departmentalized approach to the problem of management. Its primary objective was the efficient assignment of organization activities to individual jobs and the grouping of these

---

[5] This assumption is the basis for the "backward-bending" labor supply curve found in the literature of economics.
[6] See, for example, Andreas G. Papandreou, "Some Basic Problems in the Theory of the Firm," in *A Survey of Contemporary Economics,* ed. Bernard F. Haley (Homewood, Ill.: Richard D. Irwin, Inc., 1952), Vol. II, 183-219.

[7] James G. March and Herbert A. Simon, *Organizations* (New York: John Wiley & Sons, Inc., 1958), pp. 12ff.
[8] *Ibid.,* p. 6.

jobs by departments in such a way as to minimize the total cost of carrying on the activities of the firm. Writers of this school concerned themselves largely with the development of "principles of management" dealing with such subjects as lines of authority and responsibility, specialization, span of control, and unity of command.[9] This administrative management theory appears to have had a substantial and continuing influence on management theory and practice.

The work of Taylor and his scientific management successors led them into detailed studies of factory costs and provided an important stimulus for the development of modern cost and management accounting. Administrative management theory further contributed to this development through its emphasis on control and departmental responsibility and accountability. Finally, all of this occurred within the overall setting provided by the economic theory of the firm. In summary, it seems clear that with respect to both its philosophy and techniques, much of contemporary management accounting is a product of, and is geared to, these classical theories. This is what is referred to here as the "traditional management accounting model of the firm."

A TENTATIVE STATEMENT OF BEHAVIORAL ASSUMPTIONS UNDERLYING PRESENT-DAY MANAGEMENT ACCOUNTING

It should now be possible to draw together the several strands of the preceding discussion and attempt to postulate some of the fundamental behavioral assumptions that appear to underlie the traditional management accounting model. These assumptions were presented in Table 1 above. The parenthetical nota-

tions note the major conceptual sources of the assumptions. In some cases there appears to be a considerable overlapping of sources; however, since this is not crucial to the present investigation, the notations have been limited to the primary or most significant area.

SOME BEHAVIORAL CONCEPTS OF MODERN ORGANIZATION THEORY

The preceding paragraphs were concerned with an effort to identify a set of behavioral assumptions which could be associated with current theory and practice in management accounting. We will now attempt to develop an alternative set of behavioral assumptions for management accounting—one that is based on concepts from modern organization theory.

Of the several different modern organization theory approaches, the "decision-making model" of the firm has been selected for use here. The basis for this choice is the close relationship which appears to exist between the decision-making model and the information-system concept of management accounting discussed earlier. The decision-making approach to organization theory effectively began with the writings of Chester I. Barnard, particularly in *The Functions of the Executive*, and was further developed by Simon and others.[10] The model is primarily concerned with the organizational processes of communi-

[9] *Ibid.*, pp. 22ff.

[10] Chester I. Barnard, *The Functions of the Executive* (Cambridge, Mass.: Harvard University Press, 1938); Herbert A. Simon, *Administrative Behavior* (New York: John Wiley & Sons, Inc., 1947); March and Simon, *Organizations;* and Richard M. Cyert and James G. March, *A Behavioral Theory of the Firm* (Englewood Cliffs, N.J.: Prentice-Hall, Inc., 1963). The preceding works represent the principal theoretical sources for the decision-making model discussed here.

cation and decision making. While drawing heavily on sociology and psychology, it is distinguished from these organization theory approaches by its emphasis on the decision as the basic element of organization.

Organizations are viewed as cooperative efforts, or coalitions, entered into by individuals in order to achieve personal objectives which cannot be realized without such cooperation. These individuals are motivated to join the organization and contribute to the accomplishment of its objectives because they believe that in this way they can satisfy their personal goals. It is important to note that these personal goals include social and psychological, as well as economic, considerations. Thus, the survival and success of the organization depends on the maintenance of a favorable balance between the contributions required of each participant and the opportunities to satisfy personal goals which must be offered as inducements to secure effective participation.

It is common practice to speak of organization goals; however, to be completely precise, it is the participants who have goals. The organization itself is mindless and, therefore, can have no goals. In the sense that it is used here, the term "organization goals" is intended to mean the goals of the dominant members of the coalition, subject to those constraints which are imposed by other participants and by the external environment. This view implies an organizational goal structure which is in a constant state of change as the environment and the balances and relationships among the participants change. Under such circumstances, it seems meaningless to talk of a single universal goal, such as profit maximization. To the extent that any long-run overall objective might be identified, it appears that this objective would have to be stated in very broad and general terms, such as the goal of organization survival.

The decision-making process is usually described as a sequence of three steps: (1) the evoking of alternative courses of action, (2) a consideration of the consequences of the evoked alternatives, and (3) the assignment of values to the various consequences.[11]

It has been suggested that any behavioral theory of rational choice must consider certain limits on the decision maker.[12] These include his (1) limited knowledge with respect to all possible alternatives and consequences, (2) limited cognitive ability, (3) constantly changing value structure, and (4) tendency to "satisfice" rather than maximize. Rational behavior, therefore, consists of searching among limited alternatives for a reasonable solution under conditions in which the consequences of action are uncertain.

The behavioral concepts which flow from the decision-making model have a number of interesting implications. For example, authority is viewed as something which is accepted from "below" rather than imposed from "above."[13] In other words, there must be a *decision to accept* authority before such authority can become effective. Further, human activity is considered to be essentially a process of problem-solving and and adaptive behavior—a process in which goals, perception, and abilities are all interrelated and all continually changing.

To summarize the decision-making model, the basic element of organization study is the decision. The objective of managerial decision-making is to secure and coordinate effectively the contributions of other participants. This is accomplished by influencing, to the extent

---

[11] March and Simon, p. 82.
[12] Herbert A. Simon, *Administrative Behavior*, 2nd ed. (New York: The Macmillan Company, 1957), pp. xxv-xxvi.
[13] Douglas McGregor, *The Human Side of Enterprise* (New York: McGraw-Hill Book Company, 1960), pp. 158-60.

possible, their perception of alternatives and consequences of choice and their value structures, so that the resulting decisions are consistent with the current objectives of the dominant members of the organization.

While the theorists of the "decision-making" school have paid substantial attention to behavioral concepts, the literature does not appear to contain a detailed and complete statement of their underlying behavioral assumptions. Accordingly, it becomes necessary, as it was with the traditional accounting model, to abstract and formulate a set of assumptions. The modern organization theory assumptions presented in Table 2 represent an attempt by the present writer to identify and extend the behavioral assumptions of the decision-making model in terms of the management accounting function.

BASIC CONFLICTS BETWEEN THE BEHAVIORAL ASSUMPTIONS OF TRADITIONAL MANAGEMENT ACCOUNTING AND MODERN ORGANIZATION THEORY

An examination of the two sets of behavioral assumptions developed above suggests a number of interesting questions. Answers to these questions, however, can only be found through extended empirical analysis. Thus, whatever value attaches to the foregoing discussion appears to relate to its possible contribution in providing a theoretical framework for future empirical research. This research might be designed to explore such questions as the following:

1. What behavioral model provides the most realistic view of human behavior in business organizations? (Accountants should, perhaps, be willing to accept the research findings of

organization theorists regarding this question.)

2. Is it possible to draw any general conclusions about the view of behavior actually held by accountants (and managers) in practice?

3. What, if any, are the major differences in the behavioral assumptions of the views in Tables 1 and 2, above?

4. What, if any, are the consequences for the organization and its participants of the differences in the behavioral assumptions of the views in Tables 1 and 2?

5. Is it possible to design management accounting systems which are based on a more realistic view of behavior, and would such systems produce better results than present systems?

Lacking empirical evidence, any attempt to investigate the implications of the differences between the two views of behavior discussed in this paper must be considered highly speculative. We might, however, examine briefly a few of the major differences in order to illustrate the nature of the problem. Let us assume for the moment that the decision-making model represents a more realistic view of human behavior than the traditional management accounting model. Let us further assume that the traditional model is a reasonably accurate summary of actual management accounting views in practice. Under these circumstances, what are some of the consequences for business organizations of the use of accounting systems based on the traditional management accounting model of behavior? The system of classification used in Tables 1 and 2 will also be adopted here. Thus, this analysis will concentrate on four major areas: organization goals, behavior of participants, behavior of management, and the role of accounting.

ASSUMPTIONS WITH RESPECT TO ORGANIZATION GOALS

In comparing these two sets of assumptions, the most immediately apparent difference concerns the relative simplicity and brevity of the traditional accounting assumptions as contrasted to those of the organization theory model. This should not be particularly surprising, since such a difference seems to be consistent with the general philosophies of the two models. There can be little doubt that the view of human behavior associated with the scientific management movement and classical economics is much less complicated than the behavioral outlooks of modern organization theory. In fact, the principal conflict between modern and classical organization theories appears to rest precisely on this issue. Since traditional management accounting is closely related to the classical models, it seems reasonable to expect that it will also tend toward a relatively simple and uncomplicated view of behavior. For example, with respect to organization goals, the behavioral assumptions of the accounting model focus on a single universal objective of business activity. The organization theory assumptions, on the other hand, suggest a much broader and rather imprecise structure of goals.

The traditional management accounting view of organization goals, which appears to be directly related to the theory of the firm of classical economics, may be summarized as follows: The principal objective of business activity is the maximization of the economic profits of the enterprise; the total responsibility for the accomplishment of that objective can be divided into smaller portions and distributed to subunits throughout the organization; the maximization by each subunit of its particular portion of the profit responsibility will result in maximization of the total profits of the enterprise.

The entire structure of traditional management accounting appears to be built around this concept of profit maximization and the related (but quite different) idea of cost minimization. Management accountants have, for the most part, limited the scope of their systems to the selection, processing, and reporting of data concerning certain economic events, the effects of which can be reduced—without too many complications—to monetary terms. This approach is justifiable only if the particular class of events under consideration can be viewed as *the* critical variables affecting the organization. Thus, accountants have been able to rationalize the importance of the data flowing through their systems by relating these data and their use directly to the assumed goal of profit maximization. However, the classical economic view of profits as the universal motivating force of business enterprises has come under substantial attack in recent years. This attack has been based on two general issues. First, questions have been raised concerning the adequacy of economic profits as the sole significant explanation for what takes place within an organization. Second, it has been suggested that limitations on the decision-making process result in behavior which is best described as "satisficing" rather than maximizing.

It should be particularly emphasized that the recognition of a more complex goal structure does not mean that economic profits can be ignored. Obviously, business firms cannot survive for any extended period of time without some minimum level of profits. Nevertheless, the attempt to summarize the entire goal structure of a complex business entity through the use of one index may result in an overly simplified and unrealistic view of the organization. In short, profits may represent a necessary but not a sufficient definition of the goal structure of business organizations.

The view of organization goals, suggested by the behavioral assumptions of the decision-making model, has two major aspects. First, those objectives which are commonly referred to as goals of the organization are, in fact, the goals of the dominant group of participants. Secondly, it is suggested that these goals are the result of the interaction of a set of constantly changing forces. Thus, the goal structure of an organization is not only rather imperfectly defined at any given point in time but it is also in a continual process of change throughout time. In order to identify any truly universal goal, it may be necessary, as suggested earlier, to generalize to the very broad—and perhaps meaningless—level of an objective such as organization survival.

In view of the complex nature of organization goals, it is possible that the profit maximization assumption unduly restricts the role of management accounting to providing a limited and inadequate range of data for decision-making. It is as if the accountant were viewing the firm through a narrow aperture which permits him to observe only a thin "slice" of the total organization activity. In emphasizing this narrow view, traditional management accounting appears to ignore many of the complexities and interrelationships that make up the very substance of an organization. What is the practical implication of these observations? How would management accounting change if accountants did not concentrate exclusively on profit maximization? It is likely that this, in itself, would not involve immediate operational changes but rather a change in underlying philosophy. As this philosophy is modified, it should become apparent that a number of specific changes in procedures and systems are in order. Examples of such specific changes might be found in the depart-

mental budgeting and accounting techniques discussed below.

The traditional accounting assumption with respect to the divisibility and additivity of the responsibility for the accomplishment of organization goals seems to warrant some additional comment. Research in organization theory has indicated that individual members of an organization tend to identify with their immediate group rather than with the organization itself. This tendency appears to encourage the development of strong subunit loyalties and a concentration on the goals of the subunit even when these goals are in conflict with the interests of the organization. The usual departmental budgeting and accounting techniques, by which management accountants endeavor to measure the success of the various subunits within an organization in achieving certain goals, are based on the assumption that profit maximization or cost minimization at the departmental level will lead to a similar result for the firm as a whole. Thus, accounting reports tend to highlight supposed departmental efficiencies and inefficiencies. Reports of this type seem to encourage departmental activities aimed at "making a good showing" regardless of the effect on the entire organization. It appears to be common for departments within an organization to be in a state of competition with each other for funds, recognition, authority, and so forth. Under such circumstances it is not very likely that the cooperative efforts necessary to the efficient functioning of the organization as a whole will be furthered by an accounting system which emphasizes and, perhaps, even fosters interdepartmental conflicts.

The tendency for intraorganizational conflict appears to be further compounded by some of the common management accounting techniques for the allocation and control of costs. For example, in some organizations with relatively rigid budgeting procedures, it appears to be a normal practice for departments to attempt deliberately to use up their entire budget for a given period in order to avoid a reduction in the budgets of succeeding periods. Another example is the emphasis often placed on the desirability of keeping costs below some predetermined amount. In such cases, it is likely that, even though a departmental expenditure would be extremely beneficial to an organization, it will not be undertaken if such action would cause the costs of that department to exceed the predetermined limit.

ASSUMPTIONS WITH RESPECT TO THE BEHAVIOR OF PARTICIPANTS

The view of the individual inherent in the behavioral assumptions associated with traditional management accounting is one which has been completely rejected by most of the behavioral scientists interested in modern organization theory. To what extent this traditional view is actually held by accountants in practice is a question which, as stated earlier, can only be answered by empirical investigation. Our own limited experience suggests that it is held by a sufficient number of management accountants to be considered at least a significant view within the profession.

It is possible that the failure of management accountants to consider the more complex motivating forces which organization theory recognizes in the individual contributes to the use of accounting systems and procedures which produce "side effects" in the form of a variety of unanticipated and undesired responses from participants. For example, many management accounting techniques intended to control costs, such as budgeting and standard costing, may virtually

defeat themselves because they help to create feelings of confusion, frustration, suspicion, and hostility. These techniques may not motivate effectively because they fail to consider the broad spectrum of needs and drives of the participants.[14]

ASSUMPTIONS WITH RESPECT TO THE BEHAVIOR OF MANAGEMENT

Modern organization theory encompasses a view of the management process which differs substantially from the "classical" view associated here with management accounting. It is interesting, however, that both models appear to take essentially the same position with respect to the basic purpose of managerial activity. This purpose relates to securing effective participation from the other members of the organization. One way of emphasizing the nature of the conflict between the two models in this regard is to examine the manner in which each attempts to accomplish this basic purpose.

According to the traditional accounting model, management must control the performance of others—the principal instrument of control being authority. This model assumes that participants must be continually prodded to perform and that this prodding is accomplished through the use of authority which is applied from above. Also, it places heavy reliance on the use of economic rewards and penalties as devices to implement authority and motivate effective participation.

The decision-making model, on the other hand, assumes that management must *influence* the behavior of others. Furthermore, this approach suggests that,

[14] For a discussion of the behavioral implications of budgets, see Andrew C. Stedry, *Budget Control and Cost Behavior* (Englewood Cliffs, N.J.: Prentice-Hall, Inc., 1960).

unless individuals are willing to accept such influence, effective participation cannot be assured regardless of the extent of the formal (classical) authority available to management. Viewed in this sense, meaningful authority cannot be imposed on a participant; rather, it must be accepted by him. Finally, the decision-making model asassumes that the willingness of participants to accept authority and to make effective contributions to the organization depends not only on economic considerations but also, to a substantial extent, on social and psychological factors.

There seems to be a very close relationship between the behavioral assumptions of traditional management accounting and those associated with the classical management view of the firm. This is evidenced not only in their historical development but also by the manner in which management and management accounting currently interact in the modern business organization. It appears reasonable to expect that the effect of this interaction is to strengthen a jointly shared philosophy with respect to human behavior and the role of management. Managers who tend toward the classical view of behavior are likely to find support from traditional accounting systems which provide the kinds of data that emphasize this view. This accounting emphasis in turn probably serves to focus the attention of management on issues and solutions which are consistent with the philosophy of the classical view. Thus, a "feedback loop" is established which appears to be an important factor in perpetuating this relatively narrow view of human behavior among both management and accountants.

Since the assumptions of the traditional accounting model are so close to classical organization theory and, in fact, appear to be a reasonably good description of the classical theory itself, it would be interesting to consider two

questions. First, does the classical view of management provide an efficient solution to the problems of influencing behavior within an organization? Second, if the principal function of management accounting is to furnish relevant data for managerial decision making, should the accountant be concerned with providing the kinds of information that management actually wants or the kinds of information that management should want?

With respect to the first question, this paper has attempted to demonstrate that the classical view may not be an efficient approach in motivating organizationally desirable behavior. This premise appears to be supported by a substantial amount of theoretical and empirical research in modern organization theory. In terms of the present discussion, the important point is that traditional management accounting procedures and attitudes cannot be justified solely on the basis that they are consistent with other common management practices because serious questions have been raised regarding the desirability of many of these practices themselves.

In reference to the second question posed above, it can be argued that it is the task of management accounting to provide the information desired by management and to provide it in a manner which is consistent with existing management philosophy. In other words, it is not the responsibility of the accountant to attempt to change the viewpoint of management but only to function within the framework established by this viewpoint. The difficulty with this argument is that it treats accounting as something separate from management. This paper, on the other hand, assumes that management accounting is an integral part of management. The adoption of a more realistic model of behavior by accountants could place them in the position of leading rather than passively following the changes in management philosophy which are bound to occur as a result of the impact of modern organization theory. Thus, it might be hoped that the development of more sophisticated management accounting systems would encourage the evolution of a much more sophisticated management viewpoint in general.

ASSUMPTIONS WITH RESPECT TO THE ROLE OF ACCOUNTING

Modern economic organizations are, of course, highly complex entities. Business managers must continually operate under conditions of uncertainty and limited rationality. In addition, management accountants are subject to the same kinds of drives and needs as are other members of the organization. All of this suggests that management accounting systems could not, even under the best of circumstances, achieve the degree of certainty, neutrality, and objectivity that is often attributed to them. To the extent that management accounting fails to live up to its image in this regard, it can be anticipated that problems will arise for the organization. For one thing, organization members are often subject to evaluations based on information produced by the accounting system. These individuals are likely to be seriously confused and disturbed by a flow of seemingly precise and exact accounting data which they cannot really understand or explain, but which nevertheless imply that they are (or are not) performing their tasks properly. The better education of organization participants regarding the limitations of accounting data, while worthwhile in its own right, does not represent an adequate solution. A much more important step would be a clearer understanding of these limitations by accountants themselves.

Also, as members of the organizations which they serve, management accoun-

tants can be expected to seek such psychological and social objectives as security, prestige, and power. In some instances, they might also be expected—as suggested by the discussion of subunit goals—to view the success of the accounting department and the technical perfection of the accounting process as ends in themselves. Thus, it is possible that some management accountants tend to view their function as primarily one of criticizing the actions of others and of placing the responsibility for failures to achieve certain desired levels of performance. Where this tendency exists, it may be expected to have a significant effect on motivation and be a major source of difficulty within the organization.[15]

CONCLUSIONS

This paper has attempted to postulate a set of behavioral assumptions which could be associated with the theory and practice of "traditional" management accounting. The resulting set of fifteen assumptions represents an accounting adaptation of what might be termed the classical view of human behavior in business organizations. This view emphasizes such concepts as profit maximization, economic incentives, and the inherent laziness and inefficiency of organization participants. It is a model which is structured primarily in terms of the classical ideas of departmentalization, authority, responsibility, and control. The accounting process which has emerged in response to the needs presented by this classical model appears to treat human behavior and goals essentially as given. Further, the generally accepted measure of "good" accounting

[15]Chris Argyris, *The Impact of Budgets on People* (Ithaca, N.Y.: Prepared for The Controllership Foundation at Cornell University, 1952).

seems to be one of relevance and use-fulness in the maximization of the money profits of the enterprise.

In addition, we have examined a set of behavioral assumptions based on research in modern organization theory. It seems clear that a management accounting system structured around this second set of behavioral assumptions would differ in many respects from the accounting systems found in practice and described in the literature.

One should not infer that the traditional assumptions considered here are completely invalid. The very fact that they have endured for so long suggests that this is not the case. It should at least be recognized, however, that in many respects the extent of their validity may be subject to question. Also, it is not argued that all accountants limit themselves at all times to this traditional view. Rather, the two sets of behavioral assumptions discussed might be considered as extreme points on a scale of many possible views. The significance of the traditional point on such a scale appears to be twofold: (a) it is likely that the traditional model represents a view of behavior which is relatively common in practice, and (b) this view seems to underlie much of what is written and taught about accounting.

If the modern organization theory model does ultimately prove to be a more realistic view of human behavior in business organizations, there is little doubt that the scope of management accounting theory and practice will need to be expanded and broadened. In particular, accountants will have to develop an increased awareness and understanding of the complex social and psychological motivations and limitations of organization participants. What is urgently needed, and what we have had very little of in the past, is solid empirical research designed to measure the effectiveness with which management accounting systems do, in fact, perform their functions of motivating, explaining, and predicting human behavior.

The Effects of Accounting Alternatives on Management Decisions

Yuji Ijiri

Carnegie-Mellon University

Robert K. Jaedicke

Stanford University

Kenneth E. Knight

University of Texas

A theoretical analysis of the relationship between the accounting and decision-making processes of the firm is presented. Conditions under which variations in accounting methods produce different decisions and conditions that produce no effect are analyzed. Lack of feedback, functional fixation on the part of decision-makers, and an ill-structured environment can each contribute to misinterpretation of accounting data.

Reprinted from *Research in Accounting Measurement*, eds. Robert K. Jaedick, Yuji Ijiri, and Oswald Nielson (Chicago: American Accounting Association, 1966), pp. 186-99. Used by permission of Yuji Ijiri, Robert K. Jaedicke, Kenneth E. Knight, and The American Accounitng Association. The authors gratefully acknowledge the helpful suggestions of Professors R. Gene Brown, Oswald Nielsen, and Gerald O. Wentworth of the Stanford Graduate School of Business. The study was

supported in part by funds made available by
the Ford Foundation to the Graduate School of
Business, Stanford University. However, the
conclusions, opinions, and other statements in
this publication are those of the authors and
are not necessarily those of the Ford Foundation.

INTRODUCTION

A growing interest has arisen among
accountants in understanding accounting
in relation to the entire business decision
process. They have questioned such factors as the role of accounting in the
whole complex process of decision
making in business and what effects, if
any, different accounting methods have
on this decision process. Research has
been aimed at finding out if decisions
made in an organization can be influenced by changing its accounting system.

Until recently discussions of alternative accounting methods have been directed primarily toward how outputs
from accounting systems differ, depending upon the accounting methods
that are used. We know that in many
cases LIFO and FIFO can result in
different inventory values and, hence, will
produce different profit figures even
though the firm operates in an identical
business environment. But a more important question is whether these different
profit figures affect managers' decisions
and, if so, under what conditions? Unless
we can show that the different figures (or
more precisely different patterns of figures) lead to different decisions under a
given set of conditions, there is no point
in arguing the merits or demerits of
alternative accounting methods.

Some recent studies have been directed toward understanding how differences in the data affect the behavior of
the users. Bonini (1)* carried out a
simulation of business activity based on

*The numbers in parentheses refer to the se-
lected references at the end of this reading.

some assumptions about how business
managers behave and found that a firm
with the LIFO inventory method tends to
generate more profit under given conditions than a firm with the average cost
method of inventory valuation. The
reasoning behind this finding is that the
LIFO inventory method increases the
variability of profits from period to
period more than does the average cost
inventory method, and hence, it stimulates more attention and pressures by
managers toward better profit.

On the other hand, the experimental
study by Bruns (2) leads to contradictory
conclusions. He found that there is no
apparent relationship between inventory
valuation methods and managers' decisions on selling price, promotion, production volume, etc. An even more recent
experiment by Dyckman (7) also came to
the same conclusions.

It is, however, difficult to derive general statements from the results of these
three studies concerning the influence of
different accounting methods upon managers' decisions. We cannot conclude
from Bonini's study that the LIFO
method should be preferred to the average cost method of inventory valuation
because the former tends to generate
higher levels of profits, nor can we
conclude from Bruns's study or Dyckman's study that inventory valuation
methods have no effect on business decisions. Accounting variations may have
significant effects under some conditions,
and may have no effect under other
conditions. The basic problem in these
studies is an inability to generalize from a
single case.

Therefore, an even more important
question than whether different accounting methods have *any* effects upon decisions is: *Under what conditions do variations in accounting methods produce
different decisions,* and *why* are (or *are
not*) different decisions produced by
using different accounting methods?

In order to answer these questions, we need, in addition to empirical studies, a theoretical clarification of the mechanism by which an accounting process and a decision-making process are related. The purpose of this paper is to develop a theoretical analysis of the relationship between the accounting and decision-making processes of a firm. This analysis is then used to study the effect of alternative accounting methods on managers' decisions. Instead of analyzing one empirical situation and deriving conclusions based on that particular example, we have derived some general conditions under which alternative accounting methods do have an effect upon the decision-making process and other conditions under which different accounting methods do not have any effect. For each individual empirical situation we are then able to specify a set of variables which will allow us to predict whether or not alternative accounting methods have an effect upon management decisions. In the following section we concentrate on the role of information in the decision-making process. In Parts 3 and 4, respectively, the effects on decisions of (1) *changes* in accounting method and (2) *alternative* accounting methods are discussed.

THE ROLE OF INFORMATION IN THE DECISION PROCESS

THE DECISION PROCESS AS A FUNCTION

A decision process is characterized by three factors: (a) decision inputs, (b) decision outputs, and (c) a decision rule. Decision inputs are factors which are considered by the decision-maker in making his decision. Decision outputs are decisions made by the decision-maker. A decision rule is a rule by which a set of

decisions is associated with a set of decision inputs. For example, in an investment decision, let us assume that investments are to be based only upon the rate of return of the project (say, invest if the rate of return is greater than or equal to 15 per cent per year; otherwise, do not invest). Here the decision input is the project's rate of return, and the decision output is either "invest" or "do not invest." The decision rule is to associate all rates of return greater than or equal to 15 per cent per year with the decision output "invest" and all other rates of return with the decision output "do not invest."

Of course, an actual investment decision will be much more complicated involving many other decision inputs and outputs. However, suppose if we focus on only one input (e.g., rate of return) and one output (e.g., invest or do not invest), keeping other decision inputs constant, then it would be reasonable to assume that there is a relationship between the value of the input and the value of the output which is relatively stable for some period of time. This is what is meant by a decision rule.

If we let x represent a variable for the input and z a variable for the output, then the decision rule concerning the input x and the output z can be represented as a function h as follows:

$$z = h(x) \qquad (1)$$

In an actual decision process, the value of the output for a given value of the input may not be unique; that is, the function h may not be single-valued. For example, the decision-maker may decide to invest on a project A and decide not to invest on a project B, even though the two projects have an identical rate of return. In this case a single value of the decision input yields two different values of the decision output, i.e., "invest" and "do not invest"; that is, the decision function is not single-valued. However, we may assume that by making finer specifications on the environmental conditions (i.e., the values of the other decision inputs) under which the decision function is supposed to be applied, it can eventually be converted into a single-valued function. We shall, therefore, deal with only a single-valued function in the following analysis.

PRINCIPALS VERSUS SURROGATES AS DECISIONS INPUTS

In order to understand the role of accounting data in a decision process, it is crucial to distinguish between *principal* decision inputs and *surrogated* decision inputs. We will emphasize that accounting data are generally surrogated inputs rather than principal inputs.

By a principal input, or a principal, we mean a decision input upon which the decision-maker *wants* to base his decision ultimately. A surrogated input, or a surrogate, is a decision input upon which the decision-maker bases his decision *only insofar as the surrogate reflects a principal.*[1]

For example, a thermometer reading is a surrogate for a temperature reading. We want to base our decision upon the thermometer reading only insofar as it reflects the real temperature. Similarly, in a pricing decision the decision-maker may want to base his decision upon the cost of the product that is reported in an accounting statement only to the extent that the reported cost reflects what he considers to be the "real" cost of the item.

[1] *Webster's Seventh New Collegiate Dictionary* defines a surrogate as a substitute to be put in place of another. Also see Charnes and Cooper (3, p. 369) for a further elaboration on the relationship between the principal and its surrogates.

For a given principal, there may be a hierarchy of surrogates which reflect the principal. For instance, if the reported sales volume of the firm reflects the reported profit of the firm which, in turn, reflects the real profit of the firm, the decision-maker may base his decisions upon this indirect surrogate, the reported sales volume, as a surrogate of the real profit to the firm.

CHARACTERISTICS REQUIRED FOR A SURROGATE

Obviously, in order to effectively use a surrogate instead of a principal in a decision process, the surrogate must have certain characteristics. We now want to investigate these characteristics.

Identifiablity

The surrogate must reflect the principal input. Since the decision-maker wants to base his decision upon the principal input, it is necessary for him to be able to estimate the value of the principal input from the value of surrogated input. More precisely, the decision-maker must be able to use the surrogate to identify the key factors necessary for his decision. In the above example of the investment decision, the decision-maker can use any input as a surrogate for the rate of return if, and only if, he can identify whether the rate of return is greater than or equal to 15 per cent per year. Note that in this case it is not necessary that the decision-maker be able to identify the exact value of the rate of return. For decison purposes he only needs to know whether the rate of return is greater than or equal to 15 per ent per year. This is what we mean by the decision-maker being [able] to obtain *the key factors which affect the decision.* A surrogate which reflects the principal in this sense will be called a "satisfactory surrogate." Obviously, whether or not a surrogate is satisfactory depends not only upon the surrogate-principal relationship but also upon the decision function which defines the key factors of the principal input.[2]

The notion of *identifiability* (of the key factors for the decision) raises the question of the reliability of the surrogate-principal relationship. The surrogate-principal relationship can be represented by

$$y = f(x) \qquad (2)$$

where x is a variable representing the principal input, y a variable representing the surrogated input, and f a function representing the surrogate-principal relationship. This relationship is reliable if it is *stable* enough so that the decision-maker can *identify* the key factors of the principal input from the value of the surrogate. We can use again our earlier example of the investment decision. An unstable surrogate is one where, for example, a value of 15 per cent means that the real rate of return of the project is 19 per cent per year at one time and the same value of 15 per cent means that the real rate of return of the project is 12 per cent per year at another time. When this *unstable* condition arises, the decision-maker can no longer rely upon the value of the surrogate in making his investment decision. An example of this

situation is the use of the payback factor as a surrogate for the rate of return. That is, a payback factor of 3 gives a rate of return of 12 per cent (approximately) if the life of the project is four years. On the other hand, the same payback factor of 3 gives a rate of return of 19 per cent (approximately) if the life of the project is five years. In this case the decision-maker cannot *rely* on this surrogate only, because he cannot *identify* the key factor which affects his decision.[3]

Timing

In addition to the requirement of identifiability, a surrogate must be available to the decision-maker at the time of the decision; that is, the surrogate must meet the requirement of *timing*. The significance of this requirement is made clearer in the following discussion on the *need* for a surrogate in a decision process.

NEED FOR A SURROGATE IN A DECISION PROCESS

Why does a decision-maker need a surrogate? That is, why doesn't he always use the principal input in his decision process? The following cases summarize those instances in which the decision-maker needs a surrogated input.

Case 1. Difficulty in Obtaining the Principal. When it is too expensive (either timewise or costwise or both) for the decision-maker to use the principal input in making his decision or when it is practically impossible for him to obtain the principal input, a surrogated input will be preferred to the principal. For

---

[2]Since it is not the purpose of this paper to analyze the functional relationship between a surrogate and a principal, the above statements are not as precise as they otherwise should be. The readers who are interested in pursuing this topic in a more rigorous manner are referred to Ijiri (11), where the notions of a perfect, a satisfactory, and a reasonable measure are defined, based upon the functional relationship involved. Also refer to Ijiri (12), where the relationship between a management goal and an accounting indicator as a surrogate for the goal is analyzed. The analysis is called "goal analysis," which is an extension of break-even analysis.

[3]Refer to Ijiri and Jaedicke (13), where the reliability of an accounting system is discussed by using statistical concepts. Here, for our subsequent discussions, it is sufficient to define reliability as the possibility of identifying the *key factors* of the principal input *consistently* from the value of the surrogate.

example, a bank manager may be willing to base his lending decisions upon financial statements certified by a C.P.A. even if he has the right to perform an independent investigation and the necessary auditing talent to do so.[4]

Furthermore, when the value of a principal is not available at the time of the decision, it is necessary for the decision-maker to use a surrogate insofar as he does not want to delay the decision (time lag). For example, if the profit figure of a division cannot be made available until the end of the month, the division manager may want to base his decision upon a surrogate, such as the sales volume to date (which may be available on the daily basis). Another example is the use of a predetermined overhead rate as a surrogate for the "actual" overhead rate which is not available until the end of the accounting period.

Case 2. Difficulty in Using the Principal. A surrogate may be used to simplify a decision problem where the decision-maker may actually want to base his decision on a large number of inputs. This will occur when the number of inputs to be considered exceeds the capacity of the decision-maker. It is a well-known fact that a human being can use effectively only a limited number of inputs in making his decision.[5] If the decision environment is too complicated, the decision-maker is likely to simplify the problem by grouping or aggregating a number of factors or by simply neglecting some of them. For example, a president of a firm may be able to obtain detailed data on the activities of the firm without too much cost, but he may want to base his decision upon a summary statement prepared by an accountant. The use of a representative figure, such as a mean, median, mode, maximum, minimum, variance of a set of data, is an example of the use of a surrogate to reflect many different principal inputs.

SURROGATE-PRINCIPAL RELATIONSHIP: CAUSE AND EFFECT

In discussing the surrogate-principal relationship earlier, we avoided any mention of the cause-and-effect problem. In the case of accounting data as surrogates, it is usually the principal which determines the value of the surrogate. That is, the principal is usually the cause and the surrogate (the accounting report or reported amount) is the effect. Therefore, the usual functional relationship is

$$x \xrightarrow{f} y \qquad (3)$$

where x represents the principal input, y the surrogate input, f the functional relationship between x and y, and the arrow the fact that x is the cause of y.

However, this cause-and-effect relationship is occasionally reversed. The following two examples illustrate situations where this can occur.

Example 1. A divison manager wants to exercise more pressure upon his subordinates if the manager's supervisor feels that the performance of the manager's division is unsatisfactory. In other words, his supervisor's evaluation (x) of the division is the principal for the manager's decision as to the amount of pressure (z)

---

[4]Here again, the reliability of real world data that are used in decision making is often not as satisfactory as that defined above. Occasionally, one may use an unsatisfactory surrogate which sometimes leads to a wrong decision. We often tolerate such a case if the wrong decision does not lead to a fatal outcome and if the cost of obtaining the unsatisfactory surrogate is much cheaper than the cost of obtaining a completely satisfactory surrogate. For a discussion of the use of unsatisfactory surrogates, see Ijiri (11) and (12).

[5]See, for example, Simon (17, pp. 241-60) and Garner (8, pp. 98-187).

that he exerts on his subordinate, namely,

$$x \xrightarrow{h} z \qquad (4)$$

Suppose that the division manager knows, however, that the supervisor's evaluation (x) is based upon the reported divisional profit (y) i.e., $x = \phi(y)$. Then the division manager may want to base his decision (z) upon the reported profit as a surrogate of the supervisor's evaluation $(z = g(y))$. In this case, the surrogate (y) is the cause of the principal (x):

$$x \xleftarrow{\phi} y \xrightarrow{g,} z \qquad (5)$$

Supervisor's   Reported   Amount of
Evaluation   Profit   Pressure

whereas in an ordinary case we have

$$x \xrightarrow{f} y \xrightarrow{g} z \qquad (6)$$

Principal   Surrogate   Decision

Example 2. As another situation where the principal input is caused by a surrogate (rather than vice versa), consider the role of income taxes in decisions. The income tax is based on the reported profit which is a surrogate for the real profit. Yet the income tax may be a principal input for many decisions. If the decision-maker bases his decision (e.g., the amount of money to be borrowed from banks) upon the reported profit as a surrogate for the actual income tax, the situation may be represented as follows:

$$x \xleftarrow{\phi} y \xrightarrow{g} z \qquad (7)$$

Income   Reported   Amount of
Taxes   Profit   Loans

To summarize, we have identified two different surrogate functional relationships. One relationship is where the surrogate (y) is determined by the principal (x). That is,

$$x \xrightarrow{f} y$$

The other relationship is where the surrogate (y) causes the principal (x). That is,

$$y \xrightarrow{\phi} x$$

The value of the surrogate resulting from the former relationship represents the principal, which is a *past* state or event. In the latter case the value of the surrogate is used to *predict* the principal, which is a *future* state or event. Let us distinguish between the two types of surrogates (or more precisely the two types of uses of surrogates) by calling the former a "descriptive" surrogate and the latter a "predictive" surrogate. For example, the reported profit is a descriptive surrogate of the operations of the firm but is a predictive surrogate of its future profit.

However, whether a given surrogate is a descriptive surrogate or a predictive surrogate of a given principal may be more complicated than in the cases described above. Consider the situation in which a decision-maker wants to base his price decision on the real *future* cost. Since the real future cost is unknown at the time of his decision, he may use a measure of the real *current* cost. In this case, the real current cost would be a *predictive* surrogate and not a descriptive surrogate. On the other hand, the decision-maker may use the reported (accounting) cost as a *descriptive* surrogate of the real current cost. In this case, the reported cost is a descriptive surrogate of the real current cost, which is a *predictive* surrogate of the real future cost.

In an earlier section we stated the timing requirements for a surrogate: It must be available to the decision-maker at the time of his decision. When a decision-maker needs to base his decision upon factors in the future, the use of a predictive surrogate is obviously necessary and highly important. In fact, where it may be possible to eliminate a descriptive surrogate from the decision process by actually observing the principal, it is never possible to eliminate a predictive surrogate if the decision must be based on a factor that will occur in the future.

EFFECTS OF A CHANGE IN ACCOUNTING METHOD ON MANAGEMENT DECISIONS

ACCOUNTING AND DECISION PROCESSES

In Part 2 we analyzed the role of surrogates in the decision process. Accounting data as well as other types of business information are surrogates which the decision-maker uses to carry out the decision process. Of course, he will want to use surrogates only insofar as they reflect principal inputs (as discussed in the previous section).

To illustrate the interaction between an accounting process and a decision process, let us consider the following simplified example. Suppose that a decision-maker wants to quote a price (z) on each job so as to recover 300 per cent of the direct cost for the job (x). In the absence of a surrogate, his decision process is represented by

$$z = 3x \tag{8}$$

Suppose also that the firm's accounting process provides the full cost (y) for each job by adding to the direct cost a standard overhead which is 100 per cent of the direct cost (x). Then this accounting process is represented by

$$y = 2x \tag{9}$$

If the decision-maker wants to achieve the same result by basing his decision upon the surrogate (the full cost) instead of the principal (the direct cost), he must adjust his decision so that he quotes a price equal to 150 per cent of the full cost of the job, i.e.,

$$z = 1.5y \tag{10}$$

Therefore, the accounting process and the decision process collectively constitute the decision process that the manager would use in the absence of a surrogate. Namely, the decision process which was formerly

$$x \xrightarrow{3x} z \tag{11}$$

is now decomposed as

$$x \xrightarrow{2x} y \xrightarrow{1.5y} z \tag{12}$$

If the accounting process is changed and the full cost (y) is calculated as 150 per cent of the direct cost (x) instead of 200 per cent, the decision-maker must adjust his decision process from $z = 1.5y$ to $z = 2y$ in order to keep the overall process ($z = 3x$) unchanged.

Obviously, this is an extremely over-simplified example, but nonetheless it shows the important interaction between the accounting process and the decision process, i.e., *the decision-maker must, in general, adjust his decision process* (g) *when the accounting process* (f) *is changed if he wants to keep the overall process* (h) *unchanged.*

THE DECISION-MAKER'S ADJUSTMENT TO A CHANGE IN AN ACCOUNTING METHOD

Using the relationship between the accounting process and the decision process as described above, we can now discuss the central question to be investigated. Under what conditions can (or cannot) a decision-maker adjust his decision process (g) to a change in the accounting process (f)? We will discuss this question by considering two different factors that would indicate when the manager cannot adjust. One is the lack of feedback on the performance of the accounting process, and the other factor is the possibility of "functional fixation" on the accounting concepts and measurements that are used in the decision process.

Lack of Feedback

A key factor which will determine whether or not the decision-maker can adjust to a change in the accounting process is simply whether or not he receives appropriate feedback on the performance of the accounting process. That is, he must be able to determine whether the process is performing as he expects it to perform. A type of direct feedback is for the decision-maker to observe the value of the principal input and compare it with the value of the surrogate. A cash count or a physical inventory is a good example of direct feedback. In addition to direct feedback, a decision-maker often has a means of obtaining indirect feedback. Instead of checking the process by himself, he may have somebody who checks the process for him. The use of an auditor to check any significant change in the accounting process is one way which might be used to discover when the accounting method is performing differently from what it is supposed to perform. Stockholders who, in their decisions, use profit figures as reported in financial statements are protected by auditors who report any significant changes in the accounting method used in generating profit figures. The decision-maker may have a number of surrogates which will collectively indicate any irregular performance of the accounting process, or an unexpected outcome from a decision may cause him to investigate the accounting process in detail.

It seems almost inconceivable to have a situation in business where a decision-maker has absolutely *no* feedback what-

soever on the performance of the accounting process. Therefore, it is highl[y] unlikely to have a decision change whic[h] results solely from a change in an ac[-] counting process, where this is *caused only by the lack of feedback to the decision-maker.* This is especially true if we exclude a possible short-run effect due to the time lag between the change in the accounting process and the indication of the change to the decision-maker through feedback.

Therefore, if a modification in the accounting process results in any change in the decisions even though proper feedback exists for the decision-maker, it must be attributable to his inability to *use* the feedback in order to adjust to the alteration. No matter how good the feedback is in indicating the change, if the decision-maker cannot effectively use this feedback, he cannot hope to make the same decisions as before. There do appear to be instances in which decision-makers are unable to adjust. We believe the inability to adjust, when it exists, can be explained by a psychological factor called "functional fixation."

Functional Fixation

Psychologists have found that there appears to be "functional fixation" in most human behavior in which the person attaches a meaning to a title or object (e.g., manufacturing cost) and is unable to see alternative meanings or uses. People intuitively associate a value with an item through past experience and often do not recognize that the value of the item depends, in fact, upon the particular moment in time and may be significantly different from what it was in the past. Therefore, when a person is placed in a new situation, he views the object or term as used previously.[6] If the outputs from different accounting methods are called

---

[6] This phenomenon was discussed by Duncker (6).

by the same name, such as profit, cost, etc., people who do not understand accounting will tend to neglect the fact that alternative methods may have been used to prepare the outputs. In such cases, a change in the accounting process clearly influences the decisions.

When accounting data are used as predictive surrogates, the accounting process represented by the function f does not come directly into the principal-surrogate decision relationship, as shown below:

Principal   Surrogate   Decision

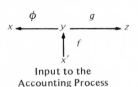

Input to the
Accounting Process

However, if the functional fixation occurs on the ϕ-function (i.e., if the ϕ-function remains the same even after the f-function has been changed), then a change in the f-function affects the principal (x); this, in turn, affects the decision (z). For instance, in Example 1 in this article if the supervisor is unable to adjust to the change in the accounting process which generates the reported profit and continues to evaluate the division in the same manner (specified by the ϕ-function) as before, even though the meaning of the reported profit has now been changed significantly, then the change in the accounting process of generating the reported profit will influence the amount of pressure exerted by the division manager. Such an influence occurs even if the division manager himself is perfectly capable of adjusting his decision function (g) to the change in the accounting process (f), since what he is concerned with is not the performance of his division per se (which is the input x' to the accounting process) but his supervisor's evaluation (x) of his divisional performance.

EFFECT OF ACCOUNTING ALTERNATIVES ON MANAGEMENT DECISIONS

In the preceding section we discussed the question of whether or not a *change* in accounting methods affects management decisions. Our conclusion is that an accounting change will not affect decisions if there is feedback on the performance of the accounting system and if there is no functional fixation; i.e., the manager is able to effectively *use* the feedback information. A second question of great importance is whether or not the *choice* of one method from a set of accounting alternatives has any influence on the management decisions.

As a first step we will analyze one set of environmental conditions where existing research shows us that the choice of accounting method definitely affects decisions. This set of conditions can be referred to as an "ill-structured environment."

DECISION MAKING IN AN ILL-STRUCTURED ENVIRONMENT

Authors who write about the management decision environment point out the ill-structured nature of the problems that confront business managers. That is, in today's business world, managers face problems for which there is great uncertainty about which alternatives are available and what constitutes an acceptable solution. Leavitt explains that in most managerial situations the decision-makers do not have a decision criterion that enables them to know exactly when they have made the correct decision.[7] Some of the reason for the ambiguity is that there is usually a long delay between a positive step (a decision) and the

[7]Leavitt (15, pp. 352-54).

recorded outcome. Then, too, there are many events that occur simultaneously in the organization which makes it almost impossible to determine the results of one particular decision. Therefore, as the manager views his world, he is always faced with the question—would another action have worked better? This difficulty means that the manager cannot unambiguously determine the decision function [in (1) $z = h(x)$] that he *should* use.

Recent research describing how people behave in ill-structured or uncertain situations has shed some light on how people probably use accounting information in the ill-structured situations.[8] The results show that when a person is confronted by such a situation, it is unlikely that he will remain in it very long. He will use his previous experience, available data, friends, etc. to define and structure his situation.[9] This problem is closely related to the one presented previously, where we discussed the limits of the human decision-making capacity. There we emphasized that the human mind can handle only a limited amount of information. We mentioned that humans simplify their problems by using surrogates which are aggregates of a number of principals or by neglecting some of the principals. These procedures represent two of the methods which the individual uses to define and structure his world.

Studies that have described a manager's actual decision-making behavior have found that he tries to avoid uncertainty and arrange the environment so that it has a predictable future. This is usually done in an organization by creating and following "standard operating procedures" in order to perform roles "safely."[10] The "standard operating pro-

cedures" are used to operationally define the decision-maker's environment and thus remove him from the previously ill-structured situation. We will now show how accounting information will sometimes be used to determine a decision-maker's "standard operating procedures," that is, *to define the goals and decision procedures of the manager.*

We find that the surrogates generated by accountants often become used as predictive surrogates to define the decision-maker's environment, his goals, and decision procedures. We mentioned (in the initial presentation of the concept of predictive surrogates earlier) the example in which the reported profit determined the goals of the division manager ($x = \phi (y)$), since the supervisor used the reported profit as a basis for the evaluation of the division manager, and not what he considers as the "real" profit.

Another way than an accounting system determines the goals for a manager is by defining an area for him to pay attention to. For example, let us assume the accountants suddenly report scrap cost for the first time. The manager now modifies his goals in that he creates a new goal that specifies his objectives in regard to the control of scrap cost. In this example, the manager's *g*-function changes to incorporate the new piece of accounting data. Furthermore, the accounting procedure, in addition to specifying goals for a manager, may also be used by him to help define his decision function. If the accountant chooses to report a given set of surrogates, this set may provide a basis around which the manager structures his decision process. In these cases, we expect that alternative accounting methods will affect the manager's decisions.

There are examples in the behavioral science literature that describe situations where accounting information has been used in the way we have just described

[8] See, for example, Knight (14) and Cyert and March (4).
[9] Refer to Knight (14) for a further elaboration of this topic.
[10] See Cyert and March (4).

and has been found to influence both the goals of the decision-maker and the alternatives which he considers in making his decisions. Ridgway, studying the problem of accounting measures and behavior in American industry, found that "even where performance measures are instituted purely for purposes of information, they are probably interpreted as definitions of the important aspects of that job."[11] The results of Ridgway's study represent direct support for the theoretical framework that we have presented in this section.

Additional support for our analysis comes from studies of the behavior in Russian industrial firms. These studies show that when specific performance surrogates are provided, they are used by the decision-maker to structure his uncertain world. Smolinski reports how "the project of the Novo Lipetsk steel mill . . . comprises 91 volumes totaling 70,000 pages. (One is not surprised to learn that the designers are paid by sheet. . . .) Literally, everything is anticipated in these blueprints, the emplacement of each nail, lamp, or washstand. Only one aspect of the project is not considered at all: its economic effectiveness."[12] What Smolinski shows is, that by measuring and recording the number of pages in a report, this surrogate has become a factor that defines the decision-maker's world. The decision-maker then restricts his goals and alternatives to ones other than those which are most useful for the organization.[13]

In a study of the Russian executive, Granick points out several dramatic shortcomings of a system where pressures result in the decision-maker receiving a limited number of performance surrogates, and these are then used to determine his goals and alternatives. Granick discusses the "standard operating practice" of "storming," the phenomenon of getting everything possible out at the end of the month because monthly bonuses are determined by the volume produced.[14] He found that the volume of production was used as a descriptive surrogate of other principals that should have been considered by the decision-maker in determining his overall effectiveness. The result of the limited accounting information available to the Russian managers shows how these accounting systems greatly influence the behavior of the decision-maker in an ill-structured situation. Phenomena similar to that observed in Russia frequently are found in the United States, where surrogates, such as direct cost as a percentage of total cost, scrap costs, maintenance costs, return on investment, etc., are used to define the manager's goals and alternatives. In the examples just described, the choice of an accounting method becomes very important in view of the fact that alternative accounting systems will tend to produce different decisions.

AREA FOR FURTHER RESEARCH

Our analysis in the last section leaves unanswered the question of whether or not the choice of accounting methods will affect decisions as we consider the infinite number of possible environments between ill-structured and well-structured. We have not been able to specify the general environmental con-

---

[11]Ridgway (16, p. 377).
[12]Smolinski (18, pp. 602-13).
[13]Note that many of the arguments in support of transfer pricing have been based on arguments about their psychological advantages or disadvantages. (See Hirshleifer (10) and Dean (5).) See also Ijiri (12), where the degree of the divergence between the organizational goal and the goals of its subsystem is analyzed by means of a "goal indicator chart" and a "goal indicator divergence coefficient."

[14]Granick (9, pp. 227-47).

ditions to predict when a choice of accounting methods would (or would not) affect decisions.

To establish a description of these general conditions, we need to investigate many issues in addition to the ill-structuredness of the environment, such as (1) the extent to which good or poor timing of accounting data affects decision, (2) the degree to which different methods of presentation of accounting data affect decisions, and (3) the extent to which the reliability (or lack thereof) of an accounting process affects decisions. In this paper we have begun to outline the variables that determine the effects of alternative accounting methods on management decisions. There is a need for extensive additional research both to find other important variables and to test empirically hypotheses already proposed.

SUMMARY

We now summarize our above analysis as follows:

1. A decision process may be characterized by three factors: decision inputs, decision outputs, and a decision rule.

2. A surrogate may be used in place of a principal input if a surrogate is available at the time of the decision (timing) and if it is possible for the decision-maker to identify the key factors of the principal input which affect his decision (identifiability). The notion of a satisfactory surrogate is introduced in connection with the requirement of identifiability.

3. A decision-maker may need to use a surrogate (a) if it is difficult for him to obtain the principal input (cost consideration, time lag, etc.) or (b) if it is difficult for him to use the principal input due to the limit in his

capacity to consider it in making his decision.

4. The two types of surrogates are: (a) a descriptive surrogate and (b) a predictive surrogate. A descriptive surrogate is one which is caused by a principal. A descriptive surrogate succeeds the principal timewise, such as in the case where the reported cost is used as a surrogate for the real cost.

On the other hand, a predictive surrogate is one which causes the principal. A predictive surrogate precedes the principal timewise. An example is the use of the current cost as a predictive surrogate for the future cost.

5. The intimate relationship between the accounting process which produces a surrogate (y) from a principal (x) and the decision process which generates a decision (z) based upon a surrogate (y) is explained by means of a simple example,

$$x \xrightarrow{f} y \xrightarrow{g} z$$

6. Then, the question, "Under what condition can (or cannot) a decision-maker adjust his decision process to change in the accounting process?" is considered in terms of (a) lack of feedback and (b) functional fixation upon accounting concepts and measurements.

7. Finally, as an important case where the *choice* of accounting method does affect decisions, we considered the role of accounting processes in supplying operational goals and alternatives for a decision-maker who is confronted with an ill-structured environment.

CONCLUSION

We set out to explore the condition under which alternative accounting methods

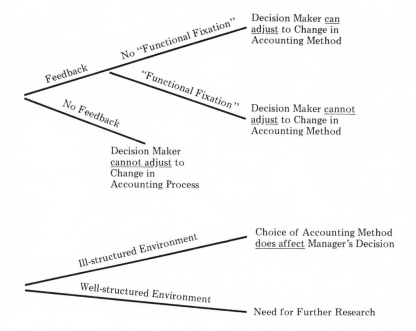

affect decisions. We did this by proposing a theoretical clarification of the mechanics by which the accounting process and the decision process are related. Of course, the relationship between the two processes is a complicated one. We do not claim, by any means, that all variables and their relationships involved in the problem are indentified in the above analysis. We believe, however, that at least the *key factors* in the relationship between the accounting process and the decision process are clarified in our theoretical analysis.

Much research still needs to be done before we can make more precise statements concerning the relationship between the accounting process and the decision process and before we can state in precise terms the effects of accounting alternatives on management decisions.

SELECTED REFERENCES

1. Bonini, Charles P., *Simulation of Information and Decision Systems in the Firm.* Englewood Cliffs, N.J.: Prentice-Hall, Inc., 1963.
2. Bruns, William, "A Simulation Study of Alternative Methods of Inventory Valuation," Unpublished Ph.D. dissertation, University of California, Berkeley, 1962.
3. Charnes, A., and W. W. Cooper, *Management Models and Industrial Applications of Linear Programming,* Vol. I. New York: John Wiley & Sons, Inc., 1961.
4. Cyert, R., and J. March, *A Behavioral Theory of the Firm.* Englewood Cliffs, N.J.: Prentice-Hall, Inc., 1963.

5. Dean, Joel, "Decentralization and Intra-Company Pricing," *Harvard Business Review,* XXXIII, No. 4 (1955), 65-74.

6. Duncker, Karl, "On Problem Solving," *Psychological Monographs,* LVIII, No. 5, Whole No. 270 (1945).

7. Dyckman, Thomas R., "The Effects of Alternative Accounting Techniques on Certain Management Decisions," *Journal of Accounting Research,* II (Spring, 1964).

8. Garner, Wendell R., *Uncertainly and Structure as Psychological Concepts.* New York: John Wiley & Sons, Inc., 1962.

9. Granick, David, *The Red Executive.* Garden City, N.Y.: Doubleday & Company, Inc., 1961, pp. 227-47.

10. Hirshleifer, J., "On the Economics of Transfer Pricing," *The Journal of Business,* XXIX (1956), 172-84.

11. Ijiri, Yuji, *Functional Analysis of Aggregation,* Working Paper No. 21. Graduate School of Business, Stanford University, August, 1964. Presented at the Tenth Annual, First International, Meeting of the Western Section of the Operations Research Society of America held on September 14-18, 1964, in Honolulu, Hawaii.

12. _____, *Management Goals and Accounting for Control.* Amsterdam and Skokie, Ill.: North-Holand Publishing Company; Rand McNally & Co., 1965.

13. _____, and Robert K. Jaedicke, *Reliability and Objectivity of Accounting Measurements,* Working Paper No. 55. Graduate School of Business, Stanford University, April, 1966.

14. Knight, Kenneth E., *The Organization as an Ill-Structured Problem Solving System,* Working Paper No. 56. Graduate School of Business, Stanford University, 1965.

15. Leavitt, Harold J., *Managerial Psychology,* rev. ed. Chicago: University of Chicago Press, 1964, pp. 352-54.

16. Ridgway, V. F., "Dysfunctional Consequences of Performance Measurements," in *Some Theories of Organization,* eds. A. H. Rubenstein and C. J. Haberstroh. Homewood, Ill.: Richard D. Irwin, Inc., 1960, p. 377. Reprinted in this volume, pp. 395-400.

17. Simon, Herbert A., *Models of Man.* New York: John Wiley & Sons, Inc., 1957.

18. Smolinski, Gern, "What Next in Soviet Planning?" *Foreign Affairs,* XLII (July, 1964), 602-13.

Organizational Communications Systems and the Decision Process*

Thomas P. Ference†

Columbia University

The emergence and solution of organizational problems are examined from the framework of the communications system. A general model is developed based on the information-processing activities of the individual members of a communications network. The model describes the problem-solving process as a sequence of five stages: problem recognition, identification procedures, information acquisition and integration, definition of constraint set, and comparison and adaptation. The relations among the critical variables of the model are then specified in a series of propositions. The main purpose of the model, as exemplified in the propositions, is to provide a testable framework for the empirical analysis of the decision process in organizations.

Reprinted from *Management Science*, October 1970, B-83-96. Used by permission of Thomas P. Ference and *Management Science*.

The purpose of this paper is to provide a thematic description of the organizational decision-making process, focusing on the operation of individual cognitive processes within the structure of the organization. The model proposed in later sections deals with the manner in which problems are identified and defined, information is gathered and evaluated, and solutions are developed and tested for acceptability. The model is developed from an analysis of the organizational communications system. Several factors

*Received February 1967; revised January 1970.
†I would like to thank R. M. Cyert and H. A. Simon for their helpful criticisms of earlier drafts of this paper.

influence the information-processing behavior of the members of the communications system. The delineation of these factors, which emphasize the effects on individual cognitive behavior of structural relationships within the organization, provides a basis for elaborating on the decision process. The analysis developed in the paper has two main components, therefore; the first establishes a general framework describing the handling of information by the members of the communications systems. The second, and major, component, utilizing this general framework, deals specifically with the decision-making process.

The working model proposed in the paper is intendedly general; it presents the dimensions of the decision-making or problem-solving process and stresses the interaction of critical variables. The model contains three levels of description. At the first level, the model proposes a sequence of five stages in the organization's problem-solving efforts. At the second level, the variables which are relevant to the process are identified and, at the third level, a series of propositions are made about the specific effects of the variables.

These propositions, while supported in part by existing theory and evidence, are admittedly speculative; they are presented as examples of the possibilities for operationalizing the model.[1] The propositions are intended, therefore, to stimulate the research needed to add precision to the processes described in the first two levels of the model. Subsequent research indicating that the relations among variables are different than suggested by the propositions would not necessarily invalidate the general model; the refinements provided by such research would more than justify the speculative nature of the initial propositions. It should be emphasized that the specification of variables in the general model, as well as the formal propositions, provide the practicing manager with a conceptual framework for analyzing the manner in which decisions are made in his organization.

THE COMMUNICATIONS STRUCTURE: DEFINITIONS AND PROPOSITIONS

The *communication system* of an organization consists of the process by which

requests for information proceed to the point of collection and by which that information is transmitted back to the person requesting it. A *communications network* refers to a particular set of persons or groups within the communications system who may gather, combine, transmit, apply or otherwise manipulate information. Information relates both to events within the organization and to aspects of the external environment. Certain information must be specifically requested such as a five-year forecast of industry sales, while other flows may be provided at regular intervals, for example, a forecast of sales for the next month.

In general, the term 'information' includes any input to a person in the communications system. In this sense relatively objective items such as profit and loss figures and sales and subjective items such as performance evaluations and personal opinions constitute information for the recipient.[2] In general, the processing of a particular item of information is dependent on the characteristics of the information-processor and his relation to his sources and on the characteristics of the information itself; these factors are discussed below. In addition, the choice and interpretation of information in the decision process is dependent on its relevance; this factor is developed more fully in the next section (see Propositions 10, 11).

A person filling a position in a communications network may be distinguished by the number of his sources of information, his relation (superior, peer, subordinate) to these sources, and the location (external, internal) of these sources in the organization.[3] Each of

[2] Cravens (3) defines an "information element" as the "smallest identifiable unit of relevant information processed for a particular task", and cites technical reports, verbal interchanges, and operating data as examples of information utilized in the problem-solving process.

[3] A position is any juncture in the communications network. Examples would

these factors contributes to the interpretation and subsequent use of the information provided by each source.

Persons in the communications network may also be distinguished by their functions; purchasing agents and engineers will perceive and react differently to information received from the same source (21).* Particular interests or concerns will determine if information is to be eliminated, modified or added to before being transmitted (4). In addition, personal motivations may influence what is transmitted. Read found that for a group of middle managers the accuracy of upward communications was inversely related to their desires for advancement (16). Particularly, the men refrained from reporting anything that might limit their mobility.

Finally, persons may be distinguished by the persons to whom they transmit. Information will be tailored to the needs of the person or group to whom it is being sent. If the recipient is a superior, there will be a tendency to make the information consistent with the transmitter's perception of what the recipient wants to hear.[4]

Thus, when evaluating information from a source, each person in the communications network, must decide the amount of integration performed by that source. He then must perform his own integration, combining this information with that received from other sources or developed by himself (6).[5] The following propositions are concerned with this process.

Proposition 1. *When information is evaluated and integrated at a position in a communications network, only the decision or inferences drawn from the information are transmitted; the information or evidence leading to the decision or inferences is not transmitted.*[6]

Proposition 2. *When information is evaluated and integrated at a position in a communications network, the weight given to the information will depend on the source providing the information.*

Proposition 2.1. *More weight will be given to information provided by a source if the source has been used more often in the past, if the source has a high position in the organization, or if the source is inside, rather than external to, the organization.*

Proposition 3. *When information is evaluated and integrated, the function of the person doing the processing will exert more influence than his personal motivation on the choice and interpretation of information.*

Propostition 3.1. *Information, once evaluated and integrated, will tend to fit the transmitter's perceptions of the recipient's needs.*

The information carried by the communications network has several critical characteristics such as the manner by which it is collected, the position at which it enters the system, and how far it travels before it is integrated with other information. Information may be ob-

---

include individuals, groups, and increasingly, computing machinery. The notion of communication networks includes the several forms described by Leavitt (12). This paper is concerned primarily with individuals who hold positions in a network

*Numbers in parentheses refer to selected references at the end of this reading.

[4]This does not necessarily imply transmitting false information or withholding vital but unpleasant facts. The tailoring may require only a shift in emphasis and an underplaying of undesirable matters.

[5]Integration implies more than simple

condensation of a number of reports. Integration may include interpretation, reconciling conflicting reports, discarding information, and applying weights to information from different sources.

[6]March and Simon (13) refer to this process as 'uncertainty absorption'. It is central to the exercise of power since it provides a means for controlling the behavior of others (1).

tained through observations of the external environment, or it may be generated at various points within the organization. Depending upon the locus of pertinent positions in the net, certain types of information may not be brought to bear upon a problem until the problem has already been processed by several other positions. For example, it is conceivable that a research development may undergo many tests and modifications before a consideration of the firm's ability to produce the new product with present equipment is made. The attributes which distinguish information which passes along a net essentially unaltered from that which is incorporated and modified at an earlier position are considered in the following propositions.

Proposition 4.   *The extent to which information is altered as it is carried through a communication network will depend on the source, content, and point of entry of the information.*

Proposition 4.1.   *To the extent that influence is differentially distributed among the members of an organization, the susceptibility of information to alteration will vary directly with the influence of the source providing the information.*

Proposition 4.2.   *Information indicating success in the pursuit of overall goals will be altered less than equally reliable information indicating failure.*[7]

Proposition 4.3.   *The later information enters in the decision process, the less that information will be altered.*

As a final distinction, the *formal* communications systems generally is highly

specific as to who initiates messages, the proper form of communication, and the degree of commitment implied by utilization of official channels. The *informal* system results from such diverse factors as the physical contiguity, sub-group affiliations, professional group membership, or even sharing in a car pool. Design engineers, for example, are more likely to be aware of problems on the production floor if their work area is located near the shop rather than in another building. Likewise, economists in different divisions of a large corporation share a common professional affiliation and are likely to converse informally on mutually relevant questions. An individual holding a position in more than one network may informally transmit information between persons who are information sources or recipients for him but who are not themselves members of the same formal communications network. Further, information transmitted in a casual conversation does not enter into formal communications files and does not necessitate an irreversible commitment to subsequent action on the part of the participants; this would suggest that informal contacts would predominate in the initial stages of problem-solving activity.

Proposition 5.   *To the extent that problems are ill defined, information obtained through informal communications systems will be preferred to information obtained through formal communication systems.*

Given these characteristics of information-processing behavior within an organizational communication system, it becomes necessary to specify the process by which certain persons, positions, and networks become involved in a particular decision while others do not. In the next section, a general model of this process will be presented.

---

[7]This is most likely to occur when the report of success or failure reflects in some way upon the performance of the transmitting position. These are probably circumstances in which a person would find it desirable to transmit reports of failure by other organizational members.

A GENERAL CONCEPTUAL MODEL

The model contains five main stages. These are outlined in flow-chart format in Figure 1 and will be developed in depth in the following sections. In overview, the first stage centers on the alternative ways that problems are recognized. Two specific behaviors are then proposed, the search for decision control and a check for existing solutions.

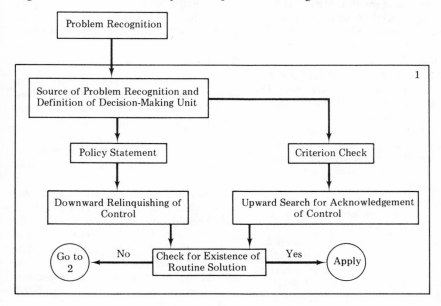

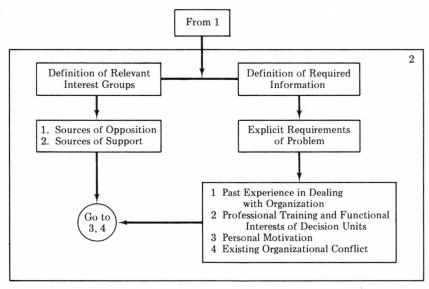

FIGURE 1.

Given that a routine solution does not exist, the next stage involves establishing the dimensions of the problem-solving process. Relevant interest groups are identified, and an initial attempt is made to specify the information that will be needed. A variety of interpersonal and structural variables are proposed as affecting the outcome of these identification procedures.

The third and fourth stages are presented as proceeding concurrently. The third stage is concerned with the factors affecting the acquisition, interpretation, and integration of information. A series of conditions are proposed as influencing the process of data collection, and criteria for evaluating and combining information are indicated.

The fourth stage focuses on the parallel process of establishing the limits of an acceptable solution. Constraints are provided by the various organizational members as well as by the specific attributes of the problem. It is proposed that the effective constraint set develops from the decision unit's perception of these factors.

In the final stage, solutions and constraints are compared. The process then either terminates or feeds back upon itself in order to locate a better fit between available actions and organizational requirements. The redefinition of the system is proposed as proceeding from simple definitional adaptations through extensive structural modifications. Each of these stages will now be examined in greater detail.

STAGE ONE:
PROBLEM RECOGNITION

The first consideration in an analysis of a decision-making system is how a problem comes to be acknowledged.

Proposition 6. *Problem-solving will ensue only when the performance of the firm is judged to be unsatisfactory by some criterion.*

The problem activating this process will generally be a specific one and efforts will be directed toward a solution for that problem. There are several ways through which the existence of a problem is signaled to the organization:

(1) *Criterion checks:* Most firms employ a series of standardized indicators of performance such as market share, inventory level, production rate, etc., which represent the overall goals or constraints upon operations. A failure to satisfy the criteria specified by this constraint set serves as a signal of some malfunction and will initiate an organizational search, first, to locate the problem, and, second, to correct it. Other indicators, internal and external, would include standard industry practices, budgets, and governmental regulations. This general system of constraints or criteria has been referred to as a negotiated environment (5).

(2) *Policy statements:* These emanate from the upper levels of the organization and represent constraints imposed on the firm from above. Examples might be a management directive to investigate the potential value of computer systems for a firm (7), an order to increase sales even though the existing sales criteria were being met, or pressure applied by management for increased research output.[8]

(3) *Repetitive procedures:* Certain types of choice behavior, such as re-

---

[8]Problem-solving may be stimulated by random encounters with the environment. A change in tactics by a competitor, a technical innovation, or opportunities provided by changes in the political or financial worlds may well lead to problem-solving activity.

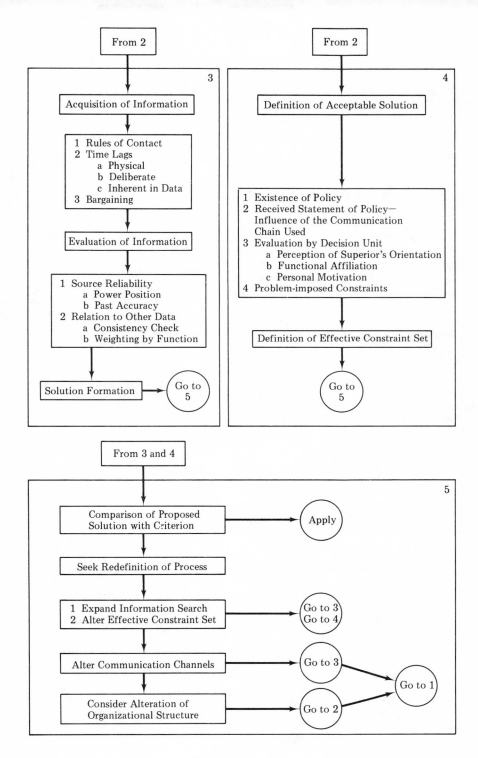

From 2

3

Acquisition of Information

1 Rules of Contact
2 Time Lags
    a Physical
    b Deliberate
    c Inherent in Data
3 Bargaining

Evaluation of Information

1 Source Reliability
    a Power Position
    b Past Accuracy
2 Relation to Other Data
    a Consistency Check
    b Weighting by Function

Solution Formation → Go to 5

From 2

4

Definition of Acceptable Solution

1 Existence of Policy
2 Received Statement of Policy—
    Influence of the Communication
    Chain Used
3 Evaluation by Decision Unit
    a Perception of Superior's Orientation
    b Functional Affiliation
    c Personal Motivation
4 Problem-imposed Constraints

Definition of Effective Constraint Set

Go to 5

From 3 and 4

5

Comparison of Proposed
Solution with Criterion → Apply

Seek Redefinition of Process

1 Expand Information Search
2 Alter Effective Constraint Set → Go to 3 / Go to 4

Alter Communication Channels → Go to 3

Consider Alteration of
Organizational Structure → Go to 2

Go to 1

sources acquisition, occur at periodic intervals.

(4) *Residual sources:* There are members of most organizations who have been defined as problem-solvers. Research engineers and college professors fit into this category. In this sense, problem-solving or innovative behavior becomes institutionalized (13).

The nature of the search process initiated by these types of problem recognition will differ in several ways. Problems signaled by policy statements will be more vague and less directly related to the day-to-day operations of the firm than those problems first noticed by means of criterion checks. Search activated by criterion checks or repetitive procedures will be limited, at least initially, to the specific area where the problem symptom emerged. Further, a solution will be sought which will not differ greatly from the current solution. Only when such efforts fail will the range of the search be extended to other parts of the organization and to noticeably different alternatives. Search ensuing from policy statements, on the other hand, will commonly involve more than one area of the organization and may, by its very nature, require innovative behavior.

Proposition 7. *The extent of the search process activated by the recognition of a problem will depend on the manner in which the problem was signaled.*

Proposition 7.1. *The search process for criterion check and repetitive problems will be limited to the immediate area of the problem signal (5).*

Proposition 7.2. *Search resulting from policy statements will be broader and more innovative than that for criterion check and repetitive problems.*

Given that a problem is recognized, the next step is to locate the level or

position in the organization at which the final decision on acceptance of a solution will be made.[9] Obviously, not all decisions are made at the top; decision-making authority will be distributed in some manner throughout the organization. There may be several bases for decision making 'power' such as expert knowledge, access to critical information, a past record of accurate decisions, or simply being assigned the responsibility by a superior.

The *decision-making* unit may be defined as the lowest level or position which has access to the necessary information and is aware of the decision rule; the unit may be one person or a group. Access to necessary information implies that the problem-initiated search first locates the relevant communication network and then proceeds through it until a position is determined which is granted decision authority by the next higher position and will not relinquish it to the next lower position. Awareness of the decision rule refers to a knowledge of the relevant constraint set which includes an interpretation of the interests and desires of superiors. Further, this concept of a decision unit is consistent with the division of a problem into several segments, each of which is handled by a different unit.

In general, when a problem is signaled by a policy statement, each position in the communications network will be more reluctant to relinquish decision control to subordinate positions than it would be for criterion check problems. Participants in the analysis of a policy statement problem will be accountable directly to the top levels for their decision while most criterion check problems

[9]This initial assignment of decision responsibility may be altered by subsequent search activity. This complication is minor, however, and merely requires that the organization retrace its steps through this process one more time.

probably are recognized and solved without their existence ever being communicated to the top.

This concept of decision control suggests that the information-processor, who performs the necessary integration of information, may well be the actual decision-maker even though the decision may bear the name of a superior. This highlights the critical nature of the integrative function described earlier and is supported by observation of the increasing influence acquired by various staff specialists in most organizations. The person who has access to vital information and prepares it for use by superiors can exert considerable if not exclusive influence on the final decision (14). Management control can be maintained in such cases, by requiring that the final decision must be acceptable to all levels above the decision-maker who are aware of the decision.

Proposition 8. *The search for decision control or responsibility will proceed upward through the organization for criterion check and repetitive problems and downward for policy statement problems.*

Proposition 8.1. *Decision control will be retained at a higher level for policy statement problems than for other problem signals.*

Once the decision-making unit is defined for a particular problem, its first task is to determine whether or not a routine or programmed solution exists (13). If such a solution exists, it will be immediately applied and the problem-solving effort terminated at this point. If the problem is unprogrammed, that is, a new problem for which no solution is contained in the organization's repertoire, actual problem-solving behavior, or search, will ensue.

Proposition 9. *Problem-solving behavior will proceed only when programmed solutions do not exist.*

STAGE TWO: IDENTIFICATION PROCEDURES

As long as a routine solution cannot be found, the organization will initiate problem-solving activity. The next step taken by the decision unit will be to ascertain which groups and individuals will have an interest in the solution and to determine what information will be required. The solution formulated will affect various groups within the organization in different ways. Some will benefit from the solution; some will suffer. The decision unit must attempt to assess both the interests and the relative power of these groups.[10] In order to have a solution accepted, the decision unit must attempt to determine ahead of time which groups will oppose a particular solution and then either alter the solution to make it acceptable or gain sufficient power through coalitions with other areas to overcome the influence of opposing factions (9).

There are two main paths through which a particular person comes to be included in the problem-solving process. The first concerns the substantive nature of the problem. Certain sources are included because they are seen by the decision unit as possessing information required to solve the problem. The second path to inclusion lies in the existing organizational environment. The inclusion of certain sources is required by the organization. Both the designation of

[10]These concepts might be operationalized for purposes of research as follows: define an *interest group* as one which either (a) possesses needed data, (b) explicitly seeks to influence the decision process, or (c) must cooperate for implementation to be successful. Define *power* as it affects the decision-maker to be his perception of the ability of other groups to countermand his decisions. The several combinations of type of interest and perceived power then provide a basis for classifying field observations or establishing an experimental design.

decision units and of information sources are mediated by procedural consider-ations. Rules of precedence and existing affiliations operate to structure the prob-lem-solving process. The questions of who shall participate and to what extent must be answered by appeal to both procedural and substantive aspects of the problem. This distinction, which does not arise in the analysis of individual problem-solving, is relevant to an understanding of in-fluence and decision processes at the organizational level.

Proposition 10. *Information from sources included for substantive reasons will be given more weight than that from sources included for procedural reasons.*

With regard to the substantive aspects of the problem, an initial definition of required information undoubtedly pre-cedes the actual acquisition stage.[11] Part of the information will be required by the problem in question; a second part will depend upon the inclinations and past experiences of the decision unit. Selznick has described the effect of past problem-solving experiences in this way, "Day-to-day decisions, relevant to the actual problem met in the translation of policy into action, create precedents, alliances, effective symbols, and personal loyalties which transform the organization from a profane, manipulable instrument into something having a sacred status and thus resistant to treatment simply as a means to some external goals" (17, pp. 258-259). Each person, each decision unit, will contain in his memory a record of those who are knowledgeable on cer-tain topics and of those whose infor-mation is unnecessary. The links created by the formal communication network

may require the usage of certain sources and types of information, but the deci-sion unit may also tap other sources it has come to regard as useful. A sales manager may regularly seek information from the purchasing agent on advertising decisions even though the formal system does not define these two positions as members of the same network for this problem.[12] The interaction between required information and experience with possible sources is developed in the following propositions.

Proposition 11. *Information defined as required by the nature of the problem is more likely to be sought from fre-quently used sources than from infre-quently used sources.*

Proposition 11.1 *Information avail-able from frequently used sources is more likely to be defined as required than that from infrequently used sources.*

The decision unit's definition of rel-evant information may also arise from the professional training and functional in-terests of the decision-maker. A financial officer may interpret the essence of a problem differently than a market analyst (8). Personal hopes and motives may lead the individual to shape the information collection in such a way as to show himself most favorably and either to ignore or 'show up' his rivals. Finally, unresolved conflicts carrying over from earlier problems may eliminate some organizational units from consideration as information sources (see Proposition 3).

STAGE THREE: INFORMATION ACQUISITION AND INTEGRATION

Once the search process has been struc-tured and initiated, the information

---

[11] This is not to say that this is the only way that information enters the systems. As discussed above, both random and planned encounters with the environment may stimulate problem-solving activity. Data may enter the process through a variety of accidents or unplanned mechanisms.

[12] Gullahorn and Gullahorn (10) provide an interesting attempt to model the impact of the past experience based on the work of Homans (11).

called for must be acquired and evaluated before solutions may be constructed. The acquisition of information identified as necessary is subject to three major factors: the rules of contact, bargaining, and time lags. The first two factors emphasize the role of procedural considerations.

The rules of contact constitute the protocol system of the organization. Different persons will require different approaches; for some, a telephone call will elicit the necessary material, for others, a written request might be needed. Bargaining occurs when concessions involving promises of future cooperation or acceptance of additional constraints in the current situation must be made to sources in order to obtain information. Time lags may be introduced by the physical limitations of the communications system, by the deliberate actions of individuals or groups, and by the nature of the required data which may require time-consuming efforts to collect.

Proposition 12. *Information will be acquired only when the rules of contact, formal and informal, are observed in the acquisition process.*

Proposition 12.1. *Information which can be obtained without bargaining will be preferred to that which requires bargaining.*

Proposition 12.2. *Information which can be obtained without time lags will be preferred to that which will require time to collect.*[13]

Once the information has been acquired, it will be evaluated and interpreted in order to construct a solution. The evaluation will proceed along two lines: the first is the reliability of the source. The credence given to information emanating from any source will depend upon the prestige of the source in terms

of its position in the power structure and upon the accuracy of previous information it has supplied. These two variables will be assigned for every source prior to obtaining new information. The second line of evaluation concerns the relation of the data to that received from other sources. Information will first be compared with other information for consistency, and the reliability variables just described will be employed to choose among inconsistent elements.

Proposition 13. *The later that information is acquired in the problem-solving process, the more likely it is to be either totally rejected or totally accepted (see Proposition 4.3).*

Proposition 13.1. *Information that is inconsistent with information acquired earlier in the problem-solving process in likely to be rejected.*

Proposition 13.2 *The more reliable a source has been, or the more power a source has, the less likely it is that the information it provides will be rejected, even if inconsistent with information acquired earlier in the problem-solving process.*

Once the evaluation has been completed, the accepted information will be shaped by the decision-maker and proposed as a solution. Before being accepted and applied to the problem, this solution must be compared against the criteria defining an acceptable solution.

STAGE FOUR: DEFINING THE CONSTRAINT SET

In recognizing relevant interest groups, the decision-maker has accepted a partial constraint or goal set (19). The constraint set that is perceived to be imposed by organizational policy will be dependent upon several factors including the extent

[13]There is a danger here and with bargaining that inferior data might be employed simply because they are available.

to which there is a clear statement of policy, the form in which statements of policy reach the decision unit, and the decision-unit's perception of received constraints.

For the unprogrammed type of problem considered here, there may often arise cases in which there is no explicit company policy on a particular matter. The decision unit, therefore, may acquire considerable discretion in its solution of these problems.[14] When policy does exist at some higher level, however, the decision unit will strive to act in accordance with it. The form in which this policy is communicated to the decision unit will depend upon the number and nature of the positions through which it is transmitted before reaching the unit. It remains for the decision unit to interpret the information that it receives from superiors.[15] The decision unit will attribute an orientation or a set of interests and desires to the firm and to its superiors. The validity of this assumption will depend upon the accuracy of policy transmission and the perceptual framework of the decision-maker.

Proposition 14. *The range of discretion available to the decision unit will depend on the explicitness of existing policy.*

Proposition 14.1 *The discretion of the decision unit will be greatest on problems signaled by policy statements.*[16]

[14]The decision unit may be said to be exercising *discretion* whenever its processing of information is not controlled by constraints imposed by others. The *range* of discretion, therefore, refers to the degree of processing which can take place without reference to imposed constraints.
[15]Note that constraints might also be imposed by subordinates. The process by which these constraints would be incorporated into the effective constraint set is essentially the same as that described here for superiors (14), (19).
[16]Problems signaled in this manner are likely to be broadly stated, ill-defined, and innovative, thus leading to greater discretion (see Proposition 7.2 and preceding discussion).

Proposition 14.2 *Constraints perceived by the decision unit as deriving from policy will be given more weight than constraints imposed from other sources.*

Constraints will also be imposed by the nature of the problem. This is, perhaps, the most obvious factor. Physical limitations in productive capacity or ability, external cost restraints, government regulations, accepted standards, and other relatively objective matters constrain possible solutions.

The effective constraint set formed by these factors serves to define the nature of an acceptable solution (19). It should be noted that, while the behavior of competing organizations has not been explicitly considered, it is assumed that information obtained from the external environment enters the communication network at some position and is then available to the decision unit in the same manner as internal information.

STAGE FIVE: COMPARISON AND ADAPTATION

The proposed solution will now be compared with the effective constraint set. If it satisfies all the constraints, the solution will be accepted and the decision process terminated at this point.[17]

Proposition 15. *A solution will be accepted if and only if it satisfies all components of the effective constraint set.*

Proposition 15.1. *If more than one proposed solution satisfies the effective*

[17]This is the direct application of the satisfying criteria proposed by Simon (18). If several satisfactory solutions were found, some further choice rule would have to be invoked. The relevant point here is the evaluation of solutions by comparison to a constraint set as opposed to a maximization criterion.

constraint set, the solution which best satisfies the constraints imposed by policy will be chosen (see Proposition 14.2).

Proposition 15.2. *If the constraints imposed by policy are inconsistent, the problem-solving process will be repeated in order to obtain a clarification of policy (see Proposition 8.1 and Proposition 10).*

If the available solution (or solutions) is not acceptable, a further search process is called for. In this process, the decision unit will seek to redefine the problem-solving process in order to develop a satisfactory solution. The redefinition process will proceed through several stages similar to those discussed above and will be described only briefly at this time.

The first step is to expand the search process; present information will be re-evaluated and recombined and further information will be sought. Additional segments of the organization may be drawn into the process. The next step will be to attempt to relax or alter the effective constraint set (20). Perhaps initial aspirations were too high, or perhaps the interests of certain parties were misinterpreted or overemphasized. These two attempts at redefinition suggest that the organizational behavior represents a feedback system wherein the ground covered in earlier periods of the decision process is re-examined. The scope of such a feedback system would initially be small; first attempts revert back to the most recent stages, those of solution formation and criteria definition. If these attempts are not successful, however, the range of redefinition will expand.

The manner in which further restructuring will develop would probably vary among organizations. It seems safe to assume, however, that the next effort would be directed at an alteration of the communication system in order to improve the information-collection and pro-

cessing system. Failing here, the firm would have to consider more basic adjustments, requiring either a change in the organizational structure, such as a move to decentralization or the combination of two product lines, or a shift in the power or influence system. If certain groups or persons are blocking the solution, it may be necessary to force them to alter their positions or to minimize their influence relative to the current problem. A final step in the redefinition process would be a complete revamping of the organization or, possibly, the collapse of the organization.

Proposition 16. *A failure to develop an acceptable solution, will lead to an expansion of the search process by including more information and more sources of information.*

Proposition 16.1. *In redefining the search process, changes in the constraint set will be preferred to the changes in positional (structural) or interpersonal relations* (20).

SUMMARY

This paper has examined the organizational decision process from the perspective of the organizational communication system, and the pertinent factors of this system were developed. Briefly, they include the order and number of positions in a communications network, functional commitments, the point of entrance of information, and the influence and attributed reliability of information sources. The role of positions was seen to be that of integration and transmittal. In particular, this integrative behavior was seen to be a critical factor in determining the subsequent nature of the decision process.

The decision process itself was then examined and a five-stage model proposed. In the first stage, the problem source is specified, and the point at which the decision will be initiated. After determining the organizational groups whose interests must be considered, the information required for the formation of a solution is specified. Several factors other than the explicit nature of the problem were considered. The next two stages are processed concurrently. The effective constraint set is defined, and the acquired information is translated into a proposed solution. In the final stage, this solution is tested against the relevant criteria and is either accepted or rejected. If it is rejected, a redefinition process is activated which attempts to arrive at an acceptable solution, first, by expansion of the search process and by relaxing the constraint set, and, if necessary, seeking more basic structural alterations.

The patterns of communication and interaction within organizations are complex and affected by many diverse variables. A theory of decision-making in organizations must take these variables into account. The propositions incorporated in this paper should provide a starting point for the empirical analysis of decision-making within the complex of people and machines constituting an organization. It would seem that simulation techniques would be most useful in testing the model as a whole; examples of previous work simulated by related models may be found in the several studies of heuristic decision processes reported by Cyert and March (5) and in

the complex model of social behavior developed by Gullahorn and Gullahorn (10). An alternative approach, coupling simulation with a carefully controlled laboratory experiment is exemplified by Clarkson (2) who examined an adaptive model of individual information-processing in a group situation. Field studies of decision-making processes in a complex organizational environment would also be useful in testing both specific propositions and the model as a whole; related examples include the study of a computer-selection decision reported by Cyert, Simon, and Trow (7) and the recent study by Cravens (3) of the information-processing behavior of engineers. It should be noted that the variables and models examined in these earlier studies are generally analogous to specific components of the present model.

The conceptual framework provided by the model should also be of assistance to the practicing manager in identifying inefficiencies in his information-processing system by focusing on key interactions. For example, the propositions concerned with the factors governing the choice, acquisition, and subsequent use of information should provide clear guides for the manager who wishes to understand the circumstances leading to existing decisions or who wishes to guarantee the inclusion of certain information in future problem-solving efforts. Similar examples could be drawn for other propositions and for the model as a whole.

REFERENCES

1. Bendix, R., "Bureaucracy and the Problem of Power," *Public Administration Review.* (Summer, 1945).

2. Clarkson, G. P. E., "Decision Making in Small Groups: A Simulation Study," *Behavioral Science,* Vol. 13 (1968).

3. Cravens, D. W., "An Exploratory Analysis of Individual Information Processing," *Management Science,* Vol. 16, No. 10 (1970).

4. Cyert, R. M., and March, J. G., "Organizational Structure and Pricing Behavior in an Oligopolistic Market," *American Economic Review* (March 1955).

5. _____ and _____ , *A Behavioral Theory of the Firm,* Prentice-Hall, Englewood Cliffs, 1963.

6. _____ , _____ and Starbuck, W. H., "Two Experiments on Bias and Conflict in Organizational Estimation," *Management Science,* Vol. 8 (1961).

7. _____ , Simon, H. A. and Trow, D. B., "Observation of a Business Decision," *Journal of Business,* Vol. 29 (1956).

8. Dearborn, D. O. and Simon, H. A., "Selective Perception: A Note on the Departmental Identifications of Executives," *Sociometry,* Vol. 21 (1958).

9. Gore, W., *Administrative Decision Making,* Wiley, New York, 1954.

10. Gullahorn, J. T. and Gullahorn, J. E., "A Computer Model of Elementary Social Behavior," in E. A. Feigenbaum and J. Feldman (Eds.), *Computers and Thought,* McGraw-Hill, New York, 1963.

11. Homans, G. C. *Social Behavior: Its Elementary Forms,* Harcourt, Brace and World, New York, 1961.

12. Leavitt, H. J., "Some Effects of Certain Communication Patterns on Group Performance," *Journal of Abnormal & Social Psychology* (1949).

13. March, J. G. and Simon, H. A., *Organizations,* Wiley, New York, 1958.

14. Mechanic, D., "Sources of Power of Lower Participants in Complex Organizations," in W. W. Cooper, H. J. Leavitt, and M. W. Shelly, *New Perspectives in Organization Research,* Wiley, New York, 1964.

15. Menzel, M., "Planned and Unplanned Scientific Communication," in B. Barber and W. Hirsch (Ed.), *The Sociology of Science,* Free Press, New York, 1963.

16. Read, W. H., "Upward Communication in Industrial Hierarchies," *Human Relations* (January 1962).

17. Selznick, P., *TVA and the Grass Roots,* University of California Press, Berkeley, 1953.

18. Simon, H. A., "A Behavioral Model of Rational Choice," *Quarterly Journal of Economics* (February 1955).

19. _____ , "On the Concept of Organizational Goal," *Administrative Science Quarterly* (June 1964).

20. Starbuck, W. H., "Organizational growth and development," in J. G. March, *Handbook of Organizations,* Rand-McNally, 1965.

21. Strauss, G., "Tactics of Lateral Relationship: The Purchasing Agent," *Administrative Science Quarterly,* Vol. 7 (1962).

SELECTED REFERENCES FOR CHAPTER 8

BOOKS

Argyris, Chris, *The Impact of Budgets on People.* New York: The Controllership Foundation, 1952.

Barnard, Chester I., *The Functions of the Executive.* Cambridge, Mass.: Harvard University Press, 1938.

Bonini, Charles P., *Simulation of Information and Decision Systems in the Firm.* Englewood Cliffs, N.J.: Prentice-Hall, Inc., 1963.

Bowers, Raymond V., ed., *Studies on Behavior in Organizations.* Athens, Ga.: University of Georgia Press, 1966.

Bruns, William J., Jr. and Don T. DeCoster, *Accounting and Its Behavioral Implications,* New York: McGraw-Hill, Inc., 1969.

Burns, Thomas J., ed., *The Use of Accounting Data in Decision Making.* Columbus, O.: The Ohio State University Press, 1967.

Cooper, W. W., H. J. Leavitt, and M. W. Shelly, *New Perspectives in Organization Research.* New York: John Wiley & Sons, Inc., 1964.

Cyert, Richard M., and James G. March, *A Behavioral Theory of the Firm.* Englewood Cliff, N.J.: Prentice-Hall, Inc., 1963.

Dahl, Robert A., Mason Haire, and Paul F. Lazarfield, *Social Science Research on Business: Product and Potential.* New York: Columbia University Press, 1959.

Gellerman, Saul W., *Motivation and Productivity.* New York: American Management Association, 1963.

Ijiri, Yuji, *Foundation of Accounting Measurement.* Englewood Cliffs, N.J.: Prentice-Hall, Inc., 1967.

Katz, Daniel, and Robert L. Kahn, *The Social Psychology of Organizations.* New York: John Wiley & Sons, Inc., 1966.

Leavitt, Harold J., *Managerial Psychology,* 2nd ed. Chicago: University of Chicago Press, 1964.

Likert, Rensis, *New Patterns of Management.* New York: McGraw-Hill Book Company, 1961.

Lorsch, Jay W. and Paul R. Lawrence, *Studies in Organization Design.* Homewood, Ill.: Richard D. Irwin, Inc., 1970.

McGregor, Douglas, *The Human Side of Enterprise.* New York: McGraw-Hill Book Company, 1960.

March, James G., and Herbert A. Simon, *Organizations.* New York: John Wiley & Sons, Inc., 1958.

Rubenstein, Albert H., and Chadwick J. Haberstroh, eds., *Some Theories of Organization,* rev. ed. Homewood, Ill.: Richard D. Irwin, Inc., 1966.

Simon, Herbert A., *Administrative Behavior,* 2nd ed. New York: The Macmillan Company, 1957.

———, Harold Guetzkow, George Kozmetsky, and Gordon Tyndall, *Centralization vs. Decentralization in Organizing the Controller's Department.* New York: The Controllership Foundation, 1954.

Stedry, Andrew C., *Budget Control and Cost Behavior.* Englewood Cliffs, N.J.: Prentice-Hall, Inc., 1960.

Vickers, Geoffrey, *The Art of Judgment.* London: Chapman and Hall Ltd., 1965.

Wildavsky, Aaron, *The Politics of the Budgetary Process.* Boston: Little, Brown and Company, 1964.

ARTICLES

Argyris, Chris, "Human Problems with Budgets," *Harvard Business Review,* XXXI (January-February, 1953).

———, "Management Information Systems: The Challenge to Rationality and Emotionality," *Management Science,* XVII (February 1971).

Becker, Selwyn and David Green, Jr., "Budgeting and Employee Behavior," *The Journal of Business,* XXXV (October 1962).

Birnberg, Jacob C., and Raghu Nath, "Implications of Behavioral Science for Managerial Accounting," *The Accounting Review,* XLII (July, 1967).

———, "Laboratory Experimentation in Accounting Research," *The Accounting Review,* XLIII (January, 1968).

Bruns, William J., Jr., "Inventory Valuation and Management Decisions," *The Accounting Review*, XL (April, 1965).

_____ , "Accounting Information and Decision-Making: Some Behavioral Hypotheses," *The Accounting Review*, XLIII (July, 1968).

Carter, E. Eugene, "The Behavioral Theory of the Firm and Top-Level Corporate Decisions." *Administrative Science Quarterly.*

Churchman, C. West, "Managerial Acceptance of Scientific Recommendations," *California Management Review*, VII (Fall 1964).

Churchman, C. W., and A. H. Schainblatt, "The Researcher and the Manager: A Dialectic of Implementation," *Management Science*, XI (February, 1965).

Cyert, Richard M., H. A. Simon, and D. B. Trow, "Observation of a Business Decision," *Journal of Business*, XXIX (October, 1956).

_____ , W. R. Dill, and J. G. March, "The Role of Expectations in Business Decision Making," *Administrative Science Quarterly* (December, 1958).

DeCoster, Don T. and John P. Fertakis, "Budget-Induced Pressure and Its Relationship to Supervisory Behavior," *Journal of Accounting Research*, VI, (Autumn 1968).

Dutton, J. M., and R. E. Walton, "Operational Research and the Behavioral Sciences," *Operations Research Quarterly*, XX (September, 1964).

Dyckman, Thomas R., "The Effects of Alternative Accounting Techniques on Certain Management Decisions," *Journal of Accounting Research*, II (Spring, 1964).

Fertakis, John P, "On Communication, Understanding, and Relevance in Accounting Reporting," *The Accounting Review*, XLIV, (October 1969).

Brummet, R. Lee, Flamholtz, Eric G., and Pyle, William C., "Human Resource Measurement—A Challenge for Accountants," *The Accounting Review* XLIII (April 1968).

Flamholtz, Eric, "A Model for Human Resource Valuation: A Stochastic Process with Service Rewards," *The Accounting Review*, XLVI (April 1971).

Golembiewski, Robert T., "Accountancy as a Function of Organization Theory," *The Accounting Review*, XXXIX (April, 1964).

Hawkins, David F., "Behavioral Implications of Generally Accepted Accounting Principles," *California Management Review*, XII (Winter 1969).

Hofstedt, Thomas R. and James C. Kinard, "A Strategy for Behavioral Accounting Research," *The Accounting Review*, XLV, (January 1970).

Jasinsky, Frank J., "Use and Misuse of Efficiency Controls," *Harvard Business Review*, XXXIV (July—August, 1956).

Jensen, Robert E., "Empirical Evidence From the Behavioral Sciences: Fish Out of Water," *The Accounting Review*, XLV, (July, 1970).

Likert, Rensis, and Stanley E. Seashore, "Making Cost Control Work," *Harvard Business Review*, XLI (November—December, 1963).

McGregor, Douglas, "Do Management Control Systems Achieve Their Purpose?" *Management Review*, LVI (February, 1967).

Miles, Raymond E., and Roger C. Vergin, "Behavioral Properties of Variance Controls," *California Management Review*, VIII (Spring, 1966).

Onsi, Mohamed, "Factor Analysis of Behavioral Variables Affecting Budgetary Slack," *The Accounting Review*, XLVIII, (July, 1973).

Revsine, Lawrence, "Change in Budget Pressure and Its Impact on Supervisor Behavior," *Journal of Accounting Research*, VIII (Autumn, 1970).

Schlosser, Robert E., "Psychology for the Systems Analyst," *Management Services*, I (November—December, 1964).

Stedry, Andrew C., "Budgeting and Employee Behavior; A Reply," *The Journal of Business,* XXXVII, (April, 1964).

Toan, Arthur B., Jr., "Power, Influence, Persuasion and Management Reports," *Financial Executive,* XXXIII (August, 1965).

Trull, Samuel G., "Some Factors Involved in Determining Total Decision Success," *Management Science,* XII (February, 1966).

Wallace, Michael E., "Behavioral Considerations in Budgeting," *Management Accounting,* XLVII (August, 1966).